WOMEN

A Feminist Perspective

FOURTH EDITION

Edited by Jo Freeman

Mayfield Publishing Company
Mountain View, California

Copyright © 1989 by Mayfield Publishing Company

Library of Congress Cataloging-in-Publication Data

Women : a feminist perspective / edited by Jo Freeman. —
4th ed.
     p.   cm.
  Includes bibliographies and indexes.
  ISBN 0-87484-801-6
  1. Women — United States — Social conditions.
2. Feminism — United States.   I. Freeman, Jo.
HQ1426.W62   1989
305.4′2′0973 — dc19   88-34582
                                                              CIP

Manufactured in the United States of America
10 9 8 7 6 5 4 3 2 1

Mayfield Publishing Company
1240 Villa Street
Mountain View, California 94041

Sponsoring editor, Franklin C. Graham; production editor,
Linda Toy; manuscript editor, Lyn DuPre; cover designer,
Ingbritt Christensen. The text was set in 10/12 Meridien
Light by Digitype and printed on 50# Finch Opaque by
R. R. Donnelley & Sons.

Contents

Preface

The first edition of this book was put together as a labor of love and published primarily as an act of faith. It had its genesis in 1968, at the first national conference of what was to become the younger branch of the women's liberation movement. Many of us at that conference had just begun reading everything we could find on women, and in that traditional era we were appalled at the scarcity of perceptive writings and only occasionally delighted by a gem that sparkled with new ideas. There were no books or anthologies presenting a feminist perspective on women's status, and those books about women that were not written from a wholly traditional view generally discounted feminism as outmoded, extreme, or both.

Ironically for a group that has since produced so much writing, most of us then felt unable to express our rising consciousness in words. Why not, we thought, do the next best thing? Why not bring together those few existing pieces that were worthwhile and save other women the task of seeking them out? That was a job I took on. Unfortunately, at the same time, I started working for my Ph.D. in political science. It took two years longer to publish the anthology than it did to get the degree.

During the years I worked on the book it grew and changed with the movement. Of the earliest selections, only two made it to the first edition. The rest represented the new research of that time, the new thinking, and the new interpretations of old research inspired by the women's liberation movement.

The first-edition articles came from a variety of sources. I placed ads in most of the burgeoning feminist media, and some organizations, notably the Women's History Research Library of Berkeley and KNOW of Pittsburgh, included special notices with their regular mailings. The response was overwhelming. Hundreds of articles and proposals poured in, and well over a year was spent reading and editing them.

From the beginning the standards were high. This book was to contain pieces that were comprehensive, lucidly written, and well grounded in scholarly research. Needless to say, the submissions I received in response to ads were not uniform in style and approach; nor did they cover all the topics needed. Hence I also collected movement pamphlets and other publications on women, attended feminist meetings, and audited panel discussions on women at professional meetings to find potential authors.

During this period both scholarly and popular writing on women was increasing exponentially, with feminist insights sparking analysis of the contradictions in women's lives in every conceivable sphere. Simultaneously, it was becoming harder and harder to interest a publisher in the book. Some who had expressed tentative interest when I first began sending out the prospectus decided as the book took shape that "this women's thing" was a fad and what market there was, was already glutted. Then one of my authors discussed the book with the traveling editor of a small house on the West Coast. That editor was Alden Paine. He wrote to me; I sent the manuscript; and after I agreed to decrease its length by one-third, National Press Books (soon to become Mayfield Publishing Company) sent me a contract.

As the book went to press, almost everything about it (except the quality of the articles) was an unknown. Owing to its size and recent name change, the publisher was unknown. I was an unknown. All but a few of the authors were unknowns. The potential readership was unknown. All publishing involves some risk, but this was extraordinary. Within two years we knew that love and faith had carried the day. Women's studies courses grew and spread, and both teachers and students found the volume an appropriate introductory text. The reason the courses spread, even in an atmosphere of skepticism and a period of declining college enrollments, is that feminism is not a fad, but a national consciousness that is fundamentally changing the fabric of all our lives.

The first edition took seven years to complete. The second, third, and fourth editions took only about two and a half years each. All have required hard decisions about what to delete and what to add. In each revision, some decisions have made themselves: Not all authors were available to update their contributions; a few articles no longer had the same impact as they had earlier; feedback from users of the text identified some articles that were not widely assigned in class. And, as much as possible, I wanted to replace reprints with original articles and to survey the current issues.

Despite the many problems that remain, the women's liberation movement has been a very successful endeavor. The fourth edition of this book is as much a testament to what the movement has accomplished as it is a critique of what still needs to be done. For the fourth edition as in previous ones we ran calls for papers in approximately twenty newsletters and journals. New authors and topics emerged from this process. Still other new contributors were proposed by the publisher. Some authors of classics that we wanted revised had gone on to other things. Recognizing the importance of educating the next generation, they solved this problem by taking on co-authors. In other cases I did the revision myself. The process made me acutely conscious of how much has changed in the twenty years since this book was first conceived.

The evolution of this book also illustrates some of the developments of feminist scholarship. Papers submitted for the first edition tended to be light on data and heavy on expression of personal feelings. Most authors tried to say a little bit about everything because women were so conscious of the interconnections between the various facets of their existence. Papers for the second edition were well substantiated but still dealt with broad themes (thus it was the easiest edition to edit). In contrast, papers sent in for consideration for the third edition sometimes drowned in data and were too narrow for this particular book. Many of the fourth edition submissions were less interested in analyzing institutions and presenting basic facts than they were in exploring the usefulness of different theoretical frameworks.

Through all these changes I have tried to maintain the standards set in the first edition of providing solid, accurate and up-to-date information along with a critical analysis that interpreted the facts from a feminist perspective. As in previous editions, authors were encouraged to use the most recent data and to double-check them for accuracy. Often I checked the data myself. During the editing of the second edition, I had an office in the Department of Labor in Washington, D.C. and learned how to locate and use the tons of statistics the government produces each year. Before editing the third edition I finished law school. Consequently, the statistics and legal citations in this edition have all been carefully scrutinized and often revised. For this edition I spent many days in the documents department of Brooklyn College Library, whose cooperative staff were extremely resourceful in locating obscure government publications. As in the previous two editions, Howard Hayghe of the Bureau of Labor Statistics was a gold mine of information; he never failed to come through with a necessary number or an explanation of why there wasn't one. All references to "unpublished data from the Bureau of Labor Statistics" in the different chapters are a tribute to his efforts. In addition, I phoned many different subunits in the Bureau of the Census, the Bureau of Justice Statistics, the Department of Education, and the Department of Health and Human Services to find the best sources. As I had learned in previous years, there is often a lot of valuable information around that isn't in university libraries or isn't catalogued in a way that makes it readily accessible. Networking through the telephone is often the only way to find it.

The book that has emerged from this effort contains not only an enormous amount of painstaking research and original thinking but some information that cannot easily be found anywhere else. The reader will find this a useful reference book as well as a general text. What can't be found in the articles can probably be found in sources cited in the footnotes. But while accuracy, thoroughness, and the use of the most recent data are stressed throughout, the true strength of the book rests not in its facts but in its ideas, and in the comprehensive orientation provided by a feminist perspective.

Introduction

The feminist perspective can best be understood in contrast to the traditional view, for each arises from a dramatically different set of premises. The traditionalist view looks at the many ways in which women differ from men and concludes that these differences reflect some basic intrinsic difference that far transcends reproductive capacities. The traditionalist notes that historically women have always had less power, less influence, and fewer resources than men, and assumes this must accord with some natural order. The feminist perspective looks at the many similarities between the sexes and concludes that women and men have equal potential for individual development. Differences in the realization of that potential, therefore, must result from externally imposed restraints, from the influence of social institutions and values. The feminist view holds that so long as society prescribes sex roles and social penalties for those who deviate from them, no meaningful choice exists for members of either sex. Such roles and restraints are incisively examined and challenged in this book, in the belief that only by first understanding their origins and manifestations can we gain the wisdom to dismantle them and create a more just society.

The organization of the book allows readers to begin by looking at their own lives, then moves out in widening circles to bring in the social and historical context of women's present-day status. The book concludes with a section on feminism as the historical and contemporary challenge to that status. Nonetheless, owing to the scope of many of the pieces and the very nature of their topics, the global and the personal are often combined.

In Part One, Carole J. Sheffield provides an overview of the different ways in which a woman's body is controlled and, through it, women as a group. Beginning with Lucy Stone's admonition that a woman's right to herself is the most fundamental one of all, Sheffield argues that such practices as rape, wife assault, the sexual abuse of children, and sexual harassment form a system of *sexual terrorism* "by which males frighten, and by frightening, control and dominate females." Nonetheless, women are perceived as perpetrators rather than as victims of this system because, as

Dianne Herman argues, we live in a "rape culture" in which women are held responsible for the sex act even when it is against their will. Susan Ehrlich Martin shows that this is also true of sexual harassment, which has never been a crime and only recently has been held to be a form of illegal sex discrimination. Nadean Bishop chronicles the twists and turns in the abortion controversy, and Barbara Katz Rothman points out how both reproductive and mothering functions have been co-opted by the medical establishment. Together these authors illuminate how something as personal as a woman's body has been used and misused for political purposes.

The family has been the primary social institution to inform women's lives, and the patriarchal family has been perhaps the single most pervasive and effective means of confining and controlling women's activities. In Part Two, Naomi Gerstel and Harriet Engel Gross put the family in a historical context, showing how different family forms and different systems of production have interacted with patriarchical norms about woman's place. The other contributions to this section look at the different phases of the family. Letitia Anne Peplau and Susan Campbell show how power is wielded in the mating game called dating; Janice M. Steil argues that the inequity in marital relationships has psychic as well as tangible costs for women; Janet Chafetz analyzes the social structural factors which make marriage a very different experience for men than for women; Michele Hoffnung explores the contradictions of the motherhood mystique and the conflict it creates with other important aspects of women's lives. Jill Norgren concludes this section by analyzing why the United States is the sole industrial nation for which child care is primarily a private responsibility.

It is through socialization and education that women are steered away from participating in the major social and economic institutions of our society. In Part Three, Hilary Lips summarizes the sex role socialization literature, with a particular emphasis on how the experience of growing up female differs by race and class. Lois M. Greenwood-Audant argues that this socialization creates, along with the financial dependence and the norms and values resulting from working primarily in the home, a sense of powerlessness in housewives that incapacitates them when they become displaced homemakers. Mary Frank Fox looks at higher education, which has opened many opportunities for women but still does not treat them as the equals of men. Inge Powell Bell examines the consequences for older women of accepting the social norms of the female life cycle.

In Part Four, the economic consequences of society's channeling are clearly delineated by Francine D. Blau and Ann Winkler who point out that there are two distinct labor markets—one male and one female—and the female market is economically depressed. Woman's share of the total income earned in this country, by and large, is not proportionate to her productive contribution. Evelyn Nakano Glenn and Roslyn L. Feldberg focus on clerical work to show how increased employment of women in clerical occupations has led to decreased benefits. It is clear that income is more directly related to the sex of the employee than to the requirements of the job. Anne Nelson, a colleague of the late Barbara Wertheimer, updated Wertheimer's exploration of labor history which documents women's valiant, but often unwelcome, contribution to the labor movement. Debra Renee Kaufman profiles the professions and how they are structured around the typical male lifestyle, while Judith Lorber looks at some of the noneconomic reasons why women are excluded from male domains in the work world. Looking at different types of work, Shelly Coverman shows how domestic work interacts with paid work to create burdens and stresses on women that men, no matter what their class, values or education, do not experience.

More overt institutions of social control are analyzed in Part Five. Jo Freeman looks at the history of women's constitutional rights and public policy on women, which were significantly increased after the emergence of the women's liberation movement. Martha Reineke analyzes how myths, rituals, and symbols are used to socialize and control women. Elizabeth McTaggart Almquist examines eight minority groups to show how ethnicity and sex interact in shaping the everyday lives of women. Rose Weitz calculates the price of independence by looking at the fate of women who would live without men: spinsters, widows, nuns, and particularly lesbians. More subtle spheres of control are charted by two complementary pieces, one by Nancy Henley and Jo Freeman on nonverbal communication and the other by Karen L. Adams and Norma C. Ware on language; both reveal the pervasiveness of sexism in interpersonal dealings, as well as the ways in which everyday conversation constantly reinforces prescribed sex-role behaviors in our society. Less subtle spheres of control are described by two other complementary pieces that address the increasing impoverishment of women. Kathleen Shortridge asks who the female poor are and why they are in poverty. Diana M. Pearce examines why welfare has not only failed to eliminate women's poverty but is locking women into it. Nancy Theberge shows how control of women's sports and athletic activities has been used to control their bodies and to reinforce traditional definitions of what is appropriate for women. Jan Yoder examines how tokenism affects women's performance and evaluations in a particularly male dominated institution — West Point.

The last section, Part Six, is devoted to feminism past and present, a subject well worth a book in itself. Jo Freeman chronicles feminist activities after Suffrage through the current feminist movement. Pauline Terrelonge advocates the relevance of feminism for black women and identifies barriers to its active acceptance. Finally, Susan E. Marshall looks at the rhetoric of the anti-feminist backlash to both the suffrage and the women's liberation movements, and Michael S. Kimmel looks at the ways in which men have responded to feminism.

The articles in this book are not merely a critique of society; implicitly, they take to task the scholarly disciplines whose research and concepts they draw upon. These disciplines, like the institutions and agencies of society at large, are dominated by those on the inside. They still reflect, to a great degree, the traditionalist point of view, and with it a desire to explain, justify, and maintain the status quo of human and institutional relationships. The result is too often a consistency of approach that is almost stifling. It may be politically convenient to view the world through the most comfortable lenses, but the resulting distortion is scientifically unacceptable. Only when one changes position, views the world from another stance, and relaxes one's claim to a monopoly on truth can new knowledge be gained.

The papers in this book show how feminist thought can contribute to this process by providing a new perspective from which to reexamine basic concepts in many spheres of learning. They not only point out the sexist prejudices of old research but show how new human opportunities can be created by changing outworn institutions and values. A feminist perspective is practical as well as theoretical; it illuminates possibilities for the future as well as criticizes the limitations of the present.

Yet these new ideas can have real meaning only within the context of a political movement organized to put them into practice. They will not be adopted merely because they appear in print. For proof of this fact, we need only look at what happened during and after the last feminist movement. We are, after all, not the first scholars to challenge traditional attitudes toward women. Within the limits of the scholarly tools then available to them, our feminist forebears did this once before. One has only to visit the library of the National Woman's Party in Washington or the Schlesinger Library in Cambridge, Massachusetts, or the library of the Fawcett Society in London to realize the magnitude of their work. And one has only to think about how this work was relegated to dusty shelves and ignored after the last wave of feminism ended to feel a certain amount of despair: Clearly new ideas are not espoused by society on the basis of merit alone.

Thus we are in the position of calling "new" what is in fact very old. The feminist ideas of today are "new" only in the sense that most people now alive have not been exposed to them until recently, and in the sense that the more advanced methodology of the scholarly disciplines can "renew" their significance. But if we are not to repeat history—if we are not to see our own volumes ultimately join those others on the dusty shelves—we cannot complacently assume that they will be readily embraced. Instead we must recognize the political context in which such ideas thrive, and we must work to maintain that context until they are thoroughly incorporated into the everyday frame of mind.

The Contributors

JO FREEMAN is the author of *The Politics of Women's Liberation* (winner of a 1975 American Political Science Association prize as the Best Scholarly Work on Women and Politics) and the editor of *Social Movements of the Sixties and Seventies* (1983). She has a Ph.D. in Political Science from the University of Chicago (1973) and a J.D. from New York University School of Law (1982). Her articles on feminism, social movements, law, public policy, sex-role socialization, organizational theory, education, federal election law, and party politics have been published in *The Nation, Ms., Valparaiso Law Review, Trans-action, School Review, Liberal Education, American Journal of Sociology, Intellect, Political Science Quarterly, Acta Sociologica, Prospects, Signs, Pace Law Review,* and numerous anthologies.

KAREN L. ADAMS is an assistant professor in the English department of Arizona State University. She has a Ph.D. in linguistics from the University of Michigan. Her research and teaching interests deal with the relationship between language and society. She has recently given courses and organized conferences on the relationship of language to power. Her recent publications and research are concerned with the structure of political debates and style differences between male and female candidates from different regions of the U.S.A.

ELIZABETH MCTAGGART ALMQUIST is Regents Professor of sociology at the University of North Texas, where her research centers on the intersections of gender, race, and social class. She heads a study group, sponsored by the American Sociological Association, which is assessing the status of women from minority groups in fifteen countries. Her articles have appeared in *Gender and Society, Signs: Journal of Women in Culture and Society, Sex Roles, Journal of Marriage and the Family,* and *Social Science Quarterly.* She is writing a book which describes research on gender inequality in occupations and political offices in the United States.

INGE POWELL BELL, formerly professor of sociology at Pitzer College, is now retired and gardening in Northern California. Her published works include *Core and the Strategy of Nonviolence* (1967), "The Double Standard" (*Transaction,* Nov. 1970), "Buddhist Sociology" (In Scott McNall, ed., *Theoretical Perspectives in Sociology,* 1979), and *This Book Is Not Required,* 1984. The latter is a sociologist's advice to undergraduates on how to get an education, though in college.

NADEAN BISHOP is professor of English literature and women's studies at Eastern Michigan University at Ypsilanti. She has contributed poetry and articles to such journals as *The Wordsworth Circle, Literature and Psychology, Labyris, Corridors,* and *Human Behavior,* and she is editor of *Lovers and Other Losses: Poetry by Seven Women* (1981). She is a former co-ordinator of Women's Studies at EMU and contributed the chapter on Women in Literature to the textbook, *American Women: Their Past, Present, and Future,* edited by Marie Richmond-Abbott. At age fifty she went to seminary at Pacific School of Religion; and after receiving the M. Div. degree, she became pastor of the Northside Community Church in Ann Arbor. In addition to teaching and pastoring, she is director of Isis House, a retreat center for the study of women and spirituality in Ann Arbor.

FRANCINE D. BLAU is professor of economics and labor and industrial relations at the University of Illinois at Urbana-Champaign where her teaching includes courses on women in the labor market. She is the author of *Equal Pay in the Office* (1977) and, with Marianne A. Ferber, *The Economics of Women, Men, and Work* (1986). She has contributed widely to professional journals and is a member of the editorial boards of *Signs: Journal of Women in Culture and Society, Social Science Quarterly,* and *Women and Work.* She is a member of the Executive Board of the Industrial Relations Research Association and a former vice president of the Midwest Economics Association.

SUSAN MILLER CAMPBELL is a doctoral student in social psychology at the University of California, Los Angeles. She is currently working on an investigation of women's reactions to involuntary infertility. She is also involved in a study of the power strategies utilized in negotiations about the use of a condom. Previous work includes a study of children's memory for gender-inconsistent information.

JANET SALTZMAN CHAFETZ is professor of sociology at the University of Houston, where she has taught since 1971. Her areas of teaching and research concentration are gender and sociological theory, interests she has recently combined in several articles and three books: *Sex and Advantage* (1984), *Female Revolt* (with A. G. Dworkin, 1986), and *Feminist Sociology* (1988). She is currently working on an integrated theory, which will be published in 1990 as *Stability and Chage in Gender Systems.* She served as president of Sociologists for Women in Society between 1984–1986.

SHELLEY COVERMAN was an associate professor of sociology at Tulane University. Much of her work concerned the connections between work and family, specifically how gender inequality in the home and in the labor force reinforced each other. In a brief seven year academic career, she published more than a dozen scholarly works, among them "Role Overload, Role Conflict, and Stress: Assessing Consequences of Multiple Role Demands" (*Social Forces,* 1988); "Change in Men's Housework and Child Care Time, 1965–1975," with Joseph F. Sheley (*Journal of Marriage and the Family,* 1986); and "Gender, Domestic Labor Time, and Wage Inequality" (*American Sociological Review,* 1983). She worked actively to foster an academic environment sympathetic to women chairing both the Tulane Faculty Salary Pay Equity Study and the Newcomb College Center for Research on Women Faculty Committee. She died in August 1988.

ROSLYN L. FELDBERG is a sociologist who studies women's employment and works in coalitions to promote pay equity and policies that make it easier to encompass the work-family connection for the varying configurations of contemporary families. Her recent publications include *Hidden Aspects of Women's Work* (co-edited by Chris Bose and Natalie Sokoloff) and articles on comparable worth. As associate director of labor relations at the Massachusetts Nurses Association, Dr. Feldberg is beginning a study of the origins and meanings of part-time work among nurses.

MARY FRANK FOX is associate professor of sociology and women's studies at Pennsylvania State University. Her research focuses upon stratification processes in science and academia and gender stratification in organizations and occupations. She has published in over twenty different scholarly journals and collections. She is an Associate Editor of *Gender & Society,* Editorial Board Member of *Work and Occupations,* and past Chair of the Sex and Gender Section of the American Sociological Association. She is a Council Member and the Publication Chair of the Society for the Social Studies of Science.

EVELYN NAKANO GLENN teaches at the State University of New York, Binghamton, where she is professor of sociology and women's studies. Her research focuses on women's work, with particular emphasis on race and gender hierarchies and technology. In addition to co-authoring many articles on transformations in clerical work, she has written extensively on the work and family lives of racial/ethnic women. She is the author of *Issei, Nisei Warbride: Three Generations of Japanese American Women in Domestic Service,* and she is a member of the Women and Work Research Group, which recently published a collection of articles, *Hidden Aspects of Women's Work.*

LOIS M. GREENWOOD-AUDANT received her Ph.D. in political science in 1980 from the University of California at Berkeley. She has worked as an organizational evaluation consultant for Berkeley Planning Associates and for the Displaced Homemakers Center in Oakland, California. She was the principal investigator for a national evaluation of demonstration projects for displaced homemakers funded by the U.S. Department of Labor; this evaluation resulted in a five-volume study of displaced homemaker programs throughout the nation. For five years, she taught political science and women's studies courses as a lecturer at the University of California at Berkeley and at Davis. She is a member of the Women's Caucus for Political Science and served as its San Francisco Bay Area coordinator for three years. In 1984 she was the director of a Cross-Cultural Communication Program for U.C. Berkeley Extension and lectures on the subject of women, work, and power.

NAOMI GERSTEL is an associate professor of sociology at the University of Massachusetts, Amherst. With a grant from the Rockefeller Foundation, she is currently conducting research on changes in the meaning and practice of "charity work" and caregiving that occur with women's entrance into the labor force. She is co-author (with Harriet Gross) of *Commuter Marriage* and co-editor of *Families and Work.* Her articles on marriage and divorce have appeared in such journals as *Gender & Society, Journal of Marriage and the Family, Social Forces, Social Problems,* and a number of anthologies.

HARRIET ENGEL GROSS is professor of sociology at Governors State University, where she is responsible for the graduate program in Family Studies. She is currently engaged in research with Professor Grace Budrys of DePaul University on physicians' responses to alternative health care delivery systems. She is co-editor with Naomi Gerstel, of *Families and Work* (1987) and *Commuter Marriage* (1984).

NANCY HENLEY is professor of psychology at the University of California at Los Angeles. Her research in recent years has focused on gender and communication, both verbal and nonverbal. Dr. Henley's published works include *Body Politics: Power, Sex and Nonverbal Communication* (1977), *Language and Sex: Difference and Dominance* (co-edited with Barrie Thorne, 1975), *Gender and Nonverbal Behavior* (co-edited with Clara Mayo, 1981), and *Language, Gender and Society* (co-edited with Barrie Thorne and Cheris Kramarae, 1983).

DIANNE HERMAN is Director of Community Mental Health Services for the Montgomery County Board of Mental Health in Dayton, Ohio. She is a Licensed Social Worker in the State of Ohio. At Family Service Association, she managed the SCAN Program, which provides prevention and treatment for victims and perpetrators of child abuse and neglect. She also directed a shelter for victims of domestic violence and their children. She teaches a course on Family Violence and produced a television edition of the course for Sinclair Community College. She has presented at numerous workshops on sexual assault, incest, and battered women.

MICHELE HOFFNUNG is professor of psychology at Quinnipiac College in Hamden, Connecticut. Since 1969, she has been teaching psychology of women, psychology of motherhood, and other women's studies courses. She is the editor of *Roles Women Play: Readings Toward Women's Liberation* (1971) and the author of articles about childbirth, child care, motherhood, and feminist teaching. Her current research focuses on the experience of motherhood for contemporary women; she is also active in revising the liberal arts curriculum to integrate women. She is mother of three children.

DEBRA RENEE KAUFMAN is professor of sociology and the coordinator of the women's studies program at Northeastern University in Boston, Massachusetts. Her book length scholarly works include: *Achievement and Women: Challenging the Assumptions* (1982, co-authored with B. Richardson and nominated for the C. Wright Mills Award for notable contributions to sociological thought); *Public/Private Spheres: Women Past and Present* (edited volume to be published by Northeastern University Customs Textbooks, Spring 1989); *Coming Home: The Feminine Awakening Among Newly Orthodox Jewish Women* (forthcoming Rutgers University Press, 1990). She has published numerous articles on related topics. She regularly reviews for *Gender and Society,* actively supports Sociologists for Women in Society, and is a member of the Princeton Advisory Board on women's studies. She was the twenty-third annual Robert D. Klein lecturer at Northeastern University in recognition of her outstanding scholarly achievement, professional contribution, and creative classroom activity. Her lecture was entitled: ''Religious Revival in America: Awakening the Feminine'' (published by Northeastern University Press, Annual Publication Series, 1987).

MICHAEL S. KIMMEL is a sociologist at State University of New York at Stony Brook, where he teaches courses on gender, social movements, sexuality, and social theory. His books include *Against the Tide: Pro-Feminist Men in America, 1830–1987,* a documentary history co-edited with Tom Mosmiller (Beacon Press, in press), *Changing Men: New Directions in Research on Men and Masculinity* (Sage Publications, 1987), *Men Confronting Pornography* (Crown Books, in press), and *Men's Lives: Readings on Men Through the Life Course,* co-edited with Michael Messner (Macmillan, in press). He is currently working on *Gender and Desire* with John Gagnon (Basic Books), which is a study of the ways in which sexual experience is organized by and filtered through masculinity and femininity. He is the book editor of the magazine, *Changing Men,* and he has served on the National Council of the National Organization for Changing Men.

HILARY M. LIPS received her Ph.D in social psychology from Northwestern University in 1974. Currently, she is a professor of psychology at the University of Winnipeg, where for fourteen years she has been teaching undergraduate courses in social psychology, social conflict, and the psychology of sex and gender. During that time, she has also been active in the development and administration of the women's studies program. Her research interests lie mainly in the social psychology of gender. She is currently engaged in a series of studies examining the processes through which gender differences emerge in students' avoidance or pursuit of university-level science and mathematics. She recently completed a textbook for undergraduate courses in the psychology of sex and gender (*Sex and Gender: An Introduction*, Mayfield, Publishing Co., 1988), and she is working on a new book, *Women, Men, and Power*.

JUDITH LORBER is professor of sociology at Brooklyn College and at the Graduate Center, City University of New York, where she directs the women's studies certificate program. She is the author of *Women Physicians: Careers, Status, and Power*, published in 1984 by Tavistock/Methuen, New York and London, and numerous articles on helps and hindrances in the careers of professional women. She is the founding editor of *Gender & Society*, official publication of Sociologists for Women in Society. Her current research is on couples' experiences with *in vitro* fertilization.

SUSAN E. MARSHALL is associate professor of sociology at the University of Texas at Austin, where she is also affiliated with the women's studies program. She has published numerous articles on the impact of Islamic revivals on women and on the relationship between underdevelopment and gender inequality. Her research on American antifeminist movements has also appeared in *Social Forces* and *Social Problems*. Her current research projects include analyses of gender, class, and race differences in gender consciousness. She is also writing a social history of the antisuffrage movement in the United States.

SUSAN EHRLICH MARTIN is a project director at the Police Foundation. She is currently conducting studies of the status of women in policing and of the police handling of child abuse and neglect cases. She is author of *"Breaking and Entering": Policewomen on Patrol* (1980) and co-editor of *Research on Sentencing: the Search for Reform* (1983). She has published articles on women in policing, law, and criminal justice policy issues in *Symbolic Interaction, Criminology*, and *Justice Quarterly*. She is a chair of the Task Force on Domestic Violence of the Montgomery County, Maryland National Organization for Women and a member of Sociologists for Women in Society.

ANNE H. NELSON is director of the Institute for Women and Work of Cornell University's School of Industrial and Labor Relations. She is a commissioner of the National Commission on Working Women, past president of the University and College Labor Education Association, and a founding member of the Coalition of Labor Union Women. She is co-author of *Trade Union Women: A Study of Their Participation in New York City Locals (1975)* and of the chapter "Policy Implications," (in *The Worth of Women's Work: A Qualitative Synthesis*, 1988). In addition, she co-edited *Women as Third-Party Neutrals* with Barbara M. Wertheimer. A contributor to numerous journals, most recently to the Women's Bureau, U. S. Department of Labor publication, *Flexible Workstyles* (1988), where she wrote on the temporary labor force and its effect on women.

JILL NORGREN is professor of government and public administration at John Jay College, The City University of New York. She has been interested in issues of family policy for many years. In addition to popular and scholarly articles on family policy, Norgren has participated in neighborhood efforts to establish child care programs. She received a Rockefeller Foundation Humanities Fellowship in 1980. Her reviews and articles have appeared in the *New York Times, The Nation, Howard Law Journal, The American Political Science Review, Western Political Quarterly,* and several anthologies. In the summer of 1983 she traveled throughout Japan interviewing women and men about their attitudes concerning family roles.

DIANA M. PEARCE received her Ph.D. in sociology and social work from the University of Michigan in 1976. Her research has addressed such subjects as women in poverty, housing discrimination, school desegregation, and urban inequality. She is currently director of the Women and Poverty Project, which she started in 1985, and which is now located at the Institute for Women's Policy Research in Washington, DC. In addition to teaching and research, she has testified before Congress, served as expert witness in civil rights cases, consulted with fair housing groups, helped organize the National Coalition on Women, Work, and Welfare Reform, and has spoken widely on women's inequality and poverty. Her published works include "The Feminization of Poverty: Women, Work, and Welfare" (1978), *Women and Children: Alone and in Poverty* (co-authored with Harriette McAdoo, 1981) and, as a member of the Women's Economic Agenda Working Group, co-author of *Towards Economic Justice: A National Agenda for Change.* Her current work focuses on women and federal and state welfare reform, women and housing and homelessness, and the marginal status of women in the labor force.

LETITIA ANNE PEPLAU is professor of social psychology at the University of California, Los Angeles. At UCLA, she has been active in the women's studies program, has served as the Associate Director of the Center for the Study of Women, and teaches courses on the psychology of gender. Her research has focused on the impact of gender and changing gender roles on intimate relationships, including studies of dating, friendship, and lesbian/gay relationships. Her publications include *Close Relationships* (co-authored with Harold Kelley et al., 1983), *Loneliness* (co-edited with Dan Perlman, 1982) and *Social Psychology* (co-authored with David Sears, Shelley Taylor, and Jonathan Freedman, 1988).

MARTHA J. REINEKE received her Ph.D. from Vanderbilt University in 1983. She is an assistant professor of religion at the University of Northern Iowa where she teaches courses in women's studies, religion and society, and world religions. Her published works include articles in *Philosophy and Theology, Feminist Ethnics,* and *Soundings.* She is currently working on a book, influenced by Julia Kristeva and René Girard, in which she will probe the coincidence of violence and the sacred in the history of Western culture from a feminist perspective.

BARBARA KATZ ROTHMAN is professor of sociology at Baruch College and the Graduate Center of the City University of New York. She is the author of *In Labor: Women and Power in the Birthplace*, also published in paperback as *Giving Birth*, a comparison of the medical and midwifery models of childbirth; and of *The Tentative Pregnancy: Prenatal Diagnosis and the Future of Motherhood*, a study of women's experiences with amniocentesis and selective abortion; and most recently, *Recreating Motherhood: Ideology and Technology in a Patriarchal Society*, a feminist analysis of changing ideas about motherhood in America.

CAROLE J. SHEFFIELD is an associate professor of political science and women's studies at the William Paterson College of New Jersey. She was a founding member of the college's women's studies program and teaches in both the Women's Studies and the Race and Gender Programs. She was the architect for the college's sexual harassment policy and is presently co-chairing a project on campus violence. Sheffield lectures widely and continues to publish on issues of feminism and violence against women. Her current work focuses on sexual terrorism in a global perspective.

KATHLEEN K. SHORTRIDGE became involved in the women's movement in 1970 when, as a graduate student in journalism, she undertook a study of the status of women at the University of Michigan. The study's findings provided a basis for women's groups to begin to demand change in the institution. Shortridge has worked with numerous local and university women's and civil rights groups in Michigan and in Kentucky. She has been employed as an editor, a university administrator, a farmer, and as director of affirmative action at the University of Louisville. She completed her law degree at the University of Louisville and now practices law in Indianapolis, Indiana.

JANICE M. STEIL received her Ph.D. from Columbia University. She is currently an associate professor of social psychology at the Institute of Advanced Psychological Studies at Adelphi University in New York. Her primary research interests are in the area of the psychology of justice and the psychology of women. Her publications include review chapters in several books as well as the reporting of her research in major psychology journals. A study testing the hypotheses of the chapter in this volume was published in 1987 in the *Applied Social Psychology Annual*.

In 1984, PAULINE TERRELONGE was an assistant professor of political science and Afro-American and African studies at the University of Michigan at Ann Arbor. She holds advanced degrees in law and political science. She has taught courses on women in political theory, black women in America, and legal policy. She is the author of articles in a number of scholarly journals on the subject of black politicians in American society and has done research on women in the Caribbean. Her current work is on United States immigration policy.

NANCY THEBERGE is an associate professor at the University of Waterloo in

Canada, where she holds a joint appointment in the Departments of Kinesiology and Sociology. She has a Ph.D. in sociology from the University of Massachusetts at Amherst. She has published extensively on the subjects of women in sport, feminist theory and sport, and the organization of amateur sport in Canada. A co-editor (with Peter Donnelly) of *Sport and the Sociological Imagination,* she is also a founding member of the Canadian Association for the Advancement of Women and Sport.

NORMA C. WARE is a research fellow in the program in medical anthropology at Harvard Medical School. She received the Ph.D. in Anthropology and Linguistics from the University of Michigan. She has done research on factors predicting the choice of a scientific major for college men and women, on the prevalence and correlates of bulimia in college women, and on the present life patterns of men and women who graduated from college in the mid-seventies. Her present research interests center on the relationship between culture and mental health.

ROSE WEITZ is an associate professor of sociology at Arizona State University. With Deborah A. Sullivan, she recently published the book *Labor Pains: Modern Midwives and Home Birth* (Yale University Press, 1988). Her current research focuses on the sociology of AIDS.

BARBARA M. WERTHEIMER was professor at the New York State School of Industrial and Labor Relations, Cornell University, and director of the Institute for Education and Research on Women and Work. A long-time labor educator and the author and editor of many books and articles in this field and on the subject of women's role in the work force, she died in 1983. Her books include *We Were There: The Story of Working Women in America* (1977), *Women as Third-Party Neutrals* (co-edited with Anne H. Nelson, 1978), and *Labor Education for Women Workers* (1980).

ANNE E. WINKLER is a Ph.D. candidate in economics at the University of Illinois at Urbana-Champaign specializing in labor economics. Her dissertation focuses on the incentive effects of Medicaid on women's labor supply. As a research assistant at the Bureau of Economics and Business Research at the University of Illinois, she has written articles on public aid in Illinois which have appeared in Bureau publications.

JANICE D. YODER, presently a Business Analyst for M&I Data Services, Inc., was an associate professor of psychology and coordinator of women's studies at Webster University in St. Louis when much of this research was conducted. She was one of the first civilian women to teach at West Point as a distinguished visiting professor in 1980. Her work on the social psychology of gender appears in journals such as *Psychology of Women Quarterly, Sex Roles, International Journal of Women's Studies, Gender and Society,* and the *Journal of Social Issues.* She co-authored the book, *Effective Leadership for Women and Men* (1985).

Part One

The Body and Its Control

Sexual Terrorism*

CAROLE J. SHEFFIELD

No two of us think alike about it, and yet it is clear to me, that question underlies the whole movement, and our little skirmishing for better laws, and the right to vote, will yet be swallowed up in the real question, viz: Has a woman a right to herself? It is very little to me to have the right to vote, to own property, etc., if I may not keep my body, and its uses, in my absolute right. Not one wife in a thousand can do that now.

Lucy Stone, in a letter to Antoinette Brown, July 11, 1855

The right of men to control the female body is a cornerstone of patriarchy. It is expressed by their efforts to control pregnancy and childbirth and to define female health care in general. Male opposition to abortion is rooted in opposition to female autonomy. Violence and the threat of violence against females represent the need of patriarchy to deny that a woman's body is her own property and that no one should have access to it without her consent. Violence and its corollary, fear, serve to terrorize females and to maintain the patriarchal definition of woman's place.

The word *terrorism* invokes images of furtive organizations of the far right or left, whose members blow up buildings and cars, hijack airplanes, and murder innocent people in some country other than ours. But there is a different kind of terrorism, one that so pervades our culture that we have learned to live with it as though it were the natural order of things. Its targets are females — of all ages, races, and classes. It is the common characteristic of rape, wife battery, incest, pornography, harassment, and all forms of sexual violence. I call it *sexual terrorism* because it is a system by which males frighten and, by frightening, control and dominate females.

The concept of terrorism captured my attention in an "ordinary" event. One afternoon I collected my laundry and went to a nearby laundromat. The place is located in a small shopping center on a very busy highway. After I had loaded and started the machines, I became acutely aware of my environ-

---

ment. It was just after 6:00 P.M. and dark; the other stores were closed; the laundromat was brightly lit; and my car was the only one in the lot. Anyone passing by could readily see that I was alone and isolated. Knowing that rape is a crime of opportunity, I became terrified. I wanted to leave and find a laundromat that was busier, but my clothes were well into the wash cycle, and, besides, I felt I was being "silly," "paranoid." The feeling of terror persisted, so I sat in my car, windows up, and doors locked. When the wash was completed, I dashed in, threw the clothes into the drier, and ran back out to my car. When the clothes were dry, I tossed them recklessly into the basket and hurriedly drove away to fold them in the security of my home.

Although I was not victimized in a direct, physical way or by objective or measurable standards, I felt victimized. It was, for me, a terrifying experience. I felt controlled by an invisible force. I was angry that something as commonplace as doing laundry after a day's work jeopardized my well-being. Mostly I was angry at being unfree: a hostage of a culture that, for the most part, encourages violence against females, instructs men in the methodology of sexual violence, and provides them with ready justification for their violence. I was angry that I could be victimized by being "in the wrong place at the wrong time." The essence of terrorism is that one never knows when is the wrong time and where is the wrong place.

Following my experience at the laundromat, I talked with my students about terrorization. Women students began to open up and reveal terrors that they had kept secret because of embarrassment: fears of jogging alone, dining alone, going to the movies alone. One woman recalled feelings of terror in her adolescence when she did child care for extra money. Nothing had ever happened and she had not been afraid of anyone in particular, but she had felt a vague terror when being driven home late at night by the man of the house.

The men listened incredulously and then demanded equal time. The harder they tried the more they realized how very different — qualitatively, quantitatively, and contextually — their fears were. All agreed that, while they experienced fear in a violent society, they did not experience terror; nor did they experience fear of rape or sexual mutilation. They felt more in control, either from a psychophysical sense of security that they could defend themselves or from a confidence in being able to determine wrong places and times. All the women admitted fear and anxiety when walking to their cars on the campus, especially after an evening class or activity. None of the men experienced fear on campus at any time. The men could be rather specific in describing when they were afraid: in Harlem, for example, or in certain parts of downtown Paterson, New Jersey — places that have a reputation for violence. But they could either avoid these places or, if not, the men felt capable of self-protective action. Above all, male students said that they *never* feared being attacked simply because they were male. They *never* feared going to a movie or to dinner alone. Their daily activities were not characterized by a concern for their physical integrity.

As I read the literature on terrorism it became clear that both sexual violence and nonviolent sexual intimidation could be better understood as terrorism. For example, although an act of rape, an unnecessary hysterectomy, and the publishing of *Playboy* magazine appear to be quite different, they are in fact more similar than dissimilar. Each is based on fear, hostility, and a need to dominate women. Rape is an act of aggression and possession, not of sexuality. Unnecessary hysterectomies are extraordinary abuses of power rooted in man's concept of woman as primarily a reproductive being and in his need to assert power over reproduction. *Playboy,* like all forms of pornography, attempts to control women through the power of definition. Male pornographers define women's sexuality for their male customers. The basis of pornography is men's fantasies about women's sexuality.

COMPONENTS OF SEXUAL TERRORISM

The literature on terrorism does not provide a precise definition.[1] Mine is taken from Hacker, who says that "terrorism aims to frighten, and by frightening, to dominate and control."[2] Writers agree more readily on the characteristics and functions of terrorism than on a definition. This analysis will focus on five components to illuminate the similarities of and distinctions between sexual terrorism and political terrorism. The five components are ideology, propaganda, indiscriminate and amoral violence, voluntary compliance, and society's perception of the terrorist and the terrorized.

An *ideology* is an integrated set of beliefs about the world that explains the way things are and provides a vision of how they ought to be. Patriarchy, meaning the "rule of the fathers," is the ideological foundation of sexism in our society. It asserts the superiority of males and the inferiority of females. It also provides the rationale for sexual terrorism. The taproot of patriarchy is the masculine/warrior ideal. Masculinity must include not only a proclivity for violence but also all those characteristics necessary for survival: aggression, control, emotional reserve, rationality, sexual potency, etc. Marc Feigen Fasteau, in *The Male Machine,* argues that "men are brought up with the idea that there ought to be some part of them, under control until released by necessity, that thrives on violence. This capacity, even affinity, for violence, lurking beneath the surface of every real man, is supposed to represent the primal untamed base of masculinity."[3]

Propaganda is the methodical dissemination of information for the purpose of promoting a particular ideology. Propaganda, by definition, is biased or even false information. Its purpose is to present one point of view on a subject and to discredit opposing points of view. Propaganda is essential to the conduct of terrorism. According to Francis Watson, in *Political Terrorism: The Threat and the Response,* "Terrorism must not be defined only in terms of violence, but also in terms of propaganda. The two are in operation together. Violence of terrorism is a coercive means for attempting to influence the thinking and actions of people. Propaganda is a persuasive means for doing the same thing."[4] The propaganda of sexual terrorism is found in all expressions of the popular culture: films, television, music, literature, advertising, pornography. The propaganda of sexual terrorism is also found in the ideas of patriarchy expressed in science, medicine, and psychology.

The third component, which is common to all forms of political terrorism, consists of "indiscriminateness, unpredictability, arbitrariness, ruthless destructiveness and amorality."[5] Indiscriminate violence and amorality are also at the heart of sexual terrorism. Every female is a potential target of violence—at any age, at any time, in any place. In her study of rape, Susan Brownmiller argues that rape is "nothing more or less than a conscious process of intimidation by which all men keep all women in a state of fear."[6] Further, as we shall see, amorality pervades sexual violence. Child molesters, incestuous fathers, wife beaters, and rapists often do not understand that they have done anything wrong. Their views are routinely shared by police officers, lawyers, and judges, and crimes of sexual violence are rarely punished in American society.

The fourth component of the theory of terrorism is "voluntary compliance." The institutionalization of a system of terror requires the development of mechanisms other than sustained violence to achieve its goals. Violence must be employed to maintain terrorism, but sustained violence can be costly and debilitating. Therefore, strategies for ensuring a significant degree of voluntary compliance must be developed. Sexual terrorism is maintained to a great extent by an elaborate system of sex-role socialization that in effect instructs men to be terrorists in the name of masculinity and women to be victims in the name of femininity.

Sexual and political terrorism differ in the final component, perception of the terrorist and the victim. In political terrorism we know who is the terrorist and who is the victim. We may condemn or condone the terrorist depending on our political views, but we sympathize with the victim. In sexual terrorism, however, we blame the victim and excuse the offender. We believe that the offender either is "sick" and therefore in need of our compassion or is acting out normal male impulses.

TYPES OF SEXUAL TERRORISM

Many types of sexual terrorism are crimes. Yet when we look at the history of these acts we see that they came to be considered criminal not so much to protect women as to adjust power relationships among men. Rape was originally a violation of a father's or husband's property right; consequently, a husband by definition could not rape his wife. Wife beating was condoned by the law and still is condemned in name only. The pornographic presentation of sexual violence serves to direct male violence against women and girls and to contain male violence toward other men.[7] Although proscriptions against incest exist, society assumes a more serious posture toward men who sexually abuse other men's daughters. Sexual harassment is not a crime, and only recently has it been declared an actionable civil offense. Crimes of sexual violence are characterized by ambiguity and diversity in definition and interpretation. Because each state and territory has a separate system of law in addition to the federal system, crimes and punishments are assessed differently throughout the country.

Rape

The most generally accepted definition of rape is "sexual intercourse with a female, not the wife of the perpetrator, without the consent of the female."[8] Seventeen states punish rape within marriage.[9]

Because rape is considered a sexual act, evidence of force and resistance (that is, nonconsent) plays a major role in the conviction or acquittal of rapists. Proof of nonconsent and resistance is not demanded of a victim of any other crime. If one is stopped on the street and robbed one never has to justify nonresistance or prove resistance and nonconsent. Females are expected to resist rape as much as possible, otherwise "consent" is assumed.

John M. MacDonald, in *Rape Offenders and Their Victims,* offers the following advice to law enforcement officials: "To constitute resistance in good faith it must have been commenced at the inception of the advances and continued until the offense was consummated. Resistance by mere words is not sufficient, but such resistance must be by acts, and must be reasonably proportionate to the strength and opportunities of the woman."[10] Passive resistance or compliance, even in a situation that is perceived to be life-threatening, is not, to many prosecutors, clear evidence that the rape was against one's will.

Wife Assault

For centuries it has been assumed that a husband had the right to punish or discipline his wife with physical force. The popular expression, "rule of thumb," originated from English common law, which allowed a husband to beat his wife with a whip or stick no bigger in diameter than his thumb. The husband's prerogative was incorporated into American law. Several states had statutes that essentially allowed a man to beat his wife without interference from the courts.[11]

In 1871, in the landmark case of *Fulgham v. State,* an Alabama court ruled that "the privilege, ancient though it be, to beat her with a stick, to pull her hair, choke her, spit in her face or kick her about the floor or to inflict upon her other like indignities, is not now acknowledged by our law."[12] The law, however, has been ambiguous and often contradictory on the issue of wife assault. While the courts established that a man had no right to beat his wife, it also held that a woman could not press charges against her abusive husband. In 1910, the U.S. Supreme Court ruled that a wife could not charge her husband with assault and battery because it "would open the doors of the courts to accusations of all sorts of one spouse against the other and bring into public notice complaints for assaults, slander and libel."[13] The courts virtually condoned violence for the purpose of maintaining peace.

Laws and public attitudes about the illegality of wife assault and the rights of the victim have been evolving slowly, and attempts are being made to resolve the contradictions. Only three states (California, Hawaii, and Texas) define wife abuse as a felony.[14] In other states, laws applicable to wife battery include assault, assault and battery, aggravated assault, intent to assault or to commit murder, and possession of a deadly weapon with intent to assault.

Sexual Abuse of Children

Defining sexual abuse of children is very difficult. The laws are complex and often contradictory. Generally, sexual abuse of children includes statutory rape, molestation, carnal knowledge, indecent liberties, impairing the morals of a minor, child abuse, child neglect, and incest. Each of these is defined and interpreted differently in each state. Convictions run the gamut from misdemeanors to various degrees of assault and felony. Punishments vary widely from state to state as well.

The philosophy underlying statutory-rape laws is that a child below a certain age — arbitrarily fixed by law — is not able to give meaningful consent. Therefore, sexual intercourse with a female below a certain age, with or without the use of force, is a criminal act of rape. Punishment for statutory rape, although rarely imposed, can be as high as life imprisonment. Coexistent with laws on statutory rape are laws on criminal incest. Incest is generally interpreted as sexual activity, most often intercourse, with a blood relative. The difference, then, between statutory rape and incest is the relation of the offender to the child. Statutory rape is committed by someone outside the family; incest, by a member of the family. The penalty for incest, also rarely imposed, is usually no more than ten years in prison. This contrast suggests that sexual abuse of children is tolerated when it occurs within the family and that unqualified protection of children from sexual assault is not the intent of the law.

Sexual Harassment

Sexual harassment is a new term for an old phenomenon. The research on sexual harassment, as well as the legal interpretation, centers on acts of sexual coercion or intimidation on the job and at school. Lin Farley, in *Sexual Shakedown: The Sexual Harassment of Women on the Job*, describes sexual harassment as "unsolicited nonreciprocal male behavior that asserts a woman's sex role over her function as a worker. It can be any or all of the following: staring at, commenting upon, or touching a woman's body; requests for acquiescence in sexual behavior; repeated nonreciprocated propositions for dates; demands for sexual intercourse; and rape."[15]

Sexual harassment is now considered a form of sex discrimination under some conditions and is therefore a violation of Title VII of the 1964 Civil Rights Act, which prohibits sex discrimination in employment, and of Title IX of the 1972 Education Amendments, which prohibits sex-based discrimination in education.

CHARACTERISTICS OF SEXUAL TERRORISM

Those forms of sexual terrorism that are crimes share several common characteristics. Each will be addressed separately, but in the real world these characteristics are linked together and form a vicious circle, which functions to mask the reality of sexual terrorism and thus to perpetuate the system of oppression of females. Crimes of violence against females (1) cut across socioeconomic lines; (2) are the crimes least likely to be reported; (3) when reported, are the crimes least likely to be brought to trial or to result in conviction; (4) are often blamed on the victim; (5) are generally not taken seriously; and (6) are not really about sex.

The question "Who is the typical rapist, wife beater, incest offender, etc?" is raised constantly. The answer is simple: men. Even among those who commit incest, women are exceedingly rare. The men who commit acts of sexual terrorism are of all ages, races, and religions; they come from all communities, income levels, and educational levels; they are married, single, separated, and divorced. The typical sexually abusive male does not exist.

One of the most common assumptions about sexual violence is that it occurs primarily among the poor, uneducated, and predominately nonwhite populations. Instead, violence committed by the poor and nonwhite is simply more visible because these people lack the resources to ensure the privacy that the middle and upper classes can purchase. Most rapes, indeed most incidents of sexual assault, are not reported, and therefore the picture drawn from police records must be viewed as very sketchy.

The data on sexual harassment in work situations indicate that it occurs among all job categories and pay ranges.[16] Sexual harassment is committed by academic men, who are among the most highly educated members of society.

All the studies on wife battery testify to the fact that wife beating crosses socioeconomic lines. Wife beaters include high government officials, members of the armed forces, businessmen, policemen, physicians, lawyers, clergy, blue-collar workers, and the unemployed.[17] According to Maria Roy, founder and director of New York's Abused Women's Aid in Crisis: "We see abuse of women on all levels of income, age, occupation, and social standing. I've had four women come in recently whose husbands are Ph.D.s— two of them professors at top universities. Another abused woman is married to a very prominent attorney. We counseled battered wives whose husbands are doctors, psychiatrists, even clergymen."[18]

Similarly, in Vincent De Francis's classic study of 250 cases of sexual crimes committed against children, a major finding was that incidents of sexual assault against children cut across class lines.[19]

Since sexual violence is not "nice," we prefer to believe that nice men do not commit these acts and that nice girls and women are not victims. Our refusal to accept the fact that violence against females is widespread on all levels of society strongly inhibits our ability to develop any meaningful strategies directed toward the elimination of sexual violence. Moreover, because of underreporting, it is difficult to ascertain exactly how widespread it is.

Crimes of Sexual Violence Are the Least Likely to Be Reported

The underreporting issue, often called the "tip-of-the-iceberg theory," is common to all crimes against females. The FBI recognizes that rape is the most frequently committed violent crime that is seriously underreported. According to FBI data for 1987, 91,111 rapes were reported.[20] The FBI and other criminologists suggest that this figure be multiplied by at least a factor of ten to compensate for underreporting. The FBI *Uniform Crime Report* for

1987 estimates that a forcible rape occurs every six minutes.[21] This estimate is based on reported cases; to account for the high rate of underreporting the FBI estimates that a rape occurs every two minutes. The number of forcible rapes reported to the police has been increasing every year. Between 1978 and 1987, there was a 21 percent increase in reported forcible rapes.[22] It is estimated that one-half of all rape victims are under eighteen years of age and 25 percent of rape victims are under twelve years of age.[23]

The FBI's *Uniform Crime Report* indexes 10 million reported crimes a year but does not collect statistics on wife abuse. Since statutes in most states do not identify wife beating as a crime, incidents of wife beating are usually classified under "assault and battery" and "disputes." However, the FBI estimates that wife abuse is three times as common as rape. Estimates that 50 percent of American wives are battered are not uncommon in the literature.[24]

"The problem of sexual abuse of children is of unknown national dimensions," according to Vincent De Francis, "but findings strongly point to the probability of an enormous national incidence many times larger than the reported incidence of physical abuse of children."[25] He discussed the existence of a wide gap between the reported incidence and the actual occurrence of sexual assault against children and suggested that "the reported incidence represents the top edge of the moon as it rises over the mountain."[26]

Incest, according to author and researcher Florence Rush, is the *Best Kept Secret.*[27] The estimates, however speculative, are frightening. Alfred Kinsey, in a study involving 4,441 female subjects, found that 24 percent had been approached sexually by an adult male prior to their adolescence; in 23 percent of the cases that adult male was a relative.[28] Significantly, all the respondents in the Kinsey study were white and predominately middle class. The Child Sexual Abuse Project in San Jose, California, estimates that there are approximately 26,000 cases of father–daughter incest each year. This estimate excludes incestuous behavior by grandfathers, uncles, brothers, cousins.[29] Cases reported to the Santa Clara Child Sexual Abuse Treatment Program increased from 31 in 1974 to 269 in 1976, suggesting that the incidence of incest may be grossly underestimated.[30] Child-protection organizations estimate that the number of reported incidents of child sexual abuse ranges from one hundred thousand to 1 million and that the majority of sexual assaults against children are not reported.[31]

Accurate data on the incidence of sexual harassment are impossible to obtain. Women have traditionally accepted sexual innuendo as a fact of life and only recently have begun to report and analyze the dimensions of sexual coercion in the workplace. Research indicates that sexual harassment is pervasive. Lin Farley found that accounts of sexual harassment within the federal government, the country's largest single employer, are extensive and that surveys of working women in the private sector indicate "a dangerously high rate of incidence of this abuse."[32]

In 1976, over nine thousand women responded to a survey on sexual harassment conducted by *Redbook* magazine. More than 92 percent reported sexual harassment as a problem; a majority of the respondents described it as serious; and nine out of ten reported that they had personally experienced one or more forms of unwanted sexual attentions on the job.[33] The Ad Hoc Group on Equal Rights for Women attempted to gather data on sexual harassment at the United Nations. The questionnaire was confiscated by UN officials, but 875 staff members had already responded; 73 percent were women, and more than half of them said that they had personally experienced or were aware of incidents of sexual harassment at the UN.[34] In May 1975, the Women's Section of the Human Affairs Program at Cornell University, Ithaca, New York, distributed the first questionnaire on sexual harassment. Of the 155 respondents, 92 percent identified sexual harassment as a serious problem; 70 percent had personally experienced some form of sexual harassment; and 56 percent reported incidents of physical harassment.[35]

A pilot study conducted by the National Advisory Council on Women's Educational Programs on Sexual Harassment in Academia concluded:

> The sexual harassment of postsecondary students is an increasingly visible problem of great, but as yet unascertained, dimensions. Once regarded as an isolated, purely personal problem, it has gained civil rights credibility as its scale and consequences have become known, and is correctly viewed as a form of illegal sex-based discrimination.[36]

Crimes of Violence Against Females Have the Lowest Conviction Rates

The common denominator in the underreporting of all sexual assaults is fear. Females have been well trained in silence and passivity. Early and sustained sex-role socialization teaches that women are responsible for the sexual behavior of men and that women cannot be trusted. These beliefs operate together. They function to keep women silent about their victimization and to keep other people from believing women when they do come forward. The victim's fear that she will not be believed and, as a consequence, that the offender will not be punished is not unrealistic. Sex offenders are rarely punished in our society.

Rape has the lowest conviction rate of all violent crimes. On a national average, one rapist in twenty is arrested, one out of thirty prosecuted, and one in sixty is convicted.[37] In *Forcible Rape: The Crime, the Victim, and the Offender,* the authors report that the conviction rate for Los Angeles County is less than 10 percent[38] and that "in no recent year have more than eight percent of rape arrests resulted in rape convictions" in New York City. The authors conclude that rapists in New York City have enjoyed "almost complete immunity" from prosecution.[39]

Data on prosecution and conviction of wife beaters are practically non-existent. According to Roger Langley and Richard Levy, authors of *Wife-Beating: The Silent Crisis,* "the vast majority of wife-beaters are never prosecuted. In fact, they are seldom even charged. The battered wife has to overcome an incredible array of roadblocks and detours built into the legal system before she can prosecute her husband."[40]

The roadblocks are both technical and attitudinal. The laws on wife beating are confusing and vary from state to state. Their application varies with the attitudes and beliefs of law-enforcement personnel. Police indifference to wife beating has been extensively documented by victims.

Dee Zurbrium of Laurel, Maryland, says she called police for help and was told, "We can't get involved in a domestic quarrel, Lady. The best thing you can do is get out of there because next time you may be dead."

The *Detroit Free Press,* in an article headlined "Emergency Number Still Has Kinks," reports: "A near-breathless woman, beaten by her husband, dialed 911 to ask for police assistance. 'Does he have a weapon?' the operator asked.
"She answered he did not.
" 'Then I am sorry. We won't be able to help you,' the operator said to the dismayed woman."

One woman called the police after her husband broke her nose. They took her to the hospital, bleeding and with both eyes swelling shut, but they refused to arrest her husband. "You don't want to do that, honey," said the cop, reassuringly. "It's something that happens in every man's life."[41]

It is routine policy for police officers and lawyers to discourage women from filing charges against an abusive husband. The instructors at the Police Training Academy in Michigan use the following guidelines in teaching police officers how to convince a woman not to press charges:

a. Avoid arrest if possible. Appeal to their vanity.
b. Explain the procedure of obtaining a warrant.
   (1) Complainant must sign complaint.
   (2) Must appear in court.
   (3) Consider loss of time.
   (4) Cost of court.
c. State that your only interest is to prevent a breach of the peace.
d. Explain that attitudes usually change by court time.
e. Recommend a postponement.
   (1) Court not in session.
   (2) No judge available.
f. Don't be too harsh or critical.[42]

It is also common practice for police officers and lawyers to use outright intimidation to convince battered women not to pursue the matter legally. Battered wives are confronted with statements or questions such as these: "You know he could lose his job." "Who will support you if he is locked up?" "Why don't you just kiss and make up?" "What did you do to make him hit you?" "Lady, why do you want to make trouble?"[43]

It is ironic that police officers do not view what they call a "domestic disturbance," "lover's quarrel," or "family spat" as serious. The category of "answering family disturbance calls" accounts for about 20 percent of the incidents of police killed on duty.[44]

According to Detroit Police Commander James Bannon:

The attrition rate in domestic violence cases is unbelievable. In 1972, for instance, there were 4,900 assaults of this kind which had survived the screening process long enough to at least have a warrant prepared and the complainant referred to the assault and battery squad. Through the process of conciliation, complainant harassment and prosecutor discretion, fewer than 300 of these cases were ultimately tried by a court of law. And in most of these the court used the judicial process to attempt to conciliate rather than adjudicate.[45]

Mr. Bannon argues: "You can readily understand why the women ultimately take the law into their own hands or despair of finding relief at all. *Or why the male feels protected by the system in his use of violence*" (emphasis mine).[46]

In his study of child sexual abuse, Vincent De Francis found that plea-bargaining and dismissal of cases were the norm. The study sample consisted of 173 cases brought to prosecution. Of these, 44 percent (seventy-six cases) were dismissed; 22 percent (thirty-eight cases) voluntarily accepted a lesser plea; 11 percent (six cases) were found guilty of a lesser charge; and 2 percent (four cases) were found guilty as charged. The remaining thirty-five cases were either pending (fifteen); terminated because the offender was committed to a mental institution (five) or because the offender absconded (seven); or no information was available (eight).

Of the fifty-three offenders who were convicted or pleaded guilty, thirty offenders escaped a jail sentence. Twenty-one received suspended sentences and were placed on probation; seven received suspended sentences without probation; and two were fined a sum of money. The other 45 percent (twenty-three offenders) received prison terms from under six months to three years; five were given indeterminate sentences — that is, a minimum term of one year and a maximum term subject to the discretion of the state board of parole.[47]

Most of the victims of sexual harassment in the Cornell University study were unwilling to use available procedures, such as grievances, to remedy their complaints, because they believed that nothing would be done. Their perception is based on reality; of the 12 percent who did complain, over half found that nothing was done in their cases.[48] The low adjudication and punishment rates of sexual-harassment cases are particularly revealing in light of the fact that the offender is known and identifiable and that there is no fear of "mistaken identity," as there is in rape cases. While offenders accused of familial violence — incest and wife abuse — are also known, the courts' posture is heavily in favor of keeping the family intact, or so they say. There is no such motivation in cases of sexual harassment.

Blaming the Victim of Sexual Violence Is Pervasive

The data on conviction rates of men who have committed acts of violence against females must be understood in the context of sociopolitical attitudes about women. The male-dominated society has evoked powerful myths to justify male violence against females and to ensure that these acts will rarely be punished. Victims of sexual violence are almost always suspect. We have developed an intricate network of beliefs and attitudes that perpetuate the idea that "victims of sex crimes have a hidden psychological need to be victimized."[49] We tend to believe either that the female willingly participated in her victimization or that she outright lied about it. Either way, we blame the victim and excuse or condone the offender.

Consider, for example, the operative myths about rape, wife battery, incest, and sexual harassment.

Rape

All women want to be raped.

No woman can be raped if she doesn't want it (you-can't-thread-a-moving-needle argument).

She asked for it.

She changed her mind afterwards.

When she says no she means yes.

If you are going to be raped you might as well enjoy it.

Wife Battery

Some women need to be beaten.

A good kick in the ass will straighten her out.

She needs a punch in the mouth every so often to keep her in line.

She must have done something to provoke him.

Incest

The child was the seducer.

The child imagined it.

Sexual Harassment

She was seductive.

She misunderstood, I was just being friendly.

Underlying all the myths about victims of sexual violence is the belief that the victim causes and is responsible for her victimization. Underlying the attitudes about the male offender is the belief that he could not help himself; that is, he was ruled by his biology and/or he was seduced. The victim becomes the offender and the offender becomes the victim. Clearly, two very important processes are at work here: blaming the victim and absolving the offender. These serve a vital political purpose: to protect our view of the world as orderly and just and to help us make sense of sexual violence. The rationale is that sexual violence against an innocent female is unjustifiable; therefore, she must have done something wrong or it would not have happened. Making a victim believe she is at fault erases not only the individual offender's culpability but also the responsibility of the society as a whole. Sexual violence becomes an individual problem, not a sociopolitical one.

One need only read the testimony of victims of sexual violence to see the powerful effects of blaming the victim. From the National Advisory Council on Women's Educational Programs Report on Sexual Harassment of Students:

I was ashamed, thought it was my fault, and was worried that the school would take action against me (for "unearned" grades) if they found out about it.

This happened seventeen years ago, and you are the first person I've been able to discuss it with in all that time. He's still at_____, and probably still doing it.

I'm afraid to tell anyone here about it, and I'm just hoping to get through the year so I can leave.[50]

From *Wife-Beating: The Silent Crisis,* Judge Stewart Oneglia comments:

Many women find it shameful to admit they don't have a good marriage. The battered wife wraps her bloody head in a towel, goes to the hospital, and explains to the doctor she fell down the stairs. After a few years of the husband telling her he beats her because she is ugly, stupid, or incompetent, she is so psychologically destroyed that she believes it.[51]

A battered woman from Boston relates:

I actually thought if I only learned to cook better or keep a cleaner house, everything would be okay. I put up with the beatings for five years before I got desperate enough to get help.[52]

Another battered woman said,

When I came to, I wanted to die, the guilt and depression were so bad. Your whole sense of worth is tied up with being a successful wife and having a happy marriage. If your husband beats you, then your marriage is a failure, and you're a failure. It's so horribly the opposite of how it is supposed to be.[53]

Katherine Brady shared her experience as an incest survivor in *Father's Days: A True Story of Incest.* She concluded her story with the following:

I've learned a great deal by telling my story. I hope other incest victims may experience a similar journey of discovery by reading it. If nothing else, I would wish them to hear in this tale the two things I needed most, but had to wait years to hear: "You are not alone and you are not to blame."[54]

Sexual Violence Is Not Taken Seriously

Another characteristic of sexual violence is that these crimes are not taken seriously. Society manifests this attitude by simply denying the existence of sexual violence, denying the gravity of these acts, joking about them, and attempting to legitimate them.

Many offenders echo the societal norm by expressing genuine surprise when they are confronted by authorities. This seems to be particularly true in cases of sexual abuse of children, wife beating, and sexual harassment. In her study of incest, Florence Rush found that child molesters very often do not understand that they have done anything wrong.[55] This is true as well for men who beat their wives. Many men still believe that they have an inalienable right to rule "their women." Batterers, for example, often cite their right to discipline their wives; incestuous fathers cite their right to instruct their daughters in sexuality. Clearly, these men are acting on the belief that women are the property of men.

The concept of females as property of men extends beyond the family unit, as the evidence on sexual harassment indicates. "Are you telling me that this kind of horsing around may constitute an actionable offense?" queried a character on a recent television special on sexual harassment.[56] This represents the typical response of a man accused of sexual harassment. Men have been taught that they are the hunters, and women — all women — are fair game. The mythology about the workaday world abounds with sexual innuendo. Concepts of "sleazy" (read "sexually accessible") nurses and dumb, big-breasted, blond secretaries are standard fare for comedy routines. When the existence of sexual violence can no longer be denied, a common response is to joke about it in order to belittle it. "If you are going to be raped, you might as well enjoy it" clearly belittles the violence of rape. The public still laughs when Ralph threatens Alice with "One of these days, POW — right in the kisser." Recently, a television talk-show host remarked that "incest is a game the whole family can play." The audience laughed uproariously.

Sexual Violence Is Not Motivated by Sex

The final characteristic common to all forms of violence against females is perhaps the most difficult to comprehend. Sexual assault, contrary to popular belief, is not about sex. The research that has been done in every area of sexual assault suggests that while the motivation is complex, it is not rooted in sexual frustration or sexual prowess. Rather, the motivation for the violent abuse of women has to do with the need to assert a masculine image or a masculine privilege as defined by the culture. In an article in *Ms.* magazine, "I Never Set Out to Rape Anybody," a rapist talked about his motivation to rape. He said that the image of men (masculinity) as hypersexual, violent, and dominant and the image of women (femininity) as liking tough men made him feel compelled to live up to this standard.[57]

A rapist is usually regarded as a healthy male who was the victim of a seductive and vengeful woman, a sexually frustrated man who was no longer able to control his desires, or a "pervert" or "sex fiend." These views all suggest that the rapist's behavior is motivated by sexual desire. The assumption that rape, forceful and often violent, is about the satisfaction of sexual need or desire is entirely false. In his study *Men Who Rape: The Psychology of the Offender*, A. Nicholas Groth reports that "careful clinical study of offenders reveals that rape is in fact serving primarily nonsexual needs. It is the sexual expression of power and anger."[58]

Men do not rape for sexual pleasure. They rape to assert power and dominance. Jack Fremont's interviews with several rapists revealed the notion of masculine privilege as a dominant motive. For example:

Interviewer: Do you think many men commit rape?
Jimmy: Oh, yes, I know damn well they do! With no more feeling involved and no more neurosis than just, I want you, and I can't have you, so I'll take you.[59]

David Finkelhor, in his study *Sexually Victimized Children,* argues that the sexual exploitation of women and children is made easier in a society that is dominated by men. "Sex in any society is a valuable commodity, and a dominant group—such as men—will try to rig things to maximize their access to it."[60] He maintains that "the cultural beliefs that underpin the male-dominated system contribute to making women and children sexually vulnerable. For example, to the extent that family members are regarded as possessions, men can take unusual and usually undetected liberties with them."[61] Research by Robert Geiser supports the conclusion that sexual gratification is not the dominant motive in the abuse of children. A daughter asked her father, "Why did you do it to me?" He replied, "You were available and you were vulnerable."[62] Research on offenders suggests that men turn to children because their adult relationships are complicated, unsatisfying, stressful, or anxiety-laden. According to Geiser, child molesters need to exercise authority and to avoid rejection: "The child's vulnerability and helplessness make her easier to overpower and dominate."[63]

Husbands who batter their wives are often trying to prove their superiority. Del Martin found that wife beating is unquestionably an example of power abuse. Martin characterized the battering husband this way:

> He is probably angry with himself and frustrated by his life. He may put up a good front in public, but in the privacy and intimacy of his home he may not be able to hide, either from himself or his wife, his feelings of inadequacy and low self-esteem. The man who is losing his grip on his job or his prospects may feel compelled to prove that he is at least the master of his home. Beating his wife is one way for him to appear a winner.[64]

Sexual harassment is also not about sex but about power. Farley argues that the sexual harassment of women at work arose from men's need to maintain control of women's labor.[65] Sexual harassment serves to keep women (individually and collectively) economically inferior and ensures the system of male dominance.[66]

Conclusion

Sexual terrorism is a system that functions to maintain male supremacy through actual and implied violence. Violence against the female body (rape, battery, incest, and harassment) and the perpetuation of fear of violence form the basis of patriarchal power. Both violence and fear are functional. If men did not have power to intimidate and to punish, their domination of women in all spheres of society—political, social, and economic—could not exist.

NOTES

1. Yonah Alexander, "Terrorism and the Mass Media: Some Considerations," in Yonah Alexander, David Carlton, and Paul Wilkinson, eds., *Terrorism: Theory and Practice* (Boulder, Colo.: Westview Press, 1979), 159; Ernest Evans, *Calling a Truce to Terrorism: The American Response to*

International Terrorism (Westport, Conn.: Greenwood Press, 1979), 3; Charmers Johnson, ''Perspectives on Terrorism,'' in Walter Laquer, ed., *The Terrorism Reader* (Philadelphia: Temple University Press, 1978), 273; Thomas P. Thornton, ''Terror as a Weapon of Political Agitation,'' in Harry Eckstein, ed., *The Internal War* (New York: Free Press, 1964), 73; Eugene Walter, *Terror and Resistance* (New York: Oxford University Press, 1969), 6; Francis M. Watson, *Political Terrorism: The Threat and the Response* (Washington, D.C.: R. B. Luce Co., 1976), 15; Paul Wilkinson, *Political Terrorism* (New York: John Wiley and Sons, 1974), 11.

2. Frederick F. Hacker, *Crusaders, Criminals and Crazies: Terrorism in Our Time* (New York: W. W. Norton and Co., 1976), xi.

3. Marc Feigen Fasteau, *The Male Machine* (New York: McGraw-Hill Book Co., 1974), 144.

4. Watson, 15.

5. Wilkinson, 17.

6. Susan Brownmiller, *Against Our Will: Men, Women and Rape* (New York: Simon and Schuster, 1975), 5.

7. Phyllis Chesler, ''Men and Pornography: Why They Use It,'' in Laura Lederer, ed., *Take Back the Night: Women on Pornography* (New York: William Morrow and Co., 1980), 157. Andrea Dworkin, *Pornography: Men Possessing Women* (New York: Perigee Books, 1981), 55–57.

8. Diana E. H. Russell, *The Politics of Rape* (New York: Stein and Day Publishers, 1975), 13.

9. National Clearinghouse on Marital Rape, 2325 Oak Street, Berkeley, CA 94708 (send stamped, self-addressed envelope for more information).

10. John M. MacDonald, *Rape Offenders and Their Victims* (Springfield, Ill.: Charles C. Thomas, Publisher, 1975), 266.

11. *Bradley v. State,* 1 Miss. (7 Walker) 150 (1824); *State v. Black,* 60 N.C. (Win.) 266 (1864).

12. *Fulgham v. State,* 46 Ala. 143 (1871).

13. *Thompson v. Thompson,* 218 U.S. 611 (1910).

14. Roger Langley and Richard C. Levy, *Wife-Beating: The Silent Crisis* (New York: E. P. Dutton, 1977), 153.

15. Lin Farley, *Sexual Shakedown: The Sexual Harassment of Women on the Job* (New York: McGraw-Hill Book Co., 1978), 14–15.

16. Ibid., 18.

17. Langley and Levy, 43.

18. Ibid., 44.

19. Vincent De Francis, *Protecting the Child Victim of Sex Crimes Committed by Adults* (Denver: American Humane Society, 1969), vii.

20. U.S. Department of Justice, Federal Bureau of Investigation, *Crime in the United States,* Uniform Crime Reports 1987 (Washington, D.C.: U.S. Government Printing Office, 1987), 13.

21. Ibid., 6.

22. Ibid., 14.

23. Florence Rush, *The Best Kept Secret* (Englewood Cliffs, N.J.: Prentice-Hall, 1980), 5.

24. Langley and Levy, 3.

25. De Francis, vii.

26. Ibid.

27. Rush.

28. Alfred C. Kinsey and Paul H. Gebhard, *Sexual Behavior in the Human Female* (Philadelphia: W. B. Saunders Co., 1953), 121.

29. Hirsch, 111.

30. Ibid.

31. "Studies Find Sexual Abuse of Children Is Widespread," *New York Times*, May 13, 1982, C10.

32. Farley, 31.

33. Ibid., 20.

34. Ibid., 21.

35. Ibid., 20.

36. Frank J. Till, *Sexual Harassment: A Report on the Sexual Harassment of Students* (Washington, D.C.: National Advisory Council on Women's Educational Programs, 1980), 3.

37. Robert L. Geiser, *Hidden Victims: The Sexual Abuse of Children* (Boston: Beacon Press, 1979), 24.

38. Duncan Chappell, Robley Geis, and Gilbert Geis, eds., *Forcible Rape: The Crime, the Victim, and the Offender* (New York: Columbia University Press, 1977), 266.

39. Ibid., 245–46.

40. Langley and Levy, 173.

41. Ibid., 160, 171–72.

42. Del Martin, *Battered Wives* (New York: Pocket Books, 1977), 94.

43. Langley and Levy, 171.

44. Ibid., 165.

45. James Bannon, as quoted in Martin, 115.

46. Ibid.

47. De Francis, 190–91.

48. Farley, 22.

49. Georgia Dullea, "Child Prostitution: Causes Are Sought," *New York Times*, Sept. 4, 1979, C11.

50. Till, 28.

51. Langley and Levy, 117.

52. Ibid., 115.

53. Ibid., 116.

54. Katherine Brady, *Father's Days: A True Story of Incest* (New York: Dell Publishing Co., 1981), 253.

55. Rush, 14.

56. Till, 4.

57. "I Never Set Out to Rape Anybody," *Ms.*, Dec. 1972, 22–23.

58. A. Nicholas Groth, *Men Who Rape: The Psychology of the Offender* (New York: Plenum Press, 1979), 2.

59. Jack Fremont, "Rapists Speak for Themselves," in Russell, 243.

60. David Finkelhor, *Sexually Victimized Children* (New York: Free Press, 1979), 29.

61. Ibid., 29–30.

62. Geiser, 52.

63. Ibid., 34.

64. Martin, 46.

65. Farley, 208.

66. Ibid., xvi.

The Rape Culture

DIANNE F. HERMAN

When Susan Griffin wrote, "I have never been free of the fear of rape," she touched a responsive chord in most women.[1] Every woman knows the fear of being alone at home late at night or the terror that strikes her when she receives an obscene telephone call. She knows also of the "minirapes"—the pinch in the crowded bus, the wolf whistle from a passing car, the stare of a man looking at her bust during a conversation. Griffin has argued, "Rape is a kind of terrorism which severely limits the freedom of women and makes women dependent on men."[2]

Women live their lives according to a rape schedule.

There is what might be called a universal curfew on women in this country. Whenever a woman walks alone at night, whenever she hitch-hikes, she is aware that she is violating well-established rules of conduct and as a result, that she faces the possibility of rape. If in one of these situations she *is* raped, the man will almost always escape prosecution and the woman will be made to feel responsible because she was some-how "asking for it."[3]

Underlying this view of rape is a traditional concept of male and female sexuality, one that assumes that males are sexually aggressive and females are sexually passive. Those sharing these assumptions conclude that rape is a natural act that arises out of a situation in which men are unrestrained by convention or threat of punishment. Thus, the only way to stop rape is to prevent the opportunity for it to happen by insisting that women avoid "dangerous" situations or by providing a deterrent through stiff penalties. An example of this mentality is Judge Archie Simonson's 1977 explanation when he released on probation a fifteen-year-old boy who had raped a girl in a high-school stairwell. "This community is well-known to be sexually permissive," he said. "Should we punish a fifteen- or sixteen-year-old boy who reacts to it normally?"[4] (Simonson's comment provoked a successful recall campaign by his Madison, Wisconsin constituents. He was replaced by a female lawyer who won the judgeship with the support of local feminist groups.)

RAPE IS NOT NATURAL

Most studies on rape take as a given the aggressive nature of male sexuality. Hans von Hentig wrote in the early fifties that the incidence of rape reflects a demographic imbalance, where there are too many males compared to females in the population. Yet studies sympathetic to his basic premise have found no relationship between rape and a lack of females for male sexual outlet.[5] Studies of incarcerated rapists have also demonstrated that a significant number — 42 percent in one recent research project — were either married or cohabitating at the time of their offense.[6]

Along the same lines, proposals have been offered to make prostitution legal in the hope that the incidence of rape will decrease. However, as researchers point out, "Three cities that had allowed open prostitution actually experienced a decline in rape and other sexual assaults after prostitution was prohibited."[7] Because rape is frequently believed to be a natural behavior, there have been few attempts to understand the cultural conditions that give rise to this crime.

Animals in their natural habitat do not rape, and many societies have existed where rape was not known. According to Margaret Mead in *Sex and Temperament*, the Arapesh do not have "any conception of the male nature that might make rape understandable to them."[8] Among the Arapesh, men and women are both expected to act with gentleness and concern. Thus, there is no reason to maintain the assumption that rape is a natural act. Certain social conditions do seem to contribute to a higher incidence of rape. Peggy Sanday, in a cross-cultural study of 186 tribal societies, found rape to be more frequent in male-dominated and violent societies.[9]

Anthropological studies like those of Margaret Mead have demonstrated that sexual attitudes and practices are learned, not instinctual. In this country people are raised to believe that men are sexually active and aggressive and women are sexually passive and submissive. Since it is assumed that men cannot control their desires, every young woman is taught that she must be the responsible party in any sexual encounter. In such a society, men and women are trained to believe that the sexual act involves domination. Normal heterosexual relations are pictured as consisting of an aggressive male forcing himself on a female who seems to fear sex but unconsciously wants to be overpowered.

Because of the aggressive–passive, dominant–submissive, me-Tarzan–you-Jane nature of the relationship between the sexes in our culture, there is a close association between violence and sexuality. Words that are slang sexual terms, for example, frequently accompany assaultive behavior or gestures. "Fuck you" is meant as a brutal attack in verbal terms. In the popular culture, "James Bond alternately whips out his revolver and his cock, and though there is no known connection between the skills of a gun-fighter and love-making, pacifism seems suspiciously effeminate."[10] The imagery of sexual relations between males and females in books, songs, advertising, and films is frequently that of a sadomasochistic relationship thinly veiled by a romantic facade. Thus, it is very difficult in our society to differentiate rape from "normal" heterosexual relations. Indeed, our culture can be characterized as a rape culture because the image of heterosexual intercourse is based on a rape model of sexuality.

LEGAL DEFINITIONS OF RAPE

If healthy heterosexuality were characterized by loving, warm, and reciprocally satisfying actions, then rape could be defined as sex without consent, therefore involving either domination or violence. Instead, rape is legally defined as sexual intercourse by a male with a female, *other than his wife,* without the consent of the woman and effected by force, duress, intimidation, or deception as to the nature of the act. The spousal exemption in the law, which still remains in effect in most states, means that a husband cannot be guilty of raping his wife, even if he forces intercourse against her will. The implication of this loophole is that *violent, unwanted* sex does not necessarily define rape. Instead, rape is *illegal* sex — that is, sexual assault by a man who has no legal rights over the woman. In other words, in the law's eyes, violence in legal sexual intercourse is permissible, but sexual relations with a woman who is not one's property is not.

From their inception, rape laws have been established not to protect women, but to protect women's property value for men.

Society's view of rape was purely a matter of economics — of assets and liabilities. When a married woman was raped, her husband was wronged, not her. If she was unmarried, her father suffered since his investment depreciated. It was the monetary value of a woman which determined the gravity of the crime. Because she had no personal rights under the law, her own emotions simply didn't matter.[11] Because rape meant that precious merchandise was irreparably damaged, the severity of the punishment was dependent on whether the victim was a virgin. In some virgin rapes, biblical law ordered that the rapist marry the victim, since she was now devalued property.[12] The social status of the victim was also important, as a woman of higher social status was more valuable.

Until the feminist movement compelled a change in the 1970s, special circumstances surrounded the legal definition of rape.[13] Rape complaints were assumed to be charges easily proved, often falsely made, and very difficult to defend against. To establish that the woman had not consented to intercourse, some states required proof of injury or resistance sufficient to show that the victim preferred death to rape. A victim's prior sexual history was allowed as evidence, based on the assumption that a general propensity to consent to sexual intercourse would make it more likely that a woman would consent on any given occasion. Some states required corroboration rules, or evidence other than the victim's testimony, to substantiate a charge of rape. (In 1971, before New York amended its corroboration statute, New York City had 2,415 prosecutable rape complaints but only 18 convictions.)[14] It was also formerly common practice for judges to instruct juries to evaluate the victim's testimony with caution, a procedure not common in other types of criminal trials. Provisions for psychiatric examinations of complaining witnesses also were common in many states. Polygraph, or lie-detector, tests are still widely used by prosecuting attorneys as screening devices for false rape complaints.

Due to pressure from feminist groups, the legal definition of rape has been broadened in many states over the last decade.[15] Evidentiary rules requiring corroboration, cautionary instructions, psychiatric examinations, and prior sexual history have been eliminated or revised in most states. A survey of 151 criminal-justice professionals in Florida, Michigan, and Georgia found that these types of reforms in rape-law legislation have received widespread acceptance and approval. "Further, the findings suggest that law reform need not generate the confusion, uncertainty, or antagonism predicted by some early analysts."[16]

Some jurisdictions have established categories of sexual offenses that allow for sex-neutral assaults, taking into account that men and children, as well as women, can be victims. Others have allowed prosecution when sexual assaults include acts other than penetration of the vagina by the penis, such as sodomy or oral copulation. The latest struggle has been to remove the spousal exemption in the laws, so that husbands are not immune to prosecution for rape by their wives. Each of these changes reflects an evolving understanding that rape laws should not be in existence to regulate control of virginal female bodies for sole ownership by one man; rather, rape should be defined as a sexual assault and crime of violence by one person against another.[17]

HOW COMMON IS RAPE?

There was a steady increase in the rape rate between the mid-sixties and 1980, when it leveled off. In 1964, 11.2 rapes and attempted rapes were reported nationally per 100,000 inhabitants. That figure climbed to 26.2 reports per 100,000 by 1974, and, in the 1980s, has fluctuated between 33.5 and 37.9.[18] Since male victims rarely report rape, this means that, in 1987, 73 of every 100,000 females in the United States reported that they were victims of rape or attempted rape.[19]

These statistics are based on *reported* rapes. Victimization surveys indicate that for every reported rape, an additional one to three rapes have occurred but have not been reported.[20] Diana E. H. Russell's 1978 study of 930 San Francisco women found that 44 percent reported at least one completed or attempted rape.[21] Only 8 percent, or less than one in twelve, of the total number of incidents were ever reported to the police. Using Russell's findings, the actual incidence of rape is 24 times higher than F.B.I. statistics indicate.

In addition, a woman is probably less safe from rape in this country than she is in any other developed nation. The United States has one of the highest rape rates in the world.[22] In 1984, the United States had 35.7 rapes per 100,000 people. The Bureau of Justice Statistics found European nations had an average of 5.4 rapes per 100,000 inhabitants in that same year.[23]

Many myths surround the crime of rape, but perhaps most common are those that imply that the victim was responsible for her own victimization. Projecting the blame on the woman is accomplished by portraying her as a seductress. The conventional scenario is one of a man who is sexually aroused by an attractive, flirtatious woman. But the image of the rape victim as seductive and enticing is at odds with reality. Rapes have been committed on females as young as six months and as old as ninety-three years. Most victims tend to be very young. In one study in Philadelphia of reported rapes in 1958 and 1960, 20 percent of the victims were between ten and fourteen years of age; another 25 percent were between fifteen and nineteen.[24] According to data compiled in 1974 by Women Organized Against Rape, 41 percent of rape victims seen in hospital emergency rooms in Philadelphia were sixteen or younger. The category with the highest frequency of victims was the range between thirteen and sixteen years of age.[25] A comprehensive review of the literature on rape victimization published in 1979 noted that the high-risk ages are adolescents (aged thirteen to seventeen) and young adults (aged eighteen to twenty-four).[26] In 1985, The National Crime Survey, based on findings from a continuous survey of a representative sample of housing units across the United States, reported that the rape rate is highest for those white women between ages sixteen and nineteen, and for those black women between ages twenty-five and thirty-four.[27]

In Denver in 1973, almost one in four rapes reported to Denver General Hospital for treatment or to the police were committed on children under the age of 16.[28] The author of this study found, "Rape is said to be the most unreported crime and while there are many reasons which keep adults from reporting it, there are many more which keep the child from doing so."[29] Among the reasons for underreporting by child victims are (1) children do not know that rape is a crime, (2) they do not know how and to whom to report rape, (3) they are not believed, (4) they are easily intimidated, and (5) the assailant is most likely to be a family member or friend of the family.[30] In addition, the criminal justice system may not treat the assault as a rape because the crime is classified as child abuse, the child is not considered a credible witness, and the sexual damage is seldom physical and overtly visible.[31] David Finkelhor reported that 19 percent of all American women and 9 percent of American men were sexually abused as children.[32] Russell's survey found that 16 percent of women reported being sexually abused by a family member before the age of eighteen and another 31 percent had experienced child sexual abuse by a nonrelative.[33]

Even among adult victims, there is considerable evidence to suggest that a most likely assailant is someone who is trusted, and even loved, by the victim. In Russell's survey of San Francisco women, only 115 out of 606 rapists were strangers to their victims. In addition, whereas 70 percent of stranger rapists were not reported to the police, 89 percent were not reported when the attacker was a boyfriend, and 99 percent were not when the rapist was a date.[34] *Cosmopolitan* magazine found in its September 1980 survey that, of the more than 106,000 women who responded, 24 percent stated that they had been raped at least once: 51 percent of those had been raped by friends, 37 percent by strangers, 18 percent by relatives, and 3 percent by husbands.[35]

Studies such as these, in which women report anonymously to researchers instead of to legal authorities, seem to indicate that rape is a crime commonly committed by an assailant who is known to the victim. Even in cases where women do report to the police, victim and offender are frequently acquainted. In a study of 146 persons admitted to the emergency room of Boston City Hospital during a one-year period from 1972 to 1973 with a complaint of rape, 102 of these rapes were reported to police. Forty of these victims who reported the assault knew their assailant.[36] Burgess and Homstrom believe that victims who know their rapists are less apt to report the crime. Their study found that victims who reported rapes by assailants known to them had more difficulty establishing their credibility than did victims raped by strangers, and these cases had a higher likelihood of dropping out of the criminal-justice system.[37]

The myth that rape is committed by only a stranger serves to keep many women from reporting an unpleasant sexual episode with a man known to them — or even from defining such an incident as attempted rape. It also serves to keep the men involved from construing their actions to be those of a rapist.

> The male learns the same basic mythology of rape as the woman. He is aware of the notion that rape can only be committed by a stranger. This definition can serve as a justification since it precludes the possibility that he can be called a rapist after an encounter with a woman who knew his name.[38]

The fact that victim and offender are acquainted in such a high percentage of reported cases has sometimes been interpreted to mean that large number of rapes are precipitated by the victim. Amir classified rape cases as victim-precipitated when

> the victims actually — or so it was interpreted by the offender — agreed to sexual relations but retracted before the actual act or did not resist strongly enough when the suggestion was made by the offenders. The term applies also to cases in which the victim enters vulnerable situations charged with sexuality, especially when she uses what could be taken as an invitation to sexual relations.[39]

Despite such a broad definition, Amir found that only 19 percent of all rapes in his comprehensive study of rape in Philadelphia were victim-precipitated. Some of the factors characteristic of rapes labeled as victim-precipitated were situations where the victim had a "bad" reputation; the victim had met the offender in a bar, at a picnic, or at a party; or the victim and the offender were involved in a "primary relationship."

It is difficult to imagine, however, that offenders could misinterpret the sexual signals they thought they were receiving given the finding that the closer the relationship between the participants in rape, the greater is the use of physical force. In fact, in Amir's study, neighbors and acquaintances were the most likely to engage in brutal rape. Amir was forced to conclude that rape involving people who know each other is not the result of a sexual encounter in which a woman "teases" a man.

> In general, the analysis of the interpersonal relations between victim and offender lent support to those who reject the myth of the offender who attacks victims unknown to him. But equally rejected is the notion that rape is generally an affair between, or a result of intimate relations between, victim and rapist.[40]

Once it is understood that rape occurs quite commonly between people who are acquainted, other findings about this crime start to make sense. Most studies, for example, report that about half of all rapes occur in the victim's or rapist's home.[41] Another 15 percent occur in automobiles.[42] Car rapes are especially likely to involve participants who are intimate. Many rapes occur on dates.

In Kirkpatrick and Kanin's study of male sexual aggression in dating and courtship relations in the late 1950s, first-semester college women were asked to report forceful sexual attempts they considered offensive. Behavior considered repugnant to the women included forced necking, forced petting above and below the waist, attempted intercourse, and rape. Of the 291 responding women, 56 percent reported themselves offended at least once during the academic year at some level of erotic intimacy.[43] About one out of five of these incidents involved serious sexual assaults. Those women most likely to experience forced petting or intercourse were regular dates, "pinned" or engaged to their attackers.[44]

In 1982, *Ms.* magazine reported a series of studies on college campuses confirming that, even given new and more liberal attitudes about premarital sex and women's liberation, date rape and other forms of acquaintance rape may be reaching epidemic proportions in higher education. In some cases, women have even been assaulted by men ostensibly acting as protective escorts to prevent rape.[45] A 1985 study of over 600 college students found that three-quarters of the women and more than one-half of the men disclosed an experience of sexual aggression on a date. Nearly 15 percent of the women and 7 percent of the men said that intercourse had taken place against the woman's will.[46] The victim and offender had most likely known each other almost one year before the sexual assault. Date rape occurred most frequently when the man initiated the date, when he drove to and from and paid for the date, when drinking took place, and when the couple found themselves alone either in a car or indoors. In these instances, it appears that college men may feel they have license to rape.

In explaining date rape, one set of authors have stated,

> women are often seen as legitimate objects of sexual aggression. Rape can be viewed as the logical extension of a cultural perspective that defines men as possessors of women. The American dating system, in particular, places females in the position of sexual objects purchased by men. Women are groomed to compete for men who will shower them with attention and favors, men are socialized to expect sexual reward (or at least to try for that reward) for their attention to women. This perspective presents the woman as a legitimate object of victimization: If a

man is unable to seduce a woman, and yet has provided her with certain attention and gifts, then he has a right to expect sexual payment. Only the situation of rape by a total stranger escapes the influence of this reasoning. In any other case, if a woman knows her attacker even slightly, she is likely to be perceived as a legitimate victim of a justified aggressor.[47]

The tendency to dismiss rape allegations when victim and offender know each other has contributed to the silence that surrounds marital rape. Finkelhor and Yllo in their study of marital rape found that only one textbook on marriage and the family of the thirty-one they surveyed mentioned rape or anything related to sexual assault in marriage.[48] These authors cite studies that indicate that at least 10 percent of all married women questioned on this topic report that their husbands have used physical force or threats to have sex with them.[49] Marital rape may be the most common form of sexual assault: more than two times as many of the women interviewed had been raped by husbands as had been raped by strangers.[50] In her 1978 study of San Francisco women chosen at random, Diana E. H. Russell reports that

> Eighty-seven women in our sample of 930 women eighteen years and older were the victims of at least one completed or attempted rape by their husbands or ex-husbands. This constitutes 14 percent of the 644 women who had even been married. . . . This means that *approximately one in every seven women who has ever been married in our San Francisco sample was willing to disclose an experience of sexual assault by their husbands that met our quite conservative definition of rape.*[51]

For most people, forced sex in marriage has little to do with what they would call "real" rape. When they think of real rape, they think of a stranger, a weapon, an attack, or a threat to a woman's life. Forced marital sex, on the other hand, conjures up an unpleasant, but not particularly serious, marital squabble over sex. On the contrary, marital rape frequently involves *more* serious physical injury and psychological trauma than do stranger rapes. Russell found that 19 percent of all marital rapes involved beating, and another 16 percent involved hitting or kicking.[52] Finkelhor and Yllo cite, for example, a case where a woman suffered a 6-centimeter gash in her vagina when her husband attempted to rip out her vagina.[53] These authors found that disagreements over sex were not the reason husbands rape their wives. Husbands' desires to frighten, humiliate, punish, degrade, dominate, and control their spouses were found to be the most common motivations for the sexual assaults. In their 1980–1981 study of Boston area mothers, Finkelhor and Yllo found that about half of the marital rape victims were also battered.[54] Many cases were uncovered in which wives were tortured through sadistic sexual assaults involving objects. Many more were humiliated by being forced to engage in distasteful or unusual sexual practices. One-quarter of the victims in their survey were sexually attacked in the presence of others — usually their children.[55] Many times, the rape was the final violent act in a series of physical and emotional abuses or the payback when a woman filed for separation or divorce. Sadly, many woman suffer years of abuse thinking that the assaults are caused by their failure to be good wives or feeling that they have no way out and that this is the lot of the married woman. Too often, their husbands justify their attacks on their wives by blaming the wives for causing their loss of control, or by saying that they are entitled to treat their spouses any way they choose.

Because rape so frequently involves people who know each other, most rapists and their victims are of the same race and age group. In 1985, approximately 80 percent of all rapes and attempted rapes were intraracial.[56] One reason that the myth that rapes are interracial dies hard is that cases of this type frequently receive the most publicity. In a study of rape in Philadelphia, researchers discovered that the two major newspapers, when they reported on rape cases, mentioned mainly interracial offenses. Intraracial rapes were only occasionally mentioned.[57] Gary LaFree examined the effect of race in the handling of 881 sexual assaults in a large midwestern city. He found that black males who assaulted white women received more serious charges, longer sentences, and more severe punishment in terms of executed sentences and incarceration in the state penitentiary.[58] Although black women are three times more likely to be raped than are white women, rape is least prosecuted if the victim is black.[59] The rape of poor, black women is not an offense against men of power.

WHY MEN RAPE

Russell has stated, "rape is not so much a deviant act as an overconforming one. It is an extreme acting out of qualities that are regarded as masculine in this and many other societies: aggression, force, power, strength, toughness, dominance, competitiveness."[60] In a 1979 study of high-school students, one group of researchers found that 50 percent of high-school males who were interviewed believed it was acceptable "for a guy to hold a girl down and force her to have sexual intercourse in instances such as when 'she gets him sexually excited' or 'she says she's going to have sex with him and then changes her mind.' "[61] When questioning college males, a 1981 study by Briere, Malamuth, and Ceniti found that 60 percent of the sample indicated that if no one knew and they would not be punished, there was some likelihood that they would use force to obtain sex.[62] In this study, the authors believed that attitudes about sex and women were more important in explaining these pro-rape responses than were sexual frustration or sexual maladjustment.[63] Russell concludes from studies such as these that

> The considerable percentage of men who acknowledge some likelihood that they might rape if they could get away with it, plus the widespread prevalence of actual rape victims . . . suggest that continued efforts to explain rape as a psychopathological phenomenon are inappropriate. How could it be that all of these rapes are being perpetrated by a tiny segment of the male population? Clearly, rape must be seen as primarily a social disease.[64]

One of the most surprising findings of studies on rape is that the rapist is normal in personality, appearance, intelligence, behavior, and sexual drive.[65] Empirical research has repeatedly failed to find a consistent pattern of personality type or character disorder that reliably discriminates the rapist from the nonrapist. According to Amir, the only significant psychological difference between the rapist and the normal, well-adjusted male appears to be the greater tendency of the former to express rage and violence. But this finding probably tends to overemphasize the aggressive personality characteristics of rapists, since generally only imprisoned rapists have been studied. Those few rapists who are sentenced to prison tend to be the more obviously violent offenders. In fact, studies by some researchers have found one type of rapist who is fairly meek and mild-mannered.[66] What is clear is that the rapist is not an exotic freak. Rather, rape evolves out of a situation in which "normal" males feel a need to prove themselves to be "men" by displaying dominance over females.

In our society, men demonstrate their competence as people by being "masculine." Part of this definition of masculinity involves a contempt for anything feminine or for females in general. Reported rapes, in fact, are frequently associated with some form of ridicule and sexual humiliation, such as urination on the victim, anal intercourse, fellatio, and ejaculation in the victim's face and hair. Insertion into the woman's vagina of broomsticks, bottles, and other phallic objects is not an uncommon coup de grace.[67] The overvaluing of toughness expresses itself in a disregard for anything associated with fragility. In the rapist's view, his assertion of maleness is automatically tied to a violent repudiation of anything feminine.

Most rapes are not spontaneous acts in which the rapist had no prior intent to commit rape but was overcome by the sexual provocations of his victim. Statistics compiled from reported rapes show that the overwhelming majority are planned. In one study, 71 percent of all reported rapes were prearranged, and another 11 percent were partially planned. Only 18 percent were impulsive acts.[68] Planning is most common in cases of group rape. Even when the rapist is acting alone, a majority of the rapes involves some manipulations on the part of the offender to place his victim in a vulnerable situation that he can exploit.

Perhaps this need of some men to prove their masculinity to themselves and to others explains why rape is so common in war. The U.S. military has generally eulogized the values of masculinity and has emphasized aggressiveness: the Marines built their image on their ability to form "men" out of adolescent youths. For those who lead armies, stressing that soldiers are "real men" is a perfect mechanism by which to keep in line those who might otherwise question the validity of a military conquest. Cowardice in the face of the enemy is equated with femininity. At the same time, however, the real dangers of combat cause many men to question their masculinity. Such situations are ripe for rape.

> In 1966, an American patrol held a 19-year-old Vietnamese girl captive for several days, taking turns raping her and finally murdering her. The sergeant planned the crime in advance, telling the soldiers during the mission's briefing that the girl would improve their "morale." When one soldier refused to take part in the rape, the sergeant called him "queer" and "chicken," and another testified later that he joined in the assault to avoid such insults.[69]

Nothing supports more convincingly the premise that rape in our society is the act of a male attempting to assert his masculinity than the studies that have been conducted on homosexual rapes in prisons. Interestingly, researchers have discovered that aggressors in prison-rape cases usually have little or no prior history of homosexual behavior.[70] They do not consider themselves homosexuals, and neither do the other inmates. Rather, they equate their actions with those of an aggressive, heterosexual male. They are often called "jockers" or "wolves" by other inmates, terms that characterize them as males. One researcher commented with some astonishment:

> We were struck by the fact that the typical sexual aggressor does not consider himself to be a homosexual, or even to have engaged in homosexual acts. This seems to be based upon his startlingly primitive view of sexual relationships, one that defines as male whichever partner is aggressive and as homosexual whichever partner is passive.[71]

Although the other inmates and the aggressors consider their behavior normal under circumstances of heterosexual deprivation, Davis has noted that sexual release is not the primary motivation of the prison rapist. Rather, the motive appears to be the need of some males in prison to exercise control and domination over others.

> A primary goal of the sexual aggressor, it is clear, is the conquest and degradation of his victim. We repeatedly found that aggressors used such language as "Fight or fuck," "We're gonna make a girl out of you."[72]

The attempt to control other men, and in fact to transform them into women (passive, sexual objects), demonstrates to the rapist himself and to others of the prison population that he is in fact a "real man." Genet wrote, "A male that fucks another male is a double-male."[73] Being removed from the heterosexual world, the prison rapist needs to affirm his identity as a male by being dominant over less "masculine" men. "A man who has become accustomed to validating his masculinity through regular interaction with members of the opposite sex may suddenly find his ego-image in grave jeopardy once a prison sentence consigns him to an all-male world."[74] Imprisonment knocks out whatever props the rapist may have established to prove his masculinity. Only the demonstration of sexual and physical prowess can stave off feelings of emasculation in the limited environment of the prison.

Many prison rapists display little, if any, concern for the attitudes or feelings of their partners. One study reported that a group of seventeen men raped one inmate over the course of four hours.[75] Another prisoner was raped repeatedly even after he was bleeding from his rectum, had become ill, and had vomited. But the callousness of the rapist's attitude toward his victim is required by the prison culture. For, in the narrow view of sexuality subscribed to by most inmates, one is either a "woman" or a "man." If any member of the prison population displays emotion or vulnerability, he is likely to be tagged a "woman" and is therefore open to sexual attack. It is for this reason that many inmates refuse to aid the victim and may explain why they take part in a gang-bang themselves. In a world where one is either dominant and a rapist or submissive and a victim, the pressures to be the former are so great that many men find themselves forced to be the sexual violators of others.

Aside from the need to demonstrate "masculine" competence, rapists tend to hold certain values. The rapist's attraction to dominance and violence stems from his interpretation of sexuality—"man ravishes, woman submits."[76] Many rapists believe that women enjoy sadomasochistic sex. One group of authors has said of the rape offender:

> He sees her struggle and protestation not as a refusal but as part of her own sexual excitement. "Women like to get roughed up, they enjoy a good fight." This belief is maintained even when the victim is literally fighting for her life and the offender has to brutally injure her to force her to submit to intercourse.[77]

In one instance where a sixty-three-year-old woman was robbed and raped at gunpoint by a twenty-four-year-old man, her assailant threw her a kiss and said before running away, "I bet I made your day."[78] Some offenders have been incredulous when arrested, complaining that they may have been a little rough but that the women enjoyed their advances. According to Russell's study, men who rape often see themselves as lovers, not as rapists. She reports cases where victims received requests for dates and even marriage proposals from their rapists.[79] A study by David Lipton and colleagues compared convicted rapists with both violent and nonviolent criminals in their abilities to identify social cues. They found that, when shown scenes of actors expressing five feelings from very positive to extremely negative, rapists demonstrated little ability to recognize negative feelings when expressed by women, especially in a dating situation.[80] The rapist may be the guy who simply cannot take "no" for an answer.

Most convicted rapists tend to project the blame on others, particularly the victim. Schultz found that the sex offender is twice as likely to insist on his innocence as is the general offender.[81] "In two-thirds of the cases one hears, 'I'm here on a phoney beef,' or 'I might have been a little rough with her but she was asking for it,' or 'I might have done it but I was too drunk to remember.'"[82] They also rationalize the act by labeling their victims "bad" women. Some rapists excuse and deny their crime by portraying the victim as a woman of questionable sexual reputation or as a person who has placed herself in a compromising position, thus "getting what she deserved."[83]

Interviews with convicted rapists often reveal that these men subscribe to what Pauline Bart has labeled the notion of male entitlement. "The assumption is that a woman's body is a man's *right*, and if violence occurs while the rapist is exercising that right (the act itself not being defined as violence, remember) it is because the woman attempts to deny him his due."[84]

Psychologists David L. Mosher and Ronald D. Anderson, in a study of college males, found that men who scored high on a hypermasculinity questionnaire also tended to score high on a questionnaire designed to measure sexually coercive behaviors. Callous sexual attitudes appear to go in hand with sexually coercive acts. When asked to imagine a rape scene, the macho males were more likely to report sexual arousal, but they also reported feelings of anger, distress, fear, guilt, shame, and disgust.[85]

Nicholas Groth, in his book *Men Who Rape,* has stated that rape is a pseudosexual act in which components of power, anger, and sexuality are fused. Different offenders will display these factors with different intensities. For the rapist, sex becomes a weapon used to express his aggression and his needs to dominate and control.[86] Studies of relapsed sexual aggressives have found that 75 percent of repeated sexual assaults committed by rapists after treatment were precipitated by situations that evoked negative emotional states, such as frustration, anger, anxiety, or depression. Another 20 percent of a group of relapsed clients involved situations of interpersonal conflict.[87]

American culture produces rapists when it encourages the socialization of men to subscribe to values of control and dominance, callousness and competitiveness, and anger and aggression, and when it discourages the expression by men of vulnerability, sharing, and cooperation. In the end, it is not only the women who become the victims of these men, but also the offenders themselves, who suffer. These men lose the ability to satisfy needs for nurturance, love, and belonging, and their anger and frustration from this loss expresses itself in acts of violence and abuse against others. The tragedy for our society is that we produce so many of these hardened men.

SOCIETY'S RESPONSE TO RAPE

Women have often complained that their veracity is questioned when they report charges of rape. The first public agency with which a woman makes contact when she reports a rape is usually the police department, and it has often been less than sympathetic to rape complaints. Some officers have actually asked victims questions such as "How many orgasms did you have?" and "Didn't I pick you up last week for prostitution?"[88] A 1971 California police textbook, *Patrol Procedure,* begins its discussion on sexual assaults with the statement, "Forcible rape is one of the most falsely reported crimes."[89]

The police have considerable discretion in determining whether a crime has been committed. In 1976, according to a study by the F.B.I., 19 percent of all forcible rapes reported to the police were unfounded.[90] *Unfounding* simply means that the police decide there is no basis for prosecution.

A study conducted in 1966 of the procedures used by the Philadelphia Police Department in unfounding rape cases discovered that one of the major factors for the unfounding of a case was the moral appraisal of the victim by the police. For example, if the woman had been drinking, the police in most instances dismissed her charges.[91] The police were also most likely to unfound cases involving black participants and least likely to do so when victim and offender were both white.[92] In a study of institutional reactions to rape victims, Holmstrom and Burgess found that the police tended to treat prostitutes, women with emotional or psychiatric problems, and persons with drug or alcohol addictions with humor, hostility, distain, and impatience.[93] In a more recent study in a large midwestern city, involving an analysis of 905 sexual-assault complaints over a six-year period, the investigators found that police practices have become less discriminatory. But when the police thought that the victim had been guilty of "misconduct," they were still reluctant to pursue charges.[94] One reason for the judgmental attitudes expressed by the police about some rape complainants may be that the police are concerned with making a "good case." If the victim cannot give consistent information and be shown to be of upstanding character, the quality of the police investigation may be questioned, which may reflect negatively on the officers involved.[95]

According to many studies, one of the most frequent causes of unfounding rape is a prior relationship between the participants. In the Philadelphia study, 43 percent of all date rapes were unfounded. The police, according to the researcher, seemed to be more concerned that the victim had "assumed the risk" than they were with the fact that she had not given consent to intercourse.[96]

Another common reason police unfound cases is the apparent lack of force in the rape situation. The extent of injuries seems to be even more important in the decision to unfound than is whether the offender had a weapon.[97] There is no requirement that a male businessperson must either forcibly resist when mugged or forfeit protection under the law. But proof of rape, both to the police and in court, is often required to take the form of proof of resistance, substantiated by the extent of injuries suffered by the victim. Yet local police departments frequently advise women not to resist if faced with the possibility of rape.

> In a confusion partially of their own making, local police precincts point out contradictory messages: they "unfound" a rape case because, by the rule of their own male logic, the woman did not show normal resistance; they report on an especially brutal rape case and announce to the press that the multiple stab wounds were the work of an assailant who was enraged because the woman resisted.[98]

The victim is told that if she was raped it was because she did not resist enough. But if she fights back and is raped and otherwise assaulted, police blame her again for bringing about her own injuries because of her resistance.

The number of unfounded rapes is probably underestimated because of police practices. Police may turn away a complaint and not file an incident report at all. Or rape complaints may be categorized as "investigations of persons" — a catchall for incidents requiring an investigation report but for which there is insufficient information for reclassification into other crime categories. If further investigation confirms police doubts and the case is closed, then the incident is not recorded as an unfounded-rape complaint. Because of these police practices, one author estimates that the F.B.I.'s 19 percent unfounding rate is far too low and that the true figure is probably at least 50 percent.[99] Other investigators who have interviewed police personnel have found from the latter's comments that the police believe that 80 to 90 percent of the rapes reported to them are not really rapes. In addition, the Philadelphia study found that the prosecutor's office was even less likely than were the police to believe that the victim had been forced against her will to have intercourse.[100]

Police and prosecuting practices that are demeaning to rape victims have been criticized in the past decade, and there are indications that some changes are being made. A study in 1974, for example, found that about half of the police departments surveyed had, in the last three years, instituted some innovations in their methods of handling rape cases — notably in providing specialized training to officers or in assigning women to investigate.[101] Prosecutors have established special victim-assistance programs, primarily to provide support and services for rape complainants. In 1975, however, after a fifteen-month nationwide investigation, the U.S. Law Enforcement Assistance Administration concluded that the response by police, prosecutors, and hospitals to rape victims is "generally poorly coordinated and inadequate."[102] Studies continue to find that "the credibility of the rape victim is questioned more than that of any other victims of crime."[103] In 1974, almost half of the prosecutors' offices surveyed in a national study admitted using polygraph examinations in many instances because they suspected that the alleged rape victim was lying.[104]

Of all professionals who routinely work with rape victims, law-enforcement officers are the most favorably evaluated by women reporting the crime. In one study, over 30 percent of victims reported positively about police handling of their case and could cite some specific action of the police that made them feel better.[105] While police and prosecutors appear to be developing a more sympathetic response to rape victims, the medical profession has been described as less willing to make changes.[106]

Holmstrom and Burgess point out that historically the medical bias in examination of the rape victim has been centered on the issue of false accusation and not on the victim's right to have evidence accurately recorded. They cite the following:

> In one rape case, the gynecologist announced that "nothing happened," even though there was a bruise to the perineum and tears of the hymen. Asked why he made this statement, he explained that it was because he did not find any sperm.[107]

One reason physicians are reluctant to diagnose injuries as caused by a sexual assault is due to their reluctance to have to give up their valuable time to testify on behalf of the prosecution. In the early seventies, the District of Columbia newspapers reported that doctors at D.C. General Hospital were intentionally giving negative medical reports of rape victims so they would not be called to court. In one case that reached the appeals court, the doctor had reported absolutely no injuries even though police photographs showed bruises and scratches on the victim's face. As a result, the trial court dismissed the rape charges and the defendants were only found guilty of assault with intent to commit rape.[108]

For many women, the experience of having their account of the events scrutinized, mocked, or discounted continues in the courtroom. Women have often said that they felt as though they, not the defendants, were the persons on trial. According to Burgess and Holmstrom, "Going to court, for the victim, is as much of a crisis as the actual rape itself."[109] They quote one victim shortly after she appeared in district court: "I felt like crying. I felt abused. I didn't like the questions the defense was asking. I felt accused— guilty 'til proven innocent. I thought the defense lawyer made it a big joke."[110] They relate how one twelve-year-old girl had a psychotic break-down during the preliminary court process.[111]

The victim, by taking the case to court, incurs extensive costs, both psychological and financial. Expecting to testify just once, she is likely to have to repeat her story at the hearing for probable cause, to the grand jury, and in superior-court sessions. To convey the discomfort of such a process, feminists have recommended that individuals imagine having to tell an audience all the details of their last sexual experience. In addition to expos-ing themselves to public scrutiny, rape victims may be subject to harassment from the friends or family of the perpetrator.

Financially, the time away from work nearly always stretches beyond expectations. According to Burgess and Holmstrom, the victims they accom-panied to court were often forced to sit three to four hours in the courthouse, only to be told that the case had been continued. After they and their witnesses had taken time off from work and, in some cases, traveled great distances, they were less than enthusiastic about the idea of seeing justice done.[112] Wood has said, "Due to the traumatic experience which a victim must go through in order to attempt to secure the attacker's successful prosecution, it is amazing any rape cases come to trial."[113]

Even if the victim is resilient enough to pursue her case, she may encounter prejudicial attitudes from judges and juries. Thirty-eight Philadel-phia judges were interviewed by Carol Bohmer in 1971 with the following results.

> The judges seemed to feel that there were three basic categories of women in rape trials. One was the "genuine" victim, the victim of the stereotype crime with a stranger committing the assault and her at-tempting to resist. In these situations they were generally sympathetic. But if the woman fell into the classification of vulnerability because she had met the man before, they termed those "friendly rapes" or "assault with failure to please." Their understanding diminished accordingly. The third heading was the "vindictive" female. This was often the case when victim and assailant were acquainted or when she might have some personal reason for "getting back at him." In these, they assumed either intercourse was agreed to or it did not take place.[114]

Kalven and Zeisel conducted an analysis of jurors' reactions to many crimes, including rape, in over 3,500 trials. They found that in rape cases the jury does not consider solely the issue of consent during intercourse but also includes as relevant to conviction any suggestions of contributory behavior on the part of the victim. The jury convicted defendants of rape in only three of forty-two cases of nonaggravated rape, whereas the judge would have convicted in twenty-two of these.[115] Shirley Feldman-Summers and Karen Lindner investigated the perceptions of victims by juries and found that, as the respectability of the victim decreased, the jury's belief that the victim was responsible for the rape increased.[116] In a sense, juries have created an extralegal defense. If the complainant somehow "assumed the risk" of rape, juries will commonly find the defendant guilty of some lesser crime or will acquit him altogether.[117] "A seventeen-year-old girl was raped during a beer-drinking party. The jury probably acquitted, according to the judge, because they thought the girl asked for what she got."[118] In one case, according to Medea and Thompson, "a woman who responded with 'fuck off' when approached lost her case because 'fuck' is a sexually exciting word."[119] If the victim knew the offender previously, especially as an intimate, juries will be reluctant to convict.

> In one case of "savage rape," the victim's jaw was fractured in two places. The jury nevertheless acquitted because it found that there may have been sexual relations on previous occasions, and the parties had been drinking on the night of the incident.[120]

As a consequence of these practices, rape is a crime that is very rarely punished. In reported rape cases where the police do believe the victim, only about half of the rape offenders are actually arrested. As Russell has pointed out, one reason for this low arrest rate may be that the police tend to take less seriously rapes perpetrated by persons known to the victim and to pursue stranger-rape cases, where the offender is most difficult to identify and apprehend.[121] Even if the police catch up with an accused rapist, however, he is unlikely to be convicted. Many times prosecutors will fail to file charges despite knowing that the suspect is in custody. In Denver in 1973, for example, although the police cleared by arrest almost 45 percent of rape complaints, the prosecutor accepted the case by filing on only about 15 percent of the incidents.[122] Of those police agencies reporting to the F.B.I. in 1971, only 65 percent of those arrested for rape or attempted rape were prosecuted. Of these, 40 percent were acquitted or had the charges dismissed, and another 13 percent were found guilty of lesser offenses.[123]

Using 1970 F.B.I. statistics, LeGrand calculated that

> a man who rapes a woman who reports the rape to police has roughly 7 chances out of 8 of walking away without any conviction. Assuming only one women in five reports the rape, his chances increase to 39 out of 40. If these figures take into account the high percentage of those who receive probation or suspended sentences, his chances of escaping incarceration are in the vicinity of 98 to 99 out of 100.[124]

There is some evidence to suggest that legal reform has improved the rate of convictions for rape. Michigan was one of the states where there was a significant attempt to treat rape complainants with fairness and in the same manner as other victims of crime are treated. The result has been an improvement in prosecutions from 10 percent in 1975 to 19 percent of rape arrests leading to convictions in 1985.[125]

Most individuals convicted of rape serve a sentence of no longer than four years, except when the victim is white and the offender is black. Of the 455 men executed for rape from 1930 to 1967, 405 were black.[126] Black males, however, do not uniformly receive the most severe punishment. If their victims are black females, they are likely to receive the most lenient sentences. According to a study of rape convictions in Baltimore in 1967: "Of the four categories of rapist and victim in a racial mix, blacks received the stiffest sentences for raping white women and the mildest sentences for raping black women."[127]

Despite attempts to educate the public about the dynamics of rape, myths still persist. Martha Burt, in a study of almost 600 Minnesota residents, found that most believed that "Any healthy woman can resist a rapist"; "In the majority of rapes, the victim was promiscuous or had a bad reputation"; "If a girl engages in necking or petting and she lets things get out of hand, it is her fault if her partner forces sex on her"; "One reason that women falsely report a rape is that they frequently have a need to call attention to themselves." Burt found that rapists also subscribed to these myths in attempts to excuse and rationalize their behavior.[128] The implication of her study is that the general population's attitudes toward women who are raped is very similar to the rapist's view of his victim.

During the 1986–1987 school year, a survey was taken of over 1500 sixth to ninth graders who attended the Rhode Island Rape Crisis Center's assault-awareness program in schools across the state. The results of the survey strongly indicated that even the next generation of Americans tends to blame the victim of sexual assault. For example, 50 percent of the students said a woman who walks alone at night and dresses seductively is asking to be raped. In addition, most of the students surveyed accepted sexually assaultive behavior as normal. Fifty-one percent of the boys and 41 percent of the girls stated that a man has a right to force a woman to kiss him if he has spent "a lot of money" on her. Sixty-five percent of the boys and 57 percent of the girls in junior high schools said it is acceptable for a man to force a woman to have sex if they have been dating for more than six months. Eight-seven percent of the boys and 79 percent of the girls approved of rape if the couple were married. Interestingly, 20 percent of the girls and 6 percent of the boys taking the survey disclosed that they had been sexually abused.[129]

In cases of rape, judges, juries, police, prosecutors, and the general public frequently attribute blame and responsibility to the victim for her own victimization. Unfortunately, these negative responses are often compounded by reactions from family and friends. Encounters with parents, relatives, friends, and spouses many times involves either anger at the victim for being foolish enough to get raped or expressions of embarrassment and shame that family members will suffer as a result of the attack.

Many men perceive a sexual assault against a woman with whom they have been intimate as an attack against themselves. One husband whose wife was raped said, for example, "It's a matter of territorial imperative. I fantasized ways of getting back at him, like shoving a shot-gun down his throat and pulling the trigger until it quit clicking."[130] Another husband admitted, "I wanted to kill that bastard. I wanted to destroy him for what he'd done to me."[131] The overwhelming desire for revenge reflects two strong needs: Revenge would not only allow these men to express their anger at being humiliated but also serve to restore their self-esteem in socially prescribed ways (acting in a "manly," aggressive fashion).[132] The husband whose wife has been sexually violated not only may question his masculinity but also may believe that his wife participated in some way in her own victimization or enjoyed the experience. His self-esteem is thus lowered by his wife's presumed complicity as well as by the rapist's act. Husbands who blame their wives may view the rape as marital infidelity. Victims have reported that their husband's inability to "adjust" to the fact that the rape had occurred was the cause of their divorce.[133]

Much of the psychological harm of rape comes from the lack of support the victim receives and the tendency of victims to blame themselves. Women frequently ask themselves why they "let it happen." "There is a strong desire for the victim to try and think of how she could undo what has happened. She reports going over in her mind how she might have escaped from the assailant, how she might have handled the situation differently."[134] For many women, the aftermath of the rape is worse than the physical pain and psychological trauma of the actual rape. These women are plagued by feelings of guilt, shame, loss of self-esteem, and humiliation. Many rapes go unreported because victims have been unjustifiably convinced that they were guilty of precipitating the attack.[135] This is even more probable in cases where the victim knows the offender. Some women have confessed that it was only when they were involved in more healthy relationships that they realized that their initial introduction into sex was rape.

The attitude of victims of rape can be characterized more as despair than as resentment or anger. These women have been taught to assume the responsibility for male sexuality — and many have done so. When they are raped, they feel that they have failed and that they are at fault. Medea and Thompson have argued that many female rape victims feel like sentinels who fell asleep while on guard duty.

> The male is the aggressor, the soldier laying siege to the castle; the woman is the guardian of the gate, and defender of the sacred treasure. If the male forces his way in with a battering ram and captures the treasure, he has succeeded in his purpose. There is no cause for guilt or remorse. The woman, on the other hand, has failed in her purpose. She has allowed the treasure to be taken and feels herself to be at fault. She suffers from feelings of guilt, besides the feelings of violation, humiliation and defeat.[136]

In a rape culture, even the victims believe that men are naturally sexual aggressors. Their response to the rape is to blame themselves for not taking proper precautions, rather than to demand a change in the behavior of men.

THE RAPE CULTURE

Exposure to sexual violence in the media has been shown to increase male acceptance of rape.[137] Unfortunately, violent descriptions of male and female sexual encounters are all too common. In a content analysis of adult paperbacks published between 1968 and 1974 that *were not pornographic*, Don

Smith found that one-fifth depicted sexual episodes involving a completed rape. In addition, almost 100 percent of these rape scenes portrayed the victim as sexually stimulated to the point of orgasm.[138] Perhaps most men are educated through nonpornographic, but violent, depictions of sex in the common culture to become aroused at a description of a rape scene. It is little wonder that Malamuth and his colleagues find that "there are considerable data showing that within the general population a substantial percentage of men show arousal patterns similar to those of known rapists."[139]

As long as sex in our society is construed as a dirty, low, and violent act involving domination of a male over a female, rape will remain a common occurrence. The erotization of male dominance means that whenever women are in a subordinate position to men, the likelihood for sexual assault is great. We are beginning to see that rape is not the only way in which women are sexually victimized, and that other forms of sexual exploitation of women are rampant in our society.[140] Feminists have raised our consciousness about rape by developing rape crisis centers and other programs to assist victims and their families, by reforming laws and challenging politicians, by training professionals in medicine and in the criminal-justice system, and by educating women and the general public on the subject. They are also enlightening us about pornography; sexual harassment on the job and in higher education; sexual exploitation in doctor, dentist, and therapist relations with patients; and sexual assault in the family, such as incest and rape in marriage.

Rape is the logical outcome if men act according to the "masculine mystique" and women act according to the "feminine mystique." But rape does not have to occur. Its presence is an indication of how widely held are traditional views of appropriate male and female behavior, and of how strongly enforced these views are. Our society is a rape culture because it fosters and encourages rape by teaching males and females that it is natural and normal for sexual relations to involve aggressive behavior on the part of males. To end rape, people must be able to envision a relationship between the sexes that involves sharing, warmth, and equality, and to bring about a social system in which those values are fostered.

NOTES

1. Susan Griffin, "Rape: The All-American Crime," *Ramparts*, 10 (Sept. 1971), 26.

2. Ibid., 35.

3. Andrea Medea and Kathleen Thompson, *Against Rape* (New York: Farrar, Straus and Giroux, 1974), 4–5. See also Mark Warr, "Fear of Rape among Urban Women," *Social Problems*, 32 (Feb. 1985).

4. "Judge in Wisconsin Calls Rape by Boy 'Normal' Reaction," *New York Times*, May 27, 1977, A9.

5. Menachem Amir, "Forcible Rape," *Federal Probation*, 31 (1967), 51.

6. Diana Scully and Joseph Marolla, "Convicted Rapists' Vocabulary of Motive: Excuses and Justifications," *Social Problems*, 31 (1984), 532.

7. Paul M. Kinsie, ''Sex Crimes and the Prostitution Racket,'' *Journal of Social Hygiene,* 36 (1950), 250–252.

8. Margaret Mead, *Sex and Temperament in Three Primitive Societies* (New York: Dell, 1968), 100. See also Susan Brownmiller, *Against Our will: Men, Women and Rape* (New York: Simon and Schuster, 1975), 12–13.

9. Peggy Reeves Sanday, ''The Socio-Cultural Context of Rape: A Cross-Cultural Analysis'' (Washington, D.C.: Department of Health, Education and Welfare, 1979).

10. Griffin, 27.

11. Carol V. Horos, *Rape* (New Canaan, Conn.: Tobey Publishing Co., 1974), 4.

12. Ibid., 5.

13. National Institute of Law Enforcement and Criminal Justice, *Forcible Rape: An Analysis of Legal Issues* (Wash. D.C.: U. S. Government Printing Office, 1978), 5–33.

14. Pamela Lakes Wood, ''The Victim in a Forcible Rape Case: A Feminist View,'' *American Criminal Law Review,* 7 (1973), 372.

15. Rosemarie Tong, *Women, Sex and the Law* (Totowa, N.J.: 1984), 90–123.

16. Barbara E. Smith and Jane Roberts Chapman, ''Rape Law Reform Legislation: Practitioner's Perceptions of the Effectiveness of Specific Provisions,'' *Response,* 10 (1987), 8.

17. Tong, *Women, Sex and the Law,* 90–123.

18. *Forcible Rape: An Analysis of Legal Issues,* 2. Table 1 reports the rape rate for each year from 1960 to 1975. Figures for subsequent years can be found in *Uniform Crime Reports: Crime in the United States* (Federal Bureau of Investigation, U. S. Department of Justice, Washington, D.C.) for each year.

19. 1987 *Uniform Crime Reports for the United States* (Wash. D.C.: U. S. Department of Justice, 1987), 14.

20. Duncan Chappell, ''Forcible Rape and the Criminal Justice System: Surveying Present Practices and Reporting Future Trends,'' in Marcia J. Walker and Stanley L. Brodsky, eds., *Sexual Assault* (Lexington, Ma.: Lexington Books, 1976), 22. Annual surveys by the federal government report that from 1973 to 1986, between 41 and 61 percent of all rapes and attempted rapes were reported to the police. Bureau of Criminal Justice Statistics Bulletin, *Criminal Victimization 1986,* Table 5, p. 4. However, the National Institute of Law Enforcement and Criminal Justice reported in *Forcible Rape: Final Project Report,* March 1978, that ''the *actual* number of rapes in the United States is approximately four times the reported number'' (p. 15).

21. Diana E. H. Russell, *Sexual Exploitation* (Beverly Hills, Ca.: Sage Publications, 1984), 35–36.

22. Diana Scully and Joseph Marolla, '' 'Riding the Bull at Gilley's': Convicted Rapists Described the Rewards of Rape,'' *Social Problems,* 32 (Feb. 1985), 252.

23. *International Crime Rates* NCJ-110776 (Special Report by the Bureau of Justice Statistics), May 1988, Table 1, p. 2.

24. Menachem Amir, *Patterns in Forcible Rape* (Chicago: University of Chicago Press, 1971), 341.

25. Women Organized Against Rape, *W. O. A. R. Data* (Philadelphia: mimeo., 1975), 1.

26. Russell, *Sexual Exploitation,* 79.

27. U. S. Department of Justice, Bureau of Justice Statistics, *Criminal Victimization in the United States, 1985,* NCJ-104273, May 1987, Table 9, p. 18.

28. Carol J. Hursch, *The Trouble with Rape* (Chicago: Nelson-Hall, 1977), 22.

29. Ibid.

30. Ibid., 25.

31. William Krasner, Linda C. Meyer, and Nancy E. Carroll, *Victims of Rape* (Washington, D.C.: U. S. Department of Health, Education and Welfare, 1976), 7.

32. ''A Hidden Epidemic,'' *Newsweek,* May 14, 1984, 31.

33. Russell, *Sexual Exploitation,* 83.

34. Ibid., 101.

35. Timothy Beneke, "Male Rage: Four Men Talk About Rape," *Mother Jones,* July 1982, 13. However, the National Crime Survey reports that 57.2 percent of all rapes and attempted rapes involved strangers in 1985 (Table 29, p. 34). The NILECJ (see note 20) reported in 1978, based on 1261 complaints in five cities, that from 32 to 57 percent of all victims knew their assailants (pp. 17–18).

36. Lynda Lytle Holmstrom and Ann Wolbert Burgess, *The Victim of Rape* (New Brunswick, N.J.: Transaction, 1983), xxi.

37. Ibid.

38. Kurt Weis and Sandra S. Borges, "Victimology and Rape: The Case of the Legitimate Victim," *Issues in Criminology,* 8 (Fall 1973), 87.

39. Amir, "Forcible Rape," 57.

40. Ibid.

41. Medea and Thompson, *Against Rape,* 134.

42. Amir, "Forcible Rape," 57.

43. Clifford Kirkpatrick and Eugene Kanin, "Male Sex Aggression on a University Campus," *American Sociological Review,* 22 (Feb. 1957), 53.

44. Eugene J. Kanin, "Male Aggression in Dating–Courtship Relations," *American Journal of Sociology,* 63 (Sept. 1957), 200.

45. Karen Barrett, "Date Rape, a Campus Epidemic?" *Ms.,* 11 (Sept. 1982), 130.

46. "Date Rape: Familiar Strangers," *Psychology Today* (July 1987), 10.

47. Susan H. Klemmack and David L. Klemmack, "The Social Definition of Rape," in Marcia J. Walker and Stanley L. Brodsky, eds., *Sexual Assault* (Lexington, Ma.: Lexington Books, 1976), 136.

48. David Finkelhor and Kersti Yllo, *License to Rape, Sexual Abuse of Wives* (New York: Holt, Rinehart and Winston, 1985), 6.

49. Ibid., 6–7.

50. Ibid., 8.

51. Diana E. H. Russell, *Rape in Marriage* (New York: Macmillan Publishing Co., 1982), 27.

52. Russell, *Rape in Marriage,* 57.

53. Finkelhor and Yllo, *License to Rape,* 18.

54. Ibid., 22, 113.

55. Ibid., 133.

56. *Criminal Victimization—1985,* Table 37, p. 39.

57. Comment, "Police Discretion and the Judgment that a Crime Has been Committed—Rape in Philadelphia," *University of Pennsylvania Law Review,* 117 (1968), 318.

58. Gary D. LaFree, "The Effect of Sexual Stratification by Race on Official Reactions to Rape," *American Sociological Review,* 45 (1980), 842.

59. *Criminal Victimization—1985,* Table 7, p. 17.

60. Russell, *Sexual Exploitation,* 88.

61. Ibid., 64.

62. Ibid., 122.

63. Ibid., 123.

64. Ibid., 65.

65. Menachem Amir, *Patterns in Forcible Rape* (Chicago: University of Chicago Press, 1971), 314. See also Benjamin Karpman, *The Sexual Offender and His Offenses* (New York: Julian Press, 1954), 38–39.

66. See, for example, Camille E. LeGrand, ''Rape and Rape Laws: Sexism in Society and Law,'' *California Law Review,* 61 (1973), 922; and Marray L. Cohen, Ralph Garofalo, Richard Boucher, and Theoharis Seghorn, ''The Psychology of Rapists,'' *Seminars in Psychiatry,* 3 (Aug. 1971), 317.

67. Brownmiller, *Against Our Will,* 195.

68. Amir, *Patterns in Forcible Rape,* 334.

69. Lucy Komisar, *Violence and the Masculine Mystique* (Pittsburgh: KNOW, Inc., n.d.), 6.

70. George L. Kirkham, ''Homosexuality in Prison,'' in James M. Henslin, ed., *Studies in the Sociology of Sex* (New York: Appleton-Century-Crofts, 1971), 340.

71. Alan J. Davis, ''Sexual Assaults in the Philadelphia Prison System,'' in John A. Gagnon and William Simon, eds., *The Sexual Scene* (Chicago: Aldine Publishing Co., 1970), 122–123.

72. Ibid., 123.

73. Jean Genet, *Our Lady of the Flowers,* Bernard Frechtman, trans. (New York: Grove Press, 1963), 253.

74. Kirkham, ''Homosexuality in Prison,'' 327.

75. Davis, ''Sexual Assaults in Prison,'' 110.

76. Cohen, ''The Psychology of Rapists,'' 322.

77. Ibid.

78. Horos, *Rape,* 22.

79. Diana E. H. Russell, *The Politics of Rape, the Victim's Perspective* (New York: Stein and Day, 1975), 258.

80. ''Public Sector,'' *Psychology Today* (Oct. 1986), 4.

81. Leroy Schultz, ''Interviewing the Sex Offender's Victim,'' *Journal of Criminal Law, Criminology and Police Science,* 50 (Jan./Feb. 1960), 451.

82. R. J. McCaldon, ''Rape,'' *Canadian Journal of Corrections,* 9 (Jan. 1967), 47.

83. Scully and Marolla, ''Convicted Rapists' Motive,'' 542.

84. Les Susman and Sally Bardwell, *The Rapist File* (New York: Chelsea House, 1981), 5.

85. ''Crosstalk,'' *Psychology Today* (April 1987) 12.

86. A. N. Groth, *Men Who Rape: The Psychology of the Offender* (New York: Plenum Press, 1979).

87. William D. Pithsers and others, ''Relapse Prevention with Sexual Aggressives: A Self-Control Model of Treatment and Maintenance of Change,'' in Joanne G. Greer and Irving L. Stuart, eds., *The Sexual Aggressor: Current Perspectives in Treatment* (New York: Van Nostrand Publishing Co., 1983).

88. Pamela Lakes Wood, ''The Victim in a Forcible Rape Case: A Feminist View,'' *American Criminal Law Review,* 7 (1973), 348.

89. Brownmiller, *Against Our Will,* 364.

90. *1976 Uniform Crime Reports,* 16.

91. Comment, ''Police Discretion,'' 292.

92. Ibid., 304.

93. Lynda Little Holmstrom and Ann Wolbert Burgess, *The Victim of Rape: Institutional Reactions* (New York: John Wiley and Sons, 1978), 38–41.

94. Gary D. LaFree, ''Official Reactions to Social Problems: Police Decisions in Sexual Assault Cases,'' *Social Problems,* 28 (June 1981), 180.

95. Holmstrom and Burgess, *Institutional Reactions,* 41–44.

96. Comment, ''Police Discretion,'' 304.

97. See, for example, Duncan Chappell et al., ''Forcible Rape: A Comparative Study of Offenses Known to the Police in Boston and Los Angeles,'' in James M. Henslin, ed., *Studies in the Sociology of Sex* (New York: Appleton-Century-Crofts, 1971), 180.

98. Ibid., 291.

99. Chappell, "Forcible Rape," 199.

100. Brownmiller, *Against Our Will,* 402.

101. Comment, "Police Discretion," 279.

102. National Institute of Law Enforcement and Criminal Justice, *Forcible Rape, A National Survey of the Response by Prosecutors,* vol. 1 (Washington, D.C.: U. S. Government Printing Office, 1977), 46.

103. Jerrold K. Footlick, "Rape Alert," *Newsweek,* Nov. 10, 1975, 70.

104. Lisa Brodyaga et al., *Rape and Its Victims: A Report for Citizens, Health Facilities, and Criminal Justice Agencies* (Washington, D.C.: U. S. Government Printing Office, 1975), 15. See also E. Galton, "Police Processing of Rape Complaints," *American Journal of Criminal Law,* 4 (Winter 1975–76), 15–30.

105. Holmstrom and Burgess, *Institutional Reactions,* 51.

106. William B. Sanders, *Rape and Woman's Identity* (Beverly Hills, Ca.: Sage Publications, 1980), 31.

107. Holmstrom and Burgess, *Institutional Reactions,* 92.

108. Janet Bode, *Fighting Back* (New York: Macmillan Publishing Co., 1978), 130–131; *United States v. Benn* 476 F. 2d. 1127, 1133 (1973).

109. Ann Wolbert Burgess and Lynda Lytle Holmstrom, *Rape: Victims of Crisis* (Bowie, Md.: Robert Brady Co., 1974), 197.

110. Ibid.

111. Ibid., 211.

112. Ibid., 200.

113. Wood, "The Victim in a Rape Case," 335.

114. Bode, *Fighting Back,* 167–168.

115. Harry Kalven, Jr. and Hans Zeisel, et al., *The American Jury* (Boston: Little, Brown and Company, 1966), 250–251.

116. Shirley Feldman-Summers and Karen Lindner, "Perceptions of Victims and Defendants in Criminal Assault Cases," *Criminal Justice and Behavior,* 3 (1976), 327.

117. Note, "The Rape Corroboration Requirement: Repeal Not Reform," *Yale Law Journal,* 81 (1972), 1379.

118. Wood, "The Victim in a Rape Case," 341–342.

119. Medea and Thompson, *Against Rape,* 121.

120. Wood, "The Victim in a Rape Case," 344–345.

121. Russell, *Sexual Exploitation,* 102.

122. Hursch, *The Trouble with Rape,* 122.

123. *1977 Uniform Crime Reports,* 14–15.

124. LeGrand, "Rape and Rape Laws," 927.

125. "Rape and the Law," *Newsweek,* May 20, 1985, 62.

126. Angela Davis, "Joanne Little: The Dialectics of Rape," *Ms.,* 3 (June 1975), 106.

127. "Negroes Accuse Maryland Bench: Double Standard Is Charged in Report on Rape Cases," *New York Times,* Sept. 18, 1967, CA33.

128. Martha R. Burt, "Cultural Myths and Supports for Rape," *Journal of Personality and Social Psychology,* 38 (1980), 855.

129. Jacqueline J. Kikuchi, "What Do Adolescents Know and Think about Sexual Abuse?" (Paper presented at the National Symposium on Child Victimization, Anaheim, Calif., April 27–30, 1988.)

130. Footlick, "Rape Alert," 71.

131. Horos, *Rape,* 96.

132. Beneke, *Men on Rape.*

133. Weis and Borges, "Victimology and Rape," 105.

134. Burgess and Holmstrom, *Rape: Victims of Crisis,* 41.

135. Julia R. Schwendinger and Herman Schwendinger, "Rape Myths: In Legal, Theoretical, and Everyday Practice," *Crime and Social Justice,* 1 (1974), 18.

136. Medea and Thompson, *Against Rape,* 24–25.

137. Russell, *Sexual Exploitation,* 132.

138. Ibid., 129–130.

139. Neil M. Malamuth, "Predictors of Naturalistic Sexual Aggressions," *Journal of Personality and Social Psychology,* 56 (1986), 960.

140. See, for example, Lin Farley, *Sexual Shakedown* (New York: Warner Books, 1978); Kathleen Barry, *Female Sexual Slavery* (New York: Avon Books, 1979); Andrea Dworkin, *Pornography: Men Possessing Women* (New York: Putnam, 1981).

Abortion: The Controversial Choice

NADEAN BISHOP

"Reproductive freedom" has been a major demand of the women's liberation movement for most of its existence, as well as one of its most controversial issues. In fact, whether or not reproductive freedom was even a women's rights issue was a subject of major debate at the 1967 national convention of the National Organization for Women, and the vote to include it in the Women's Bill of Rights cost NOW its conservative wing a year later.

Although reproductive freedom includes an entire gamut of issues, such as sex education, access to contraception, and an end to forced sterilization of poor and minority women, at its core is the question of abortion. Controversy over abortion preceded the women's movement by many years, and its resurgence as a contemporary issue was not initiated by feminists. The American Civil Liberties Union was the first national organization to support it publicly, in 1965, and the ACLU has sponsored the key court cases since then. National organizations to repeal abortion laws have developed independently of the feminist movement, but the issue has nonetheless become thoroughly identified as a feminist issue. Consequently, an argument that was originally expressed in terms of the right to privacy and medical safety is now primarily debated in terms of a woman's right to control her own body.

The result is that the pro and con sides do not speak to the same issue or from the same concerns. *Pro* does not mean pro-abortion; it means prochoice. Many who would not choose to terminate a pregnancy of their own argue that every woman should have the right to choose when and under what circumstances she will bear a child. Birth-control measures sometimes fail, victims of rape and incest must have some recourse, tests may show deformity of the embryo, or the number of children already born may be too many (and unwanted children may become neglected or beaten children). Regardless of the reasons, the choice should be that of the pregnant woman. It is her body and her right to make that choice. Society should not penalize her by forcing her to bear an unwanted child or to take the risk of an illegal

Copyright © 1989 by Jo Freeman. This article was revised by Jo Freeman, who would like to thank Susan Tew for supplying most of the current data.

abortion, which can usually be had only under medically unsafe conditions. From this perspective, reproductive freedom cannot be separated from any of the other women's rights issues; every woman must be free to determine her own life and she cannot do so with the fear of an unplanned, possibly unmanageable, disruption for childrearing.

Those opposed are more concerned with the "right to life" than the "right to choose." They argue that life exists from conception and that "abortion forfeits and very basic right to life from which all other rights proceed."[1] Because this argument makes an as-yet-unproved assumption about when life begins, it is basically a religious argument and is highly identified with religious forces. Although the right to life has been strongly supported by fundamentalist Protestants and Orthodox Jews, the Catholic hierarchy (although not necessarily the laity) has been a major backer of efforts to ban or restrict abortion.

Thus, it is worth comparing what the major religious faiths have to say, even though pro-choice advocates would say that any legislation that imposes a single interpretation of when life begins denies the religious freedom guaranteed by the First Amendment.

The testimony of Jewish Rabbi Balfour Brickner before a House subcommittee in March of 1976 provides a succinct history of the position of Judaism on abortion. Many Orthodox Jewish authorities advise against abortion except "when a woman is impregnated through rape or incest or when it is clear that continuation of pregnancy to birth would constitute a clear danger to the life and/or health of the mother." But the official position differs. "In Judaism, the fetus in the womb is not a person (lav nefesh hu) until it is born. . . . Thus there is no capital liability for foeticide. By this reckoning, abortion cannot be considered murder." This interpretation is made from the scriptural admonition in Exodus 21:22: "If a man strike, and wound a pregnant woman so that her fruit be expelled, but no harm befall her, then shall he be fined as her husband shall assess, and the matter placed before the judges." Talmudic commentators on this passage conclude that the one responsible "is not culpable for murder, since the unborn fetus is not considered a person."[2]

In direct contrast to the Jewish position that life begins at birth is the official pronouncement of the Roman Catholic church that life begins at the moment of conception. Thus, for the Roman Catholic hierarchy, any aborting of the fetus is condemned as murder. Pope John Paul II has maintained a hard line on abortion, asserting that the life of the fetus takes precedence over the life of the mother. The fetus is to be carried to term even if the pregnancy resulted from incest or rape and even if the life or mental health of the mother is in jeopardy.

It is startling in the light of theological rigidity and expected conformity that so many Catholics disagree with this official position and have maintained their opposition despite over a decade of pressure from the hierarchy. All the public opinion surveys that have been done before and after the Supreme Court made most abortions legal show that Catholics and Protestants have pretty much the same opinion on the circumstances under which women should be able to get abortions. The response varies with the wording of the question, but differences by religion have not changed appreciably over time for any possible circumstance. Jews, atheists, and "others" tend to be more liberal, but 80 to 90 percent of both Catholics and Protestants approve of abortion in cases of rape, danger to the health of the mother, or strong likelihood of a serious birth defect. Forty to fifty percent approve if the mother cannot afford a child, is unmarried, or does not want any more children. Rather than religion, it is education that has the most effect on people's opinions. People with some college education are much more likely to approve of a woman's right to choose than are those with only a high-school diploma, and they in turn are more approving than those without one.[3]

Catholic theologians have not always opposed abortion on the grounds that life begins with conception. Saint Jerome, translator of the Vulgate Bible, said in a letter to a female student, Algasis, "Seeds are gradually formed in the uterus, and it [abortion] is not reputed homicide until the scattered elements receive their appearances and members." Saint Augustine also said, "The law does not provide that the act [abortion] pertains to homicide, for there cannot yet be said to be a live soul in a body that lacks sensation when it is not formed in flesh and so not yet endowed with sense." Pope Gregory XIV in 1591 in the Codicis Juris Fontes returned to the practice of allowing abortions up to forty days, following the Aristotelian ruling on ensoulment, thus overturning the 1588 prohibition of abortion by Sixtus V.[4]

It was not until 1869 that the Catholic church, under Pope Pius IX, forbade all abortions. This dogma has been reaffirmed since, most strongly in the 1974 Declaration on Procured Abortion, which states: "The First Right of the Human Person is his life. Never, under any pretext, may a woman resort to abortion. Nor can one exempt women from what nature demands of them." This dogma is vehemently opposed by many Catholic women, such as Dr. Janet Furlong-Cahill, former professor at Saint Mary's, Notre Dame: "Such a stand is designed to leave woman at the mercy, not only of her biological makeup, but also at the mercy of a celibate hierarchy, who claim the right to damn her eternally if she uses methods such as artificial birth control, sterilization or abortion to protect herself against unwanted or dangerous pregnancies."[5]

Protestant denominations have a diversity of opinion regarding when life begins and whether abortion should be allowed. The testimony of Theressa Hoover, associate general secretary of the United Methodist church, before a House subcommittee may be taken as representative of the sentiments of many Protestants regarding abortion. Ms. Hoover stresses the strong Protestant tradition of "advocating individual responsibility in matters concerning family, sexuality, and community."[6] This belief is rooted in the teachings of Jesus, which admonish Christians to take responsibility for their own lives and to make responsible personal decisions. The right to privacy and the autonomy of the individual are basic doctrines, which are violated by governmental interference in matters of family planning.

Protestants would almost universally choose the life of the mother over the life of the fetus. As Ms. Hoover expresses it:

A woman suffering from heart disease, diabetes, or cancer, could suffer grave, if not fatal risks if she continued a pregnancy to term. And a woman who is the carrier of a genetic disease, such as sickle cell anemia or Tay-Sachs, which may be transmitted to the fetus, should not be compelled to bear that fetus if she does not choose to after medical tests have confirmed that the fetus is affected. We cannot in good conscience force a woman who has been raped to carry the possible resulting pregnancy to term. To do so would be to totally disregard the anguish which women suffer in such circumstances.[7]

Leaders from eighteen religious persuasions, including Protestants, Jews, and Roman Catholics, joined in 1973 to found the Religious Coalition for Abortion Rights to safeguard the option of legal abortion. The current crusade of RCAR is to counteract the anti-choice minority, headed by the National Conference of Catholic Bishops, the Moral Majority, and the National Right to Life Committee. The stance of the RCAR is not pro-abortion but pro-choice, a position that parallels the one taken by the American Civil Liberties Union: "The union itself offers no comment on the wisdom or the moral implications of abortion, believing that such judgments belong solely in the province of individual conscience and religion."[8]

LEGAL AND LEGISLATIVE STATUS OF ABORTION

On January 22, 1973, the Supreme Court handed down two landmark decisions regarding abortion, *Roe v. Wade* and *Doe v. Bolton*. *Roe* is the anonymous label given a pregnant unmarried woman in a Texas case, and *Doe* is the name given a pregnant married woman, mother of three, in a Georgia referral. In both cases the Court voted seven to two in support of the right to privacy of the women involved. It found that neither Texas nor Georgia had established any "compelling state interest" to restrict abortions during the first trimester of pregnancy, and it limited the legal control a state could exert over abortions in the second trimester to measures to protect the health of the mother.[9]

The ruling in *Roe v. Wade* surveyed medical, religious, moral, and historical material before concluding that the Fourteenth Amendment's protection of personal liberty "is broad enough to encompass a woman's decision whether or not to terminate her pregnancy."[10] Having decided this, the Supreme Court set different standards according to the trimester. During the first trimester, abortion presents very little danger to the mother, and thus no state interference is warranted in the decision to terminate an unwanted pregnancy: It is a matter between the patient and her doctor. After the first trimester, the state has the right to specify certain standards for the facilities where the abortion occurs, as well as for aftercare services in case of complications, which are more frequent during the second and third trimesters. But even then the state must not limit the reasons for which a woman may obtain an abortion.

In *Roe v. Wade,* the Supreme Court declined to intervene in the theological debate on when life begins: "We need not resolve the difficult question of when life begins. When those trained in the respective disciplines of medicine, philosophy, and theology are unable to arrive at any consensus, the judiciary, at this point in the development of man's knowledge, is not in a position to speculate as to the answer."[11] Addressing the state's interest in the right of the fetus, the Court in *Roe v. Wade* concluded that the potential life is not itself a person, implying that it is not entitled to precisely the same Fourteenth Amendment guarantees as the pregnant woman but that the state has some interest in potentiality of life.[12] Thus, after viability, which usually occurs between the twenty-fourth and twenty-eighth weeks, at which point the fetus may have hope for "meaningful life outside the mother's womb," the state may regulate or even forbid abortion unless it is required to save the pregnant woman's life or mental health.

A history of earlier abortion legislation may put recent decisions in perspective. The restrictive provisions of the ruling for the final trimester echo the wording of all abortion laws in the United States for the hundred years prior to 1973. For the first two hundred years of American history, abortion before the first movement of the fetus was not considered a crime of any kind, and during colonial times, in keeping with the English common law, willful abortion of a quickened fetus was accounted a simple misdemeanor. In 1803 the British revised their criminal code and made abortion a crime, although with lesser penalties before quickening. Exceptions were normally made if the abortion was necessary to save the life of the pregnant woman. In the United States the first abortion legislation was not passed until 1821, and it was not until after the Civil War that most states created statutes superseding British common law. Thereafter the restrictive provisions applied.[13]

Liberalization of these restrictions was proposed in 1959 in the Model Penal Code of the American Law Institute. The ALI code said that a licensed physician could terminate a pregnancy (1) if the life or mental health of the mother was threatened; (2) if the child was likely to be born with "a grave, permanent, and irremediable mental or physical defect" (such as those caused by the drug thalidomide); or (3) if the woman became pregnant as a result of rape or incest. Colorado in 1967 was the first state to adopt this code for therapeutic abortion; twelve other states adopted variations of it in the ensuing years. The removal of nearly all legal controls on abortion followed in 1970 in four states: New York, Washington, Alaska, and Hawaii.[14]

Georgia was one of the states adopting the ALI code, and in a companion case to *Roe,* the Court addressed its regulations. Georgia required that abortions be performed in hospitals approved by the Joint Commission on Accreditation, even though only 54 of its 159 counties had such hospitals. The court found this requirement invalid on the basis of lack of equal access as well as lack of compelling state interest. Also struck down were provisions requiring approval at all stages of pregnancy by two state-licensed physicians and a hospital review committee.[15]

The Supreme Court has addressed the right of the state to regulate the abortion decision several times since 1973; each time, it has reaffirmed its original ruling. On June 15, 1983, the Court ruled provisions of an Akron, Ohio, ordinance regulating abortion to be unconstitutional. In a decision written by Justice Lewis F. Powell, Jr., the Court ruled that second-trimester abortions may not be limited to performance in hospitals, since extensive experience shows that such abortions may be done as safely in an ambulatory surgical facility or in an outpatient clinic. Further, the Court ruled that governments may not impose a blanket provision "requiring the consent of a parent or person in loco parentis as a condition for abortion of an unmarried minor." The provision of the Akron ordinance that required the physician to inform the pregnant woman that "the unborn child is a human life from the moment of conception" violates "the Court's holding in *Roe v. Wade* that a state may not adopt one theory of when life begins to justify its regulation of abortions." This was also unacceptable because it was seen as an "intrusion upon the discretion of the pregnant woman's physician." A waiting period was also struck down, although the dissenting opinion written by Justice O'Connor argued forcefully that "the waiting period is surely a small cost to impose to insure that the woman's decision is well-considered in light of its certain and irreparable consequences on fetal life."[16]

The issue of state regulation was addressed again on June 11, 1986, when the Court struck down a Pennsylvania law whose sponsors admitted was designed to discourage women from choosing abortions. This law required that a woman be informed about the characteristics of the fetus at two-week intervals throughout gestation, the availability of agencies willing to help her bear the child, and the "detrimental and psychological effects" of abortion. The law also required that if there was a possibility that the aborted fetus could be viable, a second physician be present to preserve its life. The Court objected, pointing out that

> The states are not free, under the guise of protecting maternal health or potential life, to intimidate women into continuing pregnancies. Appellants claim that the statutory provisions before us today further legitimate compelling interests of the [State]. Close analysis of those provisions, however, shows that they wholly subordinate constitutional privacy interests and concerns with maternal health in an effort to deter a woman from making a decision that, with her physician, is hers to make.[17]

Although this case affirmed *Roe,* it indicated a growing gap in the Justices' views. *Roe* was decided by seven votes to two, with Justices William H. Rehnquist and Byron R. White in dissent. In the 1983 case, new Justice Sandra Day O'Connor increased the minority; in the 1986 case, Chief Justice Warren E. Burger switched sides, reducing the majority to five votes. He then resigned and was replaced by Antonin Scalia. In 1987, Justice Powell retired and on December 14, 1987, when there were only eight sitting justices, the Court split evenly on an Illinois law requiring teenage girls to notify their parents at least 24 hours before obtaining an abortion. The four-to-four vote left in place the appeals-court decision striking down the law, but set no national legal precedent. The legal future of a woman's right to decide whether or not to have an abortion may lie in the hands of the latest Reagan appointee.[18]

State restrictive laws, many of which were struck down by lower courts and never reached the Supreme Court, are just one part of an organized campaign to curtail legal abortions. In Congress, the primary efforts by opponents have been to restrict the use of federal funds to pay for abortions, and to pass a Constitutional amendment that would nullify *Roe*. The latter thrust has not met with much success, in part due to lack of consensus among its proponents on how strong an amendment to support. But the movement to limit federal funds has been extremely successful.

In 1976, Representative Henry Hyde (R. Ill.) attached an amendment to the 1977 Labor/HEW Appropriations Act that prohibited the use of federal Medicaid money to pay for abortions except where the life of the mother would be endangered. Medicaid provides federal funding for the health-care needs of people whose income falls below a certain level, provided that the states share the costs. Once federal funds were cut off, the states had the option of paying for the entire procedure with state money, and over a dozen states plus the District of Columbia have chosen to do so. Litigation delayed implementation of the cutoff, but once the Supreme Court held that Congress and the states could choose what medical care to provide, poor women in most states were left with the choice of paying for an abortion out of their own meager income, or of carrying the child to term.[19] The number of publicly subsidized abortions dropped from 295,000 in 1977 to 194,000 in 1978, and to 187,500 in 1985.[20]

Researchers have estimated that approximately 20 percent of Medicaid-eligible pregnant women bore their children, with the other 80 percent finding money to pay for an abortion from other sources. However, the lack of public funding has had a major impact both on poor women and on the public purse. Those poor women who do get abortions usually take the money out of family living expenses. Those who do not end up costing the taxpayers $4 in publicly financed medical and welfare expenses for every tax dollar not spent to pay for an abortion. Furthermore, the health risks are greater. "An estimated 22 percent of the Medicaid-eligible women who had second-trimester abortions would have had first-trimester abortions if there had been no finance-related delay. . . . [Because] the risk of complications following an induced abortion is increased if the procedure is done later in gestation"; the Center for Disease Control estimated that three deaths resulted from the funding restrictions in the first eighteen months.[21]

Since the first "Hyde Amendment," there have been dozens of fights in Congress over similar amendments every year. Although the language and the restrictions vary from year to year, the areas covered have gradually expanded. Currently, Congress prohibits the use of federal funds to pay for abortions not only of poor women, but of "federal employees, Indians served by federal health programs, military personnel, and Peace Corps volunteers."[22]

Under the Reagan administration, the move to ban federal funding for abortions spread to family-planning programs. Funded by Title X of the Public Health Service Act, several thousand clinics run by states, local health departments, and private nonprofit groups disseminate information on family planning and contraceptives. The Title X funds could not be used to perform abortions, but could support abortion counseling and referrals.

Conservatives in Congress sought to eliminate the Title X program; when that failed, they tried to prohibit the use of funds for abortion counseling and referrals.

When two years of jockeying left Title X tattered but intact, President Reagan announced that his administration would accomplish through regulations what it had failed to achieve with legislation and would bar from receipt of federal funds organizations that "encourage, promote, or advocate abortion," as well as those organizations that used their own money to provide abortions. These regulations would have eliminated Planned Parenthood, the nation's largest family-planning agency, from the program, which was a goal of the National Right to Life Committee. Planned Parenthood obtained an injunction from a federal court stopping implementation of the regulations by arguing that "restrictions on the content of counseling" violated the First Amendment and interfered with the doctor–patient relationship.[23]

Despite the intensity of the participants, as reflected in the numerous roll-call votes in Congress on abortion, the issues remain salient to only a small group in the population. Both election results and surveys indicate that very few people vote for or against a candidate or an office holder on the basis of that person's position on abortion. In 1984, less than 7 percent of the voters thought that the presidential candidates' position on abortion was important. Analyses of Congressional races showed a similar lack of salience. Although there is a relationship between party preference and attitudes on abortion, it appears to be coincidental, and not causal. Those with liberal attitudes on abortion tend to prefer Democrats, and those with traditional attitudes tend to prefer Republicans.[24]

WHO GETS AN ABORTION WHERE, AND HOW?

According to the Alan Guttmacher Institute, which is the most reliable source of abortion statistics, 30 percent of all pregnancies are terminated by abortion, 91 percent within the first trimester. The majority of women obtaining abortions over the last several years has characteristically been young (62 percent are 24 years and under), white (70 percent), and unmarried (81 percent).[25] The highest rate (abortions per 1,000 females age 15 to 44) is for women 18 to 19 years old, although the highest ratio (abortions per 1,000 pregnancies) is for girls under 15. The majority (57 percent) of women who had abortions had no children, although 3 percent had four or more. Similarly, the majority (63 percent) had never had an abortion, but almost 4 percent had had three or more.[26] Nonwhite women have twice as many abortions as white women, but this statistic partially reflects a higher fecundity rate. The ratio of abortions to pregnancies is only 50 percent higher for nonwhite women. "Nonwhite women usually use abortion to space their children or to terminate childbearing, whereas white women usually use it to postpone the onset of childbearing."[27]

Although statistics on abortion before its legalization are obviously incomplete, both the rate and the ratio rose steadily after 1973, but leveled off in the eighties (see Figure 1). Both of these measures vary widely by locality. Metropolitan areas have much higher rates than do rural areas, and the range among the states is enormous. The District of Columbia continues to lead all areas, with three times the rate of the two highest states (New York and California) and fifteen times that of the four lowest (Wyoming, Mississippi, Arkansas, and West Virginia). This wide variation is due primarily to the fact that "abortion services remain unavailable in many areas . . . particularly rural communities and small towns. Only 32,000 abortions, or two percent of the national total, were provided outside of metropolitan areas during 1985."[28]

The availability of abortion services has declined in the last few years, in part due to harassment of abortion providers.[29] According to the National Abortion Federation, which monitors incidents, 1984 saw a significant

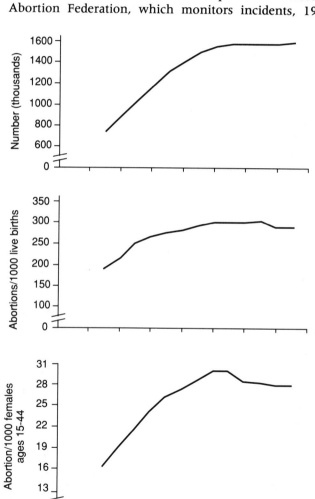

SOURCE: Alan Guttmacher Institute, as presented in *Family Planning Perspectives*, Mar./Apr. 1987, Table 1, p. 64.

FIGURE 1 *Legal abortions, by year, United States, 1973–1985.*

increase in the number and severity of antiabortion actions.[30] In 1985, 47 percent of all providers serving 83 percent of all patients were harassed in some form. The most common type of harassment was picketing, but bomb threats, death threats, sit-ins, vandalism, and arson also occurred. Not only were the centers targets, but staff members and patients were personally harassed in various ways, including picketing of their homes and threatening telephone calls. Large nonhospital facilities and clinics were the most common targets, especially in the South and Midwest, and were usually subject to an ongoing campaign, not just sporadic acts. Although there is no evidence that harassment has reduced the number of abortions performed, it has raised the costs of providing them. Facilities enduring harassment report increased security, insurance, and legal costs, as well as licensing problems and high staff turnover.[31] In addition, there is evidence that harassment has decreased the range of services available by discouraging small providers and those in small towns.[32]

By 1985, 60 percent of all abortions were performed in abortion clinics, and 23 percent in other clinics. Only 13 percent were done by hospitals. The remaining 4 percent took place in physicians' offices.[33] Some form of suction and surgical currettage is used in over 96 percent of abortions now being performed in the United States. This procedure can range from menstrual regulation in the early weeks, through suction of the embryo with a flexible cannula, to a D & C (dilation and curettage in which the womb is scraped by a sharp instrument after vacuum evacuation). Only 0.07 percent of abortions involve hysterotomy (an incision of the uterus) or hysterectomy (removal of the uterus). The remaining procedures (approximately 4 percent) are forms of medical induction of abortion, usually consisting of injecting saline into the womb or administering prostaglandins.[34]

THE UNCERTAIN FUTURE

The changing composition of the Supreme Court raises the real possibility that women throughout the United States will not always have the same right to choose as they have had since 1973. Yet an entire generation of young women has grown to maturity without any understanding of what it was like before *Roe* made legal abortions readily available.[35] During this period, the issue of reproductive control has become, if anything, even more controversial, and has spawned the issue of a woman's right to have a child as well as her right not to have one. Many unresolved issues, such as surrogate motherhood, in vitro fertilization, and the scope of family planning technologies have been caught up in the battle. What has not been debated is how to minimize abortions. Although both opponents and proponents of a woman's right to choose agree that abortion should be the strategy of last resort, there has been no agreement on strategies to prevent abortion. Yet analyses of other developed countries clearly indicate that the key to lowering the abortion rate is effective family-planning services. When services are available and young women are educated about their value, the pregnancy rate decreases. Because the services and education are not widely available in the United States, this country has one of the highest pregnancy rates, with the greatest percent of unplanned pregnancies of any developed Western country. It is also second only to Greece in both its abortion rate and abortion ratio.[36]

Should the Supreme Court decide to overrule *Roe*, this high pregnancy rate will become a major social problem. Such a decision would not prohibit abortion; it would return to the states the right to make laws curtailing or regulating the practice. There would be two consequences. One is that the state legislatures would become arenas for conflict. The other is that illegal, back-alley abortions would flourish once again, with all the risks they bring to women's health. Even more than in the pre-*Roe* era, the availability of abortion would be dependent on a woman's income. Women with some financial resources would be able to travel to those states that permit abortions; those without would not. The injustices this situation would create means there is no room for complacency. Abortion has been a controversial choice for decades; it will remain so for decades to come.

NOTES

1. National Commission on the Observance of International Women's Year, *"To Form a More Perfect Union": Justice for American Women* (Washington, D.C.: Government Printing Office, 1976), 280.

2. *Judaism and Abortion*, testimony before the Subcommittee on Civil and Constitutional Rights of the Committee on the Judiciary, U.S. House of Representatives, Mar. 24, 1976 (Religious Coalition for Abortion Rights, 100 Maryland Ave., N.E., Washington, D.C. 20002, 1976).

3. National Opinion Research Center, *General Social Survey*, Cumulative Code Book, University of Chicago. A summary of NORC data can be found in *Family Planning Perspectives*, 5 (Sept./Oct. 1987), 221. *The Gallup Report* publishes the surveys by that organization, which include questions on abortion.

4. Catholics for a Free Choice, *Theological Facts of History on Abortion* (Catholics for a Free Choice, 201 Massachusetts Ave., N.E., Washington, D.C. 20002, 1976).

5. Janet Furlong-Cahill, *Abortion: the Double Standard* (Washington, D.C.: Catholics for a Free Choice, 1974), 5.

6. *Protestantism and Abortion*, testimony before the Subcommittee on Civil and Constitutional Rights of the Committee on the Judiciary, U.S. House of Representatives, Mar. 24, 1976 (Religious Coalition for Abortion Rights, 100 Maryland Ave., N.E., Washington, D.C. 20002, 1976).

7. Ibid.

8. *Abortion: Why Religious Organizations in the United States Want to Keep It Legal* (Religious Coalition for Abortion Rights, 100 Maryland Ave., N.E., Washington, D.C. 20002, 1976).

9. For a narrative description of the story behind the case see Marian Faux, *Roe v. Wade: The Untold Story of the Landmark Supreme Court Decision That Made Abortion Legal* (New York: Macmillan, 1988).

10. *Roe v. Wade* 410 U.S. 113, 153 (1973).

11. *Roe v. Wade* at 159.

12. *Roe v. Wade* at 154, 158.

13. Harriet F. Pilpel, Ruth Jane Zuckerman, and Elizabeth Ogg, *Abortion: Public Issue, Private Decision*, pamphlet no. 527 (Public Affairs, 381 Park Ave. South, New York, N.Y. 10016, 1975), 11.

14. Ibid.

15. *Doe v. Bolton,* 410 U.S. 179 (1973).

16. *City of Akron v. Akron Center for Reproductive Health, Inc.,* 462 U.S. 416, 439 [quoting *Planned Parenthood of Central Missouri v. Danforth,* 428 U.S. 52, 74 (1976)], 444, 445, 474 (1983).

17. *Thornburgh v. American College of Obstetricians and Gynecologists,* 476 U.S. 747, 759, 760, 90 L.Ed. 2d. 779, 793, 795 (1986).

18. *CQ Weekly Report,* Dec. 19, 1987, 3132.

19. *Beal v. Doe,* 432 U.S. 438 (1977). *Maher v. Roe,* 432 U.S. 464 (1977). *Harris v. McRae,* 448 U.S 297 (1980).

20. Stanley K. Henshaw and Lynn S. Wallisch, "The Medicaid Cutoff and Abortion Services for the Poor," *Family Planning Perspectives* 16 (July/Aug. 1984), 171; Rachel B. Gold and Jennifer Macias, "Public Funding of Contraceptive, Sterilization and Abortion Services, 1985," *Family Planning Perspectives* 18 (Nov./Dec. 1986), 259–264.

21. Henshaw and Wallisch, p. 170; Aida Torres, Patricia Donovan, Nancy Dittes and Jacqueline Darroch Forrest, "Public Benefits and Costs of Government Funding for Abortion," *Family Planning Perspectives* 18 (May/June 1986), 111. J. Gold and W. Cates Jr., "Restriction of Federal Funds for Abortion: 18 Months Later," *American Journal of Public Health* 69 (1979) 929.

22. *Congress and the Nation 1981–1984,* vol. IV, p. 690.

23. *CQ Weekly Report,* Sept. 19, 1987, 2241–2; Nov. 14, 1987, 2821–2; March 5, 1988, 616–7.

24. Donald Granberg, "The Abortion Issue in the 1984 Elections," *Family Planning Perspectives* 19 (Mar./Apr. 1987), 59–62.

25. Stanley K. Henshaw, "Characteristics of U.S. Women Having Abortions: 1982–1983," *Family Planning Perspectives* 19 (Jan./Feb. 1987), 5. The Federal Center for Disease Control also collects abortion statistics, but consistently underestimates the figures from the AGI survey by about 15 percent. The CDC gets most of its data from state health departments, and some from hospitals and other medical facilities. Not all states provide data. AGI directly surveys abortion providers, and calculates an increment for nonrespondents. The Bureau of the Census relies on the AGI data in computing its tables for the annual *Statistical Abstract of the United States,* and not on those of CDC.

26. *Ibid.,* Table 1, p. 6.

27. *Ibid.,* Table 2, p. 7.

28. Stanley K. Henshaw, Jacqueline Darroch Forrest, and Jennifer Van Vort, "Abortion Services in the U.S. 1984 and 1985," *Family Planning Perspectives* 19 (Mar./Apr. 1987), Table 3, pp. 64–65.

29. *Ibid.,* 65.

30. National Abortion Federation "Incidents of Reported Violence Toward Abortion Providers" in *Abortion Clinic Violence,* Oversight Hearings before the Subcommittee on Civil and Constitutional Rights of the Committee on the Judiciary, House of Representatives, 99th Cong., Mar. 6, 12, and Apr. 3, 1985; and Dec. 17, 1986, 675.

31. Jacqueline Darroch Forrest and Stanley K. Henshaw, "The Harassment of U.S. Abortion Providers," *Family Planning Perspectives* 19 (Jan./Feb. 1987), 9.

32. Henshaw, Forrest, and Van Vort, 70.

33. Ibid., 67.

34. Henshaw, 6.

35. Some of the horror of that period is captured by Ellen Messer and Kathryn E. May, *Back Rooms: Voices From the Illegal Abortion Era* (New York: St. Martin's Press, 1988).

36. Elise F. Jones, Jacqueline D. Forrest, Stanley K. Henshaw, Jane Silverman, and Aida Torres, "Unintended Pregnancy, Contraceptive Practice and Family Planning Services in Developed Countries," *Family Planning Perspectives* 20 (Mar./Apr. 1988), 53–67.

Sexual Harassment: The Link Joining Gender Stratification, Sexuality, and Women's Economic Status

SUSAN EHRLICH MARTIN

Although jokes about the producer, the starlet, and the casting couch, or about the secretary taking dictation on the boss's lap, have long been part of our social lore, serious consideration of sexual harassment as a feminist issue is in its infancy. Until recently, if sexual harassment received any attention, it tended to be regarded as an individual problem, either a not-too-serious matter brought on by the woman of dubious virtue whose demeanor or attire "asked for it" or a complaint initiated by a woman as an illegitimate way to get ahead on the job. Until 1976, when the term *sexual harassment* apparently first came into use, the phenomenon was literally unspeakable (MacKinnon 1979). Since that time, sexual harassment has come to be recognized as a pervasive and harmful social problem and as a form of behavior prohibited by the Supreme Court as sex discrimination under Title VII of the Civil Rights Act of 1964.

Understanding sexual harassment requires recognizing that it is central to maintaining women's subordinate social, economic, and sexual statuses and thus is closely related to other feminist issues. Along with rape, wife beating, prostitution, and pornography, it is one of the ways in which male control of women's sexuality shapes women's experience.

This article reviews recent studies of the nature and extent of sexual harassment, analyzes the meaning of harassment from a feminist perspective, and examines the responses of individuals to the harassment experience. It also examines the government's responses to the issue through the development of case law and public policy.

DEFINITIONS OF SEXUAL HARASSMENT

Various definitions of sexual harassment have been proposed. For example, Safran (1976:149) defined it as "sex that is one-sided, unwelcome, or comes with strings attached"; Farley (1978:14–15) called it "unsolicited, nonreciprocal male behavior that asserts a woman's sex role over her functioning as a worker"; and Yale University defined it as "an attempt to coerce an unwilling person into a sexual relationship, to subject a person to unwanted attention or to punish a refusal to comply" (cited by Crocker, 1983:698). The definition of sexual harassment applicable throughout the federal civil service is "deliberate or repeated unsolicited verbal comments, gestures, or physical contact of a sexual nature which are unwelcome" (U.S. House of Representatives 1980:8). What is common to these definitions is that sexual harassment (1) is physical or verbal behavior that is sexual in nature (i.e., it makes the victim's sex salient over her occupational or other statuses); (2) is unwanted; and (3) implicitly or explicitly is experienced as a threat to the woman's job or ability to perform her work or educational activities.[1]

Problems arise in defining and identifying incidents of sexual harassment because harassing behavior is not always clearly different from other acts. The same action, such as a man's putting an arm around a woman's shoulder, may be regarded by its recipient either as intentionally offensive or as a friendly gesture, and may be welcome or repugnant depending on the woman's interpretation of the man's intentions, her view of him, and the situation.[2]

Two primary types of sexual harassment have been identified by MacKinnon (1979) and subsequently by the courts: *quid pro quo harassment* and *harassment as a continuing condition of work.* Quid pro quo harassment involves a more or less explicit exchange: A woman must comply sexually or forfeit an employment or educational benefit. In such instances, the harasser tends to be an employer, supervisor, or teacher because his power to punish or reward rests on his occupational status. Male coworkers, classmates, and clients, however, may use informal authority in the work or academic setting or the power to give or withhold business or sales in order to harass. Quid pro quo harassment situations involve three elements: an advance, a response, and a consequence. Four different outcomes are possible: (1) an employer or instructor makes an advance, the woman declines it, and she is punished; (2) the employer or instructor makes an advance, the woman complies, but she does not receive the promised benefit; (3) the employer or instructor makes an advance, the woman complies, and she gains the benefit; (4) the employer or instructor makes an advance, the woman declines, and she receives no subsequent harassment or reprisal. Although each situation involves harassment, all successful legal cases against quid pro quo harassment have dealt with the first type, whereas courts have identified the second type as an additional illegal "condition of work."

Sexual harassment may also occur as a condition of work. Such harassment generally does not involve outright sexual demands (but see discussion of *Meritor v. Vinson* 477 US 57 [1986] on pages 69–71), but does include a variety of behaviors, such as touching, teasing, and making comments about a woman's appearance or sexuality; these require no response but make the woman's work environment unpleasant. Often such harassing behavior is less blatant or threatening than quid pro quo harassment, is condoned by management, and is regarded as "normal" male behavior or as an extension of the male prerogative of initiation in male–female interaction. For these reasons, women often do not define such behavior as sexual harassment and, when they do, they tend to be more reluctant to make formal complaints about it than about quid pro quo harassment.

SURVEY FINDINGS REGARDING SEXUAL HARASSMENT

Knowledge is still limited about the frequency of various types of sexual harassment, the characteristics of victims and harassers, the conditions under which it occurs, its psychological and physical effects on the victims, and their responses to it. Most of the early studies involved nonrandom surveys with self-selected respondents, lacked a standard definition of sexual harassment, failed to specify the time period within which the respondent was to answer, and provided evidence that was stark but impressionistic rather than scientific (Safran 1976; Carey 1977; Kelber 1977; Silverman 1976–77). Several recent studies have used random samples that permit more conclusive statistical analyses of the distribution of harassing behavior (Loy and Stewart, n.d.; Gutek et al. 1980; Gutek 1981; MSPB 1981; Benson and Thomson 1982; McCormack 1985; MSPB, 1988). Loy and Stewart surveyed a random probability sample of 304 female and 203 male adult residents of Connecticut. Gutek et al., in 1980, pilot-tested interviews with 399 men and women, and subsequently (1981), Gutek interviewed 405 men and 827 women in the Los Angeles area using a random-digit-dialing selection procedure. Benson and Thomson sent questionnaires to a random sample of 400 female students in their senior year at the University of California at Berkeley and got 269 responses. McCormack (1985) conducted a survey of 1178 randomly selected male and female students majoring in physics, chemistry, economics, and sociology at sixteen northeastern universities. The first study by the U.S. Merit Systems Protection Board (MSPB: 1981) involved a stratified random sample of more than 23,000 civilian employees of the executive branch of the federal government and thus provides the fullest and most reliable picture of sexual harassment to date.[3]

Extent of Sexual Harassment

In the early studies estimates of the proportion of women experiencing sexual harassment on the job were so high that *Redbook* observed: "The problem is not epidemic; it is pandemic—an everyday, everywhere occurrence" (Safran 1976:217). Recent studies support this conclusion. Both the first and follow-up MSPB studies found that 42 percent of the female federal employees had experienced some form of sexual harassment in the work-place during the previous two years. The most severe type of harassment, actual or attempted rape or sexual assault, decreased from 1 percent in 1980 to .8 percent in 1987, and unwanted pressure for dates also fell (from 26 to 15 percent). The rate of all other types of harassment remained the same (9 percent faced pressure for sexual favors and 28 percent received suggestive looks or gestures in both years of the survey) or increased (the proportion of women that received unwanted letters, telephone calls, or materials of a sexual nature grew from 9 to 12 percent; deliberate touching, leaning over, cornering, or pinching increased from 15 to 26 percent; and the proportion experiencing sexual remarks, teasing, jokes, or questions grew from 33 to 35 percent) (MSPB 1988:16–17).

Loy and Stewart (n.d.:Table 3) found that almost half (49.8 percent) of the women surveyed had experienced at least one type of sexual harassment, with 37 percent reporting commentary harassment, 26 percent manhandling, 7 percent negotiation harassment, and 2 percent assault.

Benson and Thomson (1982:241) found that about 30 percent of the Berkeley seniors who responded had personally experienced at least one incident of sexual harassment during their college careers, although a larger proportion knew of incidents involving someone else and agreed that such occurrences were not rare. These incidents tended to take the form of gradual inducements not overtly linked to grades or to immediate sexual obligations. Instead, instructors displayed friendliness and offered extra help and flexible deadlines, which laid the groundwork for subsequent overtures. McCormack (1985) found only 2 percent of the male and 17 percent of the female students reported sexual harassment by a teacher.

Victim Characteristics

Women of all backgrounds and in all positions have been victims of harassment, although a woman's age, marital status, and education affect the likelihood of harassment. The first MSPB study found that the rate of harassment was directly proportional to the youth of the victim. Twice as many women between sixteen and nineteen years of age (67 percent) reported being harassed as did women between forty-five and fifty-four (33 percent) (MSPB 1981:43). More single (53 percent) and divorced (49 percent) women reported harassment than married (37 percent) and widowed women (31 percent). Surprisingly, both MSPB studies found that harassment increased with the woman's education. The higher victimization rate of the more educated female employees appears to be related both to the difference in their attitudes (i.e., they defined more behaviors as harassment) and to their presence in nontraditional jobs (MSPB 1981:44, MSPB 1988:20). The race and ethnic background of the victim, however, made virtually no difference (MSPB 1981:44–45).

Organizational Characteristics

A number of organizational characteristics were also found by the MSPB studies to be related to sexual harassment, including agency, job classification, traditionalism of the job, sex of the victim's supervisor, and sexual composition of the victim's work group. Incidents of harassment in the 1987 study varied from 29 to 52 percent of the respondents among federal agencies (MSPB 1988:18); the job classification of the victim showed only a modest relationship to victimization. The earlier study found that harassment occurred most frequently among trainees (51 percent); the proportions of women in professional and technical, clerical, and blue-collar positions that reported victimization were 41, 40, and 38 percent respectively (MSPB 1981:50). The differences between the trainees and other employees may reflect the younger age and greater powerlessness of the former. It is noteworthy that 53 percent of the women in nontraditional jobs but only 41 percent in traditional jobs reported unwanted sexual attention on the job (MSPB 1981:51). Women with a male supervisor were somewhat more likely to be sexually harassed (45 percent) than were those with a female supervisor (38 percent). In addition, the male–female ratio of the work group was strongly related to harassment. The greater the proportion of men in the work group, the more likely the women were to be harassed: 55 percent of those who worked in virtually all-male groups and 49 percent of those in predominantly male groups were subjected to harassment; 37 percent in predominantly female and only 22 percent in all-female work groups were victims of harassment (MSPB 1981:52). This difference may be related both to the statistically greater number of men in jobs that are nontraditional for women and to deliberate harassment by men as an expression of resentment of the presence of women in these jobs. Differences among salaries and grade levels and by region were minor, as were several other organizational characteristics, including privacy on the job, length of federal service, work schedule, typical working hours, and the size of the immediate work group (MSPB 1981:52–54).

The Harassers

The typical harasser of federal female employees was a male coworker who was married, older than the victim, of the same race or ethnic background, and likely to have harassed others at work, according to descriptions of the victims (MSPB 1981:59–60). In the 1987 study, in 29 percent of the cases, women reported harassment by an immediate or higher-level supervisor (down from the 37 percent who reported victimization by supervisors in the 1980 study); 69 percent were bothered by a coworker or other federal employee with no supervisory authority over the victim (an increase from the 65 percent figure reported in 1980); and only 2 percent were bothered by a subordinate (a decrease from the 4 percent reported in 1980) (MSPB, 1988: 20). The 1980 study found that for the victim of rape or sexual assault, however, the supervisor was the perpetrator in 51 percent of the cases (MSPB 1981:60).

Loy and Stewart report somewhat different proportions of harassment by coworkers and supervisors. They found that 48 percent of the women reporting harassment had been victimized by an immediate or higher-level supervisor, and 50 percent reported harassment by a coworker (Loy and Stewart, n.d.:Table 8).

Sexual harassment has psychological, social, and physical effects on its victims. Like rape victims, sexually harassed women feel humiliated, ashamed, and angry. In one survey in which women could report more than one reaction, 78 percent reported feeling angry, 48 percent feeling upset, and 23 percent feeling frightened; an additional 27 percent mentioned feeling alienation, aloneness, helplessness, guilt, or some other negative emotion. Only 7 percent reported feeling indifference (Silverman 1976–77). The harassed women tended to feel that the incident was their fault and that they were individually responsible as well as demeaned. Some women reported strained relations with men, including their husbands, as a result of the harassment (Safran 1976; Lindsey 1977). Others reported development of physical symptoms and attitude changes, including loss of ambition and self-confidence and a negative view of their work (Safran 1976; Silverman 1976–77; New Responses, Inc. 1979). One-third of all the victims—and 82 percent of the victims of rape/assault—reported suffering emotional or physical consequences (MSPB 1981:81).

Sexual harassment also had harmful effects on female students. One study found that it disrupted the process of intellectual development and caused confusion, uncertainty, self-doubt, and distrust of male faculty in general (Benson and Thomson 1982:246–47). It also led to feelings of helplessness—that nothing was likely to be done about a complaint, that the student was not likely to be believed when a tenured professor denied a complaint, and that she would be labeled a "troublemaker" or suffer reprisals in the form of lowered grades and poor recommendations.

Although there is no way to estimate costs to individual victims, the MSPB estimated that the sexual harassment of women cost the federal government $267 million between May 1985 and May 1987. This figure encompasses the costs of job turnover, including the costs of offering a job to, doing background checks on, and training new employees; dollar losses due to emotional and physical stress, measured in terms of increased use of governmental health-benefit plans; and dollar losses due to absenteeism and lost individual and work-group productivity over a two-year period (MSPB 1988:39).

ANALYSIS OF SEXUAL HARASSMENT

Sexual harassment is traditionally explained as either biologically based, "natural" behavior or as the idiosyncratic personal proclivity of a minority of men. One variation of this traditional perspective assumes that the human sex drive is stronger in men, leading them to act in sexually aggressive ways toward women. Another variation maintains that men and women are naturally attracted to each other and therefore inevitably engage in sexually oriented behavior in the workplace. A third variation suggests that sexually harassing behavior stems from the personal peculiarities of isolated, highly sexed individuals. What these variations have in common is their denial that sexual harassment at work has the intent or effect of discriminating against women or that it reduces women's chances to achieve social equality.

This traditional approach has several notable shortcomings. Most important is the failure to see that men and women are gender groups that are socialized into learned sex roles and work behaviors. Sexual behavior, like other kinds of social behavior, is learned, shaped by social rules and norms, and best understood in a social rather than an isolated individual context. Most individuals can and do control their impulses, in conformity with existing social rules. In addition, the traditional view trivializes the problem of sexual harassment by asserting that such behavior is "normal" or that it is futile to try to change human nature, thereby making any systematic effort to remedy the problem hopeless.

A feminist approach to sexual harassment views this behavior as the use of power derived from the economic or occupational sphere to gain benefits or to impose punishments in the sexual sphere. Thus, economic inequality (i.e., the employer's control of workers) and sexual inequality (i.e., men's dominance over and control of women) reinforce each other to undercut women's potential for social equality in two interlocking ways. Women's confinement to dead-end, low-paying, sex-typed jobs and their subordination to male supervisors, employers, and instructors make them systematically vulnerable to sexual coercion. At the same time, the sex-role expectations of women as wives, mothers, and sex objects get carried into the workplace and are used to coerce women economically.

Women in the Occupational System

Women's place in the occupational world is characterized by (1) lower pay than men on the average, and lower pay for doing the same job; (2) subordination to male supervisors and dependence on their goodwill and approval for getting, keeping, and advancing on a job; and (3) concentration in sex-typed occupations considered appropriate for women with limited opportunities for mobility into other types of work or up a career ladder. Limited alternatives and subordination to male supervisors make it difficult for female workers to reject sexual advances by males in positions of authority. Occupational segregation contributes to the sexual harassment of women employed in both traditionally "female" and traditionally "male" jobs through a phenomenon termed *sex-role spillover* (Gutek and Morash 1982). Sex-role spillover occurs when gender-based expectations for behavior get carried into the workplace, so that workers in their work roles are expected to behave as males or females.

"Women's jobs" not only offer low pay, little prestige, and routine tasks, but also require women to serve, emotionally support, and be sexually attractive to men. Thus, these jobs are extensions of the female sex role into the workplace. The secretary, for example, is the "office wife," who, in addition to performing her official duties, is expected to make coffee, run her boss's personal errands, and maintain his sense of masculinity through flattery and deference (Kanter 1977). Similarly, the scanty attire required of some waitresses and the former requirement that airline stewardesses be unmarried and younger than thirty years of age indicate that female sexuality is an integral part of what is being sold by their employers. Indeed,

> the very qualities which men find sexually attractive in the women they harass are the real qualifications for the jobs for which they hire them. It is this good-girl sexiness . . . that qualifies a woman for her job that leaves her open to sexual harassment at any time and to the accusation that she invited it [MacKinnon 1979:23].

Women who enter male-dominated occupations or high-status positions, as conspicuous "token" exceptions to women's position in the occupational world, also suffer from sexual harassment. For them, too, sex-role expectations spill over into work-role expectations. But their jobs require behaviors regarded as masculine — behaviors seen as incongruent with their sex role. The tendency of male coworkers in this situation is to behave toward these women in accordance with the men's primary conception of them; i.e., as women rather than as workers. The women's sex becomes salient, and the men cast them into stereotyped female roles, including "the mother," "the sister," and "the seductress," whose sexuality blots out all other characteristics (Kanter 1977:234–35). Although similar stereotyping of women in traditionally female jobs occurs, it is less visible because the expected behavior is perceived to be a part of the woman's job.

In addition, women in "men's jobs" are sexually harassed as a condition of work. Men view the presence of these women as an invasion of male economic turf (i.e., as a challenge to the men's better pay and supervisory authority), as an invasion of their social turf (e.g., army barracks, board rooms, and police stations), and as a threat to their definition of their work and selves as "masculine." They often harass women to keep the women from working effectively, thereby "proving" women's unfitness for a "man's job" and, in some instances, driving out the female "invaders."

Sex-Role Socialization and Cultural Norms

Sexual harassment, as well as the position of women in the occupational world, rests on the social arrangements between the sexes and the perpetuation of these arrangements through sex-role socialization. Sex-role socialization is the process by which people learn the cultural norms for attitudes and behaviors appropriate to their sex; that is, they learn how to think and act as men or as women. These sex-role norms also express the relative positions of the sexes. Male and female sex roles are not simply different; they reflect sexual inequality and, in their enactment, perpetuate it. Women are not born weak, passive, dependent, and receptive to male initiation; they are socially conditioned to develop these qualities. Similarly, men learn that they are expected to be strong, dominant, independent, aggressive, and the initiators of sexual interaction. These expectations and norms permit men as a group to dominate women as a group through the privilege of initiating — and thereby controlling — intimate relationships. The social and sexual power that sex-role norms give men over women is carried into the workplace and is reinforced through male economic control of women's livelihood.

Despite folklore about "women who sleep their way to the top," there is little evidence that women advance on the job by using their sexuality to gain employment benefits. On the contrary, there is strong indication that acquiescence to sexual harassment has harmful effects on women's efforts to gain social and economic equality. Allegations of women's sexual complicity to gain employment benefits trivializes the magnitude of the problem of sexual harassment and obscures the nature of the situation faced by most women by putting it in false moral terms. For example, Phyllis Schlafly asserted that "sexual harassment on the job is not a problem for the virtuous woman except in the rarest of cases" (Rich 1981:A2). Such a statement implies that sexual harassment is the woman's fault. Rather than perceiving the woman as a victim of unwanted attention from someone with power over her livelihood, Schlafly blames the woman who "allows" herself to be harassed—or worse, elicits the harassment—because she is of dubious virtue. However, sexual harassment is not a question of "virtue"; it is a question of power. Women who acquiesce often are not in a position to refuse; their surrender is the price of survival. And while some women may gain benefits by providing "sexual favors," statistics on women's employment clearly indicate that these must be few in number, since as a group women fail to attain jobs for which they are qualified, much less to obtain undeserved advancement.

Both women and men feel injured by the benefits given to acquiescent women. But they direct their anger at the victims rather than looking at the system that permits the victimization. The acquiescence of a few women divides women as a group, thereby diminishing their ability to unite in fighting economic and sexual discrimination. Compliant women become the scapegoats for women's anger, which should properly focus on the men who offer economic rewards at a price, the work organization that permits harassment (often informally regarding it as a perquisite of male employees), or the sexual-stratification system that gives men power over women's livelihood and sexuality and perpetuates women's subordination and dependence.

Women's acquiescence to sexual harassment also reinforces the hostility of men to female coworkers. Many men who tolerate or accept a variety of other forms of favoritism in the distribution of job-related rewards, including relationships cultivated on the ball field, in the locker room, or at all-male clubs, are infuriated by the thought that women have and use "advantages" men do not have, making them feel "disadvantaged as a class" (Martin 1980). Men's anger at this form of injustice, however, is directed at both the compliant women and all women on the job, rather than at their male bosses (since it would be dangerous to express such jealousy and anger) or at the system that evades the merit principles it espouses. Such anger also serves as a convenient ego-protecting device, particularly for men of average competence. Stories or rumors about compliant women protect such men's sense of masculinity, which is threatened by the possibility that female coworkers are being advanced ahead of them because the women are more competent. By implying that the only way a woman can succeed is by using her sexuality rather than by performing better than male colleagues, the men can rationalize their failures, redirect their anger at a less threatening target, and thereby reassert their superiority as males.

INDIVIDUAL RESPONSES TO SEXUAL HARASSMENT: STRATEGIES AND OUTCOMES

Victims of sexual harassment have limited options for dealing with unwanted sexual attention. They can adopt informal approaches, which include ignoring the harassment and asking the harasser to stop. They can quit the job or seek a transfer; students can change majors or courses. They can use formal grievance and complaint procedures or take legal action. Or they can acquiesce. Each strategy has risks and costs. Informal approaches may be ineffectual and may trigger escalation of the situation or retaliation. Escapist approaches can have substantial economic consequences: the loss of seniority, accumulated job knowledge, personal work-based ties, and income during the transition; the possibility of finding a new job only at a lower salary; and the acquisition of a reputation as an unstable worker. Formal complaints risk reprisals (including failure to be promoted, reduction in duties, dismissal, or, for students, lowered grades and poor recommendations); acquisition of a reputation for being a "troublemaker" among coworkers, who often "blame the victim"; and considerable expense if legal action is taken.

Given these options, most women workers seek to handle the situation informally—by either ignoring the behavior, avoiding the harasser, or asking him to stop. In the first MSPB study (1981:67), 61 percent of the victims reported ignoring the harassment and 48 percent asking the harasser to stop. Loy and Stewart (n.d.) found 32 percent ignoring the harasser and 39 percent asking him to stop. Respondents in both studies indicated that ignoring the harassment failed to end it and often made it worse. Asking the harasser to stop was effective for 54 percent of the women (MSPB 1981:67)—but ineffective in almost half the cases.

Findings from several studies suggest that the high turnover and absenteeism rates for female workers are related to sexual harassment. In the initial MSPB study, 6 percent of all sexually harassed women (but 14 percent of the rape victims and 10 percent of the severely harassed women) reported subsequently quitting or transferring from their jobs (MSPB 1981:80). Loy and Stewart (n.d.:Table 4) found that 17 percent of victims reported quitting or transferring. Only a small proportion of victimized women sought a formal remedy by complaining through official channels (3 percent according to MSPB [1981:70] and 12.5 percent according to Loy and Stewart [n.d.:Table 4]). The vast majority of female victims did not complain through official channels due to ignorance of available remedies, the belief that formal action is less effective than informal treatment, and fear of making the situation worse. Fear of reprisals and negative outcomes appears to be well founded. Among MSPB respondents who had taken formal action, 41 percent found that their actions had no effect or made things worse (MSPB 1981:88–92).

Acquiescence is also an option. In the case of the less severely harassed women, this generally means tolerating suggestive looks, jokes, teasing, or pressure to go on dates. According to the MSPB study, 18 percent of the less severely harassed, 3 percent of the severely harassed, and 14 percent of the rape/assault victims reported that they "went along with the behavior," but only 8 percent of these women found that things had improved as a result (MSPB 1981:67).

Female students manage unwanted sexual attention in ways similar to those adopted by working women. Some, fearful of making a direct complaint, try to ignore the harassing behavior or use indirect strategies for stopping it. These strategies include directing discussion with the instructor back to the academic issue, bringing a friend to the instructor's office to avoid being alone with the instructor, and talking about a husband or boyfriend to indicate sexual unavailability. About 30 percent of the student victims did not directly communicate their displeasure to the harassing instructor; for almost all these women (thirteen out of fifteen), his unwanted behavior continued (Benson and Thomson 1982:244). The 70 percent who directly communicated their displeasure were more successful in stopping the harassment, although the professor's power tended to affect this outcome. Power was measured by three factors: whether the professor had tenure, whether he was in the student's chosen major field, and whether the student aspired to attend graduate school. The sexual harassment stopped in twenty-one of the twenty-four cases in which one or two of the three conditions were present. However, the harassment stopped in only five of the eleven instances in which all three were present (Benson and Thomson 1982:244). Even when the harassment stopped, however, students who did not reciprocate sexual attention were often punished by the instructor's withdrawal of intellectual support and encouragement, by his making critical comments about work that formerly had been praised, and by his giving lower grades.

In sum, findings from studies of women's responses suggest that ignoring sexual harassment is not likely to end it, but that both informal confrontation and formal complaints have risks and only modest success rates. Although there is no single "right way" to deal with harassment, and although victims must tailor their reaction to their individual situation, two strategies appear to be advisable across the board. Students and workers should (1) learn about their organization's formal grievance procedures and know who is responsible for handling complaints, and (2) should discuss incidents they regard as potentially harassing with a trusted confidant to avoid self-blame and to gain support both in dealing with feelings and in examining response options.

ORGANIZATIONAL RESPONSES TO SEXUAL HARASSMENT

Since the late 1970s, the federal government's response to pressure to prohibit sexual harassment in the workplace has been the relatively swift establishment of formal policy. Sexual harassment has been defined as an illegal form of sex discrimination by the Equal Employment Opportunity Commission (EEOC) and by the federal courts. Universities, often following the lead of major higher-education professional organizations, have adopted policy guidelines and grievance mechanisms for dealing with sexual harassment. Despite this clear policy mandate, however, enforcement of the law remains weak. Punishment of harassers is rare, and victims continue to suffer the triple burden of harassment, hostility and suspicion of coworkers, and reprisals by supervisors. Furthermore, the structural context of inequality in the workplace and power differentials in the university remain barely changed (Schneider, 1985).

The Federal Government and Sexual Harassment

Before 1979, no federal agency had a policy prohibiting sexual harassment. In 1979, apparently in response to adverse publicity regarding one government agency (Ripskis 1979) and to pressure from organizations representing working women, the House Committee on the Post Office and Civil Service held hearings on sexual harassment in the federal government and called on the U.S. Merit Systems Protection Board (MSPB) to conduct a study of sexual harassment in the federal workplace. In addition, the Office of Personnel Management issued a policy statement applicable throughout the federal government that defined sexual harassment, unequivocally declared that such harassment is unacceptable conduct in the workplace, and directed each federal agency to establish policies to reduce sexual harassment and grievance mechanisms to handle complaints (U.S. House of Representatives 1980:7–8).

In September 1980, the Equal Employment Opportunity Commission (EEOC) issued guidelines applicable to both federal and private employers that prohibit sexual harassment as a form of discrimination under Title VII of the Civil Rights Act of 1964. The guidelines declare that the degree of injury sufficient to support a finding of sexual harassment may occur under three sets of circumstances: (1) where the sexual conduct is made an explicit term or condition of an individual's employment (employment condition); (2) where submission to or rejection of the condition is used as a basis for employment decisions (employment consequence); and (3) where the condition creates an offensive, hostile, or intimidating work environment or interferes with job performance (offensive job interference) (Equal Employment Opportunity Commission 1980). The guidelines also make an employer liable for nonsupervisory employees if it "knows or should have known" of the harassing behavior, and liable for supervisory employees "regardless of whether the employer knew" of the offense.

Most universities receive federal funding and, therefore, must follow guidelines prohibiting discrimination on the basis of sex established by the Office of Civil Rights (OCR) of the U.S. Department of Education. Although the OCR did not promulgate guidelines regarding sexual harassment, it has maintained that sexual harassment is prohibited by Title IX of the Educational Amendments Act of 1972. In response, a number of colleges and universities have adopted explicit statements defining and condemning sexual harassment and have established grievance procedures to process sex-discrimination complaints, including those regarding sexual harassment. Some, including Harvard and the University of California system, have issued "amorous relationship" statements that define sexual relationships or sex between teachers and students directly under their supervision as unprofessional conduct, even if the act is initiated by a student (Hoffman 1986:111). Although such statements are important, and shift the burden of responsibility, how they are interpreted and applied will determine whether they signal a return to paternalistic rules or a way to empower women (Hoffman 1986).

Development of Case Law Concerning Sexual Harassment

Although women who experience sexual harassment recognize that it was done to them *as* women, acceptance of the argument that it is sex discrimination prohibited by law took time. Ten years passed between the enactment of the Civil Rights Act of 1964 prohibiting employment discrimination on the basis of sex and an action before a federal court based primarily on sexual harassment. It was not until 1986 that the U.S. Supreme Court finally ruled on a sexual-harassment case. In *Meritor Savings Bank FSB v. Vinson* (477 US 57 [1986]), the Supreme Court clearly ruled that sexual harassment in employee relations is sex discrimination prohibited by Title VII, but left unresolved the specific issues of employer liability and standards of consent as well as the basic questions how gender, sexuality, and power are related.

In the early cases, the plaintiffs argued unsuccessfully that sexual harassment is an illegal form of sex discrimination (see *Corne v. Bausch and Lomb, Inc.,* 390 F. Supp. 161 [D.C. Ariz. 1975]; *Miller v. Bank of America*, 418 F. Supp. 233 [N.D. Calif. 1976] *reversed,* 600 F.2d 211 [1979]; *Barnes v. Train,* Civ. No. 1828-73 [D.C.C. Aug. 9, 1974]; and *Tomkins v. Public Service Electric and Gas Co.* 422 F. Supp. 553 [D.J.J. 1976]). In *Corne,* for example, Jane Corne and Geneva DeVane alleged that the repeated verbal and physical sexual advances of their male supervisor made their jobs intolerable and forced them to choose between "putting up with being manhandled or being out of work" (Brief of Appellants at 17). They argued that their employer, Bausch and Lomb, Inc., was responsible because it had allowed them to be supervised by a man who sexually harassed them. The judge, however, dismissed the claim that the advances constituted sexual discrimination, stating that the supervisor's conduct was simply "a personal proclivity, peculiarity, or mannerism" (390 F. Supp. at 163) for which the employer could not be held liable. The court also found that the supervisor's behavior was not "based on sex" because the harassment might have been directed at male as well as at female employees. In addition, the judge expressed concern that granting relief in this case might lead to "a potential federal lawsuit every time an employee made an amorous or sexually-oriented advance toward another" (390 F. Supp. at 163–64). Similarly, in *Tomkins,* in denying that sexual harassment is either sex-based discrimination or employment related, the court stated:

> In this case the supervisor was male and the employee was female. But no immutable principle of psychology compels this alignment of parties. . . . While sexual desire animated the parties, or at least one of

them, the gender of each is incidental to the claim of abuse. [422 F. Supp. at 556]

A different conclusion, reached in *Williams v. Saxbe* (431 F. Supp. 654 [D.D.C. 1976] *reversed on other grounds sub. nom. Williams v. Bell*, 587 F.2d 1240 [D.C. Cir. 1978]), marked the turning of the tide. The court ruled that a male supervisor's retaliatory action against a female employee who refused his sexual advances constituted treatment "based on sex" within the meaning of Title VII of the Civil Rights Act of 1964; but whether an incident was employment related was left to be determined as a fact at trial.

The *Williams* result was followed by reversals on appeal in *Barnes* and *Tomkins* and similar rulings in several other cases (*Barnes v. Costle*, 561 F.2d 982 [D.C. Cir. 1977]; *Tomkins v. Public Service Electric and Gas Co.*, 568 F.2d 1044 [3d Cir. 1977]). In reversing *Barnes*, the Court of Appeals for the District of Columbia ruled that making sexual compliance a "job retention condition" imposed an employment requirement on a woman that would not be imposed on a man and for which the employer was held accountable. The court affirmed that, for discrimination in employment to be found, "it is enough that gender is a factor contributing to the discrimination in a substantial way" (561 F.2d at 990). In reversing *Tompkins*, the Court of Appeals for the Third Circuit affirmed that an unresponsive employer to whom a victim had complained was legally liable for the actions of its agent or supervisor. Other appellate courts, however, while agreeing that harassment involving injury to a plaintiff in the form of a tangible loss of job benefits (i.e., quid pro quo harassment) violated Title VII, differed with respect to the extent of employer liability.

In 1981, the Circuit Court of Appeals for the District of Columbia in *Bundy v. Jackson* (641 F.2d 934 [D.C. Cir 1981]) expanded coverage in sex-discrimination cases to sexual harassment as a condition of work. It extended the phrases "terms, conditions, and privileges of employment" to cover nontangible injury to the victim, thus making sexual harassment in and of itself a violation of the law. The court found conditions of employment to include the psychological and emotional work environment and reasoned that unless employers are prohibited from maintaining a "discriminatory environment," they could sexually harass a female employee with impunity by carefully stopping short of firing her or taking other action against her when she resisted.

In the *Meritor* case, Plaintiff Michelle Vinson was hired by Sidney Taylor, a vice president and branch manager of Meritor Savings Bank, in 1974. After she became a teller, Taylor invited her to dinner and suggested they have sexual relations. At first, she refused Taylor's advances but, at his insistence and out of fear of losing her job, she acquiesced. Thereafter Vinson estimated she had intercourse with Taylor forty to fifty times between 1975 and 1977. She claimed that she did not report the problem to any of Taylor's superiors or use the bank's complaint procedure out of fear of Taylor. Taylor and the bank denied all allegations of sexual misbehavior on his part. The bank also claimed that because it did not know of the situation, it could not be held responsible (477 US at 61).

The District Court (23 Fair Empl. Prac. Cas. [BNA] 37 [D.D.C. 1980]) found that if there was a sexual relationship, it was voluntary, and thus denied Vinson's claim of sex discrimination. The Court of Appeals for the District of Columbia Circuit reversed and remanded (753 F.2d 141 *reh'g denied,* 760 F.2d 1330 [D.C. Cir. 1985]), finding that Vinson was a victim not of quid pro quo sexual harassment but of harassment of the type emanating from a hostile working environment. It held that the voluntariness of the sexual relationship was immaterial and that the employer was strictly liable for the sexual harassment of an employee by its supervisor or agent even if he did not have the authority to hire, fire, or promote, since the mere appearance of influence over job decisions gives him opportunity to impose on employees.

The Supreme Court unanimously affirmed that both types of sexual harassment identified in the EEOC guidelines are prohibited by Title VII and that in hostile-environment cases the victim does not necessarily have to demonstrate economic harm (477 US at 64). For sexual harassment to be actionable, to Court ruled "it must be sufficiently severe or pervasive 'to alter the conditions of [the victim's] employment and create an abusive work environment" (*id.* at 67 quoting *Henson v. Dundee,* 682 F.2d 897, 904 [11th Cir. 1982]). In addressing the issue of employer liability, however, the Supreme Court refused to rule definitively on liability for hostile-environment–type discrimination. A slim majority held that the Court of Appeals erred when it held employers automatically liable for the sexual harassment by supervisors (*id.* at 72).

Case law prohibiting sexual harassment as sex-based discrimination against students under Title IX of the Education Amendments Act is not well established, although most of the arguments are now similar to those already established under Title VII. In a lawsuit brought against Yale University (*Alexander v. Yale University,* 459 F. Supp. 1 [D. Conn. 1977] *reversed on other grounds,* 631 F.2d 178 [2d Cir. 1980]), a student alleged that her grade was adversely affected by her refusal to submit to her professor's sexual demands. Using reasoning developed in the context of employment discrimination cases, the court held that the student had stated a cause of action under Title IX, but dismissed the suit because the complainant had failed to prove that an improper advance had been made or that the student had been adversely affected. It also dismissed the claims of coplaintiffs alleging harm resulting from "contamination" of the educational environment. The Second Circuit Court of Appeals affirmed this reasoning, thereby establishing quid pro quo harassment as illegal but leaving open the issue of environmental harm. In *Moire v. Temple University School of Medicine* (613 F. Supp. 1360 [E.D. Pa. 1985] *affirmed* 800 F.2d 1136 [3d Cir. 1986]), the district court allowed a claim for sexual harassment based solely on environmental harm, although it found no merit in the particular allegation that because of her sex the complainant had been subjected to a harassing or abusive environment. The *Moire* court's explicit recognition that the EEOC guidelines are equally applicable to Title IX suggests that the courts will continue to decide claims of sexual harassment brought by students under Title IX using reasoning similar to that established under Title VII cases.

The turnabout of the courts has been dramatic. Although the early cases involved blatant abuses of power by supervisors, the judges treated these abuses as matters of "natural" attraction or of the personal peculiarity of the supervisors unrelated to job conditions. As legal analyses clarified the relationship between sexual harassment and sex discrimination, as research supported the claims that sexual harassment is widespread and socially patterned, as the EEOC added its authority in support of the plaintiffs in a number of cases, and as the media called public attention to the issue, the courts could no longer sustain the traditional "personal proclivity" approach. They shifted to the view that sexual harassment is an illegal, socially imposed wrong—sex discrimination—not only when the victim faces tangible economic losses, but also when the harassment is made a condition of work. Thus, the law now acknowledges the socially defined character of sexual harassment by recognizing that the unwanted sexual advances are "based on sex" and that women are sexually harassed because they are women. Nevertheless, ambiguity remains regarding standards for identifying when behavior is "unwelcome" (thereby creating a hostile environment) and it may be a while until the courts establish a "reasonable victim" perspective to protect women from offensive behavior that results from the divergent perceptions of men and women (*Harvard Law Review* 1984).

Clear prohibition of sexual harassment is an important first step toward recognition of the problem the latter poses for women. It provides victims with legal redress, establishes employer responsibility, and encourages employees to resist harassment. However, enforcement of the law is weak, litigation is expensive, and even women's willingness to invoke it remains far from complete. Existing procedures rely principally on informal mediation; if a problem cannot be resolved informally, the mechanisms for redress break down, since few employers have policies for using sanctions and the government has no mechanisms to monitor policy statements or grievance procedures (Livingston 1982; Schneider 1985).

Women often fail to define certain offensive behaviors as sexual harassment, blame other women or themselves rather than the harasser for the experience (Jensen and Gutek 1982), and, when they do label the unwanted behavior as sexual harassment, tend to treat it as an individual matter to be handled informally. Their reluctance to take more formal action for fear of making things worse, particularly at a time of economic insecurity and reduced civil-rights law enforcement, appears to be well founded.

Even more frequent complaints and fuller enforcement through formal channels, however, only provide redress on a case-by-case basis without addressing the underlying structural causes of sexual harassment—the conditions of social and economic inequality. Thus, the elimination of sexual harassment in the workplace and educational setting may not bring fundamental change unless the root of the problem—the nature and structures of the environment in which women and men work and learn—are altered.

CONCLUSION

Sexual harassment in the university and the workplace must be recognized and treated as an oppressive form of sex discrimination that undercuts women's potential for independence and equality. It disrupts women's drive for autonomy outside of the home and family by sexualizing women's work role and by making sexuality a condition of economic survival. Women as a group suffer from two inequalities: inequality based on socially defined patterns of sexual initiative and acquiescence, and economic inequality maintained by women's separate and subordinate place at work. Sexual harassment links these inequalities by expressing the unequal social power of women, sexualizing their subordination, and deepening their powerlessness as women.

NOTES

1. Although men have been victims of sexual harassment as well as women, the vast difference between the sexes in victimization rates and the meaning attached to sexual initiatives make sexual harassment primarily a problem of women. Only research findings on the sexual harassment of women are presented here, and the analysis of harassment is from the perspective of female victims.

2. One study found that more than 70 percent of the women surveyed would not call a behavior sexual harassment if the person doing it did not mean to be offensive (U.S. Merit Systems Protection Board [MSPB] 1981:29). Much of the recent psychological research on sexual harassment focuses on the cognitive processes involved in interpreting a behavior as harassing. Studies have found that (1) men tend to rate hypothetical scenarios (Gutek et al. 1983) and specific social-sexual behaviors (Gutek et al., 1980) as less harassing than do women; and (2) lesbian women workers are more likely than are heterosexual ones to label a variety of specific social sexual behaviors directed at them as sexual harassment (Schneider 1982). Other studies have found that when behaviors are inconsistent with ordinary expectations of the actor's social role and thus appear to be inappropriate (e.g., enacted by a professor rather than by a fellow student), they are more likely to be viewed as incidents of sexual harassment (Pryor 1985). In interpreting ambiguous incidents, students put more weight on personal and interpersonal aspects of a relationship between the persons involved than the actual behavior, suggesting that people tend to emphasize the positive aspects of a relationship and to deny that sexual harassment exists (Cohen and Gutek 1985).

In an effort to explain individual perceptions of sexual harassment, Konrad and Gutek (1986) tested three theories related to perceptions of sexual harassment. They postulated that differences between men and women in the perception of sexual harassment were related to (1) differences in personal orientation to sexual harassment and to the definition of it; (2) differences in sexual experiences at work; and (3) differences due to gender-role spillover. They found support for all three explanations and concluded that women label more behaviors as sexual harassment than do men because of differences in both attitudes and experiences.

3. In 1978, the Civil Service Reform Act reorganized the Civil Service Commission by dividing it into two agencies: MSPB and the Office of Personnel Management. The MSPB hears and adjudicates appeals by federal employees complaining of adverse personnel actions, resolves cases charging prohibited personnel practices, and conducts special studies on the civil service and other executive branch merit systems. The Office of Personnel Management administers a merit system for federal employees, which includes recruitment, examination, training, and promotion on the basis of people's knowledge and skill.

Donna J. Benson and Gregory E. Thomson. "Sexual Harassment on a University Campus: The Confluence of Authority Relations, Sexual Interest and Gender Stratification," *Social Problems* 29 (1982), 236–51.

Sandra H. Carey. "Sexual Politics in Business" (Unpublished paper, University of Texas, San Antonio, 1977).

Aaron G. Cohen and Barbara A. Gutek, "Dimensions of Perceptions of Social-Sexual Behavior in a Work Setting," *Sex Roles* 13 (1985), 317–327.

Phyllis Crocker, "An Analysis of University Definitions of Sexual Harassment," *Signs* 8 (1983), 696–707.

Equal Employment Opportunity Commission. "Discrimination Because of Sex Under Title VII of the Civil Rights Act of 1964, as amended: Adoption of Interim Interpretive Guidelines," *Federal Register* 29 (1980), 1604. (Washington, D.C.: U.S. Government Printing Office).

Lyn Farley, *Sexual Shakedown: The Sexual Harassment of Women on the Job* (New York: McGraw-Hill, 1978).

Barbara A. Gutek, "The Experience of Sexual Harassment: Results from a Representative Survey" (Paper presented at the American Psychological Association annual meeting, Los Angeles, August 29, 1981).

Barbara A. Gutek and Bruce Morash, "Sex Ratios, Sex Role Spillover, and Sexual Harassment of Women at Work," *Journal of Social Issues* 38 (1982), 55–74.

Barbara A. Gutek, Charles Y. Nakamura, M. Gahart, I. Handschumacher, and Diane Russell. "Sexuality in the Workplace," *Basic and Applied Social Psychology* 1 (1980), 255–265.

Harvard Law Review. "Sexual Harassment Claims of Abusive Work Environment under Title VII," 97 (1984), 1449–1467.

Frances L. Hoffman, "Sexual Harassment in Academia: Feminist Theory and Institutional Practice," *Harvard Educational Review* 56 (1986), 105–120.

Inger W. Jensen and Barbara A. Gutek, "Attributions and Assignments of Responsibility in Sexual Harassment," *Journal of Social Issues* 38 (1982), 121–136.

Rosabeth M. Kanter, *Men and Women of the Corporation* (New York: Basic Books, 1977).

Mim Kelber, "Sexual Harassment . . . the UN's Dirty Little Secret." *Ms.*, Nov. 1977, 51, 79.

Alison M. Konrad and Barbara A. Gutek, "Impact of Work Experiences on Attitudes Toward Sexual Harassment." *Administrative Science Quarterly* 31:422–438.

Karen Lindsey, "Sexual Harassment on the Job." *Ms.*, Nov. 1977, 47–51, 74–78.

Jay Livingston, "Responses to Sexual Harassment on the Job: Legal, Organizational, and Individual Actions." *Journal of Social Issues* 38 (1982), 5–22.

Pamela Loy and Lee Stewart, "Sexual Harassment: Strategies and Outcomes" (Unpublished paper, University of Hartford, W. Hartford, Conn., n.d.).

Catherine A. MacKinnon, *Sexual Harassment of Working Women: A Case of Sex Discrimination* (New Haven, Conn.: Yale University Press, 1979).

Catherine A. MacKinnon, "Feminism, Marxism, Method and the State: An Agenda for Action." *Signs* 7 (1982), 515–544.

Susan E. Martin, *"Breaking and Entering": Policewomen on Patrol* (Berkeley: University of California Press, 1980).

Arlene McCormack, "The Sexual Harassment of Students by Teachers: The Case of Students in Science," *Sex Roles* 13 (1985), 21–32.

MSPB, see U.S. Merit Systems Protection Board.

Adrienne Munich, "Seduction in Academe," *Psychology Today*, Feb. 1978, 82–108.

Letty C. Pogrebin, "Sexual Harassment: The Working Woman," *Ladies Home Journal*, June 1977, 47.

Project on the Status of Women in Education. *Sexual Harassment: A Hidden Issue* (Washington, D.C.: American Association of Colleges, 1978).

John B. Pryor, "The Lay Person's Understanding of Sexual Harassment," *Sex Roles* 5/6 (1985), 273–286.

Spencer Rich, "Schlafly: Sexual Harassment on Job No Problem for Virtuous Woman," *Washington Post,* April 22, 1981, A2.

Al Ripskis, "Sexual Harassment Rampant at HUD." *Impact* 7 (July/Aug. 1979), 1, 5, 7.

Claire Safran, "What Men Do to Women on the Job: A Shocking Look at Sexual Harassment," *Redbook,* Nov. 1976, 149, 217–223.

Beth E. Schneider, "Consciousness about Sexual Harassment among Heterosexual and Lesbian Women Workers," *Journal of Social Issues* 38 (1982), 75–97.

Beth E. Schneider, "Approaches, Assaults, Attractions, Affairs: Policy Implications of the Sexualization of the Workplace," *Population Research and Policy Review* 4 (1985), 93–113.

William C. Seymour, "Sexual Harassment: Finding a Cause of Action under Title VII," *Labor Law Journal* (Mar. 1979), 30: 170–210.

Dierdre Silverman, "Sexual Harassment: Working Women's Dilemma," *Quest: A Feminist Quarterly* 3 (winter 1976–77), 15–24.

U.S. House of Representatives. *Hearings on Sexual Harassment in the Federal Government* (Committee on the Post Office and Civil Service, Subcommittee on Investigations, Washington, D.C.: U.S. Government Printing Office, 1980).

U.S. Merit Systems Protection Board. *Sexual Harassment in the Federal Workplace: Is it a Problem?* (Washington, D.C.: U.S. Government Printing Office, 1981).

U.S. Merit Systems Protection Board. *Sexual Harassment in the Federal Government: An Update.* (Washington, D.C.: U.S. Government Printing Office, 1988).

Women, Health, and Medicine

BARBARA KATZ ROTHMAN

Women are not only people: *Woman* is a subject one can study, even specialize in within medicine. Obstetricians and gynecologists are medicine's, and perhaps society's, generally recognized "experts" on the subject of women, especially women's bodies: their health, reproductive functioning, and sexuality.[1] *Obstetrics* is the branch of medicine concerned with the care of women during pregnancy, labor, and the time surrounding childbirth,[2] and is similar in some ways to midwifery. *Gynecology* is the "science of the diseases of women, especially those affecting the sex organs."[3] There is no comparable "science" of the study of men, *their* diseases, and/or reproductive functions. An attempt by urologists in 1891 to develop an "andrology" specialty came to nothing.[4]

At its simplest, a medical specialty can be seen as arising out of preexisting needs. People have heart attacks: The medical specialty of cardiology develops. Or the amount of knowledge generated in a field grows so enormously that no one person can hope to master it all: Physicians "carve out" their own areas of specialization. Increasing knowledge about cancer thus led to the specialty of oncology and subspecialties within oncology.

But the development of a medical specialty is not necessarily the creation of a key for an already existing lock. Medical needs do not necessarily predate the specialty, even though the specialty is presumably organized to meet those needs. This has been made quite clear in the work of Thomas Szasz on the relatively recent expansion of medicine into such "social problem" areas as alcoholism, gambling, and suicide.[5] Medicine does not have the "cures" for these problems, but by defining them in medical terms, as sickness, the physician gains political control over the societal response: Punishment becomes "treatment," desired or not, successful or not. Similarly, medical control over childbirth, lactation, menopause, and other women's health issues was not based on superior ability to deal with these concerns.

The case of Jacoba Felice de Almania, a woman tried for the illegal practice of medicine in 1322, illustrates this point. In her defense Almania had witnesses who testified that she never charged unless she cured and that her cures were successful where other, "legal" (male) practitioners had failed. However, since she had not attended a medical school (medical schools being closed to women), she was not licensed to practice medicine. That she saw women who did not want to go to a male practitioner and that she was successful did not matter. "Efficacy of treatment was not the criterion for determining who was or was not a legitimate medical practitioner, but the educational requirements and membership in the faculty of an organized group were the most important factors."[6] In essence, the statement behind professional control over medicine is: "We may not be able to help you, but we are the only ones qualified to try."

Vern Bullough, in his analysis of the development of medicine as a profession, writes about the situation during the Middle Ages: "One obvious group outside of the control of the university physician was the midwife, but during the period under study the university physician generally ignored this whole *area of medicine.* Midwives might or might not be qualified, but this *was not a matter of public concern*"[7] (emphasis added). More accurately, one might state not that physicians ignored this "area of medicine" but that midwifery and its concerns were outside the area of medicine, just as other matters that were undoubtedly of concern to women existed outside of the "public" concern. Until pregnancy and childbirth were defined as medical events, midwifery was in no sense a branch, area, or interest of medicine as a profession.

Medical expansion into the area of childbirth began before the development of asepsis, surgical techniques, or anesthesia — all of which are now considered the contributions of obstetrics. And yet, even without the technology, medicine had begun to redefine childbirth by the beginning of the nineteenth century. Childbirth came to be seen not as a family or religious event, but as a medical one, needing medical presence for its safe conduct.[8]

Midwives treated childbirth in the larger context of women's lives. Midwives did not and do not "deliver" babies. They teach women how to give birth. Brack has called the role of the midwife "total" — she helped both as teacher and as role model in the socialization of the mother to her new status. "The midwife's relation to the woman was both diffuse and affective, while the physician role demanded specificity and affective neutrality."[9] Midwives taught how to birth babies, how to nurse them, how to care for them and for the mother's own body. Physicians deliver babies and move on. The physician "isolated the laboring woman and her delivery of the infant from the rest of the childbearing experience, and defined it as a medical and surgical event which required specialized knowledge."[10] As one modern nurse-midwife has said of obstetrics residents: "They want us to stay with the woman in labor and just call them when she's ready to deliver. To them, that's the whole thing."

At the time that physicians were taking over control of childbirth, it is virtually unarguable that the noninterventionist, supportive techniques of the midwives were safer for both the birthing woman and her baby. The physicians' approaches included bleeding to "syncope" (until the woman fainted), tobacco infusion enemas, frequent nonsterile examinations, and other surgical and chemical interventions.[11] In the 1910s and 1920s, as American physicians successfully ousted midwives, the midwives' safety records remained better than the physicians'. In Newark from 1914 to 1916, a midwifery program achieved a maternal mortality rate as low as 1.7 per thousand, while in Boston, where midwives were banned, the rate was 6.5 per thousand. Similarly, the infant mortality rate in Newark was 8.5 per thousand, contrasted with 37.4 in Boston.[12] In Washington, as the percentage of births reported by midwives shrank from 50 percent in 1903 to 15 percent in 1912, infant mortality in the first day, first week, and first month of life all increased. New York's dwindling corps of midwives did significantly better than did New York doctors in preventing both stillbirths and postpartum infection.[13]

The physician's separation of the delivery of the baby from its larger socioemotional context has its roots as far back as René Descartes's concept of mind–body dualism. To Descartes, the body was a machine whose structure and operation fall within the province of human knowledge, as distinguished from the mind, which God alone could know. Although even the Hippocratic principles state that the mind and body should be considered together, "most physicians, . . . irrespective of their professional activities and philosophical views on the nature of the mind, behave in practice as if they were still Cartesian dualists. Their conservative attitudes are largely a matter of practical convenience."[14]

The medical models used for convenience are that diseases are the bad guys that the good-guy medications can cure; that the body breaks down and needs repair; that the body can be repaired in the hospital like a car in the shop; and that once "fixed" the person can be returned to the community. The earliest models were largely mechanical; later models worked more with chemistry; and newer, more sophisticated medical writing describes computerlike programming. But the basic points remain the same. These models were useful when dealing with the problems facing medicine at the turn of the century: primarily bacterial and viral disease-causing agents and simple accidents and trauma. They have never worked well for understanding the problems that women face in dealing with doctors, including those encountered during the experience of childbirth. While midwives learned by apprenticeship, doctors were instructed in the use of forceps, as well as in the techniques of normal delivery, by "book learning," by discussion, by the use of wooden models, and infrequently by watching another doctor at work. Dorothy Wertz, in her study of the development of obstetrics, has pointed out that "by regarding the female body as a machine, European doctors found that they could measure the birth canal and predict whether or not the child could pass through."[15] Stories of women giving birth while their doctors scrub for a cesarean section are part of the lore of midwifery. Among the stories midwives tell one another are tales of women who were told that they could never deliver vaginally and then went on to have normal births of oversized babies.

In the nineteenth and early twentieth centuries midwives and physicians were in direct competition for patients, and not only for their fees. Newer, more clinically oriented medical training demanded "teaching material," so that even immigrant and poor women were desired as patients.[16] The displacement of the midwife by the male obstetrician can be better understood in terms of this competition than as an ideological struggle or as "scientific advancement." Physicians, unlike the unorganized, disenfranchised midwives, had access to the power of the state through their professional associations. They were thus able to control licensing legislation, restricting the midwife's sphere of activity and imposing legal sanctions against her in state after state.[17]

The legislative changes were backed up by the medical establishment's attempt to win public disapproval for midwifery and support for obstetrics. Physicians accused midwives of ignorance and incompetence and attacked midwifery practices as "meddlesome." Rather than upgrading the practice of midwifery by teaching the skills physicians thought necessary, the profession of medicine refused to train women either as midwives or as physicians.[18] Physicians argued repeatedly that medicine was the appropriate profession to handle birth because "normal pregnancy and parturition are exceptions and to consider them to be normal physiologic conditions was a fallacy."[19] Childbirth was redefined as a medical rather than a social event, and the roles and care surrounding it were reorganized to suit medical needs.[20]

Once professional dominance was established in the area of childbirth, obstetrics rapidly expanded into the relatively more sophisticated area of gynecology. The great obstetricians of the nineteenth century were invariably gynecologists (and of course were all men).[21] Among other effects, this linking of obstetrics and gynecology further reinforced the obstetrical orientation toward pathology.

One of the earliest uses of the developing field of gynecology was the overt social control of women through surgical removal of various sexual organs. Surgical removal of the clitoris (clitoridectomy) or, less dramatically, its foreskin (circumcision), and removal of the ovaries (oopherectomy or castration) were used to check women's "mental disorders." The first gynecologist to do a clitoridectomy was an Englishman, in 1858.[22] In England, the procedure was harshly criticized and was not repeated by others after the death of the originator in 1860. In America, however, clitoridectomies were done regularly from the late 1860s until at least 1904,[23] and then sporadically until as recently as the late 1940s.[24] The procedure was used to terminate sexual desire or sexual behavior, something deemed pathological in women. Circumcisions were done on women of all ages to stop masturbation up until at least 1937.[25]

More widespread than clitoridectomies or circumcisions were oopherectomies for psychological "disorders." Interestingly, the female gonads were removed not when women were "too female"—i.e., too passive or dependent—but when women were too masculine—assertive, aggressive, "unruly." Oopherectomies for "psychiatric" reasons were done in America between 1872 and 1946.[26] (By the 1940s, prefrontal lobotomies were gaining acceptance as psychosurgery.)

The developing medical control of women was not limited to extreme cures for psychiatric problems. The physical health and stability of even the most well-adjusted, ladylike women were questioned. Simply by virtue of gender, women were (and are) subject to *illness labeling.*

One explanation for women's vulnerability to illness labeling lies in the functionalist approach to the sociology of health. Talcott Parsons has pointed out that it is a functional requirement of any social system that there be a basic level of health of its members.[27] Any definition of illness that is too lenient would disqualify too many people from fulfilling their functions and would impose severe strains on the social system. System changes, such as war, can make changes in standards of health and illness generally set for members. This works on an individual level as well, standards of health and illness being related to social demands: A mild headache will excuse a student from attending class but not from taking final exams. A logical extension of this is that the less valued a person's or group's contribution to society, the more easily are such people labeled ill.

Women are not always seen as functional members of society, as people doing important things. This has historically and cross-culturally been especially true of the women of the upper classes in patriarchal societies, where it is a mark of status for a man to be able to afford to keep a wife who is not performing any useful function. A clear, if horrifying, example of this is the traditional Chinese practice of foot-binding. By crippling girls, men were able to show that they could afford to have wives and daughters who did nothing. It is a particularly disturbing example of conspicuous consumption. But we do not have to turn to faraway places to see women defined as useless. In their historical analysis of the woman patient, *Complaints and Disorders,* Barbara Ehrenreich and Deirdre English speak of the "lady of leisure" of the late nineteenth and early twentieth centuries. "She was the social ornament that proved a man's success; her idleness, her delicacy, her childlike ignorance of 'reality' gave a man the 'class' that money alone could not provide."[28]

The practice of creating physical deformity in women can be seen in our history as well. A woman researcher who studied menstrual problems among college women between 1890 and 1920 found that women in the earlier period probably were somewhat incapacitated by menstruation, just as the gynecologists of the day were claiming. However, the researcher did not attribute the menstrual problems to women's "inherent disabilities" or "overgrowth of the intellect" as did the male physicians; she related it to dress styles. Women in the 1890s carried some fifteen pounds of skirts and petticoats, hanging from a tightly corseted waist. As skirts got lighter and waists were allowed to be larger, menstruation ceased to be the problem it had been.[29] In the interest of science, women might try the experiment of buckling themselves into a painfully small belt and hanging a fifteen-pound weight from it. One might expect weakness, fatigue, shortness of breath, even fainting: all the physical symptoms of women's "inherent" disability. And consider further the effects of bleeding as a treatment for the problem.

It follows from Parsons's analysis that, in addition to suffering created physical disabilities (the bound feet of the Chinese, the deforming corsetry of our own history), women were more easily *defined* as sick when they were not seen as functional social members. At the same time in our history that the upper-class women were "delicate," "sickly," and "frail," the working-class women were well enough to perform the physical labor of housework, both their own and that of the upper classes, as well as to work in the factories and fields. "However sick or tired working class women might have been, they certainly did not have the time or money to support a cult of invalidism. Employers gave no time off for pregnancy or recovery from childbirth, much less for menstrual periods, though the wives of these same employers often retired to bed on all these occasions."[30] The working-class women were seen as strong and healthy; for them, pregnancy, menstruation, and menopause were not allowed to be incapacitating.

These two factors—the treatment of the body as a machine and the lesser functional importance assigned to women—still account for much of the medical treatment of women. Contemporary physicians do not usually speak of the normal female reproductive functions as diseases. The exception, to be discussed below, is menopause. The other specifically female reproductive functions—menstruation, pregnancy, childbirth, and lactation—are regularly asserted in medical texts to be normal and healthy phenomena. However, these statements are made within the context of teaching the medical "management," "care," "supervision," and "treatment" of each of these "conditions."

Understood in limited mechanical terms, each of these normal female conditions or happenings is a complication or stress on an otherwise normal system. Medicine has fared no better than has any other discipline in developing a working model of women that does not take men as the comparative norm. For example, while menstruation is no longer viewed as a disease, it is seen as a complication in the female system, contrasted to the reputed biological stability of the supposedly noncycling male.[31] As recently as 1961, the *American Journal of Obstetrics and Gynecology* was still referring to women's "inherent disabilities" in explanations of menstruation:

> Women are known to suffer at least some inconvenience during certain phases of the reproductive cycle, and often with considerable mental and physical distress. Woman's awareness of her inherent disabilities is thought to create added mental and in turn physical changes in the total body response, and there result problems that concern the physician who must deal with them.[32]

Research on contraception displays the same mechanistic biases. The claim has been made that contraceptive research has concentrated on the female rather than the male because of the sheer number of potentially vulnerable links in the female chain of reproductive events.[33] Reproduction is clearly a more complicated process for the female than the male. While we might claim that it is safer to interfere in a simpler process, medicine has tended to view the number of points in the female reproductive process as distinct entities. Reproduction is dealt with not as a complicated organic process but as a series of discrete points, like stations on an assembly line, with more for female than for male.

The alternative to taking the female system as a complication of the "basic" or "simpler" male system is of course to take female as the working norm. In this approach, a pregnant woman is compared only to pregnant women, a lactating breast compared only to other lactating breasts. Pregnancy and lactation are accepted not only as nominally healthy variations but as truly normal states. To take the example of pregnancy, women *are* pregnant; pregnancy is not something they "have" or "catch" or even "contain." It involves physical changes; these are not, as medical texts frequently call them, "symptoms" of pregnancy. Pregnancy is not a disease, and its changes are no more symptoms than the growth spurt or development of pubic hair are symptomatic of puberty. There may be diseases or complications of pregnancy, but the pregnancy itself is neither disease nor complication.

In contrast, medicine's working model of pregnancy is a woman with an insulated parasitic capsule growing inside. The pregnancy, while physically located within the woman, is still seen as external to her, not a part of her. The capsule within has been seen as virtually omniscient and omnipotent, reaching out and taking what it needs from the mother-host, at her expense if necessary, while protected from all that is bad or harmful.

The pregnancy, in this medical model, is almost entirely a mechanical event in the mother. She differs from the nonpregnant woman only in the presence of this thing growing inside her. Differences other than the mechanical are accordingly seen as symptoms to be treated, so that the woman can be kept as "normal" as possible through the "stress" of the pregnancy. Pregnancy in this model is not seen necessarily as inherently unhealthy, but it is frequently associated with changes other than the growth of the uterus and its contents, and these changes are seen as unhealthy. For example, hemoglobin (iron) is lower in pregnant women than nonpregnant, making pregnant women appear (by nonpregnant standards) anemic. They are then treated for this anemia with iron supplements. Water retention, or edema, is greater in pregnant women than nonpregnant ones, so pregnant women are treated with limits placed on their salt intake and with diuretics. Pregnant women tend to gain weight over that accounted for by the fetus, placenta, and amniotic fluid. They are treated for this weight gain with strict diets, sometimes even with "diet pills." And knowing that these changes are likely to occur in pregnant women, American doctors generally have tried to treat all pregnant women with iron supplements, with limits on salt and calorie intake, and sometimes with diuretics. This attempt to cure the symptoms has brought up not only strict diets to prevent normal weight gain and diuretics to prevent normal fluid retention but also the dangerous drugs, from thalidomide to Bendectin, to prevent nausea. Each of these "cures" has had devastating effects: Fetal malformation, maternal and fetal illness, even death.

What is particularly important to note is that these "treatments" of entirely normal phenomena are frequently not perceived by the medical profession as interventions or disruptions. Rather, the physician sees himself as assisting nature, restoring the woman to normality. Janet Bogdan, in her study of the development of obstetrics, reports that in the 1800s, a noninterventionist physician, as opposed to a "regular" physician, would give a laboring woman some castor oil or milk of magnesia, catheterize her, bleed her a pint or so, administer ergot, and use poultices to blister her. "Any of these therapies would be administered in the interests of setting the parturient up for an easier, less painful labor and delivery, while still holding to the belief that the physician was letting nature take its course."[34] Dorothy Wertz says that medicine currently has redefined "natural childbirth," in response to consumer demand for it, to include any of the following techniques: spinal or epidural anesthesia, inhalation anesthesia in the second stage of labor, forceps, episiotomy, induced labor.[35] Each of these techniques increases the risks of childbirth for mothers and babies.[36] Under the title "Normal Delivery," an obstetric teaching film shows "the use of various drugs and procedures used to facilitate normal delivery." Another "Normal Delivery" film is "a demonstration of a normal, spontaneous delivery, including a paracervical block, episiotomy . . ."

As both the technologies of "curing" and of "diagnosis" grow more powerful, the danger increases. The extraordinary rise in cesarean sections starting in the 1970s in the United States provides a striking example of this. Refinements in anesthesiology, and to a lesser extent in surgery itself, have made the cesarean section a much safer procedure in recent years. While it is not, and cannot be, as safe as an unmedicated vaginal birth—a section is major abdominal surgery, and all anesthesia entails risks—it is unquestionably safer today than it was twenty or forty years ago. Thus, the "cure" is more readily used. But what is the disease? The disease is labor, of course. While medicine now claims that pregnancy and labor are not diseases per se, they are always considered in terms of "riskiness": labor is at best "low risk" and is increasingly often defined as "high risk." At first only labors defined as high risk, but now even low-risk labors, are routinely being monitored electronically. The electronic fetal monitor has a belt that wraps around the pregnant belly, thus preventing normal walking and movement, and an electrode that goes into the vagina and literally screws into the top of the baby's head. Contractions, fetal heartbeat, and fetal scalp blood are all continuously monitored. With all of this diagnostic sophistication, "fetal distress" can be detected—and presumably cured, by cesarean section. The National Center for Health Services Research announced as far back as 1978 that electronic fetal monitoring may do more harm than good, citing among other things the dangers of the rapidly increasing cesarean section rate, but monitoring is still receiving widespread medical acceptance.[37]

The use of estrogens provides an even better example of how medicine views the body as a machine that can be "run" or managed without being changed. Estrogens are female hormones; in medicine they are seen as femininity in a jar. In the widely selling *Feminine Forever,* Dr. Robert A. Wilson, pushing "estrogen-replacement therapy" for all menopausal women, calls estrogen levels, as detected by examination of cells from the vagina, a woman's "femininity index."[38] As estrogen levels naturally drop off after menopause a woman, according to Wilson, is losing her femininity. Interestingly, estrogen levels are also quite low while a woman is breast-feeding, something not usually socially linked to a "loss of femininity."

Menopause remains the one normal female process that is still overtly referred to as a disease in the medical literature. To some physicians, menopause is a "deficiency disease," and the use of estrogens is restoring the woman to her "normal" condition. Here we must reconsider the question of women's functional importance in the social system. Middle-aged housewives have been called the last of the "ladies of leisure," having outlived their social usefulness as wife-mothers and having been allowed no alternatives. While oopherectomies and clitoridectomies are no longer being done on upper-class women as they were a hundred years ago, to cure all kinds of dubious ills, older women are having hysterectomies (surgical removal of the uterus) at alarming rates.[39] Much more typical of modern medicine, however, is the use of chemical rather than surgical "therapy." Because the social changes and demands for readjustment of middle age roughly coincide with the time of menopause, menopause becomes the "illness" for which women can be treated.

Estrogens have been used in virtually every stage of the female reproductive cycle, usually with the argument that they return the woman to normal or are a "natural" treatment. Estrogens are used to keep adolescent girls from getting "unnaturally" tall; to treat painful menstruation; as contraception, supposedly mimicking pregnancy; as a chemical abortion in the "morning after" pill; to replace supposedly missing hormones and thus to prevent miscarriages; to dry up milk and return women to the "normal" nonlactating state; and to return menopausal women to the "normal" cycling state. For all the claims of normality and natural treatment, at this writing approximately half of these uses of estrogens have been shown to cause cancer. The use of estrogens in pregnancy was the first to be proved carcinogenic: Daughters of women who had taken estrogens (notably DES, a synthetic estrogen) are at risk for the development of a rare cancer of the vagina.[40] The sequential birth-control pill was taken off the market as the danger of endometrial cancer (cancer of the lining of the uterus) became known,[41] and, similarly, estrogens taken in menopause have been shown to increase the risk of endometrial cancer by as much as fourteen times after seven years of use.[42]

The model of the body as a machine that can be regulated, controlled, and managed by medical treatments is not working. "Femininity" or physical "femaleness" is not something that comes in a jar and can be manipulated. Nor are women accepting the relegation to secondary functional importance, as wives and mothers of men. In rejecting the viewpoint that women bear men's children for them, women are reclaiming their bodies. When pregnancy is seen not as the presence of a (man's) fetus in a woman but as a condition of the woman herself, attitudes toward contraception, infertility, abortion, and childbirth all change. When pregnancy is perceived as a condition of the woman, then abortion, for example, is primarily a response to that condition.

The women's health movement has grown as an important part of the contemporary women's movement. In some of its work, the health movement has been geared toward consumerism within medicine, seeking better medical care and a wider ranger of services for women. While better trained, more knowledgeable, and more humane physicians are a high priority, what the self-help and lay midwifery groups are doing goes much deeper than that. I believe that these women are reconstructing the preobstetrics and pregynecology model of women's health. They are redefining women's health in fundamentally women's terms. The extraordinary scope and power of this redefinition can be seen in the two-volume proceedings of a 1979 conference on "Ethical Issues in Human Reproductive Technology: Analysis by Women." This work demonstrates the fundamental reevaluations that come with feminist insight.[43]

On a more pragmatic level, feminist clinics and self-help groups are teaching women how to examine their own bodies, not in the neverending search for pathology in which physicians are trained, but to learn more about health. Medical technology and physicians are clearly useful in treating illness, but do we really want physicians to be "treating" health? It is entirely possible for a woman to fit herself for a diaphragm, do a pap smear and a breast examination (all with help and instruction if she needs it), and never adopt the patient role. It is also possible for a woman to go through a pregnancy and birth her baby with good, knowledgeable, caring help, without becoming a patient under the supervision of a physician.

Redefining normality within the context of the female reproductive system will take time. Women have been imbued with the medical model of women's bodies and health, and it is hard to work past that. Redefining women in women's terms is not a problem unique to health. It is an essential feminist issue.

NOTES

1. Diana Scully and Pauline Bart, "A Funny Thing Happened on the Way to the Orifice: Women in Gynecology Textbooks," *American Journal of Sociology* 78 (1971), 1045–50.

2. *Gould Medical Dictionary,* 3d ed. (New York: McGraw-Hill, 1972), 1056.

3. *Gould Medical Dictionary,* 658.

4. G. J. Barker-Benfield, *The Horrors of the Half-Known Life* (New York: Harper and Row, 1976), 88.

5. Thomas Szasz, *The Theology of Medicine* (New York: Harper Colophon, 1977).

6. Vern Bullough, *The Development of Medicine as a Profession* (New York and Switzerland: Karger, 1966), 101.

7. Bullough, *Development of Medicine,* 102.

8. Janet Carlisle Bogdan, "Nineteenth Century Childbirth: Its Context and Meaning" (Paper presented at the third Berkshire Conference on the History of Women, June 9–11, 1976), 2.

9. Datha Clapper Brack, "The Displacement of the Midwife: Male Domination in a Formerly Female Occupation" (unpublished, 1976), 4.

10. Brack, "Displacement of the Midwife," 5.

11. Bogdan, "Nineteenth Century Childbirth."

12. Frances E. Kobrin, "The American Midwife Controversy: A Crisis in Professionalization," *Bulletin of the History of Medicine* (1966), 355.

13. Ibid.

14. René Dubos, *Man, Medicine and Environment* (New York: New American Library, 1968), 79.

15. Dorothy C. Wertz, "Childbirth as a Controlled Workspace: From Midwifery to Obstetrics" (Paper presented at the 71st annual meeting of the American Sociological Association, 1976), 5.

16. Barbara Ehrenreich and Deirdre English, *Witches, Midwives and Nurses* (Old Westbury, N.Y.: Feminist Press, 1973), 33.

17. Brack, "Displacement of the Midwife."

18. Bogdan, "Nineteenth Century Childbirth," 8.

19. Kobrin, "American Midwife Controversy," 353.

20. Brack, "Displacement of the Midwife," 1.

21. Barker-Benfield, *Horrors of the Half-Known Life,* 83.

22. Ibid., 120.

23. Ibid., 120.

24. Barbara Ehrenreich and Deirdre English, *Complaints and Disorders* (Old Westbury, N.Y.: Feminist Press, 1973).

25. Barker-Benfield, *Horrors of the Half-Known Life,* 120.

26. Ibid., 121.

27. Talcott Parsons, "Definitions of Health and Illness in Light of American Value Systems," in E. Gartly Jaco, ed., *Patients, Physicians and Illnesses* (New York: Free Press, 1958).

28. Ehrenreich and English, *Complaints and Disorders,* 16.

29. Vern Bullough and Martha Voght, "Women, Menstruation and Nineteenth-Century Medicine" (Paper presented at the 45th annual meeting of the American Association for the History of Medicine, 1972).

30. Ehrenreich and English, *Complaints and Disorders,* 47.

31. Estelle Ramey, "Men's Cycles (They Have Them Too, You Know)," *Ms.* (1972), 8–14.

32. Milton Abramson and John R. Torghele, *American Journal of Obstetrics and Gynecology* (1961), 223.

33. Sheldon Segal, "Contraceptive Research: A Male Chauvinist Plot?" *Family Planning Perspectives* (July 1972), 21–25.

34. Janet Carlisle Bogdan, "Nineteenth Century Childbirth: The Politics of Reality" (Paper presented at the 71st annual meeting of the American Sociological Association, 1976), 11.

35. Wertz, "Childbirth as a Controlled Workspace," 15.

36. Doris Haire, *The Cultural Warping of Childbirth* (Hillside, N.J.: International Childbirth Education Association, 1972).

37. See Barbara Katz Rothman, *In Labor: Women and Power in the Birthplace* (New York: Norton, 1982), for a fuller discussion of the medicalization of the maternity cycle and developing alternatives.

38. Robert A. Wilson, *Feminine Forever* (New York: Pocket Books, 1968).

39. John Bunker, "Surgical Manpower," *New England Journal of Medicine* 282 (1970), 135–44.

40. Arthur Herbst, J. Ulfelder, and D. C. Poskanzer, "Adenocarcinoma of the Vagina," *New England Journal of Medicine* 284 (1971): 871–81.

41. Barbara Seaman and Gideon Seaman, *Women and the Crisis in Sex Hormones* (New York: Rawson Associates, 1977), 78.

42. Harry Ziel and William Finkle, "Estrogen Replacement Therapy," *New England Journal of Medicine* 293 (1975), 1167–70.

43. Helen B. Homes, Betty B. Hoskins, and Michael Gross, *Birth Control and Controlling Birth: Woman Centered Perspectives* (Clifton, N.J.: Humana Press, 1981), and *The Custom Made Child? Woman Centered Perspectives* (Clifton, N.J.: Humana Press, 1981).

Part Two

In and Out of the Family

Women and the American Family: Continuity and Change

NAOMI GERSTEL AND HARRIET ENGEL GROSS

The family, we like to think, is, or at least should be, about love. Whatever we like to think, however, the realities of family life suggest otherwise. For women, men, and children alike, the family is, and long has been, an institution based on economic dependence. Despite women's unprecedented entry into the labor force, most women depend financially on husbands. Despite men's apparent financial independence, most depend on wives not only for "invisible" and unpaid household work, but also for the income provided by their wives' paychecks. Despite children's growing assertions of independence, most offspring still depend on their parents for current and future class positions. Yet, although a division of labor links husband with wife and children with parents, ideologies transmute and mystify the economic significance of these exchanges, casting them in terms of love and companionship.

This chapter examines the economic bonds of family life and the ideologies that have grown up around them. First, we trace the historical origins and transformations of economic interdependence in colonial and industrial America. Next, we show how the historical legacy of nineteenth-century families, in both ideology and practice, continues to shape contemporary families. Finally, we discuss both how the growing participation of women in the labor force and current trends in the structure of families have altered, but not eliminated, the economic dependencies of men, and women, and children.

THE FAMILY AS AN ECONOMIC UNIT: AN HISTORICAL PERSPECTIVE

Colonial Families

In colonial America, economic and family life were merged. The majority of husbands, wives, and children lived on farms or in artisan households. The colonial family was not self-sufficient, especially in New England: Colonial farmers engaged in a constant exchange of domestic goods and work with their neighbors and kin. Yet, in broad comparison to contemporary families, the colonial family depended primarily on goods it produced for itself and by itself.[1] A self-governing entity — or, more accurately, an entity governed by a patriarchal father — it formed a little "commonwealth."[2]

In ideology, if not always in practice, the colonial family was multigenerational. To be sure, extended kin did not typically share a household throughout the life course: Few people lived long enough to reside in a three-generation household, and inheritance practices forced children who did not inherit the family farm to leave when they married. Thus, at any one time in colonial America, most households were nuclear families.[3] Yet, ties between the generations were strong and important: The long-term security of family members and the continuity of family lineage took precedence over individual advancement.[4]

Despite the fact that most households were nuclear, a significant proportion of elderly parents lived with their children. One study found that although only 9 percent of households contained grandparents, 80 percent of persons over sixty-five who had living children resided with those children. A high adult-mortality rate, rather than a distaste for multigenerational households, explains the predominance of nuclear households.[5]

The authority of parents — vested mainly in fathers — typically overrode individual rights or claims to independence. In the North, male parents normally retained legal control of much of the family estate until death, in order to ensure their material well-being in old age.[6] That control ensured the long-term obedience of children, which, in turn, shaped patterns of marriage. Sons had to wait for grants of land from their fathers before they could marry, whereas fathers delayed turning over that land as a way to determine when, and perhaps whom, their sons would marry.[7] So, too, fathers preferred daughters to marry in the order of their birth (otherwise, a prospective suitor might well think something was wrong with an unmarried older daughter); and, indeed, New England older daughters typically married before their younger sisters.[8] However, even though the prescriptive literature of the day, written in scriptures and repeated in sermons of early New England, expressed the widespread injunction to "honor old age," such honor often was limited to those elderly parents who commanded economic resources. Only those with both productive land and economically dependent family members actually commanded much respect. For other elderly — often women — old age brought poverty and dishonor.[9]

Neither the nuclear family nor even extended kin defined the boundaries of colonial families. Servants who lived and worked in a household, whether or not they were related by blood, were viewed and treated often as family members by those with whom they shared a home. They provided labor, and in return they were taught productive skills, religious doctrine, and moral values. They were family members *because* they shared and worked in a household, and were subject to the authority of its head, not because they were treated with nurturance, affection, or love. In fact, in colonial New England towns, the term "love" was reserved for the ideal relationship with persons outside the family.[10]

Most important, the nuclear family was a unit of production. Unlike the contemporary family, which purchases many of the goods and services it consumes, the colonial family shared in the production of most (although not all) of what it consumed. Wives usually took care of the kitchen garden, animals, and house — by cleaning and preparing food, cloth, and candles. Husbands plowed, planted, and harvested the fields. Yet, husbands sometimes helped with the making of cloth, as wives sometimes helped with the hoeing.[11]

Just as colonial husbands and wives shared in production for household use, so, too, they shared in childrearing. Both fathers and mothers were deeply involved in caring for children who were welcomed for their labor and for the security they promised in their parents' old age. Children did not simply "help"; they were an essential source of labor. These children rather quickly became "little adults": If not bound out as servants, daughters learned from and worked side by side with their mothers; sons, with their fathers.[12]

Living and working together, husbands and wives, parents and children, may well have developed strong feelings for one another. Yet, to imagine that such feelings were the primary bonds of colonial family life would be to distort these people's experience. Productive ties — among spouses and their children, extended kin, and even boarding servants — were explicitly the ties that bound colonial American families. This agrarian society was a "family economy," or a "family system of production."[13]

The Rise of Industrial Capitalism and the Birth of New Family and Gender Ideologies

The late eighteenth and early nineteenth centuries were pivotal periods in the transformation of the family. From the "family economy" characterizing colonial America, industrial capitalism gradually fractured job site and household into separate spheres. A growing commercialization of agriculture, an increasing number of itinerant traders, and improvements in transportation made possible links to expanding national markets. At first, however, most families still lived in rural areas and still produced primarily for family consumption or local exchange. Fathers and their mature sons still farmed crops and raised livestock for the use of their own families. Mothers and daughters prepared the family's food and turned their talents and energies to the home production of textiles that they made into clothes for household use. Only when there was a surplus were crops, livestock, and textiles put up for sale in the expanding market.[14]

Gradually, at different rates in different locales, land became more difficult to acquire, at least for those unwilling to migrate west. With the rise of
factories, stores, and centralized workshops "manned" by a newly land-poor
labor force, production slowly moved out of the home. No longer making all
of their own clothes, often not growing much of their own food, families
came to depend on cheap ready-made goods available for purchase. Without
sufficient land to provide support or work for an entire family, and newly
dependent on cash-producing pursuits, families had little choice but to send
their children (in particular their young, single daughters who, unlike sons,
neither inherited land nor migrated west) to work in the new industrial and
commercial enterprises owned and run by a growing entrepreneurial elite.[15]

As the century progressed, a number of forces in both the working and
middle class converged to produce new images of family and gender relations common to both classes. The young "native" women factory operatives were gradually pushed out by employers who speeded up production
and hired cheaper immigrant labor, by working-class men who fought for a
male family wage, and by elite reformers who began to elaborate an ideology of a privatized "affectionate family" with clearly differentiated gender
roles. These developments slowly became the basis for a new vision of the
family, one not only spatially and temporally but also normatively distinct
from work. This vision included new prescriptions for the roles of husbands,
wives, and children. Although to some extent these roles were rooted in the
preindustrial past, they were also a forced adaptation to the emerging realities of industrial capitalism.

At the same time, at least among the growing urban elite, a new ideology for married women began to take hold. The Victorian "domestic code"
or "cult of true womanhood," outlined in the prescriptive literature of the
nineteenth century, cast women as moral guardians — pious, nurturant, and
naturally domestic.[16] Wives' "proper place" became the home; their proper
duties, "housework" and mothering.

Over the course of that century, "manliness became equated with success in the economic competition; indeed man's position in the household
came to be described as bread*winner*."[17] Popular literature by midcentury
created a mythology of the "self-made man": he no longer followed in his
father's footsteps, but worked in jobs requiring "manly independence" and
"individual exertions."[18] Simultaneously, because these urban men ventured
daily into competitive and tension-filled jobs away from home, they and
their wives increasingly believed home-based wives were essential to supply
husbands with emotional support and children with care and guidance.

Changing views of husbands and wives operated in concert with changing images of parents and children. Over the course of the nineteenth
century, urban middle-class children became "economically worthless"[19] as
they, like their mothers, were thought best removed from paid employment.
Not incidentally, during the same period, fertility was cut in half: In 1800,
women gave birth to an average of 8.0 children; by 1900, that average had
dropped to 3.7.[20] These declining birth rates, in concert with declining
infant-mortality rates and changing cultural conditions, increased the emotional (as contrasted to economic) value of each child.

Children's work in the home, like their play, became increasingly construed as acts of character development, anticipating future—rather than embodying current—productive activity. So, too, girls' and boys' games became clearly differentiated. Whereas competitive play was promoted for little boys, the nineteenth century saw the creation of "playing house" as the preferred pastime of little girls.[21] Here, children were taught at an early age that women's family work was really play.

Having become "emotionally priceless," these middle-class children, boys and girls alike, were increasingly presented in the growing literature of child-rearing advice as needing their mother's homebound influence in order to maintain their innocence while developing a conscience or a sense of *self*-control.[22] At the same time, fathers' presumed and actual preoccupation with an increasingly separate occupational sphere conspired to reduce their prescribed contribution to the daily care of children.[23] Children's new innocence, their delicately balanced self-control, their differentiated gender "natures," and their father's absence required that mothers should focus all the more on the home. Middle-class women's domestication and purification, then, went hand in hand with new "sentimentalization" of childhood.

With changes in its members' roles, the nineteenth-century family and home was increasingly heralded as secluded and subdued, cut off from the "public" world. Middle-class wives' residence in and guardianship of the home was proclaimed necessary to preserve the family as a private haven and, as important, to civilize the increasingly distant, harsh, and competitive world of commerce and politics. Not only the middle-class woman, but also the middle-class man, "was being enticed into the same darkened corner of history. The popular literature of the 1850's courted men away from their male associations—from taverns, political clubs, lodges—into the feminine world of the home."[24] To be sure, the husband was not expected to contribute to the care of house or children. But his nightly presence as companion to his wife and children in the newly private home was touted as essential to that home's emotional mission.

The conjugal unit gradually became, at least in the prescriptive literature of the day, a privatized emotional unit that produced an "affectionate family." In contrast to the colonial American family, which was defined in terms of productive contribution, nineteenth-century spouses were expected to unite on the basis of love, sexual attraction, and affection; husbands and wives were to become one another's primary companions, complementing one another with their special personalities as well as skills; and parents (especially mothers) were to become nurturant and self-sacrificing for their innocent children.[25]

Ideology versus Practice in the Middle Class

The development in the nineteenth century of an ideology of the family as a private emotional unit, and the concomitant sentimentalization of its members' ties, masked the actual relations among those members. The obscured reality was that marriages were based on economic exchange.

A telling indicator that women were oriented to marriage as an economic resource can be found in the records of those relatively few women who became financially independent. A study of over 100 spinsters from the northeastern United States found that these women self-consciously chose "single blessedness" if they could afford to do so.[26] Based on a survey of single women's reasons for their spinsterhood, a nineteenth-century reporter summarized her findings in the following way:

> I have a good job;
> I earn a good living;
> I am contented and happy;
> Why be encumbered?[27]

In addition, those well-educated women who eventually wed increasingly chose to marry late and to postpone childbearing.[28] Finally, nineteenth-century widows whose husbands left them a substantial inheritance were much less likely to remarry than were those left without means.[29] In practice, then, women seemed to marry for material consideration as much as, if not more than, for respect and emotional concern.

In fact, whatever they married for, the distinctly separate spheres of women and men led more to their emotional segregation than to their union. Women's common domestic location engendered sisterhood.[30] Because they inhabited the same worlds, women empathized with one another. Close relationships flourished outside the home: Middle-class women formed intense loyalties and deeply loving and dependent ties with women friends and kin. These often competed with conjugal ties for women's affection.[31] Although dependent on their husbands for economic support, many women did not, or could not, turn to those husbands for empathy or emotional care. Although middle-class men increasingly returned to the home as a nightly haven, working-class men spent their evenings in saloons, lodges, and clubs where male camaraderie prevailed.[32] Ironically, for most women and some men, the separation of spheres impeded the very emotional ties that the ideology of marriage promised.

So, too, the ideology of marriage suggested that couples were bound by sexual attraction and physical love. Using diaries and a nineteenth-century survey on sexuality, recent research does show that Victorian women, at least in the middle class, viewed sexual intercourse as a normal part of married life and were orgasmic.[33] But most of these same women believed procreation, not pleasure, was the purpose of marital intercourse.[34] Women achieved freedom and autonomy—from the pain of childbearing, burden of childrearing, and unsatisfactory sex lives—by denying these sexual desires.[35] Thus, the ideal of companionate marriage, with its promise of emotional and sexual pleasure, was undermined by the actual conditions of adult lives.

Just as was true in their parents' generation, the family remained an important economic resource for middle-class children, albeit in an altered way. Although the inheritance of land was no longer an essential prerequisite for independence, their fathers' income provided these nineteenth-century children (especially sons) with the formal schooling and time necessary for preparation for high-status jobs.[36] So, too, parents, especially mothers, continued to provide the cultural background and training in conduct and language, as well as in physical appearance, that prepared their children to assume the family's class position.[37]

The family, broadly defined, remained an economic unit in still another sense. Like their colonial counterparts, elderly widows often moved in with their adult children and helped with domestic chores. If they could afford to, elderly parents remained an important source of financial assistance for their offspring.[38] Thus, extended kin were themselves central to the material well-being of the married pair.[39]

In sum, then, the ties binding nineteenth-century bourgeois families remained, at least in large part, material rather than emotional. The creation of separate spheres had transformed the character of, but had hardly sundered, their economic bonds.

Variations by Class, Ethnicity, Region, and Race

Just as the ideology of the "affectionate family" masked material dependence in the nineteenth-century middle class, a family ideology with similar consequences took root in other social classes. No less than in the middle class, the ideology masked as it transformed family members' economic dependence.

In the urban working class, the reorganization of the family took place around the idea of the male earner's entitlement to a "family wage." Beginning in the 1830s, demands for a male "family wage" first served the working-class struggle to obtain for itself a decent standard of living. Yet, in the end, working men joined their industrial bosses to make the "family wage" an affirmation of men's market, and of women's and children's nonmarket, roles.[40] Although men no longer contributed to the household as a productive unit, their paychecks were essential to a family increasingly viewed as a unit of consumption, whose buying power was determined by the husband's income.

At the same time, the economic well-being of the family continued to depend on the unpaid work of wives at home. Hidden in the home, women's unpaid domestic efforts were rarely recognized as "real" work, but instead came to be viewed as pure and simple acts of love. Yet wives and mothers not only produced many services on which husbands depended (from cooking their meals to cleaning their homes and mending their clothes), but also reproduced—both literally and metaphorically—the very labor force on which industry depended. Receipt of the domestic services of wives helped to make it possible for husbands, working- and middle-class alike, to work outside the home; at the same time, the wives' provision of such services made it more difficult for the wives to do so.[41] The ideology that exalted and sentimentalized wives' domestic roles condemned those women forced to do wage work. It allowed and supported the establishment of low wage rates for women: "working" women, in this conception, were only waiting for marriage and were working for "pin money."[42] Thus, both wives and husbands came to rely on each other for gender-based material support, even as the material basis of this mutuality was mystified.

Yet, the romantic veneer overlaying practical realities and material dependence was even thinner for those who were not privileged members of the urban bourgeoisie. As Stansell writes of nineteenth-century New York: "Like other family relationships, the marriages of laboring men and women harbored little explicit, articulated tenderness. Courting was a time for private strolls and seductions, but its end was a practical household arrangement based on reciprocal obligations."[43] This description characterizes most marriages and families outside of the privileged class.

Foreign immigrants to the northeast. Most foreign immigrants—albeit with differences by regions from which they came—practiced some aspects of the family- and gender-role patterns found in the middle class even as they diverged from others. Although their domestic work was often more strenuous and demanding than it was among their middle-class counterparts, immigrant women—whether Irish, German, Italian, or Polish—assumed primary responsibility for the care of their homes and children.[44] So, too, these women relied on the incomes, typically greater than their own, of fathers and husbands. The all-too-frequent loss of a man's economic support —whether through death or through desertion—often left them in devastating poverty.[45]

However, given hard times, low wages, and the instability of employment, an immigrant husband's income was rarely enough to support an entire family. Immigrant wives, like their single and widowed counterparts, were often forced to earn a wage in order to help support their families.[46] The paid work they performed was shaped both by their gender and by their particular ethnic group. Thus, Polish wives often took in paying boarders for whom they cooked and cleaned. Italian wives took sewing into their homes. Irish wives, at least compared to other white ethnic groups, were particularly likely to work for pay outside of the home: Many of them took jobs working as domestics in the homes of white "natives."[47] Thus, it was the very presence of a large reservoir of such poor women who sewed, washed, cleaned, cooked, and served that made possible the Victorian "true womanhood" of the privileged class.

Neither were nineteenth-century children of the immigrant poor "sentimentalized." As Early found of the children of French Canadians newly immigrated to nineteenth-century Massachusetts: "Family survival was— literally—in their [the children's] hands."[48] In the big cities of the northeast, immigrant children helped their mothers with domestic work by not only sewing and cleaning but also toting water and scavenging for fuel.[49] These children also endured great misery as they worked in the mines, factories, and streets for low wages that they contributed to their families. Like their preindustrial counterparts, poor immigrant parents thought of childhood not as a separate stage of life, but rather as a time to begin to shoulder the burdens of labor. They struggled against elite reformers who believed the development of children's morality depended on the mothers' protection of children within the home.[50]

These immigrant families often relied quite heavily on the material contributions of kin and neighbor. Nineteenth-century relatives were a vital resource for one another—they often moved close to one another, and helped one another to find and keep jobs. Employers used kin ties for industrial recruitment and training.[51] Immigrants, especially those not residing near kin, engaged in a constant exchange with neighbors that was often crucial for survival. Kin and neighbors alike helped one another with housing as they borrowed and loaned household goods.[52] Thus, these immigrant families typically lived a dense communal existence in which all, regardless of age or gender, who could contribute materially were called on to do so.

Southern rural families. Nineteenth-century southern rural white families—especially those not members of the planter elite—established a "family economy" resembling in many ways that of their preindustrial counterparts. Although husbands and fathers were patriarchs and household heads, all family members were deeply involved in producing primarily for household use. Men were largely responsible for field work, and women were responsible for tending gardens, dairying, cooking, and producing cloth. Yet women often helped men, and men often helped women, with their respective labors. Economically valuable children were incorporated into the family's effort at survival, and vital exchange relationships were formed with kin. Here, the explicit link among family members was economic rather than emotional.[53]

In contrast, southern elite planters were "strongly influenced by the sentimentalization of family life and children that swept like a tidal wave over the wealthy . . . during the eighteenth and nineteenth centuries."[54] But only when white farmers owned a number of slaves did white women become fragile, sentimentalized "ladies of leisure." Just as Victorian womanhood in the North depended on the labors of poor immigrants, the leisured lady of the South depended on the labor of slaves. Yet even this lady of leisure worked to nurture her children and manage the domestic routines of slaves as her planter husband managed the routines of fieldwork.[55]

Among nineteenth-century black slaves, everyone—woman, man, boy, girl—who could work was put to work. Insofar as it did not interfere with black women's capacity to bear a future work force, slave owners—who upheld the ideology of virtue, innocence, and delicacy for their white wives and children—downplayed gender and age differences in the work assignments meted out to slaves.[56]

Owners sometimes presented (and perhaps viewed) themselves as authoritarian fathers; their plantations, as big families.[57] Yet most owners acted to encourage stable family life among slaves only insofar as it increased fertility, producing children who could be put to work or sold, or insofar as family ties provided labor incentive for adult slaves (who, when living with family, were less likely to run away and often worked harder to protect or hide the feebleness of kin).[58] But even this attenuated commitment to the slaves' family life broke down in many stages of the plantation owners' lifespan. When a young planter got married and was setting up a work force for a newly established plantation, many slave families were broken up when their members were proffered as wedding gifts. So, too, when an owner died, his slaves were often dispersed by sale or inheritance. Only in the middle phase of the plantation cycle would many slave owners encourage stability of slave families for both economic and moral reasons, finding these families to be a source of fertility and an incentive conducive to labor discipline.[59]

In contrast, among slaves themselves, the family became a basis for "resistance to dehumanization": they used it to create an organization of work and relationships different from that imposed by slave masters.[60] Often, slaves managed to keep up extensive kin networks and remained committed to marriage.[61] The strength of slaves' attachment to families was amply shown in their anguish when families were sold apart. Ironically, it was among blacks—denied economic resources—that family attachment may have attained the fullest expression of pure sentiment.

Yet, as part of this resistance, slaves, men as well as women, upheld gender-based division of labor in their own quarters: Wives and daughters cooked and sewed while husbands and sons fished and hunted for prey.[62] Whether from their own cultural heritage or because of the conditions of their lives as slaves (in which owners encouraged the authority of males and handed out resources through them), slaves came to value husbands and fathers as heads of their households.[63] Overall, then, there were clear indications of the tenacity of the black family, with a commitment to gender-differentiated roles, despite the great adversity of slavery.

When freed, large numbers of blacks obtained marriage licenses to gain official recognition that they were legally wed even though doing so used up most of the few resources they had.[64] Freed blacks reestablished the authority of black men over black women and removed black women from field work to their own homes whenever they had the opportunity to do so. Only at planting and harvest time did these wives join their husbands in the fields.[65] Other freed black women, particularly widows, became heads of their own households and had to seek employment, often as domestics, to support them.[66] Usually, such work only ensured that many black women and their children would survive on the edges of poverty, dependent on the support of extended kin just as most white women were dependent on the incomes of husbands.

Nineteenth-century industrial capitalism, then, wrought massive changes in the ideology and practices of American families as it fractured job site and household into separate spheres and provided a new basis for the segregation of women and men. The implementation of these changes varied by class, ethnicity, region, and race. Yet, overall, although the economic bonds of family members were transformed, among no group were they eliminated entirely.

CONTEMPORARY FAMILIES: CONTINUITY AND COMMONALITY

Nineteenth-century developments set in place the basic scaffolding undergirding twentieth-century families. As the following sections will show, gender-linked material dependencies remain very much alive. Women retain their primary responsibility for care of home and children and most remain economically dependent on husbands (or on husbands' counterparts in subsidies upheld or generated by the state.) However, the majority of wives and mothers — across race and class — have added paid employment outside the home to their work inside of it. This twentieth-century addition, and its ideological repercussions, have again transformed but not eliminated the economic dependencies of women and men.

Getting Married

The most fundamental continuity between the nineteenth century and the present is that marriage remains a near universal experience for American women. Just as 95 percent of women married in 1800,[67] 95 percent of both black and white women born before the end of World War II married. Although demographers now predict that a somewhat smaller proportion of women born recently will marry, they nonetheless expect that about 90 percent of young white and 80 percent of young black women are likely to do so.[68] To be sure, women now delay marriage.[69] And certainly, given these delays in concert with increased rates of divorce,[70] women of all races spend less time in first marriages than they did previously.[71] Yet, reduced mortality and high rates of remarriage (at least among whites) mean women spend more time in marriage than they did in the nineteenth century: In 1800, women spent about 27 years in marriage; now, after a peak of 42 years during the baby boom, they are married for an average total of 35 years.[72]

The slight decline in the rate of marriage has been accompanied by a steady rise in the rate of cohabitation. The number of unmarried cohabiting couples has gone from 439,000 in 1960 to over 2.2 million by 1986; 30 percent of these couples have children.[73] A number of factors, including increased sexual freedom and growing tolerance of singlehood, encourage cohabitation. Cohabitation, however, is not so much an alternative to marriage as a stage on the way to marriage: a great majority (over 90 percent) of cohabiting women expect to marry and "cohabitation seems to be most common among those who use or intend to use it as a stepping stone to marriage."[74]

Contemporary women's decision to marry, like that of their historical predecessors, is very much affected by economic considerations. Women with more financial resources, whether personal income or educational credentials likely to command future income, are less likely to get married than are other women, whereas the rate of marriage increases among men with greater financial resources.[75] Thus, as Goldscheider and Waite recently found, women use resources, whether from their own employment or from their parents, to "buy out of marriage."[76] Most, however, do not have the resources to "buy out."

When they choose a spouse, young women today are aware of their likely financial dependence. Thus, one survey of college students showed that 65 percent of men but only 24 percent of women said they would not marry unless they were in love, even if a relationship had all the other qualities they desired.[77] Similarly, another study found that young women do more "feeling work" on love, as they seek to redirect it in "realistic" or "practical" directions. Hochschild explains these differences by suggesting: "Young men hold hegemony over the courtship process while at the same time women, *for economic reasons*, need marriage more."[78]

Being Married: Housework

Although women look to husbands for financial support more than men look to wives for such support, wives nonetheless continue to make important contributions to the economic well-being of families through their labors in the home. After getting married, contemporary wives—like their nineteenth-century counterparts—cook, clean, shop, and manage domestic routines. As much quantitative research has shown, domestic work, across race and class,[79] remains women's work. Husbands "help." But they do far less than their wives.[80] Although employed wives devote fewer hours to domestic labor than do housewives, they—no less than farm women— labor from dawn to dusk.[81]

Although its nature is obscured by popular and legal ideas, housework consists of economically valuable services. An increasing number of household tasks have their analogue in the marketplace. Prepared food is for sale in restaurants; transportation is available from buses and taxis; cleaning and child care are available from paid housekeepers and baby-sitters. Researchers who calculate the dollar value of housework, pricing it at its equivalent market price, estimate that such compensation would increase the family's income by as much as 60 percent.[82] In reality, then, husbands continue to rely on wives' family work just as wives rely on husbands' greater income.[83]

To be sure, the character of women's domestic work has changed over the course of the twentieth century. Women put less time into laundry and cooking but more into marketing. Much domestic labor has become "consumption work" that pulls women outside the home into shopping malls, supermarkets, and bank lines.[84] As Ruth Schwartz Cowan writes: "The automobile brought with it the woman driver and the suburbs. The peddler disappeared and so did the milkman, replaced by the supermarket—and the woman who drove to the shop."[85] And since the early part of the century, the reorganization of stores has intensified the efforts of shoppers. For example, in grocery stores, a known customer aided by helpful clerks who gave advice, knew products, and packed and delivered them has gradually been replaced by an unknown consumer who now "memorizes the location of goods, makes selections without consulting a clerk, loads the cart and pushes it to the checkout stand [where she] loads the goods onto the counter, placing purchases in bags and portering them home."[86] Such "self-service shopping" may not reduce costs but it does intensify women's unpaid efforts outside the home.[87] Thus, the family's ability to function as the unit of consumption increasingly depends on the labors of wives.

Women themselves experience contradictory impulses with regard to their continued responsibility for housework. On the one hand, many women often resent the time-consuming, isolating, boring, and repetitive chores that much housework involves.[88] When they can find and afford it, many take advantage of alternatives available in the market by "subcontracting"[89] out part of the housework to poorer, often immigrant or black, women or to the growing number of firms that employ such women.[90] So, too, newly created food services—from the caterers serving the elite to the fast-food restaurants serving the many—now provide a good number of the meals once cooked at home. And, notably, women seem to be lowering their standards for housework; one telling indicator is that in the last few years, the sale of paper plates has increased markedly while the sale of floor waxes has declined.[91]

On the other hand, some women find satisfaction in some of the work they do for their families; it is still both constituted and experienced as a "labor of love." Given the availability of commercial services and products, at least part of what was once compulsory is now voluntary: sewing, cooking, and gardening are sometimes freely chosen by women, who find such work enjoyable to themselves as well as useful to their husbands and children. Many believe that purchased services are not always equivalent to homemade ones; they lack the personal touch. Wives and mothers also gain a sense of control by managing a home and the routines of its members. Moreover, doing housework validates womanhood: Adult women create and experience their gender identity in the very process of doing domestic chores.[92] Finally, they know it will create conflict—and possibly more work for themselves—if they ask their husbands to take a greater share. Thus, recent studies show, often to the surprise of the researchers, that although there has been an increase in the proportion of women desiring greater help from their husbands, many women themselves do not want to give up, or fully to share, housework.[93] To understand all of women's family work simply as "oppressed labor" or to view women who choose to do housework as victims of false consciousness is to miss the point: Some housework produces a sense of achievement and harmony, just as women's control over their families' well-being affirms their gender identity.[94]

Women, then, resent their work in the home *and* resist forfeiting it. Yet, however they feel about housework, such work constrains women's ability to achieve financial independence. The more housework they do, the lower their wages;[95] the greater the household demands, the lower their labor-force participation.[96] Moreover, as economist Barbara Bergmann notes: "If she stops doing the housework, the marriage will probably end. So there is in reality an exchange of the wife's housework for the husband's continuance in the marriage, and for his continuing to supply her with room, board and other benefits."[97]

Parenting

Just as wives continue to do most of the housework, they also continue to do most of the parenting. Here, too, husbands "help." Even women employed full-time in demanding careers spend far more time with their children than do their husbands. When fathers do spend time with children, their primary activity is playing. Mothers are much more likely to engage in "custodial activities" such as diapering, bathing, and feeding.[98]

Although women today have fewer children than they did in the past,[99] childrearing remains a central activity in their lives. It is often a primary arena in which wives exercise power, express creativity, as well as work out unconscious desires rooted in their own experience as children being mothered.[100] Whether for reasons conscious or unconscious, parenting is a source of satisfaction that many women do not want to give up. Fewer than 10 percent of young women become adults with no expectation of having or desire for children.[101] Even career women, who often plan to give birth at a time that will not interfere with their careers, find that it is their jobs, rather than their children, they see as the interference.[102] Children, then, continue to be seen as "emotionally priceless."

Yet the very parenting women cherish imposes constraints on other areas of life — on marriage, leisure, and employment — which these women also value. Both black and white wives with children, especially those with young children, are less satisfied with their marriages and friends than are those without children.[103] More important, even when they have similar education and work experience, women who give birth to children while still in their early twenties have lower wages than do those who delay childbirth.[104] Although parenting may be seen as standing outside a system of economic exchange, mothering nonetheless reinforces wives' economic dependence on their husbands. At the same time, husbands are able to maintain full involvement in their jobs or careers because their wives assume primary responsibility for child care.

Emotion Work

Although women continue to perform much labor in the home, many think that what distinguishes the modern family (with its roots a century old) and what now binds family members is the provision of emotional support. Thus, we say marriage and the family have become newly "companionate." Yet, in fact, if the modern family provides emotional support, it does so primarily for husbands and children. To be sure, many married women — especially in the middle class — turn to their husbands and children for emotional support and security. But they are much more likely to give than to receive.

Husbands turn to their wives as their only confidant — the person to whom they disclose their personal feelings and concerns. In contrast, like their nineteenth-century counterparts, wives typically have more than one confidant: they have close women friends and kin to whom they turn for emotional support.[105] At the same time, wives sustain marital conversations: They do more listening, more questioning, and less interrupting than do their husbands.[106] Perhaps for these reasons, husbands are more likely than are wives to say that their spouse is appreciative and affectionate and that their spouse understands them well.[107] So, too, women more often respond to their children's emotional demands, and thereby shield their husbands from those demands. Both by shielding and by comforting her husband, a wife makes an economic contribution in that "the emotional gratification provided by her enables the husband to devote himself more effectively to his role as the family breadwinner."[108]

The emotional work that women do is not limited to nurturing their husbands and children. The work of "kinkeeping" depends on the efforts and resources of wives far more than on those of husbands, as both husbands and wives believe that it is wives who should keep in touch with kin.[109] Many studies demonstrate that they do: Wives call, write, visit, and invite both their own and their husbands' kin far more often than do men.[110] At least some studies suggest that because women do such caretaking, their own employment suffers. Thus, women postpone entry into the labor force, limit their hours of work, take time off, and even quit jobs entirely in order to provide care for aged kin.[111] Moreover, because wives do such work, husbands can invest themselves in their jobs.

In sum, like their nineteenth-century counterparts, wives make the "home a haven" by doing not only most of the housework and parenting but also the emotion work. An ideology still attaches to this work, turning it into pure and simple acts of love. Yet, such work contributes much to both the husband's economic success and the wife's economic dependence.

CONTEMPORARY FAMILIES: DISCONTINUITY AND DIVERSITY

The patterns that contemporary families share with their historical counterparts are matched by an equally important difference. While husbands and fathers continue to take little part in "women's sphere," wives and mothers are increasingly entering men's. We might expect these changes to make women economically independent of husbands. As we shall see, only a minority is. At the same time, these changes might make men—at least to some extent—dependent on the incomes of their wives. As we shall see, a majority is. If nineteenth-century marriage was based on the exchange of husbands' income for wives' domestic service, twentieth-century marriage is increasingly becoming one in which the economic bond of husband and wife is extended to the pooling of incomes.

Two oft-cited and connected demographic trends are particularly important for understanding this transformation. First, except for a brief period after World War II, the proportion of women in the labor force has increased steadily during the twentieth century. Before World War II, women in the labor force were primarily single. After that, although the unmarried were still more likely to be employed, the number and proportion of married women in the labor force increased steadily. By 1987, over half of married women were in the labor force (making up about half of all employed women), whereas only one-fifth of married women were in the labor force in 1950 (when they made up only 24 percent of employed women).[112] Among married women, the most rapid increase took place among mothers of preschool children: In 1950, only about 11 percent of these women were in the labor force, but since then the proportion has increased steadily, reaching 63 percent in 1987.[113]

Second, as we have seen, the early stages of industrial capitalism developed with — perhaps even depended on — married women's labor, paid and unpaid labor in and outside of the home. But, the logic of capitalism is to extend markets into previously excluded areas. Women's exit from the home both provides a new source of cheap labor and generates demands for the products of new industries. As employed wives necessarily do less household labor than do unemployed ones, their families must either do without the products of such labor or purchase them. Thus, the labor force expands as two-earner families provide a new market for prepared food, child care, and cleaning services. Indeed, since World War II, the fastest-growing sector of the economy has consisted not of products but of services — including, for example, retail trade, personal and business services, and food and health industries. Between 1970 and 1980, the service sector grew by close to 14 million jobs — a 31 percent growth in this sector's share of the labor market.[114] Of note, women assumed 75 percent of these new jobs.[115] This sector's growth, then, relied on a relatively large number of low-paid women workers, many of whom (especially when compared to their male counterparts in manufacturing) needed or were willing to work intermittently or part-time, with limited fringe benefits and chances for advancement.[116]

These two demographic trends are linked not only to one another but also to the family. The nineteenth-century construction of the husband as the family's breadwinner has set the stage in the twentieth century for the inferior position of women in the labor force. As Joan Smith writes: "The nature of jobs offered them in the growing service sector is shaped by the presumption that women still have access to sufficient support beyond their own earnings and are at best only partially committed to wage labor."[117] Thus, the growth of a service-dominated economy — based on the inclusion of women — depended on those very features of family life created by the exclusion of married women from employment in the industrializing economy of the nineteenth century.

In this sense, the twentieth century's economy inherited and made use of the nineteenth century's expectations for women's and men's family life. Yet, although these presumptions are made use of, the very conditions on which they were based have been transformed by women's labor force participation. This transformation takes different forms at different levels of the class structure and in different types of families.

Dual-Earner Families

Today, two or more jobs are typically required to meet a family's financial needs and, in the modal family, both husband and wife are employed: More than half (56 percent) of married couples were dual-earners in 1987, while ten years earlier the proportion was only 48 percent.[118] The family's financial status is closely linked to wives whose earnings contribute, on average, 29 percent of family income. White married couples, for instance, had a median income in 1986 of $26,421 when the wife was a full-time homemaker, compared to $38,972 when she was employed. For blacks, the median income was $16,766 when the wife was a full-time homemaker, compared with $31,949 when she was in the labor force.[119]

Thus, while they have contributed little additional work at home, most husbands have become dependent on the earnings of their wives. At the same time, completely dependent wives now constitute a minority of all wives.[120] Yet, women's lower average earnings mean that wives still rely more than husbands do on their spouses for financial support, and that unmarried mothers often face poverty.

Divorce and Female-Headed Households

While the labor force expanded, the two-parent family declined. By 1986, over half of all black families with children, and one-sixth of white families, were headed solely by women.[121]

The increase in female-headed families is due in large part to the increase in the divorce rate. The incidence of divorce in the United States more than doubled between 1970 and 1980, to more than 1 million divorces annually.[122] In 1973, for the first time, the number of marriages ending in divorce exceeded the number ending in widowhood.[123] What has not changed much is the placement of children: In 1986, 89 percent of children in single-parent families lived with their mothers;[124] in the last few decades, there has been almost no change in the proportion of children living only with fathers.[125]

The economic dependence of wives and mothers, particularly white ones, on marriage becomes especially clear when marriages dissolve. Growing divorce rates, accompanied by negligible alimony and unreliable child-support payments, have led an increasing number of women to rely on their own, typically low, earnings.[126] Whereas both marriage and divorce have relatively little effect on the economic status of black and white men, divorce is a key event accounting for a decline in the economic status, often even impoverishment, of white women. Although divorce is also associated with a drop in the economic status of black women, it is less important in accounting for these women's poverty. Recent national evidence suggests that white, but not black, men also suffer a drop in their family income in the first year following a divorce. However, the decline at this point for white men is much smaller than that for white or black women. Moreover, by the third year after divorce, men's family income, white as well as black, has increased, while the family income of still-divorced white and black women remains much lower than it was when they were married.[127]

The primary way poor white women, especially if they head households, can improve their economic situation is through remarriage.[128] Most divorced women—especially those who are uneducated, young, poor, and white—remarry if they have the opportunity to do so. On remarriage, these women regain a standard of living almost equal to that of divorced men or women who stayed married.[129] The situation is quite different for black women.

Variants on a Theme: The Black Family and Poverty

Given the greater likelihood of poverty among black men, marriage does not serve as the economic safeguard for black women in the way it can for white women. The differences between white and black families are tied to both the poorer labor market prospects of black women and the decreasing labor-market status of black men.[130] Since 1960, the number of black men out of the labor force—because they are unemployed, are discouraged workers, are in correctional facilities, or are unaccounted for—has more than tripled. Thirty percent of working-aged black men are unemployed, discouraged workers, or unaccounted for compared to only 11 percent in these categories for working-aged white men.[131] Analysts of black family life suggest this worsening economic position of black males has been a major, if not the single, factor contributing to an increase in black female-headed households. Developing an "index of marriageable males" (which includes not only labor-force participation but also mortality and incarceration rates), Wilson and Neckerman reveal a long-term decline in the proportion of black men who are in a position to support a family. Their work, and the analyses of others, suggest that the economic position of black males, in concert with discriminatory political and cultural forces, forces many black women to leave or forego marriage.[132]

As a result, black women have higher divorce rates than do white women.[133] However, an even more striking feature—and the factor most different from those for whites—is the increase over the last two decades in the proportion of never-married black mothers.[134] The increase in the rate of never-married mothers is not a result of increasing rates of adolescent pregnancy. In fact, the rate of teenage pregnancy and child birth has declined sharply since the late 1950s. Rather, what has happened, particularly among black women, is a separation of childbearing from marriage.[135] Although most of these women will eventually marry, childbearing often comes several years before marriage.[136] In 1980–1981, fewer than 10 percent of black women who conceived a firstborn child out of wedlock married before the birth of the child, whereas 51 percent of such white women did so.[137]

Although both divorce and out-of-wedlock birth are *associated* with high rates of poverty,[138] recent research makes clear these are not the *cause* of poverty for blacks. As Mary Jo Bane found, three-quarters of whites who were poor in the first year after forming a female-headed or single-person household became poor simultaneously with that transition. In contrast, of the blacks who were poor after the transition, about two-thirds had also been poor before.[139] As Bane concludes: "Although there has indeed been a dramatic and shocking increase in female-headed households among blacks and an equally dramatic feminization of black poverty, one cannot conclude that much of the poverty could have been avoided had families stayed together."[140] Whereas for white women, divorce is both cause and consequence of poverty, for black women, poverty is a cause of divorce.

The primary way poor white women can improve their economic situation is through remarriage; among poor blacks, the situation is very different. Because of the lower earnings of black men, poor black women can expect fewer economic gains from remarriage than can white women. And, in fact, black women remarry far less often than do white women.[141]

In the absence of an economically viable marital bond, poor black women, like the nineteenth-century poor more generally, regularly turn to friends, neighbors, and extended kin for economic support. Since relations with friends and extended kin compose dense networks of exchange, these relationships are more stable than is marriage. Moreover, poor black women turn friends into "fictive kin," which means that these friends can be counted on to exchange money, goods, and services—not simply love. In the face of failure of the conjugal ties, blacks, then, adapt the language of kinship to the friends and neighbors on whom they rely.[142]

Overall, then, the economic bonds of black families—at least among the poor—differ from those of white families. Disadvantaged black men are, for whatever reasons, unable to provide women with economic security. Yet, this is not to say that economic ties among black families disappear altogether. Rather, they are reconstituted along different lines, emphasizing extended and fictive kin ties rather than conjugal ties.

Professional Women and Dual-Career Families

As the high unemployment rate among black men has loosened the economic ties binding black families, so too has the growing (although still small) number of women who have well-paying careers loosened the economic ties binding affluent families. For these women, new career options provide alternatives to a forced marital dependency. Compared to those with fewer resources, better-educated and better-paid women are less likely to marry, or to have children if they do. They are also more likely to divorce, and are less likely to remarry.[143] Ironically, then, although for very different reasons, the nineteenth-century bargain that marriage promised is collapsing for these professional women just as it is for poor black women.

But the parallels between these groups should not overshadow important differences. While poor black women reconstitute family as an economic unit around kin, professional wives may reconstitute marriage as a productive unit, albeit in a sense quite different from that of their historical counterparts. Thus, as recent research indicates, dual-career husbands and wives often bring their work home to get help from, and to give help to, a knowledgeable spouse.[144] In doing so, they may increase their own productivity. Not only are married men more productive in their professions than are their single counterparts, but also at least some married women professionals—including academics, research scientists, and lawyers—are more productive than are unmarried ones.[145] Thus, in relying on their mates, these dual-career spouses fortify an economic as well as emotional bond between each other. However, because of their ability to earn a good income, it is for such well-paid women that marriage and family can most readily be "freely chosen," based on and sustained by emotional dependence. They can be tied by emotional attachment precisely because they are least economically driven.

Yet we cannot be too sanguine about the combination of career and family for these women. Along with career gains, these married professional women often experience the anxiety that accompanies high expectations and token status. Typically, these women feel desperately pressed for time, giving up their own leisure and sleep to meet demands of both employment and family. Unlike men, these women discover that their job and family constantly intrude on each other.[146] Notwithstanding the media's celebrated creation, the "superwoman" who does it "all" is as unrealistic and pernicious an image as is her predecessor, the "supermom."[147]

CONCLUSION

We have shown how the nineteenth-century construction of different spheres for men and women, and its attendant romanticization of family ties, account for both changing and enduring features of contemporary families. Our analysis of the relationship between that heritage and the realities of women's and men's lives over the course of this century highlights the fact that ideology never exerts its influence in a social vacuum. Instead, people's everyday experiences in given historical circumstances reverberate on ideology, revealing the interplay between them. But even more, we have seen how ideology and practice mutually constitute and reconstitute each other over time, so transformations in both develop out of the realities created by each.

Day-to-day realities in the "new" families of the eighties—female-headed, dual-earner, and dual-career—derive from the legacy of the nineteenth-century relegation of woman to the home and the ideological celebration of her presence there. Trivialization of the considerable remaining work women do for their families—a residue of the devaluation that this work underwent over the course of the last century—hides that work's economic value and even conceals that it is work. Most family responsibilities, in turn, whether willingly pursued or begrudgingly resented, vitiate women's continued attachment to jobs, or, at the very least, keep employed wives and mothers perpetually exhausted.

Moreover, woman's relative economic disadvantage on the job—also a throwback to nineteenth-century definitions of the worth of her labor both at home and in the market—ensures that women are likely to be poor if they head their own household, and that they probably will be obliged to subordinate job demands to family if they marry. In such ways have ideologies set in place and nourished the reality of gender inequality in the twentieth century.

At the same time, however, the new realities of women's lives in the twentieth century—their increasing labor-force participation, higher educational achievements, and growing necessity to manage a family alone—have in turn challenged prevailing ideologies and transformed the basis of women's personal identities, as well as the social landscape available to them. Now that women are no longer confined to the family, women's experiences in families, and in social life more generally, are changing beliefs and practices both in the home and away from it. In such ways have demographic and economic developments in this century produced new realities that constrain old ideologies and at least offer the promise of mitigating gender inequality.

An important conclusion results from this analysis. Some people argue. that recent changes—from the decrease of single-earner families and the rising employment of women to the declining fertility and increasing divorce rates — are evidence for the imminent demise of the family. Many more believe that while families of the past were linked by strong economic bonds, the ties that bind contemporary families are made of a weak emotional twine. In contrast, we have argued that far from having lost its economic significance, the family is still the predominant economic lifeline for most women. Unfortunately, however, the premium put on the modern family's emotional life has eclipsed the family's remaining economic significance.

In fact, the family remains economically significant for all its members. Although it is true that men's economic fortunes do not plummet, as women's do, on divorce, married men and their children are increasingly relying both on their wives' unpaid domestic services and on their wives' wages to maintain their family's economic status. And even (perhaps especially) among those women spurning marriage — black impoverished and white affluent women — it is underlying economic exigencies that explain, as they constrain, such options. A common productive effort no longer constitutes family ties, but a common economic fate is still very much a family affair — even if this common fate, based as it is on exchange, is an unequal exchange. Whether affluent or poor, white or black, husbands, wives, and children are still economically intertwined — for better or worse — even as that union is mystified by notions of romantic and maternal love. These mystifications must be made visible if they are to be resisted effectively.

Moreover, the increasing requirement that there be two earners to ensure a family's economic solvency suggests that economic ties among family members will continue to shape emotional ones, just as the reverse will remain true. Thus, spouses and parents in dual-career marriages who put in long hours required by their jobs may find it harder and harder to fulfill the emotional goals they set for their families.[148]

Thus, we see a dialectic, as well, in the relative economic versus emotional tilt assigned to the family. While we have come to emphasize the family's emotional significance, we may have changed the conditions that could sustain such an emphasis. As others have suggested, the fifties may have been the last decade in which women's behavior and social norms coincided.[149] If this is so, we must come to terms with the new realities inhering in the fact that women need jobs and that our society needs their labor, just as that labor necessarily changes families. We can no longer afford to sustain an ideological eclipse of such economic realities if for no other reason than that such views so influence the state policies we get and ask for.

NOTES

1. James A. Henretta, ''Families and Farms: Mentality in Pre-Industrial America.'' *William and Mary Quarterly*. 35 (January, 1978), 15–17; Laurel T. Ulrich, *Good Wives, Image and Reality in the Lives of Women in Northern New England. 1650–1750* (New York: Oxford University Press, 1980), 51–68.

2. For use of the concept ''little commonwealth'' to describe the colonial family, see John

Demos, *A Little Commonwealth: Family Life in Plymouth Colony* (New York: Oxford University Press, 1970). Although most people agree the colonial family was a "little commonwealth," historians have disagreed about the relative power of men and women in colonial America. In the 1970s, some feminist historians (including Mary Ryan and Joan Wilson) argued that because women made essential contributions to household production, they wielded considerable power. In the 1980s, others (including Nancy Folbre and Mary Beth Norton) argued that such contributions did not ensure that women exercised family authority or control over economic resources. In a recent and insightful review of the data and argument, Toby Lee Ditz suggests that while colonial women may have had considerable influence and respect, these are not equivalent to power: "control over resources is the crux of the matter. There was nothing in the wife's role as producer per se to dilute the husband's position as the ultimate arbiter of household business." (p. 128) See Mary Ryan, *Womanhood in America: From Colonial Times to the Present* (New York: Franklin Watts-New Viewpoints, 1979), 3–40; Joan Hoff Wilson, "The Illusion of Change: Women and the American Revolution," in Alfred Young, ed. (Dekalb, Ill.: Northern Illinois University Press, 1976), 383–445; Nancy Folbre, "Patriarchy in Colonial New England," *Review of Radical Political Economics* 12 (1980), 4–13; Mary Beth Norton, "The Evolution of White Women's Experience in Early America," *American Historical Review* 89 (June 1984), 593–619; Toby L. Ditz, *Property and Kinship* (Princeton, N.J.: Princeton University Press, 1986), 118–127.

3. Andrew Cherlin, "Changing Family and Household: Contemporary Lessons from Historical Research," in Ralph Turner and James Short, eds., *Annual Review of Sociology*, vol. 9 (Palo Alto, Calif.: Annual Reviews Inc., 1983), 52–54.

4. Michael Merrill, "Cash is Good Enough to Eat: Self-Sufficiency and Exchange in the Rural Economies of the United States," *Radical History Review* 4 (Winter 1977), 42–71; Henretta, "Families and Farms," 3–32.

5. Tamara K. Haraven, "American Families in Transition: Historical Perspectives on Change," in Arlene S. Skolnick and Jerome H. Skolnick, eds., *Family in Transition*, 5th ed. (Boston: Little Brown and Co., 1986), 75.

6. Philip J. Greven, "Family Structure in Seventeenth-Century Andover, Massachusetts," 136–154 in Michael Gordon, ed., *The American Family in Social Historical Perspective* (New York: St Martin's Press, 1983), 136–154; Robert A. Gross, *The Minute Men and Their World* (New York: Basic Books, 1976), 210–213.

7. Greven, "Family Structure in Seventeenth-Century Andover, Massachusetts," 154–168.

8. Daniel S. Smith, "Parental Power and Marriage Patterns: An Analysis of Historical Trends in Hingham, Massachusetts," *Journal of Marriage and the Family* 35 (Aug. 1973), 219–28.

9. John Demos, "Old Age in Early New England," in Michael Gordon, ed., *The American Family in Social Historical Perspective* (New York: St Martin's, 1983), 269–305; Maris Vinovskis, "Aged Servants of the Lord: Changes in the Status and Treatment of the Elderly in Colonial America," in Matilda W. Riley, Ronald P. Abelews, Martin S. Teitelbaum, eds., *Aging from Birth to Death: Sociotemporal Perspectives* (Boulder, Colo.: Westview, 1982), 105–138.

10. Mary Ryan, "The Explosion of Family History," *Reviews in American History* 19 (Dec. 1982), 180–195.

11. Alice Kessler-Harris, *Out to Work* (New York: Oxford University Press, 1982), Chapter 1.

12. Recent research has suggested that some of the characteristics associated with "the little adult" child were exaggerated in earlier research. Although children were certainly important for production, parents were not (as some had proposed) formal, distant, or particularly punitive toward their children, but instead were affectionate and kind. Although parents sometimes resorted to physical punishment and even to serious abuse, such offending adults were severely punished. See Linda Pollock, *Forgotten Children: Parent–Child Relations from 1500–1800* (New York: Cambridge University Press, 1983).

13. Although economy and family were merged throughout the colonies, the circumstances of these families varied considerably by geographic region. For example, the Chesapeake colonists of Maryland and Virginia experienced high mortality at a relatively young age (due to epidemics of typhoid and dysentery, and later, malaria), a severely imbalanced sex ratio (with men far outnumbering women), and an immigrant-dominated population consisting of single, often indentured, servants. These demographic facts had profound consequences for family life. Because the people immigrated as singles rather than in family groups, and because they died so young, kin networks remained small and underdeveloped compared to their northern counterparts. In the absence of older generations to control them, sons and daughters obtained relatively early autonomy in marriage decisions. Because parents, especially fathers, died young, many children were orphaned, and unstable family units were often held together by impoverished widows. Because there were so many available single men, after the death of a husband these widows remarried quickly and reinstated the same division of labor found in the North to ensure the economic survival of themselves and their progeny. Overall, although surviving family members worked together to provide for their needs, these southern colonists had far less developed family systems and controls. For a discussion of these southern colonists, see Lois Green Carr and Lorena S. Walsh, "The Planter's Wife: The Experience of White Women in Seventeenth Century Maryland," in Michael Gordon, ed., *The American Family in Social Historical Perspective* (New York: St. Martin's Press, 1983), 321–339; Daniel Blake Smith, "Mortality and Family in the Colonial Chesapeake," *Journal of American History* 8 (1978), 403–427; Daniel Blake Smith, "The Study of Family in Early America: Trends, Problems and Prospects," *William and Mary Quarterly* 39 (Jan. 1982), 3–28; Norton, "The Evolution of White Women's Experience in Early America," 597–601.

14. To be sure, these forces—the commercialization of agriculture, the growth of external markets, and the availability of transportation—varied in their force even within the northeast. Some communities were primarily subsistence-plus—they did not rely heavily on production for nonlocal markets—whereas others became highly commercialized. And, of course, these different rates of development were highly consequential for the development of family life. For a good discussion of such differences in the northern countryside, see Ditz, *Property and Kinship*, 3–14, 61–102, 157–173.

15. For good overviews of this transition, see Christopher Clark, "Household Economy, Market Exchange, and the Rise of Capitalism." *Journal of Social History* 13 (winter 1979), 1800–1860; Kessler-Harris, *Out to Work*, 20–45.

16. A rich body of works documents the rise of this cult of domesticity or true womanhood. See, for example, Barbara Welter, "Cult of True Womanhood: 1820–1860," in Gordon, ed., *The American Family in Social Historical Perspective*, 372–392; Nancy Cott, *The Bonds of True Womanhood* (New Haven, Conn.: Yale University Press, 1977); Kathryn Kish Sklar, *Catherine Beecher: A Study in American Domesticity* (New Haven, Conn.: Yale University Press, 1973).

17. Julie Matthaei, *An Economic History of Women in America* (New York: Schocken Books, 1982), 105.

18. Mary Ryan, *Cradle of the Middle Class: The Family in Oneida County, New York, 1790–1865* (New York: Cambridge University Press, 1981), 146–147.

19. Viviana A. Zelizer, *Pricing the Priceless Child: The Changing Social Value of Children* (New York: Basic Books, 1985).

20. Susan C. Watkins, Jane A. Menken, and John Bongaarts, "Demographic Foundations of Family Change," *American Sociological Review* 52 (June 1987), 346–358.

21. Ryan, *Womanhood in America*, 134.

22. Ryan, *Cradle of the Middle Class*, 155–178.

23. Pleck and Rothman note that nineteenth-century middle-class fathers were still expected to take responsibility for the inculcation of practical skills, especially among their sons; but, when compared with colonial fathers, they were expected to be "far less involved" with their children. Elizabeth Pleck and Ellen Rothman, *The Legacies Book* (New York: Corporation for Public Broadcasting Project, 1987), 195. See also Ryan, *Cradle of the Middle Class*, 156–158.

24. Ryan, *Cradle of the Middle Class*, 147.

25. Carl Degler, *At Odds*, (New York: Oxford University Press, 1980), 8–86; Ryan, *Womanhood in America*, 134–159. For an overview of the "affectionate family," see Pleck and Rothman, *The Legacy Book*, 180–195.

26. Lee V. Chambers-Schiller, *Liberty, A Better Husband: Single Women in America; The Generations of 1780–1840* (New Haven, Conn.: Yale University Press, 1984).

27. Cited in Ruth Freeman and Patricia Klaus, "Blessed or Not? The New Spinster in England and the United States in the Late Nineteenth and Early Twentieth Century," *Journal of Family History* 9 (winter 1984), 404.

28. Gerda Lerner: "Single Women in Nineteenth Century Society: Pioneers or Deviants?" *Reviews in American History* 15 (Mar. 1987), 94–100.

29. Suzanne Lebsock, *The Free Women of Petersburg* (New York: W.W. Norton, 1984), 26–27.

30. Cott, *The Bonds of Womanhood*, 160–196.

31. Caroll Smith-Rosenberg, "The Female World of Love and Ritual: Relations between Women in Nineteenth Century America," in Gordon, ed., *The American Family in Social Historical Perspective*, 411–435.

32. Herbert Gutman, "Work Culture and Society in Industrializing America: 1815–1919," *American Historical Review* 78 (1973), 531–588; Kathy Peiss, *Cheap Amusements* (Philadelphia, Penn.: Temple University Press, 1986), 11–34; Ryan, *Cradle of the Middle Class*, 145–179.

33. Carl N. Degler, "What Ought to Be and What Was: Women's Sexuality in the Nineteenth Century," *American Historical Review* 79 (1975), 1468–1491; Carol Z. Stearns and Peter N. Stearns, "Victorian Sexuality: Can Historians Do it Better?" *Journal of Social History* 18 (summer 1985), 625–634.

34. Estelle B. Freedman, "Sexuality in Nineteenth Century America: Behavior, Ideology and Politics," *Reviews in American History* 10 (Dec. 1982), 196–215.

35. Linda Gordon, *Women's Bodies, Women's Rights: A Social History of Birth Control in America* (New York: Grossman, 1976), 104–115.

36. Ryan, *Cradle of the Middle Class*, 155–179.

37. For an interesting analysis of this work, see Dorothy Smith, "Women's Inequality and the Family," in Naomi Gerstel and Harriet Gross, eds., *Families and Work* (Philadelphia: Temple University Press, 1987), 35–37.

38. Susan M. Juster and Maris A. Vinovskis, "Changing Perspectives on the American Family in the Past," in W. Richard Scott and James F. Short, eds., *Annual Review of Sociology*, vol. 13 (Palo Alto, Calif.: Annual Reviews, Inc., 1987), 210.

39. A substantial minority of Americans did share a home with nonkin, whether they were servants, apprentices, employees, boarders, or friends. Some scholars even suggest that if we compare the early twentieth century to any earlier period, the changing composition of households can more properly be described as the increasing exclusion of nonkin rather than kin. See, for example, Barbara Laslett, "Production, Reproduction, and Social Change: The Family in Historical Perspective," in James Short, ed., *The State of Sociology* (Beverly Hills, Calif.: Sage Publications, 1981) 167.

40. Martha May, "The Historical Problem of the Family Wage: The Ford Motor Company and the Five Dollar Day," in Naomi Gerstel and Harriet Gross, eds., *Families and Work* (Philadelphia, Penn.: Temple University Press, 1987), 111–113.

41. Smith, "Women's Inequality and the Family," 23–54.

42. Kessler-Harris, *Out to Work*, 53.

43. Christine Stansell, *City of Women, Sex and Class in New York, 1789–1960* (Urbana and Chicago, ILL: University of Illinois, 1987), 77.

44. Matthaei, *An Economic History of Women in America*, 120–141.

45. For a discussion of the high rates of poverty among unmarried immigrant women in New York, see Stansell, *City of Women, Sex and Class in New York, 1789–1860*, especially 11–18, 43–52, 106–120.

46. Kessler-Harris, *Out to Work*, 45–73.

47. Degler, *At Odds*, 132–143.

48. Francis H. Early, "The French-Canadian Economy and the Standard of Living in Lowell, Massachusetts, 1870," in M. Gordon, ed., *The American Family in Social Historical Perspective* (New York: St. Martin's Press, 1983), 491.

49. Stansell, *City of Women*, 50–52.

50. Christine Stansell, "Women, Children and the Uses of the Street: Class and Gender Conflict in New York City: 1850–1860," *Feminist Studies* 8 (summer 1982), 309–336.

51. Tamara Haraven, "The Dynamics of Kin in an Industrial Community," in Naomi Gerstel and Harriet Gross, eds., *Families and Work*, 55–83.

52. Stansell, *City of Women*, 41–62.

53. Jean E. Friedman, *The Enclosed Garden: Women and Community in the Evangelical South, 1830–1900* (Chapel Hill, N.C.: University of North Carolina Press, 1985), 21–38. While we have focused here on the rural south, western migrants also recreated the preindustrial division of labor characteristic of colonial America and of the nineteenth century south. The "affectionate family" with its cult of domesticity collapsed with migrations to the West. Men had more power (indeed, men typically decided when a family would move west, often against the protestations of their wives). Yet both husbands and wives contributed what became once again a family explicitly united by the productive labors of its members. On reaching their destinations, these western wives cared for the home, dairy, hen house, and garden, and spun the clothes their families wore while husbands cleared and plowed the fields, cared for the tools, and hauled wood. However, this was a diminished family, whether compared to its colonial predecessor, southern rural families, or to the eastern industrializing families that these women and men abandoned. In the West, the family had become a relatively isolated unit, with few external supports for its primary mission of economic survival. John Mack Farragher, *Women and Men on the Overland Trail* (New Haven, Conn.: Yale University Press, 1979), especially Chapters 3, 4, 5, and 7.

54. Jane Turner Censer, *North Carolina Planters and Their Children: 1800–1860* (Baton Rouge, La.: Louisiana State University Press, 1984), xiv.

55. For a discussion of work roles of planters' wives, see Anne Firor Scott, *The Southern Lady* (Chicago: University of Chicago Press, 1970), 28–33; Catherine Clinton, *The Plantation Mistress* (New York: Pantheon Books, 1984), 30–35. There is some disagreement about the relationship of these elite southern women to their children. Some, such as Phillip Greven, argue that the presence of slave nursemaids promoted and allowed distant, formal relationship between white parents and children. However, Jean Censer in her study of North Carolina planter families found an affectionate relationship between parent and children, as she found mothers who focused on their offspring. See Phillip Greven, *The Protestant Temperament: Patterns of Child Rearing, Religious Experience and Self* (New York: Basic Books, 1977), 274–276; Censer, *North Carolina Planters*, 20–41.

56. Jacqueline Jones, *Labor of Sorrow, Labor of Love* (New York: Basic Books, 1983), 11–43.

57. Eugene D. Genovese, *Roll, Jordan, Roll-The World Slaves Made.* (New York: Vintage Books, 1974), 70–75.

58. For the argument that slave-family ties produced incentives for labor, see Genovese, *Roll, Jordan, Roll*, 477–481; Degler, *At Odds*, 112–113.

59. Herbert G. Gutman, *The Black Family in Slavery and Freedom: 1750–1925* (New York: Pantheon, 1976), 129–137, 284–291, 310–317. In one study, only 13.6 percent of recently freed exslave couples said they had lived together without some disruption. And one-third of these disruptions were caused by sales. See John W. Blassingame, *The Slave Community* (New York: Oxford University Press, 1972), 90–92.

60. Genovese, *Roll, Jordan, Roll*, 319.

61. Gutman, *The Black Family in Slavery and Freedom*, 129–137, 284–291, 310–317.

62. Jacqueline Jones, "My Mother was Much of a Woman: Black Women, Work and the Family under Slavery," in Naomi Gerstel and Harriet Gross, eds., *Families and Work* (Philadelphia, Penn.: Temple University Press, 1987), 95–96.

63. John E. Goldthorpe, *Family Life in Western Societies* (New York: Cambridge University Press, 1987), 191–192.

64. Gutman, *The Black Family in Slavery and Freedom*, 455–456.

65. Jones, *Labor of Love, Labor of Sorrow*, 63.

66. Lebsock, *The Free Women of Petersburg*, 90.

67. Susan Watkins, Jane A. Menken, and John Bongaarts, "Demographic Foundations of Family Change," *American Sociological Review* 52 (June 1987), 348.

68. Arthur J. Norton and Jean E. Moorman, "Current Trends in Marriage and Divorce Among American Women," *Journal of Marriage and the Family* 49 (Feb. 1987), 3–14.

69. In 1800, the median age at first marriage for females was twenty, but it had risen to twenty-two by 1890, when the first reliable census data became available. For the next fifty years it remained stable, with half of all eligible women marrying before the end of their twenty-first year. During the "baby-boom" years after World War II, the median age dropped steadily until it bottomed out at 20.1 in 1956. Thereafter women married at a later and later age; the median age peaked in 1985 at 23.3. The figure for 1800 comes from Susan Watkins, Jane A. Menken, and John Bongaarts, "Demographic Foundations of Family Change," *American Sociological Review* 52 (June 1987), 346–358. The other figures can be found in U.S. Bureau of Labor Statistics, "Marital Status and Living Arrangements: March 1985," *Current Population Reports*, Series P-20, No. 410 (November 1986), Table A-1, p. 67. "Median Age at First Marriage" is also graphed on p. 2. The 1986 report (Series P-20, No. 418, Table B) shows that the median age declined in 1986 to 23.1. The 1987 report does not contain any information on age at first marriage. These sources give only aggregate figures for males and females. Other sources indicate that blacks used to marry earlier than did whites. Andrew J. Cherlin, *Marriage, Divorce, Remarriage* (Cambridge, Mass.: Harvard University Press, 1981), 94. Black women now delay marriage—although not motherhood, a point we return to—even longer than do whites. Suzanne M. Bianchi and Daphne Spain, *American Women in Transition* (New York: Russell Sage, 1986), 15.

70. For data on increases in divorce and declines in remarriage, see section "Divorce and Female-Headed Households."

71. The average time spent in first marriages has declined by ten or eleven years over the last three decades. Suzanne M. Bianchi and Daphne Spain, *American Women in Transition* (New York: Russell Sage, 1986), 85.

72. Watkins, Menken, Bongaarts, "Demographic Foundations of Family Change." 351.

73. U.S. Bureau of the Census, "American's Marital Status and Living Arrangements." *Current Population Reports*, Series P-20, No. 418 (Washington, D.C.: U.S. Government Printing Office, 1986), Table I, p. 11.

74. Koray Tanfer, "Patterns of Premarital Cohabitation among Never-Married Women in the United States," *Journal of Marriage and the Family* 49 (Aug. 1987), 483–497 (quote on 493).

75. Hugh Carter and Paul C. Glick, *Marriage and Divorce: A Social and Economic Study*, 2d edition (Cambridge, Mass.: Harvard University Press, 1976); Sharon K. Houseknecht, Suzanne Vaughan, Anne Statham, "The Impact of Singlehood on the Career Patterns of Professional Women," *Journal of Marriage and the Family* 49 (May 1987), 353–366.

76. Francis K. Goldscheider and Linda J. Waite, "Sex Differences in the Entry into Marriage," *American Journal of Sociology* 92 (July 1986), 91–109.

77. William Kephart, "Some Correlates of Romantic Love," *Journal of Marriage and the Family* 29 (1967), 470–474.

78. Arlie R. Hochschild, "Attending to, Codifying and Managing Feelings: Sex Differences in Love, " in Laurel Richardson and Vera Taylor, eds., *Feminist Frontiers* (Reading, Mass.: Addison-Wesley, 1983), 250–262.

79. Most studies of housework do not specify class and race differences. However, of the studies that examine racial differences, two report that black husbands do more housework than do white husbands, and two studies show the opposite. The same inconsistency characterizes studies of class differences: High-income husbands do the least housework in one sample and the most in another. Overall, studies show that husbands, across class and race, do far less housework than their wives do. Peter Stein, "Men in Families," in Beth Hess and Marvin Sussman, eds., *Women and the Family, Two Decades of Change* (New York: Haworth Press, 1984), 151–152.

80. Estimates suggest that men spend only from 15 to 50 percent as much time doing domestic work as women do. For a review, see Shelley Coverman and J. Shelley, "Changes in Men's Housework and Child Care Time," *Journal of Marriage and the Family* 48 (May 1986), 413–422.

81. See Myra Marx Ferree's review essay: "Housework: Rethinking the Costs and Benefits," in Irene Diamond, ed., *Families, Politics and Public Policy: A Feminist Dialogue on Women and the State* (New York: Longman, 1983), 148–169; Sara F. Berk, *The Gender Factory: The Apportionment of Work in American Households* (New York: Plenum Press, 1985); Dana Hiller and W. W. Philliber, "The Division of Labor in Contemporary Marriage: Expectations, Perceptions, and Performance," *Social Problems* 33 (Feb. 1986), 191–201; Donna Hodgkins Berardo, Constance L. Shehan, and Gerald R. Leslie, "A Residue of Tradition: Jobs, Careers, and Spouses' Time in Housework," *Journal of Marriage and the Family* 49 (May 1987), 381–390.

82. Researchers have used a number of different techniques for assessing the dollar value of housework. Few suggest that the salary of a paid housecleaner is equivalent to the value of homemakers' labor. Some economists do suggest the use of a "shadow wage" (in which the value of housework is the wage the homemaker herself could earn on a full-time job). Others use the occupational-components approach, in which the hours a housewife puts into particular jobs (e.g., her work as a nurse, chauffeur, dietician, housecleaner, etc.) are multiplied by the wages for those particular jobs. However, each of these techniques had its own flaws (e.g., the shadow-wage method pays highly educated women more than less-educated women for the same job of housework; the occupational components method gives all women the same wage for similar tasks, although skill levels vary enormously). For a discussion of these different methods, see Bergmann, *The Economic Emergence of Women*, (New York: Basic Books, 1986), 206–209.

83. See Naomi Gerstel, Catherine Riessman, and Sarah Rosenfield, "Explaining the Symptomatology of Separated and Divorced Women and Men," *Social Forces* 64 (Sept. 1985), 84–101.

84. Batya Weinbaum and Amy Bridges. "The Other Side of the Paycheck: Monopoly Capital and the Structure of Consumption," *Monthly Review* 28 (July–Aug. 1976), 88–103.

85. Ruth Schwartz Cowan, "Women's Work, Housework and History: The Historical Roots of Inequality in Work-Force Participation," in Gerstel and Gross, eds., *Families and Work*, 171.

86. Nona Y. Glazer, "Servants to Capital: Unpaid Domestic Labor and Paid Work," in Gerstel and Gross, eds., *Families and Work*, 241.

87. Ibid., 246–248.

88. Catherine White Berheide, "Women's Work in the Home: Seems Like Old Times," in Beth Hess and Marvin Sussman, eds., *Women and The Family: Two Decades of Change* (New York: Haworth Press, 1984), 38–55.

89. Rosanna Hertz uses this term "subcontracting" and discusses hired help in *Dual-Career Couples in the Corporate World* (Berkeley, Calif.: University of California Press, 1986), 160–184.

90. Because so much of domestic work is not reported, reliable figures on it are difficult to obtain. However, census reports provide some data that are useful, at least for comparative purposes. In 1987, the census showed that 16,000 men and 284,000 women were employed as full-time "private-household" service workers (U.S. Department of Labor, "Weekly Earnings of Wage and Salary Workers" *News Release* #87-165 [1987], Table 3). However, as other occupations have become available to women, the proportion of women doing domestic work—either full- or part-time—has declined steadily; at the turn of the century, in 1900, 29 percent of women in the labor force were domestics; before World War II, in 1940, the proportion had declined to 18 percent; by 1950, it was again cut in half to 9 percent; by 1970, the proportion had declined to 4 percent; and by 1985, it was down to 1.2 percent. (Figure for 1987 from *Employment and Earnings* [Jan. 1988], 159, 179. Remaining data from U. S. Bureau of the Census, *Historical Statistics of the United States from the Colonial Times to the Present*, Series D [1976], 140, 182–232). As Judith Rollins (*Between Women: Domestics and Their Employers* [Philadelphia, Penn.: Temple University Press, 1985], 56–59) points out, the representation of immigrants in domestic service is increasing as that of blacks is declining: she claims that 38 percent of all domestic workers were black in 1970, only 32 percent were in 1979, and 22.6 percent were in 1987.

Employment and Earnings [Jan. 1988] 187. Figures on commercial cleaning services are not available, but as Rollins writes: "It may be assumed that if the number of women doing domestic work continues to decrease, such companies will proliferate" (p. 58).

91. These figures are from SAMI-Burke, Inc., a New York marketing research company, cited in "Housekeeping Today: Just a Lick and a Promise," *New York Times*, Aug. 20, 1987, C6.

92. Berk, *The Gender Factory*, 201.

93. Joseph H. Pleck found a small increase in the proportion of women who now desire greater help from their husbands. *Working Wives/Working Husbands* (Beverly Hills, Calif.: Sage Publications, 1985), 82–90. Moreover, although polls show that most women do not want more "help" in housework, increasing numbers of highly educated, younger women are more likely to want such help. See Joseph Pleck, "The Work-Family Role System," in Rachel Kahn-Hut, Arlene Kaplan Daniels, and R. Colvard, eds., *Women and Work: Problems and Perspectives* (New York: Oxford University Press, 1982), 105. See also Ferree's specification of the circumstances under which women feel justified in asking their husbands to help with housework. Myra Marx Ferree, "The Struggles of Superwoman," in Christine Bose, Roslyn Feldberg, and Natalie Sokoloff, eds., *Hidden Aspects of Women's Work* (New York: Praeger, 1987), 161–180. For other discussions of women's resistance to asking husbands for more help, see Joanne Vanek, "Household Work, Wage Work, and Sexual Equality," in A.S. Skolnick and J. Skolnick, eds., *Families in Transition* (Boston: Little Brown and Co., 1983) 176–189; Sara Yogev, "Do Professional Women Have More Egalitarian Marital Relationships?" *Journal of Marriage and the Family* 43 (Nov. 1981), 865–871.

94. See the concluding chapter in Berk's, *The Gender Factory*, for an insightful analysis of the ways women manufacture gender identify by doing housework.

95. As Shelley Coverman has shown, the number of hours men or women spend in housework is negatively associated with wages from jobs. "Gender, Domestic Labor, and Wage Inequality," *American Sociological Review* 48 (1983), 623–636.

96. Berk, *The Gender Factory*, 199–211.

97. Bergmann, *The Economic Emergence of Women*, 210.

98. Ralph LaRossa, *Becoming a Parent* (Beverly Hills, Calif.: Sage Publications, 1986), 106–114.

99. In 1900, wives had an average of 3.7 children. By the 1940s, the rate had fallen to fewer than 3 births. In the "baby-boom" years that followed the war, the number went back up to 3.6. But these years were followed by a "baby bust": by 1980, the total fertility rate had fallen to 1.8. 1900 and 1980 data from Watkins, Menken, and Bongaarts, "Demographic Foundations of Family Change," 346–358. Other data from Suzanne M. Bianchi and Daphne Spain, *American Women in Transition* (New York: Russell Sage Foundation, 1986), 47–48.

100. Nancy Chodorow, *The Reproduction of Mothering* (Berkeley, Calif.: University of California Press, 1978), 77–92; Judith Gardner, "Self Psychology as Feminist Theory," *Signs* 12 (summer 1987), 768–771.

101. Judith Blake, "Is Zero Preferred? American Attitudes Toward Childlessness in the 1970's," *Journal of Marriage and the Family* 41 (Aug. 1979), 245–257. Although only 10 percent of women expect to remain childless, demographers predict that a far higher proportion will end their reproductive years without giving birth. See Digest, "Fertility Rate Edges Up, but Record Proportions of Women are Expected to Remain Childless," *Family Planning Perspectives* 18 (July–Aug. 1986), 178.

102. Pamela Daniels and Kathy Weingarten, *Sooner or Later: The Timing of Parenthood in Adult Lives* (New York: W.W. Norton, 1982), 128–129.

103. Sara McLanahan and Julia Adams, "Parenthood and Psychological Well-Being," in W. Richard Scott and James Richard Short, eds., *Annual Review of Sociology*, vol. 13 (1987), 237–257.

104. Digest, "Labor Market Rewards: Women Who Postpone Families till Later Ages," *Family Planning Perspectives* 18 (Nov.–Dec. 1986), 271–272.

105. Wenda Dickens and Daniel Perlman, "Friendship over the Life-Cycle," in Steve Duck and Robin Gilmour, eds., *Personal Relationships* vol. 2. (New York: Academic Press, 1981), 91–121.

106. Pamela Fishman, "Interaction: The Work Women Do," *Social Problems* 25 (1978), 397–406.

107. Beth Vanfossen, "Sex Differences in the Mental Health Effects of Spouse Support and Equity," *Journal of Health and Social Behavior* 22 (1981), 130–143; A Campbell, Phillip Converse, and W. Rodgers, *The Quality of American Life: Perceptions, Evaluations and Satisfactions* (New York: Russell Sage Foundation, 1976).

108. Janet Finch, *Married to the Job, Wives' Incorporation in Men's Work* (London: George Allen and Unwin, 1983), 84.

109. Stephen J. Bahr, "The Kinship Role in a Contemporary Community: Perceptions of Obligations and Sanctions," in F. Ivan Nye, ed., *Role Structure and Role Analysis of the Family* (Beverly Hills, Calif.: Sage Publications, 1976), 97–112. Note that not all kinkeeping is "emotional labor." The large majority of Americans think it is the responsibility of adult women (more than men) to provide personal and household assistance to elderly parents. Women take this mandate quite seriously and provide to their aging parents an enormous amount of help. See Marjorie Cantor, "Strain among Caregivers: A Study of Experience in the United States," *The Gerontologist* 23 (Dec. 1983), 597–604.

110. Micaeli Di Leonardo, "The Female World of Cards and Holidays: Women, Families, and the Work of Kinship," *Signs* 12 (spring, 1987), 440–453; Carolyn J. Rosenthal, "Kinkeeping in the Family Division of Labor," *Journal of Marriage and the Family* 47 (May 1985), 965–974; Naomi Gerstel, "Divorce and Kinkeeping: The Importance of Gender," *Journal of Marriage and the Family* 50 (Feb. 1988), 209–221.

111. Elizabeth Abel, "Adult Daughters and Care for the Elderly," *Feminist Studies* 12 (fall 1986), 474–497; Elaine Brody, "Work Status and Parent Care: A Comparison of Four Groups of Women," *The Gerontologist* 26 (Aug. 1987), 201–208.

112. 1950 data from U.S. Department of Labor, Bureau of Labor Statistics, "Perspectives on Working Women: A Databook," Bulletin #2080 (Washington, D.C.: U.S. Government Printing Office, 1983); 1987 data from U.S. Department of Labor, "Employment and Earning Characteristics of Families," *News Release* #87-317 (July 17, 1987), Table 5.

113. 1950 and trend data from Arland Thornton and Deborah Freedman, "The Changing American Family," *Population Bulletin* 38 (Oct. 1983), 24; 1987 data from U.S. Department of Labor, "Over Half of Mothers with Children One Year Old or under in Labor Force," *News Release* #87-345 (Aug. 12, 1987), Table 1.

114. Of course, in addition to the growth that replaced women's previously directed family work, expansion of business and industry services has also been a part of the growth of this sector.

115. Joan Smith, "The Paradox of Women's Poverty: Wage Earning Women and Economic Transformation," *Signs* 10 (winter 1984), 302.

116. Ibid., 291–310. For a discussion of factors affecting women's employment since World War II, see Bergmann, *The Economic Emergence of Women*; and Natalie J. Sokoloff, "What's Happening to Women's Employment: Issues for Women's Labor Struggles in 1980–1990," in Christine Bose, Roslyn Feldberg, and Natalie Sokoloff, eds., *Hidden Aspects of Women's Work* (New York: Praeger, 1987), 14–45.

117. Smith, "The Paradox of Women's Poverty," 308.

118. U.S. Department of Labor, "Over Half of Mothers with Children One Year Old or Under in Labor Force," *News Release* #87-345 (Aug. 12, 1987), 1.

119. U.S. Bureau of the Census, Current Population Reports, Series P-60, No. 157, *Money Income and Poverty Status of Families and Persons in the United States: 1986 (Advanced Data from the March 1987 Current Population Survey)* (Washington, D.C.: U.S. Government Printing Office, 1987), Table 1, p. 8.

120. For a discussion of wives' declining dependence on husbands' income, see Annemette Sorensen and Sara McLanahan, "Married Women's Economic Dependency: 1940–1980," *American Sociological Review* 93 (Nov. 1987), 659–687.

121. U.S. Bureau of the Census, "Household and Family Characteristics: March, 1986," *Current*

Population Reports, P-20, No. 419 (Washington D.C.: U.S. Government Printing Office, Nov. 1987), Table F, p. 9.

122. Terry Arendell, "Women and the Economics of Divorce in Contemporary America," *Signs* 13 (autumn 1987), 5.

123. Paul Glick and Sung-Ling Lin, "Recent Changes in Divorce and Remarriage," *Journal of Marriage and the Family* 48 (Nov. 1986), 737–747.

124. U.S. Bureau of the Census, "American's Marital Status and Living Arrangements, March 1986," *Current Population Reports*, Series P-20, no. 418 (Washington. D.C.: U.S. Government Printing Office, 1986), 3.

125. Arendell, "Women and the Economics of Divorce in Contemporary America," 128.

126. Using a national survey, Duncan and Hoffman found the majority of both black (83 percent) and white (57 percent) women received no alimony or child support in the first year after marital dissolution, and that both the incidence and amount of such transfers declined as time passed. Greg J. Duncan and Saul D. Hoffman, "A Reconsideration of the Economic Consequences of Marital Dissolution," *Demography* 22 (Nov. 1985), 490. Moreover, as Weitzman found in her California study, only 15 percent of divorced women are awarded any alimony at all. The median child-support payment ordered by the courts covers less than half of the actual cost of raising children. Furthermore, in 53 percent of the cases, women did not receive the court-ordered payments. Leonore Weitzman, *The Divorce Revolution* (New York: Basic Books, 1985), 167–174, 270–272, 283–284. Finally, using national data, Rogers found that far fewer black (29 percent) than white (79 percent) women were awarded support. Harrell R. Rodgers, *Poor Women, Poor Families* (Armonk, N.Y.: M.E. Sharpe, 1986), 51–53.

127. Duncan and Hoffman, "A Reconsideration of the Economic Consequences of Marital Dissolution," 488–490.

128. Duncan, *Years of Poverty, Years of Plenty*. To be sure, there was a sharp decline in remarriage in the 1970s, but the rate rebounded in the 1980s.

129. Cherlin, "Women and the Family," 92.

130. For example, see William Julius Wilson and Kathryn Neckerman, "Poverty and Family Structure," in Sheldon H. Danziger and Daniel Weinberg, eds., *Fighting Poverty: What Works and What Doesn't* (Cambridge, Mass.: Cambridge University Press, 1986), 242–246, 253–259; Rose M. Brewer, "Black Women in Poverty: Some Comments on Female-Headed Households," *Signs* 13 (winter 1988), 331–339.

131. Center for the Study of Social Policy, "The 'Flip Side' of Black Families Headed by Women: The Economic Status of Black Men," in Robert Staples, ed., *The Black Family: Essays and Studies* (Belmont, CA: Wadsworth, 1986), 232–238. For a lucid summary of the factors producing the worsening economic position of black men, see Maxine Bacca Zinn, *Minority Families in Crisis: The Public Discussion* (Memphis, Tenn.: Center for Research on Women, 1987), 15–23.

132. Wilson and Neckerman, 253; Brewer, 333–339; Rodgers, 51–53; Tom Joe, "The Other Side of Black Female-Headed Families: The Status of Black Men," *Family Planning Perspectives* 19 (Mar.–Apr. 1987), 77–76; Maxine Bacca Zinn and D. Stanley Eitzen, *Diversity in American Families* (New York: Harper and Row, 1987), 237; Robert Staples, "Changes in Black Family Structure: The Conflict Between Family Ideology and Structural Conditions," in Staples, 25.

133. In 1986, the proportion of divorced women among black women was more than twice that among white women (323 versus 145 per 1,000 married women). U.S. Bureau of the Census, "Marital Status and Living Arrangements," *Current Population Reports* P-20, no. 418 (Washington, D.C.: U.S. Government Printing Office, March 1986), Table D, p. 7. For comparisons of black and white women's marital status from 1947 to 1980, see William Julius Wilson and Kathryn M. Neckerman, "Poverty and Family Structure," in Danziger and Weinberg, eds., *Fighting Poverty: What Works and What Doesn't*, 238.

134. Analyzing data from 1950 to 1980 on increases in female headed households, Garfinkel and McLanahan show that among whites, the increase in mother-only families during each decade was due primarily to the growing prevalence of formerly married mothers. (Among whites, this accounted for about 45 percent of the growth in the 1950s and 1960s, and about 57 percent in the 1970s.) In contrast, among blacks, although during the 1950s about half of the increase in families headed by women was due to increases in formerly married mothers, they accounted for less than 30 percent of the increase during the 1960s, and less than 3 percent in the 1970s. The decline in the relative importance of formerly married mothers was replaced by an increase in never-married mothers. Among blacks, never-married mothers accounted for about 9 percent of the growth in the 1950s, 20 percent in the 1960s, and 23 percent in the 1970s. Irwin Garfinkel and Sara S. McLanahan, *Single Mothers and Their Children* (Washington, D.C.: The Urban Institute Press, 1986), 53.

135. The rate of total teenage childbearing increased sharply after World War II, reached a peak in 1957, then declined, then leveled off in the 1980s. However, the birth rate for unmarried teenage women rose almost uninterruptedly from 1940 to 1980, due to the rise in premarital pregnancy and the lowered inclination to legitimize births by marriage. Black women have had much higher annual rates of out-of-wedlock childbearing than have white women since at least 1940. In 1980, the birth rate for unmarried black teenagers remained much higher than that of whites—nearly six times the rate—even though out-of-wedlock childbearing actually declined slightly among black teenagers during the 1970s. Andrew Cherlin, *Marriage, Divorce, Remarriage* (Cambridge, Mass.: Harvard University Press, 1981), 95–97; Andrew Cherlin, ''Women and the Family,'' in Sara E. Rix, ed., *The American Woman, 1987–1988* (New York: W.W. Norton, 1987), 77–78; Maris A. Vinovskis, *An ''Epidemic'' of Adolescent Pregnancy? Some Historical and Policy Considerations* (New York: Oxford University Press, 1988), 25–30. Arland Thornton, ''The Changing American Family,'' *Population Bulletin* 38 (Oct. 1983), 20.

136. Cherlin, ''Women and the Family,'' 76–78.

137. Martin O'Connell and Carolyn C. Rogers, ''Out of Wedlock Births, Premarital Pregnancies and Their Effect on Family Formation and Dissolution,'' *Family Planning Perspectives* 16 (July–Aug. 1984), 159.

138. Although most researchers suggest that poverty is a major factor causing out-of-wedlock births, there is still considerable debate about the relative impact of economic disadvantage versus other cultural and social factors. As Kenneth Clark argued about blacks in the mid-sixties: ''In the ghetto, the meaning of the illegitimate child is not ultimate disgrace. . . . On the contrary, a child is symbol of the fact that she [the mother] is a woman and she may gain from having something of her own.'' (Kenneth Clark, *Dark Ghetto* [New York: Harper and Row, 1965,] 72). For recent quantitative evidence that differences in attitudes or norms may be important in the explanation of high rates of black adolescent intercourse and childbearing, see Frank F. Furstenberg, S. Philip Morgan, Kristin Moore, James L. Peterson, ''Race Differences in the Timing of Adolescent Intercourse,'' *American Sociological Review* 52 (Aug. 1987), 511–518. However, as Carol Stack's ethnographic research has shown, favorable attitudes toward out-of-wedlock births in the black ghetto may well be tied to the economic value of children in such communities: Black children are not only symbols of their mothers' adulthood but also involve the mothers in—indeed provide access to—dense networks whose members exchange resources and information. Thus, the normative system itself may well be tied to economic disadvantage. (Carol Stack, *All Our Kin, Strategies for Survival in a Black Community* [New York: Harper and Row, 1974.] Surveys show that only a small minority of black or white teenagers today actually expect and want to become parents before marriage (William J. Wilson, *The Truly Disadvantaged* [Chicago: University of Chicago Press, 1986], 74). Other recent survey research shows that black teenagers' high level of out-of-wedlock birth is associated with a number of social conditions, including being a member of a lower social class as well as residing in an innercity ghetto neighborhood, growing up in single-parent families (rather than two-parent or two-generation ones), having a large number of siblings, and experiencing loose parental control of dating. (See Larry Bumpass and Sara McLanahan, ''Unmarried Motherhood: A Note on Recent Trends, Composition, and Black–White Differences.'' [Paper presented at the Annual Meeting of the Population Association of America, Chicago, April 29–May 2, 1987], cited and discussed in Digest, *Family Planning Perspectives* 19 [Sept.–Oct. 1987], 220; Dennis P. Hogan and Evelyn M. Kitagawa, ''The Impact of Social Status, Family Structure and Neighborhood on the Fertility of Black Adolescents,'' *American Journal of Sociology* 90 [Jan. 1985], 825–855.) Overall, then, although norms and economic status may be inextricably intertwined, no available evidence would lead us to dismiss economic disadvantage as a major factor explaining out-of-wedlock pregnancy and birth.

139. Bane, "Household Composition and Poverty," 227.

140. Ibid., 231.

141. Duncan and Hoffman, "A Reconsideration of the Economic Consequences of Marital Dissolution," 493–495.

142. Carol Stack, *All Our Kin, Strategies for Survival in a Black Community* (New York: Harper and Row, 1974).

143. Cherlin, "Women and the Family."

144. Hertz, *More Equal than Others.*

145. Although we are suggesting that some of this increased productivity may come from the reconstitution of the dual-career family, Epstein explains this seeming anomaly by suggesting: "While we might expect the obligations of marriage and family to hold women back . . . married women are simply considered more normal than single adults. They pose fewer problems to co-workers and clients. . . . Most professional men . . . are more comfortable with women colleagues who carry the protective status of being married . . . and married women make contacts through their husbands." Epstein, *Women in Law*, 342. For additional data and a discussion of greater productivity of married professional women compared to their single counterparts, see Jonathan Cole, *Fair Science: Women in the Scientific Community* (New York: Free Press, 1979), 65–66, 252; Helen S. Astin and Diane E. Davis, "Research Productivity across the Life and Career Cycles: Facilitators and Barriers for Women," in Mary Frank Fox, ed., *Scholarly Writing and Publishing* (Boulder, Colo. and London: Westview Press, 1985), 148, 153–155.

146. Rosabeth Moss Kanter, *Men and Women of the Corporation* (New York: Basic Books, 1977); Robert Rapoport and Rhona Rapoport, *Dual-Career Families Re-Examined* (New York: Harper Colophon, 1976); Colleen L. Johnson and Frank A. Johnson, "Role Strain in High-Commitment Career Women," *Journal of American Academy of Psychoanalysts* 4 (1976), 13–36.

147. Ferree, "The Struggles of Superwoman," 161–180.

148. William Kingston and Steven L. Nock, "Time Together Among Dual-Earner Couples," *American Sociological Review* 52 (June 1987), 391–400.

149. Suzanne M. Bianchi and Daphne Spain, *American Women in Transition* (New York: Russell Sage Foundation, 1986).

The Balance of Power in Dating and Marriage

LETITIA ANNE PEPLAU AND SUSAN MILLER CAMPBELL

Americans are sentimental about love. In thinking about romance, we emphasize intimacy and caring; we like to view our lover and the relationship as unique. We tend to neglect a crucial aspect of love relationships — power. This chapter investigates the nature of power in dating and marriage, and analyzes factors that can tip the balance of power away from equality.

The traditional formula for male–female relationships prescribes that the man should be the leader. In dating, he should take the initiative by asking the woman out, by planning activities, by providing transportation, and by paying the bills. In marriage, he should be the "head" of household, who has final say about major family decisions. Our society's concept of "male superiority" dictates that a woman should "look up" to the significant man in her life, a stance that is often facilitated by his being taller, older, better educated, and more experienced.

Feminists have severely criticized the idea that men should have the upper hand in love relationships. In *Sexual Politics*, Kate Millett[1] argues that patriarchal norms are pervasive and insidious. Male domination may be seen most easily in business, education, religion, and politics, but it also extends to personal relationships between the sexes. The family mirrors the power relations of the society at large and also perpetuates this power imbalance by teaching children to accept the superior status of men. In Millett's analysis, romantic love does not "put women on a pedestal" or elevate women's social status. Rather, the ideology of love hides the reality of women's subordination and economic dependence on men. As television commercials readily illustrate, "love" can be used for the emotional manipulation of women. It is "love" that justifies household drudgery, as well as deference to men. Thus, true equality would require basic changes in the intimate relationships of women and men.

Although traditional views of romantic relationships are being challenged, proponents of the old pattern remain strong. A striking example is provided by Helen Andelin,[2] author of *Fascinating Womanhood* and an advocate of a benevolent form of male dominance. Andelin urges women to accept and enjoy traditional sex roles. Male leadership is a key element. According to Andelin, women should defer to men and take pleasure in being cared for. The man is "the undisputed head of the family." The woman has a "submissive role, a supporting role and sometimes an active role. . . . But, first she must accept him as her leader, support and obey him." The popularity of *Fascinating Womanhood* and similar books suggests that many women endorse this traditional view.

Young couples today are confronted with alternative models for romantic relationships. Traditional sex roles prescribe that the man should take the lead. But contemporary thinking favors a more equal balance of power. This chapter examines the balance of power in dating and marriage today. We begin by describing in depth a study of power in the dating relationships of college students. We explore attitudes about power, consider how to assess the actual balance of power in a relationship, and analyze factors that determine whether or not couples actually achieve equal power in their relationships. Later in the chapter, we broaden our focus to consider recent research on power in marriage, and examine the accuracy of popular stereotypes that black families are "matriarchies" dominated by women and that Chicano families are "patriarchies" dominated by men.

COLLEGE COUPLES IN LOVE: A STUDY OF POWER IN DATING RELATIONSHIPS

A study by Zick Rubin, Anne Peplau, and Charles Hill[3] explored in detail the issue of power in dating relationships. This research, known as the Boston Couples Study, recruited 231 college-age couples from four colleges and universities located in the Boston area. These included a small private nonsectarian university, a large private nonsectarian university, a Jesuit university, and a state college enrolling commuter students. Participants were typically middle class in background, and virtually all were white. To be eligible for the study, a couple had to indicate that they were "going with" each other and that both partners were willing to participate. The typical couple had been going together for about eight months when the study began. Couples were studied intensively over a two-year period. In 1972, and again in 1973 and 1974, each partner in the couple independently completed lengthy questionnaires about their relationship. We found that the college students in our sample were strong supporters of an egalitarian balance of power. When we asked, "Who do you think should have more say about your relationship, your partner or you?" 95 percent of women and 87 percent of men indicated that dating partners should have "exactly equal say." Although male dominance may once have been the favored pattern of male–female relations, it was overwhelmingly rejected by the students in this study. It is possible that some students gave the answer they considered socially desirable, rather than their own true opinion. In either case, however, responses indicated a striking change in the type of male–female relationship considered appropriate.

Although students advocated equality, they seldom reported having grown up in an egalitarian family. As one student explained:

> When I was growing up, my father was the Supreme Court in our family. He ran the show. My relationship with Betsy is very different. We try to discuss things and reach consensus. And that's the way I think it should be.

Only 18 percent of the students reported that their parents shared equally in power. A 53 percent majority indicated that their father had more say; the remaining 29 percent reported that their mother had more say. Clearly, most college students were seeking a different type of relationship from the model set by their parents. Our next question was whether these student couples would be successful in achieving the equal-power relationship they desired.

Assessing the Balance of Power

Although the word *power* suggests a phenomenon that is obvious and easy to study, this is not the case. Power is often elusive, especially in close relationships. Consider a woman who appears to dominate her boyfriend by deciding what to do on dates, determining which friends the couple sees, and even selecting her boyfriend's new clothes. Is it reasonable to infer that she has a good deal of power in the relationship? Not necessarily. Further investigation might reveal that her boyfriend, a busy pre-med student, disdains such "trivial" matters, and cheerfully delegates decision making in these areas to his girlfriend. In addition, he may retain veto power on all decisions but rarely exercise it, because his girlfriend scrupulously caters to his preferences. In this instance, greater power may actually reside with the man, who delegates responsibility, rather than with the woman, who merely implements his preference.[4]

Power—one person's ability to influence the behavior of another to achieve personal goals—cannot be observed directly, but must be inferred from behavior.[5] The context in which an action occurs and the intentions of the participants largely determine the meaning of the act. Especially in close personal relationships, judgments about power may be difficult to make. One reason for this is that people can exert influence in subtle and indirect ways. Indeed, traditional sex roles have dictated that men and women should use different influence tactics—he should be direct, even bold in his leadership; she should be tactful and covert. *Fascinating Womanhood* offers several suggestions about how women should give "feminine advice":

> *Ask leading questions:* A subtle way of giving advice is to ask leading questions, such as "Have you ever thought of doing it this way?" . . . The key word is *you.* In this way you bring him into the picture so the ideas will seem like his own.
> *Insight:* When expressing your viewpoint use words that indicate insight such as "I feel." Avoid the words "I think" or "I know."

Don't appear to know more than he does: Don't be the all-wise, all-knowing wife who has all the answers and surpasses her husband in intelligence.

Don't talk man to man: Don't "hash things over" as men do and thereby place yourself on an equal plane with him. . . . Keep him in the dominant position so that he will feel needed and adequate as the leader.[6]

Sociologists have taken note of these possible differences in male and female styles of power. In fact, Jessie Bernard suggests that in many marriages male control may be only an illusion:

From time immemorial, despite the institutional pattern conferring authority on husbands, whichever spouse had the talent for running the show did so. If the wife was the power in the marriage, she exerted her power in a way that did not show; she did not flaunt it, she was satisfied with the "power-behind-the-throne" position.[7]

For these reasons, measuring the actual balance of power in relationships can be tricky.

To assess power in our couples, we asked very general questions about the overall balance of power, as well as more specific questions about particular situations and events. For instance, we asked, "Who do you think has more of a say about what you and your partner do together—your partner or you?" Subjects responded on a five-point scale from "I have much more say" to "My partner has much more say," with "exactly equal" as the midpoint. All these measures involved self-reports; that is, we asked students to describe the balance of power in their relationship as they perceived it. Most studies of power in close relationships have also used self-reports, assuming that, in the final analysis, participants in a relationship are the best judges of their own personal experiences of power.

Our results were somewhat surprising. Despite their strong support for equality, only 49 percent of the college women and 42 percent of the men in our study reported equal power in their current dating relationship. This represents a large proportion of the students, but is much less than the 91 percent who said they favored equal power. When the relationship was unequal, it was usually the man who had more say. About 45 percent of the men and 35 percent of the women reported that the man had more say, compared to 13 percent and 17 percent, respectively, who said the woman had more say. There are two points to be made about these results. First, there was much variation in students' views of the relationships. Although many students did report power equality, other patterns were also found. Second, these results suggest that at least some students who said that they wanted equal power in their relationship were not able to achieve this goal.

Tipping the Balance of Power

Why is it that some people who want an egalitarian relationship are not successful in creating one? Research had identified three important factors that affect the balance of power in relationships: the social norms dictating who "should" be more powerful, the psychological dependency of each partner in the couple, and the personal resources that partners bring to their relationship.[8]

Social norms.   Historically, social norms or rules of conduct have specified that the man should be the "boss" in male–female relationships. If couples endorse traditional roles for their relationship—believing, for example, that the man's career should be more important than the woman's, and that the woman should look up to the man as a leader—the balance of power is likely to tip away from gender equality. Our study of dating couples included a ten-item Sex-Role Attitude Scale. Students indicated their agreement or disagreement with such statements as, "If a couple is going somewhere by car, it's better for the man to do most of the driving," and "If both husband and wife work full-time, her career should be just as important as his in determining where the family lives." Responses indicated that some students advocated strongly traditional positions, others endorsed strongly feminist positions, and many fell somewhere in between. Dating partners generally held similar attitudes; it was unusual to find an ardent feminist dating a very traditional partner.

We found that endorsement of traditional sex roles was often associated with unequal power in dating relationships. For example, 59 percent of the men who had traditional sex-role attitudes believed they had greater say than did their girlfriend, compared to only 25 percent of the men with nontraditional (profeminist) attitudes. However, exceptions to this pattern did occur. For instance, over one-third of the most traditional couples reported equal power, as Paul and Peggy illustrate. For them, power was not a prominent issue. Whereas Peggy was considered the expert on cooking and social skills, Paul made decisions about what to do on dates. They divided responsibilities in a traditional way but believed that overall they had equal power. Most often, however, sex-role attitudes did have an important impact on the balance of power. Believing that men and women can perform similar tasks, acknowledging that the woman's career is as important as the man's, and other nontraditional attitudes can foster an equal-power relationship. At the same time, it is also likely that having an egalitarian relationship encourages nontraditional sex-role attitudes. The link between attitudes and power can work both ways.

Imbalance of involvement.   Social psychological theory suggests that power in a couple is affected by each partner's dependence on the relationship. In some relationships, both partners are equally in love, or equally disinterested. In other cases, however, the partners' degree of involvement differs. One partner may be passionately in love, while the other partner may have only a lukewarm interest in the relationship. Such imbalances of involvement are likely to affect the balance of power.[9] Sociologist Willard Waller[10] described this phenomenon as the "principle of least interest," which predicts that the person who is least involved or interested in a relationship will have greater influence. The more involved person, eager to maintain the relationship, defers to the partner's wishes. Thus, the less interested partner is better able to set the terms of the relationship and exert control. Being deeply in love is a wonderful experience. But unless love and commitment are reciprocated, they make a person especially vulnerable to their partner's influence.

Our questionnaire contained several measures of love and involvement. One question asked straightforwardly, "Who do you think is more involved in your relationship—your partner or you?" Less than half the students reported that their relationship was equal in involvement. The principle of least interest was strongly supported by our data, as can be seen in Table 1. In couples where the man was the least involved, it was most common for the man to have more power. In contrast, when the woman was the least involved, nearly half the couples reported that the woman had greater power.

Attraction to a partner and involvement in a relationship are affected by many factors. The degree to which we find our partner desirable and rewarding is very important, as is our assessment of the possible alternative relationships available to both of us. If our present partner is more desirable than the available alternatives, our attraction should remain high. Thus, such personal resources as physical attractiveness, intelligence, a sense of humor, loyalty, prestige, or money can affect the balance of power.

Findings concerning physical attractiveness illustrate this point. Although we may like to think that inner qualities are more important than physical appearance, there is ample evidence that beauty can be a valuable resource in interpersonal relations, at least among younger adults. As part of our study, we took full-length color photos of each participant, and then had these photos rated on physical attractiveness by a panel of student judges. As predicted, if one person was judged much more attractive than her or his partner, she or he was likely to have more power in the relationship.

Another important determinant of dependency on a relationship is the likelihood that a person could find another partner if the current relationship ended. The more options a person has about alternative dating relationships, the less dependent he or she is on a single partner. We asked students whether they had either dated or had sexual intercourse with someone other than their primary partner during the past two months. We also inquired whether there was a "specific other" they could be dating at present. For

TABLE 1
Power and involvement in dating relationships

	Relative involvement		
Relative power	Women less involved (60 couples)	Equal (57 couples)	Man less involved (100 couples)
Man more say	23%	54%	70%
Equal say	28%	20%	20%
Woman more say	49%	26%	10%

both men and women, having dating alternatives was related to having greater power in the current relationship.

Our analysis suggests that a possible way to increase one's relative power in a relationship is to acquire new personal resources or greater options. This message is conveyed, in highly different forms, by both traditionalists and feminists. *Fascinating Womanhood* promises that women can have a happier marriage by learning to be more "feminine." Women are encouraged to improve their appearance, become better cooks, learn to be more sexually alluring, pay more attention to their husband, and, in general, improve their "feminine" skills. By increasing her own desirability, the woman may indirectly increase here husband's interest in their relationship. As a result, the husband may be more willing to defer to his wife's wishes and concerns. While endorsing a pattern of male leadership and control, *Fascinating Womanhood* nonetheless suggests ways for women to work within the traditional pattern to increase their personal influence and to achieve their own goals.

Contemporary feminists have rejected inequality between the sexes and have encouraged women to become less dependent on men. Women can achieve this independence by developing closer relationships with other women and by learning new skills, especially "masculine" skills such as car repair or carpentry. The greatest emphasis has been given to women's gaining financial independence through paid employment. In the next section, data from our study bearing on the impact of women's careers on power in dating relationships are presented.

Women's career goals.   Traditionally, men divide their interest and energy between personal relationships and paid work. For women, in contrast, a family and a career have often been viewed as incompatible goals. Typically, women have given far higher priority to personal and family relationships than to paid employment. Many of the college students in our study rejected the idea that the woman's place is in the home; both men and women tended to support careers for women. What impact does this have on power in male–female relationships?

Full-time paid employment makes women more similar to men in several ways. Work provides women with additional skills and expertise, with important interests outside the relationship, and with additional resources such as income or prestige. For all these reasons, it seems likely that a woman's employment might affect power in a dating relationship.

Leonard and Felicia, two participants in our study, illustrate this effect. They met and were married in college, where both majored in music. The couple agreed that while Felicia is a competent musician, Leonard is a musical genius on his way to becoming a famous composer. After college, Felicia took a job as a music teacher to put her husband through graduate school. She acknowledged his superior ability and was willing to support his career by working. But she viewed her job strictly as a necessity. Her primary involvement was in her marriage. Leonard's job attitude was completely different. Felicia said bluntly: "For him, music comes first and I'm second. If he had to move to New York to be famous and I wouldn't go, he'd leave me." In part because of this imbalance of involvement, Leonard had greater power in their relationship. He determined where they lived, for instance, and required Felicia to tolerate his sexual infidelities.

When we reinterviewed Leonard and Felicia a year later, we learned that there had been a great deal of strain in their relationship. Partly because of this tension, Felicia took a summer-school course in a new method of teaching music. She found the course exciting, and during the summer she gained greater confidence in her abilities as a music teacher. She became seriously interested in teaching as a career. With the support of other women in the class, Felicia decided to apply for admission to a graduate program in the new instructional method. In long talks with other women, she reexamined her ideas about marriage, sex roles, and her career. She realized that "the fantasy of having a man fulfill a woman is a dangerous myth. You have to fulfill yourself." Despite some objections from Leonard, Felicia intended to start graduate school the next year. She felt that these changes had already helped her marriage and changed the balance of power. "If I'd gone on working this year to support him, as Len wanted me to, he'd be the more dominant. . . . If I hadn't decided to go to school, he'd be taking the money and running the show." Having made her decision, Felicia felt less dominated and exploited by her husband. She hoped that, as she gained more respect for her own abilities, Len would gain respect for her, too.

This is only one example. We asked all the couples about their educational and career plans. Nearly 70 percent of both men and women said they planned to go to graduate school. Among those seeking advanced degrees, women were more likely than men to desire only a master's degree (50 percent of women versus 32 percent of men). Men were more likely than women to aspire to a doctorate or the equivalent (38 percent of men versus 19 percent of women). Additional questions probed students' attitudes about full-time employment for women and their personal interest in having a dual-career marriage in which both spouses have full-time careers.

As expected, the women's educational and career plans were significantly related to the balance of power in the current relationship. For instance, in one analysis we examined the relationship between the highest degree the woman aspired to and the balance of power. The results were striking. When the woman aspired to less than a bachelor's degree, 87 percent of students reported that the man had more power in their relationship. When the woman planned to complete her bachelor's degree, about half (45 percent) reported that the man had more power. And, when the woman planned on an advanced degree, only about 30 percent reported that the man had more say. As the woman's educational aspirations increased, the likelihood of a male-dominant relationship decreased sharply. In contrast, no association was found between the man's educational aspirations or career plans and power.

In summary, we have found that power in a dating relationship is related to sex-role attitudes, to the balance of involvement, and to personal resources such as the woman's career plans. For college women in our sample, these three factors were interrelated. Women who planned on graduate school reported relatively less involvement in their current relationship, had more liberal sex-role attitudes (and tended to date men who were also more liberal), and often planned to make a major commitment to a full-time career, as well as to marriage.

For college men in our sample, educational plans, sex-role attitudes, and relative involvement were *not* interrelated. Liberal and traditional men did not differ in their educational goals or in their relative involvement in the current relationship. In American society, all men are expected to have jobs. This is as true for men who reject traditional roles as for men who support them. Although the man's educational plans did not affect the balance of power, his own sex-role attitudes and his relative involvement in the relationship were important determinants of power.

Although many women in our sample wanted to pursue a career, they did not see this as a substitute for marriage. About 96 percent of women and 95 percent of men said they expected to marry eventually, although not necessarily this partner. Further, 90 percent of women and 93 percent of men said they wanted to have one or more children. What distinguished traditional and liberal women was not their intention to marry but rather their orientation toward employment.

Finally, we should note that couples can achieve equal power in different ways. Some, perhaps most often nontraditional couples, attempt to share all decision making completely. Ross and Betsy told us that they always make joint decisions—they shop together, discuss entertainment and vacation plans together, and reach mutual solutions to conflicts. Other couples, perhaps most often traditionalists, adopt a pattern in which each partner has specific areas of responsibility. Diane told us that she and Alan have equal power, but explained that "in almost every situation, one of us is more influential. There are very few decisions that are fifty–fifty." For instance, Diane picked their new apartment, but Alan decided about moving the furniture. Diane said, "I make the aesthetic decisions and Alan makes the practical ones." Dividing areas of responsibility, sharing decision making totally, or some mixture of the two are all possible avenues to equal power in relationships.

Power and Satisfaction in Dating Relationships

Fascinating Womanhood proposed that the acceptance of traditional sex roles and male leadership is essential to a happy male–female relationship. Feminists argue that traditional sex roles oppress women and make honest male–female relationships difficult. What impact do sex-role attitudes and the balance of power have on the success of a dating relationship? Our surprising answer is that they seem to have little impact on the happiness or survival of dating relationships.

We found no association between sex-role attitudes and satisfaction with the current relationship. Liberal and traditional couples rated themselves equally satisfied with their relationships and indicated that they felt equally close to their partners. Liberal and traditional couples did not differ in reports of the likelihood of eventually marrying the current partner, of love for their partner, or of the number of problems they anticipated in the relationship. Data from our two-year followup indicated that liberal and traditional couples were equally likely to break up.

To understand these findings, we must remember that dating partners usually had similar sex-role beliefs. Sharing attitudes and values may be much more crucial to the success of a relationship than is the content of the attitudes. Mismatching on sex-role attitudes can create problems for couples, and such differences may be most important when a couple first begins to date. Since all the students in our study were already "going with" their partner, we do not have information about the impact of sex roles on first meetings or casual dating. Couples in our study had all survived the beginning of a relationship, perhaps partly because they agreed about sex roles or had managed to reconcile their differences.

Since students were nearly unanimous in their endorsement of an egalitarian ideal of power, we might expect the balance of power to affect couple satisfaction or survival. In fact, equal-power and male-dominant couples did not differ in their reports of satisfaction and closeness, or in the likelihood of breaking up by the time of our two-year followup. In contrast, however, both men and women reported *less* satisfaction in relationships where the woman had more say. It is apparently easier to follow a traditional pattern or to adhere to the new pattern of equality than to experience a female-dominant relationship.

Currently, there is much controversy over proper behavior for men and women. Whether to adopt traditional standards, to attempt to modify them, or to reject old patterns outright are decisions we all must face. The results of this study suggest that traditional and egalitarian patterns are equally likely to lead to a satisfactory dating relationship or to a miserable one. Consensus between a woman and a man may be more important for couple happiness than is the particular pattern a couple follows. Feminists, however, might raise a further question. Even if individuals are able to find personal happiness in unequal relationships, is it good for society to perpetuate male dominance in marriage?

POWER IN MARRIAGE: MYTHS AND REALITIES

How many American marriages today are equal in power? Current research cannot yet answer this question. It is clear that there is much variation among marriages, from couples in which one spouse (usually the husband) makes virtually all decisions, to relationships in which spouses share fully in power and decision making. Many contemporary American couples describe their marriages as relatively equal in power.

For instance, in a recent large-scale survey, Philip Blumstein and Pepper Schwartz[11] recruited a sample of over 3,500 married couples. These couples learned about the research from announcements on television, on the radio, or in newspapers, and then volunteered to participate. They were virtually all white, and many were college graduates. The median age was 36 for husbands and 34 for wives. A 64 percent majority said that the balance of power in their marriage was equal. When power was not equal, 27 percent of husbands and 28 percent of wives said that the husband was more powerful. Only 9 percent of husbands and 8 percent of wives described the wife as more dominant. As in our study of dating couples, the balance of power in these relationships was affected by norms and personal resources. Male dominance was most common in marriages where partners endorsed the belief that the husband should be the provider in the family, and where the husband's income was substantially larger than the wife's. We should note, however, that although this sample was unusually large, those who volunteered tended to be relatively young, urban, well educated, and white. Their experiences are not representative of those of all married Americans.

Feminist researchers have emphasized the importance of expanding the scope of research to include women and men from diverse ethnic and cultural backgrounds. In research on marital power, several studies have investigated the experiences of black and Chicano couples. The results may surprise you.

Black Matriarchy: The Myth of Female Domination in Marriage

Black families in the United States have often been described as "matriarchal," or female dominated. The term *matriarchy* can refer to two different situations. Some have used *matriarchy* to refer to the greater frequency of female-headed households among black Americans as compared to other ethnic groups. Thus, a family is described as matriarchal because the mother is raising children without a husband present. A second meaning of the term *matriarchy*, and the one of relevance to our discussion of husband–wife power, is the suggestion that in black marriages, the wife is typically the dominant spouse.[12] For many years, the stereotype of black matriarchy went untested and was used as an explanation for the problems faced by black families in America. In a controversial report published in 1965, Daniel Patrick Moynihan[13] contended that the black "matriarchal structure . . . is so out of line with the rest of American society [that it] seriously retards the progress of the group as a whole."

Controversial statements such as this spurred researchers to study the actual balance of power in black marriages. A substantial body of research refutes the matriarchy stereotype.[14] For example, in one large-scale study, Dietrich[15] studied lower-class black families from urban and rural areas. She classified 62 percent of the relationships as egalitarian, 24 percent as wife dominant, and 14 percent as husband dominant. In another study of both middle- and lower-class blacks from Los Angeles, DeJarnett and Raven[16] found a similar pattern. Based on questionnaire responses, they rated 68 percent of couples as egalitarian, 25 percent as husband dominant, and 8 percent as wife dominant. Socioeconomic class was unrelated to the balance of power in this study. This finding is important because it shows that perceptions of equal power in marriage are not limited to middle-class couples, but are also true of lower-income couples.

In a comparative study, Dolores Mack[17] recruited 80 married couples, evenly divided among black working class, black middle class, white working class, and white middle class. Mack examined not only what couples *said* about power in their relationship, but also how couples behaved in power-relevant situations. In one phase of the study, each spouse individually filled out a questionnaire about their relationship. Results showed that the four groups did *not* differ significantly in their perceptions of marital power. Next, couples went over the questionnaire together, and if they disagreed about their answers, they had to discuss and resolve them for the joint questionnaire. Mack assessed the number of disagreements resolved in favor of the husband versus the wife as another indication of power. In all groups, the wives and husbands were equal or nearly equal on this measure of power, and no racial differences were found. On this measure, working-class husbands (both black and white) were slightly more powerful than were middle-class husbands.

As a second task, couples were asked to discuss two topics—politics (a traditionally masculine topic) and childrearing (traditionally feminine). Mack was not interested in the content of these discussions, but rather in the amount of time each person spent talking. She found that there were no significant gender, racial, *or* class differences; husbands and wives held the floor for the same amount of time, whether they were black, white, working class, or middle class.

For the last part of the study, Mack devised a clever method of measuring power differences in a bargaining situation. The husband and wife were asked to play the roles of a salesperson and a customer in an African boutique. The salesperson (played by the husband) was given four African items to sell (a ring, a dress, a wood carving, and a gourd) and was told that the four items had cost him a total of $73. The higher the price he could get for the items, the higher his profit. The customer (played by the wife) was told that she had $150 to spend on the four items. The lower the price paid by the wife, the more money she would get to keep. The couple was then allowed to bargain over the items. Power was measured as the total price that the customer paid for the four items. The less money she spent, the more powerful the wife was. Again, Mack found no racial differences, but she did find class differences. Middle-class wives spent more on the items (an average of $102) than did working-class wives (an average of $91). While this result might indicate that the middle-class husbands are more powerful, it might also indicate that the middle class are more comfortable spending a larger amount of money.

Mack measured power in three quite different ways, and found no racial differences in any of the three. Black wives were no more powerful than their white counterparts in any of the three situations. Small social-class differences were found in two of the three situations. The results of the study do *not* support the notion of a black matriarchy.

In summary, many studies have found that equal power is the most common pattern among black couples. Studies that have directly compared power patterns in black and white couples have found strong similarities.[18] Dietrich appears to be correct in concluding that "the black matriarchy has been exposed as a myth."[19]

Machismo: The Myth of Male Dominance in Chicano Marriages

Popular stereotypes depict the Chicano or Mexican-American family as patriarchal; that is, as dominated by the husband. Skolnick summarized ethnic stereotypes about marital power this way: "While the black family was seen as pathological because of its presumed female dominance, the Mexican-American family was viewed as unhealthy because of its patriarchy. In contrast, the ideal middle-class Anglo family was seen as egalitarian and democratic."[20]

According to this image of Chicanos, the husband "is seen as the absolute head of the family with full authority over the wife and children. All major decisions are his responsibility, with part of the wife's role involving seeing that the father's decisions are carried out. Power and prestige are the absolute perogatives of the male head."[21] This alleged Chicano male dominance is part of a broader pattern of *machismo*, a Spanish word meaning "strong or assertive masculinity, characterized by virility, courage, or aggressiveness."[22]

Hawkes and Taylor[23] studied Mexican and Mexican-American farm-laborer families to test the "macho" stereotype. They interviewed seventy-six women whose families lived in one of twelve migrant-worker family camps in California. The interviewers were women who themselves lived in the camps and had been trained by the researchers to do the interviewing. Power was measured by responses to two different kinds of questions: questions about decision making and questions about action taking. That is, the researchers were interested not only in who made decisions, but also in who then acted on the decisions. Decision-making questions assessed who decided how to spend the money, how many children the family should have, how to raise the children, and so on. Action-taking questions asked who paid the bills, who took steps to control the number of children the family had, who handled the children, and so on. The questions could be answered in three ways: the husband usually decides or acts, the wife usually decides or acts, or they both decide or act together. Based on the answers to these questions, couples were classified according to their family power pattern.

The families fell into six pattern types, which are summarized in Table 2. Families classified as *husband dominant* were characterized by the husband deciding and acting on the decisions. *Husband semidominant* referred to fami-

T A B L E 2
Marital power in Mexican and Mexican-American families

Family power type	Definition	Percent of total (76 couples)
Husband dominant	He decides and he acts	7
Husband semidominant	He decides and both act, or Both decide and he acts	9
Husband decides — wife acts	He decides and she acts	3
Egalitarian	Both decide and both act	62
Wife semidominant	She decides and both act, or Both decide and she acts	17
Wife dominant	She decides and she acts	3

SOURCE: Based on research by Hawkes and Taylor that *interviewed* 76 wives living in farm labor camps in California.

lies where the husband decides and both act, or both decide and the husband acts. *Husband decides — wife acts* was the third category. (No couples showed the reverse pattern, in which the wife decides and the husband acts.) When the husband and wife both decide and act, the family was considered *egalitarian*. *Wife semidominant* referred to families where the wife decides and both act, or both decide and the wife acts. The last category, *wife dominant*, consisted of families in which the wife both decides and acts. The results were quite clear. Most couples (62 percent) were classified as egalitarian. Only 7 percent were classified as husband dominant, and 3 percent as wife dominant. There is thus no evidence for the stereotype that most Chicano husbands have complete power at home.

Many other studies[24] have replicated Hawkes and Taylor's findings that Chicano husbands and wives report relatively equal power. In a review of this research, Staples and Mirande[25] conclude that "virtually every systematic study of conjugal roles in the Chicano family has found egalitarianism to be the predominant pattern across socioeconomic groups, educational levels, urban–rural residence, and region of the country." The popular myth that Chicano marriages are typically dominated by a dictatorial, "macho" husband is clearly false.

DISCUSSION

Our review of research on power in male–female relationships leads to several general conclusions. First, there is much diversity among contemporary American couples. Many couples — the majority in most of the studies we examined — describe their relationship as egalitarian. But other couples report male dominance or, less frequently, female dominance. All three patterns coexist in contemporary society. Partners who report an equal balance of power do not necessarily share all decision making or divide responsibilities in a nontraditional way. Equal power can be based either on sharing, or on "separate but equal" areas of influence. Many couples have different spheres of influence within a relationship, and these are often linked to traditional sex roles. For example, a couple may perceive their relationship as egalitarian because the husband makes financial decisions, the wife makes decisions about household matters, they share decisions about leisure activities, and they believe that overall their power balances out evenly. In other words, couples often describe relationships that combine power equality with traditional sex roles.

Second, among the many factors that can determine the balance of power in dating and marriage, existing research has emphasized three. Research suggests that relationships are most likely to be equal in power when the partners endorse egalitarian norms for male–female relations, have roughly equal personal resources, and are equally dependent on the relationship. No single factor alone is sufficient to guarantee an equal-power relationship. Thus, for example, some couples who value equality are unable to achieve it in their relationship; other couples who endorse traditional values nonetheless perceive their actual relationship as equal in power.

Third, empirical research has refuted the myth that black marriages are matriarchal and that Chicano marriages are patriarchal. In general, the balance of power in marriage has not been shown to differ among whites, blacks, and Chicanos. These findings should encourage us to question other ethnic stereotypes about male–female relations as well.

Finally, it is worth considering a question that skeptics might raise about these research findings; namely, whether the majority of American marriages are *really* equal in power. Dair Gillespie,[26] for example, has argued that truly egalitarian marriage is a "myth."

Some criticisms of current research findings are methodological. Since most studies are based on self-reports of power, it is possible that research participants have deliberately exaggerated the degree of equality in their relationships, perhaps in an effort to present themselves positively to the researchers. This seems unlikely in most cases, however, because of the consistency of findings across many independent studies and also because participants often revealed themselves to be traditional in other aspects of their relationships. Another methodological concern is that studies of marital power have not included a representative sample of American marriages; those who volunteer for research may come from the more liberal segments of society. In particular, there is reason to believe that men with traditional sex-role attitudes may be reluctant to volunteer for studies about personal relationships.[27] As a result, existing power research may paint an overly egalitarian portrait of American marriages.

Another important issue is that "insiders" often have a perspective on their own relationship that is different from that of an "outsider." Power is difficult to evaluate in intimate relationships, so it is reasonable that partners might view their relationship in a way different from the way outside observers would. For instance, as outsiders we might judge a relationship as male-dominant because the husband's professional career determines where the family lives, sets the family's lifestyle, and makes many demands on the wife's time. But both the husband and wife might ignore the influence of his work decisions on the marriage, and focus instead on their equal sharing of decisions about the children and leisure activities. They might view the relationship as equal in power.

In close relationships, partners' judgments of the balance of power are not strictly rational assessments based on objectively counting specific decisions or influence attempts. Although these "facts" are important in assessments of power, other factors also come into play. People are probably more likely to see their relationship as equal in power if the relationship generally seems "fair," if they do not feel "exploited," if they are able to do the things that they personally want to do, and, more broadly, if they feel they can trust their partner and believe they have a good relationship. In a recent study, Elizabeth Grauerholz[28] provided evidence that dating couples were more likely to report equal decision making if they trusted their partner and were strongly committed to the relationship. In the psychological algebra that lovers use to evaluate equality, factors such as trust and commitment may counteract or reduce power imbalances.

Some outside observers, however, might interpret these patterns differently. Critics might suggest that, in many close relationships, love and intimacy serve to disguise the reality of male dominance. A couple's perception that their relationship is equal in power might be viewed as a convenient illusion. Indeed, Gillespie goes so far as to suggest that true equality in marriage cannot be achieved until women as a social group have equal status in society. As long as social institutions provide men with greater opportunities to develop their competence and personal resources, women will be at a power disadvantage in male–female relations. For those interested in understanding power in dating and marriage, it is important to consider both insiders' and outsiders' perspectives.

NOTES

We are grateful for the help of Monique Watson and Eileen Davis in preparing this manuscript. We received valuable bibliographic suggestions from Steven Gordon, Vickie Mays, Hector Myers, Amado Padilla, and Belinda Tucker.

1. Millett, Kate. (1970). *Sexual politics*. Garden City, NY: Doubleday.

2. Andelin, Helen. (1963). *Fascinating womanhood*. New York: Bantam. Quotations are from pp. 134–135.

3. For more information on this large-scale study, see: Hill, Charles T.; Rubin, Zick; Peplau, Letitia A.; & Willard, Susan G. (1979). The volunteer couple: Sex differences, couple commitment and participation in research on interpersonal relationships. *Social Psychology Quarterly, 42*(4), 415–420; and Peplau, Letitia A.; Rubin, Zick; & Hill, Charles T. (1976, November). The sexual balance of power. *Psychology Today*, 142.

4. Safilios-Rothschild, Constantina. (1970). The study of family power structure: A review 1960–1969. *Journal of Marriage and the Family, 32*, 539–552.

5. Huston, Ted L. (1983). Power. In Harold H. Kelley, et al., *Close relationships*, pp. 169–219. New York: Freeman.

6. Andelin, Helen. (1963). *Fascinating womanhood*, pp. 145–146. New York: Bantam.

7. Bernard, Jessie. (1972). *The future of marriage*, p. 155. New York: Bantam.

8. For other discussions of factors affecting the balance of power, see: Brehm, Sharon S. (1985). *Intimate relationships*. New York: Random House; Husten, Ted L. (1983). Power. In Harold H. Kelley, et al., *Close relationships*, pp. 169–219. New York: Freeman; McDonald, Gerald W. (1980). Family power: The assessment of a decade of theory and research, 1970–1979. *Journal of Marriage and the Family, 42*(4), 841–854.

9. Safilios-Rothschild, Constantina. (1976). A macro- and micro-examination of family power and love: An exchange model. *Journal of Marriage and the Family, 38*, 355–362.

10. Waller, Willard. (1938). *The family: A dynamic interpretation*. New York: Cordon.

11. Blumstein, Philip, & Schwartz, Pepper. (1983). *American couples: Money, work, sex*, pp. 51–77. New York: Pocket Books.

12. Hyman, Herbert H., & Reed, John S. (1969). ''Black matriarchy'' reconsidered: Evidence from secondary analysis of sample surveys. *Public Opinion Quarterly, 33*, 346–354.

13. Moynihan, Daniel P. (1965). *The Negro family: The case for national action*. Washington, DC: U.S. Government Printing Office.

14. See: Cromwell, Vicky L., & Cromwell, Ronald E. (1978). Perceived dominance in decision-making and conflict resolution among Anglo, black, and Chicano couples. *Journal of Marriage and the Family, 40*, 749–759; DeJarnett, Sandra, & Raven, Bertram H. (1981). The balance, bases, and modes of interpersonal power in black couples: The role of sex and socioeconomic circumstances. *The Journal of Black Psychology, 7*(2), 51–66; Dietrich, Katheryn T. (1975). A re-examination of the myth of black matriarchy. *Journal of Marriage and the Family, 37*, 367–374; Gray-Little, Bernadette. (1982). Marital quality and power processes among black couples. *Journal of Marriage and the Family, 44*(3), 633–646; McDonald, Gerald W. (1980). Family power: The assessment of a decade of theory and research, 1970–1979. *Journal of Marriage and the Family, 42*(4), 841–854; Myers, Hector F. (1982). Research on the Afro-American family: A critical review. In Bass, Barbara; Wyatt, Gail, & Powell, Gloria J., eds., *The assessment and treatment of Afro-American families: Selected lectures*, pp. 35–60. New York: Grune and Stratton; Willie, Charles V. (1981). Dominance in the family: The black and white experience. *The Journal of Black Psychology, 7*(2), 91–97; Willie, Charles V., & Greenblatt, Susan L. (1978). Four "classic" studies of power relationships in black families: A review and look to the future. *Journal of Marriage and the Family, 40*, 691–694.

15. Dietrich, Katheryn T. (1975). A re-examination of the myth of black matriarchy. *Journal of Marriage and the Family, 37,* 367–374.

16. DeJarnett, Sandra, & Raven, Bertram H. (1981). The balance, bases, and modes of interpersonal power in black couples: The role of sex and socioeconomic circumstances. *The Journal of Black Psychology, 7*(2), 51–66.

17. Mack, Delores E. (1971). Where the black-matriarchy theorists went wrong. *Psychology Today, 4,* 24, 86–87.

18. See: Cromwell, Vicky L., & Cromwell, Ronald E. (1978). Perceived dominance in decision-making and conflict resolution among Anglo, Black and Chicano couples. *Journal of Marriage and the Family, 40,* 749–759; Hyman, Herbert H., & Reed, John S. (1969). "Black matriarchy" reconsidered: Evidence from secondary analysis of sample surveys. *Public Opinion Quarterly, 33,* 346–354; Mack, Delores E. (1971). Where the black-matriarchy theorists went wrong. *Psychology Today, 4,* 24, 86–87; Middleton, Russell, & Putney, Snell (1960). Dominance in decisions in the family: Race and class differences. *American Journal of Sociology, 65,* 605–609.

19. Dietrich, Katheryn T. (1975). A re-examination of the myth of black matriarchy. *Journal of Marriage and the Family, 37,* p. 367.

20. Skolnick, Arlene S. (1987). *The intimate environment: Exploring marriage and the family*, p. 179. Boston: Little, Brown & Co.

21. Alvirez, David, & Bean, Frank D. (1976). The Mexican American family. In Charles H. Mindel & Robert W. Habenstein, eds., *Ethnic families in America: Patterns of variation*, pp. 277–278. New York: Elsevier.

22. Guralnik, David B. (1984). *Webster's new world dictionary*, p. 848. New York: Simon and Schuster.

23. Hawkes, Glenn R., & Taylor, Minna. (1975). Power structure in Mexican and Mexican-American farm labor families. *Journal of Marriage and the Family, 37,* 807–811.

24. See: Cromwell, Ronald E., Corrales, Ramon, & Torsiello, Peter M. (1973). Normative patterns of marital decision making power and influence in Mexico and the United States: A partial test of resource and ideology theory. *Journal of Comparative Family Studies, 4,* 749–759; Cromwell, Vicky L., & Cromwell, Ronald E. (1978). Perceived dominance in decision-making and conflict resolution among Anglo, black and Chicano couples. *Journal of Marriage and the Family, 40,* 749–759; Cromwell, Ronald E., & Ruiz, Rene A. (1979). The myth of macho dominance in decision making within Mexican and Chicano families. *Hispanic Journal of Behavioral Sciences, 1*(4), 355–373; Zamudio, Anthony. (1986). *Power structure in Mexican and Mexican-American couples: A multi-dimensional perspective.* Unpublished doctoral dissertation, University of California, Los Angeles; Zapata, Jesse T., & Jaramillo, Pat T. (1981). Research on the Mexican-American family. *Journal of Individual Psychology, 37,* 72–85; Zinn, Maxine B. (1980). Employment and education of Mexican-American women: The interplay of modernity and ethnicity in eight families. *Harvard Educational Review, 50*(1), 47–62.

25. Staples, Robert, & Mirande, Alfredo. (1980). Racial and cultural variation among American families: A decennial review of the literature on minority families. *Journal of Marriage and the Family, 42*(4), 894.

26. Gillespie, Dair L. (1971). Who has the power? The marital struggle. *Journal of Marriage and the Family, 33,* 445–458.

27. Hill, Charles T., Rubin, Zick, Peplau, Letitia A., & Willard, Susan G. (1979). The volunteer couple: Sex differences, couple commitment and the participation in research on interpersonal relationships. *Social Psychology Quarterly, 42*(4), 415–420.

28. Grauerholz, Elizabeth (1987). Balancing the power in dating relationships. *Sex Roles, 17,* 563–571. See also John Scanzoni. (1979). Social processes and power in families. In Wesley R. Burr, et al., eds., *Contemporary theories about the family*, Vol. 1, pp. 295–316. New York: Free Press, 1979.

Marital Relationships and Mental Health: The Psychic Costs of Inequality

JANICE M. STEIL

The status of married women in relation to their husbands has been described as extending along a continuum from wife as property to wife as equal partner, with wife as complement and wife a junior partner as intermediary steps.[1] Many people would assert that wives, historically, were situated on the property end of this continuum.[2] Consistent with this characterization, prior to the Civil War married women had many duties but few rights. They were not permitted to control their property, even when it was theirs by inheritance. A husband had the right to collect and use his wife's wages, to decide on the education and religion of their children, and to punish his wife if she displeased him. The wife's property status was based on the English common law, which declared that

> the legal existence of the wife is merged in that of the husband so that, in law, the husband and wife are one person. . . . The husband's dominion over the person and property of the wife is fully recognized. She is utterly incompetent to contract in her own name. He is entitled to her society and her service; to her obedience and her property. . . . In consideration of his married rights the husband is bound to furnish the wife a home and suitable support.[3]

Today, both popular and social-science literature lead us to believe that married women have moved to the other end of the continuum, wife as equal partner. As early as 1960, the authors of a singularly influential study concluded that "the average American family has changed its authority pattern from one of patriarchal male dominance to one of egalitarian sharing."[4] In this well-known study, 731 urban and suburban wives and 178 farm wives living in the Detroit area were asked:

Who usually makes the final decision about . . .
1. what job the husband should take
2. what car to get
3. whether or not to buy life insurance
4. where to go on a vacation
5. what house or apartment to take
6. whether or not the wife should go to work or quit work
7. what doctor to have when someone is sick
8. how much money the family can afford to spend per week on food

Scores were assigned on the basis of the wives' responses, which ranged from "husband always" to "wife always" makes the final decision, and these scores were then summed. The results are summarized in Table 1. The scoring procedure was based on the assumption that all the decisions were equally important. Common sense, however, suggests that this is unlikely. A husband's job is likely to have a singular impact on the family's life (certainly in terms of geographic location, standard of living, and time available to spend with family members). Many of the other decisions, such as the food budget, where to go on vacation, and the kind of home, may well be determined by the husband's job. Keeping this differential importance in mind, we note that 90 percent of the respondents reported that the husbands always made the final decision regarding the husband's job, and 41 percent reported that the wives always made the final decision regarding food. Food is the area in which wives reportedly have the most decision-making power. The two areas that seem most equal in importance are what job the husband should take and whether or not the wife should go to work or quit work. While 90 percent of the husbands were reported to have the final say regarding their own job, only 39 percent of the wives were reported to have the final say regarding whether they should or should not work. Looking at

T A B L E   1
Allocation of power in decision-making areas (731 Detroit families)

Who decides	Decision							
	Husband's job	Car	Insurance	Vacation	House	Wife's work	Doctor	Food
(5) Husband always	90%	56%	31%	12%	12%	26%	7%	10%
(4) Husband more than wife	4%	12%	11%	6%	6%	5%	3%	2%
(3) Husband and wife exactly the same	3%	25%	41%	68%	58%	18%	45%	32%
(2) Wife more than husband	0%	2%	4%	4%	10%	9%	11%	11%
(1) Wife always	1%	3%	10%	7%	13%	39%	31%	41%
No answer	2%	1%	2%	3%	1%	3%	3%	3%
Total	100%	99%	99%	100%	100%	100%	100%	99%
Husband's mean power[a]	4.86	4.18	3.50	3.12	2.94	2.69	2.53	2.26

SOURCE: Robert O. Blood and Donald M. Wolfe, *Husbands and Wives: The Dynamics of Married Living* (Glencoe, Ill.: Free Press, 1960), 21. Copyright © 1960 by The Free Press, a Corporation.

[a]The mean for each column is computed on the basis of the weights shown; e.g., "husband always" = 5.

the responses from the other direction, we find that only 1 percent of the wives reportedly had the final say regarding their husband's job, but 26 percent of the husbands were reported to have the final say on whether their wives should work. Husbands were more than twice as likely to have the final say regarding their wives' working (26 percent) as they were regarding the food budget (10 percent). Not only do the decisions differ in terms of their relative importance, but it also seems that some decisions (such as the food budget) are relegated to the less powerful partner simply because the decisions are less important.[5] Giving equal weight to the less important and delegated decisions inflated the wives' scores and biased the findings. Yet, despite this bias, the overall mean scores still reflected husband dominance.

Other investigators have studied the power structure of American marriages by asking husbands and wives, "When there's a really important decision on which you two are likely to disagree, who usually wins out?" In the findings of one such study, 50 percent of middle-class housewives and 53 percent of their husbands reported that the husband had greater influence. By comparison, none of the middle-class housewives reported that they had more influence than their husbands. One-half reported that the influence of each spouse was equal. White middle-class husbands were more likely to have "greater influence" than working-class husbands, but the tendency for greater influence declined for both groups when their wives were employed outside the home.[6] In another study, a sample of 336 Canadian households was asked, "Who is the real boss in your family?" Only wives' responses were reported. Of these, 76 percent said that the husband was the boss. Only 13 percent said that power was equally shared.[7] Despite the variability of the findings, the assertion of equality as the normative condition of marital relationships seems unwarranted. Neither the early studies nor those conducted more recently support the conclusion of equality.

THE DUAL-CAREER FAMILY

Recent investigations have focused on the dual-career family, defined as "one in which both heads of household pursue careers (as compared to jobs) and at the same time maintain a family life together."[8] The dual-career couple has been perceived as the most egalitarian marriage situation and the harbinger of future family patterns. Even among such couples, however, there is a consistent pattern of inequality in the home and at work. Only the husband's occupational characteristics, and particularly his occupational prestige, affect the probability that the family will move in response to job opportunities. Neither the wife's occupational prestige, nor her relative contribution to the family income, nor opportunities for employment in her field elsewhere in the country affect the relocation of dual-career couples.[9] Further, "when employment pressures require, the wife's career is more likely to be considered as secondary, her job is more likely to be part-time or (in academic settings) non-tenure track, and her pay and level are likely to be less than her husband's."[10] In the domestic sphere, household management and work are not evenly shared. Wives are more likely than their husbands to have to curtail career involvements in favor of family demands, and both partners seem to accept as inevitable that women have to bear the brunt of child care and domestic organization.[11] Further, as some investigators have noted, tension lines often develop. In one well-known study, the investigators observed that "the main tension lines for men were in the area of how much responsibility (as distinct from participation) to take in the home, and how much occupational achievement to *tolerate* [emphasis added] in their wives."[12] Despite the husbands' supportive orientation, both partners seem to endorse some level of male dominance. Thus, the authors report that "Mr. O encourages his wife to pursue her career . . . but the amount of income relative to his is a point of some tension between them. . . . With the X's the central issue is authority. . . . he did not wish actually to have her in authority over the job on which he himself was working."[13] Wives, it seems, collude in this process. They consider themselves fortunate in being able to combine a career with traditional responsibilities and thus report little dissatisfaction with having to assume a disproportionate share of the domestic tasks.[14] In addition, wives tend to deemphasize their work positions while they are in the home context. They may portray their careers as secondary and their successes as accidental, rather than assert the importance of their own competence.[15] Dual-career couples, then, are not egalitarian. As Bryson and Bryson concluded, "they tend to divide household responsibilities along sex-stereotypic lines and to place differential values on their careers. It also seems clear that the pressure for such differentiation falls disproportionately on the wife."[16]

FACTORS ASSOCIATED WITH HUSBAND DOMINANCE

Family size, social class, ethnicity, husband's income, and wife's employment status have consistently been associated with the extent of a husband's dominance. Blood and Wolfe found that black husbands had less power than white husbands.[17] Centers, Raven, and Rodriquez found Asian husbands had more influence than white ones and found black husbands had the least.[18] Scanzoni and Szinovacy suggested that black couples may be more egalitarian about sex roles than whites.[19] Working-class husbands have less power than do middle-class husbands.[20] White middle-class housewives who do not work outside the home may well have less power in their marital relationships than any other group. The better educated and more successful the husband, the less power the wife is likely to have.[21] This finding seems to counter hypotheses that higher levels of education and social class are usually associated with more egalitarian ideologies. As Goode points out, however, "lower class men concede fewer rights ideologically than their women in fact obtain; and the more educated men are likely to concede more rights ideologically than they, in fact, grant."[22] It may well be a two-way street. Housewives are more likely to endorse traditional sex-role ideologies than are women who work for pay.[23] It has also been reported that, the higher a husband's income, the more likely his wife is to endorse the legitimacy of his power on the basis of traditional male authority.[24]

Employed wives are consistently shown to be less likely to endorse traditional ideologies, to have more say in decision making, and to enjoy a somewhat more egalitarian division of family roles than nonemployed wives.[25] Among employed wives, influence and task sharing tend to be greater for those who work full-time. Yet, even under optimal conditions, it has been noted that working wives do five times as much domestic work as their spouses — and usually more.[26] Further, studies that ask who has prime *responsibility* for domestic tasks show no difference between full-time and part-time women workers.[27] Number of years worked and continuity and pattern of employment may also be associated with an increase in the wife's influence but not with increased sharing of child-care responsibilities.[28] Finally, two studies note that the husband's influence is greatest in first marriages and is least when both partners have remarried.[29]

The marital influence of the wife, then, is inversely related to her husband's income, his occupational prestige, and the number of young children, and is directly related to the extent of her participation in the paid labor force. Although various explanations for these findings have been and can be suggested, both ideological and economic factors seem particularly pertinent. Ideologically, many of the elements of the early English common law persist in today's value structure. The "ideal" husband still heads the household and assumes the financial responsibility of providing for his family. In return, it seems, he is still entitled to his wife's "society and service." Thus, the "ideal" wife still assumes primary responsibility for care of the home and children. She is expected to put the needs and interests of her husband and his occupation as well as the needs and interests of the children above her own. Consistent with this ideology, the likelihood of the wife's employment decreases as family size, husband's income, and husband's occupational level increase. The more the husband is able to provide economically for the family, the more likely it is that the wife will be at home. Yet, nonparticipation in the paid labor force is likely to increase the wife's economic and emotional dependence, as well as to decrease her influence in the family. As the wife withdraws from the labor force, the husband becomes the sole economic provider and primary source of family prestige. Thus, he is perceived as entitled to increasing authority over and deference from his family. Whether or not a wife works for pay, then, may be the single most important factor in determining her power status relative to her husband.

Yet, the empirical literature clearly shows that even employed professional wives are unlikely to achieve equality. The economic realities of a society in which women earn significantly less than men make it unlikely that the wife will contribute equally to the family finances. In fact, the average employed wife earns considerably less than her husband. Her reduced earning power is exacerbated by society's gender-specific ascriptions of family responsibilities. Thus, as one investigator notes, "even when the wife is well educated and working, and the husband is not successful, she tends to do more around the house than he does, and were our measurement of role sharing strict enough to include only absolutely equal patterns, we would lose all our cases."[30] Thus these authors suggest that relationships in which the husband performs 50 percent of the household tasks and the wife contributes 50 percent of the family income are so rare they defy study.

THE COSTS OF INEQUALITY

Bernard was one of the first to note that there is now a considerable body of research showing that there are really two marriages in every marital union, "his" and "hers." These two marriages do not always coincide, and, according to Bernard, "his" marriage is better than "hers."[31] Statistically speaking, marriage is good for men. Married men are less likely to show serious symptoms of psychological distress and to suffer mental health impairments than are men who were never married. Married men live longer on the average than never-married men, experience greater career success, and are less likely to be involved in crime. The fact seems unassailable that, for men, the married fare far better than the unmarried. Why this is so is less clear. Some have asked whether it is marriage that is so beneficial to men, or whether the more vulnerable men never marry. In fact, we cannot know unequivocally which is cause and which is effect. Yet most attempts to address the question suggest that marriage is indeed beneficial to men.[32]

On the other hand, marriage is not as good for women as it is for men. Although married women generally fare better than unmarried women, they "suffer far greater mental health hazards and present a far worse clinical picture" than married men.[33] An analysis of seventeen studies examining the relationship between sex, marital status, and mental illness showed that, even with wide variations in definition, married women consistently showed higher rates of mental disorder than married men.[34] This is not the case for single women compared to single men. For every category of the unmarried (i.e., never married, divorced, and widowed), the majority of studies show higher rates of mental illness for males than for females. It is only among the married, then, that women have higher rates of mental illness than men do.

The greater incidence of mental illness in married women does not seem to be a consequence of greater biological vulnerability or of differential patterns of help-seeking behavior.[35] Some have suggested that it may be due to characteristics of the female role, particularly the married woman's role as housewife.[36] Bernard reviewed the incidence of poor mental and emotional health among housewives (all of whom were presumed to be married) and working women (three-fifths of whom were married). In terms of eleven of twelve symptoms of psychological distress, the working women were found to be overwhelmingly better off than the housewives. This is really rather surprising, given the disproportionate demands that are placed on the employed/married woman. As we have seen, she continues to carry the responsibilities of housewife and mother and simply adds the responsibilities of paid work to them. Why then should the housewife fare more poorly? Bernard concluded that the major reason was the status denigration that marriage brings to housewives.[37] Other authors, particularly Gove, suggest that housework not only is accorded low status but also is invisible and unstructured. Further, the absence of paid employment deprives housewives of alternative sources of gratification when the housewife role is unsatisfying.[38] These authors suggest that, if marriage fails to bring satisfaction, the employed woman can turn to an alternative source of satisfaction, her job, whereas the housewife cannot.

Following publication of Bernard's book, two studies explicitly examined the relationship between roles and mental illness among the married.[39] In the first, Radloff assessed the prevalence of depressive symptoms among the employed married men and both employed and unemployed married women. In the second, Gove and Geerken asked employed husbands, employed wives, and unemployed housewives a series of questions assessing the extent to which they felt subjected to incessant demands, desired to be alone, and often felt lonely. In the findings of both studies, unemployed housewives consistently fared the worst, employed husbands fared the best, and employed wives scored somewhere in between. Unemployed housewives were most likely to report that they felt confronted by incessant demands, desired to be alone more frequently, and felt lonely more frequently. Housewives also reported the highest prevalence of fourteen general psychiatric symptoms and experienced the highest incidence of depression. As Radloff points out, the dual-role hypothesis that working women can turn to other sources of gratification more easily than housewives can, explains the poor position of housewives compared to employed wives but not the difference between employed wives and employed husbands.[40] Since employed wives continue to assume more responsibility for child care and housework than their husbands do, it has been suggested that this burden of double duty may cause the difference in mental states between employed husbands and employed wives. Consistent with the literature, Radloff's study showed that married female workers did in fact spend significantly more time on housework than the married men. Yet this did not seem to explain the difference in depression. Thus, the role of housewife seems to explain only part of the greater incidence of mental symptoms in married women. Further, as Radloff reports, "neither working nor happiness with jobs and/or marriage makes married women as healthy as comparable married men."[41]

Because the incidence of mental illness is lower for married women than for unmarried women, it cannot be said that marriage per se is detrimental to women's health. Yet married women clearly do not fare as well as married men, and among married women unemployed housewives do not fare as well as the employed. The pattern, we suggest, mirrors the societal and marital pattern of inequality. It is consistent with the findings reviewed earlier which show that husbands typically have more influence than wives in marital relationships, and wives who are employed typically have more influence and status than those who are not. From this perspective, women's responses to Gove and Geerken's measure of incessant demands may reflect feelings of powerlessness, just as the desire to be alone may reflect a wish to escape a situation that feels both controlling and uncontrollable. It may be that poor emotional well-being and mental health are associated less with marriage per se than they are with a relationship of relative inequality of status and power between the partners. As yet, this hypothesis remains untested. Some studies, however, have shown that those in relatively more egalitarian marriages report greater satisfaction on the part of the wives, more instances of behavior that is conducive to building self-esteem and esteem from others, and more adaptive responses to simulated crises.[42]

FROM EQUITY TO EQUALITY

Equity, equality, and need have been identified as distinct principles by which the conditions and goods that affect individual well-being are distributed.[43] Each principle represents a distinct value system and has differential implications for the course of human interaction. The equity principle prescribes that people's outcomes should be determined by their inputs; that is, by the extent to which they make valued contributions. According to some, equity-based distributions tend to undermine mutual respect and self-respect by signifying that the different participants in a relationship do not have the same value. This is because equity is associated with the goal of economic productivity, and under an equity system people come to be regarded primarily in terms of their economic utility. The principle of equality, by contrast, prescribes that conditions and goods should be equally shared. Equality is associated with the goal of fostering and maintaining enjoyable relationships and, unlike equity, does not evoke the deleterious emotions that undermine them.[44]

Contemporary marriage relationships seem to be based primarily on principles of equity. This orientation reflects the institution's historical economic roots and a societal ideology that values economic worth. Why else would women who relinquish positions of paid employment to stay home and nurture their children suffer a decline in influence? Because of this differential valuing, gender roles, which ascribe particular spheres of responsibility on the basis of sex, are not separate but equal. Rather they are separate and unequal.

We began this article with a description of a hypothetical status continuum extending from wife as property to wife as equal partner. Equality is characterized on this continuum by equal rights and equal duties for the partners in both the economic and the domestic spheres. Yet, this cannot be achieved in a system that ascribes differential responsibilities and entitlements on the basis of sex. Consequently, role specialization, as currently prescribed, must be replaced by role interchangeability and free choice. But, how is this to be achieved in a society that socializes women and men differently?

Family structures both reflect and perpetuate societal norms and values. If equality is to be achieved change must take place not only within marital relationships but also within the society as a whole. Yet change will not occur until stereotypic gender roles are perceived as unjust. Women will not see their position as unjust, however, until specific conditions have been established: women must be aware that other possibilities exist; they must want such possibilities for themselves; and, most important, they must believe they are entitled to these possibilities.[45] Those women who still support husband dominance do so because they believe in the appropriateness and importance of both the male role as breadwinner and the female role as nurturer (both to her husband and to her children).[46] Clearly, this belief has important consequences for women's perceptions of their possibilities, their responsibilities, their wants, and their entitlements.[47]

For women to achieve quality, they must perceive it as something they are *entitled* to and be willing to assume the concordant responsibilities. This involves assuming equal responsibility in the economic sphere and accepting only equal responsibility in the familial sphere. The psychological and practical difficulties of such a reorientation are indeed great, and the single most important enabling factor may be husband support.[48] Yet, just as women disproportionately bear the costs of inequality (as our review of the studies suggests), so they will have to assume the initiative disproportionately in eliminating it. Although the move toward equality may be facilitated by highlighting the benefits that will accrue to men as well as women, males overall "are not about to upset the status quo that provides them with such a favorable position."[49] The reorientation is likely to lead to an increase in the number of women who remain unmarried. In the short term, it will produce increased stress among the married, and, as long as society provides so little support to families with employed mothers, the reach for equality will exacerbate current trends toward smaller families and voluntary childlessness. As equality is achieved, however, there should be obvious improvements for all.

NOTES

1. J. Scanzoni, *Sexual Bargaining: Power Politics in the American Marriage* (Englewood Cliffs, N.J.: Prentice-Hall, 1972).

2. S. Brownmiller, *Against Our Will: Men, Women, and Rape* (New York: Simon and Schuster, 1975); Scanzoni, *Sexual Bargaining*.

3. *Phillips v. Graves* (1870), quoted in J. M. Krauskopf, "Partnership Marriage: Legal Reforms Needed," in J. Chapman and M. Gates, eds., *Women into Wives: The Legal and Economic Impact of Marriage* (Beverly Hills: Sage Publications, 1977), 94.

4. R. O. Blood and D. M. Wolfe, *Husbands and Wives* (Glencoe, Ill.: Free Press, 1960), 47.

5. C. Safilios-Rothschild, "Family Sociology or Wives' Family Sociology? A Cross-Cultural Examination of Decision Making," *Journal of Marriage and the Family* 31 (1969), 290–301; C. Safilios-Rothschild, "The Study of Family Power Structure: A Review, 1960–1969," *Journal of Marriage and the Family* 32 (1970), 539–52.

6. D. M. Heer, "Husband and Wife Perceptions of Family Power Structures," *Marriage and Family Living* 24 (Feb. 1962), 65–67.

7. J. L. Turk and N. W. Bell, "Measuring Power in Families," *Journal of Marriage and the Family* 34 (1972), 215–23.

8. R. Rapoport and R. N. Rapoport, "Further Considerations on the Dual Career Family," *Human Relations* 24 (1971), 519–33.

9. R. P. Duncan and C. C. Perrucci, "Dual Occupation Families and Migration," *American Sociological Review* 41 (1976), 252–61.

10. J. Bryson and R. Bryson, "Salary and Job Performance Differences in Dual Career Couples" in F. Pepitone-Rockwell, ed., *Dual Career Couples*, (Beverly Hills: Sage Publications, 1980), 241–60.

11. H. Lopata, D. Barnewolt, and K. Norr, "Spouses' Contributions to Each Other's Roles," in Pepitone-Rockwell, ed., *Dual Career Couples*, 111–42.

12. R. Rapoport and R. N. Rapoport, *Dual Career Families Re-examined* (New York: Harper and Row, 1976), 310.

13. R. Rapoport and R. N. Rapoport, "The Dual Career Family," *Human Relations* 22 (1969), 3–30, especially 16–17.

14. M. M. Paloma and T. N. Garland, "The Married Professional Woman: A Study in Tolerance of Domestication," *Journal of Marriage and the Family* 33 (1971), 531–40.

15. R. Rapoport and R. N. Rapoport, "The Dual Career Family," 18.

16. Bryson and Bryson, "Salary and Job Performance Differences," 256.

17. Blood and Wolfe, *Husbands and Wives.*

18. R. Centers, B. Raven, and A. Rodriques, "Conjugal Power Structure: A Re-examination," *American Sociological Review* 30 (1971), 264–76.

19. J. H. Scanzoni and M. Szinovacy, *Family Decision-making: A Developmental Sex Role Model* (Beverly Hills: Sage Publications, 1980); also J. H. Scanzoni, *The Black Family in Modern Society* (Boston: Allyn and Bacon, 1971).

20. D. M. Heer, "Dominance and the Working Wife," *Social Forces* 36 (1958), 341–47; and Heer, "Husband and Wife Perceptions."

21. Blood and Wolfe, *Husbands and Wives*; J. A. Ericksen, W. L. Yancey, and E. P. Ericksen, "The Division of Family Roles," *Journal of Marriage and the Family* 41 (1979), 301–13; Heer, "Dominance and the Working Wife"; Heer, "Husband and Wife Perceptions"; L. W. Hoffman, "Effects of the Employment of Mothers on Parental Power Relations and the Division of Household Tasks," *Marriage and Family Living* 22 (Feb. 1960), 27–35.

22. W. J. Goode, *World Revolution and Family Patterns* (New York: Free Press, 1963–70), 21.

23. L. J. Beckman and B. B. Houser, "The More You Have, the More You Do: The Relationship between Wife's Employment, Sex-Role Attitudes, and Household Behavior," *Psychology of Women Quarterly* 4 (winter 1979), 160–74; Hoffman, "Effects of the Employment of Mothers"; K. O. Mason and L. L. Bumpass, "Women's Sex Role Ideology, 1970," *American Journal of Sociology* 80 (1975), 1212–19.

24. Scanzoni, *Sexual Bargaining.*

25. Beckman and Houser, "The More You Have"; R. O. Blood and R. I. Hamblin, "The Effect of the Wife's Employment on the Family Power Structure," *Social Forces* 36 (1958), 347–52; Blood and Wolfe, *Husbands and Wives*; F. Crosby, *Relative Deprivation and Working Women* (New York: Oxford University Press, 1982); Heer, "Husband and Wife Perceptions"; Hoffman, "Effects of the Employment of Mothers"; Mason and Bumpass, "Women's Sex Role Ideology"; L. Radloff, "Sex Differences in Depression: The Effects of Occupation and Marital Status," *Sex Roles* 1 (1975), 249–65.

26. S. Model, "Housework by Husbands: Determinants and Implications," in J. Aldous, ed., *Two Paychecks: Life in Dual Earner Families* (Beverly Hills: Sage Publications, 1982), 193–205.

27. Lopata, Barnewolt, and Norr, "Spouses' Contributions."

28. Blood and Wolfe, *Husbands and Wives*; K. Weingarten, "The Employment Pattern of Professional Couples and Their Distribution of Involvement in the Family," *Psychology of Women Quarterly* 3 (fall 1978), 43–52.

29. Centers, Ravey, and Rodriques, "Conjugal Power Structure"; Scanzoni and Szinovacy, *Family Decision-making.*

30. Ericksen, Yancey, and Ericksen, "The Division of Family Roles," 311.

31. J. Bernard, *The Future of Marriage* (New York: World Publishing Co., 1972).

32. Ibid.

33. Ibid., 29–30.

34. W. R. Gove, "The Relationship between Sex Roles, Marital Status and Mental Illness," *Social Forces* 51 (Sept. 1972), 34–45.

35. Ibid.; M. Weissman and G. L. Klerman, "Sex Differences and the Epidemiology of Depression," *Archives of General Psychiatry* 34 (1977), 98–111.

36. Gove, "The Relationship between Sex Roles."

37. Bernard, *The Future of Marriage*, 53.

38. Gove, "The Relationship between Sex Roles"

39. Radloff, "Sex Differences in Depression"; and W. R. Gove and M. R. Geerken, "The Effect of Children and Employment on the Mental Health of Married Men and Women," *Social Forces* 56 (Sept. 1977), 66–76.

40. Radloff, "Sex Differences in Depression."

41. Ibid., 259.

42. R. G. Corrales, "Power and Satisfaction in Early Marriage," in R. Cromwell and D. Olson, eds., *Power in Families* (New York: John Wiley and Sons, 1975), 197–216; L. Rainwater, *Family Design* (Chicago: Aldine Publishing Co., 1965); S. J. Bahr and B. C. Rollins, "Crisis and Conjugal Power," *Journal of Marriage and the Family* 33 (1971), 360–67.

43. M. Deutsch, "Equity, Equality and Need: What Determines Which Value Will Be Used as the Basis of Distributive Justice?" M. J. Lerner, ed., *Journal of Social Issues* 31 (1975), 137–50.

44. Ibid.

45. F. Crosby, "A Model of Egoistical Relative Deprivation," *Psychological Review* 83 (1976), 85–133; and Crosby, *Relative Deprivation and Working Women*.

46. A. Sanders and J. Steil, "Women, Marital Status and Careers: Paradoxes and Parallaxes" (Paper presented at the meetings of the Eastern Psychological Association, Philadelphia, 1983); also available as A. Sanders, J. Steil, and J. Weinglass, "Taking the Traditional Route: Some Covert Costs of Traditional Decisions for the Married Career Woman," in R. Unger, ed., Special Issue on Gender, *Journal of Imagination, Cognition and Personality* 3 (1983–4), 327–336.

47. J. Weinglass and J. Steill, "When Is Unequal Unfair: The Role of Ideology" (Paper presented at the meeting of the American Psychological Association, Los Angeles, 1981; Resources in Education document no. ED218530, ERIC/CAPS Clearinghouse, University of Michigan, Ann Arbor).

48. L. Bailyn, "Career and Family Orientations of Husbands and Wives in Relation to Marital Happiness," *Human Relations* 23 (1970), 97–113; S. Houseknecht and A. Macke, "Combining Marriage and Career: The Marital Adjustment of Professional Women," *Journal of Marriage and the Family* 43 (1981), 651–61; R. Rapoport and R. N. Rapoport, "The Dual Career Family."

49. Scanzoni, *Sexual Bargaining*, 137.

Marital Intimacy and Conflict: The Irony of Spousal Equality

JANET SALTZMAN CHAFETZ

       Scholars and practitioners who deal with families appear generally to assume that spousal intimacy and conflict alike follow primarily from personal attributes of those involved, including modes of interaction and communication between marital partners (Lewis, Spanner 1979). Magazine articles, popular books, and family therapies purport to teach people how to experience more intimacy and less conflict or hostility within their marriage. The message seems to be that if the *individuals* can be taught better communication and conflict resolution skills, then marital intimacy and harmony will increase. As to "why marriages break up. . . . It often happens because we are not generally taught the arts of 'getting along' intimately with others, solving problems and conflicts as they arise." We are advised that this could be prevented by learning "skills of open communication and problem solving" (Cox 1978 117).

    While not denying this psychological approach on the individual level, I suggest that a more macro level and sociological view of these phenomena may shed important light on the contemporary American marriage. To the extent that *social structural* factors contribute substantially to the process of marital communication, conflict resolution, and the development of mutual respect and basic understanding between spouses, then individual-level intervention or education is unlikely seriously to reduce the problems that are creating an extremely high divorce rate in this and most other industrialized societies.

CONCEPTUAL DEFINITIONS

The term *intimacy* is defined in many ways (Kieffer 1977; Biddle 1976). Here it is used to mean relatively open communication on a broad range of topics salient to the lives of each spouse, including substantial empathy for one another's joys, concerns, and problems. Emphasis is on communication rather than sexual and other activities, and feelings. I contend that intimate communication stands at the root of sexual intimacy, as distinct from simple sex coupling, and of joy in joint activities and experiences. Stress is placed on the *breadth* of concerns communicated by each partner. Spouses who conceal major worries or joys from their partners, whatever the reason, are not high in intimacy. And emphasis in this definition is placed on *reciprocity* of communication. Open communication from one spouse that is not reciprocated by the other does not constitute high spousal intimacy. Finally, *empathic* reactions by each spouse to the concerns of the other are fundamental to spousal intimacy. This does not mean that the partners must always agree. It only means that each must attempt to understand the concerns of the other through the other's eyes.

Conflict refers to any situation at a point in time where spouses disagree on what should occur. Conflict may or may not be overt, verbalized, or even consciously recognized by both partners. It may be quickly settled or never essentially settled, remaining latent and periodically resurfacing. It may be "won" by one party, or some form of compromise may be reached. The issues may be as minor as what movie to see or as major as whether to move to another country.

I will consider the variables of gender differentiation and sex equality. *Gender differentiation* refers to the extent to which males and females, on the basis of biological sex alone, are socially expected to manifest very different traits or emotions, personality, interest, and intellect. It concerns the extent of gender-role stereotyping or polarization. The term *sex equality* refers to the extent to which males and females, as general categories, have equal access to the scarce and valued resources of society. It concerns the extent to which males are advantaged over females in power, financial resources, education, social status, and opportunities for psychic gratification (Chafetz 1984 ch 1).

In general, the degree to which societies differentiate the genders is positively related to the degree of sex inequality; the greater the differentiation, the greater the inequality (Sanday 1974). Where females are highly disadvantaged compared to males, the sexes also tend to be perceived as fundamentally different types of people—as "opposites" to each other. Conversely, in societies where they are more equal, there is more stress on similarities between males and females (Chafetz 1984 ch 2).

THE CASE FOR INCREASED INTIMACY

Americans commonly refer to persons not of their own sex as the "opposite" sex. Since the closing decades of the nineteenth century, and until the last few decades, masculinity and femininity have been conceived as polar opposites (Chafetz 1984 ch 2; Williams, Bennett 1975; Heilbrun 1976). Females were assumed to be emotionally expressive, males stoical; females passive and dependent, males active and dominant; males rational, females intuitive and not rational; males (as breadwinners) playing instrumental social roles in the public sphere, while females play expressive social roles in the private domestic sphere. Since the advent of the new feminist movement over 20 years ago, these polar definitions have begun to break down as stereotypes. This does not deny their relevance to individuals' behavior and expectations and appraisals of self and others, but I do argue that there is a reduction in the polarity of gender roles, especially among the younger and better-educated segments of society, and most especially a reduction of stereotyped definitions of femininity (Giele 1979; Lipman-Blumen 1976; Mason et al 1976; Spitze, Huber 1980).

Virtually all texts on marriage and family and most marriage counselors and laypersons describe mate selection in the United States as marked by considerable endogamy by race, age, religion, socioeconomic status, and ethnic identification. They also suggest, either explicitly or implicitly, a positive value to this, since similarity on these values tends to produce similar values, which, in turn, enhances the probability of marital success. Despite the birds-of-a-feather logic, most observers have traditionally stressed the logic of "opposites attract" regarding gender roles, often under the guise of "complementarity of needs." Structural–functional sociologists explicitly mandated such differences as "prerequisites" for marital survival (Parsons 1954; Martinson 1970; Ehrlich 1971). This supposition is also common to helping professionals of the Freudian tradition.

I suggest that the general principle of similarity applies to traits normally associated with gender roles, as well as to other traits; and that communication, understanding, and empathy, as the components of intimacy, are directly related to the overall degree of similarity between spouses, without the traditional exception.

My hypothesis is predicated on a long-standing and substantial body of social-psychological and race-relations research literature often ignored by marriage and family specialists. These research and theoretical traditions all speak of the need for maximal similarity between actors to maintain stable interaction patterns (Blau 1964; Thibault, Kelly 1959; Homans 1974; Dworkin, Dworkin 1982; Pettigrew 1971; Ehrlich 1973; Heider 1958).

Intimacy requires that partners share common goals and values; that they have sufficient common experiences to be able to empathize with each other; that they care about the same things generally. Extensive gender differentiation produces males and females who inhabit radically different worlds (Bernard 1981), share few common experiences, care most about substantially different things, and may not share a common language or mode of communicating (Lakoff 1975). The stoic is scarcely able to communicate feelings symmetrically with an emotionally expressive person. The workers' daily joys and aggravations may be little comprehended by the full-time homemaker with little or no labor-force experience. A rich folklore of jokes depicts a bored husband listening with stupefaction to his wife's account of trials in decorating the bedroom or taking Johnny to the pediatrician. This is complemented by images of a bewildered housewife listening with half an ear to accounts of financial mergers or office politics. More serious are the tales of widows whose husbands *protected* them from practical financial concerns, only to face utter confusion and calamity which emerged after the death of their husband. Perhaps our most common folk image is the old married couple, out to dinner, sitting silently with nothing to say.

As males and females become more similar, they share common worlds, hence common concerns and values—prime requisites for intimacy. When he is more involved in parenting and the household, discussions of wall paper and pediatrician visits are neither foreign nor boring. When she is more involved in the public sphere of life, discussion of work-related issues is no longer baffling. And when she is not perceived as a frail scatterbrain in need of protection, the sometimes-harsh realities of living can be shared by both rather than stoically shouldered by only one.

Younger couples today, and many older ones, are characterized by substantially greater involvement of the wife in the labor force, and somewhat greater involvement of the husband in domestic and especially in parental functions than in previous generations. There is a decreasing perception of wives as requiring "protection" from economic reality. I suspect that couples talk together about a greater range of topics and have more shared experiences on which to understand each other than did their parents and grandparents. I am positing an overall increase in marital intimacy over the past generation. This increased intimacy results primarily from general societal changes that have substantially altered the roles of women, serving in turn to alter those of men in the direction of less gender differentiation. Subsequently, altered roles are reflected in altered interpersonal relations.

THE CASE FOR INCREASED CONFLICT

Traditionally, males and females have had extremely unequal access to the scarce and valued resources of society, and this reflects substantial inequality in the marriage relationship. Law, custom, and religion all granted males almost total authority within the family (Kanowitz 1969 ch 3; Bernard 1972 10). Husbands provided their families with all or nearly all of their economic resources. Superior economic resources undergirded power even in the absence of authority (Blood, Wolfe 1960; Blood 1963). Law, custom, and religion served generally to convince both spouses of the husband's legitimate right to make decisions binding on the wife, as a form of "legitimate power." Lacking such legitimacy, the one who controls the financial resources on which the other depends can usually dominate by threatening to withdraw support or to bribe in a form of "reward power" or "coercive power" (French, Raven 1959). Some males delegate part or much of their authority to the wife in household and childrearing matters, but that which can be delegated can usually be retrieved when the more powerful person chooses (Safilios-Rothschild 1970).

In recent decades, changes in law, custom, and many religions have eroded male authority in the home. Erosion of male power is probably more recent and has resulted mainly from the vast influx of married women into the labor force (Scanzoni, Scanzoni 1976 313). Males still tend to have more say in familial decision making than do their wives. Males won 67 percent of the conflicts according to spouses interviewed separately (Bell et al 1982). Among those couples where only the husband was employed, males won 75 percent of the conflicts, compared to 38 percent where both spouses were employed in the labor force.

Unequal status in any type relationship does not foster honest and open communication and intimacy (Allport 1954; Dworkin, Dworkin 1982; Blau 1964). Those with superior status often believe that trust and openness exists, but as a means of self-protection the relatively powerless develop mechanisms to manipulate the more powerful, to dissemble, to hide things thought to displease their superiors (Lipman-Blumen 1984 30). The more unequal the marital relation, the less intimacy.

Marital inequality does foster relatively low levels of conflict and marital dissolution for two reasons. (1) The bases of marital inequality lie outside the family and in the public domain of law, custom, religion, and the economy. Where women cannot earn a decent livelihood, they are forced to remain in marriage almost regardless of the quality of the marital relationship (Lee 1977 249). Legal restrictions in such societies may make it difficult for them to leave, and custom can make life unpleasant for the divorced women. Such societies are apt to socialize girls to defer to male authority. Friends, relatives, and others are likely to give little sympathy to a wife in conflict with her husband. She is likely to be told to "try harder." Marital failure becomes *her* failure. In this condition, conflicts tend to remain covert or submerged, at least while the husband fulfills his minimal responsibility as provider. (2) There is a positive relation between marital stability and spousal inequality due to the processes by which conflicts that do surface are resolved. With extensive inequality, conflict resolution processes are well defined and simple. The husband may simply assert his authority, or failing that, may exercise his power. Given the wife's limited options, the conflict will typically be resolved readily, subject only to such temporary "rear guard actions" as sulking, denial of sex, or poorly prepared meals.

In recent decades many marriages have become more equalitarian, as wives begin to approximate their husbands in financial contributions, educational attainment, and public-sphere experience. This lays the foundation for increased intimacy. But it also generates more conflict, increases the difficulty of the conflict-resolution process, and enhances the wife's ability to leave and to support herself.

When marriage is not satisfactory, women who can support themselves are much more likely to leave than are those who cannot. Knowing that their wives are or can be self-sufficient may make it easier for some husbands to leave the marriage as well. As more married women participate in the labor force, more divorces can be expected, expedited by changing customs that stigmatize divorced women less than before, and changing laws that facilitate divorce (Kenkel 1977 ch 12; Lee 1977 249). Where wives are more equal to their husbands, they may also have less motive to conceal differences of opinion, resulting in more frequent overt conflicts. Ironically, the very intimacy that equality fosters probably encourages honesty and openness, which demand expression of disagreement as well as support and agreement. Once conflicts emerge, there is no simple resolution process available. Authority is no longer automatically granted to one spouse, and the power resources of spouses who are equal essentially cancel each other out. In such situations, spouses must attempt to influence one another—to convince the other of an appropriate outcome. Given mutual respect, compromise is often the solution, further cementing the marital bond, despite the fact that the process of reaching a compromise may have been arduous. However, compromise is not always possible—a fact that marriage counselors and specialists sometimes overlook.

The resources available to any couple—material, time, and energy—are scarce to a variable degree. They are finite, and are limited in comparison to wants. Given this, just as conflict over scarce resources is ubiquitous at the organizational, community, and societal levels, so it is at the familial level. Both spouses cannot always get what they want, nor will they always be able to reach a compromise equitable to both. There are many instances where conflict is not a zero-sum game, not just in the eyes of the participants, but also in reality. A couple cannot both move for one person's job opportunities and remain stationary to maximize those of the other. They cannot simultaneously spend a sum of money on a computer needed for work purposes by one spouse and a much-needed vacation from work pressures needed by the other. Even among dual-earner families, where income may be increased, material wants may expand to consume or surpass the added financial resources. Nor can a couple simultaneously devote "enough" time and energy to two children, two jobs, a household, and each other, except possibly among an elite few whose joint incomes are so high that all manner of child care and household help can be hired. And it is often not simply a question of the good intentions, communication skills, or maturity of the individuals involved that prevents reasonable compromise. Sometimes, the problem is rooted in the fundamental reality that most people live in a world of scarcity. In such a situation, "compromise" may mean that one or both partners fail to have very basic needs met. And among the dual-earner couples, while financial scarcity may be reduced, the scarcity of time and of energy probably increases markedly (Holmstrom 1976 ch 6).

CONCLUSION

Overt conflict is probably both more frequent and more difficult to resolve in equalitarian relationships, while divorce is more feasible as an alternative. Conversely, intimacy in its fullest sense is probably only possible in such relationships, and the overall level of intimacy is probably greater than in marriages based on extensive gender differentiation and sex inequality.

At the aggregate or societal level, spousal intimacy, conflict, and marital dissolution vary together. This is not to say that at the level of the individual couple, the more intimate the partners, the higher their probability of divorce. It is only to point out the irony that the same set of social forces that produces what most of us define as a social "good"—increased intimacy among spouses—also produces a phenomenon many define as a major social problem—heightened levels of marital conflict and divorce. I seriously doubt whether it will be possible to develop strategies—micro-therapeutic or macropolitical—that can resolve this irony at the societal level. Ultimately, a host of human "goods" rely on freedom and equality, but stability and harmony do not seem to be among them.

REFERENCES

Allport G 1954 *The Nature of Prejudice*. Cambridge MA. Addison Wesley

Bell D, J S Chafetz, L H Horn 1982 Marital conflict resolution: A study of strategies and outcomes. *Journal of Family Issues*. 3 111–131

Bernard J 1972 *The Future of Marriage*. New York. Bantam

1981 *The Female World*. New York. Free Press

Biddle BJ 1976 *Role Theory: Expectations, Identities, and Behaviors*. Chicago. Dryden

Blau P 1964 *Exchange and Power in Social Life*. New York. Wiley

Blood R 1963 The husband–wife relationship. 282–308 F Nye, L Hoffman eds. *The Employed Mother in America*. Chicago. Rand McNally

Blood R, D Wolfe 1960 *Husbands and Wives*. New York. Macmillan

Chafetz J S 1978 *Masculine/Feminine or Human?* Itasca Illinois. Peacock

Chafetz J S 1984 *Sex and Advantage*. Totowa NJ. Rowman Allenheld

Cox F D 1978 *Human Intimacy: Marriage, the Family and its Meaning*. St Paul MN. West

Dworkin A G, R Dworkin 1982 *The Minority Report*. New York. Holt Rinehart Winston

Ehrlich C 1971 The male sociologists' burden: The place of women in marriage and family texts. *Journal of Marriage & Family*. 33 431–450

Ehrlich H J 1973 *The Social Psychology of Prejudice*. New York. Wiley

French J, B Raven 1959 The bases of social power. 150–167 D Cartwright ed. *Studies in Social Power*. Ann Arbor MI. Michigan U. Press

Giele J Z 1979 Changing sex roles and family structure. *Social Policy* 9 32–43

Heider F 1958 *The Psychology of Interpersonal Relations*. New York. Wiley

Heilbrun A 1976 Measurement of masculine and feminine sex role identities as independent dimensions. *Journal of Consulting & Clinical Psychology* 44 183–190

Holmstrom L L 1972 *The Two-Career Family*. Cambridge MA. Schenkman

Homans G C 1974 *Social Behavior: Its Elementary Forms*. New York. Harcourt Brace Jovanovich

Kanowitz L 1969 *Women and the Law*. Albuquerque. New Mexico U. Press

Kenkel W F 1977 *The Family in Perspective*. Santa Monica CA. Goodyear

Kieffer C 1977 New depths in intimacy. 267–293 R Libby, R Whitehurst eds. *Marriage and Alternatives: Exploring Intimate Relationships*. Glenview IL. Scott Foresman

Lakoff R 1975 *Language and Woman's Place*. New York. Harper & Row

Lee G R 1977 *Family Structure and Interaction*. Philadelphia. Lippincott

Lewis R, G B Spanier 1979 Theorizing about the quality and stability of marriage. 268–294 W Burr ed. *Contemporary Theories About the Family*. New York. Macmillan

Lipman-Blumen J 1976 Implications of family structure on changing sex roles. *Social Casework* 57 67–79

Lipman-Blumen J 1984 *Gender Roles and Power*. Englewood Cliffs NJ. Prentice-Hall

Martinson F M 1970 *Family in Society*. New York. Dodd Mead

Mason K O, J Czajka, S Arber 1976 Change in United States women's sex role attitudes, 1964–1974. *American Sociological Review* 41 573–596

Parsons T 1954 Age and sex in the social structure of the United States. 89–103 *Essays in Social Theory*. New York. Free Press of Glencoe

Pettigrew T F 1971 *Racially Separate or Together?* New York. McGraw Hill

Safilios-Rothschild C 1970 The study of family power structure: A review 1960–1969. *Journal of Marriage & Family* 32 539–551; 80–90 C Broderick ed. *A Decade of Family Research and Action.* Minneapolis. National Council of Family Relations

Sanday R R 1974 Female status in the public domain. 189–206 M Rosaldo, L Lamphere eds. *Women, Culture and Society.* Stanford CA. Stanford U. Press

Scanzoni L, J Scanzoni 1976 *Men, Women, and Change: A Sociology of Marriage and Family.* New York. McGraw Hill

Spitze G, J Huber 1980 Changing attitudes toward woman's non-family role 1938 to 1978. *Sociology of Work & Occupation* 7 317–335

Thibault J W, H H Kelly 1959 *The Social Psychology of Groups.* New York. Wiley

Williams J, S Bennett 1975 The definition of sex stereotypes via the adjective check list. *Sex Roles* 1 327–337

Motherhood: Contemporary Conflict for Women

MICHELE HOFFNUNG

The power of ideology is demonstrated forcefully in the contemporary concept of motherhood. We all know about motherhood —or, at least, we think we know. We hold a set of assumptions and beliefs that is founded on the premise that the mother–child unit is basic, universal, and psychologically most suited for both the healthy development of the child and the fulfillment of the mother. "The experts have no doubts: they are unanimous in their statement that only the mother, and no one else, should take care of her child. No other question is answered so definitely and plainly. The mother is the person to look after her child."[1] Since raising children is useful work, necessary for the continuation of society, satisfying to human generative impulses, and highly valued in the lives of women who mother, it is easy for us to believe these "experts" and to accept the motherhood mystique.

Yet mothering within this narrow definition conflicts with other important aspects of women's lives—productive work, companionate marriage, economic independence. Mothering is done at home, outside the world of achievement, power, and money. It consequently pulls women who mother away from the public world back into the private world, for at least part of their adult lives.

It is this aspect of motherhood—its limiting effect on women's public participation at a time when women have won access to the public world— that must inform the next stages of feminist activity for social change. It is not enough for women to be able to do men's work as well as women's; it is necessary to reconsider the value of mothering and to reorder public priorities so that caring for children counts in and adds to the lives of women and men. Until children are valued members of society and child care is considered work important enough to be done by both men and women, the special burdens and benefits of motherhood will keep women in second place.

Mothering has not always been the same. Recent work by social historians indicates that our modern notion of motherhood has its roots in the nineteenth century.

> The most important function of the morally superior nineteenth-century woman was bearing and raising children. In the Victorian period motherhood came to have the emotional and semisacred connotations that tempt one to write it with a capital "M." The mother's task was to care for her children physically, preserve their moral innocence, protect them from evil influences, and inspire them to pursue the highest spiritual values. If woman failed in this duty, she jeopardized the whole progress of civilization, an awesome responsibility indeed. . . . This glorification of motherhood and exaggeration of its responsibilities was as new an element in Anglo-American culture as the opinion that females were particularly virtuous. Indeed, the two ideas evolved together and reinforced one another in eighteenth and nineteenth century thought.[2]

Prior to this glorification of motherhood by the nineteenth-century middle class, the bearing and rearing of children was integrated into the other work women did and was not women's most important work. In a subsistence farm economy, survival required women as well as men to place productive work before reproductive concerns. Women and men worked side by side, in and around the home. Women were responsible for food and clothing production for the family, which involved many complicated skills, as well as cooking, laundering, cleaning, and child care.[3] Infants were tended when possible, and were sometimes played with, but were never the center of their mothers' attention. Their care was largely the task of older siblings. Those children who survived infancy quickly took their places in the social and economic life of the family.[4]

Industrialization simultaneously disrupted the unity of home and workshop, decreased patriarchal power, and devalued women's work within the family. Life in industrial society is characterized by distinct separations: work from play, production from reproduction, adulthood from childhood. Adults work, children play. Work takes place in the office or factory, relaxation in the home. Activities outside the home are done for money; inside the home, activities are done for love. Within this new set of values, which emerged during the nineteenth century, women were assigned to the home as nonproducing housewives. In this context, mother-work became the focus of their attention. As work transformed into wage labor in factory or office, the family took on new meaning. It became a refuge, the place to which dad and kids would come to recover from the pressure and pain of alienated work and school.[5] The burden of providing the comforts of home was assigned to women.

The combination of homemaking and child care was a full-time job, but it carried none of the economic benefits that employment outside the home provided. Although these reproductive tasks were more physically demanding in days gone by, they were not severed from the productive work of the family or imbued with heavy psychological significance. In contrast to the economic value of women's work in the past, today a woman's devotion to "women's work" makes her dependent on the people she tends. It results in an economic dependence on her husband—a man chosen for love—and a psychological dependence on her children as products of her mothering.

Other historic changes have also made more choices possible for women. Prior to the nineteenth century, abstinence was the only effective method of controlling fertility.[6] Technological improvements and political struggles have made contraception relatively safe, effective, and available in the twentieth century. With the repeal of restrictive birth-control legislation in the 1960s, heterosexual intimacy is no longer inseparable from maternity. Although worldwide most babies are still unplanned,[7] in our country the birth rate has been decreasing steadily since 1880;[8] in the last two decades alone, the fertility rate of American women has fallen more than 50 percent.[9] Women have made a dramatic choice to have fewer children, to end their childbearing earlier, or to start their families later.

This steady decrease in the births per woman reflects more than the availability of contraception. It also reflects a perception on the part of more women that life has exciting and rewarding experiences to offer in addition to childbearing, and that these are within their reach. "Decreased fertility rates are a consequence of increased educational and occupational aspirations and pressures by women. To regulate her reproductive life a woman must also come to believe that it is morally right to control her own body and she must acquire knowledge regarding how best and most safely to so do."[10]

These increased educational and occupational opportunities are also consequences of economic and political changes. Although sex differences persist in education, today girls, like boys, are educated to compete to get ahead, to believe in and strive for individual success—first in school and then in a competitive labor market—and to value persistent independence. Coeducation, contraception, and the need for wage laborers have promoted the integration of women into the economic system; feminism has promoted the integration of women into the political system. At the same time, women are still trained to be the foundation of the family as wives and mothers. The nineteenth-century notion that "women's place is in the home" lingers on as "women's *essential* place is in the home."

PSYCHOLOGICAL CONFLICT AND MATERIAL COST

There are two sets of expectations for women. There are those made possible by industrialization—individuality, successful accomplishment, equality. Then there are those born of the patriarchal tradition—the public domain belongs to men, wives and their services belong to their husbands, and family life is the responsibility of women. Although these expectations conflict, the conflict is not always acute. Most girls learn to compartmentalize, to keep separate the feelings associated with achievement from those associated with femininity, and to handle the two as mutually exclusive.[11] Separation is one strategy for coping with essentially contradictory expectations.[12] Indeed, the very structure of modern life makes this distinction appear "natural." Girls succeed in school; then, at home, as daughters and sisters, they assist in feminine pursuits.

Daughters are encouraged to prepare for work, but they are also expected to become mothers later. Through school, during the early years on a job, or in a childless marriage, middle-class women may notice contradictions, feel anger about sex discrimination at work or about unequal responsibility for housework at home, or feel guilt about their shortcomings; but to a large extent they can manage to fulfill both sets of expectations.

The selection of a career, however, expresses clearly the consequences of this contradiction. Almost all college women expect to work at some time in their lives, almost all desire marriage and children, and almost all stress the centrality of family life to their future plans. The way they accomplish this goal is by remaining flexible in their career choices. For men, career is the central choice; by contrast, Shirley Angrist and Elizabeth Almquist, in a study of college women, found that

> choices are not so concrete, not so specific, and far from wide-ranging. The extreme changeability of occupational choices, the lack of decisiveness in their plans, the resort to a short list of predominately "women's" fields, the tendency to postpone a definite choice and to vacillate—all these tell us that while [women] students perceive pressure to make decisions about their post-college lives, the particular occupation chosen is only one and perhaps not even the central component of their thinking about the future.[13]

In a recent study of Barnard College undergraduates, Mirra Komarovsky found that occupation was an important part of these young women's self-image; the students were highly motivated to find high-status and high-paying occupations. Almost all wanted motherhood as well; 85 percent said they wished in fifteen years to be married career women with children. In spite of the increased importance of career, however, these women students exhibited indecision and dramatic shifts in occupational decision making similar to that found by Angrist and Almquist.[14]

In interviews with thirty middle-class suburban women who had at least one preschool child, I found that those who remembered having career aspirations as children were those who were employed.[15] Their particular fields of employment, however, were not necessarily related to their early aspirations or to their academic training. Most of them wanted to work, but, for most, family responsibilities came first, so work had been adjusted. Some had enjoyed working, had stopped to raise their children, and were considering career changes when they returned to the ranks of the employed in the future. Others had given up careers (such as teaching) for jobs (such as waitressing) while their children were small. Still others had continued their careers while tending their children with the help of their husbands, paid mother substitutes, or day-care centers. Yet in every case there were signs of job flexibility on the part of the employed mothers. They had rearranged hours, or changed jobs, or changed pace to encompass the demands of children as well as work. Faced with the two sets of expectations at the same time, they had readjusted work.

Both work and family require emotional investment, time, and energy;

there are many external and internal pressures that push women to devote their major energies to the family. As a result, women often shy away from commitment to high-powered careers. As mothers, they often are employed outside their homes, but they select jobs around the scheduling needs of their families rather than according to their own career development.

The conflict between individual achievement and feminine responsibility, therefore, is not just internal. It places constraints on women's commitment to employment. It pushes women to limit the careers they consider possible to less lucrative female occupations, to give up what they have accomplished for mother-work, or to spread themselves very thin. The resulting part-time or intermittent employment patterns contribute to the large wage differential between women and men.[16] Motherhood, as we know it, has substantial material costs for women.

Infant care is a twenty-four-hour-a-day job. Although no particular part of it is especially difficult, child-centered care is constantly demanding. The feeding, bathing, and laundry routine involves a lot of physical labor. Beyond the child's infancy or with additional children, the job becomes much more difficult. For women who have been working, as most women have before their first child is born,[17] the changes from a work schedule to being in demand constantly, from adult to infant company, from feeling competent to feeling like a novice require a great deal of adjustment. Although many mothers try, few accomplish this transition without suffering tension, depression, or emotional trauma. Postpartum depression is one of the first signs of difficulty. The excitement and rewards of the new mothering role partially offset the disruption. Motherhood, a very special aspect of being a woman, opens up the joy of intimate contact with a growing, developing infant, the sense of importance that nurturing holds for most women, and the personal growth that comes from facing and mastering a new developmental stage. Modern mothering ideals, however, require selflessness from women who have been socialized by their experiences at school and at work to be selves. This conflict of values is why the early mothering years are characterized by pain and conflict.

The difficulties are heightened by the fact that, while many lofty phrases are penned in tribute to mother-work, that work is accorded very low prestige. Our society values money, power, and achievement, none of which are associated with child care.[18] Women who are used to achieving in their own right and earning their own paychecks become defined as someone's wife and someone's mother. They also become financially dependent on the income of their husbands. Later, when the children leave home, there are new costs. Mothers still have half or more of their lives ahead of them, but their "priority" role, raising the children, is over.[19] Their years of full-time work in the home leave them unprepared for life after active mothering; their work skills are rusty, their training is dated, and they are unsure of themselves. Alternatively, mothers who choose to continue their employment face the difficulties peculiar to this option: double demands, two jobs at once, and guilt.

Mother-work, therefore, extracts a great cost from women. Although it carries heavy responsibility, it brings none of the material rewards of employment. It is demeaned and trivialized in the mass media, which use it to sell a multitude of housekeeping products. It is not integrated with productive work; rather, it conflicts with work or career, thereby limiting a woman's independence, achievement, earnings, and status.[20]

THE MOTHERHOOD MYSTIQUE

Motherhood, as we know it, is only one possible child-rearing arrangement. It has the aura, however, of being "natural" and unchanging. Because of this aura, our contemporary definition has been referred to as the *motherhood mystique*.[21] It has four aspects: (1) ultimate fulfillment *as a woman* is achieved be becoming a mother; (2) the body of work assigned to mothers—caring for child, home, and husband—fits together in a noncontradictory manner; (3) to be a good mother, a woman must like being a mother and all the work that goes with it; (4) a woman's intense, exclusive devotion to mothering is good for her children.

Becoming a mother introduces a woman into a new league, the league of "real" women. Once a pregnancy begins to show, women who may never have spoken to the expectant mother before become friendly and offer helpful advice. Giving birth proves womanhood, as combat proves manhood. Successful combat, however, requires physical training and intellectual rigor; successful birth requires only conception and the unfolding of the physiological processes. Endeavors that a woman has been devoted to for years tend to be overlooked in the general excitement created by pregnancy and birth. Hospitals and families act as though all else the woman has done or been is now unimportant; being a mother will absorb her, interest her, and define her.[22] This is very different from the view of fathers, who are expected to be interested in and delighted by their children but whose other interests and employment are expected to continue. This aspect of the motherhood mystique is a denial of a woman as a multifaceted person.

In spite of strong social approval for childbearing, women find that giving birth does not provide ultimate fulfillment. Fulfillment comes not from the experience of a biological event, but rather from development of and dedication to values, interests, and competencies over time. Nor does giving birth ensure a perfect relationship with a new and perfect being. Relationships are never perfect and always require time and energy. The gap between many a new mother's expectations of fulfillment and the reality of exhaustion and distraction is often shocking. Whereas almost everybody gets excited about pregnancy and birth, no one gets excited about colicky babies and dirty diapers. After being the center of attention during labor and delivery, a new mother soon finds herself very much alone at home. The birth of a first child is, therefore, "an event causing the greatest discontinuity of personality in American middle-class women," especially if the birth is not followed by full-time involvement outside the home.[23]

The second aspect of the motherhood mystique is the assumption that care of the child, home, and husband consists of complementary roles. For middle-class women this is not true; conflict exists among the roles of

mother, homemaker, and wife. Although couples usually expect the birth of
their baby to enhance their relationship, in fact the first baby's birth has
been shown to cut conversation time between parents almost in half and to
shift the topics of conversation from the parents' relationship, their inner
feelings, or sex, to the child. The two become parents first and marriage
partners second.[24] The child becomes the focus of the wife's attention, often
causing the husband to resent being ousted from first place in her consideration. There is conflict between the needs and demands of children for
attention, their noise, and their activity, and a husband's need for order,
peace, and food at the end of a workday. In addition, the modern companionate marriage assumes a strong common bond between husband and wife
in the preparental stage. The traditional wife–mother–homemaker and
husband–father–breadwinner division of labor that often follows the birth
of the first child dramatically changes the former quasiegalitarian relationship between the parents. With the child come new problems, worries, and
inner conflicts, and because their roles are now so different the husband and
wife are often pulled apart. Some of the role changes bring tension. The wife
may envy the husband's freedom. The husband may feel additional financial
pressure and envy his wife's self-regulated schedule.

In a study of infant care in which more than 700 mothers of infants
were interviewed, John and Elizabeth Newson found significant dissatisfaction with the mother role among middle-class women in Nottingham, England.[25] These women expected to be social assets to their husbands. Babies
and young children, however, interfered with this goal by disturbing the
cleanliness of their homes, their intellectual pursuits, and their previously
well-ordered lives. Mary Boulton also found differences between white middle-class and working-class English families in their expectations of the
conjugal relationships. Middle-class mothers expected companionate marriages and less sex-typed division of labor, and were less happy with the
marital changes that children brought. In both groups, however, the husbands' degree of help and of understanding had a str ng positive influence
on the women's experience of motherhood.[26]

Motherhood, therefore, is a complicated set of roles that results in
ambivalent feelings on the part of women. There are the love, intimacy, and
caring that make it personal, intense, and special, but there are also the very
real changes in women's bodies, free time, work, and marriage relationships.
This leads to conflicting feelings in most mothers: feelings of intense need
and suffocation; of sublime selflessness and supreme selfishness.[27]

Since the third aspect of the motherhood mystique is that, to be a good
mother, a woman must like being a mother, ambivalent feelings lead to guilt
and worry about mothering adequacy. Angela McBride writes of "the anger-
depression-guilt-go-round" that is a "normal-crazy" part of the motherhood
experience.[28] As people, women have different personalities, talents, and
temperaments, but as mothers they are expected to be continually patient,
even-tempered, and consistent. When they fail to meet these impossible
expectations, they fear that they are bad mothers, that they are failing their
children. In the past, when child care was not expected to be the focus of a
mother's life, there was less self-consciousness and guilt associated with the

role. Now women turn to experts—pediatricians, psychologists, social workers—to tell them what to do, and try to measure their behavior in terms of the pundits' advice.[29] The whole experience becomes more tormented and less satisfying; it loses the spontaneity and genuine warmth of unmediated intimate relations.

This self-conscious, guilt-ridden striving might be justified if the fourth aspect of the mystique—that exclusive, full-time mothering is best for child development—were true, but that is not at all clear. Having one person on twenty-four-hour duty is not optimal for meeting the developmental needs of a child. The most even-tempered mother will at times be tired, self-absorbed, occupied with other things, or under the weather. The child is then subject to adult anger, annoyance, or inattention when she or he may have real needs. On the other hand, when mom feels chipper, she may shower attention on the child at a time when the child needs most to be left alone. Assigning child care to a single adult leaves both the adult and the child subject to the needs, feelings, and demands of the other without relief. Children are consequently overmothered and undermothered by turns. When mothers feel guilty or worried, they pour attention on their children; when they feel angry or preoccupied, there is no one else to whom the child can turn. In each situation, the children are bound into the personality dynamics of the mothers. "The result of the exclusiveness of the mother–child relationship is that no one can prevent this relationship from becoming too narrow. It makes personality absorption practically unavoidable."[30]

This is the aspect of the mother–child relationship that has led to the concept of "momism." *Momism* has become a catchword for blaming a mother for living out her needs through her children, for being overbearing and overabsorbing.[31] Blaming mom, however, is blaming the victim. Because a mother gives up so much to be a mother, because she is educated and achievement-oriented, because there is so little family or community support for the contemporary mother, the child has come to mean too much to her. The child cannot grow freely but must succeed for the mother, to show that she has done a good job and that her sacrifices have been worth it. Since a woman often puts aside any personal ambition for motherhood, the child may be expected to succeed in her stead, to act out her ambitions for her. Or the child may become a substitute for them, a product she can be proud of as well as a child. The workplace values of achievement and success are extended to the kin relationship.

Women sacrifice to do what is "best" for their children, but it simply is not best.

> The way we institutionalize motherhood in our society—assigning sole responsibility for child care to the mother, cutting her off from the easy help of others in an isolated household, requiring round-the-clock tender, loving care, and making such care her exclusive activity—is not only unique, but not even a good way for either women or—if we accept as criterion the amount of maternal warmth shown—for children. It may, in fact, be the worst. It is as though we had selected the worst features of all the ways motherhood is structured around the world and combined them to produce our current design.[32]

A longitudinal study of New York City and suburban families with moms at home and dads at work clearly demonstrates this point. Sylvia Brody and Sidney Axelrod found that very few women "mothered adequately." Adequate mothering required mothers who were emotionally stable *and* educated *and* not distressed by their economic conditions *and* who had satisfactory marriages. As we know, most mothers do not have all these advantages. The majority of the mothers they studied did not, and these mothers almost had "to ignore signs of distress in the child, to make too hasty judgments of the child's behavior, or to rationalize that it is the child's unalterable nature to act as he does."[33]

THE CONTEMPORARY PROBLEM

In spite of the contradictions, most women want to be mothers and most mothers want at least two children.[34] The contemporary problem is how to fit motherhood into their lives without relinquishing their other activities, or narrowing their ambitions. Women have many reasons for wanting children — liking for children, desiring to experience pregnancy and childbirth, demonstrating being an adult, establishing a family like their family of origin, resolving an uncertain identity, conforming to social expectations. Some of these have to do with pronatalist social pressure — pressure from family, church, and media that pushes women to have children.[35] Liberation for women means freedom from the single, socially assigned role of mother, freedom to choose whether to be mothers. But self-fulfillment for most contemporary women includes a sexual relationship and motherhood as well as ego-creative work that expresses individuality.[36] Motherhood is a very limited choice, if a woman must accept the entire motherhood mystique, which denies the importance of nonmaternal pursuits. The contemporary question is: How can motherhood be organized so that it will be better for both women and children than is currently the case?

There is a related problem for men. In this world of largely contractual work relationships, the responsibility for nurturing one's offspring — some of the time — has its special rewards. Being in intimate physical and emotional contact with a child develops a father's loving and caring feelings, establishes a closeness between himself and his child, and keeps him in tune with the experiences of his child's mother. Our current assignment of childrearing responsibilities denies these rewards to men. In addition, changing the "exclusive mother" ideal can relieve some of the pressure on a couple to switch from shared roles before the birth of a child to the sex-stereotyped roles discussed earlier when the first child is born.

Given the biological demands of pregnancy and lactation, however, as well as the historical connection between mothers and children, it would be a mistake to take the focus off mothers while examining the problems of childrearing. How can a mother fit childrearing into her life? A good place to begin the examination is with the last generation of mothers. Pauline Bart, in a pioneering study of depression in middle-aged women, found that it was "women who play the traditional feminine role — who are housewives, are not aggressive, are centered on their children, who in short, have 'bought' the cultural proscriptions—who are most prone to depression when their children leave."[37] Utilizing anthropological and epidemiological data, as well as interviews with twenty hospitalized middle-aged women, she found that overinvolved and overprotective relationships with their children could be pathological for mothers in middle age.

"Today's midlife women had lived by the old rules—rules that promised [a woman] kudos, congratulations, and fulfillment of self for giving up her own life to meet her responsibilities to others."[38] Lillian Rubin conducted a series of interviews with normal middle-aged women who had devoted themselves to the responsibilities of childrearing and now were in the post-parental stage of the lives. Rubin found that the women were unprepared for life after children; neither they nor their husbands had looked ahead. The problems of these midlife women suggest a way of considering the issue of motherhood for young women. Active mothering is a stage in life, not an ultimate fulfillment or a lifelong job. Women's life expectancies are long, family size is typically small, and children grow up and move away. Young women must prepare for satisfying employment and must not consider childrearing their life work. As one of Rubin's interviewees said, "motherhood self-destructs in twenty years."[39]

Louise Kapp Howe has identified three major employment patterns that women follow after leaving school. The first is to work for a few years and then to give up employment and become a homemaker. This pattern used to be the dominant one. The second is to follow the same pattern as men, to begin work after leaving school and to continue working until retirement. This pattern is most frequent among women who have no children, black women, and women in professional and managerial careers. The third pattern is to work until having children, take time off to raise them, and then return or try to return to work. The time off for full-time mothering used to be five to ten years, but the interval has been getting shorter. This is the pattern that has grown the fastest during this century.[40]

Kathleen Gerson argues, however, that a growing percentage of young women (those born after 1944) are joining the work force with a commitment that resembles that of male workers; namely, "steady, long-term, full-time workplace attachment." The career woman, whether she combines motherhood and employment or forgoes motherhood, is no longer unusual.[41] Based on conversations with my college students and teenaged children and their friends, contemporary young women do expect to have careers.

Clearly, several life plans are possible. Each has its attendant problems; only choosing to be childless avoids this conflict.

The women Lillian Rubin spoke with, who had devoted themselves to full-time mothering, had many fears and doubts to overcome in going to work. They also had to deal with resistance on the part of their husbands and the lack of interesting, challenging, decently paying jobs for inexperienced middle-aged women.[42] Women may reduce these problems somewhat by planning to work in the future, but staying home full-time for twenty or so years to tend to the needs of others is not good preparation for successful accomplishment in much of the public world.[43] It tracks women into service jobs, extensions of mothering, when they are ready for employment. This path of "family first, then career" has been a difficult one for women to follow, in part because these women have not planned ahead. I suspect it will become even more difficult to follow when women do plan ahead, because it will push them to get childbearing out of the way early, and that decision has been shown to have particularly limiting effects on women's educational and occupational achievement.[44] In practice, first births are rarely planned; I found that when they were planned it was usually in conjunction with an active career, never with a future one.[45]

Establishing a career and then taking time out works well for some women. It is this option that attracts many women to teaching or nursing, because these careers offer some flexibility for fitting in families. For many women, however, it is frustrating and boring to be home once they have established a career, and many careers (particularly those that are less traditionally "female") do not allow for a time-off period long enough to raise a child or two to school age. This pattern of career choice results in severe limitation of the areas of women's public participation to a few sex-stereotyped jobs.

Many contemporary mothers are living out the "both" option; they cannot or do not choose to stay home with their young children. Since World War II, there has been a dramatic shift in the patterns of employment for married women in the United States. Before 1940, if a woman worked, she did so prior to marriage. After 1940, married women in their late thirties started to return to work.[46] In recent years, this trend for married women to be in the labor force has expanded to include women with children, even women with preschool children. In 1985, 61 percent of married mothers with children under eighteen were in the labor force, and 54 percent of married mothers with at least one child under six were in the labor force. Of divorced, widowed, and never-married mothers, 68 percent with children under eighteen were in the labor force; and 53 percent with at least one child under six were in the labor force.[47] For a variety of reasons, more than half the mothers with preschoolers are now employed.

When midlife comes and children go, women who have jobs or careers are better prepared for the postparental stage of life. But, during the years when a woman simultaneously works and cares for a young family, her life is physically demanding and involves constant compromise. Mothers who work full-time report more hassles with work, family, achievement, and individual concerns than do other mothers, although the reported intensity of their hassles is no greater.[48] In the past, the extended family—primarily grandmothers and aunts—shared child care, providing variety for children and relief, as well as sociability, for mothers, but today many families are geographically isolated from relatives. When female relatives are nearby, women often have their help, but they then have less help from their husbands.[49]

The most pressing problem for working mothers is lack of time—there are more tasks to be done than there are hours in the day. Working mothers have less leisure time than do other adults, full-time mothers, fathers, or nonparents. They have child-care help during their working hours, but they continue to do housework—research indicates that they have no more paid household help than do full-time mothers. The amount of paid household help a family has appears to depend on the husband's income, not on the wife's employment status. In other words, when the husband's salary is high, the couple is more likely to hire help than they are when it is low, regardless of whether the wife has a job or is a full-time homemaker.[50]

Families in which fathers are present have the option of sharing responsibilities between husband and wife. There is considerable evidence that, when the wife is employed, the husband does more house and child care than when the wife is home, although he does not do half of this work. Kathryn Walker found that husbands of working wives assisted one to three hours per day, whereas the wives spent four to eight hours on housework.[51] I found that husbands of working mothers took more responsibility for child care than did those of nonemployed mothers; most helped, and a few shared the responsibility. None of the husbands of nonemployed mothers shared responsibility, and some did not help either.[52] Joseph Pleck found that the full-time employed wife's share of the domestic tasks was three times as great as that of her full-time employed husband.[53] Although the father will often help, the working mother is typically the one responsible for making the arrangements and assigning the tasks. She usually has the "executive decision-making responsibilities over child and family matters."[54] And, of course, many working mothers have no husbands.

Although many fathers help, child care and housework are done for the most part by women, mothers, or mother substitutes. Women choosing or being forced by circumstances to do "both" are faced with serious constraints. A few have the option of hiring a full-time housekeeper–mother substitute to keep household and child well tended, while they vigorously pursue their careers. This is the female equivalent to having a wife.[55] Many others give their careers less than they would if they did not have a family to care for as well.[56] Lydia O'Donnell has distinguished between "labor-force attachment" and "labor-force involvement." She found that the seventy-four mothers in her study limited their employment so that they could continue to spend time with their children. They saw paid work as playing a limited role in their lives. They were "involved" but not "attached."[57] In an earlier study, Poloma interviewed fifty-two married women doctors, lawyers, and professors and found that they rejected the view of themselves as "career" women. They experienced very little strain between their professional and family roles because they routinely resolved any role conflicts in favor of home.[58] In these studies, we see employed women whose commitment is first and foremost to family.

Nonetheless, many mothers do work and many are committed to careers. For women who are in professional and managerial jobs, the time pressures are even more intense. These careers are structured for the lives that men lead; they assume that one is not hampered by home and child-care responsibilities. They require enormous time and energy, as well as the flexibility to leave work late or to come in early. Such demands conflict with the needs of a family. Professional and managerial women report major concern over conflicts between their careers and children. Their concerns include fatigue, emotional depletion, and, in many cases, guilt.

Not all career commitments are consistent with active mothering or fathering. An active parent must be willing to give up some of the other pursuits that engage adults, at least for a while. This continues to be a major barrier to women's achievement. There is no reason, however, why only mothers should be active parents.

A QUESTION OF VALUES

The role of mother brings with it benefits as well as limitations. Children affect parents in ways that lead to personal growth, enable reworking of childhood conflicts, build flexibility and empathy, and provide intimate, loving human connections. "Little People are more curious than cautious," they expand their caretakers' worlds by their activity levels, their imaginations, and their inherently appealing natures.[59] Although motherhood is not enough to fill an entire life, for most mothers it is one of the most meaningful experiences in their lives.

The option that most reduces the costs for young women who want to be mothers is to prepare to combine work and family. Accepting the continuing importance of employment in their lifetimes enables women to take their career choices and training seriously, to select mates who are more inclined to share the responsibility of family care, and to resist the pressures of the motherhood mystique. This option provides the most opportunity for women, men, and children. It is also the option most associated with better health for women. Women with several key roles, such as employment, marriage, and parenthood, are more likely to be healthy than are women with few roles. Multiple roles provide more privileges, more resources, and more avenues for self-esteem and social involvement. Women without multiple key roles are more subject to boredom, social isolation, and stress. Employment is the single most important factor. Employed women have the best health; full-time homemakers have the worst health.[60]

For women, relinquishing sole responsibility for childrearing and family care is necessary if they are to become equal participants in the productive activities of the public world. By defining ultimate fulfillment for women through maternity, the motherhood mystique limits all women, not just mothers, to secondary status outside the home; maternal responsibilities, or potential ones, are always expected to come first. When mothers reject the mystique, and take their productive lives as seriously as they do their family responsibilities, they help to create a different view of women.

For women to do this, however, men must change as well. Fathers must be more active as caretaking parents. Sharing responsibility for both family life and financial support enables men to be closer to their children, less at the mercy of their employers, and better friends with their wives. In fact, many critics of the masculine sex-role stereotype consider that "being with children and joining in the immediacy of their emotional life may be a route toward reclaiming the spontaneous emotional awareness that . . . masculine training drove into hiding so long ago."[61]

Children, perhaps, will gain the most if they are released from their intense one-to-one relationships with their mothers. Having two, or more, involved caretakers broadens a child's experience and makes him or her less dependent on a single personality.[62] Nurture by men, as well as by women, can alter the formation of sex-typed personality structures in young children that have been associated with exclusively women-nurtured girls and boys.[63] Two caretaking parents provide the child with a more accessible dad and a more balanced view of mom.

Many individual women and couples have forged ahead and have created their own alternatives. They split shifts, or job share, or find good day care, or form cooperatives with other couples like themselves.[64] For the most part, however, women have been trapped. They have borne the burden of rearing their children, because as individuals they lacked the insight or resources to alter the traditional arrangement.

Support services for parents of young children, fathers, and mothers, are needed. Nonprofit, neighborhood-based child-care centers, flex-time work schedules, and reliable after-school programs are a few solutions that have been implemented in some places. But there is no way to accomplish these changes on a large scale without an accompanying change in social values.[65] Our society does not value children. Children are viewed as enjoyable objects, necessary to complete a family, but not as valuable or inspiring members of society. There is little recognition on the part of adult society that children contribute something special to the family, the neighborhood, and the community. Children traditionally were valuable as additional productive members of the family; now they are costly. Women traditionally had few options outside of marriage and motherhood, but they were important economic contributors to the family. Now women have more options, but there is no place for kids in the lives of two independent spouses—unless they share responsibilities or hire a nanny. That situation requires a change in social values.

WHAT IS TO BE DONE

Changing social values is necessary, but it hardly serves as an answer to women who are now facing or contemplating motherhood. While there is accumulating evidence that employed mothers feel better about themselves, report more satisfaction with their lives, and have higher self-esteem than do their nonemployed counterparts, it is helpful to consider what factors contribute to the satisfactory combination of work and family roles.[66]

A woman's attitude toward her work is perhaps most important. Women who are more deeply committed to the work force seem to be more satisfied with their jobs. They also have high self-esteem and attach importance to intrinsic aspects of their work, viewing it as a source of enrichment.[67] They consider their employment a legitimate priority.

Family support is another important factor. Women with families supportive of their employment report greater job satisfaction, whereas women who perceive their husbands to be unfavorable toward their working report less job satisfaction, as do those whose children are unfavorable. Husbands' and children's attitudes, not surprisingly, are correlated.[68] Unfavorable family attitudes result in more conflict between home and work responsibilities.

Child care is the most important support service employed mothers require. Mothers with high-quality, reliable child care are content; those without it are subject to anxiety and guilt.[69] Whether the child care is provided in the form of a baby sitter, a neighbor's home, a licensed home, or a day-care center, when the mother is comfortable with the style of care, she has little guilt or regret.

Women who are career-oriented do not necessarily fit the stereotype of absent, uninvolved mothers. Nor are they generally less family-oriented than are their homebound counterparts. In a recent study comparing working and nonworking mothers of infants, both groups saw the mother role as important. They differed in the predictable directions, however, in *how* important they considered the homemaker role and the work role. They also differed in their perceptions of their children's needs. Career-oriented working mothers were less anxious than were home mothers about separation from their infants, were only moderately apprehensive about alternate care, and were unlikely to believe that infant distress at separation was due to their absence.[70] Career-oriented women consider their need to work as legitimate, which places the needs of their families in a somewhat different light. This, with support from their families, enables them to reduce the amount of conflicting responsibilities at home and at work and consequently to increase their life satisfaction.

In a recent effort to understand how women cope effectively in the "male" professions, Janet Gray distributed questionnaires to 232 married women doctors, lawyers, and professors. She found that these women took their careers very seriously. They worked hard to avoid limiting their professional involvement. Five of the coping strategies that they reported using were positively related to satisfaction with their lives. First was having family members share household tasks. Second was reducing standards within certain roles, such as standards of household cleanliness. Third was careful scheduling and organizing of activities. Fourth was having family members help to resolve conflicts between roles. And fifth was considering personal interests important. Strategies that were negatively related to satisfaction were eliminating roles, keeping roles totally separate, attempting to meet fully all expectations, overlapping roles, and having no conscious strategy for dealing with role conflicts. Almost all the women studied felt that the rewards of combining career and family were well worth the associated strain.[71]

Social values have to change if motherhood is to be a less conflictual part of women's lives, as do the values of individual women and men. Rejecting stereotypical roles and relationships, and putting careers and family—as well as husband and wife—on more equal footing, can make the both options more successful. These changes can reduce, although they cannot eliminate, the costs of motherhood for contemporary women.

NOTES

1. Jan Hendrick van den Berg, *Dubious Maternal Affection* (Pittsburgh: Duquesne University Press, 1972), 9–10.

2. Barbara Harris, "Careers, Conflict, and Children: The Legacy of the Cult of Domesticity," in Alan Roland and Barbara Harris, eds., *Career and Motherhood: Struggles for a New Identity* (New York: Human Sciences Press, 1979), 71.

3. See John Mack Faragher, *Women and Men on the Overland Trail* (New Haven, Conn.: Yale University Press, 1979), Chapter 2, for a detailed description of the division of labor between the sexes in subsistence farm families of the Midwest.

4. Phillipe Aries, in *Centuries of Childhood* (New York: Knopf, 1962), has pointed out that childhood itself is a relatively recent invention.

5. Eli Zaretsky, *Capitalism, the Family, and Personal Life* (New York: Harper Colophon, 1976).

6. Bernice Lott, *Becoming a Woman* (Springfield, Ill.: Charles C. Thomas, 1981), 206. James Mohr, in *Abortion in America* (New York: Oxford, 1978), Chapter 4, points out that from 1840–1880 abortion was widely used by native-born women to limit family size.

7. Linda Gordon, *Women's Body: Women's Right* (New York: Grossman Publishers, 1976), 403.

8. Robert Wells, "Women's Lives Transformed: Demographic and Family Patterns in America, 1600–1970," in Carol Ruth Berkin and Mary Beth Norton, eds., *Women of America: A History* (Boston: Houghton Mifflin, 1979), 18.

9. In 1960, the fertility rate per woman was 3.7 children; in 1970, it was 2.5; in 1980, it was 1.8. See National Center for Health Statistics, "Advance Report on Final Natality Statistics, 1980," *Monthly Vital Statistics Report*, 31(8), Supp., DHHS Pub. no. (PHS)82-1120, Nov. 1982, 13.

10. Lott, *Becoming a Woman*, 213.

11. Matina Horner, "Femininity and Successful Achievement: A Basic inconsistency," in Michele Hoffnung Garskof, ed., *Roles Women Play* (Monterey, Calif.: Brooks/Cole, 1971), 98. Although Horner's empirical work has not been successfully replicated, her descriptions of the problems for women are still apt.

12. Janet Dreyfus Gray, in "The Married Professional Woman: An Examination of Her Role Conflicts and Coping Strategies," *Psychology of Women Quarterly*, 1983, 7(3), 235–243, points out that this is a less effective coping strategy among married professional women.

13. Shirley S. Angrist and Elizabeth M. Almquist, *Careers and Contingencies* (New York: Dunellen, 1975), 67.

14. Mirra Komarovsky, *Women in College: Shaping New Feminine Identities* (New York: Basic Books, 1985), Part II.

15. Michele Hoffnung, "Working Mothers: Alternatives to Stereotyped Mothering" (Paper presented to the National Conference on Feminist Psychology, Dallas, Mar. 1979).

16. Jacquelynne S. Eccles, "Gender Roles and Women's Achievement-Related Decisions," *Psychology of Women Quarterly*, 1987, 11, 135–172.

17. In a recent study (Michele Hoffnung, *Mothers: Women Talk About Their Choices and Conflicts*, in preparation), I found that twenty out of thirty mothers had worked at least one year before having a child; fifteen of these twenty had worked more than one year.

18. Grace Hechinger, "Happy Mother's Day," *Newsweek*, May 11, 1981, 19.

19. These women are in their forties and fifties. In earlier times, active mothering would span forty years, rather than the current twenty, and the average woman's life was shorter. See Mary P. Ryan, *Womanhood in America: From Colonial Times to the Present*, 2d ed. (New York: New Viewpoints, 1979), 26.

20. Shirley L Radl, in *Mother's Day Is Over* (New York: Charterhouse, 1973), discusses many of the costs to women based on her own experience.

21. Angela Baron McBride, *The Growth and Development of Mothers* (New York: Harper and Row, 1973), Chapter 1.

22. Michele Hoffnung Garskof, "The Psychology of the Maternity Ward: A Study in Dehumanization," in *Proceedings of the First International Childbirth Conference* (Stamford, Conn.: New Moon Publications, 1973).

23. Helena Znaniecki Lopata, *Occupation Housewife* (New York: Oxford University Press, 1971), 200. Lopata's extensive interviews with women in the Chicago area led her to the conclusion that only full-time involvement outside the home reduced this discontinuity, since it prevented the abrupt and complete change in life activity that usually accompanies the birth of the first child.

24. Unpublished data by Feldman (1962) as reported in Edward Pohlman, *Psychology of Birth Planning* (Cambridge, Mass.: Schenkman, 1969), Chapter 6.

25. John Newson and Elizabeth Newson, *Infant Care in an Urban Community* (London: George Allen and Unwin, 1963).

26. Mary Georgina Boulton, *On Being a Mother* (London: Tavistock Publications, 1983).

27. Jane Lazarre, in *The Mother Knot* (New York: McGraw-Hill, 1976), gives an excellent personal account of these ambivalent feelings.

28. McBride, *The Growth and Development of Mothers*, Chapter 3.

29. Norman K. Denzin, *Children and Their Caretakers* (New Brunswick, N.J.: Transaction Books, 1973). See also Elaine Heffner, *Mothering* (New York: Anchor, 1980), which stresses the need to trust oneself as a mother.

30. Van den Berg, *Dubious Maternal Affection*, 74.

31. Philip Wylie, *Generation of Vipers* (New York: Farrar, 1942); Hans Sebald, *Momism: The Silent Disease of America* (Chicago: Nelson Hall, 1976).

32. Jessie Bernard, *The Future of Motherhood* (New York: Penguin, 1974), 9.

33. Sylvia Brody and Sidney Axelrod, *Mothers, Fathers, and Children* (New York: International Universities Press, 1978), 238–239.

34. Pohlman, *Psychology of Birth Planning*, 36. Judith Guss Teicholz, in "Psychological Correlates of Voluntary Childlessness in Married Women" (Paper presented to the Eastern Psychological Association, Washington, D.C., Mar. 1978), reports that, although fertility rates have decreased, statistics do not indicate an increase in the number of married couples that have chosen to remain childless. Throughout the twentieth century, a constant 5 percent of the married population has chosen childlessness.

35. Pohlman, in *Psychology of Birth Planning*, Chapter 4, presesnts a detailed discussion of reasons. See Ellen Peck and Judith Lenderowitz, *Pronatalism* (New York: Crowell, 1974), for a full discussion of pronatalism.

36. Esther Menaker, "Some Inner Conflicts of Women in a Changing Society," in Roland and Harris, *Career and Motherhood*, 90.

37. Pauline Bart, "The Loneliness of the Long-Distance Mother," in Jo Freeman, ed., *Women: A Feminist Perspective*, 2d ed. (Palo Alto, Calif.: Mayfield Publishing Co., 1979), 257.

38. Lillian B. Rubin, *Women of a Certain Age: The Midlife Search for Self* (New York: Harper and Row, 1979), 6.

39. Ibid., 120.

40. Louise Kapp Howe, "The World of Women's Work," in Jeffrey P. Rosenfeld, ed., *Relationships: The Marriage and Family Reader* (Glenview, Illinois: Scott, Foresman and Co., 1982), 216–217.

41. Kathleen Gerson, *Hard Choices: How Women Decide about Work, Career, and Motherhood* (Berkeley: University of California Press, 1985), 7.

42. Rubin, *Women of a Certain Age*, Chapters 7 and 8. Gail Sheehy, in *Passages: Predictable Crises of Adult Life* (New York: Dutton, 1976) also discusses these problems.

43. Tillie Olson's "Tell Me A Riddle," in Olson, *Tell Me A Riddle* (New York: Dell Laurel Edition, 1976), 72–125, is a wonderful story about how the assignment of full-time home and child care changes the character of a woman.

44. Harriet B. Presser, "Social Factors Affecting the Timing of the First Child," in Warren B. Miller and Lucille F. Newman, eds., *The First Child and Family Formation* (Chapel Hill: University of North Carolina, Carolina Population Center, 1978), 159. See also Pamela Daniels and Kathy Weingarten, *Sooner or Later: The Timing of Parenthood in Adult Lives* (New York: Norton, 1982).

45. Hoffnung, *Mothers*.

46. Valerie Kincade Oppenheimer, *The Female Labor Force in the United States: Demographic and Economic Factors Governing Its Growth and Changing Composition* (Westport, Conn.: Greenwood Press, 1970), Chapter 1.

47. Howard Hayghe, "Research Summaries—Rise in Mother's Labor Force Activity Includes Those with Infants," *Monthly Labor Review*, February 1986, 43–45.

48. Dona Alpert and Amy Culbertson, "Daily Hassles and Coping Strategies of Dual-Earner and Nondual-Earner Women," *Psychology of Women Quarterly*, 1987, 11, 359–366.

49. Michele Hoffnung, "Teaching About Motherhood: Close Kin and the Transition to Mother-hood," *Women's Studies Quarterly*, in press.

50. Myra H. Strober, "Market Work, Housework and Child Care: Buying Archaic Tenets, Building New Arrangements," in Phyllis W. Berman & Estelle R. Ramey, eds., *Women: A Developmental Perspective* (Bethesda, Maryland: U.S. Department of Health and Human Services, 1982), 210–214.

51. As reported in Alice H. Cook, *The Working Mother* (Ithaca, N.Y.: Cornell University Press, 1978), 29.

52. Hoffnung, "Working Mothers," 9–11.

53. Joseph Pleck, "The Work–Family Role System," in R. Kahn-Hut, A. Daniels, & R. Colvard, eds., *Women and Work* (New York: Oxford University Press, 1982), 101–110.

54. S. Shirley Feldman and Sharon C. Nash, "The Effects of Family Formation on Sex-Stereo-typic Behavior: A Study of Responsiveness to Babies," in Warren B. Miller and Lucille F. Newman, eds., *The First Child and Family Formation* (Chapel Hill: University of North Carolina, Carolina Population Center, 1978), 159.

55. Gail Sheehy, in *Pathfinders* (New York: Morrow, 1981), describes this as her personal solution.

56. Barbara Harris, in "Two Lives, One 24-Hour Day," in Roland and Harris, eds., *Careers and Motherhood*, presents a personal and intelligent discussion of these problems.

57. O'Donnell, *Unheralded Majority*, 58–60.

58. Cited in Janet Dreyfus Gray, "The Married Professional Woman," 236. Margaret M. Poloma, Doctoral Dissertation, Case Western Reserve University, 1970.

59. Richard Q. Bell and Lawrence V. Harper, *Child Effects on Adults* (Hillsdale, N.J.: Lawrence Erlbaum Associates, 1977), 65, 214.

60. Lois M. Verbrugge, "Women's Social Roles and Health," in Berman and Ramey, eds., *Women*, 58–59; Paula R. Pietromonaco, Jean Manis, and Katherine Frohardt-Lane, "Psycholog-ical Consequences of Multiple Social Roles," *Psychology of Women Quarterly*, 1986, 10, 373–382.

61. Joseph H. Pleck and Jack Sawyer, *Men and Masculinity* (Englewood Cliffs, N.J.: Prentice-Hall, 1974), 53. See also Marc Feign Fasteau, *The Male Machine* (New York: McGraw-Hill, 1974); Deborah S. David and Robert Brannon, eds., *The Forty-Nine Percent Majority* (Reading, Mass.: Addison-Wesley, 1976); Joe L. Dubbert, *A Man's Man* (New York: Random House, 1974), for discussions of weaknesses in the male role definition and the positive value of child care in men's lives.

62. Bruno Bettelheim, *The Children of the Dream* (London: Macmillan, 1969), 305–306.

63. See Dorothy Dinnerstein, *The Mermaid and the Minotaur: Sexual Arrangements and Human Malaise* (New York: Harper and Row, 1976); and Nancy Chodorow, *The Reproduction of Mothering: Psychoanalysis and the Sociology of Gender* (Berkeley: University of California Press, 1978).

64. Robert Rapoport and Rhonda Rapoport, *Working Couples* (New York: Harper Colophon, 1978); and Feinstein, ed., *Working Women and Families.*

65. See Alan Pifer, "Women Working: Toward a New Society," in Feinstein, ed., *Working Women and Families,* 13–34, for fuller discussion of this issue.

66. Eccles, "Gender Roles," 135–172.

67. Paul J. Andrisani, "Job Satisfaction among Working Women," *Signs: Journal of Women in Culture and Society,* 1978, 3, 588–607.

68. Nancy M. Rudd and Patrick C. McKenry, "Family Influences on the Job Satisfaction of Employed Mothers," *Psychology of Women Quarterly,* 1986, 10, 363–372.

69. Hoffnung, *Mothers.*

70. Ellen Hock, Karen Christman Morgan, and Michael D. Hock, "Employment Decisions Made by Mothers of Infants," *Psychology of Women Quarterly,* 1985, 9, 383–402.

71. Gray, "The Married Professional Woman," 235–243.

Child Care

JILL NORGREN

Child care is an economic issue, a family issue, and, in some countries, a population issue. But in the United States child care is first and foremost a women's issue. Despite the enormous number of mothers who have entered the labor force in recent years, and some restyling of family responsibilities, women remain the primary agents of child rearing.

Not surprisingly, public child-care policies have been determined most often by factors other than the needs of women. In the United States, opposition to maternal employment and fear of government intervention in the life of the family have created a deep current of opposition to public child-care initiatives. As a result of this broad suspicion, the episodic acceptance of child-care legislation reflected special historical circumstances, such as war or economic depression. More recently, child care has been used as a means of manipulating welfare participation and as a poultice for social pathologies such as mentally ill or absent parents and educational disadvantages. In the 1990s, child-care programs may increase if a projected shortage of adult workers does, in fact, occur.

In Europe, child-care programs have been associated with labor policy or used as countermeasures to population decline. Recently, a few governments have broadened the rationale underlying their child-care legislation to include specifically aiding women as mothers. Nonetheless, passage of child-care legislation—with the exception of countries such as Sweden—generally does not reflect a commitment to sexual equality or even an acknowledgment of the greater parental burden placed on women.

Child-care policy refers to a cluster of public programs and benefits offered, or mandated, by a government to influence the care of children. Most prominent—particularly in the United States—are group and family day-care programs, but child-care policy also encompasses tax credits, paid and unpaid child-care leave for parents, flexible parental work schedules, and various cash allowances to facilitate child rearing. Until Congress passed child-care tax-credit legislation in 1976, the major child-care benefits and services available in the United States were day-care and family allowances based on means tests (families below certain income levels qualify): only mothers on welfare are "paid" to rear their children (Aid to Families with

Dependent Children), only poor families receive categorical program benefits (food, housing, medical care), and income-eligible families constitute much of the client population of public day-care centers. For the working- and middle-class parent, help comes primarily through the limited mechanism of the income-tax laws.[1] In the United States, child care is largely a private responsibility.

THE NEED

Women have always worked in the United States. Historically, working-class women and women of color have participated in the labor force more than have wealthier women of European descent. Woman have not, however, always had to work away from their children. Today's workers generally are employed outside of their homes. Thus, today when a mother makes the decision to go to work, or to school or to a training program, she must find child care. In 1987, about 53 percent of children under the age of six years—more than 10.5 million in number—had working mothers.[2] The number of working mothers has been increasing steadily since the late 1940s, but the most dramatic surge has been among women with the greatest child-care needs—mothers with children under six and, in the past decade, those with children under one year of age. Moreover, today unlike even a decade ago, a majority of women go back to work immediately after having a child.[3]

Households have changed in other ways that matter a great deal when it comes to child-care needs. Foremost is the growing number of single-parent homes created after divorce or death, or when parents do not marry. In 1960, one in ten children lived in a single parent home; by 1987 that figure had risen to one in four.[4] In 1987, over 5.5 million women, and 984,000 men, were single parents working or looking for work. Their need for child care is obvious, enhanced by their often having low incomes, and sometimes being homeless.[5] Academic and government surveys demonstrate that the lack of affordable day care prevents many single parents from working,[6] although government figures also indicate that the labor-force participation rate of divorced mothers in 1987 was an impressive 80 percent.[7]

Public and private day-care programs have not expanded to meet the needs of these millions of children and parents. Licensed centers have places for about 1 million, or less than one-eighth, of the children under six who have working mothers.[8] There has been much discussion of employer-supported centers. Many employees urge the creation of workplace centers as a necessary benefit for parents, but other workers think that workplace centers require taxing commutes for small children, or hold out the possibility of tying a parent to a bad job because of a child-care program. Right now, very few day-care programs are corporate-financed: There are approximately 600 such programs in the United States, of which about 450 are hospital-based.[9] Public and private centers are supplemented by a limited number of licensed family day-care homes, where care is provided in particular for children under three.

Clearly, a majority of families cannot make child-care arrangements in a licensed program and must settle for something less formal in their own home or in someone else's. A 1984 survey of child-care arrangements for preschool children with working mothers indicated that 37 percent of such youngsters were cared for in someone else's home; 23 percent of the children attended an organized day-care facility; 31 percent of preschoolers were cared for in their own homes (half by their fathers), while the remaining number are looked after by the working mother on the job.[10] An unknown number of preschool children, and 2 million children between the ages of five and eleven cared for themselves. They are called "latchkey" children, in reference to the house keys many wear on strings around their necks.[11]

Child-care arrangements follow patterns associated with the length of a mother's workday, her marital, educational, and financial status, the age and number of her children, and her racial background. Some of these patterns have changed significantly over the past twenty years, along with women's participation in the work force. Use of group day care, for example, has increased threefold, a trend that is particularly pronounced among children of well-educated, full-time working mothers, and mothers with relatively high family incomes.[12] A marked change has also occurred in the use of care provided in a home other than that of the child's family: 27 percent of children under six with full-time working mothers received care in someone else's home in 1958; this figure rose to 47 percent in 1977 and continues to climb.[13] The trend among full-time working women clearly has been to establish out-of-home care.

Women who work part-time, on the other hand, use in-home care more often. They are twice as likely to depend on child care by the child's father, and they are able to keep their children with them on the job more frequently.[14] All mothers experience particular difficulty arranging for care for infants. The number of group centers that will take children under two years is extremely small, and even neighbors and relatives are often reluctant to take on the work and responsibility of caring for a very young child.[15] Of children under one year of age, 78 percent are cared for in their own home, or in someone else's, rather than in a day-care center.[16]

In the past, women relied on older siblings, fathers, neighbors, and in-laws to provide child care; this is less possible today. Smaller families have diminished the number of older children available as caretakers, neighboring women and female in-laws are now more likely to be out working, and divorce often results in the loss of help from the father — and from in-laws. Yet these patterns of child care differ among white and black working women, reflecting both historical differences in the strength of social networks,[17] and attitudes toward child care and neighborhoods. Black mothers, who are more likely to be employed than are white mothers,[18] are far less likely to leave their children on their own. Black mothers rely on relatives for child care more than do white parents.[19] This may reflect preference, or may be the result of the high cost of child care by nonrelatives and day-care centers.

There is no question that parents want more day-care programs: the increased use of group centers and nonrelatives demonstrates this demand.

So do the waiting lists common at centers, nursery schools, and family day-care programs. Conveniently located quality programs do not experience underenrollment. The problem, then, is our failure to expand programs and, even more astonishing in light of increased maternal employment, to reverse the funding cutbacks of the 1970s and 1980s that have resulted in the closing of centers and the termination of child-care subsidies for thousands of families.[20]

The insistence that child rearing be primarily a mother's responsibility, combined with the failure to provide adequate child-care programs, places a heavy and unequal burden on women. Job opportunities, job advancement, and lifetime earnings remain lower for women than for men, in part because of unreliable and inadequate child care. A 1981 report from the U.S. Commission for Civil Rights acknowledges this inequity and points to government responsibility: "women as workers and students, especially minority women, continue to be disadvantaged when compared with men" because federal child-care programs are "inadequate to meet the current or projected need."[21]

The inequality of opportunity experienced by all mothers in need of child care is particularly acute among low-income women. While the Civil Rights Commission speaks out about the devastating impact of the government's child-care policy, other public officials continue to support such discriminatory policy. With myopic vision, officials repeatedly conclude that, when its cost exceeds the immediate earning power of a woman, the provision of child care is a poor (and therefore unacceptable) investment. The long-term social and financial opportunities lost to the woman, her family, and society are ignored. A study carried out in New York City found public day-care to be an important factor in helping low-income women to maintain self-sufficiency. When the city closed seventy-seven day-care centers in the 1970s, 40 percent of the affected low-income mothers experienced new problems with job punctuality, and 30 percent could not avoid increased absenteeism. As a result, some women who were previously considered good employees were fired. The authors conclude that, lacking reliable, low-cost day care, the women under study had to create "elaborate schemes for survival."[22] Throughout the country, mothers in need of child care face these dilemmas every day.

AMERICAN DAY CARE IN THE NINETEENTH AND TWENTIETH CENTURIES

Contemporary attitudes toward day care, including the continued use of a means test, reflect its origins as a charitable service for the children of destitute and poor working mothers. Wealthy women began day nurseries in this country during the nineteenth century, borrowing from the European institution of the *garderie* or *creche*. The first center in the United States was opened in 1838 to provide care for the children of seamen's wives and widows.[23] In 1854, the first New York City center was started at the Nursery and Child's Hospital. Following the Civil War, the number of nurseries expanded, as veterans' widows and an increasing number of immigrant women found themselves the sole supporters of their families. These nurseries were bleak institutions, reflecting the class distinctions of the society and the belief that those who accepted charity were inferior and morally weak.

In the second half of the nineteenth century, a quite separate program, kindergarten, made its appearance in the United States. Inspired by the work of Friedrich Froebel and Maria Montessori, kindergartens stressed the social and intellectual development of the child, not custodial care. Day-care centers and kindergartens grew out of two fundamentally different traditions and came to be thought of quite distinctly. Day nurseries served the children of working parents; kindergartens provided for preschool educational and developmental needs. These functions are not mutually exclusive, yet two distinct institutions were formed in the late nineteenth century and were maintained separately until the 1970s, when the unmet demand for day care and the positive influence of Project Headstart led to reevaluation of old biases toward day care.

One reason why day-care centers did not evolve into all-day kindergartens with a positive public image was the influence of the newly professionalized social workers hired by centers in the 1920s. Although the client families thought of themselves as normal, hard-working people with a fair share of life's problems, these professionals emphasized social pathologies among parents and children. They thought of the families as abnormal—not Americanized—and insisted on the use of intake procedures (gathering data on their lives) and of formal social casework. Eventually, this imparted the aura of a social-welfare service to day care. The public fixed a negative image on day care, thinking the centers were for "troubled" families only. Reputation and reality reinforced each other. Teachers perceived the difference and chose to work in kindergartens and elementary schools rather than in day nurseries. The middle class, which did not approve of having mothers work outside the home, simply did not use the day nurseries.[24]

Until the Depression, group day care evolved locally according to the need and the response of community philanthropic and social-welfare organizations. The Depression, and later World War II, provided new reasons for day care and the opportunity to redefine both its purpose and its clientele. In 1933, the Federal Emergency Relief Administration (FERA), later known as the Works Progress Administration (WPA), anxious to create work for unemployed school personnel, authorized state departments of education to open centers offering full day care at federal expense. Nearly 2,000 centers, some with preschool education programs, were established. After meeting a means test, thousands of children were enrolled.[25]

As the economy improved in the early 1940s, the rationale for Washington's involvement diminished. During the phaseout, however, wartime labor shortages prompted a reappraisal of federally subsidized day care. Suddenly, the government found it necessary to encourage millions of women to enter the work force as part of the war effort.[26] Care of the children of these new workers became a compelling public issue. Initially, grants for child-care centers were made from the President's Emergency Fund, but, in 1941, the

Community Facilities Act, better known as the Lanham Act, was amended to permit appropriations for day care—in "war-impacted" areas only. Until 1946, the states and Washington shared, 50–50, the cost of child care for women engaged in war-related work. Nationwide, 1,600,000 children attended centers financed with funds from Washington, while their mothers worked in wartime industries.[27] Every state except New Mexico had some day-care centers; California headed the list with nearly 400.[28]

The WPA and Lanham Act programs each contained the seeds of change. By hiring teachers, the WPA centers had inadvertently mixed an educational curriculum with custodial care. Because wartime day care was part of the national labor policy, child care was dissociated in the public eye from the earlier means-tested, social-welfare context. But, although short-term events (a depressed economy and the war) had caused the government to project, and the public to perceive, day care in a positive light, deep-seated assumptions continued to hamper the redefinition of day care. The biases of professionals and of other opinion leaders who did not believe that mothers should be employed were clear even during the war. Staff members at the Children's Bureau in Washington, for example, fought the placement of centers in convenient locations, because mothers might be tempted to maintain their employment after the war emergency.[29]

At the conclusion of the war, these biases emerged forcefully once more. Officials urged that traditional roles be reestablished and argued that women would not want to take jobs away from returning soldiers. Mothers belonged at home; only "troubled" families needed day care. Good parents understood the (implied) destructiveness of unnecessary, whimsical maternal employment. Moreover, while post–New Deal politics were grounded in the philosophy of government as a growth industry, the family—at least in rhetoric—remained an institution not to be violated by the hand of the state. Publicly sponsored day care was thought too intrusive.

With the end of the Depression and of World War II, federal support for day care died. Parents, labor leaders, and child-care professionals were unable to capitalize on the existence of a program to keep it going. In Chicago, there had been twenty-three centers during the war; by 1968, there were none in all of Illinois. Eighty centers operated in Detroit in the early 1940s; ten years after the conclusion of the war, just three remained.[30] Publicly funded centers survived only where local governments agreed to subsidize them, as they did in New York and California.

The federal government did not fund day care again until 1962. Responding to strong pressure from social-work professionals and socially concerned women allied in the National Committee for Day Care, Congress authorized several million dollars to aid local day-care agencies. The focus of this 1962 Public Welfare Amendments legislation, however, continued to be on child care as a social-welfare service for troubled families. None of the lobbyists or legislators argued for a more comprehensive policy that would help women as mothers or working parents. A pamphlet put out in the mid-1960s by the Children's Bureau highlights this bias:

Who needs day care?
Giorgi does. When his father deserted the family. . . .

Esther does. She is 4 and mentally retarded. Her parents want her to live at home but are finding this . . . difficult. . . .

Paul does . . . and so do his (8) brothers and sisters. . . . Their father is unemployed, their mother hospitalized. The family lives in two rooms in a slum tenement. . . . [31]

Shortly after passage of this day-care bill, Congress approved the funding of a new preschool program, Project Headstart, as part of the 1964 Economic Act. Designed to give poor children a "head start" by means of an enriched preschool experience, the program continued the means-tested tradition but, for the first time, consciously provided comprehensive rather than merely custodial preschool child care. It is not surprising that Project Headstart was an immediate success. The centers resembled the nursery schools of the middle class, whose social and educational benefits had long been appreciated by families too poor to afford them. Less predictably, the middle class also formed a positive image of Headstart. Better-off parents and educators began to suggest that the United States should have widely available, non-means-testing child care based on Headstart's principle of comprehensive care.

Legislators neither were ready for comprehensive child care, nor were prepared to eliminate income-eligibility tests. Using the politically safe label of "welfare reform," however, Congress significantly expanded federal appropriations for day care as part of the 1967 Social Security Amendments. This legislation provided unlimited matching funds to the states for day-care services (1) to participants in the government's Work Incentive Program (WIN), and (2) to past, present, and potential recipients of welfare. While they still thought it desirable for mothers to stay at home, in the case of poor women Congress and the president decided to make an exception.

The blunt goal of the 1967 legislation was to reduce the public-welfare burden, but the eligibility requirements proved so flexible (who cannot present herself as a "potential" welfare recipient?) and the funding so generous that publicly sponsored day care blossomed all over the country. Working-class mothers and even aggressive middle-class mothers benefited from the expansion of facilities.[32]

Families liked what they found at these centers: reliable, increasingly high-quality, inexpensive child care. As more and more women returned to work and the incipient women's movement demanded child care as a social right, parents, educators, union leaders, and antipoverty spokeswomen pressed Congress for a comprehensive child-care bill (loosely modeled on Headstart). In 1971, sponsors agreed on the Comprehensive Child Development Act (Title V of the Economic Opportunity Amendments). Although the act still relied on means tests, it defined a program of cognitive and social development for children, accompanied by medical support services. For most of the twentieth century, Americans had thought of day-care centers as bleak, unhealthy places to be used only in desperation. It now appeared that public attitudes had finally changed and that the tremendous need for inexpensive—even free—child care would be addressed.

Optimism over the bill ran too high. Although Congress approved the legislation, President Nixon vetoed it, arguing that it would "sovietize" American families.[33] The Nixon veto not only killed this legislation but also tipped the delicate political balance away from a comprehensive child-care policy. Americans had long thought negatively about day care, although the success of Headstart and the nurseries of the kibbutzim had done much to alter middle-class images. By playing on powerful cold-war fears of a sovietized society, Nixon had recast the debate, and day care was newly stigmatized. Despite the increasing visibility of the women's movement, the rise in maternal employment, and the arguments of child-development experts, the tone of Nixon's message skillfully touched on just those aspects of the American political ethos that had impeded child-care legislation in the past.

The 1971 veto did more than temporarily halt legislative action; it also abetted opposition. In 1972, child-care supporters tried to revive the comprehensive bill but were unsuccessful; that same year, they also failed to block imposition of a funding ceiling on social services, including day care. Subsequent bills, including the Mondale–Brademas Child and Family Services Act, 1975, and the Cranston Child Care Act of 1979, also failed, as "new-right" lobbying against day care and public worry about expenditures for social programs increased. Although congressional support for additional funds rose in the mid-1970s, the executive branch remained cool. President Ford vetoed an important supplemental appropriation bill for day care but was persuaded to sign a revised version in 1976 after congressional Republicans convinced him that a second veto would be politically dangerous eight weeks before the national elections. Although not actually put to the test, President Carter also indicated that he would veto any major day-care bill. Child-care supporters in Congress, in particular the Congressional Caucus on Women's Issues, attempted to keep the issue alive in the early years of the Reagan administration but found virtually no support for day-care and unpaid-parent-leave legislation outlined, for example, in the family section of the Economic Equity Act (a major legislative program first introduced in 1981 and not yet enacted in its entirety). Rather, they found themselves contending with a 25 percent cut in federal day-care assistance.[34] Renewed interest in the problems of family life as well as concern for welfare costs resulted in the introduction of day-care and parent-leave bills in the closing period of the Reagan administration. To date, however, none of the bills have been passed.

As a result, although more than half of all American mothers with preschool children now work, the federal government, as we discuss next, provides only scanty, means-tested day care. Amazing as it may seem, since 1967 there has been no major legislation providing directly for an expanded program of publicly funded child care. Congress initiated a child-care tax credit as part of the Tax Reform Act of 1976, but this attempt at social policy through taxation is both inadequate and inequitable. For a variety of reasons, among them the strong opposition of the U.S. Chamber of Commerce, even legislation that would only provide employees a guaranteed right to unpaid child-care leave of 18 weeks without loss of job has so far also been blocked in Congress.[35]

CHILD-CARE BENEFITS AND SERVICES:
THE UNITED STATES AND EUROPE

In the United States, parents who work have to create "elaborate schemes for survival" because child-care benefits and services are not widely available. The variety and extensive coverage of many national child-care policies in Europe make a striking contrast to those of the United States. Many observers believe that there is a great deal to be learned from the range of child-care options available to European women and their families.

In Europe, there is also a large and growing population of working mothers. The numbers, of course, differ from country to country. Unlike the United States, however, these countries agree on the acceptability of government intervention in the life of the family. Thus, although no European government has been able to provide all the child care that is needed—or that has been promised—there exists a public commitment to make child care available regardless of family income. Ironically, the development of child-care policies in Europe has often been a function of the need for labor or the desire to encourage population growth, not of concern for the equality of women. Nonetheless, European women of all backgrounds have access to programs and benefits not available to American mothers and their families.

Child-care programs and services fall into six categories: family and group day care; maternity and child-care leaves; short-term sick-child leaves and housework days; family allowances; tax credits; and flexible work schedules.

Family and Group Day Care

In the United States, parents who meet fairly rigid income qualifications can try to place their child in a government-sponsored group or family day-care program or in a Headstart program. They are often placed on waiting lists. Since Headstart generally enrolls children for only half of the day, parents who work full-time must make additional child-care arrangements. Public programs for infants and toddlers are sorely inadequate relative to need, and the overall number of children cared for in government-sponsored programs is limited. It has been estimated that, before child-care budget cuts made by the Reagan administration, 750,000 children attended government-funded group or family day-care programs, and 372,000 children were enrolled in Headstart.[36] In 1987, the former figure had declined to 500,000 and the latter had increased to 460,000. Inadequate public funds limit the expansion of child-care facilities, but continuing use of a means test also excludes many families who would otherwise clearly use public day-care centers.

No country in Europe has been able to build a day-care program large enough to meet parental demand. France and East Germany provide the most extensive preschool-center programs. In East Germany, nearly half of all children under three years and 90 percent of children three to six are cared for in centers. Maintaining an adequate work force remains at the core of East German child-care policy. France has nearly equaled the East German record. The popularity of the free *ecoles maternelles* has caused overcrowding despite the fact that the days and hours do not match the requirements of working parents, and that these nurseries close for lunch.

A pattern of dual child-care systems—one for children up to age two or three years and another for older children—appears all over Europe. Infant day care is more difficult and expensive to provide and, as a result, enrollment capacity for it is lower everywhere.

In West Germany, where grandmothers are still the primary caretakers in the absence of mothers, there have been only modest efforts to provide more public day care. Grandmothers are also important in the Soviet Union, where a young woman's mother may take her pension early in order to become a child-minder. The Hungarians, unable to meet the demand for center care, particularly for children under three, have become increasingly tolerant of privately paid baby-sitting arrangements, although private-market arrangements were previously frowned on. Even the Swedes make extensive use of paid baby-sitters.

Maternity and Child-Care Leaves

Europeans believe that children are a major resource of the society and that the entire society should share the cost of child rearing. This attitude is expressed most consistently across Europe through the policy of paid maternity leave or, in a few countries, unpaid leave with job protection. Generally, paid maternity leave permits a woman to withdraw from her job several weeks before the birth of her child and to remain at home as long as five months after the child's arrival. Maternal child-care leave is most liberal (in terms of time) in Hungary, where mothers may stay out of the labor force for three years while receiving a cash grant of one-third to one-half an average woman's salary. Encouraging *women* to stop work and to stay at home, however, is an expression of conservative social biases whose implications must be examined by feminists. I will come back to this issue at the conclusion of this article.

Only Sweden permits a *father* to take paid leave. A total of nine months can be shared with the mother. The fact that barely 10 percent of Swedish father have taken this leave disappoints, and even worries, some Swedish feminists.[37]

In contrast to the policies of these European governments, the United States does not grant paid maternity or child-care leave as a matter of social right. Indeed, neither federal equal-opportunity legislation nor the Equal Employment Opportunity Commission (EEOC) guidelines that prohibit sex discrimination as part of Title VII require that mothers be permitted to take unpaid nonmedical maternity or child-care leave without penalty.[38] As a result of pressure from feminists, however, a number of private businesses grant unpaid, and occasionally paid, maternity leave—this despite staunch opposition to national parental-leave legislation by the U.S. Chamber of Commerce. Similarly, some public-sector employees have won such benefits, including the protection of seniority while on parental leave, through local and state government legislation, and through labor agreements. These arrangements, however, fall short of a national policy that would grant these rights to all women.[39]

Short-Term Leaves

Although sick-child or housework leave is not as common as maternity leave, in many European countries mothers or fathers receive a fixed number of days of paid leave to care for a sick child. Several countries also have a separate policy of paid personal leave days. In West Germany, for example, once a month mothers with children under the age of fourteen years may take a paid day off from work as a "housework day." A single father challenged this mothers-only policy, asserting that it constituted a denial of equal protection.[40]

In the United States, there is no public benefit equivalent to sick-child leave or housework days. Here too, however, some union contracts and company policies permit employees personal leave days that can be used for child care. The number of personal leave days, however, is considerably smaller than the average sick-child leave granted European parents.

Family Allowances

Direct cash allowances and subsidies for families in the United States are means tested. Aid to Families with Dependent Children (AFDC) and government programs of subsidized food, housing, and medical care are not available to families whose incomes rise above designated income levels. European family-benefit programs tend to be more liberal, since they were designed both to achieve income redistribution and to provide societal support for child rearing regardless of income. Because child allowances were used in the past to encourage population growth, several European countries provide this benefit only after the birth of the second child. In Europe, the family allowance is most often a cash allowance, calculated according to the number of children, but it may include subsidies for housing, food, clothing, and medical care.

Tax Credits

Government-sponsored child-care programs and benefits in the United States that give direct help are usually income related and thus are not widely available to middle-class families. As a result of pressure from the women's movement, Congress approved a tax measure in 1976 that provides indirect child-care aid to parents who work or go to school, regardless of income. This child-care tax credit helps parents to recover part of the cost of care for children under fifteen. A tax credit proved more attractive to lawmakers than did expanded funding for day-care centers, because a credit requires neither visible appropriations (the cost is all in lost tax revenue) nor a proliferation of public centers that might leave legislators open to charges of "sovietizing" American children.

Many feminists contend that the tax credit puts the cart before the horse by providing reimbursement for a service that is in short supply. The credit helps families who succeed in finding child care, but it does nothing to make day-care services more abundant. A tax credit also fails to help parents whose income is too low to be assessed for taxes and those not sufficiently sophisticated to know how to apply for the credit. Still other parents cannot claim the credit because they have hired baby-sitters who refuse to have their income reported for tax or social-security purposes. In baby-sitting, where the pay is low, such informal arrangements are common.

In Europe, tax deductions and credits are a far less important component of child-care policy than in the United States, because European governments use more direct forms of aid. In West Germany, tax exemptions for children were replaced in 1975 with a flat-rate, tax-free child allowance. France combines an extensive family-allowance package with tax benefits.[41]

Flexible Work Schedules

Flexible schedules for parents have received considerable attention both in the United States and in European countries. Some child-care problems of working parents, it has been argued, could be addressed by permitting parents of young children to work shorter days or to telescope a regular workweek into three or four long days. However, implementation of government policies mandating the right to a flexible work schedule have had only minimal success. Swedish parents have won an option for a six-hour day with decreased compensation.[42] Both here and abroad, flex-time and shorter workdays more often result from private arrangements between employer and employee.

Private Employers

Government-mandated and state-provided cash child-care benefits diminish the importance of the private-sector policy in Europe. In the United States, employers' decisions regarding whether to include child-care benefits in employee benefits' packages are far more critical. American employers vary enormously in their policies: More than 10 percent do provide specific services or benefits to help their workers arrange for child care,[43] and 50 percent have established work practices such as leave policies, flexible hours, job sharing, and voluntary part-time schedules that aid parents in caring for their children.[44] Very few businesses—and those almost all ones with more than 250 employees—sponsor day-care centers or provide specific financial assistance for day care; the service sector, drawing fully half of its employees from women, provides more child-care benefits than do the male-dominated manufacturing industries.[45]

THE IMPACT OF TRADITIONAL ATTITUDES

With the number of working mothers in the United States so large, why has the government failed to meet the need for day care or to provide other child-care options that might aid women? Part of the answer lies with the cost as well as with concern over government telling parents which child-care programs to use. Resistance to providing adequate child care has also occurred because of traditional social and political attitudes concerning mothers and child rearing.

In the past, many Americans were brought up to believe that women, and in particular mothers, belong at home. Until a decade ago, opinion leaders not only supported this point of view, but also ignored the obvious evidence that mothers were joining the labor force in record numbers. Armed with their beliefs and the myth of mother-at-home, most policy-makers simply failed to acknowledge that a public child-care policy was necessary.

The general belief that mothers should not work outside the home has been systematically nurtured by social workers, educators, and psychologists. Aided by the media, these professionals have told women and their families that the physical and mental health of children depends on the continuous presence of mother: "the rearing environment of the child was presumed to be altered by her unavailability to her family and by the various child care figures substituted for her."[46] The work of John Bowlby on maternal deprivation among British children during World War II has been repeatedly drawn on to support the importance of having mothers stay at home. But Bowlby's study, and those of other researchers, analyzed the problems of children who were living twenty-four hours per day in an institution. These studies tell us little about the effects on children of being placed in child care eight hours per day.[47] As Milton Willner has pointed out, Bowlby's study was concerned with maternal deprivation, not separation.[48] Moreover, it tells us nothing about the importance of the quality of the care.

Work by B. M. Caldwell and other investigators on the effects of day-care center attendance does not support the drastic predictions of maternal-deprivation theory. Quite to the contrary, according to Caldwell, children of all ages on the average thrive both socially and intellectually when placed in quality child-care programs.[49]

Psychologist Jay Belsky, previously a strong supporter of day care, has recently challenged the belief that even the best day care is without problems for infants. Using data from the so-called Strange Situation test (a test that examines an infant's response to her mother after she has been momentarily abandoned), Belsky now argues that children under one year of age left more than twenty hours per week at a day-care center, or with a sitter, will suffer from insecurity and aggression.[50] Belsky's conclusions have created a great stir among child-development experts, and have occasioned a flurry of media attention. The work has been criticized for failing to consider differing quality of care, differing family background, and the likelihood that, given children's plasticity, any negative effects will disappear by the time the children reach age four.[51] Clinical doubts have been raised about the ability of the short, simple test to judge a complicated child–mother relationship. What Belsky's research also does not show is what happens to infants whose parents, without child care, have no options for organizing their lives and providing physically and emotionally stable homes.

Moreover, the debate occasioned by Belsky's research fails to consider the role of fathers in the lives of young children. Given the current nature of the dialogue, and the influence of these psychologists in congressional testimony, it is likely that any child-care–leave policy legislated by Congress will permit (admonish) mothers to stay at home, and will ignore the possibility of a larger parental role for fathers. If choice—for women and men—is a central value of the feminist movement, we need to insist on research that does not persistently view the health of young children as solely dependent on interaction with mothers.

CONCLUSION

In the early part of the twentieth century, maternal-health legislation and child labor laws were attacked by some Americans as "a socialist plot that would lead to control over the family."[52] Sixty years later, the issue of whether—or to what degree—the family is a private social institution remains unresolved. As political scientist Jean Robinson has observed, there is still an assumption that the family is a "natural construction and not subject to social manipulation."[53]

Betty Friedan has written that "dispelling the mystique of the family" —the recently described "classical family of Western nostalgia"—"may be even more threatening to some than unmasking the feminine mystique was a decade ago."[54] Advocates of a public child-care policy in the United States have had to fight both mystiques: the feminine mystique that insisted on only a domestic role for women, and the mystique of the family that glorified this institution as a self-sufficient unit that would be debilitated by government intervention. By instituting the child-care tax credit, the government has tacitly acknowledged women's—in particular, middle-class women's— changing roles, but the lack of any comprehensive child-care policy confirms the government's fundamental unwillingness to date to change public responsibilities vis-à-vis the family.

In Europe, governments have been more responsive to demands for child-care policy, although European attitudes on the place of women are similar to those of Americans. Wars and political revolutions have made child-care programs a means of stimulating both population growth and labor-force participation, and they are less often identified with aid to the needy. As a result, negative attitudes toward working women and state intervention have been neutralized more readily.

The accelerated use of child-care leave raises an important question about the future direction and impact of European child-care policy, and of American policy, if such a program should become popular here. Through such policies, working mothers are increasingly permitted, even encouraged, to stay at home. By paying these mothers, providing job security, and continuing pension entitlements, European governments have made it easier for women to drop out of the labor force. Because such leave is generally designated for mothers only, and because benefits are often considerably less than a regular salary, these policies can easily reinforce traditional attitudes identifying women as primary nurturers and secondary wage earners. Feminists should not lose sight of this possibility as they propose child-care options.

Child-care policy decisions reflect societal attitudes toward female roles and influence future opportunities for women. In the United States, the women's movement is, perhaps only today, beginning to give extensive attention to child-care policy. With heightened media interest in policies of day care and parental leave, now is time for feminists to define a defensible child-care policy and to demand it as a social right. Both Republicans and Democrats are sponsoring day-care bills in Congress and both political parties supported increased child care in their 1988 platforms.[55]

Large-scale social programs were out of favor in the late 1970s and 1980s. Unfilled jobs, particularly in the service sector, and a growing awareness that cutbacks in service for children and their families have gone too far, both contribute to new assessments of policy needs. Recently, Senator Christopher Dodd (D. Conn.) said, "Before the issue was if there should be a federal role in child care, and now it's not if, but what the role should be."[56] The speeches of the major party candidates in the 1988 presidential campaign verify Dodd's conclusion: Bush and Dukakis debated not whether the nation needs more child-care programs, but rather how extensive a role the federal government should play in the provision and regulation of existing and new programs. Women—and men—must now work with legislators, and employers, to obtain the comprehensive child-care policies without which women will never gain equality in the United States. The issue is not a simple one: Because of the severe financial cutbacks sustained during the Reagan era, child-care supporters must be certain that new government programs do more than simply bring back public funding to pre-1980 levels. Far more important is the need for new child-care programs to be fair and flexible. They should meet the needs of a culturally pluralistic society, avoiding the imposition of one dominant cultural notion of correct child rearing and family life.

In the United States, the role of mother has always been glorified. Without child-care policies that acknowledge the needs of women and their children, that talk will continue to be a rhetoric that mocks us in its lack of a substantive national commitment.

NOTES

1. In some states, need is considered in addition to income eligibility, permitting working parents and parents in training to place children in public day-care programs. Current legislation includes the income-tax deduction for dependent children, the child-care tax credit, and the deduction for extensive medical expenses. See Tax Reform Act of 1986, P.L. 99–514, 26 Sec. 21.

2. U.S. Department of Labor, Bureau of Labor Statistics, *News*, August 12, 1987, 1, and Table 2.

3. Ibid. In 1977, 32 percent of mothers with infants worked; in 1982, the figure climbed to 43 percent with the trend continuing until, in 1987, 52 percent of women with children one year or younger were in the labor force. Statistics on women returning to work in 1988 immediately after childbirth vary—in some cases dramatically—by age, race, ethnicity, and education. For example, 63 percent of women with college degrees returned to jobs immediately after giving

birth, as compared with 38 percent whose schooling ended with high school. Fifty-three percent of black women resumed employment immediately, as did 51 percent of white women, in contrast to the much lower figure of 38 percent of Hispanic women. "A Threshold Is Crossed on Mothers Who Work," *New York Times*, June 16, 1988, All. U.S. Bureau of the Census, "Fertility of American Women: June 1987," *Current Population Reports*, Series P-20, No. 427 (May 1988), Table C.

4. U.S. Bureau of the Census, Arlene F. Saluter, "Americans' Marital Status and Living Arrangements: March 1987," *Current Population Reports*, Series P-20, No. 423 (April 1988), Table 4. Among white children, 19 percent lived with one parent in 1987 compared with 31 percent of Hispanic children and 53 percent of black children.

5. U.S. Bureau of Labor Statistics, unpublished data from the March 1987 Current Population Survey.

6. Martin O'Connell and David E. Bloom, *Juggling Jobs and Babies: America's Child Care Challenge* (Washington, D.C.: Population Reference Bureau, No. 12, February 1987).

7. U.S. Department of Labor, *News*, August 12, 1987, 1. This is the highest labor-force participation rate of any group—defined by sex and marital status—in the population.

8. U.S. Commission on Civil Rights, *Child Care and Equal Opportunity for Women* (Washington, D.C.: U.S. Commission on Civil Rights, 1981), 14.

9. U.S. Bureau of Labor Statistics, *News*, January 15, 1988. But see, Barbara Reisman's letter to the editor, "Labor Dept. Child-Care Study Misleads Public," *New York Times*, Feb. 11, 1988, A34.

10. U.S. Bureau of the Census, "Who's Minding the Kids? Child Care Arrangements: Winter 1984," *Current Population Reports*, Series P-70, No. 9 (May 1987), pp. 3, 5.

11. Determining the number of children who care for themselves is difficult. First, parents underreport leaving children on their own because of guilt and because, in some states, it is illegal. Second, the standard question asked by the Current Population Survey—"Who takes care of your child most of the time while you are at work?"—doesn't capture emergency situations. The latest figures available are for 1984. At that time, no one admitted to leaving preschool children alone. U.S. Bureau of the Census, "After School Care of School Age Children: December 1984," *Current Population Reports*, Series P-23, No. 149 (January 1987), p. 1. Glenn Collins, "Latchkey Children: A New Profile Emerges," *New York Times*, Oct. 16, 1987, C16.

12. U.S. Bureau of the Census, "Trends in Child Care Arrangements of Working Mothers," *Current Population Reports*, Series P-23, No. 117, (June 1982), 3, 7; and U.S. Bureau of the Census, "Who's Minding the Kids?" 6–8. But women with higher education and professional status are also likely to leave children alone after school. "2 Million Children Stay Home Alone," *New York Times*, Feb. 6, 1987, A19.

13. U.S. Bureau of the Census, "Trends in Child-Care Arrangements of Working Mothers," 6–7.

14. Ibid., 7.

15. Ibid., 7–8.

16. "Jobs and Child Care Studied," *New York Times*, May 11, 1987, C11; see also, U.S. Bureau of the Census, "Who's Minding the Kids?"

17. Carol B. Stack, *All Our Kin: Strategies for Survival in a Black Community* (New York: Harper & Row, 1974); see also, Gloria I. Joseph and Jill Lewis, "Black Mothers and Daughters: Their Roles and Functions in American Society," in *Common Differences: Conflicts in Black and White Feminist Perspectives* (Garden City, N.Y.: Anchor Books, 1981), 76.

18. Howard N. Fullerton, "The 1995 Labor Force: BLS' Latest Projections," *Monthly Labor Review*, Nov. 1985, 19, 21–23.

19. "2 Million Children Stay Home Alone," A19. Evelyn Nakano Glenn argues that white society in the United States has historically viewed the domestic life, and therefore the child-care obligations, of women of color quite differently from that of white women: "Where racial ethnic women diverge from other working class women is that, as members of colonized minorities, their definition as laborers in production took precedence over their domestic roles. Whereas the wife-mother roles of white working class women were recognized and accorded

respect by the larger society, the maternal and reproductive roles of racial ethnic women were ignored in favor of their roles as workers. The lack of consideration for their domestic functions is poignantly revealed in the testimony of black domestics . . . who were expected to leave their children and home cares behind while devoting full-time to the care of the white employer's home and children." "Racial Ethnic Women's Labor: The Intersection of Race, Gender, and Class Oppression," *Review of Radical Political Economics* 17 (1985): 102.

20. As a result of the fiscal crisis in New York City in 1975, seventy-seven day-care centers were closed and 5,000 places terminated. Compounding the problem, the federal government began a series of significant funding cutbacks for child care in 1981 when Title XX funds that provided child-care funds for low- and moderate-income families were made a block grant program. The funds targeted for child care were cut $200 million. Georgia L. McMurray and Dolores P. Kazanjian, *Day Care and the Working Poor* (New York: Community Service Society of New York, 1982), 4; Children's Defense Fund, *A Children's Defense Budget: An Analysis of the President's Budget and Children* (Washington, D.C.: Children's Defense Fund, 1982), 111–16; Martin O'Connell and David E. Bloom, *Juggling Jobs and Babies: America's Child Care Challenge*, 13–14.

21. U.S. Commission on Civil Rights, *Child Care and Equal Opportunity for Women*, 50–51, and Chapters 1 and 2.

22. McMurray and Kazanjian, *Day Care and the Working Poor*, ii, 7, 8, and 13. For national data showing the disruption to parental employment, see U.S. Bureau of the Census, "Who's Minding the Kids?" Table E.

23. Sources differ on the date of the earliest European day nursery. According to Ethel Beer, *Working Mothers and the Day Nursery* (New York: Whiteside, Inc., 1957), 27, a Swiss minister opened a nursery in 1767 for children whose mothers worked in the fields. Others trace the day nursery to the Industrial Revolution and mention a discussion of it in Robert Owen, *Life of Robert Owen* (New York: Augustus M. Kelley Publishers, 1857–58). See Bernice Fleiss, *The Relationship of the Mayor's Committee on Wartime Care of Children to Day Care in New York City* (Ph.D. dissertation, New York University, 1962), 1. For a discussion of the earliest American day nurseries, see Ethel Beer, *The Day Nursery* (New York: E.P. Dutton, 1930); and William L. Pierce, "Day Care in the 1970's: Planning for Expansion," *Child Welfare* 50 (Mar. 1971), 160.

24. Florence A. Ruderman, *Child Care and Working Mothers: A Study of Arrangements Made for Daytime Care of Children* (New York: Child Welfare League of America, 1968), 13, 19.

25. Rosalyn Baxandall, Linda Gordon, and Susan Reverby, *America's Working Women* (New York: Random House, 1976), 293.

26. Ibid.

27. Anna Mayer, *Day Care as a Social Instrument: A Policy Paper* (New York: Columbia University School of Social Work, Jan. 1965), 24.

28. Rosalyn F. Baxandall, "Who Shall Care for Our Children? The History and Development of Day Care in the United States," in Jo Freeman, ed., *Women: A Feminist Perspective*, 2d ed. (Palo Alto, Calif.: Mayfield Publishing Co., 1979), 138.

29. Mayer, *Day Care as a Social Instrument*, 27.

30. Baxandall, "Who Shall Care for Our Children?" 138.

31. U.S. Department of Health, Education and Welfare, Children's Bureau, Welfare Administration, *What Is Good Day Care?* (Washington, D.C.: U.S. Department of Health, Education and Welfare, 1964).

32. In New York City, for example, numerous day-care centers organized by professional families received public funds after arguing that child care was a social right regardless of income status. The Agency for Child Development subsidized these centers because the families had lobbied persistently and noisily.

33. See Richard Nixon, "Veto of Economic Opportunity Amendments of 1971," *Weekly Compilation of Presidential Documents*, Dec. 13, 1971, 1635–36. For a more comprehensive analysis of the politics of child care in the 1970s, see Jill Norgren, "In Search of a National Child-Care Policy: Background and Prospects," in Ellen Boneparth and Emily Stoper, eds., *Women, Power and Policy*, 2d ed. (New York: Pergamon Press, 1988), 168–189.

34. Sylvia Ann Hewlitt, "Feminism's Next Challenge: Support for Motherhood," *New York Times*, June 17, 1986, A27.

35. "Women's Groups to Press for Parental Leave," *New York Times*, May 8, 1987, A19.

36. Children's Defense Fund, *A Children's Defense Budget*, 110. 1987 Figures are an unpublished estimate by the Children's Defense Fund. "Project Headstart: A Statistical Fact Sheet," Administration for Children, Youth, and Families, Office of Human Development, Health and Human Services, January 1988.

37. Kathleen Teltsch, "Swedish Feminists See a New Sense of Apathy," *New York Times*, July 8, 1982, B6; Ruth Sidel, "What Is To Be Done? Lessons From Sweden," in *Women and Children Last: The Plight of Poor Women in Affluent America* (New York: Viking Press, 1986), 182.

38. U.S. Commission on Civil Rights, *Child Care and Equal Opportunity for Women*, 44–46. The Supreme Court has ruled unconstitutional the mandatory termination of employment for pregnant women. See *Cleveland Board of Education v. La Fleur*, 414 U.S. 632 (1974). Earlier, the Court had ruled that the refusal of employers to hire women with preschool children was a violation of Title VII of the 1964 Civil Rights Act. See *Phillips v. Martin Marietta Corporation*, 400 U.S. 542 (1971).

39. Some of these state laws provide for leave through pregnancy-disability legislation. One such California law was subject to legal challenge on the grounds that it constituted special treatment of women inconsistent with federal laws prohibiting sex discrimination. A divided U.S. Supreme Court decided, in *California Savings and Loan Association v. Guerra*, 479 U.S. 272, 107 S.Ct. 683, 93 L.Ed. 2d 613 (1987), that the California law requiring private employers with five or more workers to give women unpaid pregnancy disability leave of up to four months did not discriminate because it "allows women, as well as men, to have families without losing their jobs." Some observers believe that such laws will have a backlash, reinforcing sexist stereotypes and leading employers simply not to hire women. "Pregnancy Leave for Women, and Men," *New York Times*, Jan. 18, 1987, A21; and Stuart Taylor, "Job Rights Backed in Pregnancy Case," *New York Times*, Jan. 14, 1987, A1.

40. "Single Fathers Are Entitled to 'Housework' Days," *The Week in Germany*, Nov. 27, 1981, 41.

41. Sheila B. Kamerman and Alfred J. Kahn, *Child Care Family Benefits and Working Parents: A Study in Comparative Policy* (New York: Columbia University Press, 1981), 57–58, 64.

42. Ibid., 18.

43. "Employers Offer Aid on Child Care," *New York Times*, Jan. 17, 1988, A29.

44. Ibid.

45. Ibid.

46. Milton Willner, "Day Care: A Reassessment," *Child Welfare* 44 (Mar. 1965), 126. Also, Barbara Tizard and Judith Rees, "A Comparison of Adoption, Restoration to the Natural Mother, and Continued Institutionalization on the Cognitive Development of Four-Year-Old Children," *Child Development* 45 (Mar. 1974), 92. Biases against day care show up in the wording of survey research questions. A mid-1970s General Mills American Family Report survey attempted to assay parental attitudes toward day care with the following item: "Parents can never be sure of how well children are being cared for in day-care centers." Why not cast the item in the positive: "Children are generally well cared for in day-care centers"? See General Mills American Family Report, 1976–1977, *Raising Children in a Changing Society* (Minneapolis: General Mills, 1977), 112.

47. See John Bowlby, *Mental Care and Mental Health* (Geneva: World Health Organization, 1951). For a contemporary statement of maternal deprivation theory, see Selma Fraiberg, *Every Child's Birthright: In Defense of Mothering* (New York: Basic Books, 1977). At the same time Bowlby wrote, certain professionals did argue that individual motherly care was not necessarily the only, or best, approach. Psychologist Thomas Scott of the University of Delaware, in a personal communication, points out that American psychologist B.F. Skinner advocates "a fully socialized child care system, one that replaces mother love with community love." (Scott to J. Norgren, Jan. 15, 1984).

48. Willner, "Day Care: A Reassessment," 126–127.

49. Among Caldwell's publications, see B. M. Caldwell and J. B. Richmond, "The Children's Center in Syracuse," in Laura L. Dittmann, ed., *Early Child Care: The New Perspectives* (New York: Atherton, 1968), 326–58; B. M. Caldwell, C. M. Wright, A. S. Honig, and J. Tannenbaum, "Infant Day Care and Attachment," *American Journal of Orthopsychiatry* 40 (1970), 397–412.

50. Jay Belsky, "Infant Day Care: A Cause for Concern?" *Zero to Three* (Sept. 1986).

51. Deborah Phillips, Kathleen McCartney, and Carollee Howes, "Selective Review of Infant Day Care Research: A Cause for Concern!" *Zero to Three* (Feb. 1987); Stella Chess, "Comments: Infant Day Care: A Cause for Concern'," *Zero to Three* (Feb. 1987); and response, Jay Belsky, "Risks Remain," *Zero to Three* (Feb. 1987). For popular-press reporting, see Betty Holcomb, "Where's Mommy?" *New York Magazine* (Apr. 1987).

52. Ellen Boneparth, ed., *Women, Power and Policy* (New York: Pergamon Press, 1982), ix.

53. Jean Robinson, "The State and Family Policy in a Marxist-Leninist Society: Manipulating the Public–Private Dichotomy in the People's Republic of China" (Paper presented at the annual meeting of the American Political Science Association, Washington, D.C., 1980), 4.

54. Betty Friedan, "Feminism Takes a New Turn," *New York Times Magazine*, Nov. 18, 1979, 92.

55. *Congressional Quarterly* Weekly Report (Feb. 27, 1988), 514–15.

56. Julie Johnson, "Deaths of Unattended Children Spur Day Care Bills in Congress," *New York Times*, Nov. 25, 1987, B9.

Part Three

Growing Up Female

Gender-Role Socialization: Lessons in Femininity

HILARY M. LIPS

Recently, two researchers examined the creative writing of elementary-school children attending a "young authors conference" in Michigan. Their findings with respect to gender roles were striking: Male characters outnumbered female ones in stories written by both girls and boys, and male characters were credited with more attributes—both positive ones, such as courageous and determined, and negative ones, such as mean and nasty—than were female characters (Trepanier & Romatowski, 1985). Most striking of all was the difference in the occupational roles assigned to female and male characters: Of 127 occupations assigned by the young authors to their protagonists, 111 (87 percent) were assigned to males and only 16 (13 percent) to females. The occupational assignments clearly reflected the assumption that females' capabilities limited them to gender-stereotypic jobs: The few roles allotted to female characters included those of princess, cook, hula dancer, teacher, babysitter, nurse, and housekeeper.

It is early indeed that children show an awareness of the message that males are active while females watch from the sidelines, and that females are generally less interesting and less important than males are, and have narrower horizons and less impact on the world than males do. The (often inadvertent) bearers of this message include parents, peers, and teachers, with reinforcement from a variety of media sources and cultural institutions.

CHILDHOOD SOCIALIZATION

Parents

Perhaps because it is one of the earliest distinguishing pieces of information available about a child, gender appears to be an important dimension of socialization for parents in virtually every cultural, ethnic, and class group.

Among white, middle-class North American parents, female infants are viewed, as early as twenty-four hours after birth, as softer and more delicate than are their male counterparts (Rubin, Provenzano, & Luria, 1974). Mothers playing with another woman's six-month-old infant have been found to offer gender-stereotypic toys and to smile at and hold the baby more closely when told it is a girl than when told it is a boy (Will, Self, & Datan, 1976). Furthermore, parents provide their daughters and sons with different kinds of toys, games, and environmental surroundings (Bradbard, 1985; Peretti & Sydney, 1985; Rheingold & Cook, 1975).

Parental gender-role socialization has a more global impact than does the communication of a particular set of "gender-appropriate" behaviors. Girls and boys are taught by their parents to take different approaches to problem solving, to challenge, and to life in general. Noting the research showing that parents give male infants more stimulation and varied responses than they give to females, give more contingent responses to boys than to girls, and allow boys more freedom to explore than they do girls, Jeanne Block (1984) argued that boys are socialized to "develop a premise system that presumes or anticipates mastery, efficacy, and instrumental competence" (p. 131). The socialization practices directed at girls tend toward "fostering proximity, discouraging independent problem solving by premature or excessive intervention, restricting exploration, and discouraging active play" (p. 111). Speaking in even stronger terms, Block suggested that the end result of the differing patterns of socialization for females and males is that boys develop "'wings'—which permit leaving the nest, exploring far reaches, and flying alone" (p. 137), while girls develop "'roots'—roots that anchor, stabilize and support growth" (p. 138), but allow fewer chances to master the environment.

Block's conclusions are supported by a wealth of research besides her own. For example, one study showed that parents used different strategies when working on jigsaw-puzzle and memory tasks with their six-year-old sons and daughters. They were more likely to try to teach general problem-solving strategies to their sons and to make specific solution suggestions to their daughters. With a daughter, parents were more likely to work with the child cooperatively and to provide her with information about whether her performance was correct. With a son, parents were more likely to be physically uninvolved in the task but to direct and order the child's activities and to give him praise (such as "You did well") or negative reactions (such as "Stop acting silly") (Frankel & Rollins, 1983). What these parents seemed to be communicating to their children is that it is more important for the sons than for the daughters that they not only solve this problem, but also learn how to solve others like it—and that they do it, as far as possible, on their own.

Other research also shows that parental behavior toward children may lay the groundwork for gender differences in patterns of thinking and problem solving. North American mothers' speech to their female and male toddlers differs significantly on dimensions thought to stimulate cognitive development. In one study, mothers used more questions, more numbers, more verbal teaching, and more action verbs when talking to their sons than they did when talking to their daughters (Weitzman, Birns, & Friend, 1985). Moreover, parents tend to expect more of their children in gender-stereotypic areas of performance, and to communicate these differential expectations to children at a young age. For example, after tracking 1,100 children semester by semester over the first three grades of school, one research team found that boys developed higher expectations for their performance in mathematics than girls did, despite the fact that arithmetic marks and general aptitude were similar for girls and boys in the first grade. Boys' higher expectations for their own performance seemed to be related not to past performance or to teachers' evaluations, but rather to parents' expectations for their children's performance (Entwisle & Baker, 1983).

Even the different toys and play activities parents encourage for girls and boys influence not only children's conceptions of what activities are appropriate for females and males, but also what thinking, problem solving, and social skills these children develop. For example, when mechanical toys such as models and tools are defined as "boys' toys" and are not given to girls, the outcome is a chance for boys to develop both their spatial ability and the attitude that this ability is a peculiarly masculine one. A study by Cynthia Miller (1987) used adults' ratings to classify children's toys on twelve functional dimensions, illustrating that the toys selected as appropriate for boys and girls do differ in the kinds of skills they promote. Toys rated as "boys' toys" were also rated as high in the promotion of symbolic or fantasy play, competition, constructiveness (adding pieces or combining with another toy to create something new), handling, sociability, and aggressiveness; "girls' toys" were rated higher on manipulability (ease of removing and replacing parts), creativity, nurturance, and attractiveness.

Although parents in various cultural groups differ in the rules they attach to gender, it is not unusual to find that parents (particularly fathers, according to some research) pay more attention to boys than to girls, emphasize cooperation and nurturance more for girls and achievement and autonomy more for boys. For example, a study of Mexican families by Phyllis Bronstein (1984) showed that, when interacting with their school-aged children, fathers but not mothers listened more to boys than to girls and were more likely to show boys than to show girls how to do things. On the other hand, they treated girls especially gently, but with a lack of full attention and a readiness to impose opinions on them. Overall, these fathers were communicating to their children that what boys have to say is more important than what girls have to say, and that boys are more capable than girls are of learning new skills.

Within North American society, there are variations among groups in gender-role socialization. A number of studies has shown that gender stereotyping tends to be stronger and restrictions on girls greater in working-class than in middle-class families (McBroom, 1981; Rubin, 1976). Perhaps as a result, middle-class children's ideas about gender roles reflect more sharing of characteristics between the sexes than do those of working-class children (Romer & Cherry, 1980). Ethnicity is also linked to variations in parental gender-role socialization. Studies of both Mexican-American (Mirande, 1977) and Puerto Rican (Fitzpatrick, 1971) families suggest that these families emphasize the wife–mother role for women more than non-Hispanic white families do. One study of American upper-middle-class black and white fathers found that black fathers were more likely than were white fathers to emphasize femininity for their daughters and masculinity for their sons (Price-Bonham & Skeen, 1982). Pollard (1982), who interviewed black parents, found that fathers were more likely than were mothers to expect different behaviors from daughters and sons. In general, however, research on black families suggests that they are *less* likely than are white families to polarize behavioral expectations according to gender (Lewis, 1975; Reid, 1985). Romer and Cherry (1980) found that black children differed from Jewish and Italian children in their conceptions of the masculine role: Black children viewed men and women as being equally emotionally expressive, whereas children from the other two groups thought that emotional expressivity was more characteristic of women than of men. Particularly noteworthy in black families, however, is the way that the conception of the *female* role differs from that to which white children are socialized. Girls in black families are socialized toward a female role that is defined as one of strength, independence, and resourcefulness rather than of weakness (Reid, 1985).

Peers

As soon as they are old enough to have peers outside the home, children begin to rely heavily on these peers as a source of information and approval about social behavior. Peer interactions promote gender-role socialization first of all by a tendency to segregate the sexes. School-aged children tend to play in same-sex groups (Katz & Boswell, 1984), thus minimizing contact between girls and boys and promoting an "us–them" rhetoric that contributes to the exaggeration of female–male differences, self-serving gender prejudice on the part of both groups, and a tendency to react negatively to children who "break the rules" by behaving in non–gender-stereotypic ways. There is some evidence that peers even help to shape girls' and boys' different orientations toward mastery and power.

Researchers have found consistently that children evaluate their own gender group more positively than they do the other (Etaugh, Levine, & Mennella, 1984; Olsen & Willemsen, 1978). There is also strong evidence that preschoolers, kindergartners, and elementary-school children are active and effective at maintaining gender-stereotypic behavior in their peers. Very young children make harsh judgments about and punish other children, especially boys, who violate gender stereotypes (Fagot, 1977, 1984, 1985; Langlois & Downs, 1980). The girl who tries to join a boys' game is likely to be told "You can't play — you're a girl"; the boy who picks up a girls' toy is likely to be taunted "now you're a girl." Young children are also active in reinforcing peers who engage in gender-appropriate behavior, and the peers do adjust their behavior to conform to the gender roles thus enforced (Lamb, Easterbrooks, & Holden, 1980; Lamb & Roopnarine, 1979). When researchers interviewed children in kindergarten and in the second, fourth, and sixth grades about their attitudes toward hypothetical peers who violated gender-role norms, the vast majority of the children, while indicating that cross-gender behavior was not wrong, said that they would prefer not to associate with children who violated these norms (Carter & McCloskey, 1983/84). Reactions to cross-gender behavior were more negative among older than among younger children, suggesting that children become more sure of their gender stereotypes as they progress through elementary school. These children also reported that would react more negatively toward males than toward females who exhibited cross-gender behavior. The negative reactions listed by children in the interviews indicate just how strong the gender stereotypes can be at a young age: "I would push him and call him a weirdo"; "I'd probably hit him and take away the doll"; "I'd call him a sissy and make fun of him"; "I wouldn't go anywhere near him." Other research indicates that same-sex peers are the most effective socializers: Girls respond more to the pressures of female peers, boys to those of male peers (Fagot, 1985). It is not clear whether children are aware of their power to keep their peers "in line" with gender-role expectations, or even exactly what motivates them to exert these pressures. It is evident, however, that peers do act as strict enforcers of gender-role norms in the areas of activities, toy preference, friendship choices, and traits.

Not only do peers enforce gender roles in specific content areas, but they also play an important part in the creation and maintenance of gender-differentiated approaches to power, mastery, and influence. Among toddlers, the beginnings of gender differences in power and effectiveness can be noted in the finding that girls paired with male playmates behave more passively than do girls paired with other girls or than boys paired with either girls or boys, and that vocal prohibitions (such as "Stop! Don't do that!") are most likely to be ignored when addressed to a boy by a girl (Jacklin & Maccoby, 1978). Power is still problematic for females, even in elementary school. A study of first and second graders in same-sex groups showed that, although both the female and male groups were structured by power hierarchies that were maintained in essentially similar ways, reactions to power holders differed in female and male groups. Boys who held top positions in the hierarchy were liked and accepted by their peers; powerful girls, on the other hand, were rejected (Jones, 1983).

Among preschoolers, boys make a greater number of influence attempts on their male and female peers than girls do—a difference that is almost entirely due to boys' greater use of "direct" requests and that becomes more pronounced with age (Serbin, Sprafkin, Elman, & Doyle, 1982). Between the ages of three and five years, boys become more likely to use influence attempts, such as ordering a peer to "give me the truck," announcing "you have to give me the truck," or specifying roles, as in "pretend you're the doctor." Across the same ages, girls become more likely to use "indirect" requests, in which either the request is implied rather than clearly spelled out (e.g., "I need the truck"), or it is bracketed in polite phrases (e.g., "May I please have the truck?"). Furthermore, boys become less and less responsive with age, from three to five, to peer influence attempts, particularly indirect requests, whereas the responsiveness of girls to influence attempts seems to be relatively stable across the same ages. Another interesting finding is that girls in this age range are more effective in their direct requests of other girls than in those of boys. The researchers suggest that the social effectiveness that girls experience with other girls, relative to boys, helps to perpetuate the high levels of same-sex play found in preschool classrooms, and that this sex segregation, in turn, fosters the development of increasingly differentiated verbal social influence styles and perhaps differences in cognitive and social problem-solving skills.

Even the way that children talk to one another underlines and reinforces differences in gender roles with respect to power. Research by Austin, Salehi, and Leffler (1987), who studied the discourse of samples of mainly white children from working- and middle-class homes, uncovered gender differences in the degree to which children "took charge" of conversations as opposed to simply facilitating continuing interaction. Boys of all ages studied (preschool, third, and sixth grades) were more likely than were girls to initiate conversations, and to use verbal (e.g., "Hey, look at me") and non-verbal (e.g., tapping another child on the arm) attention-getting devices. Girls, on the other hand, were more likely than were boys to say things that facilitated an ongoing conversational theme and to use reinforcers, especially positive ones, that acknowledged their partner's speech or behavior. These gender differences are similar to those that have been found for adults, and suggest that peers play a role in the early development of patterns of conversational dominance by males.

Peers may play a more important role in socialization for some groups than for others. For example, Ladner (1971), studying girls in a lower-class black American inner-city community, noted that the peer group had a broader function for these children than for their middle-class counterparts. The girls tended to have a lot of unsupervised contact with peers, and began at an early age to rely heavily on them for company, emotional support, advice, comfort, and other intangible resources that might, in other groups, be expected to come from parents. Thus, according to Ladner, in poor inner-city communities, peers are an extremely important force in shaping black American girls' images of womanhood.

Teachers

Teachers' behavior adds to gender-role–socialization pressure as soon as children enter the educational system. Part of teacher influence occurs through the teachers' choice of textbooks and other curriculum materials that depict gender in traditional ways and present females as invisible or incompetent (e.g., Marten & Matlin, 1976; United States Commission on Civil Rights, 1980; Weitzman & Rizzo, 1974). Moreover, teachers reinforce sex-differentiated activity patterns by introducing toys and play activities in gender-stereotypic ways (Serbin, Connor, & Citron, 1981; Serbin, Connor, & Iler, 1979). In one study, researchers asked teachers of preschoolers to introduce one of three toys to their classes each day: a magnetic fishing set, a set of sewing cards, and a number puzzle. To introduce the toy, they were to show it to the class and then call on four to six children to assist in demonstrating the toy and to try it out. When the toy in question was a fishing set (a stereotypically masculine toy), these teachers were far more likely to call on boys than on girls to demonstrate it, thus effectively restricting the play experience of the girls. For the other two toys, rated by observers as feminine and neutral respectively, the teachers showed no overall preference for either girls or boys as demonstrators (Serbin, Connor, & Iler, 1979). In a second study, the same researchers showed that gender-stereotyped introductions of toys to preschoolers leads the children to make gender-stereotypic toy choices. For example, when a teacher introduced a set of trucks and cars by saying ''Daddies can go to work and drive a trailer truck'' and then called on only boys to demonstrate the trucks, girls were much less likely to play with the trucks than they were when the teacher introduced the toys by saying ''We can pretend to be policemen and policewomen driving the police car'' and called on children of both sexes to demonstrate.

Perhaps the most important influence of teachers on the development of gender roles, however, is that teachers respond differently to girls and boys. Even in preschool, teachers, apparently unaware of the differential treatment they are handing out, pay more attention to boys, and respond more to boys who act aggressive and to girls who act dependent (Serbin & O'Leary, 1975). Moreover, these researchers found that teachers actually teach boys more than they teach girls, with boys twice as likely as girls to receive individual instruction in how to do things. For example, in one classroom where the children were making paper baskets, it was necessary to staple the paper handles onto each basket. The teacher circulated through the room, helping each child individually to do this task. With boys, she held the handle in place and allowed the child to staple it; for girls, unless the child spontaneously stapled the handle herself, the teacher simply took the basket and stapled it for her rather than showing her how to do it.

Even teachers' evaluations of the intellectual competence of children is biased by gender-role considerations. For example, a preschool child's compliance to teachers does not significantly predict teachers' evaluations of that child's competence, providing the child is a boy. However, for girls, compliance to teachers is a significant factor in teacher evaluation of intellectual competence, with the less compliant girls being viewed as less competent (Gold, Crombie, & Noble, 1987). Even gender stereotypes with respect to physical appearance affect teachers' reactions to their young students. For example, the stereotype that females should be dainty and petite disadvantages girls who do not fit this mold. In one study, teachers of children in kindergarten through fourth grade rated each child's academic, athletic, and social skills. Girls who were larger and heavier than their peers were rated by teachers as lower in all three areas of skill. Moreover, teachers gave lower grades to these large girls. The same pattern was not found for teachers' ratings of boys (Villimez, Eisenberg, & Carroll, 1986).

In elementary-school classrooms, girls and boys are treated in ways that tend to produce relatively more feelings of control among boys and relatively more feelings of helplessness among girls. Teachers allow boys to talk and to interrupt them more than they do girls, thus ensuring that more time will be spent on boys' than on girls' questions and that children will learn that male concerns take first priority. In addition, teachers punish girls and boys for different kinds of behaviors: girls for academic mistakes and boys for being disruptive. On the other hand, when teachers praise students, they are more likely to be responding to good appearance or conduct for girls and good academic performance for boys (Dweck, 1975; Dweck, Goetz, & Strauss, 1980). Teachers also encourage girls and boys to react differently to the children's own mistakes. Boys are given more precise feedback and are encouraged to keep trying until they get the right answer; girls are more often told not to worry about a mistake, and teachers spend less time with them suggesting new approaches and encouraging them to keep trying. In fact, girls are often simply left in the dark about whether their answers are right or wrong (Sadker & Sadker, 1985).

Studies of teacher–student interactions that have included race as a variable suggest strongly that the classroom is a place where white middle-class conceptions of gender roles are enforced. Among elementary-school students, Irvine (1985) found that white females received significantly less total communication from teachers than did white males or black females or males. Moreover, when teacher–student interactions are examined across grade levels, it becomes clear that black females are being socialized by teachers to join their white sisters in invisibility. In early elementary school (grades K through 2), black girls do not receive less teacher feedback than do their male counterparts; by later grades (3 through 5), however, they fit the pattern of inconspicuousness and low salience to the teacher that holds for white girls from the beginning (Irvine, 1986). Irvine suggests that it is because black girls are not socialized to the passive and submissive behaviors encouraged in white girls that they receive more teacher attention than do white girls in the early grades. As noted by Lightfoot (1976), black female students in the classroom may be more likely to be seen as ''assertive and bossy'' rather than as fitting the white-female-student image of ''submissive and cuddly'' (p. 259). However, as found by Irvine (1986), as black girls move from lower to upper elementary-school grades, there is a significant decline in the total amount of teacher feedback they receive, in the amount of positive teacher feedback they receive, and in the number of opportunities to respond in class they are given. As Irvine notes, ''Black female students present an active, interacting and initiating profile in the early grades but join their white female counterparts in the later grades in what appears to be traditional female sex role behaviors'' (p. 20). The teachers in Irvine's study were predominantly white and female; this research leaves unanswered questions as to the importance of teacher race and sex, and of the race and gender composition of the classroom, in producing the patterns Irvine found.

Other research supports the notion that children's approach to school achievement is influenced by gender-role socialization, and that these gender roles vary among ethnic groups. Studies of white middle-class children show that, as early as the third grade, boys begin to predict more successful performance for themselves than do females (Erkut, 1983;

Vollmer, 1984). However, when samples include a high proportion of black and low-socioeconomic-status children, gender differences in expectations for success on specific tasks are not found (Fulkerson, Furr, & Brown, 1983). Even when it comes to actual achievement, the mediation of gender roles by cultural and ethnic factors is evident. In mathematics achievement, where studies of white middle-class children have generally shown an advantage for boys, some studies of black American children show no gender differences (Fulkerson, Furr, & Brown, 1983), and research on children of a number of different racial backgrounds in Hawaii shows a consistent advantage for females (Brandon, Newton, & Hammond, 1987).

Specific Consequences of Childhood Socialization

Aggression. Researchers generally agree that boys are more likely than are girls to behave in aggressive ways. The difference was noted by Maccoby and Jacklin (1974), after an extensive review of the literature, as one of the few female–male behavioral differences that is found consistently. Since then, the greater tendency of male than of female children toward such physical aggression as hitting and pushing has been demonstrated repeatedly in free-play situations (e.g., Archer & Westeman, 1981; Di Pietro, 1981), and boys have also been found to surpass girls in the use of verbal aggression such as insults (Barrett, 1979). Although well established, however, gender differences in aggression are neither large nor completely consistent. Janet Hyde's (1984) analysis of 143 studies indicated that the amount of variation in the aggressive behavior measured in these studies that can be attributed to gender is about 5 percent. As well, some researchers have noted that the apparent overall gender difference can sometimes be traced to extremely aggressive behavior by a few boys (Archer & Westeman, 1981).

It is clear that socialization plays an important part in the formation of whatever gender differences in aggression exist. For example, while cross-cultural research shows that, within any given society, boys tend to be at least slightly more aggressive than girls, the variation *among* societies in children's aggressive behavior is far more dramatic than is the gender difference. In some societies, children of both sexes have violent temper tantrums and learn to scream insults as soon as they learn to speak; in others, children tend not to quarrel at all. In fact, in any particular society, the level of aggression displayed by children of one sex is strongly and positively related to the level of aggression displayed by the other (Rohner, 1976, pp. 61–62). Clearly, social reactions to and tolerance of aggression affect the likelihood that children of either sex will engage in it.

Researchers have shown that, when girls and boys are similarly rewarded for aggressive behaviors, girls are as aggressive as boys (Bandura, 1973). It has been established, however, that boys are more rewarded by their peers than females are for aggressive behavior, and that aggression in females meets with disapproval, even among children. One study showed that aggression by girls in the classroom was far more likely to be ignored, by both peers and teachers, than was aggression by boys. For the girls in this study, more than 50 percent of their aggressive actions received no response whatsoever (Fagot & Hagan, 1985). Since any response, either positive or negative, is better than none at all for maintaining a behavior, it is easy to see the large part that the social environment plays in making boys more aggressive than girls.

Performance on cognitive tests: language and mathematics. Small but consistent gender differences in performance on tests of verbal, quantitative, and spatial ability have been reported in the psychological literature (Maccoby & Jacklin, 1974; Hyde, 1981). By the onset of adolescence, girls tend to outperform boys on a variety of language-related tasks, whereas boys tend to outscore girls on mathematics tests and tests of visual–spatial ability. Despite the small size of these differences and the wide individual variation among children, the differences have sometimes been cited as evidence that girls and boys are naturally suited for different kinds of tasks and should prepare for different kinds of work. In particular, it has been said that boys' apparent superiority in quantitative and visual–spatial ability gives them an advantage in mathematics and science and explains why so many more males than females choose to study and work in these areas. Because the differences are so small, the argument misses the point. For example, Hyde (1981), making the initial assumption that a person would have to be in the top 5 percent of the range of spatial abilities to be qualified for a profession such as engineering, calculated that, if spatial ability were the only determining factor, the ratio of males to females in such professions would be 2 to 1. Since, the ratio of men to women in engineering has never been less than 20 to 1, gender differences in spatial ability could conceivably explain only a small part of the male dominance of the engineering professions.

The gender difference in mathematics achievement is linked more strongly to gender-role socialization than to ability differences. Parents and teachers have differing expectations for girls and boys, and these expectations are communicated early. One study of the parents of mathematically gifted children in the Johns Hopkins Talent Search found that the boys' parents were considerably more likely than were the girls' parents even to be aware that their child was mathematically talented (Tobias, 1982), and parents of boys were more likely than were parents of girls to have given their children science-related gifts, such as science kits, telescopes, and microscopes (Astin, 1974). Furthermore, even within the same mathematics class, girls and boys tend not to get the same education. When one team of researchers observed thirty-three second-grade teachers in the classroom, they found that these teachers spent more time teaching reading than mathematics to individual girls and more time teaching mathematics than reading to individual boys (Leinhardt, Seewald, & Engel, 1979).

A large-scale study of Baltimore first graders indicates that, even as children enter school, girls and boys have already begun to learn that different things are important (Entwisle, Alexander, Pallas, & Cardigan, 1987). At this stage, academic competence and the student role formed a more important and distinct aspect of self-concept for boys than for girls. Boys were more concerned with learning quickly; girls were more concerned with obeying rules and being honest. Being able to do arithmetic was an important aspect of the academic self-concept for boys; for girls, it was irrelevant. The girls did not view their ability in mathematics as relevant to their academic self-image, even though they did as well in mathematics as the boys did and were exposed to the same mathematics instruction classes as the boys. Where do these differences come from? The study suggests that, for girls at least, they originate partly in parental expectations — and parental expectations of girls focus strongly on "being good" rather than on academic achievement. However, when data for black children and white children in this study are examined separately, it appears that black parents give a less gender-stereotypic message about mathematics to their daughters than white parents do. For black girls, but not for white girls, parents' mathematics-acheivement expectations were significant predictors of their daughters' academic self-image.

SOCIALIZATION IN ADOLESCENCE

By adolescence, the impact of gender-role socialization centers on two major issues: vocational decisions and sexuality. For girls much more than for boys, these two issues are linked, since the girls have observed by this time that adult women make a lot more compromises between work and family relationships than men do. As girls struggle with decisions in these areas, parental, peer, and teacher socialization influences continue to be important. A theme from childhood that continues to be present is that girls are frequently given the message that they have little control over their lives.

For girls, physical maturation — such as the development of breasts and a more sexually mature appearance — is associated with early pressures in the direction of the traditional female role. Parents, worried about pregnancy, often place new restrictions on girls at this stage, so that growing up is associated with a feeling of loss of freedom rather than with one of expanding horizons (Golub, 1983; Katz, 1986). Under such conditions, early marriage, or even pregnancy, is sometimes idealized by the young girl as an escape from parental pressures and a chance to take control of her life and to prove that she is grown up and responsible. This kind of situation can tip the balance of the career versus family conflict in the direction of family at such an early age that the girl does little exploration of occupation-related possibilities. A girl who is physically well developed at an early age faces especially strong pressure to emphasize relationships at the expense of achievement. She receives reinforcement earlier than do her peers for following a traditional feminine "script," reducing the likelihood that she will explore less traditional alternatives, such as a career (Katz, 1986). Also, to the extent that males keep the role of initiator in the heterosexual dating arena, a girl often finds herself in a situation where she is passively waiting to be "asked out" rather than feeling that she has active control over her relationships or her leisure time. In the realm of sexuality also, girls have traditionally been taught that whatever control they have is of a reactive (and negative) nature — the power to say no (or, in special circumstances, yes), but not that to initiate sexual interactions. Thus, even if a girl has survived childhood with her sense of control and effectiveness intact, the interpersonal issues she encounters in adolescence are likely to shake her feelings of efficacy.

A common gender stereotype is that women are less motivated than are men by a need for achievement, but research has not supported this notion. What the research does suggest is that women, from adolescence onward, are faced with pressures to balance their achievement needs against their desire for relationships, and for marriage and family. For female adolescents planning their future, the potential conflict between work and family life can be intense. Young women are more likely than are young men to expect to have to be flexible in their work roles in order to have a family life (Herzog & Bachman, 1982). Thus, even a young woman with high occupational aspirations and commitment has probably learned to consider her future parental and spouse-support roles as more important than, or even incompatible with, her future work role. Such considerations are frequently encouraged by parents and teachers, and they may snowball as female adolescents watch their peers and siblings begin to marry. A girl is led to feel at this stage that she cannot, or should not, assert the independent control of her life that choosing a demanding occupational path entails. She is encouraged to prepare for a variety of options and to remain flexible, rather than to become committed to a particular personal goal (Angrist, 1969). The message received by adolescent girls is often that they will have to adapt their career goals to the needs of a future spouse and family. Moreover, the pressure to make marriage and family a primary concern increases as these young women approach the end of their schooling, or when they become involved seriously with a particular boyfriend (Weitzman, 1984).

Children list parents as one of the primary sources of information about education and occupations (Farmer, 1985; Kidd, 1984). Furthermore, parental encouragement and expectations, and the values parents place on achievement and on the homemaker role for women, are influential for educational and occupational plans. It has long been acknowledged, for example, that parental encouragement to attend college is linked to high occupational aspirations among teenage girls (Picou & Curry, 1973). In a rare longitudinal study that followed adolescents and their parents from seventh to twelfth grades, Perrone (1973) showed that changes in the behavior parents valued in their daughters seemed to precede changes in the daughters' occupational values. When the daughters reached early high school, many parents began to value their development of home-making skills and domestic orientation. The communication of these values may have been important in the development of new occupational values among the daughters, for by late high school these girls' most frequently voiced occupational values had changed from self-fulfillment to working with people and helping others. At this stage, for the first time in this study, their occupational aspirations were lower than were those of their male counterparts.

By the end of high school, many girls have finally accepted the message that having a marriage, home, and family will conflict with occupational goals—and they reduce their occupational goals accordingly. In fact, gender-role socialization apparently leads women to lower their vocational goals even before they begin the process of choosing a specific occupation. According to a model proposed by Corder and Stephan (1984), young women plan their future in two stages: First they decide how they will combine family and work roles, then they decide on an occupation. In the first stage, because they perceive that men dislike career-oriented women and because they have been taught to value marriage and family more than a career, most adolescent women rule out occupations that are high in prestige or in required commitment. Then, in the second stage, the choice of a specific occupation is made from a range that has been drastically limited by decisions made in the first stage. Corder and Stephan's research supports not only their notion of a two-stage process in adolescent women's vocational decisions, but also the validity of the young women's perceptions of men's preferences. The adolescent men in their sample showed a definite lack of enthusiasm for future marriage to career-oriented women.

Research indicates that young women are continuing to base their occupational choices on gender-stereotyped perceptions of family roles (Leslie, 1986). Such choices, rather than reflecting a lack of awareness of the options available to women, may, as Jane Gaskell (1985) argues, indicate their realistic assessment of the situation. In her study of high-school girls from working-class families, Gaskell (1981) found that many of them were choosing business courses and planning for clerical jobs, even though they readily admitted that they found the courses boring. They persisted in this choice, however, because they knew it would lead to employment, and finding a job after graduation was crucial. Moreover, these young women were reluctant to plan for demanding occupations, since their own family experiences led them to believe that, if they married, they would have the primary responsibility for domestic work, and that their paid work outside the home would have to take second priority. Thus, a young woman's realistic assessment of a gender-unequal labor market and family support system may lead her to make traditional choices when planning her future work. The employment situation may be assessed somewhat differently by girls from upper middle-class families, who do have more options for continuing their education. Among these young women, there has been an increase in the percentage who aspire to high-status, nontraditional occupations (Geller, 1984).

An important factor in socialization for achievement is the presence of models. Where girls are provided with achieving female models, their attitudes toward success and career attainment seem to be favorably affected. The literature on maternal employment indicates that, in middle-class families, daughters of employed mothers have higher educational and occupational aspirations than do daughters of women who are full-time homemakers (Etaugh, 1974; Hoffman, 1984; Stein & Bailey, 1973). Daughters of employed women also regard the professional competence of women more highly than do daughters of women who are full-time homemakers (Baruch, 1972), and there is a correspondence between mothers' and daughters' career interests and aspirations (Zuckerman, 1981). Among black female university students, those pursuing nontraditional careers were more likely than were their more traditional counterparts to have mothers who were well educated and were working in nontraditional fields themselves (Burlew, 1982).

Parental socialization of daughters for work is an area in which race and class differences in the conception of gender roles are substantial. For example, most researchers agree that in white working-class families, the pressures on daughters to conform to the traditional female role are greater than those that exist in white middle-class families (McBroom, 1981). However, in black working-class families, the notion of what is "traditional" for women is quite different from the notion of the full-time homemaker role idealized by working-class whites. For black women, it is, in fact, "traditional" to participate in the labor force, and some researchers have argued that black women's long-term experience in the work force has profoundly influenced these black women's ideology of gender (Gump, 1980; Malson, 1983). For example, in a heterogeneous sample of urban black women interviewed by Malson (1983), 95 percent had mothers who had been employed, usually full-time, when they were children. As Malson quotes one of these women, "I'd never known a woman who stayed home with children . . . I did not know any housewives. That form of life was kind of alien. I did not even know that was possible. When I found out that people actually only stayed home and did nothing but raise children and clean house, I thought it was fascinating. . . . I always assumed I'd work and have children" (p. 107).

Research suggests that black females are socialized to assume that they must take some economic responsibility for family support (Peters & de Ford, 1978; Smith, 1982). It is sometimes assumed that this means that these women place less value on family roles than on work roles, but this assumption is not supported by evidence. Young black women have been found to be equally predisposed toward work and homemaking–childrearing (Engram, 1980; Gump, 1975). In fact, a recent study of gender-role attitudes among southern college students revealed that blacks were more likely than were whites to believe that a woman's real fulfillment in life comes from motherhood, *and* that blacks were more likely than whites to believe that it was appropriate for a mother with school-aged children to work outside the home (Lyson, 1986). It is clear that the black students had not been socialized as strongly as had the white students to see motherhood and employment as mutually exclusive.

Black women are not the only group for whom cultural traditions and some isolation from mainstream middle-class socialization pressures have resulted in less gender-sterotyped perceptions of work. One team of researchers studying the attitudes of seventh-grade Navajo children in reservation schools found them to have less gender-stereotyped perceptions of occupations than had any other group studied (Beyard-Tyler & Haring, 1984). The researchers attribute the lack of stereotyping to lack of information about the dominant culture; however, an additional factor is probably the longstanding tradition of flexibility in male–female work roles among the Navajo (Griffin, 1984).

In school settings, the role of teachers and counselors in guiding women toward particular occupational choices can be crucial. Unfortunately, the evidence indicates that such resource persons are generally not very good at providing students with information about options that are gender-nontraditional (Eccles & Hoffman, 1984). For young minority women, this problem is compounded by the dual effects of racism and sexism. Studies have found that black female students tend to be steered toward low-level, blue-collar jobs, while their white counterparts are oriented toward white-collar occupations (Baker & Levenson, 1975), and that counselors discourage minority women from going to college or channel them into traditional nonscientific majors (Alexander, 1979). This problem has been noted as an especially strong reason for Native American women's clustering in low-paid occupations (Metoyer, 1979; Abella, 1984). In fact, the low occupational status of both Native American women (Abella, 1984) and Hispanic-American women (Ortiz & Cooney, 1984) has been linked to low levels of education—a factor that may well reflect teacher and counselor influence.

Most of the literature on women's socialization in adolescence is characterized by a concern with the tension implicit in the role demands placed on women. According to tradition, women are supposed to be preparing to be wives and mothers, yet increasingly they are also expected to be preparing for a lifetime of employment. Much of this preparation takes place in the context of expectations that, in most marriages, when work and family demands conflict, the woman will have to make more compromises than the man will and the woman will be saddled with more than half of the domestic responsibilities. If, as they contemplate this prospect, young women feel ambivalent about the wholehearted pursuit of achievement goals, as studies show they do (Weitzman, 1984), it is hardly surprising. It seems a reasonable prediction that, even if socialization pressures on girls increasingly stress achievement, girls' realistic appraisal of the difficulties of combining family and job demands in a culture that still refuses to consider women's occupational lives as comparable in importance to men's occupational lives will contribute to reluctance to pursue demanding careers. By the time young women reach the end of adolescence, they have accumulated years of experience of being less influential than males—of receiving less attention, getting less feedback, being taken less seriously. It would be surprising indeed if most of these young women, finding themselves at the point in their lives where the pressures to find a marriage partner and start a family are strongest, were to resist social expectations and to refuse to marry unless they had an agreement with their partner of complete equality, or to decide not to marry or have children at all.

Finally, there is no reason to assume that the family goals that young women have been taught to value are any less important than the achievement goals so often stressed for young men (Eccles, 1987). If members of either gender group choose at times to compromise work success in favor of family obligations, there is perhaps more cause for celebration than alarm—except that in our present society the economic costs of such choices are substantial, and they fall disproportionately on women. As young women face choices about work and family, there is much in their socialization that has prepared them for the necessary compromises and less that has prepared them for the necessary firmness in pursuit of their own goals. The challenge for them, and for society as a whole, is to find an appropriate balance.

REFERENCES

Abella, Judge Rosalie S. (1984). *Equality in employment: A royal commission report*. Ottawa: Canadian Government Publishing Centre.

Alexander, Vicki (1979). The nature of professional training for minority women: An overview. In Lucy Ann Geiselman (Ed.), *The minority woman in America: Professionalism at what cost?* (pp. 15–25). San Francisco: University of California.

Angrist, Shirley S. (1969). The study of sex roles. *Journal of Social Issues, 25*, 215–232.

Archer, John, & Westeman, Karin (1981). Sex differences in the aggressive behaviour of schoolchildren. *British Journal of Social Psychology, 20*, 31–36.

Astin, Helen (1974). Sex differences in mathematical and scientific precocity. In Julian C. Stanley, D. P. Keating, & Lynn Fox (Eds.), *Mathematical talent: Discovery, description and development*. Baltimore: Johns Hopkins University Press.

Austin, Ann M. B. A., Salehi, Mahshid, & Leffler, Ann (1987). Gender and developmental differences in children's conversations. *Sex Roles, 16* (9/10), 497–510.

Baker, Sally Hillsman, & Levensen, Bernard (1975). Job opportunities of black and white working-class women. *Social Problems, 2*, 510–533.

Bandura, Albert (1973). *Aggression: A Social Learning Analysis*. Englewood Cliffs, NJ: Prentice-Hall.

Barrett, David E. (1979). A naturalistic study of sex differences in children's aggression. *Merrill Palmer Quarterly, 25* (3), 193–203.

Baruch, Grace K. (1972). Maternal influence upon college women's attitudes toward women and work. *Developmental Psychology, 6*, 32–37.

Beyard-Tyler, Karen, & Haring, Marilyn J. (1984). Navajo students respond to nontraditional occupations: Less information, less bias? *Journal of Counseling Psychology, 31* (2), 270–273.

Block, Jeanne H. (1984). Psychological development of female children and adolescents. In Jeanne H. Block, *Sex Role Identity and Ego Development* (pp. 126–142). San Francisco: Jossey-Bass.

Bradbard, Marilyn R. (1985). Sex differences in adults' gifts and children's toy requests at Christmas. *Psychological Reports, 56*, 969–970.

Brandon, Paul R., Newton, Barbara J., & Hammond, Ormond W. (1987). Children's mathematics achievement in Hawaii: Sex differences favoring girls. *American Educational Research Journal, 24* (3), 437–461.

Bronstein, Phyllis (1984). Differences in mothers' and fathers' behaviors toward children: A cross-cultural comparison. *Developmental Psychology, 20* (6), 995–1003.

Burlew, Ann Kathleen (1982). The experiences of black females in traditional and nontraditional professions. *Psychology of Women Quarterly, 6* (3), 312–326.

Carter, D. Bruce, & McCloskey, Laura A. (1983/84). Peers and the maintenance of sex-typed behavior: The development of children's conceptions of cross-gender behavior in their peers. *Social Cognition, 2* (4), 294–314.

Corder, Judy, & Stephan, Cookie White (1984). Females' combinations of work and family roles: Adolescents' aspirations. *Journal of Marriage and the Family, 46*, 391–402.

Di Pietro, Janet A. (1981). Rough and tumble play: A function of gender. *Developmental Psychology, 17* (1), 50–58.

Dweck, Carol S. (1975). The role of expectations and attributions in the alleviation of learned helplessness. *Journal of Personality and Social Psychology, 31*, 674–685.

Dweck, Carol S., Goetz, Therese E., & Strauss, Nan L. (1980). Sex differences in learned helplessness: IV: An experimental and naturalistic study of failure generalization and its mediators. *Journal of Personality and Social Psychology, 38*, 441–452.

Eccles, Jacquelynne S. (1987). Gender roles and women's achievement-related decisions. *Psychology of Women Quarterly, 11* (2), 135–172.

Eccles, Jacquelynne S., & Hoffman, Lois W. (1984). Sex roles, socialization, and occupational behavior. In H. W. Stevenson & A. E. Siegel (Eds.), *Research in Child Development and Social Policy:* Volume 1 (pp. 367–420). Chicago: University of Chicago Press.

Engram, E. (1980). Role transition in early adulthood: Orientations of young Black women. In La Frances Rodgers-Rose (Ed.), *The Black Woman,* Beverly Hills, CA: Sage Publications.

Entwisle, Doris R., Alexander, Karl L., Pallas, Aaron M., & Cadigan, Doris (1987). The emergent academic self-image of first graders: Its response to social structure. *Child Development, 58* 1190–1206.

Entwisle, Doris R., & Baker, D. P. (1983). Gender and young children's expectations for performance in arithmetic. *Developmental Psychology, 19* (2), 200–209.

Erkut, Sumru (1983). Exploring sex differences in expectancy, attribution, and academic achievement. *Sex Roles, 9,* 217–231.

Etaugh, Claire (1974). Effects of maternal employment on children: A review of recent research. *Merrill Palmer Quarterly, 20,* 71–98.

Etaugh, Claire, Levine, Diane, & Mennella, Angela (1984). Development of sex biases in children: 40 years later. *Sex Roles, 10,* 911–922.

Fagot, Beverly I. (1977). Consequences of moderate cross-gender behavior in preschool children. *Child Development, 48,* 902–907.

Fagot, Beverly I. (1984). Teacher and peer reactions to boys' and girls' play styles. *Sex Roles, 11,* 691–702.

Fagot, Beverly I. (1985). Beyond the reinforcement principle: Another step toward understanding sex role development. *Developmental Psychology, 21* (6), 1097–1104.

Fagot, Beverly I., & Hagan, Richard (1985). Aggression in toddlers: Responses to the assertive acts of boys and girls. *Sex Roles, 12* (3/4), 341–351.

Farmer, Helen S. (1985). Model of career and achievement motivation for women and men. *Journal of Counseling Psychology, 32,* 363–390.

Fitzpatrick, J. (1971). *Puerto Rican Americans: The Meaning of Migration.* Englewood Cliffs, NJ: Prentice-Hall.

Frankel, Marc T., & Rollins, Howard A., Jr. (1983). Does mother know best? Mothers and fathers interacting with preschool sons and daughters. *Developmental Psychology, 19* (5), 694–702.

Fulkerson, Katherine Fee, Furr, Susan, & Brown, Duane (1983). Expectations and achievement among third-, sixth-, and ninth-grade black and white males and females. *Developmental Psychology, 19* (2), 231–236.

Gaskell, Jane (1981). Sex inequalities in education for work: The case of business education. *Canadian Journal of Education, 6* (2), 54–72.

Gaskell, Jane (1985). Course enrollment in the high school: The perspective of working-class girls. *Sociology of Education, 58,* 48–59.

Geller, Gloria (1984). Aspirations of female high school students. *Resources for Feminist Research, 13* (1), 17–19.

Gold, Dolores, Crombie, Gail, & Noble, Sally (1987). Relations between teachers' judgments of girls' and boys' compliance and intellectual competence. *Sex Roles, 16* (7/8), 351–358.

Golub, Sharon (1983). Menarche: The beginning of menstrual life. *Women & Health, 8* (2/3), 17–36.

Griffin, J. (1984). Culture contact, women and work: The Navajo example. *Social Science Journal, 21* (4), 29–39.

Gump, Janice (1975). A comparative analysis of black and white women's sex-role attitudes. *Journal of Consulting and Clinical Psychology, 43,* 858–863.

Gump, Janice (1980). Reality and myth: Employment and sex role ideology in black women. In F. Denmark & J. Sherman (Eds.), *The psychology of women.* New York: Psychological Dimensions.

Herzog, A. R. & Bachman, J. G. (1982). *Sex-Role Attitudes Among High School Seniors*. Ann Arbor, MI: Institute for Social Research, University of Michigan.

Hoffman, Lois W. (1984). Maternal employment and the young child. In M. Perlmutter (Ed.), *Mother/Child Interaction and Parent/Child Relations in Child Development* (pp. 101–128). Hillsdale, NJ: Lawrence Erlbaum Associates.

Hyde, Janet S. (1981). How large are cognitive gender differences? A meta-analysis using ω and δ. *American Psychologist, 36,* 892–901.

Hyde, Janet S. (1984). How large are gender differences in aggression? A developmental meta-analysis. *Developmental Psychology, 20* (4), 722–736.

Irvine, Jacqueline Jordan (1985). Teacher communication patterns as related to the race and sex of the student. *Journal of Educational Research, 78* (6), 338–345.

Irvine, Jacqueline Jordan (1986). Teacher–student interactions: Effects of student race, sex, and grade level. *Journal of Educational Psychology, 78* (1), 14–21.

Jacklin, Carol Nagy, & Maccoby, Eleanor Emmons (1978). Social behavior at thirty-three months in same-sex and mixed-sex dyads. *Child Development, 49,* 557–569.

Jones, Diane C. (1983). Power structures and perceptions of power holders in same-sex groups of young children. *Women and Politics, 3,* 147–164.

Katz, Phyllis A. (1986). Gender identity: Development and consequences. In R. D. Ashmore & F. K. Del Boca (Eds.), *The Social Psychology of Female–Male Relations* (pp. 21–67). Orlando, FL: Academic Press.

Katz, Phyllis A., & Boswell, S. L. (1984). Sex-role development and the one-child family. In T. Falbo (Ed.), *The Single-Child Family*. New York: Guilford Press.

Kidd, J. M. (1984). Young people's perceptions of their occupational decision-making. *British Journal of Guidance and Counseling, 12,* 15–38.

Ladner, Joyce A. (1971). *Tomorrow's Tomorrow: The Black Woman*. Garden City, NY: Doubleday.

Lamb, Michael E., Easterbrooks, M. Ann, & Holden, George W. (1980). Reinforcement and punishment among preschoolers: Characteristics, effects, and correlates. *Child Development, 51,* 1230–1236.

Lamb, Michael E., & Roopnarine, Jaipaul L. (1979). Peer influences on sex-role development in preschoolers. *Child Development, 50,* 1219–1222.

Langlois, Judith H., & Downs, A. Chris (1980). Mothers, fathers, and peers as socialization agents of sex-typed play behaviors in young children. *Child Development, 51,* 1237–1247.

Leinhardt, G., Seewald, A. M., & Engel, M. (1979). Learning what's taught: Sex differences in instruction. *Journal of Educational Psychology, 71,* 432–439.

Leslie, Leigh A. (1986). The impact of adolescent females' assessments of parenthood and employment on plans for the future. *Journal of Youth and Adolescence, 15,* 29–50.

Lewis, Diane K. (1975). The black family: Socialization and sex roles. *Phylon, 36* (3), 221–237.

Lightfoot, S. L. (1976). Socialization and education of young black girls in school. *Teachers College Record, 78,* 239–262.

Lyson, Thomas A. (1986). Race and sex differences in sex role attitudes of southern college students. *Psychology of Women Quarterly, 10* (4), 421–428.

Maccoby, Eleanor E., & Jacklin, Carol N. (1974). *The Psychology of Sex Differences*. Stanford, CA: Stanford University Press.

Malson, Michelene Ridley (1983). Black women's sex roles: The social context for a new ideology. *Journal of Social Issues, 39* (3), 101–114.

Marten, Laurel A., & Matlin, Margaret W. (1976). Does sexism in elementary school readers still exist? *The Reading Teacher, 29,* 767–776.

McBroom, William H. (1981). Parental relationships, socioeconomic status, and sex role expectations. *Sex Roles, 7,* 1027–1033.

Metoyer, Cheryl A. (1979). The Native American woman. In Eloise C. Snyder (Ed.), *The study of women: Enlarging perspectives of social reality* (pp. 329–335). New York: Harper & Row.

Miller, Cynthia L. (1987). Qualitative differences among gender-stereotyped toys: Implications for cognitive and social development in girls and boys. *Sex Roles, 16* (9/10), 473–487.

Mirande, Alfredo (1977). The Chicano family: A reanalysis of conflicting views. *Journal of Marriage and the Family, 39,* 747–756.

Olsen, Nancy J., & Willemsen, Eleanor W. (1978). Studying sex prejudice in children. *The Journal of Genetic Psychology, 133,* 203–216.

Ortiz, Vilma, & Cooney, Rosemary Santana (1984). Sex-role attitudes and labor force participation among young Hispanic females and non-Hispanic white females. *Social Science Quarterly, 65* (2), 392–400.

Peretti, Peter O., & Sydney, Tiffany M. (1984). Parental toy choice stereotyping and its effect on child toy preference and sex-role typing. *Social Behavior and Personality, 12* (2), 213–216.

Perrone, Philip A. (1973). A longitudinal study of occupational values in adolescents. *Vocational Guidance Quarterly, 22,* 116–123.

Peters, M., & de Ford, C. (1978). The solo mother. In R. Stables (Ed.), *The Black Family: Essays and Studies.* Belmont, CA: Wadsworth.

Picou, J. Steven, & Curry, Evans W. (1973). Structural, interpersonal and behavioral correlates of female adolescents' occupational choices. *Adolescence, 8,* 421–432.

Pollard, D. S. (1982, November). Perspectives of black parents regarding the socialization of their children. Paper presented at the Seventh Conference on Empirical Research in Black Psychology, Hampton, Virginia.

Price-Bonham, Sharon, & Skeen, Patsy (1982). Black and white fathers' attitudes toward children's sex roles. *Psychological Reports, 50,* 1187–1190.

Reid, Pamela Trotman (1985). Sex-role socialization of black children: A review of theory, family, and media influence. *Academic Psychology Bulletin, 7,* 201–212.

Rheingold, Harriet L., & Cook, Kaye V. (1975). The contents of boys' and girls' rooms as an index of parents' behaviors. *Child Development, 46,* 459–463.

Rohner, Ronald P. (1976). Sex differences in aggression: Phylogenetic and enculturation perspectives. *Ethos, 4* (1), 57–72.

Romer, Nancy, & Cherry, Debra (1980). Ethnic and social class differences in children's sex-role concepts. *Sex Roles, 6,* 245–263.

Rubin, Jeffrey Z., Provenzano, Frank J., & Luria, Zella (1974). The eye of the beholder: Parents' views on sex of newborns. *American Journal of Orthopsychiatry, 44,* 512–519.

Rubin, Lillian (1976). *Worlds of Pain: Life in the Working Class Family.* New York: Basic Books.

Sadker, Myra, & Sadker, David (1985, March). Sexism in the schoolroom of the '80s. *Psychology Today, 19,* 54–57.

Serbin, Lisa A., Connor, Jane M., & Citron, Cheryl C. (1981). Sex-differentiated free play behavior: Effects of teacher modeling, location and gender. *Developmental Psychology, 17,* 640–646.

Serbin, Lisa A., Connor, Jane M., & Iler, Iris (1979). Sex-stereotyped and non-stereotyped introductions of new toys in the preschool classroom: An observational study of teacher behavior and its effects. *Psychology of Women Quarterly, 4,* 261–265.

Serbin, Lisa A., & O'Leary, K. Daniel (1975, December). How nursery schools teach girls to shut up. *Psychology Today, 9* (7), 56–58, 102–103.

Serbin, Lisa A., Sprafkin, Carol, Elman, Meryl, & Doyle, Anna-Beth (1982). The early development of sex-differentiated patterns of social influence. *Canadian Journal of Behavioural Science, 14* (4), 350–363.

Smith, Elsie J. (1982). The black female adolescent: A review of the educational, career, and psychological literature. *Psychology of Women Quarterly, 6* (3), 261–288.

Stein, Aletha H., & Bailey, Margaret M. (1973). The socialization of achievement orientation in females. *Psychological Bulletin, 80* (5), 345–366.

Tobias, Sheila (1982, January). Sexist equations. *Psychology Today*, 14–17.

Trepanier, Mary L., & Romatowski, Jane A. (1985). Attributes and roles assigned to characters in children's writing: Sex differences and sex-role perceptions. *Sex Roles, 13* (5/6), 263–272.

U.S. Commission on Civil Rights (1980). *Characters in textbooks.* Washington, D.C.: U.S. Government Printing Office.

Villimez, Carolyn, Eisenberg, Nancy, & Carroll, James L. (1986). Sex differences in the relation of children's height and weight to academic performance and to others' attributions of competence. *Sex Roles, 15* (11/12), 667–681.

Vollmer, Fred (1984). Sex differences in personality and expectancy. *Sex Roles, 11,* 1121–1139.

Weitzman, Lenore J. (1984). Sex-role socialization: A focus on women. In Jo Freeman (Ed.), *Women: A Feminist Perspective,* third edition (pp. 157–237). Palo Alto, CA: Mayfield.

Weitzman, Lenore J., & Rizzo, Diane (1974). *Images of Males and Females in Elementary School Textbooks.* New York: National Organization for Women's Legal Defense and Education Fund.

Weitzman, Nancy, Birns, Beverly, & Friend, Ronald (1985). Traditional and nontraditional mothers' communication with their daughters and sons. *Child Development, 56,* 894–898.

Will, Jerrie, Self, Patricia, & Datan, Nancy (1976). Maternal behavior and perceived sex of infant. *American Journal of Orthopsychiatry, 46,* 135–139.

Zuckerman, Diana M. (1981). Family background, sex-role attitudes, and life goals of technical college and university students. *Sex Roles, 7,* 1109–1126.

Women and Higher Education: Gender Differences in the Status of Students and Scholars

MARY FRANK FOX

In the nineteenth-century movement for women's rights, feminists thought that higher education would lead not only to equal suffrage, but also to widespread political, legal, and economic reforms of benefit to women (Antler, 1982:15). It is unclear whether gains in education lead or follow women's progress in other areas. And increased levels of education have not resulted ''as a matter of course'' in political or social gains for women (Schwager, 1987:335). However, women's educational attainment is related to their participation and role in the economy. To begin with, the more education a woman has, the more likely she is to be employed. Of all women sixteen years of age or over who had completed just eight years of school, only about one in five—or 22 percent—were in the labor force in 1987. With higher levels of education, rates of labor-force participation rose sharply, so that among women who had completed high school, well over half (59 percent) were employed; among those with four years of college, 72 percent were employed; and among those with five or more years of college, over three-quaters (79 percent) were in the labor force (U.S. Bureau of Labor Statistics, 1988:unpublished data).

Moreover, occupational advancement is more closely linked to education for women than it is for men. Men use their educational credentials for initial entry to jobs, and then rely on job-related ''experience'' for advancement (Featherman, 1980). For women, however, formal credentials remain critical throughout their working lives (Featherman, 1980). In other words, the direct effect of education on occupational status is stronger for women (Sewell, Hauser, and Wolf, 1980). Although women cannot expect to gain the same returns (salary, occupational rank, advancement) on their education as men do (Featherman and Hauser, 1976:481; U.S. Bureau of the Census 1987), if women's credentials are "less than the best," women can suffer even greater inequality (see, for example, Fox, 1981:81).

Finally, because higher education influences the next generation and reflects social trends in American society, the standing of women as faculty indicates the position and plight of women in the professions, and sets an example to students of the status of women in society.

WOMEN AS STUDENTS IN HIGHER EDUCATION: HISTORICAL BACKGROUND

In America's colonial era, educational opportunities were almost nonexistent for women. The town schools of New England generally excluded girls, or admitted them for just a few hours per day at inconvenient times when boys were not in attendance (Woody, 1966:177). The few colleges of this era were given over to the training of ministers; since women were barred from the ministry, they were excluded from these schools. Only in the wealthiest families, where a system of tutorial education prevailed, did girls sometimes get instruction in arts, letters, and literature. For the vast majority of women, education was simply an apprenticeship in the home, where they learned domestic arts and skills.

At the beginning of the eighteenth century, however, the seminary or academy schools began to open, and these schools became the prevailing form of education available to women. The seminary or academy schools frequently emphasized "flashy accomplishments of little substantial value" (Woody, 1966:399), and have been sorely criticized for their cursory and superficial curriculum. Still, along with courses of music, dancing, and fancy needlework, these schools provided rudimentary training in grammar, composition, rhetoric, geography, and arithmetic. Further, the seminary schools nurtured women's aspirations. The experience of taking classes, competing, and winning prizes gave these young students a taste for a new role — beyond that of merely being a daughter (or wife) (Gordon, 1979). Most important, the seminary and academy schools, which flourished throughout New England, the mid-Atlantic, and the deep South, secured public recognition of and support for female education (Woody, 1966). From the seminary schools, higher education for women got its start.

The seminary schools of the postrevolutionary, American Federal era flourished in an ideology — called Republican Motherhood — unknown in Europe at the time. That ideology assigned to women a political role as educators of the next generation of sons, and thus as educators for the independence of the nation (Kerber, 1976, 1980). This put some premium on rationality and literacy for women — within the confines of women's domestic responsibilities.

During the nineteenth century, women's education also advanced with the growth of normal schools established to train teachers for the growing system of public education. The expansion in public education during this period raised great concern about the costs it incurred. Because female teachers earned about one-quarter to one-third of the salaries of male teachers, they provided a cost-saving solution (see Woody, 1966:492–493). Thus, women were in demand for the public schools and for the institutes in which teachers trained. In consequence—and as an indicator—during the antebellum years, one out of five white women (and one out of four native-born white women) taught sometime during their lives (Bernard and Vinovskis, 1977).

These teaching institutes had several notable effects. First, they provided solid and useful preparation in principles of education and practices of teaching. Second, the development of teaching as an occupation for women marked a new phase in the lifecycle of nineteenth-century women: it added three or more years of education and, critically, made women's life cycle more complex by providing an option of remaining single (Allmendinger, 1976; Schwager, 1987). Finally, the normal schools gave an impetus to women's education throughout the nineteenth century. But the pace of progress was halting.

Before the Civil War, only three private colleges (Oberlin, Hillsdale, and Antioch) and two public colleges (Utah and Iowa) admitted women. This coeducational experiment was not one of parallel education for women and men, however; rather, it was one of women's conventional value for men on campus. The history of Oberlin College is a striking example.

Founded as a self-subsidizing school with a farm attached to it, Oberlin College enrolled men students who produced crops to help pay for their education. It became apparent, however, that a domestic labor force was necessary to clean, cook, launder, and mend clothes—and women students fit the bill. Once admitted, women students attended no classes on Mondays when they did laundry, and each day they cooked, waited on tables, and served meals. They were also regarded as a "balance" to men's mental and emotional development, altogether duplicating the conventional role of women in the family (Conway, 1974:6). Throughout the debate on the Oberlin experiment, not one serious discussion occurred on what coeducation might do for women—except to prepare them for marriage. As Conway (1974) points out, this argument of coeducation's benefit for men has a contemporary ring to it found in the rationale for admitting women to elite men's colleges during the 1970s.

Not until the later part of that century did advanced education on a par with that of men become available to women. Again, "demand" factors were important. The shortage of male students and dwindling enrollments during the Civil War encouraged administrators to open their doors to female students (Graham, 1978). First-rate women's colleges also opened—starting with Vassar College in 1865, followed by Smith and Wellesley in 1875, Bryn Mawr in 1885, and Mt. Holyoke in 1888. Modeled on a classical and literary curriculum, these women's colleges provided an education for women that was not merely "compensatory" to or for that of male students (Conway, 1974:8). Spurred on by the women's rights movement, enrollment in these women's colleges increased by 348 percent between 1890 and 1910. And at coeducational colleges, the number of women students grew by even more —438 percent—during that same period (Antler, 1982:18).

At the end of the nineteenth century, higher education for women emphasized the development of character, the pursuit of culture, and the ideals of liberal arts — especially at women's colleges (Antler, 1982). All of this was consistent with prevailing notions of femininity and traditional values of womanhood, and thus justified "the experiment in female education" (Antler, 1982:20). After the turn of the century, however, the goals of women's education took other directions — focusing first on service and utility to society and community, and later on vocational and life preparation (Antler, 1982). During the early 1920s, especially, college curricula for women began to incorporate career preparation. This shift toward career was most apparent at the women's colleges, since state schools had always emphasized vocational training as part of their mandate to the public.

Yet the focus on career preparation faltered severely in the next decades. Between the 1930s and 1960s, college women married earlier, bore more children, and turned their attention to homemaking in greater proportions than did the graduates of the early 1920s (Antler, 1982:29; Perun and Giele, 1982). Studies indicate that during this period — and especially during the 1950s — few college women had clear vocational goals, and most attended for the general education, prestige, and social life. Thus, college had come to occupy an interlude between high school and marriage (and motherhood) for young women (Antler, 1982; Chafe, 1972; Graham, 1978:770 – 771).

In the late sixties and early seventies, however, a resurgence in the women's movement, a decline in fertility, and a dramatic increase in female labor-force participation ushered in an era of changes in women's role in work, society, and education. Nonetheless, as we shall see, certain patterns — especially the sex segregation of eductional fields and the male dominance of educational institutions — continue to restrict women's prospects in higher education.

WOMEN AS STUDENTS: RECENT DATA AND TRENDS

Until recently, men were more likely to attend college than were women. Parents were more apt to encourage and finance the education of sons, and admissions standards favored males (see Frazier and Sadker, 1973:146 – 147). In the past two decades, however, the proportion of women going on to college has been growing — while the proportion of males has remained stable. Currently, women receive over half of all bachelor's and master's degrees and one-third of all doctorates and first professional degrees (Figure 1).

However, women's proportion of bachelor's degrees has not increased in a simple linear fashion over the century (see Figure 1). Before World War II, women's proportion of bachelor's degrees was higher than in the early post-War years. Their proportion of bachelor's degrees dipped particularly in 1949 – 50. During these post-War years, the G.I. Bill dramatically changed women's role in higher education. Passed by a Congress nervous about the unemployment of returning veterans, the G.I. Bill democratized higher education for men, while taking no particular notice of women. In 1946 – 47, when veterans first arrived in the classrooms, pre-War enrollment rates of colleges doubled overnight (Hornig, 1984:33). Eventually, one-third of

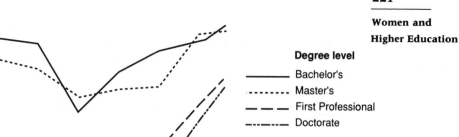

SOURCES: 1919–20 to 1949–50 data from Douglas Adkins, *The Great American Degree Machine* (Berkeley, Calif.: Carnegie Commission on Higher Education, 1975), Table A-2, and from National Center for Education Statistics, *Digest of Education Statistics, 1981* (Washington, D.C.: U.S. Government Printing Office, 1981), Table 95. 1960–61 to 1975–76 data from Mary Lou Randour, Georgia Strasburg, and Jean Lipman-Blumen, "Women and Higher Education: Trends in Enrollment and Degrees Earned," *Harvard Educational Review* 52 (May 1982): Table 4. 1979–80 data from National Center for Education Statistics, *Degrees Awarded to Women: 1979 Update* (Washington, D.C.: U.S. Department of Education), Tables 1, 3, 5, 7. 1985–86 data from Center for Education Statistics, *Bachelor's and Higher Degrees Conferred in 1985–86* (Washington, D.C.: U.S. Department of Education), Table 1.

F I G U R E 1 *Percentage of degrees earned by women, 1919–20 to 1985–86.*

America's returning veterans enrolled in college, and only 3 percent of all veterans were women (Clifford, 1983:8).

Beyond the overall proportions of women attaining degrees, gender patterns in higher education also vary with racial and ethnic status. In 1981, the last date for which data for disaggregated racial/ethnic groups are available, the proportion of degrees awarded to women compared to men was lowest among Asians and highest among blacks (Table 1). More recent data are available for blacks, although not for the other racial/ethnic groups. They indicate that in 1986 the proportion of doctorates awarded to women

T A B L E 1

Percent of Degrees Awarded to Women by Institutions of Higher Education, by Racial/Ethnic Group, 1980–81

	Degree			
Racial/ethnic group	BA	MA	Ph.D.	First Professional
White non-Hispanic	49.7	52.1	33.2	26.2
Black non-Hispanic	59.6	64.1	45.1	39.6
Hispanic	50.5	52.3	39.3	26.6
Asian or Pacific Islander	46.2	39.9	25.3	31.9
American Indian/Alaskan native	52.7	51.6	26.9	30.2

SOURCE: United States Department of Education. *Digest of Education Statistics,* 1987. Washington D.C.: U.S. Government Printing Office, 1987: Tables 159–162.

rose to 61 percent among blacks, from 45 percent in 1981 (National Research Council, 1987: Table F).

In assessing women's status in higher education, we must look beyond degrees to fields of study. Although fields of study are not as segregated as they were formerly, men and women continue to concentrate in different areas. At the bachelor's level, men are at least twice as likely as are women to concentrate in computer and physical sciences, and are seven times more likely to specialize in engineering. Women, on the other hand, are three times more likely than are men to major in education, and are five times more likely to concentrate in health fields (nursing, health services, and health technologies) (see Table 2). Over the past fifteen years, the big change has been in the proportion of women taking undergraduate business degrees. In 1986, business was the single most popular undergraduate degree for both women and men. The consequence in jobs and managerial opportunities remains to be seen.

Finally, it is important to look to the trends in professional and graduate education—since this education is a prelude to and prerequisite for employment in higher-ranking positions in professions, business, and government. Although women have made some striking gains in graduate and professional education, gender differences still prevail, especially in fields of concentration.

Twenty-five years ago, women earned only about 3 percent of all professional (e.g., medical, dental, law, veterinary) degrees awarded; throughout the 1960s and early 1970s, that proportion grew very slowly. But in the mid-1970s, women began making strides in professional education; between 1970 and 1975, the proportion of professional degrees awarded to women grew from 7 to 16 percent, and by 1979 women were earning 24 percent of all professional degrees. In 1986, women's proportion of professional degrees increased to 33 percent (see Figure 1). However, men continue to predominate in the most powerful and prestigious areas in professional education.

In medicine, for example, the highly remunerative, surgical areas are overwhelmingly male domains. Across surgical specialties (excluding obstetrics/gynecology), 97 percent of the physicians are men. Even among young (under age thirty-five) physicians, who are most recently trained, 91 percent of those in surgical areas are men (American Medical Association, 1986: calculated from Tables B-3 and B-4). The specialties with the highest proportions of women are those in the lower-status and less remunerative areas— pediatrics, child psychiatry, physical medicine, and rehabilitation, public health, and general preventive medicine. Among physicians under age thirty-five, pediatrics and child psychiatry are still the specialties with the highest proportion of female (compared to male) practitioners, but obstetrics/gynecology, dermatology, and pathology follow (American Medical Association, 1986: calculated from Tables B-3 and B-4; also see Lorber, 1984).

In law schools, the proportion of women students rose from 10 percent in 1970 to 33 percent in 1980 (Epstein, 1983); in 1986, 39 percent of all law degrees were earned by women (U.S. Department of Education, 1987c:Table 157). At the same time, the law schools with the highest proportions of

TABLE 2

Distribution of Bachelor's Degrees, by Gender and Discipline Division: 1971 and 1986

| | Percentage of degrees awarded | | | |
| | Women | | Men | |
Discipline division	1971	1986	1971	1986
Agriculture and natural resources	.1	1.1	2.5	2.4
Architecture and environmental design	.2	.7	1.0	1.2
Area studies	.4	.4	.2	.3
Biological sciences	2.9	3.7	5.3	4.1
Business and management	2.9	21.7	22.1	26.6
Communications	1.0	5.1	1.5	3.6
Computer and information sciences	.1	3.0	.4	5.5
Education	26.0	13.2	9.5	4.3
Engineering	.1	2.5	10.4	17.2
Fine and applied arts	4.9	4.5	2.6	2.9
Foreign languages	4.2	1.5	1.1	.6
Health professions	5.4	10.9	1.2	2.0
Home economics	3.0	2.8	.1	.2
Law	(*)	.2	.1	.1
Letters	12.2	5.0	6.0	3.4
Library science	.3	(*)	(*)	(*)
Mathematics	2.6	1.5	3.2	1.8
Military science	(*)	(*)	.1	(*)
Physical sciences	.8	1.2	3.9	3.2
Psychology	4.6	5.6	4.4	2.6
Public affairs and services	1.2	3.3	1.0	2.9
Social sciences	15.8	8.2	20.6	10.8
Theology	.3	.3	.6	.8
Interdisciplinary studies	1.1	3.7	2.1	3.3

SOURCE: For 1971: United States Department of Education. *Degrees Awarded to Women.* Washington, D.C.: U.S. Government Printing Office. 1981: Table 2. For 1986: United States Department of Education. Center for Education Statistics. "Bachelor's and Higher Degrees Conferred in 1985–86" Bulletin. Washington, D.C.: Office of Education Research and Improvement, December 1987: Calculated from Table 2.

* Less than .05 percent.
Note: Total may not add to 100.0 percent because of rounding

women are the newer (and less prestigious) schools, and women remain concentrated in trust, estate, tax, and family specialties (Epstein, 1983).

As with professional education, women have made gains in attainment of doctoral degrees. However, the trend is one of variable rather than steady improvement. Between the two World Wars—in 1920, 1930, 1940— women received between 13 percent and 15 percent of all doctorates. That proportion dropped to 10 percent in 1950, and did not begin to rise until about 1970. In 1970, women earned 14 percent of all doctorates, and the proportion rose to 23 percent in 1975. By 1980, women accounted for 28 percent of the doctoral degrees awarded; in 1986, they earned 35 percent (see Figure 1).

These gains notwithstanding, gender differences among doctorates prevail. In 1986, nearly half of women's doctorates were in education or psychology, which accounted for 32 and 13 percent, respectively, of the doctorates received by women. Women doctorates also clustered in literature (letters), biological science, and certain social sciences (see Table 3). Thus,

T A B L E 3
Distribution of Doctoral Degrees, by Gender and Discipline Division: 1971 and 1986

| | Percentage of degrees awarded | | | |
| | Women | | Men | |
Discipline division	1971	1986	1971	1986
Agriculture and natural resources	(*)	1.6	3.8	4.4
Architecture and environmental design	(*)	.1	(*)	.3
Area studies	(*)	.6	(*)	.4
Biological sciences	13.0	9.5	11.1	10.2
Business and management	(*)	1.8	(*)	3.5
Communications	(*)	.9	(*)	.5
Computer and information sciences	(*)	.4	(*)	1.4
Education	29.6	32.1	18.3	15.2
Engineering	(*)	1.9	13.1	14.6
Fine and applied arts	3.0	2.8	1.7	1.8
Foreign languages	6.4	2.2	1.7	.8
Health professions	1.7	5.4	1.4	2.8
Home economics	1.6	2.0	(*)	.4
Law	0	(*)	(*)	.2
Letters	12.4	6.6	6.7	4.2
Library science	(*)	.3	(*)	.1
Mathematics	2.0	1.0	4.0	2.8
Physical sciences	5.3	5.0	15.0	13.6
Psychology	9.3	13.4	4.9	6.9
Public affairs and services	(*)	1.9	(*)	1.0
Social sciences	11.0	8.3	11.4	9.0
Theology	(*)	1.0	1.0	4.9
Interdisciplinary studies	(*)	1.1	(*)	1.1

SOURCE: For 1971: United States Department of Education. *Degrees Awarded to Women.* Washington, D.C.: U.S. Government Printing Office. 1981: Table 6. For 1986: United States Department of Education. Center for Education Statistics. "Bachelor's and Higher Degrees Conferred in 1985–86" Bulletin. Washington, D.C.: Office of Education Research and Improvement, December 1987: Calculated from Table 4.

* Less than .05 percent.
Note: Total may not add to 100.0 percent because of rounding

women are being awarded doctorates largely in traditional female areas, which are already "glutted" with people holding doctoral degrees (Ekstrom, 1979:1). Men, on the other hand, are distributed in a larger number of fields, and are more likely than are women to be awarded degrees in business, engineering, physical science, and other technical fields (see Table 3) — growing and lucrative employment areas.

Among minority women, the clustering of doctorates in female-typed fields is even more marked. Minority women are concentrated specifically in the field of education. In 1986, almost three-fifths (56 percent) of the doctorates awarded to black women and nearly one-half (45 percent) of those awarded to Hispanic women were in education (National Research Council, 1987:Table F).

Beyond Enrollment: Gender-Biased Processes in Higher Education

To fully understand the disparate status of the women and men in American colleges and universities, we must look beyond simple enrollment data and trends to the socialization and experiences of students.

Even when men and women attend the same institution, occupy the same classroom, and share the same teachers, their educational experiences differ (Association of American Colleges, 1982). In faculty interaction with students, a "subtle and silent language" prevails. Studies indicate that, in their interaction with students, faculty encourage male as compared to female students by making more eye contact with the men, nodding and gesturing in response to men's questions, assuming a position of attentiveness when men speak, and taking a location near men (see Association of American Colleges, 1982:7; Thorne, 1979).

Observers frequently note that even the brightest and most talented female students tend to remain silent in the classroom, while their male counterparts dominate the discussion (Sterglanz and Lyberger-Ficek, 1977; Speizer, 1982). Faculty promote and reinforce the invisibility of women students by subtle practices such as calling directly on men but not on women, addressing men by name more often than they do women, giving men more time to answer a question before going on to another student, interrupting women more frequently or allowing them to be interrupted, and crediting the contributions of men but not those of women (Association of American Colleges, 1982). These practices convey messages about women's value and status in the classroom, and signal their exclusion as significant members of the college community. This, in turn, depresses women's intellectual development, undermines their confidence, and dampens their aspirations both in and out of school.

Such patterns are especially consequential for the undergraduates — since, at this level, education is largely a formal classroom process. Graduate education, in contrast, is an informal process of interaction, socialization, and alliance. Yet here again men's and women's experiences are very different. In their doctoral training, men and women are about equally likely to receive a research or teaching assistantship sometime during graduate school (National Research Council, 1983). But women see faculty and research advisors much less frequently than do men (Holmstrom and Holmstom, 1974; Kjerulff and Blood, 1973), and their interaction and communication with faculty are less relaxed and egalitarian (Kjerulff and Blood, 1973). Further, women tend to regard themselves as students rather than as colleagues of faculty, and report that they are taken less seriously than are male graduate students (Berg and Ferber, 1983; Holmstrom and Holmstrom, 1974; see also Freeman, 1979). In short, in graduate and professional education, women report that they are more marginal — especially outside of formal classroom proceedings. As one woman at Berkeley put it:

> have I been overtly discriminated against? Probably no. Have I been encouraged, congratulated, received recognition, gotten a friendly hello, a solicitous "can I help you out?" The answer is no. Being a woman here just makes you tougher, work harder, and hope that if you get a 4.0 GPA, someone will say "You're good." (Quoted in Association of American Colleges, 1982:1.)

To understand the implications of this pattern, one must appreciate the consequences of faculty alliance in graduate education. For their favored students, faculty provide the research training and experience necessary for professional and intellectual development. They nominate preferred students for fellowships and awards, and take a stand for them in the perennial disputes surrounding qualifying examinations and degree requirements. They provide professional visibility by introducing their protégés at meetings and conferences, and by coauthoring papers and articles with them. Faculty selectively provide students the opportunity to pose important questions, to solve problems, and to set professional goals. Ultimately, the faculty help their favored students to locate good jobs, and thus place them on the road of career mobility.

Women's limited interaction with faculty lessens their opportunities for advancement. This exclusion is not a simple function of overt discrimination. Rather, it is linked more subtly to the character of dominance and control within higher education. Like other organizations and institutions in our society, academia is largely a "male milieu." The men have grown up together, have played, learned, and competed together. They share certain language, traditions, and understandings — in and out of the work setting (see Epstein, 1970:167–176; Epstein, 1974). When these professionals choose protégés or apprentices, they look to fledglings in whom they can see a reflection of themselves. In such a system of mentor/protégé relations, women are "outsiders," and, as such, are rarely identified as successors of the men in control. Thus, in an organization that operates by way of sponsorship and support, the women students are more likely to be left to struggle along on their own.

Of course, the presence of women faculty and mentors can change the balance of interaction and support. One study reports a strong positive correlation between the proportion of female faculty and the number of women students who are subsequently cited for achievement (Tidball, 1973). And women holding doctoral degrees who had female dissertation advisors are reported to publish significantly more than do women who had male advisors (Goldstein, 1979). Moreover, since both men's and women's aspiration levels are a function of their real and perceived opportunities (Kanter, 1977), the presence and availability of female mentors can broaden women's sense of possibilities.

During the last fifteen years, the women's studies programs have been one expression of the feminist movement on college campuses. In its course offerings and its research on women, women's studies has helped to correct scholarship's long-standing oversight of the study of women—their problems, activities, and contributions. Feminist scholarship—promoted by the women's studies movement—has countered bias in the methods, conceptual schemes, and theories of academic study. In doing so, it has offered a broader and more thorough, critical knowledge base for students and scholars. Nevertheless, women faculty are few, and thus women students generally lack the interaction, identification, and support that their presence could promote.

WOMEN AS FACULTY IN HIGHER EDUCATION

As faculty, women are segregated in the tasks they perform, the places they teach, the fields they occupy, and the ranks they hold. Across each dimension (task, place, position), women receive lower rewards (Fox, 1985).

Female academics are located disproportionately in two-year and four-year (general baccalaureate) colleges—where teaching loads are heavy and service demands are high (see Table 4). In fact, among full-time teaching faculty, almost 30 percent of the women teach thirteen or more hours a week, whereas only 15 percent of the men teach this much (Ekstrom, 1979:2). Women are concentrated disproportionately in state colleges and satellite campuses rather than in the doctoral-granting universities that have resources for the research and publication on which academic eminence and recognition are based. At the top of the academic hierarchy, in the prestigious and powerful places that set the pace and dominate the standards of scholarly work, even fewer women are present (see Graham, 1978:768).

Women are located not only in less prestigious places, but also in the less powerful fields and disciplines within academia. Academic men are concentrated in the sciences, social sciences, and professional schools. Women, on the other hand, are clustered in the arts, humanities, and services associated with more marginal areas of education, public health, and welfare (Bognanno, 1987; Fox, 1981).

Moreover, the higher the rank, the fewer the women. Across fields and institutions, 38 percent of the assistant professors are women, but only 25 percent of the associate professors are women, and only 12 percent of the full professors are women (see Table 4). It is, instead, in the subprofessorial ranks where we find highly disproportionate concentrations of women: At the instructor and lecturer levels, women account for one-half of the faculty (Table 4).

These subprofessorial appointments are marginal positions that fluctuate with enrollments, unexpected leaves of absence, and other departmental

T A B L E 4

Women as a Percentage of Total Full-Time Instructional Faculty, by Institutional Type and by Rank

	Percent women
Institutional type, 1986	
Doctoral-level universities	20.4
Comprehensive institutions (diverse B.A. and post-B.A. but little doctoral education)	27.2
General baccalaureate institutions (4-year programs)	31.2
Specialized institutions (e.g., divinity, medical, engineering, business, and design institutions)	26.0
2-year institutions	38.5
Across institutions by rank, 1986	
Professor	12.3
Associate	24.6
Assistant	38.4
Instructor	53.3
Lecturer	49.5

SOURCE: For Institutional Type: United States Department of Education. Center for Education Statistics. HEGIS Survey XX. "Salaries, Tenure, and Fringe Benefits for Full Time Instructional Faculty, 1985–86." Washington D.C., 1986: Calculated from Tables 11 and 12. For Rank: United States Department of Education. Center for Education Statistics. "College Faculty Salaries, 1976–86." Bulletin. Washington D.C.: U.S. Government Printing Office, 1987: Calculated from Appendix Table A.

exigencies (see Hornig, 1979; Van Arsdale, 1978). Many of these appointments are part-time or part-year positions. For university administrators, appointing faculty to adjunct or temporary appointments provides a big benefit: It keeps salary levels down, avoids long-term commitments, and relieves "regular" faculty of tedious undergraduate courses. But for those who hold these positions, the costs are high: Part-time and adjunct appointments rarely carry fringe benefits, they never provide leaves or sabbaticals, and they offer no security or chance for tenure. Further, because these faculty are rarely represented by unions or professional associations, they are exempt from formal grievance procedures (Tuckman et al., 1978). Perhaps most important, part-time, adjunct, and subprofessorial appointees are ineligible for outside research funding—thus, reducing their chance to establish an independent scholarly record and obtain better prospects for themselves (Hornig, 1979).

As university resources have dwindled and budgets have decreased, the number of full-time faculty has declined dramatically. Between 1970–71 and 1982–83, the ratio of full-time to part-time faculty decreased from 3.5 : 1 to 2.1 : 1 (Bowen and Schuster, 1985:5)—a remarkable dive in a single decade. In two-year colleges, in particular, the number of part-time faculty grew by 80 percent between 1972 and 1977 (Tuckman et al., 1978:185), and, by 1980, a clear majority (56 percent) of all community college faculty were employed part-time (Clark, 1987:88). Across institutional types, women hold a disproportionate number of the part-time and temporary appointments: 44 percent of the female and 31 percent of the male faculty in higher education had such an appointment in 1983 (U.S. Equal Employment Opportunity Commission, 1983: calculated from Table 1, p. 1 and Table 4, p. 10).

The growth in part-time, temporary, and subprofessorial appointments creates a permanent, marginally employed faculty who exist on the fringes of academic life (see Wilke, 1979). These faculty suffer from a humiliating absence of status and from indignities, which range from denial of clerical help, to exclusion from departmental meetings and isolation from contact with "regular faculty" (see Van Arsdale, 1978). That this class of faculty is disproportionately female is an indication of, and blight on, the status of women in higher education.

Women's depressed status as faculty members is tied partially to the socialization processes and to the restrictive political and economic structures that produce gender inequalities throughout the labor force. But beyond these factors, women in higher education are disadvantaged by particular features of the academic organization itself.

First, women faculty, like women graduate students, are constrained by the male culture of academia. In this milieu, men share traditions, styles, and understandings about rules of competing, bartering, and succeeding. They accept one another; they support one another; and they promote one another. As outsiders to this male milieu, and its informal network of information and resources, women are shut off from job prospects, research information, and professional opportunities and services. As one woman in science put it:

> Sooner or later I and those around me knew I was not one of the boys. Professional identification in the absence of colleague identification gets you only so far. When somewhere along the line the boys start boosting their buddies in a kind of "quid pro quo" competition, you realize you've had it. You don't have the "quo" for the "quid." You don't have any coattails, and everyone knows it. The shift may be subtle or it may come as a jolt, but it *does* come. In school, the boys took you more or less seriously because you got the highest grades in courses and helped them study for exams. But now that everyone has degree in hand, they don't need you anymore (Tidball, 1974:56–57).

Since the academic culture is not only male but also white, these problems are compounded for nonwhite women.

In addition, the normative standards of academic work create a bias in evaluation. In scholarly and scientific work, standards are both "absolute" and "subjective." Work is measured against a standard of absolute excellence, and this, in turn, is a subjective assessment. Thus, in academia, the evaluative criteria are vague; the process of appraisal is highly inferential; and the decisions for reward are judgmental.

In such a context, stereotyped and sex-biased reactions abound. Studies indicate that the more loosely defined and subjective the criteria, the more likely white males are perceived to be and evaluated as the superior candidates, and the more likely gender bias is to operate (see Deux and Emswiller, 1974; Nieva and Gutek, 1980; Pheterson et al., 1980; Rosen and Jerdee,

1974). In academia, conditions are then prime for bias in recruitment, hiring, and promotion, and women are among the casualties of the system.

Although this bias is a violation of federal law, seeking legal redress is a costly, emotionally debilitating, and discouraging process (see Theodore, 1986). Further, an irony of academic life is that scholars and scientists have counted since childhood on their individual achievement and performance to win them recognition and reward. And, as a group, they regard the rules of their work—the standards, the evaluation, and the rewards—as legitimate. Consequently, academics tend to attribute their failure to individual performance rather than to institutional structure (Cole and Cole, 1973: 254–259; Fox, 1981:82). This process of internal attribution is especially characteristic of women compared to men (see Frieze, 1978). In this way, the norms of science and scholarship—with their emphasis on individual attainment and meritocratic reward—help to dampen collective alienation and response in academia.

Finally, women's disadvantaged status in academia is perpetuated by the very sex segregation that is an index of their subordination. Inequality in the status of the sexes is more tenable when it is less evident, and the segregation of men and women in different units, departments, and institutions makes their discrepant ranks and rewards less apparent and visible. This reduces potential strain, and in doing so, helps to perpetuate the discrepant status of the men and women without threatening academia's ideology of universalism and objectivity (Fox, 1985).

TITLE IX AND PROSPECTS FOR WOMEN IN HIGHER EDUCATION

In 1972, Congress prohibited sex discrimination in higher education by adding Title IX to the Education Amendments Act. Its key stipulation states:

> No person in the United States, shall, on the basis of sex, be excluded from participation in, be denied the benefits of, or be subjected to discrimination under any education program or activity receiving Federal financial assistance [20 U.S.C. §1681].

Because colleges and universities receive federal assistance in grants, contracts, loan programs, and student aid, the act applies to higher-education institutions along with elementary and secondary schools. Title IX covers employment in education as well as almost every aspect of student life. Thus, the Act prohibits sex discrimination in admissions to educational institutions (except admissions to private and single-sex institutions); curricular and extracurricular programs; student services and benefits such as counseling, health care, and financial aid; and hiring and promotion within educational agencies and institutions.

With this mandate, Title IX has altered the most obvious and blatant discriminatory practices in higher education, especially in admissions. As late as the early 1970s, women were subject to inequitable quota and admissions standards in colleges and universities. At Cornell University's College of Agriculture, for example, women were admitted to the program only if they had SAT scores thirty to forty points higher than those of the entering males; at Pennsylvania State University, a male applicant was five times more likely to be accepted than a female; and at the University of North Carolina, admission of female students was restricted by policies that required women to live in dormitories, of which there were only a few, whereas men could live off-campus (National Advisory Council on Women's Educational Programs, 1981:25). Title IX has eliminated the most flagrant of these practices—at least as they operate on the formal level.

Yet the area in which Title IX has been most acutely seen and felt is in athletics. Before Title IX, female athletes were a rarity on our college campuses. Men dominated the playing fields, courts, and pools; they got the athletic scholarships and awards; and they obtained public attention and acclaim for athletic accomplishment. The few female athletes, in contrast, struggled along without facilities, funding, or rewards. With Title IX, however, women's participation in college athletics greatly expanded (National Advisory Council on Women's Educational Programs, 1981; also see Theberge chapter in his book).

Beyond athletics and formal discrimination in admissions, however, Title IX has had limited impact. It has not reduced informal sources of bias in higher education—the classroom procedures, interaction processes, and systems of faculty support discussed earlier. To correct these disparities, one step would be an increase in female faculty, especially in the higher ranks. The presence and availability of female faculty would serve to broaden women's aspirations, to increase their opportunities for interaction with faculty, and most important, to reduce the male dominance of educational practices and processes.

Yet, with the stagnation of affirmative-action programs in the university and with a low public demand for redress of sex discrimination, women have not increased their proportions as faculty—particularly tenured faculty—in higher education. Between 1976 and 1986, the proportion of women among all full professors increased from 10 percent to just 12 percent (U.S. Department of Education, 1987c: Appendix Table A). Instead, women academics remain limited in number and are clustered in the lower ranks, where they have little visibility and influence. Although Title IX covers employment as well as student life, the Act has had little influence on the proportions of female faculty.

Finally, while Title IX may be one factor in the increased female enrollments in higher education, it has had limited effect on the segregation of male and female students into different areas of study. Women continue to be restricted, especially in their technical and scientific training, which has profound consequences for their occupational options. Because they have been diverted from high-school mathematics courses, in particular, many women lack the critical "filter" subject necessary for education in 75 percent of all college and university majors, including the business, medicine, science, engineering, and architecture programs (Sell, 1974), which lead to higher-paying jobs. To correct these patterns, schools must make clear to students the lifetime consequences of both technical and nontechnical preparation, and must remove the barriers that surround numbers, logic, and problem solving as male domains.

As an act for gender equity in education, Title IX has provided a broad mandate. But legislation lives and dies by its enforcement, not by its mandate (Scott, 1974:402). To achieve gender equity in education, we must confront the practices that track men and women into different curricular areas and activities, and that socialize them for different occupational outcomes. Such action requires effective monitoring, strong enforcement, and firm sanctions for noncompliance with policies of equity. These, in turn, demand the awareness, support, and effort of political institutions. Institutional action can help to break the patterns and processes that restrict women's options and constrain their possibilities throughout work and society.

NOTES

For assistance in locating data from the Higher Education General Information Survey, I thank John Boies. For help in locating recent government documents and data, I thank especially Robert Klein. In addition, I appreciate Laurie Silver's help in formatting tables for this chapter.

REFERENCES

Adkins, Douglas. *The Great American Degree Machine.* Berkeley, Calif.: Carnegie Commission on Higher Education, 1975.

Allmendinger, David. "Mount Holyoke Students Encounter the Need for Life Planning, 1837–1850." *History of Education Quarterly* 19(Spring 1979):27–46.

American Medical Association (AMA). Survey and Data Resources. *Physician Characteristics and Distribution in the U.S., 1986.* Chicago, Ill.: AMA, 1986.

Antler, Joyce. "Culture, Service, and Work: Changing Ideals of Higher Education for Women." In *The Undergraduate Woman,* pp. 15–41. Edited by P. Perun. Lexington, Mass.: Lexington, Mass., 1982.

Association of American Colleges. "The Classroom Climate: A Chilly One for Women?" Washington, D.C.: Association of American Colleges, Project on the Status and Education of Women, 1982.

Berg, H.M. and Ferber, Marianne. "Women and Men Graduate Students: Who Succeeds and Why." In *Journal of Higher Education* 54(Nov/Dec 1983):629–48.

Bernard, Richard and Vinovskis, Maris. "The Female School Teacher in Ante-Bellum Massachusetts." *Journal of Social History* 10(Spring 1977):332–45.

Bognanno, Mario. "Women in Professions: Academic Women." In *Working Women: Past, Present, Future.* Washington, D.C.: The Bureau of National Affairs, 1987.

Bowen, Howard and Schuster, Jack. *American Professors.* New York: Oxford University Press, 1986.

Chafe, William. *The American Woman: Her Changing Social, Economic, and Political Roles, 1920–1970.* New York: Oxford University Press, 1970.

Clark, Burton. *The Academic Life.* Princeton, New Jersey: The Carnegie Corporation for the Advancement of Teaching, 1987.

Clifford, Jeraldine Joncich. "Shaking Dangerous Questions from the Crease: Gender and American Higher Education." *Feminist Studies* 3(Fall 1983):3–62.

Cole, Jonathan R. and Cole, Stephen. *Social Stratification in Science.* Chicago: The University of Chicago Press, 1973.

Conway, Jill. "Perspectives on the History of Women's Education in the United States." *History of Education Quarterly* 14(Spring 1974):1–12.

Deux, K. and Emswiller, T. "Explanations of Successful Performance in Sex-Linked Tasks." *Journal of Personality and Social Psychology* 22(1974):80–85.

Ekstrom, Ruth S. "Women Faculty: Development, Promotion, Pay." *Findings: Educational Testing Service* 5(1979):1–5.

Epstein, Cynthia Fuchs. *Woman's Place: Options and Limits in Professional Careers.* Berkeley, California: University of California Press, 1970.

Epstein, Cynthia Fuchs. "Bringing Women In: Rewards, Punishments, and the Structure of Achievement." *Women and Success: The Anatomy of Achievement.* pp. 13–21. Edited by R. Kundsin. New York: William Morrow and Co., 1974.

Epstein, Cynthia Fuchs. *Women in Law.* Garden City N.Y.: Anchor Books, 1983.

Featherman, David. "School and Occupational Careers: Constancy and Change in Worldly Success." In *Constancy and Change in Human Development.* Edited by O.G. Brimm and J. Kagan. Cambridge, Mass: Harvard University Press, 1980.

Featherman, David and Hauser, Robert. "Sexual Inequalities and Socioeconomic Achievement in the U.S." *American Sociological Review* 41(June 1976):462–483.

Fox, Mary Frank. "Sex, Salary, and Achievement: Reward-Dualism in Academia." *Sociology of Education* 54(April 1981):71–84.

Fox, Mary Frank. "Location, Sex-Typing, and Salary Among Academics." *Work and Occupations* 12(May 1985):186–205.

Frazier, Nancy and Sadker, Myra. *Sexism in School and Society.* New York: Harper and Row, 1973.

Freeman, Jo. "How to Discriminate Against Women Without Really Trying." In *Women: A Feminist Perspective,* 2nd edition, pp. 217–232. Edited by J. Freeman. Palo Alto, Calif.: Mayfield Publishing, 1979.

Frieze, Irene. "Achievement and Nonachievement in Women." In *Women and Sex Roles,* pp. 234–254. Edited by Frieze, Parsons, Johnson, Ruble, and Zellman. New York: W.W. Norton and Company, 1978.

Goldstein, Elysee. "Effect of Same-Sex and Cross-Sex Role Models on the Subsequent Academic Productivity of Scholars." *American Psychologist* 34(May 1979):407.

Gordon, Ann. "The Young Ladies Academy of Philadelphia." In *Women of America: A History.* Edited by C. Berkin and M.B. Norton. Boston: Houghton Mifflin Co., 1979.

Graham, Patricia A. "Expansion and Exclusion: A History of Women in American Higher Education." *Signs* 3(Summer 1978):759–773.

Holmstrom, Engininel and Holmstrom, Robert. "The Plight of the Woman Doctoral Student." *American Educational Research Journal* 11(Winter 1974):1–17.

Hornig, Lilli S. *Climbing the Academic Ladder: Doctoral Women Scientists in Academe.* Washington, D.C.: National Academy of Sciences, 1979.

Hornig, Lilli S. "Women in Science and Engineering: Why So Few." *Technology Review* 87(Nov/Dec 1984):31–47.

Kanter, Rosabeth Moss. *Men and Women of the Corporation.* New York: Basic Books, 1977.

Kerber, Linda. "The Republican Mother: Women and the Enlightenment—An American Perspective." *American Quarterly* 28(Summer 1976):187–205.

Kerber, Linda. *Women of the Republic: Intellect and Ideology in Revolutionary America.* Chapel Hill: University of North Carolina Press, 1980.

Kjerulff, Kristen H. and Blood, Milton R. "A Comparison of Communication Patterns in Male and Female Graduate Students." *Journal of Higher Education* 44(Nov 1973):623–632.

Lorber, Judith. *Women Physicians: Careers, Status, and Power.* New York: Tavistock Publications, 1984.

National Advisory Council on Women's Educational Programs. *Title IX: The Half Full, Half Empty Glass.* Washington, D.C.: U.S. Government Printing Office, 1981.

National Research Council. Committee on the Education and Employment of Women in Science and Engineering. *Climbing the Ladder: An Update on the Status of Doctoral Women Scientists and Engineers.* Washington, D.C.: National Academy Press, 1983.

National Research Council. *Summary Report 1986: Doctorate Recipients from United States Universities.* Washington, D.C.: National Academy Press, 1987.

Nieva, Veronica and Gutek, Barbara A. "Sex Effects on Evaluation." *Academy of Management Review* 5(1980):267–276.

Perun, Pamela and Giele, Janet. "Life After College: Historical Links Between Women's Work and Women's Education." In *The Undergraduate Woman*, pp. 375–398. Edited by P. Perun. Lexington, Mass.: Lexington Books, 1982.

Pheterson, G.T.; Kiesler, S.B.; Goldberg, P.A. "Evaluation of the Performance of Women as a Function of Their Sex, Achievement, and Personal History." *Journal of Personality and Social Psychology* 19(1971):110–114.

Randour, Mary Lou; Strasburg, Georgia L.; Lipman-Blumen, Jean. "Women in Higher Education: Trends in Enrollments and Degrees Earned." *Harvard Educational Review* 52(May 1982):189–202.

Rosen, B. and Jerdee, T.H. "Influence of Sex-Role Stereotypes on Personnel Decisions." *Journal of Applied Psychology* 59(1974):9–14.

Schwager, Sally. "Educating Women in America." *Signs* 12(1987):333–372.

Scott, Ann. "It's Time for Equal Education." In *And Jill Came Tumbling After*, pp. 399–409. Edited by J. Stacey, S. Bereaud, and J. Daniels. New York: Dell Publishing, 1974.

Sell, Lucy. "High School Math as a Vocational Filter for Women and Minorities." Berkeley, California: University of California at Berkeley, 1974.

Sewell, William; Hauser, Robert; and Wolf, Wendy. "Sex, Schooling, and Occupational Status." *American Journal of Sociology* 86(1980):551–583.

Speizer, Jeanne. "Students Should be Seen *and* Heard." In *The Undergraduate Woman*. Edited by P. Perun. Lexington, Mass.: Lexington Books, 1982.

Sterglanz, Sarah Hall and Lyberger-Ficek, Shirley. "Sex Differences in Student–Teacher Interactions in the College Classroom." *Sex Roles* 3(1977):345–352.

Theodore, Athena. *The Campus Troublemakers: Academic Women in Protest.* Houston: Cap and Gown Press, 1986.

Thorne, Barrie. "Claiming Verbal Space: Women's Speech and Language in the College Classroom." Paper presented at the Research Conference on Educational Environments and the Undergraduate Woman. Wellesley, Mass.: Wellesley College, September 1979.

Tidball, M. Elizabeth. "Perspective on Academic Women and Affirmative Action." *Educational Record* 54(Spring, 1973):130–135.

Tidball, M. Elizabeth. "Women Role Models in Higher Education." In *Graduate and Professional Education of Women*, pp. 56–59. Proceedings of the Conference of the AAUW. Washington, D.C.: American Association of University Women, 1974.

Tuckman, Howard P.; Caldwell, Jaime; and Volger, William. "Part-Timers and the Academic Labor Market of the Eighties." *American Sociologist* 13(Nov 1978):184–195.

U.S. Bureau of the Census. Current Population Reports, Series P-70, no. 11. "What's It Worth?" Washington, D.C.: U.S. Government Printing Office, 1987.

U.S. Department of Education, National Center for Education Statistics. *Degrees Awarded to Women: 1979 Update.* Washington, D.C.: U.S. Department of Education, 1981a.

U.S. Department of Education, National Center for Education Statistics. *Faculty, Salary, Tenure, Benefits, 1980–81.* Washington, D.C.: U.S. Government Printing Office, 1981b.

U.S. Department of Education, National Center for Education Statistics. *Digest of Education Statistics, 1981.* Washington, D.C.: U.S. Government Printing Office, 1981c.

U.S. Department of Education, National Center for Education Statistics. HEGIS Survey XX. "Salaries, Tenure, and Fringe Benefits for Full Time Instructional Faculty." Washington, D.C.: U.S. Government Printing Office, 1986.

U.S. Department of Education, National Center for Education Statistics. *Digest of Education Statistics, 1987.* Washington, D.C.: U.S. Government Printing Office, 1987a.

U.S. Department of Education, National Center for Education Statistics. "College Faculty Salaries, 1976–1986." Bulletin. Washington, D.C.: U.S. Government Printing Office, 1987b.

U.S. Department of Education, National Center for Education Statistics. "Bachelors and Higher Degrees Conferred in 1985–86." Bulletin. Washington, D.C.: U.S. Government Printing Office, 1987c.

U.S. Equal Employment Opportunity Commission. *Job Patterns for Minorities and Women in Higher Education.* Washington, D.C.: U.S. Government Printing Office, 1983.

Van Arsdale, George. "De-Professionalizing a Part-Time Teaching Faculty." *American Sociologist* 13(Nov 1978):195–201.

Wilke, Arthur. *The Hidden Professoriate: Credentialism, Professionalism, and the Tenure Crisis.* Westport, Conn.: Greenwood Press, 1979.

Woody, Thomas. *A History of Women's Education in the United States,* Vol. I. New York: Octagon Books, 1966.

The Double Standard: Age

INGE POWELL BELL

There is a reason why women are coy about their age. For most purposes, society pictures them as "old" ten or fifteen years sooner than men. Nobody in this culture, man or woman, wants to grow old; age is not honored among us. Yet women must endure the specter of aging much sooner than men, and this cultural definition of aging gives men a decided psychological, sexual, and economic advantage over women.

It is surely a truism of our culture that, except for a few kinky souls, the inevitable physical symptoms of aging make women sexually unattractive much earlier than men. The multimillion-dollar cosmetics advertising industry is dedicated to creating a fear of aging in women, so that it may sell them its emollients of sheep's fat, turtle sweat, and synthetic chemicals, which claim, falsely, to stem the terrible tide. "Did you panic when you looked into the mirror this morning and noticed that those laugh lines are turning into crow's feet?" "Don't let your eyes speak your age!" "What a face-lift can do for your morale!"

A man's wrinkles will not define him as sexually undesirable until he reaches his late fifties. For him, sexual value is defined much more in terms of personality, intelligence, and earning power than physical appearance. Women, however, must rest their case largely on their bodies. Their ability to attain status in other than physical ways and to translate that status into sexual attractiveness is severely limited by the culture. Indeed, what status women have is based almost entirely on their sexuality. The young girl of eighteen or twenty-five may well believe that her position in society is equal to, or even higher than, that of men. As she approaches middle age, however, she begins to notice a change in the way people treat her. Reflected in the growing indifference of others toward her looks, toward her sexuality, she can see and measure the decline of her worth, her status in the world. In Simone de Beauvoir's words:

> she has gambled much more heavily than man on the sexual values she possesses; to hold her husband and to assure herself of his protection,

Reprinted from *Trans-Action* (November–December 1970), pp. 75–80, by permission of Transaction Inc. Current statistics provided by Jo Freeman.

and to keep most of her jobs, it is necessary for her to be attractive, to please; she is allowed no hold on the world save through the mediation of some man. What is to become of her when she no longer has any hold on him: This is what she anxiously asks herself while she helplessly looks on the degeneration of this fleshly object which she identifies with herself.

The middle-aged woman who thickly masks her face with makeup, who submits to surgical face and breast lifting, who dyes her hair and corsets her body is as much a victim of socially instilled self-hatred as the black person who straightens his hair and applies bleaching creams to his skin.

The most dramatic institutionalization of different age definitions for men and women is the cultural rules governing the age at which one can marry. It is perfectly acceptable for men to marry women as much as fifteen or twenty years younger than they are, but it is generally unacceptable for them to marry women more than four or five years older. These cultural rules show up very plainly in the marriage statistics gathered by the federal government. At the time of first marriage, the age differential is relatively small; the groom is on the average 1.4 years older than his bride. When widowers remarry, however, the gap is 7.6 years; and when divorced men do, the gap is 4.7 years.

These age differentials put the woman at a disadvantage in several ways. First, whatever may be the truth about age and sexual performance, our culture defines the young as sexually more vigorous and desirable. Thus, the customary age differential means that the man gets the more desirable partner; the woman must settle for the less desirable.

More important, the divorced or widowed woman is severely handicapped when it comes to finding another marital partner. Let us take, for example, a couple who divorce when both are in their thirties. What is the difference in the supply of future marriage partners for the man and for the woman? The man can choose among all women his own age or younger. This includes all those women below twenty-five, many more of whom are as yet unmarried. The woman, by contrast, is limited by custom to men her own age or older. She has access to only those age brackets in which most people are married. She is thus reduced to the supply of men who come back on the marriage market as a result of divorce or widowerhood or to those few who have not yet married. It is easy to see which of the two will have an easier time finding companionship or a marriage partner. It is also easy to surmise that the awareness of this difference makes divorce a much more painful option for women than for men and thus puts many women at a continuous disadvantage within a strained marriage.

Statistics bear out our supposition that women have a harder time remarrying than men (see Table 1). It has been estimated that, while three-quarters of divorced men remarry, only two-thirds of divorced women ever do.

Only a small proportion of this discrepancy is due to the shorter life expectancy of men and thus their relative scarcity in the upper age brackets. For example, in 1987, in the age bracket forty-five to sixty-four, there are 2.4 times as many widowed and divorced women without mates as comparable

T A B L E 1

Remarriage Rates of Widowed and Divorced Men and Women by Age Group, 1985

	Number of marriages per 1,000	
Age and marital status	Women	Men
Widowed		
45–64	11.2	52.8
65 and over	1.9	16.1
Divorced		
25–44	113.2	155.0
45–64	28.7	74.9
65 and over	4.8	23.8

men. Yet in the total population the ratio of women to men in that age bracket is only 1.1 to 1. In the over–sixty-five age bracket there are over 4.1 times as many divorced and widowed women still alone as compared to men; yet in the population as a whole, the ratio of women to men in this age bracket is only 1.4 to 1.

Still, the difference in life expectancy between the two sexes does work to a woman's disadvantage in another way. The gentleman in the ad below is making explicit an expectation made implicitly by most men:

> RECENTLY DIVORCED, 53, affectionate, virile, tall, good-looking, yearns for the one utterly feminine, loving woman in her 30s, 40s with whom he can share a beautiful new life.

In 1985, this gentleman had a life expectancy of 23.1 years. If he finds a woman of thirty-five, her life expectancy will be 44.8 more years. In other words, he is affectionately offering her a statistical chance of 21.7 years of widowhood. And she will be widowed at an age when men of her own age will be looking for women in their thirties and forties. At best, he may live to a ripe old age. When he is seventy-five she will be fifty-seven.

Now let us consider the case of a much larger group: women who have husbands. As middle age approaches, many of these married women find that they, too, are vulnerable to the difficulties posed by the different definition of age in men and women. For them, however devoutly they may wish it as they tidy their homes, take care of their teenage children, or play bridge, sexual adventure is usually out of the question. This is not just because of the more restrictive mores that bind them to fidelity; their age has already disqualified them for anything else. Not so for the husband. If he is a successful man, his virility will be seen as still intact, if not actually enhanced, and the affair becomes very much the question. Indeed, if he is engaged in a middle-class occupation, he is almost inevitably surrounded by attractive, young females, many of whom—the receptionist, the cocktail waitress at the downtown bar, and the airplane hostess—have been deliberately selected to flatter his ego and arouse his fancy. In addition, many of the women hired to fulfill more ordinary functions—the secretaries, typists, and the like—find the older man desirable by virtue of his success and wealth. Thus, the middle-aged wife, unless she is one of the statistically few whose husband is truly happy and faithful, is put into competition with the cards stacked against her. And even if her husband does not leave her for a younger woman or begin having affairs, she will probably experience anxiety and a sense of diminished self-esteem.

The mass media glamorize and legitimate the older man–younger woman relationship. Successful actors continue to play romantic leads well into their fifties and sometimes sixties (*vide* Cary Grant). Frequently they are cast opposite actresses at least half their age, and the story line rarely even acknowledges the difference. They are simply an "average" romantic couple. The question of whether the twenty-year-old heroine is out of her mind to marry the graying fifty-five-year-old hero is not even raised.

THE PRESTIGE LOSS

Occupation is man's major role, unemployment or failure in his occupational life the worst disaster that can befall him. The question "What do you do?" is seldom answered, "Well, I'm married and a father." But because men draw their self-esteem and establish their connections to others very largely through their jobs, retirement is a time of psychic difficulty and discomfort for most men. The woman faces a similar role loss much earlier. Her primary role in life is that of mother: her secondary role is that of homemaker, and her tertiary role that of sexual partner. We have already seen that the role of sexual partner, and sexually desirable object, is impaired for many women as middle age approaches. Now we must contemplate the additional fact that the woman's primary role—that of mother—also disappears during middle age.

Indeed, with decreasing family size and increasingly common patterns of early marriage, women are losing their mother role much earlier than formerly. In 1890, the average woman took care of children until her mid-fifties. Today most women see their children leave home when they are in their late forties. Whereas in 1890 the average woman lived thirty years after her last child had entered school and twelve years after her last child married, today, with longer life expectancy, the average woman lives forty years after her last child enters school and twenty-five years after her last child marries. Thus, women lose their major role long before the retirement age arrives for men.

Loss of sexual attractiveness and the maternal role comes at a time when the husband is likely to be at the peak of his career and deeply involved in satisfying job activities. Bernice Neugarten, in describing how people become aware of middle age, says:

Women, but not men, tend to define their age status in terms of timing of events within the family world, and even unmarried career women often discuss middle age in terms of the family they might have had. . . .

Men, on the other hand, perceive the onset of middle age by cues presented outside the family context, often from the deferential behavior accorded them in the work setting. One man described the first time a younger associate helped open a door for him; another, being called by his official title by a newcomer in the company; another, the first time he was ceremoniously asked for advice by a younger man.

Little research has been done on the prestige accorded men and women in different age brackets. The few studies available point to older women as the lowest-prestige group in society. In a projective test asking middle-aged persons to make up a story about a picture that showed a young couple and a middle-aged couple in conversation, Neugarten found that the older woman was seen as more uncomfortable in her role than any of the others and was the only figure who was described as often in negative as in positive terms. Mary Laurence found that respondents tended to rate women as having more undesirable personality traits than men through all age ranges, but the age group rated most severely was women over forty.

A study of characters in American magazine fiction from 1890 to 1955 found a decline in the number of older women appearing as characters. By 1955 there were none at all. The middle-aged woman almost never sees herself and her problems depicted in print or on the screen. When they are, she sees mostly negative stereotypes. Her dilemma is very similar to that of the black ghetto child who finds in the "Dick and Jane" first reader a world that is irrelevant at best, invidious at worst. To have oneself and one's experiences verified in the mythology and art of one's culture is a fundamental psychological need at every stage of the life cycle.

Women's own attitudes toward aging are shown in the interesting finding that, in the listings of the Directory of the American Psychological Association, women are ten times as likely to omit their age as men. Thus, even professional women, who presumably have roles that extend undamaged into middle age, are much more likely than men to feel that their advancing age is a serious impairment.

On the question of whether middle-aged women are actually unhappier or more maladjusted than middle-aged men, the evidence is conflicting and inconclusive. A few studies by various researchers found little or no difference between middle-aged and old men and women on such factors as personality change, engagement with life, and reported satisfaction with life. One study found older women more satisfied than older men.

One problem with these studies, however, is that some of them lump together the middle-aged group with persons past retirement age. Some of the findings may therefore be due to the fact that the retirement age is far more stressful and acute for men than for women. Women have never invested much in careers and have been adjusting to role loss for many years. In old age, an additional factor works in favor of women. Women are closer to relatives and thus are more sheltered from complete isolation.

The studies present another problem in that the respondents themselves judged how happy or satisfied they were. The trouble with this is that subordinated groups learn to expect less and therefore to be satisfied with less. A middle-aged woman whose husband has had several affairs may report that her marriage has been satisfying because society has taught her to expect infidelity from her husband. A man whose wife had behaved in similar fashion would be less likely to regard his marriage as satisfying. Indeed, social conditioning would probably dictate a more painful crisis for the cuckolded husband. Moreover, measuring the satisfaction levels of people who are already so thoroughly "socialized" does not take into account the wife's feelings the first time she saw her own mother experience such treatment from her father and realized that a similar fate was in store for herself. It does not measure the emotional cost of adjusting to the expectation of abuse. In fact, if we were to confine our evidence to degrees of self-reported satisfaction, we might conclude that a great variety of social inequities create no emotional hardships for the subjugated.

THE ECONOMIC LOSS

Discrimination against older women in employment is important because of the large number of people affected. The number of older women in the labor force has grown rapidly since World War II. By 1987, 67.1 percent of women in the age range of forty-five to fifty-four and 42.7 percent of those fifty-five to sixty-four were in the labor force. These percentages had risen sharply from 1940, when they were 24.5 percent and 18 percent respectively.

Discrimination against older workers of both sexes in industry is well documented. A 1965 Department of Labor survey concluded that half the job openings in the private economy are closed to applicants over fifty-five years of age, and one-fourth are closed to applicants over forty-five. Women are particularly disadvantaged by this discrimination because, as a result of their typical work and child-rearing cycle, many women come back on the labor market after a long period of absence (and are perhaps entering the market for the first time) during precisely these years. There is very little evidence on the question of whether older women are relatively more disadvantaged than older men. Edwin Lewis states that age is a greater detriment to women than to men but cites no evidence. A Department of Labor publication on age discrimination in employment claims that men are slightly favored, but the evidence is very incomplete. The study found that, compared to the percentage of unemployed older men and women, women were hired in somewhat greater numbers. But unemployment rates are based on self-reporting and are notoriously influenced by the optimism of a given group about the prospects of finding employment. Older women, many of whom are married, are less likely to report themselves as seeking work if they are pessimistic about the possibilities of getting any. The study also surveyed the employment practices of 540 firms and found that, although differences were slight, men were disadvantaged in a larger number of occupational categories. But in clerical work, in which 31.5 percent of women over forty-five are engaged, discrimination against women was decidedly greater.

The problem of discrimination against older men and women is complicated by the fact that a study would take into account whether discrimination was practiced because of expected lack of physical strength, long training or internship programs, or physical attractiveness. The former two considerations figure much more frequently in the case of men and certainly have more legitimacy as grounds for discriminating than the factor of physical attractiveness, which usually arises solely because the woman is seen as a sex object before she is seen as a productive worker. As long as this is the employer's orientation, it will probably do little good to cite him the studies proving that middle-aged women office workers are superior to young women in work attendance, performance, and ability to get along agreeably with others. It would also be necessary to see how much relative discrimination there is within occupational categories. There is little discrimination in certain low-paid, undesirable jobs because the supply of workers in these categories is short. Women tend to be predominantly clustered in precisely these job categories.

A check of one Sunday's *Los Angeles Times* prior to 1970, when want ads were segregated by sex, yielded a count of 1,067 jobs advertised for women and 2,272 advertised for men. For both sexes, specific upper age limits or the term *young* was attached to less than 1 percent of the job listings, and there was almost no difference between men and women. However, 97 (or 9 percent) of the female ads used the term *girl* or *gal,* while only 2 of the 2,272 male ads used the term *boy.*

To check out my hunch that *girl* is an indirect way of communicating an age limitation, in a state where discrimination by age is illegal, I called five employment agencies in southern California and asked an interviewer who handles secretarial and clerical placement what he or she thought the term *girl* meant from the employer's side and how it would be interpreted by the average job seeker. Four of the five employment interviewers stated that the term definitely carries an age connotation for employer and job seeker alike. They defined the age implied variously as ''under thirty''; ''under thirty-five —if we were looking in the thirty-five to forty-five category we would use the term 'mature'; over forty-five we don't say anything''; ''It means a youngster. I certainly don't think a forty-five-year-old would go in if she saw that ad''; ''It does mean age, which is why we always use the term 'women' in our company's ads (although we may use the term 'girl' on a specific listing).'' The last person would not state a specific age because she was obviously worried about being caught in violation of the law, to which she frequently alluded. Only one of the five replied in the negative, saying ''to me 'girl' is just another word for 'woman.' You can hardly use the term 'woman' in the wording of an ad.'' Everyone I questioned agreed that the term *girl Friday* (a tiny proportion of our cases) carries no age connotation. Several, however, mentioned that the terms *trainee, recent high-school grad,* and *high-school grad* were used to communicate an age limitation.

Along with the term *girl,* a number of ads use physical descriptions— almost entirely lacking in men's ads. ''Attractive gal for receptionist job'' is typical. More specific are the following excerpts from the columns in the *Los Angeles Times:* ''Exciting young atty seeks a sharp gal who wants a challenge''; ''Young, dynamic contractor who is brilliant but disorganized needs girl he can depend on completely''; and one headlined ''Lawyer's Pet'' which goes on to say "Looking for a future: want challenge, 'variety,' $$$? Young attorney who handles all phases of 'law' will train you to become his 'right hand.'" Few women over thirty would consider themselves qualified to apply for these jobs.

The use of the term *girl* and the reaction of one employment agency interviewer who considered this the only proper way to connote *woman* in a want ad underscore the extent to which women's jobs are still considered young girls' jobs; that is, they constitute the relatively unimportant work that a girl does before she gets married. One employment-agency interviewer stated that his agency frequently had requests for a certain age level because companies want to keep the age range in a certain department homogeneous for the sake of congeniality. It is significant that he mentioned only the "twenties" or "thirties" as examples of such desirable age ranges.

One is tempted to make a comparison between the term *girl* and the insulting racist use of *boy* for all blacks, regardless of age. In both cases, the term indicates that the species under discussion is not considered capable of full adulthood. In both cases, blacks and women are acceptable and even likable when very old, as *uncle* and *grandmother*, but somehow both are anachronistic as mature adults.

Given the scarcity and conflicting nature of the data, it is impossible to say with certainty that older women suffer more from discrimination than do older men. The question certainly merits further and more systematic exploration.

CASTE AND CLASS

The division of this article into sexual, prestige, and economic losses was taken from John Dollard's analysis of the sexual, prestige, and economic gains of whites at the expense of blacks in his classic study, *Caste and Class in a Southern Town.* The choice was not an accident; speakers for women's liberation have often drawn heavily on the analogy between the problems of blacks and those of women. Yet equally often one hears objections to the analogy. Blacks are, as a group, isolated in the lowest economic strata and physically ghettoed into the worst parts of town, whereas women, being inextricably connected to men through familial ties, do not share a drastic, common disability. It has also been suggested that to compare the plight of women with that of blacks is to belittle the importance of the need for black liberation. Most of these critics care as little for black liberation as for the liberation of women and need not be taken seriously.

Yet the intellectual objections to the analogy should be discussed. The argument actually rests on the assumption that middle-class status cushions all of life's shocks and that middle-class women are always comfortably embedded in middle-class primary groups. It assumes further that the woes of lower-class women are all essentially class-connected rather than specifically sex-connected. The loneliness of widowhood, the anguish of a woman losing her husband to a younger woman, the perplexity of the woman whose children have left home and who finds herself unwanted on the labor market—these are real hurts, and they go deep, even in the middle class. Further, the notion of the individual as being deeply rooted in primary groups certainly reflects a partial and outmoded view in a highly individualistic society where the nuclear family, usually the only long-lasting primary group, has become extremely unstable. In our society, men and women are expected to get through life essentially alone. This is true even of the woman who is able to maintain good family ties throughout her life. It is even truer for those who suffer the more common fate of having these ties weakened by discord or severed by death or separation. For the lower-class woman, of course, these difficulties are harsher and more unrelieved, but in every class the woman must bear them alone.

The differential definition of age in men and women represents a palpable advantage to men at the expense of women. It multiplies the options for emotional satisfaction on a man's side while it diminishes them on a woman's. It raises his prestige and self-esteem at the expense of hers. All men in our society benefit to some degree from this custom, while not a single woman who lives into middle age escapes bearing some of the cost. If we are ever to restructure this society into one of true equality for both sexes, this is one of the crucial points at which we must begin.

The Internalization of Powerlessness: A Case Study of the Displaced Homemaker

LOIS M. GREENWOOD-AUDANT

There is something about being married. You invent this structure for yourself. You think you are on a real solid foundation. You think you are a pillar of the community or something—somebody that can be counted on. There are all sorts of walls, floors, and ceilings. It just seems so solid.

When I was divorced, I moved and my youngest child had gone away. I had this recurring dream that was a nightmare for me. I shop at a big Safeway. In my dream, each parking place was identified by a metal archway—there was a definite place where you parked. I became my car and drove down to the Safeway and they had sawed all these things off. There was this enormous parking lot and you could park wherever you wanted. There was no way to know where you were supposed to park.

For me, this epitomized my feelings that all my structures were stripped away and no one cared. I could park wherever I wanted! I felt like Sartre's expression, "condemned to freedom."

Pat O'Hara, displaced homemaker[1]

Condemned to freedom—this is a paradoxical sentiment to have in a society where freedom and individualism are so highly valued. Yet, this woman is not alone with her dilemma. She is one of an estimated 3 million to 5 million displaced homemakers in the United States today.[2] Displaced homemakers are the traditional mothers of America before their displacement. They are typically women over the age of thirty-five, who have worked in the home as mothers and homemakers and relied on others for financial support. Due to separation, divorce, widowhood, or the coming of age of their children, they have lost that financial support from husbands or from Aid to Families with Dependent Children (AFDC). Displaced homemakers do not fit into any standard governmental classifications, and, therefore, their problems generally have been unacknowledged, their numbers are only approximations. Their dilemma often is thought to arise mainly within middle-class families where husbands can afford to support women in the home who are not bringing in outside incomes. However, displaced homemakers are found among all social classes — the working class, the poor, and the upper class — as well as among all races and ethnic groups.[3] A key identifying factor of displaced homemakers is that they view themselves primarily as mothers and homemakers, and they have not had the experience of steady work in the labor market. The result is that, when they lose their financial support for being homemakers, they face extremely limited opportunities in the marketplace. They face triple jeopardy of discrimination: because they are women, because they have been homemakers, and because they are older. When they are also from a minority group, they face a fourth jeopardy of racial or ethnic discrimination. No matter what status they held while married, they drop significantly in socioeconomic status when their marriages end. As one study points out, 25 percent of white families become poor after marital disruption; 40 percent of those poor families become relatively poor. For black women, the situation is worse: 55 to 60 percent become poor, and 70 percent become relatively poor.[4]

Some may argue that the displaced homemaker's predicament may not be typical of the inequities women face at a time when 52.8 percent of all women sixteen years and over are participating in the labor force.[5] What makes a study of displaced homemakers meaningful in this regard is that these are women in transition from a life defined by traditional sex roles to a life that neccessitates self-support and independence. Displaced homemakers are struggling to bridge the gap between work in the home and work in the marketplace, between life in the private world of the family and life in the public sphere of economics and politics. In this way, they can help us to understand a predicament common to many women. Their story highlights the dilemmas, inequities, and disparities that result from a sexual division of labor that assigns to women the primary role of child rearing and homemaking. As long as women are expected to carry primary responsiblity for child rearing, most women will be influenced by this expectation and by the experience.

Although entering the labor market is a challenging task for any woman, it is particularly so for displaced homemakers, because they seldom have many options or any preparation for their new circumstances. They usually enter when they are suffering emotional and economic upheaval. They move abruptly from dependence or interdependence to being alone, and they need jobs that pay a living wage. They have to cope with financing, housing, food, clothing, transportation, as well as with getting an education and job training.

They comprise a vulnerable segment of this nation's unemployed and, in fact, are worse off than most of the unemployed because there are few legal or institutional resources to support them. They face continuing discrimination in employment because they are older and have no recent paid work experience. They are ineligible for unemployment insurance because they have been engaged in unpaid labor in the home. They are ineligible for old-age benefits because they are too young, and many will never qualify for Social Security because they were divorced from the family wage earner too early. They have often lost their rights as beneficiaries under their husbands' employer's pension and health plans, and they are generally unacceptable to private health-insurance plans because of their age.[6] This litany of ineligibilities underscores the point made by the original proponents of displaced homemakers legislation that "these are women who fall between the cracks of our society."[7]

These women face grave obstacles to economic self-sufficiency, and they have every right to feel frustrated about their situations. However, there is more to their dilemma than these structurally imposed obstacles. Most of the women also feel powerless about their own ability to do something worthwhile after their marriages have ended. They suffer tremendous feelings of self-doubt, lack of self-confidence, and low self-esteem. Their feelings of powerlessness seem to go deeper than the feelings people generally experience when they face a life crisis such as death of a spouse, divorce, or obstacles to their advancement. Their feelings of helplessness or powerlessness pervade their lives whether they are white or black, middle class or working class.

I became aware of this phenomenon while conducting participant-observation fieldwork at the first displaced-homemaker center established in the country, in Oakland, California. As I sat in the center listening to workshop leaders encourage the women to focus on areas of power in their lives, I heard them persistently discount their strengths and emphasize their weaknesses. The women said they found it difficult to organize their lives to take positive steps toward self-sufficiency. They would talk on the telephone to friends for hours. They would stay in bed late into the morning. They felt unable to start the day until after their morning coffee or the "Today Show." They could not look for a job until they had had their teeth fixed or bought new clothes. They said they would start out as soon as they got the house organized, when they finished their diets, or after the last child had left home. They responded to suggestions for action with, "Yes, but . . . ." They went to job interviews feeling they weren't wanted—and, sure enough, they weren't. Many women openly admitted that "dependence was comfortable," even though there were costs. They found it hard to make decisions when no one shared the responsiblity. They found it hard to give up needing someone else and hard to face doing it alone.

During the four years that the Oakland Displaced Homemakers Center had been in operation, the staff had found that the majority of women coming for help experienced significant problems with powerlessness, reflected in feelings of low self-esteem and lack of self-reliance. These problems often inhibited the women from becoming job-ready and from actively seeking a job.[8]

These findings were substantiated by a national study of forty-seven displaced-homemaker demonstration projects across the country funded by the U.S. Department of Labor under the Comprehensive Employment and Training Act (CETA): The most frequently mentioned problem of displaced homemakers was a lack of self-esteem or self-confidence.[9] The study reported that the problem was the women's fears that they were incapable or not good enough.[10]

To investigate the causes of these feelings of helplessness, low self-esteem, and powerlessness that incapacitated displaced homemakers, I conducted forty in-depth interviews with displaced homemakers who had applied for services at the Oakland Displaced Homemakers Center.[11] These included life histories of the women, from childhood and family background through marriage and homemaking experiences to displacement crisis and current status.

The interview sample was randomly selected from applicants who sought service at the Oakland center in late 1978 and early 1979. I intentionally sought women who were removed from their marriages for at least one year, to mitigate the possibility that feelings of powerlessness were a result of an immediate life crisis. The women had ended their marriages an average of 6.7 years before the interview. Of these women, 75 percent were separated or divorced and 25 percent were widowed; half were working class and half middle class;[12] 75 percent were white and 25 percent were black. They ranged from forty to fifty-eight years of age. Since the end of their marriages, the women had tended to sustain themselves with some income support from their former husbands, accumulated savings from sales of their houses, life insurance in the case of widows, or other limited means of income. The center staff noted that the women often did not seek assistance until they had "spent down" to near poverty level and were beginning to panic about how they would support themselves.

POWER AND POWERLESSNESS: A THEORETICAL FRAMEWORK

Power may be defined as the ability to exercise control or direct change despite resistance.[13] Powerlessness is the inability to do so. There are objective and subjective dimensions to power. The objective dimension is access to and command over resources that contribute to people's ability to control circumstances and overcome resistance. These resources include cash, credit, wealth, or jobs; access to legitimacy, popularity, or status; control over sources of information; and control over physical force.[14] Usually the study of power concerns itself with these objective factors.

However, there is also a subjective dimension to power. People's motivation to achieve power is influenced by their belief in their ability to do so; this, in turn, is influenced by their level of self-esteem. As achievement-motivation studies have shown, people do not try to achieve unless they have some reasonable belief in their ability to succeed. This same analysis applies to power.[15] If people feel capable and worthy, they will assert themselves. Low self-esteem leads to feelings of incompetence and lack of confidence in the ability to achieve. A person with low self-esteem sets lower goals and still feels incapable of meeting them.[16]

Objective conditions of power or powerlessness influence an individual's subjective feeling of power. In turn, a subjective belief in the ability to be powerful encourages an individual's efforts to gain access to and control over objective resources. An individual with little or no control over money, legitimacy, information, or force is likely to feel powerless and incompetent. At the same time, an individual with low self-confidence is likely to be discouraged from seeking the objective resources of power. Powerlessness becomes internalized when structural constraints (the objective conditions) are translated into psychological constraints (the subjective feelings) through mediating experiences. My study of displaced homemakers identified three significant mediators of the internalization process: gender-identity formation, work in the home (thus financial dependence), and social norms.[17] How these mediate internalization of powerlessness will be discussed in greater detail later.

This concept illuminates why powerless groups may participate in their own subordination. If they have internalized their objective reality, they may feel unable to overcome the objective obstacles that prevent them from controlling their lives. As Brazilian philosopher Paulo Freire has argued, to free themselves, the disadvantaged must challenge their very self-definition as well as their objective disadvantages.[18] It is a difficult task, since it requires giving up known definitions and relationships to start anew. Such a task requires an inner strength, which is undermined by the social structures the disadvantaged are struggling against. James Baldwin expressed this problem articulately in describing his own expatriation to Europe:

> In America, the color of my skin had stood between myself and me; in Europe, that barrier was down. Nothing is more desirable than to be released from an affliction, but nothing is more frightening than to be divested of a crutch. It turned out that the question of who I was, was not solved because I had removed myself from the social forces which menaced me—anyway, these forces had become interior and I had dragged them across the ocean with me. The question of who I was had at last become a personal question, and the answer was to be found in me.[19]

Feelings of powerlessness can be an adaptive response to an objective reality. To act as if one has power when one doesn't can be an invitation to further oppression. The need to struggle against powerlessness occurs when the objective conditions that created and reinforced it allow some possibility of enacting change. But this is when the internalization of powerlessness is most debilitating. It can penetrate people's self-definition to the point that they not only feel powerless but also identify with powerless behavior. This inhibits them from successfully challenging and overcoming their disadvantage.

POWERLESSNESS IN DISPLACED HOMEMAKERS

The objective social factor creating powerlessness among displaced home-makers is the division of labor by sex, which prescribes that women are primarily responsible for child rearing and homemaking. This limits women's access to the resources that bring social power and contributes to their feelings of personal powerlessness in the public domain. The division of labor by sex generates certain mediators that translate the objective reality of powerlessness into a subjective reality: (1) gender-identity formation, (2) the personal experience of work in the home, which creates financial dependence on others, and (3) social norms and values that evolve from the experience of work in the home. These conditions influence a homemaker's subjective experience by influencing, respectively, (1) her self-image, (2) her behavior, and (3) her attitudes.

My study found that the major cause of powerlessness in displaced homemakers is dependence—both objective, structurally imposed dependence and subjective, psychologically felt dependence. This dependence develops with gender-identity formation; it is reinforced by the women's reliance on their husbands for economic support and by their sex-defined work role in the home. It affects them subjectively by influencing their self-image, behavior, and attitudes so that they often feel incapable of directing change in their lives.

Note that this study is concerned with displaced homemakers' powerlessness vis-à-vis the public domain—the world of the labor market. These women had significant strengths and often felt powerful within the private sphere of the home. But the domestic sphere is isolated from and subordinate to the public sphere, and the identity, behavior, and values that are so functional within the home do not always translate successfully into the marketplace. This lack of transferability of strength leads to experiences of dependence. As long as the women objectively are dependent and subjectively feel dependent, they are unable to assert themselves fully in the public domain.

A major debate often centers around whether objective or subjective factors are more important in perpetuating powerlessness. Simply put, do women set themselves up for failure? Or does society set women up for failure? My analysis suggests that it is too simple to blame only the individual or only the system. The truth lies in the interaction between the two. I have found that a primary cause of powerlessness for women lies in a *structure* of inequality that generates a debilitating *psychological effect*. The psychological effect of powerlessness, in turn, can reinforce the objective structure of powerlessness, thus serving as a secondary cause.

In the following discussion, I draw on the experiences of the displaced homemakers I interviewed to illustrate how the three mediators derived from the sexual division of labor—gender-identity formation, work in the home and concomitant financial dependence, and the social norms of home-making work—translate objective conditions of powerlessness into subjective ones; i.e., how powerlessness is internalized. Although the examples drawn from the women's life histories represent particular points in time, each mediator operates throughout much of a woman's lifetime.

Gender-Identity Formation

Traditionally, the father is the primary wage earner and the mother is the primary nurturer of their children. This has psychological ramifications for both girls and boys.[20] During the early years of life, girls do not differentiate their identity from their mothers as much as boys do. Because boys are almost exclusively nurtured by the opposite gender, they define themselves through differentiation.[21]

Because a girl continues to rely on and identify with her mother — her original source of nurturance — for affirmation of her being, she develops a dependence on that relationship for affirmation of her worth, approval, and love. As she grows, she extends this reliance to significant others, especially her father, boyfriend, and husband.[22] Consequently, a girl learns to be nice and pleasing to gain approval and affirmation of her self-worth. Simone de Beauvoir captures this sentiment expressively in her *Memoirs of a Dutiful Daughter* as she speaks of her mother:

> Her hold over me stemmed indeed a great deal from the very intimacy of our relationship. . . . Any reproach made by my mother, even her slightest frown, was a threat to my security; without her approval, I no longer felt I had any right to live.
> If her disapproval touched me so deeply, it was because I set so much store by her good opinion.[23]

This same dynamic appeared very strongly in the lives of the women I interviewed. According to their accounts, their mothers were traditional family-oriented homemakers, who had a strong and often controlling hold over them. Many were still struggling with their own relationships with their mothers when they, themselves, were mothers and grandmothers.[24] The following quote is from a separated, middle-class displaced homemaker:

> My relationship with my mother was mixed up as a kid. I always thought she knew everything. If I didn't wear my boots and she said it would rain, it would rain. She was hard on me verbally and emotionally. I still have ties and they are hard to break.

Because the mother's love is so important to the daughter, she does not want to jeopardize it by incurring disapproval, so she tries to be a "good girl" as much as possible. To fail to please her mother, her husband, and others who are important to her threatens her sense of self-worth. Many of the women I interviewed resented the hold their mothers had over them. They recognized that it inhibited their ability to develop an independent sense of self. But few had rebelled against their mothers' authority, because they did not want to hurt their mothers and jeopardize their love.[25] One divorced middle-class displaced homemaker explains this dynamic:

> I still have a problem of keeping in control vis-à-vis my mother. Very often I give in because I don't like to upset her. I become the

martyr. . . . I don't want to win with her. It's not important. If I win, she will lose, and it would be more difficult to live with her. *By hurting her, I only hurt myself* [emphasis added].

This initial reliance on their mothers, which results from gender identification, leads to a need to please others: the women almost unanimously put others' needs ahead of their own; they almost unanimously gave in to their husbands in times of disagreement, to maintain peace and harmony; and the majority also found themselves influenced or dominated by other people's opinions and hesitant to express their own views. All their lives they had tried to be "good" by minimizing individual self-expression in order to be loved.

The following is a typical answer to my question, "Did you find that you tended to put others' needs ahead of your own?"

> That is the story of my life, but now even my children are starting to tell me not to do it. It must be bad when your children start saying that. I just started out that way. I never wanted to upset my mother. She was sickly. I found myself doing things because she wanted me to, not because I wanted to do them. And my mother-in-law was the same. She took over from my mother. I was satisfied to do what she thought was right, and that doesn't make too much sense because I'm not a passive person. The ability to please someone else gets in the way of what you want.

To my question, "Why do you think it is more important to please others than please yourself?" this working-class widow replied:

> A need to be loved, a need to be loved! I guess I have always felt that need. You stay within the forms, you conform in order to be loved. I heard for many years from my mother-in-law, "Oh, she's just like a daughter to me," and that made me feel great, but it wasn't doing anything for my personality because I became pale in her presence. People associated me with my mother-in-law; they didn't think of me as a person.

Many of the women reiterated the same theme. As a divorced, middle-class homemaker said:

> The approval of others is absolutely important. I'm a people-pleaser.
> . . . I'm used to pleasing people. I'm used to having a pleasing personality. . . . I'm used to pleasing children. I'm far too humble a person. It makes me mad at myself to be this way. I'd like to change that and assume some role of self-importance aside from my family.

Generally, the women felt that, if they denied themselves, others would look out for them and care for them; if they made themselves vulnerable, others would come to their rescue. More often than not, they found themselves disrespected rather than loved. The hard reality they all had had to face was that, although they had cared for other in hopes of being cared for, they were left without anyone to support them.

These women gave in 70 percent of the time when they disagreed with their husbands. The main reason appeared to be to avoid conflict and disharmony. One divorced, working-class woman said:

I would get tired of arguments. . . . I would give in and, when I got low, I wished he were dead. Very seldom I won an argument. I'd usually give in and so I had low self-esteem. He'd browbeat me. I couldn't do anything right. I couldn't have any free time. Giving in was easier to do than fighting him 'cause I didn't like fighting. But I didn't know how to get out of that situation. I felt locked in it forever.

Power—the ability to bring about change despite resistance—means that one person's will may prevail over another's will. Overcoming resistance creates the risk of incurring anger, criticism, or disapproval from those who are being opposed. The women I interviewed demonstrated in a number of ways that they had no desire to run this risk.[26] As one middle-class widow put it, "I'd resist and resist and then I'd just give in to stop it 'cause I couldn't stand the conflict. I was afraid of what he'd do."

The dependence on approval was both psychological and financial; both subjective and objective conditions influenced the decision to "give in." The result was an erosion of the women's sense of self-worth, because they did not stick up for themselves. This is what a divorced, middle-class woman said:

He had a weird sense of humor, especially around our friends. He'd run me down. I wouldn't stick up for myself. I took it. I figured he needed to run someone else down in order to build himself up.

Q. Is that why you didn't stick up for yourself?

I guess I thought the most important thing was for him to maintain his ego because he was the money earner. I didn't realize people are not as fragile as I thought they were or that I was so important that I could make a difference . . . . Crazy because I sacrificed myself. So many times I wanted to say something but I didn't want to attack his strength because I needed him to be strong to take care of me, the family and the whole thing.

Each time the women gave in, they died a little and the relationship died a little. It was a price most of them were willing to pay, for a while at least, to maintain family stability and harmony. In the process, they experienced abuse and denial of their feelings, which made them lose confidence in themselves.

I presented the women with a card that listed several social communication styles. They identified 66 percent of the time with patterns that reflected some degree of "other orientation." Repeating phrases from the card that rang true for her, one middle-class widow said:

Oh, I'm "very aware of others' feelings and opinions, which makes me hesitant to speak my own mind." It's easy to identify with others. I am very aware of others' opinons. Also, I tend to "listen attentively and have things to say but rarely speak up; I'm happy to hear others' views." Listening attentively, it fits very well with the first one. It goes back to a lack of assertiveness. . . . I wonder if it's women's work in the home, as we are interdependent on others for approval. Yes, especially if there is no outside source like work . . . my part-time work did help me. It goes back to how you feel and how you like yourself. If you like yourself, then you don't need that other person.

In conclusion, the displacement crisis created an identity crisis for these women. For years, they had identified as a "we." A middle-class widow said: "The sense of worth I had was all tied up in my husband. When he died, all of a sudden I was alone. I had to find my own sense of worth which did not include another person. I had to become an 'I' instead of a 'we.'" But who is this "I"? Daughter, wife, mother, homemaker are who they have been. Now they were being forced, often for the first time in their lives, to look at themselves as individuals. It was a new and frightening experience, because years of dependence had eroded their sense of self-worth. This is why so many felt condemned to freedom. One woman expressed this sentiment directly: "I had spent my whole life being a super daughter, a super wife, a super mother—so much so that there was nothing left for me. With the divorce, I hit bottom" (Margaret Miller). Another woman (Christine Horner) expressed the feelings poetically:

> I see an unknown woman
> through her windshield
> through her tears
> it is my same face
>
> the face a man once covered
> in love, the thick and invisible
> condemnation which effaces
> it is too soon for her to guess herself
>
> out of hiding, to guess
> how the old skins peel, a map
> for unseen places rising
> from this empty mirror

Work in the Home: Financial Dependence

When women accept primary responsibility for rearing children, it is more difficult for them to become economically self-supporting. The resulting reliance on others for financial support is an objective constraint that becomes psychologically internalized over time as dependence.

Women always sacrifice some level of economic independence, success, or status when they must carry the full responsibility of child rearing. A popular article by a modern professional woman frankly states this point:

> I'm glad to be part of a generation of women who are free to make choices about careers and families. However, as far as I can tell, the seamless web of family-and-prestigious-career just doesn't work. At some point, you have to sit down and decide whether to conduct your life in pursuit of money, status, power . . . or something else. The *something else* is hard to describe, because it's not part of the official story of my generation of women. . . .
>
> The point I never see in the success stories—but that my life as a mother with a career has convinced me is true—is that you really can't have it all. . . . It's not an all-or-nothing choice, but the compromises are real.[27]

One middle-aged mother in the comparison group for this study gave some of the reasons why the compromises are real:

> Kids make it self-destructive for women to try to keep up with men. . . . Children's lives demand daily care and nurturance. And then there is the time spent arranging child care, meeting with people who will care for your child, involvement in the activities and friends of your child, the PTA . . . there's always something, and you can't act as if it's not there.

The displaced homemakers I interviewed usually were married in the 1950s, a time when society encouraged women to stay home to care for their children. Even when they worked, it was generally understood that they were merely supplementing the family income. In all but three of the marriages in this study, the men were the main income earners. In over half the cases, both working-class and middle-class husbands tightly controlled the finances, which made the wives feel dependent and often resentful. Popular notions that middle-class marriage relationships are more equal, open, and sharing than working-class relationships were not confirmed by my findings. The middle class may view equality as more desirable, but the reality is about the same amount of inequality between spouses.

The women sometimes resented the economic control their husbands exercised, but their resentment never amounted to effective resistance, as expressed by one widowed, middle-class homemaker.

> Yes, I felt very dependent on him economically. When we were both working together, he would put his paycheck in the bank and I would pay all the bills with mine. . . . Incredible! And when I stopped working, and I asked him for money for myself because I used to run the household, there was never enough for me to do anything with.

In some cases, the women did not question or challenge their economic dependence. They subjectively accepted what was objectively imposed (from a separated, middle-class homemaker):

> I felt very dependent for everything. I didn't have any life outside of the home. He controlled the money. I never kept a checkbook 'til last year. I never knew how much money he made and I never asked. I was given so much for food. I didn't have a budget and no money for clothes. My husband used to want me to buy new clothes; in fact, he would pick them out and buy them for me, like in my childhood—my mother always picked out my clothes. He took that role.

In 35 percent of the cases, the woman's feeling of economic dependence was mitigated by the fact that she shared in the financial decision making, managed the family budget, or felt free to spend money on the house and the family as she saw fit. But even these women did not feel they had a personal right to the money, and their husbands exercised veto power over any important financial decisions. They were only managing the family budget; although administration gave them some power, the final authority resided with the boss. Here is what one separated, middle-class homemaker said:

He was always generous. I wasn't aware of feeling dependent, but it did have a psychological effect by causing me to withdraw from asserting myself a lot of the time. . . . I've always had the feeling that it was his money and always had trouble rationalizing it for myself. . . . I could buy for the kids. If I had a salary coming in, I would have spent more on myself.

Because they were dependent on their husbands for financial resources, these women did not have ongoing experience in controlling their lives financially. Lacking this experience, over time they came to believe they were incapable of controlling their lives, psychologically internalizing their personal experience of financial dependence. A divorced, middle-class woman told me this:

There was a definite erosion of my self-confidence during my marriage. He is a master of it. And by nature, being dependent financially and having the children, I came more and more to doubt my feelings and feel he was it.

It goes back to my mother. Even though I had a strong mind, emotionally I couldn't stand up to them. Maybe I had a need for them to be it, never having had the opportunity to flex my own muscles. Maybe I was afraid to flex them, to find out.

Never having had the opportunity to "flex her muscles," this woman was afraid they didn't exist. This lack of experience made her vulnerable to her husband's accusations that she was incapable and inept. A majority of the women talked of this same vulnerability (from a separated, working-class woman):

He made me feel like I was nothin', just nothin'. . . . He'd always call me stupid. It got so that my name became "stupid." . . . He'd make me feel so small . . . I started to believe it! When I first got married I felt independent, but it didn't last three months.

Even women whose husbands had positive evaluations of them relied on their husbands' judgments of their abilities rather than their own. When their husbands were gone, they found it difficult to build a sense of self-esteem based on their own evaluations rather than their husbands'.

Social Norms: Home and Marketplace

Norms and values are learned from personal experiences. Because work in the home differs from work in the marketplace, it has a different set of norms, values, and behavioral patterns. Mothering develops abilities to sustain, nurture, and empathize, because mothers must learn to anticipate and identify unverbalized needs of children. This creates a self that is very responsive to outside demands. As a mother and as a wife, a woman continuously puts the needs of others ahead of her own. Such work requires administrative skill and flexibility and is characterized by continuous interruptions. The homemaker is used to being her own boss and setting her own pace within the framework of the needs and demands of her children and husband. Because there are no standardized objective criteria for measuring her success, she develops an internalized set of standards that she can apply to herself.[28] The "home culture" that evolves out of this structure of work has values and norms very different from those of marketplace work. I call it a *home* culture rather than a *woman's* culture, because its characteristics are generated by the structure of the work rather than anything that is innately female. The values it generates are beliefs in human welfare, interdependence, cooperation, service, and harmony. It emphasizes means rather than ends.

Marketplace work is characterized by task orientation and goals of self-advancement. It puts ends over means. The attributes it calls for are, in many ways, directly opposed to those needed for effective child rearing and homemaking. As one study discussing the two spheres pointed out, "the fundamental personality traits each evokes are at points diametrically opposed, so that what are assets for one become liabilities for the other, and the full realization of one role threatens defeat in the other."[29]

Moreover, it is important to recognize that the home culture is subordinate to the marketplace culture, because only in the latter is monetary value created. In a society where success is measured by the money one makes, home work and its values are not highly esteemed. Also, homemakers are less equipped to cope with the demands of what they see as "the outside world" because they have equipped themselves to deal with the demands of the private domain. They are like strangers or refugees in the world of work, and they experience entry into it as a kind of culture shock. One divorced, middle-class woman expressed this as she described her job hunt:

> I haven't had enough exposure. How can you choose when you don't know? It's like being in a foreign country. People wear different clothes and speak a different language. You have to take time and try, but I'm lacking time to figure out what I want to do. . . .
>
> What can I bring to a job? I'm willing to learn. I'm good with people. I have an organizational sense. I'm very tenacious. I work even when sick, and when things need to get done I see that they get done. But these aren't marketable skills.

In the marketplace, displaced homemakers are evaluated by a new set of criteria including punctuality, efficiency, self-reliance, competitiveness, and achieving goals established by others. Since they rarely wish to give up the very different values of the home culture, they find it difficult to win power in the world of work. During my interviews, I asked the displaced homemakers to list what priority the following items would have for them in evaluating a job—job security, good pay, self-fulfillment, flexible time schedule, room for advancement, nice environment or people, service to others, and other. They listed as the top three in priority (1) self-fulfillment, (2) service to others, and (3) nice people in the work environment. The women often equated self-fulfillment with service to others. They significantly failed to pick good pay or room for advancement. Job security trailed as a fourth choice. A full 25 percent of the women went out of their way to tell me that they were not at all interested in room for advancement. They said this in a tone that indicated it was a matter of principle. This did not mean they wanted low-level work, however. They wanted meaningful work but they didn't see the need to move up a job ladder. They tended to view advancement in terms of competitiveness, a quality they abhorred because they felt it hurt and alienated others. As one divorced, working-class woman expressed it: "To strive is not as important to me. If it was fulfilling my need, I would strive, but as things are for me, it's more gratifying for me to be helping someone else."

The values these women uphold are life-enhancing ones that have much to contribute to society. But they also mask a certain fear of power. The women are unsure of themselves and are afraid of invoking criticism or disapproval if they exercise any power that could threaten others. To the question, "How do you feel about handling a position of responsibility and making decisions?" one middle-class widow responded characteristically:

> I have a hard time with it. I don't like that feeling about myself but I have come to a point of accepting that's the way I am. In fact, I backed off from a lot of responsibility because it's easier than stepping in and worrying about it. The worry and the unsureness of doing well, of accomplishing, keeps me away from it. But I find that, with decision making, the more you are unsure of yourself . . . the more incapacitated you are to make a decision.

Generally, the women saw nothing positive about exerting power. Instead, they viewed it as "dog eat dog," hurting others, confrontational, corrupting, and alienating. A divorced, working-class interviewee explained:

> I'd like to have power for myself, but I don't want to exert it.
>
> Q. Why?
>
> Because I've seen what some people that have a little do. Those with a little power are very dangerous because they don't know how to exercise it. I wouldn't want to become a dangerous person.
>
> Q. But when you have power, you can do things for others, can't you?
>
> I've found that people resent people with power, and I don't want anybody resenting me. I try to be pleasant, try to be nice.

The women didn't think about the fact that, from a position of strength and influence, they might assert the home cultural values that were so meaningful to them. But from their position of weakness and fear, these values perpetuated their powerlessness.

CONCLUSION

Women's gender identity, their personal experience working in the home and being financially dependent, and the divergent norms and values of the home and marketplace cultures (generated by our society's sexual division of labor) induce feelings of dependence. These, in turn, reinforce the very objective conditions that hold women down. A feminine sense of self that relies on others for approval and validation evolves out of the conditions of the home where women are the primary child rearers. This reliance on others' approval led displaced homemakers to shy away from power, because they feared incurring the criticism or opposition of others. The personal experience of economic dependence in their marriages because their work was homemaking meant that they did not learn how to "flex their muscles." As a result, they came to believe that they were incompetent and incapable, a belief that was reinforced by disparaging husbands or a marketplace that devalued their work as homemakers. Convinced they had little to offer, they found it difficult to sell themselves to employers, to stick up for their rights, or to obtain what they felt was their due. Adhering to home cultural values such as concern for human welfare, interdependence, empathy, and nurturance, and developing behavior patterns that were functional for the effective accomplishment of homemaking, the women found it very difficult to adjust to the marketplace world, which called for a different set of values and behavior patterns. The objective conditions of their work in the home had created a normative and behavioral mode that was often in opposition and subordinate to the marketplace mode of action. Having internalized the home cultural values, the women were ill-prepared and often unwilling to adjust to marketplace values. This situation reinforced their position of powerlessness vis-à-vis the public domain.

The underlying structural cause of powerlessness is the sexual division of labor that relegates to women the primary responsibility for child rearing and homemaking. Displaced homemakers have been completely immersed in this traditional sex role, and so their experiences are more intense and more extreme. But they are not atypical. Women as a group are immersed in the home cultural identity, experience, and values when they are primarily raised by their mothers and when they become mothers. They have less power than men, and all women experience the consequences of this disparity. Women will not be free and equal until work in the home and the marketplace is redistributed more equitably between the sexes. This will require a significant restructuring of paid work to allow both men and women time to do both. A society that truly values the family and also develops a genuine commitment to equal opportunity for women must find the means for both parents to participate in child rearing and its related duties, so that women do not carry the primary responsibility. Only when men are as responsible as women for the care of children will women have the possibility of independence, will children have the opportunity to develop androgynously, and will home and marketplace cultural values no longer be segregated. A genuine commitment to equality of the sexes ultimately implies a restructuring of work in the marketplace and in the home so that men and women have equal access to the responsibilities and privileges of *both* worlds.

NOTES

1. In keeping with their desire to claim more power for themselves, some displaced homemakers in this study asked specifically to be identified by name.

2. This is a conservative estimate of numbers. The Women's Bureau estimate of 4 million is based on a national survey of marital status, labor force participation, and income (U.S. Department of Labor, Women's Bureau, *Survey of Income and Education, March 1976* [Washington, D.C.: Government Printing Office, 1976]). From this, approximations were developed in U.S. Department of Labor, Women's Bureau, *Tables Pertinent to Women and Displaced Homemakers by Selected Characteristics* (Washington, D.C.: Government Printing Office, July 13, 1979). The inexact numbers are due to the fact that there is no official category for counting displaced homemakers, especially since homemaking is not counted as work. Estimates in the late 1970s have ranged as high as 15 million. One study (Carol Eliason, *Neglected Women: The Educational Needs of Displaced Homemakers, Single Mothers and Older Women* [Washington, D.C.: National Advisory Council on Women's Educational Programs, 1977–78], 13) points out:

> The *Census* does not identify displaced homemakers as a group but it does show 3,164,000 widows and 2,435,000 divorced women in the 35–64 age group. Since 1968, the number of households headed by women has grown 10 times faster than traditional 2-adult families have grown.

3. A national study of displaced homemaker projects funded by the Department of Labor confirms this point. These projects served low-income (CETA-eligible) women only and participants were white, black, Hispanic, Asian, and Native American Indian, although the largest numbers served in the first year of the projects were white and black women. See Lois M. Greenwood and Deborah Kogan, *Assessment of the National Displaced Homemaker Program*, vol. I: *Overview of the 47 Displaced Homemaker Demonstration Projects, A Cross-Project Analysis,* prepared for the U.S. Department of Labor, Employment and Training Administration (Berkeley, Calif.: Berkeley Planning Associates, Sept. 30, 1981), 120–21.

4. Lois B. Shaw, "Economic Consequences of Marital Disruption," in National Commission for Manpower Policy, *Women's Changing Roles at Home and on the Job,* Special Report no. 26 (Washington, D.C.: National Commission for Manpower Policy, Sept. 1978), 197. This study refers to standard definitions of poverty and relative poverty.

5. U.S. Department of Labor, Bureau of Labor Statistics, *Employment in Perspective: Working Women,* Report no. 669 (Washington, D.C.: Government Printing Office, second quarter 1982).

6. Richard A. Batterton, Secretary, Maryland Department of Human Resources, Testimony before the U.S. Senate Subcommittee on Employment, Poverty, and Migratory Labor, September, 12, 1977, 2.

7. Since the movement began in California to initiate legislation for services to displaced homemakers, this has become an oft-quoted phrase in testimony before Congress, articles, etc. The phrase was first brought to my attention by Milo Smith, cofounder of the Oakland Displaced Homemakers Center.

8. Aliyah Stein, *Needs Assessment Study of Center Participants* (Oakland, Calif.: Displaced Homemakers Center, November 1977).

9. Greenwood and Kogan, *Assessment,* vol. I, 34.

10. Greenwood and Kogan, *Assessment,* vol. V: *Summary of Research Findings, Conclusions and Recommendations* (Oct. 30, 1981), 23.

11. Field research also included three years of participant-observation at the Displaced Homemakers Center, Oakland, California; a review of survey data on the center's participants; in-depth discussions with the center staff and other key figures active in the early period of the displaced homemakers movement; and correspondence with four displaced homemakers centers across the country about their participants' reported needs.

12. Determining the class status for married women is problematic because it is usually dependent on the class status of their fathers and husbands. I settled on the traditional method of determining class for the women by examining their husbands' levels of income, education, and types of jobs.

13. See the definitions developed by Robert A. Dahl, "Power," *International Encyclopedia of Social Sciences* (New York: Macmillan Co., and Free Press, 1968), 409; Rollo May, *Power and Innocence* (New York: Delta Books, 1972), 19; Jean B. Miller, *Toward a New Psychology of Women* (Boston: Beacon Press, 1976), Chapter 10.

14. See Dahl, ''Power.''

15. For references to achievement motivation studies, see Jacquelynne E. Parsons, ''Internal Factors Influencing Women's Career Choice,'' in Susan Golden, ed., *Work, Family Roles and Support Systems* (Ann Arbor: University of Michigan, Center for Continuing Education, 1978), 8. For the reverse dynamic, see Martin E. P. Seligman, *Helplessness: On Depression, Development, and Death* (San Francisco: W. H. Freeman and Co., 1975).

> A man . . . must begin with information about the contingency of outcome upon response. The information about contingency must be processed and transformed into a cognitive representation of the contingency. Such a representation has been variously called ''learning,'' ''perceiving'' or ''believing'' that response and outcome are independent. . . . This expectation is the causal condition for the motivational, cognitive and emotional debilitation that accompanies helplessness. [47–48]

There *are* exceptions to this rule about self-esteem. One is Lasswell's classic ''compensation theory,'' where he argues that ''a power seeker . . . pursues power as a means of compensation against . . . low estimates of the self'' (cited in Paul M. Sniderman, *Personality and Democratic Politics* [Berkeley: University of California Press, 1975], 227). Some people who have a low sense of self-esteem will have a need to prove themselves in an area that is legitimate for them. It has been more common in the past for men than women to try to prove themselves in the public domain because women traditionally have not seen this arena as a legitimate sphere of action for themselves. Jane S. Jaquette, ''Introduction: Women in American Politics,'' in Jane S. Jaquette, ed., *Women in Politics* (New York: John Wiley and Sons, 1974), xiii–xxvi.

16. See S. Coopersmith, *The Antecedents of Self-Esteem* (San Francisco: W. H. Freeman and Co., 1967), 4; Sniderman, *Personality and Democratic Politics,* 67; Patricia Wiles Middlebrook, *Social Psychology and Modern Life* (New York: Alfred A. Knopf, 1980), 56.

17. For more explanation, see my discussion of these mediators and how they operate in Lois M. Greenwood, ''Women, Work, and Powerlessness: A Case Study of the Displaced Homemaker'' (Ph.D. dissertation, University of California, Berkeley, Department of Political Science, 1980), Chapters 3 and 9.

18. Paulo Freire, *Pedagogy of the Oppressed* (New York: Seabury Press, 1968).

19. James Baldwin, *Nobody Knows My Name* (New York: Dial Press, 1961).

20. For further discussions of boys' gender identity in relationship to their mothers, see Nancy Chodorow, *The Reproduction of Mothering: Psychoanalysis and the Sociology of Gender* (Berkeley: University of California Press, 1978), Chapters 5 and 6; Margaret Mead, *Male and Female* (New York: William Morrow and Co., 1949); Karen Horney, ''The Dread of Women,'' in Karen Horney, *Feminine Psychology* (New York: W. W. Norton and Co., 1967), 133–46; Bruno Bettelheim, ''Symbolic Wounds,'' in William A. Lessa and Evon Z. Vogt, eds., *Reader in Comparative Religion: An Anthropological Approach,* 2d ed. (New York: Harper and Row, 1965), 230–40.

21. For further discussion of this subject, see Chodorow, *The Reproduction of Mothering;* Mead, *Male and Female;* Miller, *Toward a New Psychology;* Dorothy Dinnerstein, *The Mermaid and the Minotaur* (New York: Harper Colophon Books, 1977).

22. For further explanation of this dynamic, see Chodorow, *The Reproduction of Mothering,* Chapter 7; Miller, *Toward a New Psychology;* Judith Wells, ''Daddy's Little Girl,'' *Libera,* winter 1972, 43–45; Judith M. Bardwick and Elizabeth Douvan, ''Ambivalence: The Socialization of Women,'' in Vivian Gornick and Barbara Moran, eds., *Women in Sexist Society* (New York: Basic Books, 1971), 225–41.

23. Simone de Beauvoir, *Memoirs of a Dutiful Daughter* (New York: Harper Colophon Books, 1958), 39.

24. The Oakland Displaced Homemakers Center staff reported this to be one of the major issues participants struggled with as they sought new means to become self-sufficient. Chodorow cites a study based on interviews with seventy-five mothers, daughters, and granddaughters that confirms these findings. The mothers and daughters ''tend to remain emotionally bound up with each other in what might be called a semisymbiotic relationship.'' Chodorow, *The Reproduction of Mothering,* 109.

25. Naturally, this psychodynamic will vary according to the circumstances and characteristics of the mother–daughter relationship. Recent studies have shown that daughters of working mothers tend to have higher self-esteem than those of mothers who stay home. Also, women whose mothers were less affectionate were found to be high achievers. See Donna Moore, "Effects of Parental Child Rearing Attitudes and Attitudes toward Women on Female Children's Attitudes toward Women, Self Expectations and Self Esteem" (Ph.D. dissertation proposal, University of California, Davis, Department of Psychology, Nov. 1, 1976), 43. Moore notes:

> Wright and Tuska [B. Wright and S. Tuska, "The Nature and Origin of Feeling Feminine," *British Journal of Social Clinical Psychology* 5 (1966): 140–49] examined the relationship between self-stated masculinity or femininity . . . in over 2600 college Ss [students], finding that women who were rated as feminine recalled an emotionally satisfying mother and a successful father, while women rated as masculine reported an emotionally satisfying father but a frustrating, unsympathetic mother. [41]

26. For further illustration of this point, see my discussion of the women's attitudes toward responsibility, taking initiative, competition, new situations, power, and so forth, in Greenwood, "Women, Work, and Powerlessness," Chapter 10.

27. Deborah Fallows, "Mothers and Other Strangers," *Washington Monthly,* Jan. 1980, 22–24. See further accounts of this double-bind for working women who mother in Marilyn Fabe and Norma Wikler, eds., *Up against the Clock* (New York: Warner Books, 1979), and Phyllis Chesler's compelling personal story in *With Child: A Diary of Motherhood* (New York: Pantheon Books, 1974), Chapters 5 and 6.

28. See Ann Oakley, *The Sociology of Housework* (New York: Pantheon Books, 1974), Chapters 5 and 6.

29. Mirra Komarovsky, "Cultural Contradictions and Sex Roles," cited in Ann Oakley, *Woman's Work: The Housewife Past and Present* (New York: Vintage Books, 1976), 81.

Part Four

The Working Woman

Women in the Labor Force: An Overview

FRANCINE D. BLAU AND ANNE E. WINKLER

Men and women have traditionally engaged in three types of economically productive work. First, they have produced goods and services for their family's own consumption; second, they have engaged in household production for sale or exchange on the market; third, they have worked for pay outside the home. The process of industrialization has brought about a reallocation in the relative importance of these three types of economic activities, greatly increasing the absolute and relative number of men and women who seek and obtain paid employment. In this chapter, we trace the evolution of the working woman's role, examine the status of women in the labor market in terms of women's employment and earnings, and draw conclusions regarding future prospects for narrowing gender differentials in the labor market.

HISTORICAL PERSPECTIVES

In the preindustrial economy of the American Colonial period, work was frequently allocated on the basis of sex, but the work of women was as essential to the survival of the community as that of men. Unlike the experience in England and in the European countries, where women were routinely employed in reaping, mowing, and haymaking, agricultural work in the colonies was mostly in the hands of men, at least among the nonslave population.[1] This difference may have been due to the economic importance of the household industries carried on primarily by women and children, who produced most of the manufactured goods for the Colonies. In addition to caring for their children, cleaning, and cooking, colonial women spun thread, wove cloth, and made lace, soap, shoes, and candles, for the colonial economy at first provided no other source for these goods.[2]

The pressures of a struggling frontier society, faced with a continual labor shortage and imbued with a puritanical abhorrence of idleness, opened up a wide range of business activities to women. Women could be found working as tavern keepers, store managers, traders, speculators, printers, and publishers, as well as in the more traditional women's occupations of domestic servant, seamstress, and tailor.[3] However, many of the colonial businesswomen were widows, frequently with small children to provide for, who were carrying on their husband's enterprise.[4] In some cases, opportunities for women to remain single and self-supporting were curtailed, perhaps because of women's economic value in the home. For example, in early New England, female heads of households were given their portion of planting land, and in Salem even unmarried women at first also received a small allotment. "The custom of granting 'maid's lotts,' however, was soon discontinued in order to avoid 'all presedents and evil events of graunting lotts unto single maidens not disposed of.' "[5]

After the Industrial Revolution separated the home from the place of work, women generally played a less active role in the economic life of the community.[6] Although the specific tasks of men and women may have differed before the Industrial Revolution, the basic economic roles of the two sexes were the same: the production of goods and services, primarily to meet the family's own needs. But, the broad thrust of industrialization diminished the relative status of women by creating a gender division of labor in which, after marriage, women were responsible for home work and men were responsible for market work. Women thus became economically dependent on men, who were viewed as the breadwinners. However, American women played a crucial role in the development of the first important manufacturing industry, the textile industry.

During the seventeenth and early eighteenth centuries, spinning and weaving were household industries done primarily by women and children. Each household provided its own raw materials and produced chiefly to meet its own needs. But it was not uncommon for women to market part of their output, selling it directly to customers or to shopkeepers for credit against their account.[7] With the expansion of the industry in the latter half of the eighteenth century, it became more common for women to be employed by merchants to spin yarn in their own home. Under this commission system, the merchants would sell the yarn or put it out again to be woven into cloth. The first factories in America embodied no new technology. They were "merely rooms where several looms were gathered and where a place of business could be maintained." Women delivered yarn they had spun at home to these establishments and were paid for it there.[8]

The first textile factory to incorporate power machinery was established in Pawtucket, Rhode Island, in 1789 by Samuel Slater, a British immigrant. By 1800, fifteen mills had been established in New England for the carding and spinning of yarn. When the power loom was introduced in 1814, the whole process of cloth manufacture could be carried on in the new factories.[9] But cloth was still made primarily by young women and children, who constituted the bulk of the new industrial work force.

The earliest factories did not open any new occupations to women. So long as they were only "spinning mills" there was merely a transferring of women's work from the home to the factory, and by the time that the establishment of the power loom had made weaving also a profitable factory operation, women had become so largely employed as weavers that they were only following this occupation, too, as it left the home. It may, in brief, be said that the result of the introduction of the factory system in the textile industries was that the work which women had been doing in the home could be done more efficiently outside of the home, but women were carrying on the same process in the making of yarn or cloth.[10.]

Perhaps even more interesting than the pioneering role of women in the industry is the reaction of illustrious contemporaries to it. Alexander Hamilton, for example, claimed that one of the great advantages of the establishment of manufacturing was "the employment of persons who would otherwise be idle (and in many case a burthen on the community). . . . It is worthy of particular remark, that, in general, women and children are rendered more useful, and the latter more early useful, by the manufacturing establishments than they would otherwise be."[11] The notion that a farmer's masculinity might be threatened by the entry of his wife or children into paid employment apparently did not trouble American men of the time. Hamilton noted, on the contrary, that men would benefit from having a new source of income in the family.[12] Others claimed that the new factories not only opened up a new source of income but also built character in their employees:

> The rise of manufactures was said to have "elevated the females belonging to the families of the cultivators of the soil from a state of penury and idleness to competence and industry." . . . In the same spirit of unreasoning exaggeration the women in villages remote from manufacturing centers were described as "doomed to idleness and its inseparable attendants, vice and guilt."[13]

Since the economy of the United States during this period was predominantly agricultural, with an extremely favorable land-to-labor ratio, women and children were virtually the only readily available source of labor for the new manufacturing industry. This was probably an important factor in the approval accorded the entry of women into the wage-labor force. The existence of a factor of production, women, that was more productive in the new industrial pursuits than in the home, was cited as an argument for the passage of protective tariffs to encourage the development of the textile industry in a country that appeared to have a clear comparative advantage in agriculture. "To the 'Friends of Industry,' as the early protectionists loved to call themselves, it was . . . a useful argument to be able to say that of all the employees in our manufacturing establishments not one fourth were ablebodied men fit for farming."[14]

Later attitudes toward women working outside the home were not nearly as encouraging. While a careful investigation of the causes for this change remains to be undertaken, it seems reasonable to suggest that the gradual dwindling of the supply of unsettled land coupled with the waves of immigrants that provided a more abundant source of labor shifted public concern to the problem of providing sufficient employment for men. In any case, by the turn of the twentieth century, sentiment against the "intrusion" of women into the industrial work force was strong enough to compel Edith Abbott to answer this charge specifically in her classic study, *Women in Industry*. Her words add a valuable perspective to contemporary discussions of the issue as well:

> Women have been from the beginning of our history an important factor in American industry. In the early days of the factory system they were an indispensable factor. Any theory, therefore, that women are a new element in our industrial life, or that they are doing "men's work," or that they have "driven out the men," is a theory unsupported by the facts.[15]

A careful investigation of the facts also leads us further to qualify the statement that the separation of the home from the place of work during the Industrial Revolution tended to reduce the participation of American women, particularly married women, in many kinds of economically productive work. For one thing, although it is estimated that in 1890 only 5 percent of married women had jobs outside the home,[16] this pattern did not prevail among all groups in the female population. For another, various types of work done in the home continued to be important in the economy throughout the nineteenth century.

The two major groups of married women for whom work outside the home was fairly common were black women, the majority of whom still lived in the South, and immigrant women in the textile-manufacturing towns of New England. In 1890, one-quarter of black wives and two-thirds of black widows were gainfully employed. Most of these women worked either as field hands or as domestic servants — the same kinds of jobs black women had always done under slavery.[17] The greater participation in market activity of black wives compared to white wives probably can be explained by the relatively low incomes of black husbands.

The women who worked in the New England textile mills were carrying on the long tradition of the participation of women in this industry. In two Massachusetts towns, Fall River and Lowell, for example, nearly one-fifth of all married women worked outside the home in 1890. Most were first- or second-generation immigrants of French-Canadian or Irish ancestry. The low wages of men working in the textile mills frequently made it necessary for other family members, including children, to work in the mills too. Thus, Robert Smuts has suggested that it was for family reasons as well as financial ones that married women went to work: "Since many of the older children worked in the mills, mothers were not needed at home to care for them. Indeed, a mother whose children worked could look after them better if she went to work in the same mill."[18]

In addition to women from these two groups, married women from other sectors of the population were forced to seek market work when they suffered misfortunes against which there was little social protection in the nineteenth and early twentieth centuries. Some indication of the kinds of problems these women faced can be gained from the results of a study conducted by the U.S. Bureau of Labor Statistics in 1908:

Among one group of 140 wives and widows who were employed in the glass industry, 94 were widows, or had been deserted, or were married to men who were permanently disabled. Thirteen were married to drunkards or loafers who would not work. The husbands of ten were temporarily unable to work because of sickness or injury. Seventeen were married to unskilled laborers who received minimum wages for uncertain employment. Only six were married to regularly employed workers above the grade of unskilled labor.[19]

As noted earlier, some women contributed to the incomes of their families by earning money for work performed in their own homes. The types of employment and working conditions of this group varied widely. Some women took in boarders or did laundry or sewing. Others, in New York, Chicago, and other major cities, eked out a meager income doing home work in the garment industry, while Bohemian and German women in New York's upper East Side tenements provided a cheap source of labor for the cigar industry.[20]

Another element of home work, the production of goods and services for the family's own use, remained extremely important throughout the nineteenth century, even in urban areas. Women frequently kept livestock and poultry and raised fruits and vegetables in small home gardens. Even food bought at the market was usually in its natural, unprocessed form, so preserving, pickling, canning, and jelly making, as well as baking the family bread, were normal household chores. Much of the family's clothing, curtains, and linens were sewn or knit in the home. And, of course, the housekeeping tasks of cleaning, washing, and cooking were all undertaken without the benefit of modern appliances.[21]

THE LABOR FORCE SINCE 1890

While the process of industrialization took production of many goods and services out of the home and into the market, it also incorporated ever-increasing numbers of women into the paid labor force. Since fairly reliable data on the labor force did not become available until 1890, this discussion of the trends in male and female labor-force participation will be focused on the period from 1890 to 1987.

The labor force includes all those who are working (employed) or are actively seeking work (unemployed). The *labor-force participation rate* for a particular group is equal to the number of people in the group who are in the labor force divided by the total number of people in the group who are of working age. Labor-force participation rates for selected years since 1890 are shown in Table 1. The figures indicate a relatively slow rate of increase in the proportion of women that were in the labor force in the early decades of this period.[22] Between 1940 and 1987, however, more dramatic changes in women's labor-force status occurred. In 1940, the labor force included 28 percent of the female population fourteen years of age and over. By 1987, the figure had risen to 56 percent of those sixteen years old and over. The percentage of women workers increased, from one-quarter to over two-fifths

TABLE 1

Labor-Force Participation Rates, Selected Years, 1890–1987 (Total Labor Force)

Year[a,b]	Males	Females	Females as a percentage of all workers
1890	84.3	18.2	17.0
1900	85.7	20.0	18.1
1920	84.6	22.7	20.4
1930	82.1	23.6	21.9
1940	82.5	27.9	25.2
1945	87.6	35.8	29.2
1947	86.8	31.8	27.4
1950	86.7	33.9	29.0
1955	85.9	35.7	30.7
1960	83.9	37.8	32.5
1965	81.3	39.3	34.3
1970	80.3	43.4	37.2
1975	78.4	46.4	39.3
1980	77.8	51.6	42.0
1985	76.7	54.5	43.7
1987	76.6	56.1	44.3

SOURCES: U.S. Department of Commerce, Bureau of Census, *Historical Statistics of the United States, Colonial Times to 1970,* Bicentennial Edition, Part 1 (1975), pp. 131–132; U.S. Department of Labor, Bureau of Labor Statistics, *Handbook of Labor Statistics* (1985), pp. 6–7; U.S. Department of Labor, Bureau of Labor Statistics, *Employment and Earnings* (January 1988), pp. 13–14.

[a] Figures for 1947 and after include persons sixteen years old and over; for the years prior to 1947, those fourteen years old and over are included.
[b] Figures for 1950 and subsequent years include employed and unemployed civilians plus members of the Armed Forces stationed within the United States *only.*

of the total labor force. When the impact of World War II is taken into account, these changes look somewhat less impressive. Between 1940 and 1945, the female labor force expanded by 5.1 million; 36 percent of all women fourteen years of age and over were working. As the 1947 figures indicate, considerable ground was lost in the immediate postwar period. However, in the succeeding years, these losses were eventually recouped and the wartime levels were exceeded.

Underlying the long-term growth of the female labor force have been shifts in the participation patterns of women over the lifecycle. Before 1940, most female workers were young and single. As Figure 1 shows, the peak participation rate for 1940 occurred among women aged twenty to twenty-four. This pattern began to change in the 1940s and 1950s, when older married women entered or reentered the labor force in increasing numbers, while the labor-force participation rates of younger women (those under thirty-four) remained relatively constant. Married women constituted 30 percent of the female labor force in 1940 and 54 percent in 1960.

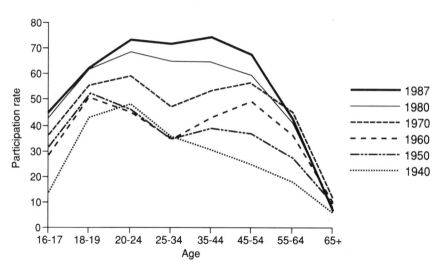

SOURCES: U.S. Department of Labor, *Employment and Earnings* (January 1988), p. 160; U.S. Department of Labor, *Handbook of Labor Statistics* (1985), pp. 18–19; and U.S. Department of Labor, Women's Bureau *1975 Handbook on Women Workers*, p. 12.

F I G U R E   1   *Civilian Labor Force Participation Rates, by Age, 1940–1987*

Since 1960, participation rates of older married women have continued to increase. Of greater note, however, have been the particularly large increases that have occurred among younger married women — a group that did not experience much growth during the earlier period. Although this trend reflects in part declining birth rates, there has also been a growing tendency of women with young children to work outside the home. The labor-force participation rate of married women with preschool-age children increased from 19 percent in 1960 to 57 percent in 1987, with nearly 53 percent of married women with infants aged one year or less in the labor force.[23] Moreover, a trend toward the postponement of marriage as well as an increase in the divorce rate have contributed to the dramatic rise in the overall labor-force participation rates of younger women. Between 1960 and 1987, the participation rate of all women twenty-five to thirty-four years of age doubled, increasing from 36 to 72 percent.[24]

These shifts in the composition of the female work force suggest that increases in women's participation have been associated with an increase in the stability of women's participation in market work. In other words, not only have women entered and reentered the labor force in increasing numbers, but also, once in the labor force, women are more likely to stay. As a result, both increased entry and decreased exit have contributed to the recent rise in women's labor-force participation rates.[25]

The source of the increase in participation rates (new entrants or "stayers") is important because each group has the opposite effect on the average work experience of women in the labor force. Work experience accumulated by women who remain continuously in the labor force (stayers) tends to increase the overall average. At the same time, the influx of new entrants into the labor market with little accumulated work experience tends to reduce average work experience. The net impact of these two groups of workers on women's average work experience affects women's economic status, because work experience is an important determinant of earnings. Evidence suggests that, before the late 1960s, growth in women's labor-force participation resulted in constant or only slow increases in women's average work experience. However, for more recent years, average experience has risen, especially among younger women, implying that the positive effect of stayers has exceeded the negative effect of new entrants on average work experience.[26]

As a result of increases in married women's labor-force participation, the two-earner family has increasingly become the norm among married couples. Families in which only the husband earned income constituted only 22 percent of married-couple families with earnings in March 1987, whereas those in which both the husband and wife earned income constituted 64 percent. (The categories comprising the remaining 14 percent were families in which only the wife, only another relative, or a relative and the husband and/or wife earned family income.) Sixty percent of American children under eighteen have mothers who work outside the home.[27]

A variety of factors has been identified to explain the growth in women's, particularly married women's, labor-force participation during the post-1940 period. Economists, such as Jacob Mincer, argue that the rising real (inflation-adjusted) wages available to women in the labor market have increased the *opportunity cost* of nonmarket activities for these women.[28] In other words, the income that women forgo by remaining out of the labor force has increased over time. This has encouraged them to substitute market work for time spent on housework and leisure — a positive *substitution effect*. On the other hand, increases in the real wages of their husbands occurring at the same time have worked to increase married women's demand for nonmarket time and to reduce their labor-force participation (a negative *income effect*). The evidence suggests that the positive substitution effect outweighs the negative income effect and that married women have continued to seek work in increasing numbers despite their husbands' rising real incomes.

Sociologist Valerie Oppenheimer has pointed out that the growing importance of service industries and white-collar work has provided greatly expanded employment opportunities in jobs traditionally held by women. Moreover, the increase in these jobs, coupled with the appearance of new female occupations between 1940 and 1960, created a demand that greatly exceeded the supply of young single women workers, once the backbone of the female labor force. Oppenheimer suggests that, under the pressures of labor shortages, employers were forced to abandon their prejudices against employing older married women.[29] It is possible that a similar process has operated to the benefit of younger married women in the period since 1960. There is some evidence that employers were reluctant to hire married women with small children, either because they feared such women would have higher rates of absenteeism or because they believed that mothers of preschool-age children should remain at home.[30] Employers may have been forced to discard these concerns in order to meet their demand for female labor, thus making possible the rapid increase in the labor-force participation of women in this group.

Other factors have contributed to the rise in women's participation rates. Social norms have changed and women's attitudes toward market work have become more favorable. Since the early 1960s, demographic trends such as declining birth rates and increasing divorce rates have also worked to increase participation rates. But it is important to point out that these factors may be *consequences* as well as *causes* of the rise in women's involvement in market work.

At the same time that female participation rates have been increasing, those of men have been declining. As shown in Table 1, the male rate fell from 87 percent in 1950 to 77 percent in 1987. This decline has been concentrated at both ends of the male age distribution, as more young men remain in school and especially as more older men retire from the labor force. As a result of the opposing trends in labor-force participation for men and women, the gender differential in labor-force participation rates has declined greatly in recent years.

WHICH WOMEN WORK

A primary determinant of a woman's decision to enter the labor force is the level of any nonlabor income available to her. It is principally for this reason that women who are married (with husbands present) are less likely to work outside the home than are single, separated, or divorced women (see Table 2). (The low labor-force participation rate of widows is largely due to widows' higher average age.) Further, within the married, husband-present group, participation has been found to be negatively related to the level of husband's income, all other factors being equal.

Another factor that influences women's participation is the presence of children. Within each marital-status category, women with small children are less likely to participate in the labor force, since children greatly increase the value of time spent within the home. It is somewhat surprising that

T A B L E 2
Labor Force Status of Women Sixteen Years Old and Over by Marital Status and Presence and Age of Youngest Child, March 1987

			With children under 18	
Marital status	Total	No. children under 18	Children 6–17 only	Children under 6
Never married	65.1	66.7	64.1	49.9
Married, husband present	55.8	48.4	70.6	56.8
Married, husband absent	61.4	57.9	72.6	55.1
Widowed	19.4	17.6	60.1	a
Divorced	75.4	71.9	84.5	70.5

SOURCE: U.S. Bureau of Labor Statistics, "Over Half of Mothers with Children One Year Old or Under in Labor Force in March 1987," *News Release,* 87–345 (August 12, 1987), Table 3.

a Insufficient data available.

within each marital-status category, with the exception of that of never-married women, women with no children under eighteen are less likely to be in the labor force than are those with school-age children. Again, this reflects the higher average age of women in those categories, since in most cases they are older women whose children are grown.

Education is another major determinant of labor-force participation. Among women who were twenty-five to sixty-four in March 1987, 45 percent of those with less than four years of high school were in the labor force, in comparison to 66 percent of those with four years of high school, and to 80 percent of those with four or more years of college.[31] Among both male and female workers, educational attainment generally affects employment opportunities and pay scales. Although the educated woman may meet with some discrimination that keeps her from better-paid, more prestigious jobs, her opportunities are still greater than are those of a less educated woman. Thus, the more education a woman has, the higher her *opportunity cost* (the level of her foregone earnings) of remaining out of the labor force. The attraction of market work is therefore greater for more educated women. The association between educational attainment and labor-force participation may also reflect a process of self-selection; those women who earn diplomas may be more strongly motivated, ambitious, and career-oriented than are those who do not.

Traditionally, proportionately more black than white women have participated in the labor force; however, the differential has been declining in recent years. In 1948, 31 percent of all white women and 46 percent of all nonwhite women were working. By 1987, 56 percent of white women and 58 percent of black women were in the labor force. The participation rate of Hispanic women in 1987, 52 percent, was lower than the rate for both white and black women.[32]

OCCUPATIONAL DISTRIBUTION

In 1987, the occupational distribution of men and women workers continued to differ substantially. As Table 3 shows, women were much more likely than were men to be employed in administrative support (including clerical)[33] and service jobs, with 47 percent of the female labor force concentrated in these occupations, and were less likely to be employed in managerial, executive, and administrative positions. Thirteen percent of men workers as compared to 10 percent of women workers held managerial jobs. Furthermore, men continued to hold a disproportionate share of the higher-status, higher-paying blue-collar jobs. In 1987, 20 percent of men as compared to only 2 percent of women held jobs in precision production, craft, and repair. Finally, while a higher proportion of women than men were employed as professional specialty workers, 48 percent of women in this category were concentrated in the predominantly (over 75 percent) female fields of librarian, registered nurse, prekindergarten and kindergarten teacher, elementary-school teacher, special-education teacher, dietician, and speech therapist. On the other hand, 44 percent of male professional specialty workers were in the relatively more lucrative, predominantly (over 80 per-

TABLE 3

Occupational Distribution of the Labor Force by Sex and Race, 1987

| | Percentage of employed labor force | | | | | |
| | Males | | | Females | | |
Occupational category	Total	White	Black	Total	White	Black
Executive, administrative and managerial	13.3	14.0	6.7	10.0	10.5	6.4
Professional specialty	11.6	11.9	6.4	14.4	14.8	10.8
Technicians and related support	2.8	2.8	1.8	3.2	3.2	3.2
Sales occupations	11.3	11.9	5.1	12.8	13.4	9.1
Administrative support, including clerical	5.9	5.5	9.2	29.0	29.5	26.4
Service occupations	9.5	8.5	18.2	18.1	16.8	28.0
Precision production, craft, and repair	20.0	20.6	15.5	2.3	2.3	2.0
Operators, fabricators, and laborers	20.9	19.7	33.3	9.0	8.2	13.7
Farming, forestry, and fishing	4.8	4.9	3.6	1.1	1.2	0.4
	100.0	100.0	100.0	100.0	100.0	100.0

SOURCE: U.S. Department of Labor, *Employment and Earnings* (January 1988), p. 180.

Note: Figures may not add to totals because of rounding.

cent) male occupations of engineer, lawyer, architect, chemist, announcer, dentist, clergy person, and physician.[34]

Although differences in men's and women's occupational status remain substantial, the occupational status of women workers relative to men workers has shown substantial, although slow, improvement in recent years. Women have made significant advances into managerial positions, with the percentage of the female labor force employed in this occupation more than doubling over the period 1972 to 1987, from 4.6 to 10 percent. Women's share of these jobs rose as well, from 20 percent in 1972 to 38 percent in 1987. Improvement in women's occupational attainment is also reflected by the decline in the proportion of women workers in administrative-support (including clerical) and service jobs, from 53 percent in 1972 to 47 percent in 1987.

Black men and women, as well, have experienced considerable recent improvement in their occupational status. Nevertheless, their employment distribution remains skewed toward the lower rungs of the occupational ladder. Both are less likely than are whites to be employed in managerial, professional, and sales jobs. Rather, black men and women tend to be overrepresented in service jobs and as operators, fabricators, and laborers. And black women, like white women, remain heavily concentrated in administrative-support positions.

Examination of the detailed occupational distribution of male and female employees highlights two additional aspects of women's position in the labor market. First, women workers were more heavily concentrated than were men in fewer occupations. Half of all working women were employed in just twenty-one of over 300 detailed occupations listed in the 1986 Current Population Survey. Men workers were more widely distributed throughout the occupational structure, with half of them employed in thirty-three occupations. Six occupations—secretary; cashier; bookkeeper, accounting, and auditing clerk; registered nurse; waitress; and other executive, administrative, and managerial worker (not elsewhere classified)—accounted for one-quarter of all employed women. Of these six occupations, the first five listed are predominately (over 75 percent) female. However, a positive sign is that the last of these six occupations—other executive, administrative, and managerial workers—is over 60 percent *male*.[35]

Second, a high degree of occupational segregation by gender exists in the labor market. That is, men still tend to work in traditionally male jobs, and women still tend to work in traditionally female jobs. We can measure the degree of occupational segregation in the labor market by constructing an "index of segregation" based on the percentage of women (or men) in the labor force who would have to change jobs in order for the occupational distribution of women workers to match that of men. In 1980, the most recent year for which census data are available, the index stood at 59.4, implying that approximately six out of ten workers would have to change jobs for women's and men's occupational distributions to be identical.[36]

Although the level of segregation is substantial, recent changes in the index reflect increasing occupational opportunities for women. Between 1950 and 1960, as predominantly female clerical and professional jobs grew in relative size, the degree of sex segregation actually increased slightly. However, from 1960 to 1970, the index declined 3.1 percentage points due to an inflow of men into female professions and of women into male sales and clerical jobs.[37] Most recently, the pace of decline accelerated as women entered formerly male-dominated occupations, particularly managerial and professional jobs. The index fell 8.5 percentage points between 1970 and 1980.[38] The index of segregation has also been computed using a second source of data, the Current Population Survey, a monthly survey conducted by the Commerce Department. Over the most recent period examined, 1972 to 1982, this index shows a 7.4 percentage point decline, from 66.9 to 59.5.[39] (Note that the *levels* of the indexes computed from the two data sources are not comparable, but changes in the indexes are.)

The detailed occupational breakdowns of the Census and Current Population Survey data do not, however, reveal the full extent of employment segregation by sex. First, the sex typing of a job may vary from one business establishment to another. One firm may hire only men as order clerks, whereas another may hire only women; many restaurants employ either waiters or waitresses, but not both. A study of employment patterns of male and female office workers in the early 1970s revealed a strong and consistent pattern of sex segregation by establishment among workers employed in the same occupational categories. Men tended to be disproportionately represented at firms that paid higher wages across the board to both male and female employees, whereas women tended to be concentrated in the relatively low-paying firms.[40] A more recent study revealed a similar pattern of segregation at the firm level based on employers' own extremely detailed job classifications. In 59 percent of the firms examined, occupations were perfectly segregated, with no men and women sharing the same job title. In the remaining firms, the mean index of occupational segregation was computed to be 84.1 percent.[41]

Second, aggregate figures may fail to reveal differences in the employment of men and women at various levels within the same occupation. For instance, men may be employed at the top of the hierarchy, in positions of greater status and authority, while women are employed at the bottom. Also, there is concern that predominantly male occupations that experience a large influx of women may become predominantly female over time, potentially resulting in lower pay and status. This occurred in the case of insurance adjusters and computer operators during the 1970s.

Despite these words of caution, the available evidence suggests that women's occupational opportunities have improved recently and should continue to improve in the future. Indeed, the pace of change may even accelerate as younger cohorts who have acquired more similar education and training relative to their male counterparts continue to take advantage of new occupational opportunities.[42]

EARNINGS

The median annual earnings of women who worked year-round, full-time was 65 percent that of men in 1987, implying that women earned 65 cents for each dollar earned by men (see Table 4). Even when men and women who have completed the same level of education are compared, women earn substantially less than men do. For example, in 1987, among those with four years of high school, the median income of full-time, year-round women workers was 65 percent of that of men; among those with four or more years of college, it was 68 percent.[43] The pay differential persists within broad occupations as well. For instance, the median earnings of full-time, year-round women workers relative to men was 61 percent for managerial workers, 68 percent for administrative-support workers; 69 percent for workers in precision production, craft, and repair; and 51 percent for sales workers (the largest differential).[44]

The substantial male–female pay gap is a consequence of several mutually reinforcing factors. First, consider women's average job qualifications compared to men's. Prior to obtaining a job, men and women tend to differ in educational attainment, in terms of length of study and fields of specialization chosen, both factors leading to the earnings differential. Once in the job market, women tend to work more intermittently and to spend less average time in the labor force and on a particular job, factors further contributing to the earnings differential.[45] For instance, in 1984, among full-time, year-round workers (aged twenty-one to sixty-four), 42 percent of the women

TABLE 4

Median Annual and Weekly Earnings of Full-Time Women Workers as Percent of Men's Earnings, Selected Years, 1955–1987

Year	Annual[a]	Weekly[b]
1955	63.9	NA
1960	60.8	NA
1965	60.0	NA
1970	59.4	62.3
1975	58.8	62.0
1976	60.2	62.2
1977	58.9	61.9
1978	59.7	61.3
1979	60.0	62.4
1980	60.2	63.4
1981	59.2	64.6
1982	61.7	65.0
1983	63.6	65.6
1984	63.7	67.8
1985	64.5	68.2
1986	64.3	69.2
1987	65.0	70.0

SOURCES: U.S. Bureau of Labor Statistics, *U.S. Working Women: A Databook 1955–1975,* Bulletin 1977 (annual earnings 1955–1975); Earl F. Mellor, "Investigating the Differences in Weekly Earnings of Women and Men," *Monthly Labor Review* 107 (June 1984), pp. 17–28 (weekly earnings 1970–1983); U.S. Bureau of the Census, *Money Income of Households, Families and Persons in the United States,"* Current Population Reports Series P-60, various issues (annual earnings 1976–1987); *Employment and Earnings* (January issues for 1986–1988), Table 54 (weekly earnings 1984–1987).

[a] Includes full-time, year-round workers only. Includes income from self-employment.
[b] Includes all full-time workers, regardless of weeks worked. Excludes income from self-employment.
NA signifies not available.

experienced one or more work interruptions lasting six months or more over the course of their labor-market careers, as compared to 12 percent of the men.[46] Men had accumulated more labor-market experience, with 40 percent of men as compared to 23 percent of women having over twenty years of work experience in the labor market, and 36 percent of men as compared to 23 percent of women having spent ten years or more in their current job.[47]

Although differences in job qualifications can explain a substantial portion of the male–female pay gap, these differences cannot fully account for the earnings differential. A growing body of research supports the view that a second factor, discrimination, accounts for as much as half or more of the male–female pay gap.[48] The magnitude of these findings is impressive given the fact that newly available data sets have permitted researchers to control for a wide array of productivity-related factors in reaching this conclusion, including formal education, work history, and labor-force attachment.

The portion of the pay gap attributed to discrimination may come about, in part, as a consequence of occupational segregation by sex. Partly due to labor-market discrimination and partly due to gender differences in socialization and preferences, women have tended to "crowd" into a small number of sex-segregated occupations. The abundance of supply relative to demand may result in lower earnings for women's jobs.[49]

Finally, women's expectations about participating in the labor force in the future may also play a role in creating the pay differential. A recent study shows that young women who had no plans to be in the work force at age thirty-five, but who ended up working at that age, had 30 percent lower earnings than did young women who had consistently anticipated working at age thirty-five, even after accounting for differences in education, work experience, and job tenure.[50]

The pay gap remains substantial, but recent evidence suggests that it is beginning to narrow. As Table 4 shows, since 1977, when the median earnings of women who worked year-round and full-time reached its most recent low of 58.9 percent, they have followed an upward trend, rising to 65 percent in 1987. Even more compelling evidence of a narrowing of the male–female pay gap is provided by the weekly earnings of women full-time workers relative to those of men full-time workers. The ratio has risen steadily, from 61.3 percent in 1978 to 70 percent in 1987.

Gains in relative income have been greatest for cohorts of younger women. The median income among year-round, full-time women workers aged twenty-five to thirty-four relative to their male counterparts increased from 62.2 percent in 1967 to 74 percent in 1987, with most of the improvement occurring in the last decade. In addition, recent evidence suggests that these women are likely to continue to fare better than did their predecessors as they age. Hence, the overall pay gap, like the differences in the occupational distribution of men and women, should diminish as younger cohorts replace older ones.[51]

Both improved job qualifications and decreased labor-market discrimination appear to have contributed to the improvement in women's relative earnings. In recent years, gender differences in education and experience have been declining, particularly for younger women.[52] Also, since 1964, an impressive array of federal antidiscrimination laws and regulations have been promulgated. One recent study found that labor-market discrimination declined from the early 1970s to the early 1980s; a second study suggested that antidiscrimination legislation was a contributing factor.[53] It has been suggested that government policies not only may have increased women's access to opportunities formerly closed to them, but also may have had the indirect effect of providing women with greater incentives to acquire job-related skills and training. Thus, women's improved job qualifications *and* antidiscrimination efforts may have reinforced each other, resulting in a long-term cumulative process that reduced the earnings differential.[54]

While the pay of all women has just begun to advance toward the level of men's, black women's pay improved significantly relative to white women's from the mid-1950s to mid-1970s. Black women's median (full-time, year-round) income increased from 51 percent of that of white women in 1955 to 96 percent in 1975. Black men also gained relative to white men. Their median full-time, year-round income rose from 61 percent of that of white men in 1955 to 73 percent in 1975.[55] The gains in the relative incomes of blacks are partially due to substantial increases in blacks' relative educational attainment, but cannot be fully explained by that factor.[56] They may in part be due to the impact of legislation on equal employment opportunity. The more rapid improvement in the relative income position of black women may reflect the large number of entry-level positions in many typically female jobs, in comparison to the higher experience and training requirements in typically male jobs. However, since the mid-1970s the data show no further improvement in the relative income of blacks. In fact, over the period 1975 to 1987, both black women and black men experienced a decline in their median full-time year-round income relative to their white counterparts. Black women's median income relative to white women's declined from 96 to 91 percent, and black men's median income relative to white men's declined from 73 to 71 percent, from 1975 to 1987.[57] Although the reasons for this recent trend are not well understood, this is an important development meriting further study.

The previous discussion of gender-related earnings differentials must be viewed against the backdrop of the large and increasing reliance of American families on the economic contributions of women workers. One indicator of this reliance is that a substantial portion of women workers are either primarily responsible for their own support or are maintaining families (family heads). In March 1987, 45 percent of women workers were single, widowed, divorced, or separated from their husbands, and 12 percent of working women were maintaining families.[58]

In 1987, 16 percent of American families and 20 percent of American families with children under eighteen were headed by women; 48 percent of black families with children under eighteen were headed by women; and 25 percent of Hispanic families with children under eighteen had female heads.[59] Such families constitute a large proportion of the poverty population. In 1987, 34 percent of the families maintained by women lived in poverty, in comparison to only 6 percent of married-couple families. Over half of the families maintained by black or Hispanic women had incomes below the poverty line.[60]

In addition, as women's labor-force attachment has increased, growing numbers of married-couple families have come to rely on the contribution of the working wife to ensure their standard of living. In 1987, among white married-couple families with wives working in the labor force, median income was 50 percent higher than it was among white married-couple families in which only the husband worked. Among black married-couple families, median income was 98 percent higher when both the husband and wife worked than it was when only the husband worked.[61]

PROSPECTS FOR THE FUTURE EMPLOYMENT OF WOMEN

Over the period 1986 to 2000, the Bureau of Labor Statistics projects that the labor-force composition will become increasingly minority and female. Blacks, Hispanics, Asians, and people from other racial/ethnic groups will comprise 57 percent of total labor-force growth. Women will constitute 64 percent of new additions to the labor force and are expected to constitute over 47 percent of the labor force by the year 2000.[62] The economy's ability to provide employment for a larger female work force depends on two factors. First, the aggregate level of economic activity must be sufficient to absorb the anticipated increase in the number of women seeking work. Second, since, despite recent progress, women remain fairly concentrated in a limited number of occupational categories, the ability of women to find employment depends not only on the aggregate number of jobs available, but also on the structure of demand as well.

Bureau of Labor Statistics projections of the occupational distribution of the work force through 2000 indicate above-average rates of increase in employment in the executive, administrative, and managerial; technical and related support; professional specialty; sales; and service occupations, which together employed 59 percent of all women in 1987. Whereas future prospects for women are extremely favorable in these broad occupations, the outlook is less bright for women employed in the administrative-support (including clerical) field, if the present concentration of women in this occupation persists into the future. From 1986 to 2000, below-average growth in administrative-support (including clerical) jobs is anticipated, with the share of all administrative-support (including clerical) jobs out of total employment expected to decline slightly.[63]

Although the aggregate statistics appear favorable for women, with the exception of jobs in administrative support (including clerical), examination of employment prospects for more detailed occupations within broad occupational categories highlights certain problem areas. For instance, although the broad category of administrative support (including clerical) is expected to experience below-average growth overall, prospects for detailed occupations within that category are expected to differ considerably. Jobs for typists and word processors, stenographers, payroll–time-keeping clerks, and several other positions are expected to decline substantially due to technological change and office automation. At the same time, the positive effect of technological change, resulting in an increased demand for computer operators, among others, will only partially offset the negative impact on traditional clerical jobs, resulting in below-average growth for the broad category as a whole.[64]

Prospects for the predominately female occupations of preschool, kindergarten, and elementary-school teacher, which constituted 21 percent of female professional workers in 1987, are brighter than are those for clerical work. According to projections by the Bureau of Labor Statistics, jobs for preschool teachers are anticipated to grow faster than average due to the increased demand for day-care services, and jobs for kindergarten and elementary-school (including junior high) teachers are expected to have average growth due to an increase in births starting in the late 1970s.[65] On the other hand, secondary-school teaching jobs, which employed an additional 9 percent of female professional workers in 1987, are expected to experience below-average growth due to small projected increases in enrollments through 2000.[66] Of course, high-school enrollments should swell in subsequent years, as children in elementary school in the year 2000 work their way into the secondary-school system.

Shifts in demand are not unusual in a dynamic and changing economy.

Under conditions of full employment, the decline in employment opportunities in one occupation should be offset by expanding employment opportunities in other areas. However, occupational mobility may be restricted to the extent that the distribution of jobs is segregated by sex. Furthermore, in the case of job displacement, workers must have sufficient education and training to facilitate the transition from one job to another. The acquisition of adequate skills will be especially important in coming years because, with the exception of service jobs, the fastest-growing occupations from 1986 to 2000 will be those that require relatively greater levels of education.[67]

According to the Bureau of Labor Statistics, women's future prospects are relatively favorable because women workers already represent a sizeable share of employment in the fastest-growing occupations, with the exception of natural scientists, and computer specialists, engineers, surveyors, and architects. Employment prospects for black and Hispanic women and men in the fastest-growing occupations are much less favorable, according to the Bureau, because there is a much greater disparity between current occupational employment of minorities and projected employment opportunities. These workers are currently overrepresented in the slowest-growing and declining occupations, with much lower representation in the fastest-growing occupations. A further problem compounding future prospects for black and Hispanic workers is that level of educational attainment lags behind that of white workers.[68]

An assessment of the future prospects of women in the labor market would be incomplete without some consideration of the impact of the level of unemployment on women's economic status. The adverse effect of periods of high unemployment on women cannot be overemphasized. First, since the unemployment rate of women is generally somewhat higher than that of men, women bear a disproportionate share of unemployment. Second, in times of high unemployment, many women become discouraged and drop out of the labor force; others postpone their entry into the labor force until economic conditions improve. This kind of "hidden unemployment" is a particular problem for women. Finally, the level of unemployment will undoubtedly affect the social acceptance of programs designed to increase the opportunities for women in what are presently predominantly male jobs.

An unavoidable consequence of the effort to expand the employment opportunities open to women is that men must face a new source of competition. Thus, some men may find that they are unable to obtain employment in their preferred occupation. However, under conditions of full employment, they can always find employment elsewhere. Further, a full-employment economy combined with a new occupational mobility for women workers should tend to reduce earnings differentials between jobs that were once predominantly male or female. Thus, the price paid by men for being unable to enter the occupation of their choice might not prove to be great. On the other hand, during a period of high unemployment, public support for a fundamental change in women's employment status may diminish. Moreover, since it is the new jobs that become available in a growing, healthy economy that are most likely to become available to women, the maintenance of full employment is particularly important if we are to improve women's occupational status rapidly.

In conclusion, employment opportunities for women in managerial, professional, technical, sales, and service jobs should expand through the year 2000, provided the economy remains strong. The decline in administrative-support jobs as a percentage of total employment does provide some cause for concern. However, as younger women, in particular, anticipate longer and more continuous work lives and acquire education and job qualifications more similar to men's, they should be less restricted to traditionally female occupations, such as administrative support, and more able to take advantage of occupational opportunities elsewhere. Furthermore, it seems likely that, as women's job qualifications continue to improve and as occupational segregation continues to decline, the male–female earnings gap will narrow further.[69] The extent and pace of women's progress may well depend, however, on society's continued commitment to antidiscrimination policies as well as on the prevalence of employer policies that make it easier for workers of both sexes to accommodate the dual demands of work and family responsibilities.

NOTES

1. Edith Abbott, *Women in Industry* (New York: Appleton, 1910), pp. 11–12.

2. Eleanor Flexner, *Century of Struggle: The Women's Rights Movement in the United States* (New York: Atheneum, 1968), p. 9.

3. Abbott, *Women in Industry*, pp. 13–18. "It should be noted that the domestic servant in the seventeenth and eighteenth centuries was employed for a considerable part of her time in processes of manufacture and that, without going far wrong, one might classify this as an industrial occupation." Ibid., p. 16.

4. Flexner, *Century of Struggle*, p. 9.

5. Abbott, *Women in Industry*, pp. 11–12.

6. Viola Klein and Alva Myrdal, *Women's Two Roles* (London: Routledge and Kegan Paul, 1956), p. 1.

7. Abbott, *Women in Industry*, pp. 18–19.

8. Ibid., p. 19, and for quote, p. 37.

9. Elizabeth Faulkner Baker, *Technology and Women's Work* (New York: Columbia University Press, 1964), p. 5.

10. Abbott, *Women in Industry*, p. 14.

11. Alexander Hamilton, *Report on Manufactures*, vol. 1, cited in Baker, p. 6.

12. Hamilton, *Report on Manufactures*, cited in Abbott, p. 50.

13. Abbott, *Women in Industry*, p. 57.

14. Ibid., p. 51. The same author noted (p. 25, n. 1) that "manufactures are lauded because of their 'subserviency to the public defense; their employment of women and children, machinery, cattle, fire, fuel, steam, water, and even wind—instead of our ploughmen and male laborers.'"

15. Ibid., p. 317.

16. Robert W. Smuts, *Women and Work in America* (New York: Columbia University Press, 1959), p. 23.

17. Ibid., pp. 10, 56.

18. Ibid., p. 57.

19. Ibid., p. 51.

20. Ibid., pp. 14–17.

21. Ibid., pp. 11–13.

22. There is some question whether there was any increase at all in female labor-force partici-pation during the 1890–1930 period. The 1910 census, in which enumerators were given special instructions *not* to overlook women workers, especially unpaid family workers, yielded a participation rate of 25 percent. Robert W. Smuts has argued that women workers were undercounted in the 1900, the 1920, and perhaps the 1930 census as well, but that, over the period, gradual improvements in technique, broader definitions of labor force status, and a redistribution of the female work force from unpaid farm work to paid employment resulted in an apparent rather than a true increase in the female participation rate. Smuts, "The Female Labor Force," *Journal of the American Statistical Association,* LV (March 1960), pp. 71–79. For a discussion of this issue see Valerie Kincade Oppenheimer, *The Female Labor Force in the United States* (Berkeley, University of California, Institute of International Studies, 1970), pp. 3–5.

23. U.S. Manpower Administration, *Manpower Report of the President,* April 1975 (Washington, D.C.: U.S. Government Printing Office); U.S. Department of Labor, Bureau of Labor Statistics, "Over Half of Mothers with Children One Year Old or Under in Labor Force in March 1987," News Release 87-345 (August 12, 1987), Tables 1 and 3.

24. U.S. Bureau of Labor Statistics, *Handbook of Labor Statistics* (1985), Table 5, p. 19; *Employment and Earnings* (January 1988), p. 160.

25. Claudia Goldin, "Life-Cycle Labor Force Participation of Married Women: Historical Evi-dence and Implications," National Bureau of Economic Research Working Paper, No. 1251 (December 1983).

26. Francine D. Blau, "Longitudinal Patterns of Female Labor Force Participation," in Herbert S. Parnes, et al., eds, *Dual Careers: A Longitudinal Analysis of the Labor Market Experience of Women,* vol. 4 (Columbus, Ohio: Center for Human Resource Research, Ohio State University, December 1978), pp. 27–55; Claudia Goldin, "Life-Cycle Labor Force Participation of Married Women: Historical Evidence and Implications"; June O'Neill, "The Trend in the Male–Female Wage Gap in the United States," *Journal of Labor Economics* (January 1985, Supp.); and James P. Smith and Michael P. Ward, "Times Series Changes in the Female Labor Force," *Journal of Labor Economics* (January 1985, Supp.).

27. U.S. Department of Labor, "Over Half of Mothers," Tables 2 and 4.

28. Jacob Mincer, "Labor Force Participation of Married Women," National Bureau of Eco-nomic Research, *Aspects of Labor Economics* (Princeton: Princeton University Press, 1962) pp. 63–97.

29. Oppenheimer, *Female Labor Force.*

30. See for example, Georgina M. Smith, *Help Wanted—Female: A Study of Demand and Supply in a Local Job Market for Women* (Rutgers, N.J.: Rutgers University, Institute of Management and Labor Relations, 1964), pp. 18–19.

31. U.S. Bureau of Labor Statistics, "Labor Market Success Continues to Be Linked to Educa-tion," News Release 87-415 (September 28, 1987), Table 1.

32. In 1948, the category "nonwhite" was predominantly black. This figure is used because more disaggregated data is not available. U.S. Department of Labor, Bureau of Labor Statistics, *Employment in Perspective: Working Women: Summary 1980,* Report 643, p. 2; *Employment and Earnings* (January 1988), Table 39, p. 203.

33. In January 1983, the Bureau of the Census changed the occupational classification system used in the Current Population Survey. Among the changes made, the former category "clerical workers" was replaced by the category "administrative support (including clerical)," which is defined slightly differently. The new category is less broad and excludes the occupations of cashier and real-estate appraiser, both previously included in "clerical workers."

34. *Employment and Earnings* (January 1988), Table 22, p. 181.

35. *Employment and Earnings* (January 1987), Table 22, pp. 179–183.

36. Suzanne Bianchi and Nancy Rytina, "The Decline in Occupational Sex Segregation During the 1970s: Census and CPS Comparisons," *Demography* 23 (February 1986), p. 81.

37. Francine Blau and Wallace Hendricks, "Occupational Segregation by Sex: Trends and Prospects," *Journal of Human Resources,* 14 (Spring 1979), p. 200.

38. Bianchi and Rytina, "The Decline in Occupational Sex Segregation," p. 81.

39. Andrea H. Beller, "Trends in Occupational Segregation by Sex and Race: 1960–1981," in *Sex Segregation in the Workplace,* Barbara F. Reskin, ed. (Washington: National Academy Press, 1984), pp. 11–26.

40. Francine D. Blau, *Equal Pay in the Office* (Lexington, Mass.: Lexington Books, D. C. Heath & Co., 1977).

41. William T. Bielby and James N. Baron, "A Woman's Place is with Other Women," in Barbara F. Reskin, ed., *Sex Segregation in the Workplace* (Washington: National Academy Press, 1984), pp. 27–55.

42. Francine D. Blau and Marianne A. Ferber, "Women's Progress in the Labor Market: Should We Rest on Our Laurels?," *Proceedings of the 39th Annual Meetings,* Industrial Relations Research Association (1987), pp. 70–76.

43. Both income and earnings data are presented because those for earnings, the preferred concept, are not always available. Income is a broader measure than is earnings, and includes transfer payments, dividends and interest, for example, as well as earnings. For those cases in which both income and earnings data are available, women's income relative to men's is very close to women's earnings relative to men's. U.S. Bureau of the Census, *Money Income and Poverty Status of Families and Persons in the United States: 1987* (Advance Report), Series P-60, No. 161 (Washington, D.C.: U.S. G.P.O., 1988), Table 7, p. 19.

44. Ibid.

45. Jacob Mincer and Solomon Polachek, "Family Investments in Human Capital: Earnings of Women," *Journal of Political Economy* 82 (March/April 1974, Part 2), pp. S76–S108. In addition, full-time hours for women tend to be less than those for men, on the average. For the effect of adjustment for this factor on the earnings differential, see *Economic Report of the President* (Washington, D.C.: U.S. Government Printing Office, January 1973), p. 104.

46. U.S. Bureau of the Census, *Male–Female Differences in Work Experience, Occupation, and Earnings: 1984,* Series P-70, No. 10 (Washington, D.C.: U.S. Government Printing Office, 1987), p. 2.

47. U.S. Department of Commerce, *Male–Female Differences,* p. 3.

48. Francine Blau, "Discrimination Against Women: Theory and Evidence," in William Darity, Jr., ed., *Labor Economics: Modern Views* (Boston: Martinus Nijhoff, 1984); Francine Blau and Marianne Ferber, "Discrimination: Empirical Evidence for the United States," *American Economic Review,* 77 (May 1987), pp. 316–320.

49. Barbara R. Bergmann, "Occupational Segregation, Wages and Profits When Employers Discriminate by Race or Sex," *Eastern Economic Journal,* 1 (April and July 1974), pp. 103–110; Francine D. Blau, "Occupational Segregation and Labor Market Discrimination," in Barbara F. Reskin, ed., *Sex Segregation in the Workplace* (Washington: National Academy Press, 1984), pp. 11–26.

50. Lois B. Shaw and David Shapiro, "Women's Work Plans: Contrasting Expectations and Actual Work Experience," *Monthly Labor Review* (November 1987), pp. 7–13.

51. Blau and Ferber, "Women's Progress in the Labor Market," p. 73.

52. O'Neil, "The Trend in the Male–Female Wage Gap in the U.S.: Smith and Ward, *Women's Wages and Work in the Twentieth Century* (Santa Monica, Calif.: Rand, October 1984); Francine D. Blau and Marianne A. Ferber, *The Economics of Women, Men, and Work* (Englewood Cliffs, N.J.: Prentice-Hall, 1986).

53. Francine D. Blau and Andrea H. Beller, "Trends in Earnings Differentials, by Gender: 1971–1981," *Industrial and Labor Relations Review* 41 (July 1988), pp. 513–529; Andrea H. Beller, "The Impact of Equal Employment Opportunity Laws on the Male/Female Earnings Differential." In Cynthia B. Lloyd, et al., eds., *Women in the Labor Market* (New York: Columbia University Press, 1979), pp. 304–330.

54. Blau and Ferber, "Women's Progress in the Labor Market," p. 75.

55. U.S. Bureau of the Census, *Money Income of Households, Families and Persons in the U.S.,* Series P-60, various issues (Washington, D.C.: U.S. G.P.O.); Bureau of the Census, *Money Income and Poverty Status of Families and Persons in the U.S.: 1975 and 1974 Revisions,* Series P-60, No. 103 (Washington, D.C.: U.S. G.P.O., 1976), Table 9, pp. 22–23.

56. Charles Brown, "The Federal Attack on Labor Market Discrimination: The Mouse that Roared?" *Research in Labor Economics* 5 (1982), pp. 33–68.

57. U.S. Bureau of the Census, *Money Income and Poverty Status: 1987* (Advance Report), Table 7, p. 19.

58. U.S. Department of Labor, "Over Half of Mothers," Table 3; U.S., *Monthly Labor Review* (September 1987), Table 6, p. 92.

59. The word "family" refers to two or more individuals related by birth, marriage, or adoption who live together. All such related individuals, including related subfamily members, are members of *one* family. Unrelated subfamilies are neither included in the count of families nor counted as family members. U.S. Bureau of the Census, *Household and Family Characteristics: March 1987,* Series P-20, No. 424 (Washington, D.C.: G.P.O., 1988), Table 1, pp. 4–6.

60. U.S. Bureau of the Census, *Money Income and Poverty Status: 1987* (Advance Report), Table 15, p. 27.

61. Ibid., Table 1, pp. 12–14.

62. Howard N. Fullerton, Jr., "Labor Force Projections: 1986 to 2000," *Monthly Labor Review* (September 1987), pp. 19–29.

63. G. T. Silvestri and J. M. Lukasiewicz, "A Look at Occupational Employment Trends to the Year 2000," *Monthly Labor Review* (September 1987), pp. 46–63.

64. Ibid., p. 58.

65. While birth rates remain low, the large size of the cohort in the child-bearing years has resulted in an increase in the number of births.

66. Silverstri and Lukasiewicz, "A Look at Occupational Employment Trends to the Year 2000," pp. 57–58.

67. Ibid., p. 62.

68. Ibid., pp. 62–63.

69. Blau and Ferber, "Women's Progress in the Labor Market," p. 76.

Clerical Work: The Female Occupation

EVELYN NAKANO GLENN AND ROSLYN L. FELDBERG

Every weekday, from nine in the morning until five in the evening, in offices all over the country, accounts are checked, correspondence typed, inventories tallied, bills prepared, appointments booked, records filed, and documents reproduced. This "paper work" is carried out in small offices of one or two persons and in corporate headquarters with hundreds of workers, in private industry and in public agencies. Some of the people are all-around workers, carrying out myriad different activities each day; others are single-function clerks, repeating the same small task over and over. Some work with paper, pencil, and perhaps a typewriter; others work with electronic equipment linking them to a computer system that automatically handles many complex clerical operations.

The five most frequently found titles among the 18.25 million people engaged in clerical activities are secretary, bookkeeper, computer operator, typist, and receptionist. These five categories account for nearly half of all clerical workers, but there are numerous other titles classified as "administrative support including clerical," including bank teller, data-entry keyer, stock clerk, reservation agent, counter clerk, keypuncher, telephone operator, and file clerk.

All of these people are engaged in what is called *white-collar* work (to contrast it with blue-collar manual labor). Features that have traditionally characterized clerical occupations include the following: the work is "clean"—it takes place indoors in relatively safe, clean, and comfortable surroundings and involves no great physical exertion; it is "mental"; it relies to some extent on a worker's judgment and requires a literate work force that is able to read, write, and manipulate symbols; and it lacks a distinctive product—its outcome is not a concrete commodity, but rather a flow of documents and communication. In addition, the clerical worker has traditionally enjoyed certain advantages in work life over the factory employee: a fixed weekly salary rather than hourly wages, more regular hours, greater job security, smaller fluctuations in salary during hard times, and greater opportunities for advancement.[1] These supposed advantages have conferred on clerical work a status above blue-collar, sales, and service occupations. At the same time, those in the other white-collar occupations—managers and professionals—have looked down on clerical work as more routine, offering less scope for independent decisions. In addition, the workers' hours, movements, and work patterns are subject to closer controls. Although there have been many changes (which will be described later), these features are still prominent in popular conceptions of clerical work.

CLERICAL WORK AS A FEMALE OCCUPATION

Aside from the work itself, the most distinctive feature of clerical work is the gender of the people who do it: They are overwhelmingly female. In the United States in 1987, four out of five clerical workers (80.0 percent) were women. In two of the largest categories, secretaries and typists, the proportions rose to 99.1 and 94.6 percent. Overall, 14.6 million women were engaged in clerical work in 1987. Over one-third (36.2 percent) of all employed women were in this category.[2] Clerical work is therefore, absolutely and proportionally, the largest single occupation for women. The degree to which clerical work is common to women was confirmed by a personal experience. Recently in an all-female discussion section of a sex-roles course, the instructors asked how many students had ever done office work. Out of twenty-five women present, twenty-three raised their hands, including the two instructors.

Considering these numbers and percentages, it can be argued that clerical work represents the prototypical female employment experience. We shall explore this tie between women and clerical work by examining a set of interrelated questions: How did clerical work become a large and predominantly female occupation? How has the concentration of women in this occupation affected wages, status, and working conditions? What has been the impact of economic and organizational changes on the role and function of clerical work? What effects have these factors had on the quality of work life for this group of women workers? What is the outlook for, and what are the possible outcomes of, organizing clerical workers? What form might a largely woman-based organizing movement take?

In addressing these questions, the following line of argument will be developed. There have been two seemingly contradictory trends in clerical work. The increased size and complexity of organizations mean that internal control, coordination, and communications become increasingly critical for organizational survival. Since these activities rely largely on clerical labor, clerical work takes on a more central role in the economy. But, while clerical work has become more important, organizations have pushed toward streamlining and mechanizing the work to increase efficiency in and control over the work process. This has degraded the work, lowered the status of clerical workers, and further restricted opportunities for advancement. Thus, clerical workers as a group have become a large and important part of the economy, while their jobs and status have become less desirable. The combination of these two trends can be expected to strengthen the impetus for workers to organize—to use the untapped power of clerical workers as leverage to improve their wages and conditions relative to other groups.

289

**Clerical Work:
The Female
Occupation**

THE FEMINIZATION OF CLERICAL WORK

The office setup of a typical large organization is structured in the following way. At the top, occupying the highest positions, are the officers and top managers, all men. Each has at least one private secretary and/or administrative assistant. Below them are other managers, mostly men, graded into many levels. Several of them may share the services of a single secretary or call on a pool of typists and/or clerks. Below them are several specialized sections, divided according to function—for example, accounting, billing, and inventory control. Each section has many women clerks engaged in the routine tasks of record-keeping, coding and processing information, and communication. The supervisor of each section is frequently a woman promoted from the ranks. In addition, there may be a photocopy or reproduction unit made up of a mixed group of young men and women and a data-processing unit where women operators enter information into the computer system via electronic terminals. An office manager, usually a man, may be responsible for overall office administration. Most large organizations also have a separate computer department, consisting of computer operators, programmers, and systems analysts who oversee the operations of the centralized data system.

In short, there are three separate groups of office jobs differing in gender composition. One group, the clerical, is clearly female (secretaries, typists, data-entry operators); the second, the managerial, is clearly male (vice-president, product manager, sales manager); the third, the technical, is mixed sex (computer operators, programmers, and systems analysts). Furthermore, each group of jobs is organized into a hierarchy that is also sex-typed.[3] Management is a male hierarchy, although it frequently includes female supervisors at the lowest levels. The clerical staff is largely a female hierarchy. The technical category is also gender-stratified, with the lower-ranked jobs filled by both men and women, while the higher-ranked jobs—upper-level programmers and systems analysts—are held almost exclusively by men. Occasionally one hears of a clerk who trains to be a systems analyst or a secretary who rises to become an officer in the company. This kind of story generates excitement precisely because it is a freak occurrence.

The segregation of jobs by sex is so universal that the office structure is frequently viewed as a "natural" situation. Does not having men in authority and women in subordinate positions reflect their places in society as a whole? Moreover, do not the requirements for clerical and managerial jobs fit the stereotypes for feminine and masculine traits? Women are said to make good clerks because they are conscientious about details, have nimble hands for operating office machines, and are sufficiently submissive to take orders well. In contrast, managerial traits—rationality, decisiveness, objectivity, and assertiveness—are seen as exclusively masculine qualities.

The appearance of naturalness is shattered by a historical survey, which reveals that the sex composition of jobs shifts over time. Jobs that were once predominantly male sometimes come to be occupied primarily by females, and vice versa. When the work force of an occupation changes from largely male or mixed sex to predominantly female, the process is called *feminization*. Accompanying the shift in sex may be a change in the actual activities of the job or in the traits that are seen as necessary for the job.

Changes in both sex composition and job activities have taken place in the office. The present division of labor in the large office is a fairly recent phenomenon. Until 1910, office work was done almost exclusively by men. Clerks were few in number, constituting only 2.6 percent of the labor force in 1900.[4] Until the last years of the nineteenth century, most businesses were small, local, family-owned enterprises.[5] The offices were made up of a handful of clerks, at most. The head clerk had extensive responsibilities, many of which would be labeled managerial today.[6] His advice might be sought by his employer, because of his familiarity with the details of the business. He might be expected to carry on the business when the owner was absent or away. Braverman notes:

> This picture of the clerk as assistant manager, retainer, confidant, management trainee, and prospective son-in-law can of course be overdrawn. There were clerks — hard-driven copyists in law offices, for example — whose condition and prospects in life were little better than those of dock workers. But by and large, in terms of function, authority, pay, tenure of employment (a clerical position was usually a lifetime post), prospects, not to mention status and even dress, the clerks stood much closer to the employer than to factory labor.[7]

The ground for women's entrance into the offices was prepared during the Civil War, when women were hired to work in the government because of the shortage of male labor. The "experiment" was successful, for the women proved to be good workers and economical, working for only one-half to two-thirds the wages paid to men.[8]

The large-scale entry of women into offices, however, did not begin until the end of the nineteenth century. This period was one of rapid growth and consolidation of corporations.[9] The economy came to be dominated by enterprises with national markets and substantial financing by banks. The size of organizations mushroomed and with it the volume of communication, record-keeping, and related activities. Hence there was a burgeoning demand for clerical labor, met by an influx of workers into the field. As shown in Table 1, the clerical work force grew from an estimated 91,000 in 1870 to more than 770,000 by 1900, doubling in the next ten-year period to 1,885,000. Except for 1929–1935, during the Depression, the clerical work force has grown substantially every decade. As impressive as the overall growth was, the most striking trend was the increasing proportion of women. While the size of the occupation increased by a factor of eight between 1870 and 1900, the proportion of women increased by a factor of 340. The number of women entering clerical work then began to exceed the number of men, so that by the late 1920s a tipping point had been reached, at which over half of all the clerical workers were women.

TABLE 1
Growth of the Clerical Force, 1870–1987[a]

	1870	1880	1890	1900	1910	1920	1930	1940	1950	1960	1970	1980	1987
Total clerical workers (in thousands)	91	186	490	770	1,885	3,311	4,274	4,847	7,635	9,783	13,714	18,105	18,256
As percentage of employed persons	.7%	1.1%	2.1%	2.6%	5.1%	8.0%	9.0%	9.1%	12.8%	14.7%	17.4%	18.6%	16.2%
Female clerical workers (in thousands)	2	8	83	204	677	1,601	2,223	2,549	4,597	6,629	10,233	14,502	14,605
As percentage of all clerical workers	2.4%	4.3%	16.9%	26.5%	35.9%	48.4%	52.0%	52.6%	60.2%	67.8%	74.6%	80.1%	80.0%

SOURCES: For total clerical workers and female clerical workers, 1870 to 1940: compiled from Janet M. Hooks, *Women's Occupations through Seven Decades*, U.S. Department of Labor, Women's Bureau, Bulletin no. 218 (Washington D.C.: U.S. Government Printing Office, 1947), Tables 11A, 11B. For employed persons, 1870 to 1940: U.S. Bureau of the Census, *Historical Statistics: Abstracts of the United States*, Series D57-71. For 1950 to 1970: U.S. Bureau of the Census, *Statistical Abstract of the United States* (Washington, D.C.: U.S. Government Printing Office, 1972), Table 366. For 1980: *Employment and Earnings* 28 (Jan. 1981) U.S. Bureau of Labor Statistics, Table 23; For 1987: *Employment and Earnings* 35 (Mar. 1988), U.S. Bureau of Labor Statistics, Table 22.

[a] Figures are not strictly comparable due to reclassifications of occupational categories. For example, after 1980, the category "clerical and kindred" was relabeled "administrative support, including clerical" and "cashiers"—the second largest occupation classified as clerical prior to 1980—was transferred to "sales occupations." If cashiers were still included in 1987, the total "clerical" would be 20,542,000 or 18.3 percent of all employed persons.

Women, far from being seen as naturally suited to office work, were at first considered an oddity. An 1875 engraving depicts the ludicrousness of women in offices by showing them crocheting, dressing each other's hair, reading *Harper's Bazaar,* and spilling ink; a man, presumably the owner, has just walked in and is dumbstruck. A lively debate was carried on in the pages of popular and business magazines from the 1890s through the 1920s by attackers and defenders of women in offices.[10] During the 1920s and 1930s, many popular novels and short stories depicted the lives and loves of the "office girl," in which the principal conflict was romance and marriage versus career and spinsterhood.[11]

Faced with this skepticism about their desirability, why did increasing numbers of women go into clerical work rather than other occupations? Clearly, the large number of jobs created by changes in corporate structure provided one necessary condition. Another important factor, according to some writers, was the impact of the typewriter, which was invented in 1873.[12] The Remington Company trained women to demonstrate the new machines, so that from the beginning the machines were operated by women. Typing in offices became identified as a feminine specialty.

Although this may have facilitated women's entry into the field, it would not have made a difference if there were not a large supply of available women to do the work.[13] Women constituted an untapped reservoir of educated and cheap labor. Women in that era were more likely to have finished high school (a requisite) than men.[14] And those men who had the requisite education could find better opportunities elsewhere. In contrast, women with high-school education had few options that were more attractive. Factory and sales jobs were lower in status and in pay.[15] There is also scattered evidence that clerical workers received higher wages, particularly in the early period, than did teachers.[16]

Part of the reason men had better opportunities was that, while clerks were growing more numerous, another category was also increasing in size. Managers were needed to help coordinate the diverse activities and departments of the new organizations. A new stratum of hired managers, replacing the old-style owner-manager, was inserted between the top officers and the clerks. Henceforth, this new stratum became the dominant group in the office, taking over the planning and decision making, leading one observer to call this the era of the "managerial revolution."[17]

The rise of managers and the feminization of clerical work fundamentally altered the meaning and status of clerical work. Increasingly, it meant that the carrying out of routine tasks was planned, set up, and supervised by others. A clerical job came to be viewed less and less as a stepping-stone to business success. A survey conducted in the late 1920s showed that 88 percent of the office managers "felt they needed 'clerks who are satisfied to remain clerks.' "[18] Thus, women entered the work force in occupations that no longer offered the traditional advantages of white-collar jobs: They found themselves in dead-end occupations that were declining in status, and, to make matters worse, wages did not rise as expected.

In fact, most writers argue that the wages of clerical workers actually declined in relation to manual labor, both in the early period and in the years following World War II.[19] Evidence on this point is scattered. Although available data indicate a fall in average office wages compared to average factory wages over the last ninety years, the degree and timing of the fall are difficult to pin down. Data from different historical periods are not comparable because the definitions of office work sometimes differ, and men's and women's wages are not reported separately.

Prior to 1920, we find no systematic evidence of decline. National wage data for the years 1890 to 1926 (shown in Table 2) indicate marked fluctuations in the relative wage advantage of clerical workers in manufacturing and steam railways over other wage earners in those industries. Overall, however, the clerical workers earned substantially more than other wage earners during the entire thirty-six-year period.[20] Data on postal employees and government employees (not shown in the table) indirectly confirm the relatively higher clerical salaries during this period.

It is only after 1920 that systematic data separate men's and women's wages. For the period from 1920 through World War II, the most systematic data were collected by New York State, which surveyed office workers employed in factories as well as all workers employed by these establishments. Table 3 presents information for five representative years. Note that clerical women during the entire period earned much less than clerical men (usually 50 to 60 percent) and somewhat less than factory men. The only group over which they have an advantage is factory women, and this declines over time.

In the post–World War II era, there is much clearer evidence of an overall decline (not due to a greater proportion of low-wage women). As Table 4 shows, clerical women's wages declined markedly in relation to men's blue-collar wages between 1939 and 1960. The advantage that clerical women enjoyed over blue-collar women also shrank. Since 1960, women clerical wages have stabilized at 70 to 72 percent of men operative wages, and have fluctuated between 116 and 123 percent of women operative wages. Because men predominate in the operatives category, and women in the clerical category, the average combined male–female clerical earning were lower than the average combined male–female blue-collar earnings.

T A B L E 2
Average Yearly Wages for Clerical and Wage Workers in Manufacturing and Steam Railways, 1890–1926

Workers	1890	1900	1910	1920	1926
Clerical, in manu-facturing and steam railways	$848	$1,011	$1,156	$2,160	$2,310
Wage, in manufacturing	439	435	558	1,358	1,309
Wage, in steam railways	560	548	677	1,817	1,613
Clerical wages as proportion of other manufacturing wages	193.2%	232.4%	207.2%	159.0%	176.5%

SOURCE: U.S. Bureau of the Census, *Historical Statistics of the United States: Colonial Times to 1970*, bicentennial ed., Part 2, Series D (Washington, D.C.: U.S. Government Printing Office, 1975), 779–93.

TABLE 3

Average Weekly Wages for Office Workers and All Workers[a] in New York Manufacturing Industries, 1914–1947

Workers	1914	1924	1934	1944[b]	1947
Office	$19.18	$33.58	$32.45	$42.99	$47.74
Women office	[c]	21.29	21.15	34.60	40.76
All factory	11.82[d]	26.22	21.97	47.71	53.96
All women factory	[c]	16.65	14.90	38.46	39.62

SOURCE: New York State Department of Labor, *Handbook of New York Labor Statistics, 1948*, Special Bulletin no. 226 (1949), Tables D4 and D12.

[a] Including office workers.
[b] Wages for years after 1939 are not comparable with earlier years because of some changes in classification.
[c] Breakdown by sex not available.
[d] Average for last seven months of the year.

RACIAL STRATIFICATION

One feature of clerical work that did not change with feminization was the overwhelmingly white racial character. Clerical work remained a white-dominated preserve through the 1950s. Historically, color bars kept blacks, Hispanics, and Asian Americans out of offices, forcing them to concentrate in low-status blue-collar jobs, especially in service — as private household workers, cleaners, food-service workers, and the like. As recently as 1950, for example, only one in twenty black women in the labor force was employed in a clerical position, making up a little over 1 percent of the total (Table 5). It was not until the 1960s, with the Civil Rights movement and the

TABLE 4

Median Yearly Wage or Salary Income for Year-Round, Full-Time Clerical Workers and Operatives by Sex, 1939–1985

Workers/Operatives	1939	1949	1960	1970	1980	1985
Clerical workers, women	$1,072	$2,235	$3,586	$5,539	$10,997	$15,157
Clerical workers, men	1,564	3,136	5,247	8,652	18,247	22,997
Operatives, women	742	1,920	2,970	4,465	9,440	12,303
Operatives, men	1,268	2,924	4,977	7,644	15,702	21,318
Women clerical workers Wages as percentage of men operatives' wages	84%	76%	72%	72%	70%	71%
Women clerical workers Wages as percentage of women operatives' wage	144%	116%	121%	124%	116%	123%

SOURCES: For 1949: U.S. Bureau of the Census, *1950 Census of the Population of the United States: Special Reports, Vol. 4*, P-E no. 1B, Table 20. For all other years: U.S. Bureau of the Census, *Current Population Reports*, Series P-60, no. 69, Table A-10 (for 1939 and 1960), no. 80, Table 55 (for 1970), no. 132, Table 55 (for 1980) and no. 156, Table 39 (for 1985). The figures given for all years except 1949 are for year-round full-time workers. Those for 1949 are for all year-round workers.

years following World War II.[19] Evidence on this point is scattered. Although available data indicate a fall in average office wages compared to average factory wages over the last ninety years, the degree and timing of the fall are difficult to pin down. Data from different historical periods are not comparable because the definitions of office work sometimes differ, and men's and women's wages are not reported separately.

Prior to 1920, we find no systematic evidence of decline. National wage data for the years 1890 to 1926 (shown in Table 2) indicate marked fluctuations in the relative wage advantage of clerical workers in manufacturing and steam railways over other wage earners in those industries. Overall, however, the clerical workers earned substantially more than other wage earners during the entire thirty-six-year period.[20] Data on postal employees and government employees (not shown in the table) indirectly confirm the relatively higher clerical salaries during this period.

It is only after 1920 that systematic data separate men's and women's wages. For the period from 1920 through World War II, the most systematic data were collected by New York State, which surveyed office workers employed in factories as well as all workers employed by these establishments. Table 3 presents information for five representative years. Note that clerical women during the entire period earned much less than clerical men (usually 50 to 60 percent) and somewhat less than factory men. The only group over which they have an advantage is factory women, and this declines over time.

In the post–World War II era, there is much clearer evidence of an overall decline (not due to a greater proportion of low-wage women). As Table 4 shows, clerical women's wages declined markedly in relation to men's blue-collar wages between 1939 and 1960. The advantage that clerical women enjoyed over blue-collar women also shrank. Since 1960, women clerical wages have stabilized at 70 to 72 percent of men operative wages, and have fluctuated between 116 and 123 percent of women operative wages. Because men predominate in the operatives category, and women in the clerical category, the average combined male–female clerical earning were lower than the average combined male–female blue-collar earnings.

TABLE 2

Average Yearly Wages for Clerical and Wage Workers in Manufacturing and Steam Railways, 1890–1926

Workers	1890	1900	1910	1920	1926
Clerical, in manu- facturing and steam railways	$848	$1,011	$1,156	$2,160	$2,310
Wage, in manufacturing	439	435	558	1,358	1,309
Wage, in steam railways	560	548	677	1,817	1,613
Clerical wages as proportion of other manufacturing wages	193.2%	232.4%	207.2%	159.0%	176.5%

SOURCE: U.S. Bureau of the Census, *Historical Statistics of the United States: Colonial Times to 1970*, bicentennial ed., Part 2, Series D (Washington, D.C.: U.S. Government Printing Office, 1975), 779–93.

Number and Percentage of Black Women Workers Employed in Clerical Occupations

	1950	1960	1970	1980	1987
Number	100,868	181,678	634,208	1,200,516	1,581,440
As percent of black women workers	5.3%	7.4%	19.2%	25.8%	28.0%
As percent of all clerical workers	1.3%	1.8%	4.6%	6.6%	8.7%

SOURCES: For 1950, U.S. Bureau of the Census. *U.S. Census of Population: 1950. Vol. IV, Special Reports,* Part 3, Chapter B, Nonwhite Population by Race (Washington, D.C., U.S. Government Printing Office, 1953), Table 9; for 1960, U.S. Bureau of the Census. *U.S. Census of Population: 1960. Subject Reports, Nonwhite Population by Race,* Final Report PC(2)1C (Washington, D.C. U.S. Government Printing Office, 1963), Table 37; for 1970, U.S. Bureau of the Census, *Census of Population: 1970, Subject Reports, Negro Population.* Final Report PC(2)1B (Washington, D.C.: U.S. Government Printing Office, 1973), Table 7; for 1980, U.S. Bureau of the Census, *1980 Census of Population. Vol. 1, Characteristics of the Population,* Chapter C, *General Social and Economic Characteristics,* Part 1, *United States Summary* PC801C1 (Washington, D.C.: U.S. Government Printing Office, 1983), Table 89; for 1987, *Employment and Earnings,* 35, March, 1988, Table 22. Last line of table computed from these sources and from Table 1, this chapter.

implementation of equal-opportunity legislation, that minorities were able to enter white-collar work in any significant numbers. With the barriers down, minority women poured into clerical work in the 1960s and 1970s; thus, by 1980, one out of every four black women workers was employed in a clerical position. Gains were slower in the 1980s, so there was still a gap of 8 percentage points between the percent of black women workers employed in clerical positions and the proportion of white women so employed in 1987. Further, if we examine where black women are located, we see that, although they are now included in the clerical ranks, they remain segregated within particular specialties and sectors. Black women are concentrated in public-sector employment (government) and are found disproportionately in lower level, "back-room," mass-production jobs as file clerks, data-entry keyers, and messengers. They are underrepresented in private industry and in higher-level jobs, especially in the more visible positions requiring contact with managers and clients—for example, bookkeepers, secretaries, and hotel clerks.[21]

THE FUNCTIONS OF CLERICAL WORK

The role of clerical work in organizations and in the economy has been altered as well as increased over time. In the early stages of industrialization, the accounting, record-keeping, and other office operations were incidental to the main productive activities of a company. The amount of clerical labor expended for a given unit of goods produced was relatively small. In more advanced stages of capitalism, however, the accounting and record-keeping functions became much more complex. The number of intermediate stages between production and consumption—wholesaling, transportation, advertising, marketing—increased, and at each stage clerical operations need to be performed. Finally,

> Just as in some industries the labor expended upon marketing begins to approach the amount expended upon the production of the commodities being sold, so in some industries the labor expended upon the mere transformation of the form of value (from the commodity form into the form of money or credit)—including the policing, the cashiers and collection work, the recordkeeping, the accounting, etc.—begins to approach or surpass the labor used in producing the underlying commodity or service.[22]

In short, in large-scale modern organizations, clerical operations are no longer incidental functions, but important processes in their own right.

An equally important trend in the past quarter-century has been a shift of economic growth from manufacturing to the service and financial sectors. These sectors rely on clerical labor in the same way that manufacturing industries rely on blue-collar labor—for the production of the main goods for exchange. The so-called office industries (principally banking, insurance, and finance) deal almost solely with the accounting and transfer of values. To a lesser but still considerable extent, service industries and public agencies—such as educational institutions and auto registration bureaus—rely heavily on office functions to do their work. Thus, they become "semiclerical" industries. The office and semiclerical industries together now employ a larger and larger share of the work force.

The sheer numbers of workers employed in clerical work have made it important to the economy. But the services that the office and semiclerical industries provide to other sectors of the economy have made these industries vital even for basic production activity. The net result is that clerical work is increasingly central to the operation of the economy as a whole.

These developments constitute what has been called a paper-work revolution. The incredible growth of these clerical occupations in turn has significance for issues of gender equality. Women have traditionally been seen as an auxiliary work force, a secondary group of workers who carry out the least essential activities, while men carry out the central ones. The paperwork revolution changes that pattern. Functions previously seen as auxiliary are now central to the running of industrial organizations, and it is women who are carrying out these functions. For the first time since the early 1800s, women predominate in a job category that is central to the industrial economy. They can no longer be viewed simply as auxiliary workers. As a collectivity, therefore, women clerical workers have a great deal of potential power, perhaps equal to that of male production workers—but as yet unrealized.

THE CHANGING CONDITIONS IN THE OFFICE

The realization of this potential power is made problematic, however, by a second and related trend. The very size and centrality of clerical operations has made managers eager to bring office work under closer managerial control.[23] As a result of their efforts to do so, the features that once distinguished clerical work are being eroded, and the line between it and manual work is becoming blurred.[24]

Most people are aware of the principle of subdivision as it applies to the organization of blue-collar production. Tasks are broken down into small segments so that each worker does one part of the overall work. An unskilled worker can be trained quickly to carry out these narrow tasks, and should the worker leave, she or he can be easily replaced by another unskilled worker. Mechanization speeds up the work by substituting machine power for human energy. The pace of the machine controls the pace of the work. With more sophisticated machinery, many operations can be carried out automatically.

These principles of subdivision and mechanization can also be applied to paper work — and have been since the rise of the large office. The initial thrust for reorganization of clerical work occurred in the office industries. Operations such as handling correspondence were studied and then standardized. Where possible, the operation was divided into subtasks assigned to different pools of workers. By the second decade of the century scientific management had been introduced into office routines.[25] Extensive time-and-motion studies were conducted on the minutest details — opening file drawers, taking off a paper clip, and so forth. Office machines, both simple and complex, were also introduced, but more slowly. Extensive mechanization and automation occurred after World War II.[26]

These changes in the office have been uneven. There are numerous small offices today that scarcely differ from their nineteenth-century counterparts. Even in large corporations, pockets of the "preindustrial office" have survived. Private secretaries have been largely exempt from the rationalizing trend, and they usually perform a variety of tasks from composing letters and answering the telephone to running personal errands. They have frequent personal contact with their superiors. Since the secretary's whole position is defined by her attachment to a particular person, some observers have labeled her the "office wife."[27] This personal tie to her boss effectively screens her from organizational scrutiny of her activities. Until recently, corporations were willing to tolerate this situation, even encouraging it for the sake of managerial morale. Having a secretary to carry out time-consuming routine chores was a perquisite of executive status.

In recent years, the drive for managerial control over employees' time and output has taken on added momentum. The first step in control is to gather the scattered secretaries and place them in a pool where they can be centrally supervised. Private secretaries are increasingly reserved for the highest ranks of managers. Lesser lights must make do with the shared services of pools.

Pools of typists and clerks have existed for some time, but now their use is more extensive and they are more highly organized. We observed an example of the new pooling system in a branch office of a firm we will call Public Utility. The office was reorganized when an IBM word-processing system was installed, and it is now typical of clerical industries in the way routine correspondence is handled.

Middle-level managers (called *clients* in this system) share the services of two major pools of clerks. The word-processing unit, made up of ten to twelve women, does all typing. Clients submit material to be typed on dial dictation equipment; the word-processing clerks transcribe the material into typed form, using semiautomatic machines. The work flow is continuous, unvaried, and fast. The administrative-service center performs all nontyping services, such as answering telephones and scheduling appointments. Instructions for carrying out tasks are written in manuals. For example, precise instructions are given for routing telephone calls and delivering the mail. A third group does all copying and reproduction work.

These new pooling arrangements have been facilitated by technological advancements. For example, output machines with memory capacity can type more than a hundred "personal" letters per hour. Canned paragraphs, stored in the memory, are melded with names, addresses, and "personal greetings" from a computer list as the letter is typed on the printer. The typist types only the names, addresses, and greetings. The impetus to subdivide the work process can best be understood, however, not as a response to technological advances but as part of a drive to attain control over the cost of clerical services and to assure reliability and standardization in the work process. Since the automated systems require workers to use standard forms, they also make it easier for management to trace errors and to assess each worker's productivity, whether it be number of lines typed or the number of telephone calls answered.[28]

Pooling breaks down personal ties and makes secretaries interchangeable. A secretary noted about the administrative-service center at her company: "Each secretary has a backup. . . . She cannot leave her workstation to go to the bathroom, get a drink, go to lunch, or whatever unless the other secretary is there. . . . Each secretary has a job description. If [a secretary] is on vacation or out ill, her backup will handle both jobs."

Even the savings made possible by having fewer secretaries servicing more managers are not enough for some companies. To further cut costs, employers are reducing the number of permanent employees by subcontracting clerical functions to outside agents. Secretaries at one company do very little typing. Smaller typing jobs are assigned to an in-house word-processing center using typists employed by a subcontractor, while large jobs are sent to an off-site subcontractor who picks up jobs to be done and drops off finished work twice each day. Some corporations are experimenting with "vendorizing" their administrative-service centers. The centers are contracted to outside vendors who hire, train, and pay the secretaries. Although these vendor-on-premise (VDP) secretaries work alongside regular employees, they are not technically employees of the corporation, which therefore has no legal liability for them. The corporation does not assume any long-term costs of permanent employees, such as medical and pension benefits. A regular employee described the case of a VDP secretary who wanted to work at a high-technology firm so much that she found out who got the contract and applied to the vendor for a job. However, she was soon disillusioned, discovering she was not entitled to the same kind of training that corporation employees received. The regular employee described her friend's experience:

I guess the transition period, the way they [the vendor] handled it, was just totally unreal. They [the secretaries] were given a job description: "Here this is your job, this is what you will do; this is your equipment, learn it." She didn't know the people; she didn't know where they were located. She went home . . . so torn because of the lack of training . . . and the noncaring attitude.[29]

THE EXPERIENCES OF CLERICAL WORKERS

What impact do conditions have on the workers themselves? How do the women feel about their jobs? For the past twelve years, we have been studying clerical work. In 1975 and 1976, we conducted in-depth interviews with thirty female clerical workers in a variety of jobs in many different organizations. Their responses were as varied as their own situations. Additional interviews, conducted in a large insurance and utility company between 1978 and 1980 as part of a larger study, revealed similar patterns of responses. We have continued to track trends in the 1980s, particularly changes growing out of office automation.

Pay

Women clerical workers are not poorly paid in comparison to other women workers, but their wages reflect the disadvantaged position of women in relation to men. In 1985, the median yearly earnings of women clerical workers employed full-time year-round was $15,157. This figure was only 71 percent of the median earnings of male operatives, whose jobs require less education and training; and it was only 65.9 percent of earnings of male clerical workers.[30]

Another important yardstick is the standard of living made possible by earnings. According to a 1985 U.S. Department of Labor Consumer Survey, a single person living independently spent an average of $13,353 for all living expenses and purchases of goods and services, exclusive of income taxes. If taxes are added in, we see that the median clerical salary was sufficient to maintain an "average" standard of living for a single individual. It was clearly inadequate for a woman head of household with dependents. For example, the average expenditure for two-person households was $22,056, and that for three-person households was $26,781.[31] Thus, most clerical women with families are dependent on another person's income to maintain a moderate standard of living.

The salaries among the women we interviewed in Boston were typical in that they averaged slightly above what the Labor Department estimated to be a budget for an "intermediate" standard of living for a single person in the Boston area, but well below what was needed for an intermediate standard for a woman head of household with two dependents.[32] Also striking was the wide range of salaries, with women doing similar work being paid very different amounts. Five of the thirty women (16.7 percent) earned *below* the intermediate standard for even a single individual. Half of the thirty women thought their wages should be higher, primarily because they believed that their work was worth more. The responses of the other half, who judged their salaries appropriate, were interesting. Nine said that the work they did or their own qualifications were not worth more, and five said that other women doing comparable work received similar wages. Perhaps these workers had internalized the low value accorded their work by society and the company, accepted other women's low wages as the appropriate comparison, or realized they had little hope of earning more. Whatever the reason, their acceptance dissipated the feeling that they deserved a living wage.

In the 1980s, wages of women clerical workers rose more rapidly than did those of male clerical workers and female blue-collar workers. However, not all workers benefited from the gains. While employers offer higher wages to attract new workers, they do not adjust the wages of long-term employees to reflect these people's contributions and experience. Thus, older employees suffer from "salary compression." During a recent union meeting, a secretary with seventeen years service complained, "The longer you work at Harvard, the lower your pay."

Deskilled Jobs

Clerical jobs have been deskilled in two ways. First, the *variety* of skills required in all-around jobs is not needed in the growing number of limited-function jobs. An administrative-services clerk, who had formerly worked in smaller offices, complained that she was unable to keep up her typing skills. All typing was done in the word-processing unit. She did not want to type full-time, so she did not get to type at all. Second, the *level* of skills required has been degraded. Complete accuracy is not essential in typing because the new equipment corrects errors semiautomatically. Even literacy, long a hallmark of clerical occupations, is being programmed out of some traditional specialties. The file clerk in automated systems does not need to know the sequence of the alphabet or numbers. She simply places the documents to be filed on the plate of the machine as quickly as possible.

Overqualified Workers

A related outcome is that many women feel that their abilities and skills go unused. Many women are simply *overeducated*. Our sample of thirty women included sixteen with at least some college education. This proportion was much higher than in the general clerical population; figures for 1976 show that 28.4 percent of all clerical workers had at least some college, and 6.7 percent had four or more years. By 1987, 40 percent of clerical workers had some college, and 12.6 percent had four or more years[33] (see Table 6). One of the college-educated women in our sample noted: "The things on the job decription, any sixth grader could do."

College-educated women are not alone in feeling that their jobs are too limited. Many of the noncollege women are *overskilled*. They have received training in stenography or other specialties in high school or in vocational

TABLE 6

301

Clerical Work:
The Female
Occupation

Educational Attainment of Clerical Workers Aged Twenty-Five to Sixty-Four,[a]
March 1987

	Total employed (thousands)	Years of school completed			
		Fewer than 12 years	12 years	1–3 years of college	4 or more years of college
Number	14,076[b]	744	7,638	3,917	1,778
Percentage	100%	5.3%	54.3%	27.8%	12.6%

SOURCE: U.S. Department of Labor, Bureau of Labor Statistics, "Labor Market Success Continues to be Linked to Education," *News,* Sept. 28, 1987.

[a] Includes men.
[b] Numbers do not add exactly to total because they were calculated from percentages.

institutions. These skills are either obsolete or in limited demand because of the new systems. The women expressed their convictions of being underused by such statements as "I could do more;" "I can handle more responsibility;" "There's no way I would not welcome more challenging work;" or "I feel misplaced."

Career Ladders

Because of the sex-segregated office hierarchies described earlier, clerical jobs do not link up to professional or managerial ladders. Many workers find themselves at the tops of their ladders in a few years, with nowhere to go. Although there are few advantages to staying in the job, there are also few benefits from changing. The worker typically finds she can move only horizontally or downward. One woman expressed frustration that she was at a dead end in her current job, then concluded: "It took me ten years of seniority to get a month's vacation. If I left and went to another job, I don't know how long it would take."

Job Security

Just as a blue-collar assembly-line worker can be easily replaced, the clerical worker in a highly rationalized clerical job finds she has a precarious hold on her position. Caplow points out the basic similarities of semiskilled factory work and clerical jobs in large offices in this regard:

> The modern technics *[sic]* of job classification and personnel selection, developed in connection with large-scale production, are designed above all to facilitate the interchangeability of personnel. One method of ensuring interchangeability is to reduce each complex operation to a series of simple operations which require no extraordinary ability. . . . At the same time, the formal qualifications required for employment are standardized by the educational process, so that there are comparatively few differences that matter between one worker and another.[34]

Many clerical workers are acutely aware that they are expendable. A worker notes: "We laugh around here and say, 'Clericals? They're the throw-aways.' I feel like clerical workers are like machines. When the machines break down, you just replace them." An insurance company clerk says, "I'm a number. That's all anybody is at *X*. If you die, they replace you the next day. You can always be replaced." A clerk in administrative services describes the manuals the clerks are required to write, listing their duties and specifying exactly how each of their clients likes to have his mail delivered. She says, "If I'm out, my fill-in should be able to do what I do. . . . It's like writing yourself out of a job."

Control over the Worker

The private secretary and the limited-function clerk provide illustrations of the two main forms of control over the office worker. The secretary experiences personal control by her immediate boss. By definition, she is doing a good job if he is pleased by her performance. By the same token, the boss screens the secretary from direct company control. Several secretaries mentioned that their bosses safeguarded their time or protected them from unpleasant company assignments. The basis of control, therefore, is highly personal, with all of the problems of arbitrariness that this entails.

In contrast, clerks in pooled arrangements are subject primarily to impersonal controls; that is, formal rules are applied (e.g., clocking in) and external checks of performance are built into the work routine. The supervisor makes no special effort to keep track of workers' performance — the worker is, for example, simply visible at her designated post. A supervisor at a large insurance company claims she can tell at a glance whether one of her charges is doing her assigned task. The total output of a clerk is automatically counted by her machine.

This automatic counting represents the latest form of impersonal control, electronic monitor. Workers have always been subject to constant surveillance by superiors, but they could contrive to look busy without actually doing assigned tasks. With electronic monitor, it is harder to avoid scrutiny; the very equipment that the worker uses is her inspector. Automated equipment can monitor work in a variety of ways. The terminals on which data-entry clerks work keep track of the number of key strokes and documents completed. Automatic call distributors used in the telephone work of reservations clerks and customer-service representatives give each call to the first unengaged line, and keep track of how long each call takes and the amount of time a line is "down." In addition to providing an electronic record of the worker's day, the equipment allows supervisors to "listen in" on calls at any time. Thus, not only the quantity, but also the quality, of the clerk's activity is open to inspection.

Stress

Whereas a secretary can get angry at her boss for exercising control, a word-processing clerk cannot easily target her resentment. She may be angry at her supervisor while realizing that the supervisor has no real power, or she may feel generally angry at "them" (the anonymous big bosses). Frequently, she experiences the anger as a pervasive sense of tension or a feeling of being in a fishbowl. The combination of close monitoring and pressure for productivity thus creates anxiety and stress. Workers in production units complain about the constant pace and the lack of slack periods or frequent-enough breaks. Responding to a checklist of health problems, women most often mentioned suffering from frequent insomnia and headaches. These responses parallel the findings of a survey conducted by the National Association of Working Women 9, to 5, which reported that, although managerial women were more likely to describe their jobs as very stressful, lower-level workers, including clerical workers, were more likely to report symptoms of stress and stress-related illnesses.[35]

The Meaning of Work

The many negative job conditions do not mean women find no meaning or satisfaction in their jobs. We found that, on the whole, the women were committed to working, if not to their specific jobs. In addition to the income, which they clearly saw as most important, the women found meaning in three areas. First, work provided opportunities to form and maintain social connections. Second, it gave direction and purpose to their lives by structuring their time and getting them involved in "useful" activity. Third, for some women, particularly married women with children, it provided an identity separate from their family roles.[36]

Coping and Resistance

Since the women sought meaning in their work, and their particular jobs sometimes frustrated this desire, they responded in a number of ways. A few, whose jobs allowed the latitude, informally expanded their jobs, gradually taking over new responsibilities (but they were not given titles or salaries commensurate with their actual activities). Some, particularly the college graduates, intended to leave the clerical field altogether. The majority, however, felt they had limited options and tried to find what satisfactions they could on the job—by being particularly "nice" to one another, by viewing the materials they typed as critical to the company, or by simply doing their often limited jobs well. At the same time, they protected themselves from attempts to exploit their eagerness to do something meaningful. They shrugged off compliments and rejected ploys designed to get them to do extra work. They also found creative ways to evade or resist control by electronic monitor. Some data-entry keyers said they pressed certain keys, such as the space bar, repeatedly to raise their key-stroke count. Telephone clerks arranged to call people back with additional information to increase their call count and to give themselves extra time to complete work.

ORGANIZING

None of the women in our original study spontaneously suggested organizing or unionization as a possible strategy for dealing with her problems. Yet in the later study, when asked about the idea of an organization for clerical workers, over 50 percent of the women working in a nonunion company said it was a good idea. The main reason given was that a union would back them up in case of a dispute with management, and would thus prevent individual workers from having to fight alone.[37] Interestingly, higher pay was not the most frequently mentioned reason, even though it is the most easily documented benefit of unionization—in 1987, clerical workers represented by unions earned 25 percent more than did nonrepresented workers. Despite clerical workers' own sentiments and the evident advantages of unionization, these workers remain the largest category of unorganized wage workers.

Experienced labor organizers generally consider clerical workers the most difficult segment of labor to organize, and they have made relatively little effort to unionize it. A variety of arguments have been put forward to explain the difficulties of organizing clerical personnel. Most explanations focus on two characteristics: their gender and their lack of worker consciousness.

One line of argument is that women see themselves as secondary workers. Their primary commitment is to their present or future family roles. Therefore, their wages and working conditions are not of sufficient importance to motivate them to join unions. A second line of argument focuses on women's socialization. Women are trained to take a subordinate position to men. Their situation in the office does not strike them as unfair; thus they are unlikely to organize in opposition to authority.[38] A related argument is that, also as a result of socialization, women accept exploitation because they have been trained to think it unladylike to fight back. According to one writer:

> A great majority of office workers are female and have been socialized into anti-militant values, militancy having been equated by their parents with unfeminine attitudes. Furthermore, the single office girl might prefer the prestige of a white collar job to the demotion in status involved in joining a union and thereby becoming less attractive (perhaps even declasse) to the young executive she had her eye on.[39]

This quote also illustrates another common view: that clerks fail to identify as workers because they identify with management. In the case of men, it is because they aspire to managerial positions.[40] In the case of women, it is because they hope to marry into management.[41] Lockwood cites a union official who says the personal relations between managers and clerical workers make it unlikely that the latter will unite to oppose management.[42] In addition, common dress, common working conditions, and overlapping job activities encourage clerks to see themselves as part of management.

Another belief illustrated by the above quote and elaborated by Lockwood is that clerical workers are particularly status-conscious.[43] Their marginal social positions make them snobbish and anxious about their status. To protect themselves, they set up artificial barriers between themselves and the working class.

More and more women see themselves as serious, long-term workers.

Out of the thirty women we interviewed, twenty-seven planned to be work-ing five years in the future, some outside the field of clerical work, but most within it. This is a realistic expectation, given the emerging pattern for women of more continuous participation in the labor force. Seven out of ten women between the ages of eighteen and fifty-four are employed.[44] Several trends indicate that women are likely to spend more years in the labor force. First, single women have traditionally high rates of employment, and more young women are remaining single today. Second, labor-force participation among married women with children has increased phenomenally over the past twenty years. Third, women are having fewer children, which means that they will be taking fewer years out for childbearing and child rearing.[45] In fact, a study of work-life expectancies indicated that the work life of women born in the 1960s can be expected to average nearly 30 years.[46] Certainly the women we interviewed took their earning power seriously. Being able to make a living—being economically independent—was an important source of pride and self-esteem.

Whether women consider union activity "unfeminine" is harder to determine directly. What is clear is that about half of the women we inter-viewed, when asked directly, supported the idea of a union. Those who opposed the idea expressed concern that unions represented another outside force, another "they," which would impose conditions the women might not want. Such an expression can hardly be taken to mean that women accept subordination easily. Moreover, we note that nationally 59 percent of clerical workers in 1988 were married.[47] It is unlikely that they reject union activity for the sake of snaring a manager into marriage.

We found little evidence that clerks identify with management in oppo-sition to their own self-interest. To be sure, private secretaries took personal pride in their bosses' successes. However, clerks in other categories were keenly aware of the dichotomy between boss and worker. Many of them resented what they perceived as attempts by management to manipulate them through false compliments. Others complained about having no say over where they worked or what they did. They could be transferred from one section to another or have their jobs changed arbitrarily. Powerlessness of the individual worker was one of the main reasons given for supporting a union. As one worker said, "If we had unions, we could stick together and help each other instead of one person defending herself." Another woman displayed a wily cynicism about managerial pronouncements. She said that when the company instituted pools, workers were told that the new systems would be more democratic. She shrewdly pointed out that pool clerks were paid 20 percent less than secretaries.

We would argue, therefore, that female character and lack of worker consciousness are not impenetrable barriers to organizing. The fact remains that clerical workers have not been organized. Why? An important part of the answer is that not much effort has been put into organizing them. Many are employed in sectors of the economy that are newer and not unionized—for example, service industries.[48] Unions have generally concentrated on improving wages and benefits and increasing membership in industries in which they are already established, rather than organizing new industries.

Another part of the answer lies in the nature of the labor market in which women work. Most explanations of the absence of unions overlook this factor. Women confront a sex-segregated labor market. They are crowded into a few sex-typed occupations. The occupations dominated by women are those in which it is difficult to control entry (i.e., monopolize jobs) and in which there is a surplus of qualified workers who are not in the labor force at a given time.[49] Any worker can be easily replaced from this available labor pool. Under these conditions, it is difficult for women to develop collective strength.

Still another part of the answer lies in the composition of the clerical work force. Clerical workers are extremely diverse; they come from widely varied educational and social backgrounds. Our own sample of thirty women reflects the range: The occupations of their fathers covered the thirteen major groupings used by the U.S. Census. Their own educations varied from less than high school to postgraduate college degrees. Because of the limited job options open to women, due to sex-typing of jobs, women with diverse qualifications end up in a common occupation. The current situations of these women were equally varied. Among the married women, some were married to professionals, others to semiskilled or unskilled workers. This fits the national picture. Of all married female clerical workers with employed husbands in 1987, 51 percent had white-collar husbands and 49 percent blue-collar husbands.[50] Since these women lack a shared class situation, it should not be surprising that they lack a sense of common identity.

Despite the barriers to organizing, there has been a great increase in organizing activity among women clerical workers. Ironically, the very changes in technology and organization that managers are introducing into offices may help to create conditions that encourage organization among workers. As common disadvantages become more widespread, they may overshadow the absence of common class background. Some evidence suggests that employed women come to judge their social class from their own occupations, rather than from that of their husbands or their fathers.[51]

In addition, there has been a general trend toward unionization among white-collar workers, and growing efforts have been made to organize clerical workers. Organized labor has stepped up its campaign to organize state and municipal employees and has also begun making inroads in the private sector. Grassroots groups have sprung up among women office and service workers in the larger cities. Ten of these groups are now affiliated in a national organization known as 9 to 5 (previously called Working Women), which has chapters in Boston, Providence, Baltimore, Atlanta, Pittsburgh, Cleveland, Cincinnati, Minneapolis, Seattle, and Los Angeles. Several other groups—Women Organized for Employment, in San Francisco; Women Employed, in Chicago; and Women Office Workers, in New York—remain independent but have reciprocal information exchanges with 9 to 5. All these groups use political and educational strategies to improve the position of women office workers. They work for changes in employer policies (such as job posting), for work-place improvements (such as back-pay settlements and training programs), to inform the public about the conditions office workers face, and to build organizations for office workers.

A second level of organization has developed in the form of new unions, separate locals of established unions, or separate unions affiliated with internationals. Boston's Local 925 of the Service Employees International Union (SEIU) began as a spin-off of the Boston chapter of 9 to 5. While the Boston 9 to 5 group continues its educational and politicizing activities, Local 925 evolved into District 925 (SEIU), an organization with a national jurisdiction and the rights of a local. Another partnership links District 65 (Distributive Workers of America) with the United Automobile Workers, while other unions—the American Federation of State, County, and Municipal Employees; the Office and Professional Employees International Union; the Hotel Employees and Restaurant Employees International Union; and the Teamsters—organize particular areas of the clerical work force.

There are two possible—and not mutually exclusive—outcomes of clerical organizing. One is that clerical workers will receive increased material benefits in the form of higher wages, shorter hours, better medical insurance, and other traditional union goals. Another is that the quality of work life will be improved through changes in the organization of work activities.

The history of organized labor indicates that the first set of goals is likely to be achieved, but the second is not. However, the degree to which issues of quality of work life are addressed will depend partly on which forms of organizing predominate and what kinds of unions are formed. At one time, it seemed that the women's movement would provide a model for a different kind of organizing among clerical workers. Although the uncertain future of the women's movement makes that prospect seem less likely, the grassroots organizing of what might be called the preunion groups continues to borrow heavily from the techniques of the women's movement. These include the use of group support to help women identify common problems, consciousness-raising activities (such as public speakouts), and interpersonal strategies for changing worker–boss relationships. The shift toward forming unions necessarily involves other methods of organizing, yet it may not signal the end of a unique kind of organizing among clerical workers.

The successful effort by Local 34 of the Hotel Employees and Restaurant Employees International Union (HERE) to organize clerical and technical workers at Yale in 1983–1984 is a model of grassroots organizing centered on women workers' concerns. The first eighteen months were devoted to building rank-and-file support through home visits and lunch meetings. A 400-member organizing committee was in place before the union even distributed membership cards. During the contract negotiations Local 34 rejected narrowing their tactics to simply withholding labor. While they had a brief strike to buttress their demands, they simultaneously worked to rally broad-based support from faculty and students and other employees within the university, as well as from outside religious and political organizations and the black community in New Haven. The union's goals were linked to larger issues of achieving economic justice for women and minorities, recognizing the value of women's work, and encouraging Yale to be a responsible citizen in the community.[52] Similarly, in May 1988, the Harvard Union of Clerical and Technical Workers won an election, the culmination of ten years of organizing efforts. Here too, much of the organizing was done in small groups, and issues of economic justice, child-care for workers' children, and the university's responsibility to the community were addressed.

The Yale drive, the Harvard drive, and other recent organizing drives in large and small work places testify to clerical workers' growing self-confidence, militance, and commitment to democratic principles.[53] These organizing drives also testify to the growing recognition among male unionists that women clerical workers are serious workers who will strengthen the union movement. In the Yale drive, members of Local 35 (HERE), the largely male blue-collar union at Yale, raised their dues to contribute to the organizing efforts of clerical and technical workers: the parent union HERE supplied considerable financial support and experienced organizers while respecting local autonomy.[54] At Harvard, despite a split between the local organizing committee and its original supporting union, the union movement remained committed to the drive; another major union, the American Federation of State, County and Municipal Employees, stepped in with substantial financial and technical support without interfering with local grassroots control.[55]

Employers obviously take clerical organizing seriously. Both Yale and Harvard delayed the union efforts at their respective schools through challenges to the National Labor Relations Board. When these challenges failed, both waged sophisticated and expensive antiunion campaigns. Only after losing its appeal to the NLRB to overturn the election did Harvard concede the results and recognize the union in November, 1988.

Clerical workers are beginning to gain recognition as workers in the popular culture too, as in the film and television show "Nine to Five." Moreover, they are including in their organizing issues that directly challenge sexist practices and identify unique aspects of women's work experience—such as pay equity (comparable worth) and protection against sexual harassment. Such organizing seems to proceed from a vision of active, autonomous locals and a full voice for workers. If the organizing succeeds on these grounds, it is more likely to lead to demands for fundamental changes in the work place than if more traditional approaches are used.

It is an exciting future to contemplate. When clerical women organize widely, they will become one of the largest groups within the union movement. They may well alter the issues and concerns addressed by organized labor.

NOTES

1. U.S. Bureau of Labor Statistics, *Trends of Earnings among White Collar Workers during the War,* Bulletin no. 783 (Washington, D.C.: U.S. Government Printing Office, 1944). Also Grace Coyle, "Women in the Clerical Occupations," *Annals of the American Academy of Political and Social Sciences* 143 (1929), 180–87.

2. U.S. Bureau of Labor Statistics, *Employment and Earnings* 35 (Mar. 1988), Table 22.

3. See Rosabeth Kanter, "Women and the Structure of Organizations," in Marcia Millman and Rosabeth Kanter, eds., *Another Voice* (New York: Anchor, 1975). Also Rosabeth Kanter, *Men and Women of the Corporation* (New York: Basic, 1977).

4. The best descriptions of the historical changes in office work are: Margery Davies, "Women's Place Is at the Typewriter: The Feminization of the Clerical Labor Force," *Radical America* 8 (1974), 1–28; Harry Braverman, *Labor and Monopoly Capital* (New York: Monthly Review Press, 1974), Chapter 15; C. Wright Mills, *White Collar* (New York: Oxford University Press, 1956).

5. Daniel Bell, "The Breakup of Family Capitalism," in Bell, *The End of Ideology,* rev. ed. (New York: Collier, 1961).

6. Mary Kathleen Benet, *The Secretarial Ghetto* (New York: McGraw-Hill, 1972).

7. Braverman, *Labor and Monopoly Capital,* 294.

8. Davies, "Women's Place Is at the Typewriter."

9. Bell, "The Breakup of Family Capitalism."

10. Davies, "Women's Place Is at the Typewriter."

11. Judith Smith, "The New Woman Knows How to Type: Some Connections between Sexual Ideology and Clerical Work, 1900–1930" (Paper presented at the Berkshire Conference on the History of Women, Radcliffe College, Cambridge, Mass., 1974).

12. Writers who have made this point include: Coyle, "Women in the Clerical Occupations"; Davies, "Women's Place Is at the Typewriter"; Janet Hooks, *Women's Occupations through Seven Decades,* Women's Bureau Bulletin, no. 218 (Washington, D.C.: U.S. Government Printing Office, 1944); Bruce Bliven, Jr., *The Wonderful Writing Machine* (New York: Random House, 1954); and Elizabeth F. Baker, *Technology and Woman's Work* (New York: Columbia University Press, 1964).

13. The introduction of new technologies is often related to changes in the sex composition of an occupation. Jo Freeman (personal communication) points out that sometimes a new labor force is introduced because the older group of workers will not or cannot use the new technology. We would argue against strictly technological determination, however. The replacement of frame-spinning machinery with mule-spinning machinery in the 1840s coincided with a changeover from a predominately female to a predominately male labor force in textiles. Mule-spinning equipment was considered unsuitable for women, partly because it was awkward to use with long skirts. Mule spinning had been widely used for many years in England prior to its use in the United States. Due to the shortage of male labor, its introduction into American factories was delayed for many years. Thus, we would argue that a changeover in labor force accompanying technological change occurs only when there is an available alternate labor pool. See Edith Abbott, *Women in Industry* (New York: Appleton, 1910), especially 91–92.

14. Valerie K. Oppenheimer, *The Female Labor Force in the United States: Demographic and Economic Factors Governing Its Growth and Changing Composition,* Population Monograph Series, no. 5 (Berkeley: University of California, 1970).

15. Robert Smuts, *Women and Work in America,* rev. ed. (New York: Schocken, 1971).

16. U.S. Bureau of the Census, *Historical Statistics of the United States: Colonial Times to 1970,* bicentennial ed., part 2 (Washington, D.C.: U.S. Government Printing Office, 1975), 168. Also Elyce Rotella, "Occupational Segregation and the Supply of Women to the American Clerical Labor Force, 1870–1930" (Paper presented at the Berkshire Conference on the History of Women, Radcliffe College, Cambridge, Mass., 1974).

17. James Burnham, *The Managerial Revolution* (New York: John Day, 1941).

18. Coyle, "Women in the Clerical Occupations."

19. For example, Braverman, *Labor and Monopoly Capital;* Mills, *White Collar;* and Coyle, "Women in the Clerical Occupations."

20. Braverman *(Labor and Monopoly Capital)* uses the 1900 data on manufacturing and steam railway workers and contrasts them with 1971 data on clerical and manual wages to illustrate the erosion of clerical wages. The contrast implies a dramatic decline over the seventy years. As Table 2 shows, the 1900 figures are the point of maximum difference, 56 percent greater than 1890, thus accentuating the apparent decline of clerical wages.

21. *Employment and Earnings,* 35 (March, 1988), U.S. Department of Labor, Table 22.

22. Braverman, *Labor and Monopoly Capital,* 302.

23. Alfred Vogel, ''Your Clerical Workers Are Ripe for Unionism.'' *Harvard Business Review* 49 (1971), 48–54.

24. Evelyn N. Glenn and Roslyn L. Feldberg, ''Degraded and Deskilled: The Proletarianization of Clerical Work,'' *Social Problems* 25 (1977), 52–64.

25. Influential proponents of scientific management in offices were William Henry Leffingwell, *Scientific Office Management* (Chicago: Shaw, 1917), and Lee Galloway, *Office Management: Its Principles and Practices* (New York: Ronald Press, 1918).

26. Jon M. Shepard, *Automation and Alienation: A Study of Office and Factory Workers* (Cambridge, Mass.: M.I.T. Press, 1972).

27. Benet, *The Secretarial Ghetto;* and Kanter, *Men and Women of the Corporation.*

28. For further discussions of technology and changing conditions in the office, see U.S. Department of Labor, Women's Bureau Bulletin, no. 218, *Women and Office Automation: Issues for the Decade Ahead* (Washington, D.C.: U.S. Government Printing Office, 1985); National Research Council, *Computer Chips and Paper Clips* (Washington, D.C.: National Academy Press, 1987); and Daniel Marschall and Judith Gregory, eds., *Office Automation, Jekyll or Hyde?* (Cleveland, Ohio: Working Women's Education Fund, 1983).

29. Interview conducted by Sue Funari, 1987.

30. U.S. Bureau of the Census, ''Money Income of Households, Families and Persons in the United States: 1985,'' *Current Population Reports,* Series P-60, no. 156 (Washington, D.C.: U.S. Government Printing Office, 1987), Table 40.

31. U.S. Department of Labor, Bureau of Labor Statistics, ''Consumer Expenditure Survey Results from 1985,'' *News,* USDL no. 87-399, September 24, 1987.

32. See U.S. Bureau of Labor Statistics, *Autumn 1981 Urban Family Budgets and Comparative Indexes for Selected Urban Areas* (Boston) (Washington, D.C.: U.S. Government Printing Office, April, 1981). Budget figures are presented for lower, intermediate, and higher budgets for families of four. Figures for single individuals and single heads of families are computed from these basic figures using equivalence scales from Table A-1, ''Revised Scale of Equivalent Income for Urban Families of Different Size, Age, and Composition,'' which is available from regional Bureau of Labor Statistics offices.

33. U.S. Bureau of Labor Statistics, ''Labor Market Success Continues to be Linked to Education'' *News* USDL no. 87-415 (Washington, D.C.: U.S. Government Printing Office, Jan. 21, 1987).

34. Theodore Caplow, *The Sociology of Work* (New York: McGraw-Hill, 1954), 85.

35. National Association of Working Women, 9 to 5, *National Survey on Women and Stress* (Cleveland, Ohio: 1984). See also Suzanne Haynes and M. Feinlab, ''Women, Work and Coronary Heart Disease,'' *American Journal of Public Health* (1980).

36. Roslyn L. Feldberg and Evelyn N. Glenn, ''Category or Collectivity: The Consciousness of Clerical Workers'' (Paper presented at the meeting of the Society for the Study of Social Problems, Chicago, 1977).

37. *Employment and Earnings* (January 1988), Table 62.

38. Albert Blum, *Management and the White Collar Union* (New York: American Management Association, 1964).

39. Elliot Krause, *The Sociology of Occupations* (Boston: Little, Brown, 1971), 86.

40. Mills, *White Collar.*

41. Krause, *The Sociology of Occupations.*

42. David Lockwood, *The Black-Coated Worker* (London: Unwin University Books, Allen & Unwin, 1958).

43. Ibid.

44. Susan E. Shank, ''Women and the Labor Market: The Link Grows Stronger,'' *Monthly Labor Review* (March 1988), 3–8.

45. Ibid; see also Allyson Sherman Grossman, ''Women in the Labor Force: The Early Years,'' *Monthly Labor Review* 98 (1975), 3–9.

46. U.S. Bureau of Labor Statistics, *Worklife Estimates: Effects of Race and Education,* Bulletin no. 2254 (Washington, D.C.: U.S. Government Printing Office, 1986), Table A-4.

47. U.S. Bureau of Labor Statistics, unpublished data from March, 1988 Current Population Survey. We thank Mary Sullivan of the Boston Regional Office of the BLS for tracking down these data.

48. Martin Oppenheimer, ''Women Office Workers: Petty-Bourgeoisie or New Proletarians?'' *Social Scientist,* Monthly Journal of the Indian School of Social Sciences, Trivandrum, Kerala, nos. 40–41. For statistics on rates of union representation by industry, see U.S. Department of Labor, Bureau of Labor Statistics, Bulletin no. 2105, *Earnings and Other Characteristics of Organized Labor, May, 1980* (Washington, D.C.: U.S. Government Printing Office, 1981); and *Employment and Earnings,* January 1988, Table 60.

49. See Caplow, *The Sociology of Work,* Chapter 10, for a discussion of these and related points. An economist, Mary Stevenson, in ''Wage Differences between Men and Women: Economic Theories,'' in Ann H. Stromberg and Shirley Harkess, eds., *Women Working* (Palo Alto, Calif.: Mayfield, 1978), 89–107, analyzes the impacts of occupational segregation and consequent crowding of women's occupations on women's wages.

50. U.S. Bureau of the Census, ''Household and Family Characteristics, March, 1986,'' *Current Population Reports,* Series P-20, no. 419 (Washington D.C.: U.S. Government Printing Office, 1987), calculated from Table 6.

51. Kathleen Ritter and Lowell Hargens, ''Occupational Positions and Class Identifications of Married Women: A Test of the Asymmetry Hypothesis,'' *American Journal of Sociology* 80 (Jan. 1975), 934–48.

52. Molly Ladd Taylor, ''Women Workers and the Yale Strike,'' *Feminist Studies,* 11 (1985), 463–465.

53. See Cynthia B. Costello, ''On the Front: Class, Gender and Conflict in the Insurance Workplace,'' Ph.D. dissertation, Department of Sociology, (Madison, WI: University of Wisconsin, 1984).

54. Taylor, ''Women Workers and the Yale Strike,'' 466.

55. Kristine Rondeau, President, Harvard Union of Clerical and Technical Workers, personal communication, 1988.

"Union Is Power": Sketches from Women's Labor History

BARBARA M. WERTHEIMER AND ANNE H. NELSON

EARLY ATTEMPTS TO UNIONIZE

Women have always worked, in the paid as well as the unpaid work force. Whenever they worked for pay, their labor has been valued at less than a man's. In the 1847 mill town of Lowell, Massachusetts, an activist group of women textile workers played a major role as writers and editors of the labor paper *Voice of Industry*. One edition carried an article that summed up the problem then. Its theme continues to be relevant now.

> It is well known that labor performed by females commands but little when compared to that what is paid to men—though the work may be of the same character. Why is this? What possible difference can it make to the employer whether he pays A or B one dollar for accomplishing a piece of work, so that it be done equally as well by one as the other? A female generally receives but about one-half as much as is paid to a man for doing the same amount of labor. It has been urged that they are the weaker sex, and are dependent upon us for resistance, and per consequence this difference in the price of labor should be made. But this very dependence is the result of inequality, and would not exist were the proper remedy applied. There are, it is well known, hundreds of families in our cities supported solely by females, who are obliged to labor with the needle twelve to fourteen hours out of the twenty-four, to gain hardly a comfortable subsistence for themselves and those dependent upon them, so trifling is the compensation they receive.[1]

Women and children made up the first factory population of the United States in the early nineteenth century. In 1814, the first power loom went into operation, and a year later the first mill opened in Waltham, Masschusetts. The agricultural sector was suffering from an acute labor shortage, and every able-bodied man was needed to work the land. The new industrialists gave assurances that, indeed, they did not mean to lure men off the land but rather to take advantage of "six hundred thousand girls in the country between the ages of ten and sixteen," not fit for agriculture because they were too young or too weak but good candidates for work in the mill.[2]

By 1830, some 55,000 workers, most of them women, worked in the growing number of mills dotting the New England landscape along the rushing streams that provided the necessary water power. By midcentury, close to 100,000 were employed by the textile industry. Home production of textiles was a thing of the past; the time of the wage-earning woman was at hand.

As early as 1824, women began to organize to fight wage cuts, the speeding up of their increasingly large and noisy machines, and the relentless stretch-out where each worker had to tend more machines for less money. "Our present object is to have union," proclaimed striking Lowell mill workers in 1834.[3] Walking out to protest another wage cut, the women vowed to "have their own way if they died for it." As in so many other *turnouts* (as strikes were called then), the women lost.

Organizing was difficult for men in the nineteenth century (and labor organizations invariably went under with each of the country's frequent economic downturns), but it was doubly hard for women. Striking against an employer violated every code society had established for women's behavior. It was daring to act in concert, to parade in the street, to protest, and to make demands. Newspapers berated the women; ministers pressured them to return to work.

In addition, in the first half of the nineteenth century, unions were primarily for craft and skilled workers and neither organized nor accepted women members. The women who struck had no national organizations to turn to for help and no prior union experience. In forming trade unions they were pioneers in uncharted territory. Moreover, their pay was so meager that they could neither withstand long strikes nor pay dues to support an organization that could make strike benefits available in time of need.

Since society frowned on women participating in labor organizations or even making public speeches, women rarely could count on the public for support. Furthermore, companies did not recognize women's unions. Strike leaders were not only fired but also blacklisted and found themselves unable to find work in any mill throughout New England. The courts, too, sided with the employers. The wonder is that women organized at all.

About the year 1836, a woman named Sarah Bagley traveled from the hills of New Hampshire to the Lowell mills to become one of the most dynamic labor leaders in American history, although we know about only ten short years of her life. The job of labor organizing was a lonely one. She spent several years laying the groundwork, training a corps of young women like herself, conducting classes in her boardinghouse room. Together, in 1845, these women formed the Lowell Female Labor Reform Association. Their motto was "Try Again!"—which is just what the women had to do. Their turnouts failed, as did the strikes a decade earlier, but these women did not stop there. Failing to win improvements through their strikes, the women tried to shorten their fourteen-hour workday by joining the ten-hour-day movement. Through the *Voice of Industry,* they publicized the worsening conditions in the mills. The Lowell Female Labor Reform Association succeeded in pressuring the Massachusetts state legislature to hold this country's first public hearings on factory conditions, at which mill women became the first to testify about the health hazards, low pay, and long hours of factory work.

As suddenly as she appeared, Sarah Bagley—labor educator, journalist, orator, public activist, organizer, and the country's first woman telegrapher—vanished. After 1846 there is no record of her life or whereabouts. But her active years in the Lowell mills, defying society's sanctions on women's proper place, attest to her courage. Criticized for speaking in public (and she could hold a crowd of 2,000 in a premicrophone era), she responded:

> For the last half a century, it has been deemed a violation of woman's sphere to appear before the public as a speaker; but when our rights are trampled upon and we appeal in vain to legislators, what shall we do but appeal to the people?[4]

By midcentury, the character of the mill work force had changed; immigrant families had replaced the farm women to form a permanent factory population. Newly arrived in a strange land and penniless, they were forced to take jobs at any wages to support themselves. They were victims not only of low pay and long hours but also of increasingly unsafe working conditions: machines with no safety guards, buildings without fire escapes or proper ventilation, poor sanitary facilities. Conditions were no better for the growing numbers of women who worked in city tenements sewing shirts and umbrellas, making flowers, or rolling cigars for a pittance. Neither group was able to organize successfully, although both tried repeatedly to raise their wages to subsistence levels.

As early as 1831, Lavinia Waight, a New York tailoress and secretary of her union, openly talked of female oppression. Tailors and tailoresses in Boston tried to organize in 1844. That same year in New York, Elizabeth Gray spoke to a meeting of 700 women and publicly named employers who were paying their workers ten to eighteen cents a day. The Female Industry Association grew out of that New York meeting, taking as members book folders, stitchers, straw-hat workers, lace makers, and sewing workers of all kinds. But again the women found themselves powerless against the employers, and their meetings drew men who circulated among the women with offers of an easier life through prostitution.[5]

ADVANCES IN WARTIME

Ironically, wartime has always meant the expansion of job opportunities for women. The Civil War saw nursing established as a profession, through the remarkable women who served on both sides.[6] On the home front, new factories in the North opened almost overnight, employing thousands of women workers to produce the uniforms and munitions the army needed. The government, giving job preference to war widows and children of soldiers who had been killed in action, hired women as clerks and copyists for the first time. In 1866, recognizing that this was not a temporary phenomenon, Congress set wages for them at $900 a year. However, men doing the same work earned $1,800. The reforms of 1870 set equal wages for men and women in each job category, but this made little difference, because men and women rarely performed the same work.

It was not long after the war that the first national union of women workers was formed; it was short-lived but was successful for a time. The Daughters of St. Crispin, organized in 1869, united women shoebinders from Lynn, Massachusetts, to San Francisco, California, and included more than forty lodges at its height. At its second convention the organization adopted this resolution on equal pay:

> Whereas the common idea among employers has been and still is that woman's labor should receive a less remuneration, even though equally valuable and efficient, than is paid men even on the same qualities of work; and
>
> Whereas in every field of human effort the value and power of organization is fully recognized: Therefore be it
>
> Resolved by this national Grand Lodge . . . that we demand for our labor the same rate of compensation for equal skill displayed, or the same hours of toil, as is paid other laborers in the same branches of business; and we regard a denial of this right by anyone as a usurpation and a fraud.[7]

Only a few years earlier in Troy, New York, shirt and collar manufacturing center of the country, the Troy Collar Laundry Union was organizing. For several years this union was one of the most successful of the period, even sending donations to men's unions on strike. Fiery Kate Mullaney, the leader, also was active in the National Labor Union and was an advocate of women's suffrage. She saw in the ballot a political tool that would win for women the respect of the local press, which, she noted, backed the men's organizing efforts while belittling those of the women. However, after a long strike that proved disastrous for the Collar Laundry Union, the women were forced to sign a pledge to give up their union in return for their jobs. In 1869, after a short but glorious six years, the Troy Collar Laundry Union folded.

CHANGES FOLLOWING THE WAR

In the decades following the Civil War a few unions, faced with growing numbers of women in their trade, began to support the admission of women to membership. The first to do so was the National Union of Cigar Makers, which opened its doors to women and black workers in 1867. Eight years later, it added a clause to its constitution forbidding any local to refuse membership to a worker because of sex. In one of the early public tributes to women as union members, the *Cigar Makers' Journal* in 1878 declared that women were as loyal to the union as any men: "[Women] picketed the factories faithfully, from early morning till late in the evening, in stormy weather, rain and snow, and piercing cold."[8] Nonetheless, locals of the national union dragged their heels about admitting women and blacks to equal membership and some went to great lengths to discourage their entrance into the industry. Since many women produced cigars in the home rather than in the factory, and the union saw the home workers as a major threat to its pay scale, the "system of working" became an important union issue as well as a human one. The conditions of home workers were described in an 1885 study by New York City:

> These people worked till twelve P.M. or one o'clock A.M., then slept by the machine a few hours, and commenced work again. [Women sat] surrounded by filth with children waddling in it, whose hands, faces and bodies were covered with sores . . . even on the lips of the workers.[9]

Organizing these tenement shops was close to impossible. At the same time, because the home workers were considered a threat, Adolph Strasser, union president, turned to protective legislation in order to keep down the numbers of women in cigar making. He urged passage of laws restricting women under eighteen to no more than eight hours of work a day, with no overtime allowed, and prohibiting women from working six weeks before or after giving birth to a child. Good as they might seem in themselves, these laws cut with more than one edge. Employers forced to follow these strict rules regarding their female employees would simply not hire them and would employ men instead. For women dependent on the few cents they could earn at cigar making to feed their families, these laws spelled disaster. Even so, by the turn of the century more than one-third of all cigar workers were women, up from 10 percent in 1870.

The second union to admit women was the International Typographical Union, which helped young Augusta Lewis organize International Typographical Union Local No. 1 for women compositors. In 1870 Lewis was elected corresponding secretary for the entire union, the first woman ever to be elected a national officer of a union made up predominantly of men. In her post as secretary she surveyed conditions in the printing industry and organized, as well as making the usual reports of that post. She tried to use her position to appeal to the men for greater acceptance of union women in the trade. Often the women could not find work because union foremen would not hire them and union printers would not back them up. While the women's Typographical Union No. 1, never very large, lasted just nine years, by the time it disbanded the doors to union membership had been opened to women in printing on an equal basis with men.[10]

BLACK WOMEN WORKERS

Black women in America have always worked, since 1619, when the first three arrived in the colony of Virginia on a Dutch frigate along with seventeen black men. If life was difficult for white women, how much more so for black, most of whom were slaves until the Civil War. Sharing the long hours of work in the fields with the men, women carried the additional burden of cooking and child care. After the official end to the slave trade in 1808, owners saw black women slaves as breeders of more slaves and often used them as such.

After the Civil War, slaves who could do so migrated to the North or the West to escape the tenant and sharecropping systems that virtually enslaved them anew. They were not welcomed in the cities by white workers, who feared—with some justification—that employers would use them as strike-breakers. In all but a very few unions they were refused membership. Black men had such a difficult time finding employment in the cities that it was the black woman, working at housework and taking in laundry, who usually kept the family from starvation. Black laundresses are credited with forming Mississippi's first labor organization, the Washerwomen of Jackson. In June 1866, they organized to set prices for their work that were uniform through-out the city; they fined members who violated the code by charging less.

That same year the National Labor Union, a loose association of local unions and lodges, voted to admit black workers (and women). However, since few member locals actually admitted blacks, not many black workers joined. Toward the end of 1869 the National Colored Labor Union was founded, from the start admitting both unskilled workers and women to membership. One woman, Mary A. S. Carey, was elected to the NCLU's first executive committee, and women attended the union's first convention. Included in convention reports was that of the committee on women's labor, which urged that the new organization profit from "the mistakes heretofore made by our white fellow citizens in omitting women" and "that women be cordially included in the invitation to further and organize cooperative societies."[11] The report was adopted unanimously, including its endorsement of equal rights for women workers. Unfortunately, the NCLU had a brief life.

KNIGHTS OF LABOR

In 1881, the first national labor federation of any substance, the Noble Order of the Knights of Labor, opened its doors to women and to black workers and called for equal pay for equal work. It was a federation made up of lodges across the country, and their favorite anthem, sung at every assembly, voiced their philosophy:

> Storm the fort, ye Knights of Labor,
> Battle for your cause;
> Equal rights for every neighbor—
> Down with tyrant laws!

Among the women who joined the Knights was Leonora Barry, a widow trying to support two children through her work in a hosiery mill in Amster-dam, New York. She rose rapidly to leadership, soon heading an assembly of almost a thousand women. At the 1886 convention of the Knights in Rich-mond, Virginia, she met and worked closely with the fifteen other women delegates to put forward a motion, unanimously passed by what must have been a startled group of male delegates, calling for the appointment of a full-time paid woman organizer (general investigator) and a secretary to assist her. Barry was chosen for the job, a new one for a woman in labor history. Her energy, enthusiasm, and zeal show in the report of her activities for the next year. In a time when communications were slow, and travel painful, she answered 537 requests for help from women wanting to organize; filled 213 appointments; visited almost 100 towns and cities; filled 100 speaking engagements; answered 789 letters seeking advice or information; distributed some 2,000 leaflets; and answered 97 telegrams.[12]

Barry charted a new course. With no road maps to guide her, she became organizer, business agent, and labor educator all in one. When women wrote to the Knights' headquarters to request that a man be assigned as their president because they found they could not conduct meetings, she ran classes in parliamentary procedure. She worked for passage of state factory-inspection laws and helped to set up two cooperative shirt factories, in line with the Knights of Labor philosophy that cooperatives were an alternative to the wage system. She launched an insurance department to help women in need, and initiated boycotts of nonunion products. A dynamic speaker, she was much in demand on the women's suffrage platform and in support of temperance. The causes for which she worked included industrial education to enable women to find jobs in other than traditionally low-paid women's work; abolition of the tenement system of labor; and prohibition of child labor. She was one of the first to point out that northern mills were relocating in the South in order to escape new northern laws limiting employment of children and that wider passage of legislation protecting children from exploitation was needed.

A traditionalist in some ways (she believed it unladylike to lobby by buttonholing state assemblymen, and left paid employment herself when she remarried), Barry was nevertheless far ahead of her time. Many of her conclusions about the role of women in unions anticipated problems that women union leaders discuss today: poor meeting attendance, low self-confidence of women members, the need for encouragement to stimulate greater involvement of women in their assemblies, and women's reluctance to try better jobs even when trained for them. She was discouraged when she found women earning good wages who failed to extend a helping hand to other women. She came to believe that women should be organized in one "industrial hive" rather than in separate women's assemblies. She saw, too, that the indifference of the men in the Knights played an important part in discouraging women's participation.

Like Sarah Bagley and other women union leaders before her, Barry suffered the wrath of society for her nontraditional role in a period when it was still deemed improper for women to travel unaccompanied on the railroads or to speak out on behalf of workers. When priests of the Catholic church dubbed her a "lady Tramp," it hurt her as much as it angered her, and she lashed back, proclaiming her right "as an Irishwoman, a Catholic, and an honest woman" to come to the support of working women.[13]

One of the most significant women of her day, she remained active in those causes in which she believed even after she remarried, left her job, and moved to Saint Louis. For example, she took an active part in the campaign for state suffrage in Colorado (1893) and continued as a popular speaker until 1928, when cancer forced her to retire.

Yet history books rarely record her contributions, just as labor history texts ignore the strikes of women members of the Knights of Labor, such as that of the Yonkers (New York) carpet weavers in 1885. Here 2,500 women walked off the job and formed a mass picket line around the mill. This time police violence against the strikers backfired, and the women found public support for their struggle. The New York labor movement joined forces to honor the bravery of the women, who held out for six months. Although they did not win the union recognition they sought, they did get important grievances resolved and a wage cut rescinded.

At its peak, the Knights claimed 50,000 women, out of a total claimed membership of 700,000. This marked a new phase in women workers' organizing. For the first time, a labor federation had recognized the importance of its women members and established a women's department, elevating its director to a post as a general officer in 1887. Even though individual men in the Knights often failed to cooperate with the women's department —or did so reluctantly—the Knights openly supported equal pay for equal work, in some cases with considerable success. After 1890 the Knights of Labor declined. It would be many years before women found the same welcome and support in a labor federation again.

THE WOMEN'S TRADE UNION LEAGUE

As the Knights declined, a new labor organization rose to take its place: the American Federation of Labor (AFL). In 1890, when the federation was in ascendance, close to 4 million women were employed outside the home in a total work force of 22 million. One in four of these working women was nonwhite, and most of the nonwhite women still lived and worked in the South.

New jobs were opening for white women as several occupations became established as "women's work": retail sales, telephone-switchboard operation, clerical and secretarial work, and garment sewing. By 1895, although many unions still refused to admit women, 5 percent of all union members were female. Officially, the policy of the AFL was to organize women and to urge equal pay. In practice, the federation did not have the power to enforce this policy on member unions and exerted little pressure on them to conform. In some cases, the AFL chartered federal locals of women workers, allowing direct affiliation with the federation, but these small, independent locals had a low survival rate.

Nonetheless, by the turn of the century, women made up more than half of all union members in five industries: women's clothing, gloves, hat and cap, shirtwaist and laundry, and tobacco. Women's wages averaged little more than half of men's, and black women, few of whom were in any industrial or office jobs, earned only half of what white women made.

Women needed to unionize. In 1903 an organization was launched that officially and unequivocally investigated conditions of women workers and sought to help them organize. The National Women's Trade Union League united, for the first time, the expertise and funds of middle-class women with a social conscience and the energy and dedication of rank-and-file women workers. Together they exerted an influence far in excess of the organization's always modest membership.

In 1909 the league issued a *Handbook* that described the industries it had investigated, those in which most women worked. This publication underscored the need for collective action to improve working conditions. For example, in describing women in steam laundries the *Handbook* reported:

> How would you like to iron a shirt a minute? Think of standing at a mangle just above the washroom with the hot steam pouring up through the floor for 10, 12, 14 and sometimes 17 hours a day! Sometimes the floors are made of cement and then it seems as though one were standing on hot coals, and the workers are dripping with perspiration. Perhaps you have complained about the chemicals used in the washing of your clothes, which cause them to wear out quickly, but what do you suppose is the effect of these chemicals upon the workers? They are . . . breathing air laden with particles of soda, ammonia, and other chemicals! The Laundry Workers Union . . . in one city reduced this long day to 9 hours, and has increased the wages 50 percent.[14]

The first major test for the league came that same year, when 20,000 New York City shirtwaist workers walked off their jobs to begin a winter-long strike that would result in shaping a major labor union—the International Ladies' Garment Workers' Union (ILGWU). This union today remains one of the top two unions in number of women members. Pauline Newman, veteran ILGWU organizer, was among those who walked out of the Triangle Shirtwaist Company in November 1909. She describes that day:

> Thousands upon thousands left the factories from every side, all of them walking down toward Union Square. It was November, the cold winter was just around the corner. We had no fur coats to keep warm, and yet there was the spirit that led us on. . . . I can see the young people, mostly women, walking down and not caring what might happen. The spirit, I think the spirit of a conqueror led them on. They didn't know what was in store for them, didn't really think of the hunger, cold, loneliness and what could happen to them. They just didn't care on that particular day; that was *their* day.[15]

The story of the strike is well known: the arrests; the days and nights women strikers spent in the workhouse; the weeks of cold and hunger; and the victories as shop after shop finally recognized the union, 339 shops in all. Some shops, including the notorious Triangle Shirtwaist Company, did not. To these the workers drifted back in defeat.

Although union conditions proved hard to maintain, the strike, viewed in context, was still a great achievement. Thousands of immigrant workers, mostly women, stood firm against employers who had all the force of law behind them. Out of their struggle and sacrifice, with the active support of the Women's Trade Union League, they laid the foundation for a strong international union that could endure.

Just a year later, these same workers rallied again, after 146 of their number lost their lives in the tragic Triangle Shirtwist Company fire. This time the struggle was for factory legislation. The owners of the Triangle Company had locked the factory doors so that there was no escape for the women trapped in the burning building. They also had never checked the fire escapes, which crumpled under the weight of workers fleeing the fire. Nevertheless, they were found innocent when brought to trial. An aroused public and a determined union and factory commission (whose chief investigator was Frances Perkins) finally succeeded in getting the New York legislature to pass factory safety and inspection laws. Again the Women's Trade Union League played an important role.

Two other major labor struggles in the first two decades of the twentieth century involved women workers: the strike of men's clothing workers in Chicago in 1910 and the Lawrence textile workers' strike of 1912. In the first, the league again was prominent. The second was one of the triumphs of the Industrial Workers of the World. This loose-knit union organized industrially, opening its doors to the women and blacks and unskilled workers that the craft unions would not take in. Although it encouraged women to join its staff as organizers, no women ever held key leadership positions, although several, including Elizabeth Gurley Flynn, achieved a national reputation.

The Chicago clothing workers' strike resulted, four years later, in the birth of the Amalgamated Clothing Workers of America, a union whose membership today is over 75 percent female. Here, as in the ILGWU, no woman has ever held a top office at the international level. Women remain a small minority of both unions' executive boards, although many women hold local and regional positions of considerable responsibility.

UNION DOORS OPEN TO WOMEN

As women moved into the same unions as men, unions of women workers became a thing of the past. What did women win or lose through this change? Unions of women workers invariably were small, independent, and financially weak. They lacked staying power, were limited in scope, and operated in isolation from the rest of the labor movement. Women needed to join with men. The combined strengths of both were necessary in the struggle to organize at a time when there were no labor laws giving workers the right to form unions or protecting them against job loss for doing so. There was no such thing as unemployment insurance, food stamps, or welfare programs to assist workers who might face weeks of joblessness through blacklisting.

On the other hand, unions of women workers had provided a chance for women to develop leadership skills, to set forth bargaining demands that represented their interests, and to have what one labor historian has called their "moment in the sun."[16] In unions run by men, women would for almost three generations, and with few exceptions, take a back seat, only gradually asserting their rights to major union leadership positions.

In 1920 women at last won the right to vote. It did not alter the political direction of the country, however, and the decade that followed World War I was difficult for men and women workers alike. The employer-sponsored American Plan to crush unions and the government's anti-Red Palmer raids combined to make the period preceding the Depression one of intense hostility to labor organizations. Union membership, not surprisingly, declined drastically. The depression that hit the southern textile industry in the later years of the decade should have served as a barometer of the unhealthy state of the economy, but not many noticed. Four major, but unsuccessful, strikes of southern textile workers in Tennessee, North Carolina, and Virginia — against low wages, the stretch-out and speed-up, and the harassing conditions of mill life — led thousands of workers, many of them women, to endure months of violence, only to return in defeat to the mills. Elizabethton, Marion, Greensboro, Danville, and Gastonia are southern towns that became names in labor history. In the Gastonia (North Carolina) strike, Ella May Wiggins — mother, worker, union activist, and songwriter — was shot and killed. In 1934, just four years later, textile workers struck again, but even in a general strike workers could not match the strength of their employers.

With the Depression, however, came the election of Franklin D. Roosevelt and the New Deal. The National Labor Relations Act, passed in 1935, for the first time wrote into law the right of workers to organize into unions of their own choosing. Out of this new spirit, industrial unionism was born: one union for all workers in the same plant or mill rather than many separate craft unions. Breaking away from the AFL, a number of unions that sought to organize this way formed the Committee for Industrial Organization (later the Congress of Industrial Organizations, or CIO). The cry "The President wants you to join the union" swept the country, as thousands of workers rushed to sign up in the new CIO. Shirt workers in Pennsylvania, store workers in five-and-dimes, "baby" strikers fourteen years of age or younger who worked for as little as five cents per week — everyone sat in where they worked or marched on picket lines until union recognition was won.

One of the most famous of the sit-down strikes — that of the auto workers in Flint, Michigan — owed its success in part to the Women's Emergency Brigade, headed by Genora Johnson, wife of a sit-down striker and mother of two young boys. When the brigade was organized to give active support to sit-down strikers in the plant, Johnson told the women: "Don't sign up for this unless you are prepared to stand in the front line against the onslaughts of the police."[17] Five hundred women responded, donning red berets and armbands with "E.B." lettered in white. They were organized in almost military fashion, with five lieutenants working under Johnson. These were women, as Johnson put it, who "could be called out of bed at any hour, if necessary, or sleep on a cot at the union hall."[18]

All through the strike the women saw to it that the men inside the plant got the food they needed. When the National Guard threw tear gas into the factory to force the men out, it was the Emergency Brigade that smashed the windows to let in the fresh air that, some say, saved the strike. Those who were there remember the sight and the sound of the Emergency Brigade as it marched over the hill and down the street to the plant singing:

> Hold the fort, for we are coming,
> Union men be strong,
> Side by side we battle onward
> Victory will come!

WOMEN IN LABOR ORGANIZATIONS TODAY

Women now represent a new force in the labor movement. Over the past twenty years, more than half of all new union members have been women. (A number of labor organizations, such as the National Education Association and the American Nurses Association, do not use the term *union* in their title, nor do many state employee associations; they function as collective bargaining organizations with signed agreements, as do labor unions.) The fastest-growing labor organizations are those that have been organizing in sectors where increasing numbers of women are employed, in particular the public sector and the health care sector. In 1987, 34.5 percent of all members of labor unions and associations were women, although only 12.6 percent of employed women (5.8 million out of 45 million) belonged to a labor organization.[19]

However, the total number of workers in unions has remained constant. Although the work force has grown, a smaller overall proportion is unionized—today only about 17.5 percent. Another 2 percent are represented by unions even though they aren't members.[20] This is a result of the decline of the relatively highly unionized manufacturing sector and the growth of the less well organized white-collar and service sectors. Since almost 80 percent of all women workers are in white-collar and service jobs, it is clear that the labor movement must organize women workers if it is to expand.

This need is recognized at the highest levels of the American Federation of Labor–Congress of Industrial Organizations (AFL-CIO). AFL-CIO President Lane Kirkland stated that "the primary concern of the AFL-CIO is [the fact] that working women continue to suffer from widespread wage discrimination in the workplace. . . . The Federation has redoubled its efforts to see that all workers are paid equally for work of comparable value, and to remove all barriers to equal opportunity for women."[21] In 1980 Kirkland appointed the first woman to the Executive Council of the AFL-CIO, and in 1981 the second, in response to growing pressure by women unionists for more adequate representation.[22] Since then, the AFL-CIO has appointed a woman to head its Education department, created a Women's Affairs section within the Civil Rights department, and a Committee on Salaried and Professional Women within the Department of Professional Employees.

The labor movement has shown its awareness of women as members and as rank-and-file leaders in other ways. Today, 98 percent of all union contracts include nondiscrimination clauses. Many unions deal with both sex discrimination and sexual harassment complaints as part of their regular grievance procedures. A number of unions that formerly had no women members now have some — such as the plumbers', electricians', and carpenters' unions. And more than 3,000 women work in the mines today.

Although women still hold only a small percentage of the top union leadership posts, they are moving into regional- and district-level positions of responsibility in most unions that have substantial numbers of women members. Five national unions have female presidents: the National Education Association; Association of Flight Attendants; Retail, Wholesale and Distributive Workers' Union; Actors' Equity Association; and Screen Actors' Guild. A 1985 poll by the American Federation of State, County, and Municipal Employees (AFSCME) found that 45 percent of its local union offices were held by women, as were 33 percent of its local presidencies. Two major locals in New York City are headed by women: the Postal Union, and the United Federation of Teachers.

Women are more frequently found in staff positions than in elected office, but here too they are still pioneering male territory. The chief counsel for the Carpenters Union is now a woman, as is the Teamsters' organizing director. These changes are a result of a new awareness among women in labor organizations — an awareness of themselves as workers with a permanent commitment to the labor force and of their importance to their unions.

In a manifestation of this new awareness, 35,000 women from across the country, from a wide cross-section of labor organizations, gathered in Chicago in March 1974 to found a new organization, the Coalition of Labor Union Women (CLUW). Its purpose was to move more women into leadership roles in the labor union structure and to work within the framework of the labor movement to achieve four major goals:

1. To increase affirmative action on the job and women's involvement in their unions at all levels.
2. To work for legislation important to women workers, on both the federal and the state levels.
3. To foster women's participation in the political process, including encouraging more women to run for office.
4. To help organize the many millions of unorganized women workers in the United States, without whom the labor movement, now at a membership standstill, cannot grow.

The structure of CLUW parallels in many ways that of the labor movement. It has an elected executive board, with 225 representatives of city chapter organizations and the unions whose members participate in CLUW. As of 1987, the organization had 75 chapters and 20,000 members, but it exerts an influence far beyond these numbers, as the voice of union women. CLUW leaders speak out nationally and locally, testify on legislative issues, and join in coalitions with other women's organizations about concerns of working women. As of 1980, CLUW's president serves on the AFL-CIO Executive Council. CLUW is supported by national membership dues, levied contributions from the AFL-CIO, and financial support from individual unions. Local chapters have separate, usually lower, dues structures established by each chapter.

CLUW's greatest potential for effecting change lies in the opportunities it provides women to meet and learn from other women with different union experiences and to develop political skills that are transferable to their own union situations. Through chapter activities, women have the chance to speak in public, run for office, chair committees, conduct chapter business — all important functions for the woman who wants to move up the leadership ladder in her own union. CLUW women often exert influence in their local unions, especially when their numbers are substantial. And the collective effect works both ways, so that unions with numerous CLUW members may have a strong voice in CLUW as well.

Several CLUW publications have strongly influenced union women. The first, *Effective Contract Language for Union Women* (1979) has been widely used as a model for antidiscrimination clauses. More recently, *Bargaining for Child Care: A Union Parents Guide* (1985) details the major issues women confront in reconciling work and family care. As a consequence of a survey CLUW conducted in 1979 on women's (lack of) representation within the leadership, *A Handbook for Empowerment of Union Women* was published in 1982.

CLUW serves to rationalize and legitimize union women's focus on issues related to equality. Many women workers, union and nonunion, strongly support equal access to jobs and training programs, equal pay for work of comparable worth, child care, maternity and paternity leave, and ways to end sexual harassment. Within CLUW, union women gain support for promoting these issues in their own labor organizations. Although the women's movement also supports these issues, and has done so for many years, working toward these goals within their unions is a more familiar route for union women, one that conforms to their strong labor loyalties.

Early fears that CLUW would siphon off the energies of capable women, leaving them unwilling or unable to tackle the political challenges of running for union office, have proved unfounded. On the contrary, women who have been active in CLUW have moved into a number of important positions in labor organizations, both elected and appointed. Another concern has been that participation in CLUW, which frequently adheres to the programs and policies of the AFL-CIO, might channel women's energies away from the organization of women's caucuses within their own unions. Clearly, union workers must be united when dealing with employers on issues of wages, health and safety, employment, or unsettled grievances. The question is whether a women's caucus in the local union, not always concurring with the union's leadership, might make union leaders more responsive to women's needs.

Indeed, CLUW women in individual unions constitute a logical core for the formation of women's caucuses, because they have gained the know-how through their participation in CLUW chapter committees. The goals of these caucuses include conducting union women's conferences, promoting contract demands, supporting women candidates for negotiating committees and union offices, and using grievance procedures more effectively for sexual harassment complaints. Pressure from women's caucuses has moved local unions to act on statewide legislative issues of special concern to women workers; to support feminist actions; and to finance scholarships for the leadership training summer schools held annually on a regional basis for union women, to encourage their participation in the unions.

While the women's caucuses have served to make some unions in some locations more responsive, they have also tended to isolate women's needs where these are separate but not yet equal. Despite some setbacks, and some problems, the political and legislative experience women are gaining is quite different from the stamp-licking and coffee-pouring roles of women in the past.

WORKING WOMEN: MOBILIZING OUTSIDE THE LABOR MOVEMENT

In city after city throughout the 1970s, clerical and other white-collar workers who do not yet belong to labor unions or associations have been forming mutual-support groups to seek raises, respect for the work they do, and an equal chance, theirs by law, to advance on their jobs.

As the technological revolution sweeps the white-collar work place, threatening to make it the assembly line of the 1980s, office workers have voiced increasing concern about the stress and even the health hazards of working at video display terminals all day. They are isolated from their fellow workers and have no voice in the way changes affect their work life.

In the early seventies, clerical workers in several cities began to organize among themselves to improve their working conditions. These groups formed a loose affiliation in 1976 and, in March 1982, took the name of 9 to 5: National Association of Working Women. Today the association has over 12,000 members and ten chapters, which conduct campaigns against banks, insurance companies, and large offices, sometimes suing under Title VII of the Civil Rights Act of 1964 for salary increases, job posting, and an end to sexual harassment on the job. The association effectively uses mass demonstrations, leaflet campaigns, television-spot announcements, and a newsletter to publicize the concerns of clerical workers.

Membership is open to office workers within each city where there is a chapter. (New chapter formation is one of the association's immediate goals.) The association holds that when enough workers within a particular office wish it, union organization is the logical next step, because it offers maximum long-range protection plus the strength of collective bargaining. In 1981, in an unusual move, 9 to 5 joined forces with the Service Employees International Union (SEIU) to organize clerical workers into the union. SEIU established a separate unit, District 925, within its international union structure. The president of District 925 is the executive director of 9 to 5. Most of the organizing staff of District 925 comes out of the working women's association. SEIU leadership sees the task of organizing clerical workers as a twenty- to thirty-year effort, and an expensive one. But the union, which already represents 50,000 office workers, believes that the time has come to mount this effort and to use the 9 to 5 chapters, wherever possible, as a base.[23]

With 20 million office workers in the work force to be organized, a number of other major unions (including the Auto Workers; Steelworkers; Food and Commercial Workers; Office and Professional Employees; Oil, Chemical, and Atomic Workers; and the Service Employees), together with the Coalition of Labor Union Women (CLUW), have mounted a joint campaign in the Washington, D.C.–Baltimore area to organize white-collar workers. This is the first time that CLUW has worked directly with international unions to organize the unorganized.[24]

The decade of the 1990s, then, well may be one of wider cooperation and work in coalitions to win gains for women workers. Those inside the labor movement are joining with those outside it to organize the unorganized and to support candidates—particularly women candidates—on state and national levels. Women understand as never before the importance of being fairly represented where decisions are made and laws enacted. The gains of the past twenty years are in great danger.

The foundation on which this new movement for collective action stands owes its existence to the working women of the past, who supplied the building blocks: the Lowell women—who held banners reading "Try Again!"—and the Lynn shoebinders—whose signs proclaimed, "American Ladies Will Not Be Slaves!" Leonora Barry, Pauline Newman, and countless others traveled a lonely road that women today travel together. Although equal pay for work of equal value is still in the future, and some unions still have no women members, women in this country and around the world today are determined to win a full partnership role in the work force, in labor unions, and in political and community life.

NOTES

1. Philip Foner, *The Factory Girls* (Champaign-Urbana: University of Illinois Press, 1977), 309.

2. Barbara Wertheimer, *We Were There: The Story of Working Women in America* (New York: Pantheon, 1977), 56; Edith Abbott, *Women in Industry* (New York: Appleton, 1910), 51–59.

3. John B. Andrews and W. D. P. Bliss, *History of Women in Trade Unions*, Bureau of Labor Report on Conditions of Women and Child Wage-Earners in the United States, vol. 10 (Washington, D.C.: U.S. Government Printing Office, 1911), 24, quoting *The Man*, Feb. 22, 1834.

4. Ibid., 71, quoting the *Voice of Industry*, June 5, 1845. For a fuller account of the early mill women, see Wertheimer, *We Were There*, Chapter 5.

5. Wertheimer, *We Were There*, 99.

6. A number of books have been written by and about Civil War nurses. For suggestions, see the bibliography of Wertheimer, *We Were There*, 408–10.

7. Andrews and Bliss, *History of Women*, 109, quoting the *American Workman*, Apr. 30, 1870.

8. *Cigar Makers' Journal*, May 10, 1878.

9. Annie Nathan Meyer, *Women's Work in America* (New York: Holt, 1891), 308.

10. For a fuller account, see Wertheimer, *We Were There*, 166–69.

11. Philip Foner, *Organized Labor and the Black Worker, 1619–1973* (New York: Praeger, 1974), 34.

12. Andrews and Bliss, *History of Women,* 118–19.

13. Philip Foner, *The History of the Labor Movement in the United States,* vol. 2 (New York: International, 1947–65), 65.

14. *Toward Better Working Conditions for Women,* Women's Bureau Bulletin no. 252 (Washington, D.C.: U.S. Department of Labor, 1953), 14, quoting the *National Women's Trade Union League Handbook,* 1909.

15. Wertheimer, *We Were There,* 301, quoting Pauline Newman, in a talk to Trade Union Women's Studies students, Cornell University, New York State School of Industrial and Labor Relations, Mar. 1975.

16. Connie Kopelov, *Women in American Labor History,* Trade Union Women's' Studies course module (Ithaca, N.Y.: Cornell University, New York State School of Industrial and Labor Relations, Mar. 1976), 16a.

17. Jeane Westin, *Making Do* (Chicago: Follett, 1976), 310.

18. Ibid., 315.

19. *Employment and Earnings,* Jan. 1988, Table 59, p. 222.

20. Ibid.

21. *AFL-CIO News,* May 22, 1982, 7.

22. By custom, Executive Council members of the AFL-CIO are presidents of unions affiliated with the federation. In order to appoint women to the council and to increase the number of minorities as well, the rules of the council had to be amended. The first woman appointed was Joyce D. Miller, a vice-president of the Amalgamated Clothing and Textile Workers Union and president of the Coalition of Labor Union Women. A year later, in 1981, Barbara Hutcheson, a vice-president of the American Federation of Government Employees, became the second woman on the council.

23. AFL-CIO, Department for Professional Employees, *Note This,* July 13, 1981, C–9, transcript of interview with John Sweeney, Labor News Conference, Apr. 1, 1981.

24. *CLUW News* 8, no. 4 (July–Aug. 1982): 2.

Professional Women: How Real Are the Recent Gains?

DEBRA RENEE KAUFMAN

Today there are just under 50 million women in the civilian labor force. Nearly 10 million women, or one out of every five of those employed, hold professional or managerial positions. In law, medicine, postsecondary education, and business, the number of women has increased significantly during the last ten years. But the gains that women have made in the professions have been hard won and may well prove even harder to maintain. As Epstein warned in 1970, "No matter what sphere of work women are hired for or select, like sediment in a wine bottle they seem to settle to the bottom" (1970b, p. 2). What women are allowed to do remains limited, and barriers still restrict their mobility in the professional world. In professions that are as male-dominated today as they were a decade ago, women are still likely to be overrepresented in low-paid and low-prestige subspecialities. However, when men enter female-dominated professions, they usually rise to the top.

Society has various expectations of and beliefs about its professionals. It assumes that they will abide by a code of ethics in dealing with their colleagues and clients and that they will belong to a professional association entrusted with enforcing this code. Since professionals are considered best qualified to judge each other's work, they are expected to submit to the judgment of their colleagues. Professionals are expected to make decisions without pressure from clients, the public, or an employing agency. It is believed that professional work benefits the public.

In many respects, professionals represent the elite cadre of society's work force. Since professions carry a high degree of honor and status in our society, their members can expect greater rewards for their services. Professional prestige is partly attributable to the fact that professionals are highly educated. Their specialized training allows them to draw on a body of knowledge unavailable to lay people. The exclusivity of the professions is also a result of their legal right to exercise a virtual monopoly over the delivery of their service. Professionals are thought to derive a great deal of fulfillment from their work and to enjoy a high degree of autonomy. It is not clear, however, that professional women enjoy these advantages to the same extent as do their male colleagues. Even when women are willing and able to make the commitment to a professional career, most find themselves located in subsidiary positions within prestige professions or in positions that do not accord them the autonomy, prestige, or pay customarily associated with the professional image (See Table 1).

Table 1 shows that, from the beginning of this century to the present, the professions have been clearly sex-segregated. Although comparable data cannot be obtained until the next decennial census of the United States is taken, there are clear indicators that the prestige professions remain male-dominated. In 1987, only 6.9 percent of the clergy, 19.7 percent of lawyers and judges, 19.5 percent of physicians, and 37.1 percent of college and university teachers were women. Conversely, the percentages of women who are social workers (65.6 percent), teachers except college and university (73.6 percent), registered nurses (95.1 percent), and librarians (85.6 percent)

T A B L E 1
Percent Female in Eight Selected Professions, 1900–1980

Profession	1980	1970	1960	1950	1940	1930	1920	1910	1900
Physicians[a]	13.4	9.3	6.8	6.5	4.7	4.4	5.0	6.0	5.6
Lawyers and judges	12.8	4.9	3.5	3.5	2.5	2.1	1.4	0.5	.8
Clergy	5.8	2.9	2.3	4.1	2.7	2.2	1.4	0.5	3.1
Professors[b]	36.6	28.6	21.9	23.3	26.5	32.5	30.2	18.9	6.3
Social workers[c]	64.9	62.8	62.7	69.1	64.3	78.7			
Nurses[d]	95.9	96.1	97.5	97.6	97.8	98.1	96.3	92.9	93.6
Librarians[e]	82.5	82.0	85.5	88.5	89.5	91.3	88.2	78.5	74.7
Teachers[f]	70.8	69.5	72.5	78.8	75.3	81.8	84.5	80.1	74.5

SOURCES: For 1980: *Supplementary Report from the 1980 Census of Population,* Table 1, "Detailed Occupations and Years of School Completed, by Age for Civilian Labor Force, by Sex, Race, and Spanish Origin: 1980," PC80-51-8. For 1970: *Nineteenth Decennial Census of the United States,* Vol. 1, *Characteristics of the Population,* Part 1, Section 2, Table 221. "Detailed Occupations of Experienced Civilian Labor Force and Employed Persons by Sex, 1970 and 1960," p. I-718. For 1960 and 1950: *Eighteenth Decennial Census of the United States,* Vol. 1, *Characteristics of the Population,* Part 1, Table 201, "Detailed Occupations of Experienced Labor Force, by Sex, for the United States, 1960 and 1950," p. I-522. For 1940: *Sixteenth Decennial Census of the United States: Population: Comparative Occupation Statistics for the United States, 1870 to 1940,* Table 2, "Persons 14 Years Old and over in the Labor Force (except New Workers), 1940," p. 49. For 1930, 1920, and 1910: *Fifteenth Decennial Census: Population: General Report on Occupations,* Table 1, "Gainful Workers 10 Years Old and over, by Occupation and Sex, with the Occupations Arranged according to the Classification of 1930, for the United States, 1930, 1920, and 1910," Vol. 5, p. 20. For 1900: *Twelfth Decennial Census: Population:* Part 2, Table 91, "Total Persons 10 Years of Age and over in the United States Engaged in Each Specified Occupation (in Detail), Classified by Sex, 1900," p. 505.

[a] Osteopaths were included with physicians in 1910, 1970, and 1980.
[b] For "professors" we have used the category "teachers, college and university" in the 1970 and 1980 censuses. "College presidents, professors, and instructors" was used for the others.
[c] From 1930 to 1960, the decennial reports use the category "social and welfare workers," but the 1930 count is not comparable to those that came afterward. Prior to 1920, social and welfare workers were included in the group "religious, charity, and welfare workers."
[d] The category used for 1970 and 1980 is "registered nurses"; that for 1950 and 1960 is "nurses, professional"; that for 1940 is "nurses and student nurses." Before 1930, the category is "trained nurses."
[e] In 1910, "librarians" includes librarian assistants.
[f] "Teachers" is a composite figure for elementary- and secondary-school teachers from 1960 to 1980. The 1940 and 1950 reports use "teachers (Not elsewhere classified)," and those for 1910 to 1930 use "teachers (school)" as the category. Prior to 1910, "teachers" included all teachers of every kind.

indicate that those professions remain female-dominated (*Employment and Earnings,* Jan. 1988, p. 181). Perhaps even more revealing about women's status in the professions is that the female-dominated occupations, although classified by the Bureau of the Census as professions, are often referred to in the sociological literature as the "semiprofessions" (Etzioni, 1969; Ritzer, 1972).

We see that this distinction is more than academic when we realize that the term *profession* seems to be reserved for only those careers structured for the lives that men lead. Such careers are predicated on the notion that the professional is relatively free from child-care and home responsibilities. This permits great investments of time, energy, devotion, and "overtime" work, which are not possible for someone whose primary obligation is to a family. Extensive, difficult, and often expensive schooling is also required for the pursuit of such careers. "Continuity is usually essential," writes Oppenheimer, "and the freedom to move or to stay put, depending on the exigencies of the career, may be an important factor in whether or not success is achieved" (1970, p. 115).

THE FEMALE-DOMINATED PROFESSIONS

While the female-dominated occupations, like other professions, require advanced education and specific credentials, they often lack the authority, autonomy, and monopoly over a knowledge base that characterize the prestige and male-dominated professions. Oppenheimer suggests that the major female-dominated professions stand in direct contrast to the male-dominated ones:

> All of [the female-dominated professions] depend on skilled but cheap labor in fairly large quantities . . . most of the training for them is acquired *before* employment, and career continuity is not essential. They exist all over the country, and hence mobility — or the lack of it — is not usually a serious handicap. Diligence and a certain devotion to the job are required, but long-range commitments and extensive sacrifices of time and energy are not necessary. Employment in most of these occupations relatively infrequently puts the female worker in a supervisory position over male employees, though she may be in a position of relative power over those outside the organization. Nurses, for example, may initiate action for patients, but their authority to do so is derived from the attending physician; furthermore, the authority and the task have a distinctly feminine flavor — that of the nurturing female. Social workers are often in power positions vis-à-vis clients, but these clients are not in the work organization and are in a notoriously poor position to effect changes anyway. (Oppenheimer, 1970, 114.)

While all women are affected by this pattern, black professional women are especially vulnerable. They are heavily concentrated in the lower-paying specialities in the female-dominated professions, serving black clients and generally poor and working-class people in the public sector (Sokoloff, 1986, pp. 24–25).

Men assume the more respected positions of authority and power in female-dominated professions, positions quite consonant with societal views about men's "natural" roles. Male nurses, for instance, tend to be promoted to administrative jobs more frequently than are female nurses (Butter, et al., 1987, p. 134). Likewise, a 1987 survey of 3,577 public- and private-school administrators showed that men are more likely than are women to be superintendents and principals (Feistritzer, 1988, p. 3). Among teachers, women are more likely to teach at less prestigious levels of education than are men. In 1987, 98.4 percent of prekindergarten and kindergarten and 85.3 percent of elementary-school teachers were women, compared to 54.3 percent of secondary-school teachers (*Employment and Earnings*, Jan. 1988, p. 181).

THE PRESTIGE PROFESSIONS

Despite the increasing number of women earning doctorates, completing professional degrees, and entering the professions, the prestige professions and the prestige specialities within them still remain male-dominated. Medicine, law, academia, and science have a similar gender hierarchy.

Medicine

Throughout the first seventy years of this century, the proportion of women among active American physicians remained essentially unchanged, at around 7 percent. Many factors have contributed to this low percentage —from early gender-role socialization to discrimination in admission practices and policies of medical schools. However, in the last two decades, changes in federal law and in custom have helped women more than quadruple their enrollment in medical schools. In 1964–1965, 7.7 percent of the first-year medical students in America were women (Association of American Medical Colleges, 1982); in 1987–1988, 36.5 percent of them were women (Association of American Medical Colleges, 1988, Table I). In 1976–1977, women accounted for 19.2 percent of all those who obtained medical degrees in America; by 1985–1986, they made up 30.8 percent of those receiving professional degrees in medicine (Vetter, B., and Babco, E., 1987, Table 3-2, p. 72). As of 1987, women constituted 19.5 percent of all practicing physicians (*Employment and Earnings*, Jan. 1988, p. 181), and 27.0 percent of all medical residents in America (Association of American Medical Colleges, 1988, Table 4.5).

However, it is after medical school that the recent gains women have made come into question. Female physicians, for instance, tend to concentrate in such specialities as pediatrics, psychiatry, public health, physical medicine (rehabilitation), and preventive medicine, while men concentrate in high-status and high-pay surgical specialities (Lorber, 1984; Butter, et al., 1987; Vetter, B., and Babco, E., 1987). Despite steady increases, women are primarily located in the less prestigious areas of the medical profession and earn less in each speciality (Bowman and Gross, 1986; Butter, et al., 1987). In part, this may be because men are more likely to practice in independent or group practices and women are more likely to be found in salaried positions (Bowman and Gross, 1986).

Law

Women have made great strides in the legal profession, increasing from 22.5 percent of those receiving law degrees in 1976–1977 to 38.5 percent in 1984–85 (Vetter, B., and Babco, E., 1987, Table 3-2, p. 72). In 1987, 19.6 percent of all lawyers were women (*Employment and Earnings,* 1988, p. 181). The figure increases only slightly (19.7 percent) when judges are included (*Employment and Earnings,* Jan. 1988, p. 181). However, as with medicine, the gains women have made are tempered by the different career patterns women lawyers face compared to those of their male colleagues. While women have been able to enter areas formerly denied to them—such as small private companies, large corporate firms, law school faculties, and the judiciary (Epstein, 1981)—they are still heavily clustered in the less prestigious areas of family law, trusts and estates, and tax. Even their Wall Street advances from associates to partners must be interpreted with caution (Epstein, 1980, 1981). Although more women are making gains in the profession, such advancements may have a different meaning now than they would have had earlier.

> For women and minority associates, there is a greater chance of becoming partner, but that position may be a junior partnership bringing a proportionately smaller share of profits at the end of the year. It may also have less power and influence attached to it. There is some suspicion on the part of older women attorneys that this is the kind of partnership young women are likely to get as the firms are feeling pressed to promote their women associates. Although this is definitely a step upward compared to the past, it does not mean that women have "made it" in relation to men who are rising in the hierarchy. (Epstein 1980, p. 308.)

Academe

Many disparities exist between male and female professors. Academic women are concentrated in lower-ranked and nontenured positions; they work mainly in less prestigious institutions and fields; they are often segregated in areas with predominantly female student bodies; and, even within the same academic rank or category of institutional affiliation, they do not earn as much as men do (Kasper, 1987, Table 4, p. 10). Even in traditional women's fields, men are more likely to be at the top of the professions within them. Men direct the libraries, schools of social work, and teacher-training institutions for elementary and secondary education (Theodore, 1986, p. xix). Outside of education departments, employment of minority women is virtually nonexistent in all types of schools (See Fox, in this book).

Women in science and math fare particularly poorly compared to men in the academic world. For instance, women are twice as likely as men are to be on a nontenure track (Vetter, B., and Babco, E., 1988). For men and women first appointed to medical school faculties in 1976, 16.6 percent of the men are currently tenured, compared to 11.5 percent of the women (Association of American Medical Colleges, 1988, Table 2, p. 2). In addition, women are more likely than are men to be located in the lower ranks of medical faculties (Association of American Medical Colleges, 1988, Table 5, p. 7). If women are disproportionately on nontenure track appointments, and if such appointments are in the lower ranks, as the data suggest, it is not certain that women, over time, will achieve either professional security or equality in ranks with men.

Science and Engineering

In 1986, women accounted for 15 percent of the science and engineering work force, up from 9 percent in 1976 (Vetter, B., and Babco, E., 1988, p. vii). Women account for a larger share of employment in science than they do in engineering. For instance, in 1986, while more than one in four scientists was a woman, only one in twenty-five engineers was a woman. Again, as with the other male-dominated professions, women are not randomly distributed in science or engineering. Among women scientists, only 5.5 percent are in the physical sciences, and only 4.9 percent are in mathematics, whereas 25.3 percent are computer specialists. In engineering, women represent 3 percent of both mechanical and electronics engineers (Vetter, B., and Babco, E., 1988, Table 1-3, p. 10). The most recent National Science Foundation report states that salaries for women are lower than are those for men in essentially all fields of science and engineering and at all levels of professional experience (Vetter, B., and Babco, E., 1988, p. vii). In 1986, the overall annual salaries for women averaged 75 percent of those for men. In that same year, the unemployment rate for women was about double for that of men (Vetter, B., and Babco, E., 1988, p. vii).

Sokoloff (1986) suggests that a split is developing in the organization of law, medicine, and university teaching. Two sets of jobs seem to be emerging: those with high prestige, good pay, autonomy, and opportunity for growth, and those that are more routinized, poorly paid, and less autonomous. She also notes that shifts in sex segregation have been often followed by declines in earnings or career possibilities (1986, p. 34). Therefore, numerical growth may not offset segregation patterns within the professions. This has led some authors to conclude that desegregation in the male-dominated professions has not substantially changed the sex-segregation patterns within those professions.

In conclusion, there are fewer women in the prestige professions than there are men, female professionals generally still occupy the least prestigious specialities within those professions, and females earn less for comparable work. These facts suggest that women still face stern barriers to their entry into and advance through the professional ranks.

Not only have the professions been segregated by sex, but also they have been greatly affected by the even more invidious process of sex-typing. When a majority of those in a profession are of one sex, the "normative expectation" develops that this is how it *should* be (Epstein, 1970b). The model of the practitioner then takes on the personality and behavioral characteristics associated with that sex. For instance, in my study of accountants, the quality most frequently cited for success and mobility by both young and old, male and female respondents was "executive presence" (Kaufman and Fetters, 1983). This term almost perfectly matches what is called in the sociological literature the *male managerial behavioral model* —characterized by aggressiveness, decisiveness, competitiveness, and risk taking. In fact, so identified is *male* with *manager* that one writer has stated: "The good manager is aggressive, authoritative, firm and just. He is not feminine" (McGregor, 1967, p. 23). The high-status professions and the prestige specialities in our society are identified with the instrumental, rigorous, "hard-nosed" qualities identified as masculine, not with the "softer," more expressive, nurturing modes of behavior identified as feminine. Since the characteristics associated with the most valued professions are also those associated with men, women fail to meet one of the most important professional criteria: They are not men.

Research on the subject has clearly shown that traits customarily associated with femininity, and consequently with women, are not as highly valued in our society as are traits stereotypically associated with men. The belief in strong sex differences persists, although leading scholars clearly state that the overlap between the sexes on most personality and behavioral measures is extensive. Jacklin and Maccoby, for instance, in a thorough review of the subject, argue that whether there are sex differences in fear, timidity, anxiety, competitiveness, and dependence among young children remains open to debate because of insufficient or ambiguous evidence (1975). They also assert that there is little scientific support for sex differences in such areas as achievement motivation, risk taking, task persistence, or other related skills. Yet these traits are typically associated with men in our society and with the pursuit of a successful professional career.

Other studies (Rosenkrantz, et al., 1968; Broverman, et al., 1970, 1972) have revealed a deep conviction in our society that men and women manifest different characteristics, as well as showing that there is a more positive valuation of those characteristics ascribed to men. Perhaps their most surprising finding was that even mental-health clinicians ascribed specific traits to each sex and agreed that a normal, healthy adult more closely reflects those traits ascribed to a healthy male than it does those ascribed to a healthy female (Broverman, et al., 1970). The clinicians portrayed healthy female adults as more submissive, less independent, less adventurous, less objective, more easily influenced, less aggressive, less competitive, more excitable in minor crises, more emotional generally, more conceited about their appearance, and more apt to have their feelings hurt. This childlike portrait led the authors to remark that "This constellation seems a most unusual way of describing *any* mature healthy individual" (p. 5, emphasis mine).

Such stereotypes follow women into the work place. Even when women do the same work as men, they are not perceived as being as competent as men, and their work is not perceived to be as prestigious. In a fine and thorough review of the social-psychological literature on sex-related stereotypes, O'Leary (1977) notes that Feldman-Summers and Kiesler (1974) were unable to find a single occupation in which women were expected to outperform males, even in elementary-school teaching and nursing. Toughey (1974a) emphasizes that anticipating greater participation by women in high-status professions has resulted in a decline in the way both males and females perceive the prestige of these occupations. However, the converse was found when men entered female-dominated professions (Toughey, 1974b). In a study by Bass, Krussell, and Alexander (1971), 174 male managers and staff personnel perceived women as unable to supervise men and as less dependable than men. In another study of managers' perceptions of sex differences, particularly perceptions relevant to the promotion of women, Rosen and Jerdee (1978) found that male managers and administrators held uniformly more negative perceptions of women compared to men on each of four scales: aptitudes, knowledge, and skills; interest and motivation; temperament; and work habits and attitudes. Generally, women were perceived as having aptitudes, knowledge skills, and interests and motivations compatible with routine clerical roles and not managerial roles (p. 841). In this study, virtually every perceived difference between male and female employees was unfavorable to women aspiring to higher-level occupations (p. 843). On the other hand, Reskin and Hartmann cite other studies that suggest that negative correlations about women supervisors are weaker among women, well-educated males, and workers with female bosses (1986).

In their study, Rosen and Jerdee (1973) found that males and females often were treated differently in their managerial roles. In a simulated situation, "supervisor" subjects promoted men more often, gave men more career development opportunities, trusted men more in handling personnel problems, and granted men leaves of absence for child-care duties less often than they did with hypothetical female counterparts. However, we need not rely on hypothetical supervisors to know that sex biases exist. Women earn less than men do for comparable work in almost every occupation and within almost all specialties (Mincer and Polachek, 1974, 1978; Sandell and Shapiro, 1978; Zincone and Close, 1978). Perhaps the best indicator that women are less valued in our society simply because they are female comes from a number of studies documenting that women possessing the *identical* qualifications and skills as men fare more poorly in obtaining professional-type jobs (Dipboye, Fromkin, and Wibac, 1975; Fidell, 1970; Shaw, 1972; Zikmund, Hitt and Pickens, 1978; Firth, 1982).

The Fidell study in 1970 was particularly eye opening for people at that time just entering graduate school and planning for an academic career. Fidell sent one of two forms to all colleges and universities that were offering graduate degrees in psychology in 1970. Each form contained ten paragraphs describing professional characteristics of ten hypothetical psychologists. The person most closely associated with departmental hiring was asked to participate in the study by judging the "candidates" and their chances of obtaining full-time positions. Form A used masculine first names; form B, feminine first names. Except for the names and pronouns, the wording on both forms was identical. Fidell found that men received higher levels of appointments; the positions were more likely to be on tenure track; and only men were offered full professorships (pp. 1096–97).

Since the prestige professions are sex-typed, the expectations for men and women differ from the moment people make a decision to train for a career. As graduate students, women are not expected to be as dedicated, ambitious, or serious about their studies as men are. It is assumed that marriage and childrearing will eventually interrupt their studies and certainly their careers. The data suggest that such interruptions are indeed more disruptive for women than they are for men. In a reanalysis of a nationwide sample of graduate students, Feldman (1975) found that divorced men were unhappier with the graduate-student role than were single or married men, whereas divorced women among all graduate students were the happiest. He concluded that "apparently divorced men are burdened with greater responsibilities than their single or married counterparts, while divorced women have reduced their responsibilities and are thus freer to pursue the student role" (p. 227).

Such disparities persist beyond graduate school. Of the twenty-four women partners on Wall Street interviewed by Epstein, nineteen were mothers, and some had serious problems arising from motherhood (1980, p. 310). While marriage for most of Epstein's sample was not regarded as an impediment to career commitment, children were often perceived as a source of problems.

The full-time employed wife–mother bears the largest burden for managing the home and children. Her share of domestic activities is three times as great as that of her full-time employed husband (Pleck 1982). These findings may not simply reflect a generation lag: in Komarovsky's study of Columbia University male students, even the "liberated" males in her sample expressed concern about the combination of motherhood and career for their future wives (1976). The majority of the men believed that home and child-care responsibilities were still primarily the concern of the wife–mother (p. 33). Professional careers are designed not for women with families, but rather for men who are free of family obligations. For the professional man, frequent absences from home, tardiness for dinner, and "overtime" work are not only expected but also accepted as evidence that he is a good provider and therefore a good parent and spouse. Such is not the case for the professional woman. (For an excellent discussion of some of these points, see Coser and Rokoff, 1971.)

Multiple-role conflict is but one area in which differences exist between men and women who pursue professional careers. Another difference has to do with the timing of that endeavor. Hochschild argues that age is measured against one's achievements. Getting there first is an important element of success. "If jobs are scarce and promising reputations important, who wants a 50 year old mother-of-three with a dissertation almost completed?" (1975, p. 61). Referring specifically to the academic arena, Hochschild states that "time is objectified in the academic vita which grows longer with each article and book, and not with each vegetable garden, camping trip, political meeting or child" (p. 62). A successful professional career requires early achievement and uninterrupted competition for continued success — timing based on a male pattern.

In almost every particular, professional life is oriented more toward males than toward females. Because women are expected to behave in a generally "softer" way than are men, they may be perceived as unsuited for the combative style expected from many professionals. Even smiling might be bad for women's business careers because it is interpreted by male co-workers as a sign of submission (Varro, 1982). This is substantiated by studies suggesting that the way women talk, gesture, smile, touch, sit, walk, and use space communicates their dependent and inferior status in our society. (For a comprehensive review see Frieze, et al., 1978, especially Chapter 16; and Thorne, et al., 1983.) Some feminists have openly challenged the "success ethic" and the values of the professional life, arguing for a more humane (if not feminine) style in the work place. However, such changes demand a total restructuring of the attitudes and behavior now common in the professions and a redefining and revaluing of what is feminine. The incentives for such change are few, particularly in a tight economy, and, as the following section shows, change generally comes quite slowly.

HISTORICAL REVIEW

The discouraging picture painted in the preceding discussion still represents an improvement over the past. The professions at the top of the American occupational hierarchy — medicine, law, and higher education — began as medieval guilds from which women were virtually excluded. In the thirteenth century, European medicine became firmly established as a secular science, and physicians were trained in the universities. Since females were excluded from the universities, they were denied the key resource to become professionals. However, there was little that we would recognize as science in the late medieval training. Physicians rarely saw any patients, and no experimentation of any kind was taught. Medicine was sharply differentiated from surgery; the dissection of bodies was considered sacrilegious. In contrast, women healers of the same time, who were often labeled witches, had an experimental and empirical base to their healing. "It was witches who developed an extensive understanding of bones, muscles, herbs, and drugs, while physicians were still deriving their prognoses from astrology"; in fact, "Paracelsus, considered the 'father of modern medicine', burned his text on pharmaceuticals, confessing that he had learned from the Sorceress all he knew" (Ehrenreich and English, 1973, p. 17).

The key point is that neither knowledge nor techniques, nor results, defined the professional. What defined the professional was access to the universities. Society barred women from practicing medicine as professionals by denying them access to university training. By the fourteenth century, the church had explicitly legitimized the professionalism of male practitioners by denouncing healing without university training as heresy. Medieval writings on the subject asserted that "if a woman dare to cure without having studied, she is a witch and must die" (Ehrenreich and English, 1973, p. 19).

The development of the American medical profession was quite different, but the results were the same — women were effectively barred from the profession. By the early nineteenth century, there were many formally trained doctors — "regular" doctors, as they called themselves. At the same time, the Popular Health Movement and numerous other groups with new medical philosophies were establishing their own schools, which were open to women and to blacks. Frightened by these new movements, the "regulars" established the American Medical Association, in 1847, thereby asserting themselves as the only legitimate spokespersons for the medical profession. Noting that by definition a profession has authority to select its own members and to regulate their practice, Ehrenreich and English (1973) emphasize that the "regular" doctors were a formidable obstacle to women. The rare woman who did make it into a "regular" medical school faced a series of "sexist hurdles" that only the most motivated women could manage:

> First there was the continuous harassment — often lewd — by the male students. There were professors who wouldn't discuss anatomy with a lady present. There were textbooks like a well-known 1848 obstetrical text which states, "She (Woman) has a head almost too small for intellect but just big enough for love." There were respectable gynecological theories of the injurious effects of intellectual activity on the female reproductive organs. . . . Having completed her academic work, the would-be woman doctor usually found the next steps blocked. Hospitals were usually closed to women doctors, and even if they weren't, the internships were not open to women. If she did finally make it into practice, she found her brother "regulars" unwilling to refer patients to her and absolutely opposed to her membership in their medical societies. (Ehrenreich and English, 1973, p. 29.)

By the early twentieth century, "irregular" schools and their students were routinely closed out of the medical profession. Tough licensing laws requiring extended college and clinical training sealed the doctors' monopoly on medical practice (Ehrenreich and English, 1973, p. 33).

Law, like medicine, began as a medieval guild and has been, until very recently, a male bastion. Women in law, until the last decade, have been "sex segregated in an occupational hierarchy: the lawyers and judges are almost invariably men, while the clerks, paralegal workers and secretaries who work for them are usually women" (Patterson and Engleberg, 1978, p. 277).

It was even more difficult for women to enter the legal profession than it was for them to become doctors. The first woman to be admitted to the practice of law in the United States was Belle Mansfield in 1869. Less than one year later, Myra Bradwell was refused admission to the bar in Illinois solely on the basis of her sex. In the nineteenth century, the legal profession was more highly organized and protected by government than was medicine (Brownlee and Brownlee, 1976, p. 264). Law schools did not admit women until the 1890s, and then did so only reluctantly. And after completing their studies, "even if women did achieve professional acceptance, they usually supported themselves through salaried positions, generally with insurance companies or government agencies, rather than through independent practice" (p. 289). Patterson and Engleberg note that even now women lawyers are still more likely than are men to turn to government positions. But what is more important, the authors find that when a man enters a government position, he uses it as a stepping-stone into private practice, whereas a woman tends to stay put, making it a career (p. 282).

Prior to 1920, women's admission to law schools was not critical because preparation to practice law could be done by apprenticeships. In 1920, the American Bar Association officially endorsed law school as the desired preparation for the practice of the profession. But it was not until 1972 that women were finally admitted to *all* law schools (Fossum 1981, p. 579). In addition, there has been evidence of "low quotas and higher entrance standards for women at many law schools" (p. 579).

The recruitment of women into the now female-dominated professions has had a different historical pattern. Shortages of cheap skilled labor—particularly during wars, recessions, and depressions—have accounted for a good deal of the recruitment of women into teaching and nursing. There were several advantages to using females as teachers. Women were available in great numbers and they were willing to work for low wages. Moreover, this profession did not challenge the cultural ideal of woman's "natural" place. Who could be more "naturally" equipped to teach children than women?

Nursing, too, began as an occupation dominated by men. But, when the Civil War created a shortage of male nurses, women entered the field in significant numbers (Brownlee and Brownlee, 1976, p. 264). The Brownlees contend that the transformation of nursing into a woman's profession did not occur until there was a "sustained entry of educated women who reduced wages below what productivity justified" (p. 264). These were, for the most part, educated women who had been closed out of the prestige professions. Ehrenreich and English, for instance, note that Dorothea Dix and Florence Nightingale did not "begin to carve out their reform careers until they were in their thirties and faced with the prospect of a long useless spinsterhood" (1973, p. 38).

In nursing, female attributes seemed more important than competence or skill; good nurses were essentially ones who looked good and possessed "character." Ehrenreich and English suggest that the "ideal lady" of the nineteenth century was simply transplanted from home to hospital.

> To the doctor, she brought the wifely virtue of absolute obedience. To the patient, she brought the selfless devotion of a mother. To the lower level hospital employee she brought the firm but kindly discipline of a household manager accustomed to dealing with servants. (Ehrenreich and English, 1973, pp. 36–37.)

Nursing itself was hard labor; therefore, while the educators remained upper class, the practitioners were mostly working-class and middle-class women. When a group of English nurses proposed that nursing model itself after the medical profession, with examinations and licensing, Nightingale claimed that "nurses cannot be examined any more than mothers" (cited in Ehrenreich and English 1973, p. 37). The occupations of nursing and teaching were extensions of women's "natural" domestic roles.

KEEPING WOMEN DOWN: THE SUBTLE ART OF PRACTICING THE PROFESSIONS

How can we explain women's continuing secondary status within the professions? As we have seen, the prestige professions are defined primarily in terms of men and the lives they lead. The processes that maintain this male model are usually well beyond a woman's control, however committed or dedicated she may be. No matter what her personal characteristics, a woman is often assigned the stereotypical characteristics of her sex, and despite her efforts to transcend these stereotypes, certain structural features of the professions work against her upward mobility.

"Interaction in professions, especially in their top echelons," Epstein points out, "is characterized by a high degree of informality, much of it within an exclusive, club-like context" (1970a, p. 968). Hughes notes that the "very word 'profession' implies a certain social and moral solidarity, a strong dependence of one colleague upon the opinions and judgments of others" (1962, p. 125). Those who bear certain characteristics (black, Jewish, female, etc.) are at an immediate disadvantage in such a collegial context. As Hughes (1945) suggested years ago, such statuses condition what is considered an "appropriate" set of characteristics for acceptance by one's peers as a professional; he describes these as "auxiliary characteristics." Such auxiliary characteristics as race, religion, ethnicity, and sex are "the bases of the colleague group's definition of its common interests, of its informal code, and of selection of those who become the inner fraternity" (p. 355). Hughes's fraternal imagery is apt; like fraternal societies, the collegial group depends on "common background, continual association and affinity of interest" (Epstein 1970a, p. 972). Almost by definition, women and other low-status groups are excluded from such brotherly associations.

Professional "standards of excellence" allegedly establish the criteria for recruitment and advancement in one's field. Excellence, however, like any other social reality, is not universally manifest, but must be defined and interpreted. As Epstein (1970a) notes, fine distinctions between good and superior performances require subtle judgments, and such judgments are rendered by one's peers. In many ways, one's acceptance into and success within the professions are contingent on one's acceptance into the informal circles.

> The professions depend on intense socialization of their members, much of it by immersion in the norms of professional culture even before entry; and later by the professional's sensitivity to his peers . . . Not only do contacts with professional colleagues act as a control system,

they also provide the wherewithal by which the professional may become equipped to meet the highest standards of professional behavior. (Epstein, 1970a, p. 972.)

Those who do not conform because they lack important "auxiliary characteristics" create dilemmas for themselves and for others. For example, the protégé system is one of the mechanisms whereby one's name and work become known in the upper echelons of one's profession. According to Epstein (1970a, 1970b) and White (1970), the men who dominate the top echelons of most professions may be reluctant to adopt female protégés. White claims that "a man . . . may believe that she is less likely to be a good gamble, a risk for him to exert himself for, or that she is financially less dependent upon a job" (p. 414). The man may also fear others' suspicion of a sexual liaison as a byproduct of such close and intense work. Although it is not unusual for a senior executive to be a mentor to a rising male star, this acceptable practice immediately becomes suspect if a young female receives it. A lack of sponsorship means a woman is more likely to be excluded from those crucial arenas where professional identity and recognition are established.

Collegial contacts are important for more than one's professional identity and acceptance into the profession. Social psychologist White (1970) interviewed women scholars at the Radcliffe Institute who had been awarded fellowships to continue their professional interests on a part-time basis while raising their families. The women thought that access to stimulating colleagues was as important as was the opportunity to be intellectually engaged in a project. White concluded that "appraisals of their work by others, coupled with acceptance and recognition by people whose professional opinions were relevant and appropriate, made a significant difference in determining whether a woman felt like a professional, and whether she in turn had a strong sense of commitment to future work" (p. 413). Furthermore, she suggests that "challenging interaction with other professionals is frequently as necessary to creative work as is the opportunity for solitude and thought" (p. 414).

Collegial contacts are also crucial for survival.

There are elaborate social systems in all parts of academic and business life, and purely technical training is rarely enough. The aspiring young scientist must be knowledgeable about many aspects of institutions, journals, professional meetings, methods of obtaining source materials, and funding grant applications. Knowing how to command these technical and institutional facilities requires numerous skills, many unanticipated by the young student. . . . This is the kind of learning we speak of as "caught," and not taught, and it is a valued by-product of acceptance and challenging association with other professionals. (White 1970, p. 414.)

If women are excluded from male networks, they remain not only marginal but also invisible when such important professional decisions as selection for promotion, tenure, research grants, coeditorships, summer teaching, and departmental privileges are under consideration (Hughes,

1973). My research (Kaufman, 1977) suggests that women academicians are less likely than are men to include people of higher rank in their collegial networks, and are more likely to claim their colleague-friends as professionally unimportant to their careers.

It is within the collegial arena that judgments are made and standards are set. It is within the collegial arena that the ongoing dynamics of professional life are carried out. If women are denied access to this arena (even if they have formed their own networks), they are left out of the power centers of their professions. Moreover, their exclusion from male networks prevents the breakdown of myths about professional women. If women and men operate in different networks, gender-role stereotypes remain unchallenged (Kaufman and Richardson, 1982).

CONCLUSION

How real are women's most recent gains in the professions? Despite their increasing numbers in male-dominated professions, women still constitute a disproportionately small percentage of those practicing the professions. Moreover, even in female-dominated professions, women are second to men in that their positions tend to carry less prestige.

Perhaps the most difficult task in assessing women's gains is measuring the "cost" of success. Even when women have been able to achieve high-pay, high-prestige positions within the professions, the costs for such success have been high. Many have had to give up or delay marriage, family, and significant relationships. Those who have not given up family have had to add to their demanding career commitments the major responsibilities of managing home and child-care tasks. In our society, both families and professional careers are "greedy" institutions. Until changes occur, women who want both can expect to face conflicting and overwhelming demands. Moreover, until we change the normative expectations about a woman's place both within the professions and within the home, so that both demands and rewards are equal to those of men, we must continue to question the gains women have made.

REFERENCES

Abel, E. 1981. "Teachers and Students on the Slow Track: Inequality in Higher Education." *Socialist Review,* 60(November–December):57–75.

Association of American Medical Colleges. 1982. *Women in Medicine Statistics.* Washington, D.C.: Association of American Medical Colleges.

Association of American Medical Colleges. 1988. *Women in Medicine Statistics.* Washington, D.C.: Association of American Medical Colleges.

Astin, H. 1969. *The Woman Doctorate in America.* New York: Russell Sage Foundation.

Bass, B.M.; Krussel, J.; and Alexander, R.A. 1971. "Male Managers' Attitudes toward Working Women." *American Behavioral Scientist* 15:77–83.

Baxandall, R.; Gordon, L.; and Reverby, S. 1976. *America's Working Women.* New York: Random House.

Bowman, M., and Gross, M. 1986. "Overview of Research on Women in Medicine — Issues for Public Policymakers." *Public Health Reports* 101 (September–October):513–21.

Broverman, I.K.; Broverman, D.M.; Clarkson, F.E.; Rosenkrantz, P.S.; and Vogel, S.R. 1970. "Sex Role Stereotypes and Clinical Judgments of Mental Health." *Journal of Consulting and Clinical Psychology* 34:1–7.

Broverman, I.K.; Vogel, S.R.; Broverman, D.M.; Clarkson, F.E.; and Rosenkrantz, P.S. 1972. "Sex Role Stereotypes: A Current Appraisal." *Journal of Social Issues* 28(3):59–78.

Brownlee, W.E., and Brownlee, M. 1976. *Women in the American Economy: A Documentary History. 1675–1929.* New Haven, Conn.: Yale University Press.

Bulletin. August, 1987. Office of Education Research and Improvement. U.S. Department of Education. Center for Education Statistics.

Butter, I.; E. Carpenter; B. Kay; and Simmons, R. 1987. "Gender Hierarchies in the Health Labor Force." *International Journal of Health Services,* Vol. 17(1):133–49.

Coser, R., and Rokoff, G. 1971. "Women in the Occupational World: Social Disruption and Conflict." *Social Problems* 18(4):535–52.

Dipboye, R.L.; Fromkin, H.L.; and Wibac, K. 1975. "Relative Importance of Applicant's Sex, Attractiveness, and Scholastic Standing in Evaluation of Job Applicant Resumes." *Journal of Applied Psychology* 60(February):39–43.

Ehrenreich, Barbara, and English, Dierdre. 1973. *Witches, Midwives, and Nurses: A History of Women Healers.* Old Westbury, N.Y.: Feminist Press.

Employment and Earnings. January, 1988.

Epstein, Cynthia. 1970a. "Encountering the Male Establishment: Sex-Status Limits on Women's Careers in the Professions." *American Journal of Sociology* 75(6):965–82.

Epstein. C. 1970b. *Woman's Place: Options and Limits in Professional Careers.* Berkeley: University of California Press.

Epstein, C. 1980. "The New Women and the Old Establishment." *Sociology of Work and Occupations* 7(3):291–316.

Epstein, C. 1981. *Women in Law.* New York: Basic Books.

Etzioni, A., ed. 1969. *The Semi-Professions and Their Organizations.* New York: Free Press.

Feldman, S. 1975. "Impediment or Stimulant? Marital Status and Graduate Education." In, *Changing Women in a Changing Society,* ed. J. Huber, 220–232. Chicago: University of Chicago Press.

Feldman, S. 1975. "Impediment or Stimulant? Marital Status and Graduate Education." In *Changing Women in a Changing Society,* ed. Joan Huber. Chicago: University of Chicago Press.

Feldman-Summers, S., and Kiesler, S.B. 1974. "Those Who Are Number Two Try Harder: The Effects of Sex on Attributions of Causality." *Journal of Personality and Social Psychology* 30(6):846–55.

Fidell, Linda. 1970. "Empirical Verification of Sex Discrimination in Hiring Practices in Psychology." *American Psychologist* 25(12):1094–1098.

Fidell, L. 1970. "Empirical Verification of Sex Discrimination in Hiring Practices in Psychology." *American Psychologist* 25:1092–98.

Firth, M. 1982. "Sex Discrimination in Job Opportunities for Women." *Sex Roles* 8(8):891–901.

Freize, I.H.; Parsons, J.; Johnson, P.; Ruble, D.; and Zellman, G. 1978. *Women and Sex Roles.* New York: W.W. Norton and Co.

Grimm, J. 1978. "Women in Female-Dominated Professions." In *Women Working,* ed. A Stromberg and S. Harkess, 293–313. Palo Alto, Calif.: Mayfield Publishing Co.

Hochschild, A.R. 1975. "Inside the Clockwork of Male Careers." In *Women and the Power to Change,* ed. F. Howe. New York: McGraw-Hill Book Co.

Hughes, E. 1945. "Dilemmas and Contradiction of Status." *American Journal of Sociology* 50:353–59.

Hughes, E. 1962. "What Other?" In *Behavior and Social Processes,* ed. A. Rose, 23–28. Boston: Houghton Mifflin Co.

Jacklin, C., and Maccoby, E. 1975. "Sex Differences and Their Implications for Management." In *Bringing Women into Management,* ed. F. Gordon and M. Strober. New York: McGraw-Hill Book Co.

Kasper, H. 1987. "The Annual Report on the Economic Status of the Profession, 1986–87." *Academe,* 73 (2):10–19.

Kaufman, D. 1978. "Associational Ties in Academe: Some Male and Female Differences." *Sex Roles* 4(1):9–21.

Kaufman, D., and Fetters, M. 1983. "The Executive Suite: Are Women Perceived as Ready for the Managerial Climb?" *Journal of Business Ethics* 2:203–12.

Kaufman, D., and Richardson, B. 1982. *Achievement and Women: Challenging the Assumptions.* New York: Free Press.

Komarovsky, M. 1976. *Dilemmas of Masculinity.* New York: W.W. Norton and Co.

Leserman, J. 1982. "Women in Law." Book review in *Social Forces* 61(2):421–26.

Lips, Hilary. 1986. *Sex and Gender.* Mountain View, Calif.: Mayfield Publishing Co.

Lorber, J. 1984. *Women Physicians: Careers, Status and Power.* New York: Tavistock.

McGregor, D. 1967. *The Professional Manager.* New York: McGraw-Hill Book Co.

Mincer, J., and Polachek, S. 1974. "Family Investments in Human Capital: Earnings of Women." *Journal of Political Economy* 82(2, part II):S76–108.

Mincer, J., and Polachek, S. 1978. "The Theory of Human Capital and the Earnings of Women: Women's Earnings Re-examined." *Journal of Human Resources* 13(1):118–34.

O'Leary, Virginia. 1977. *Toward an Understanding of Women.* Monterey, Calif.: Brooks/Cole Publishing Co.

Oppenheimer, V.K. 1970. *The Female Labor Force in the U.S.: Demographic and Economic Factors Governing Its Growth and Changing Composition.* University of California at Berkeley Population Monographs, no. 5. Berkeley: University of California.

Patterson, M., and Engleberg, L. 1978. "Women in Male-Dominated Professions." In *Women Working,* ed. A Stromberg and S. Harkess, 201–25. Palo Alto, Calif.: Mayfield Publishing Co.

Pleck, J. 1982. "The Work-Family Role System." In *Women and Work,* ed. R. Kahn-Hut, A. Daniels, and R. Colvard, 101–10. New York: Oxford University Press.

Reskin, B., and Hartmann, H. (eds.) 1986. *Women's Work, Men's Work.* Washington, D.C.: National Academy of Science.

Ritzer, G. 1972. *Man and His Work, Conflict and Change.* New York: Appleton-Century-Crofts.

Rosen, B., and Jerdee, T. 1973. "The Influence of Sex-Role Stereotypes on Evaluations of Male and Female Supervisory Behavior." *Journal of Applied Psychology* 57(1):185–218.

Rosen, B., and Jerdee, T. 1978. "Perceived Sex Differences in Managerially Relevant Characteristics." *Sex Roles* 4(6):837–43.

Rosenkrantz, P.S.; Vogel, S.R.; Bee, H.; Broverman, I.K.; and Broverman, D.M. 1968. "Sex-Role Stereotypes and Self-Concepts in College Students." *Journal of Consulting and Clinical Psychology* 32(3):287–95.

Rossi, A., and Calderwood, A. 1973. *Academic Women on the Move.* Russell Sage Foundation: New York.

Sandell, S.H., and Shapiro, D. 1978. "The Theory of Human Capital and the Earnings of Women: A Reexamination of the Evidence." *Journal of Human Resources* 13(1):103–17.

Shaw, E.A. 1972. "Differential Impact of Negative Stereotyping in Employee Selection." *Personnel Psychology* 25(2):333–38.

Sokoloff, N. 1986. "A Profile of the General Labor Force and the Professions: A Review of the

Aggregate Gender and Race Segregation Literature." Paper presented at the American Sociological Association, New York, August 1986.

Theodore, A. 1986. *The Campus Troublemakers: Academic Women in Protest.* Houston, Tex.: Cap and Gown Press.

Touhey, J.C. 1974a. "Effects of Additional Men on Prestige and Desirability of Occupations Typically Performed by Women." *Journal of Applied Social Psychology* 4(4):330–35.

Touhey, J.C. 1974b. "Effects of Additional Women Professionals on Ratings of Occupational Prestige and Desirability." *Journal of Personality and Social Psychology* 29(1):86–89.

U.S. Bureau of Labor Statistics. 1980. *Perspectives on Working Women: A Databook.* Bulletin, 2080, table 11, p. 10. U.S. Govt. Printing Office: Washington, D.C.

Varro, B. 1982. "To Smile or Not to Smile? That Is the Question." *Boston Globe,* Aug. 11, pp. 25, 27.

Vetter, B., and Babco, E. 1987. *Professional Women and Minorities.* Seventh Edition. Washington, D.C.: Commission on Professions in Science and Technology.

White, M. 1970. "Psychological and Social Barriers to Women in Science." *Science* 170(3956):413–16.

Wolf, W.C., and Rosenfeld, R. 1978. "Sex Structure of Occupations and Job Mobility." *Social Forces* 56(3):823–44.

Zikmund, W.G.; Hitt, M.A.; and Pickens, B.A. 1978. "Influence of Sex and Scholastic Performance on Reactions to Job Applicant Resumes." *Journal of Applied Psychology* 63(2):252–54.

Zincone, L.H., Jr., and Close, F.A. 1978. "Sex Discrimination in a Paramedical Profession." *Industrial and Labor Relations Review* 32(1):74–85.

Trust, Loyalty, and the Place of Women in the Informal Organization of Work

JUDITH LORBER

When a student walks into a classroom, he or she is not likely to make a particular effort to find a same-sex person to sit near, unless the person is a friend. On most college campuses today, classrooms, dormitories, extracurricular activities, and social groups are mixed by sex. Yet in the work world, job titles, work sites, promotion tracks, unions, lunch groups, coffee-break groups, and after-work leisure groups all tend to be sex-segregated. Even when sex discrimination is made illegal, the informal aspects of work perpetuate and support occupational segregation. To understand the social pressures of the informal organization of work, we must understand the power of the colleague peer group.

THE COLLEAGUE PEER GROUP

Two seemingly opposing social psychological tendencies shape work life in male-dominated American occupations and professions. The first is individual competitiveness—often fierce, bitter, and personal, even in areas supposedly objective and dispassionate.[1] The second is the development of team cohesiveness or esprit de corps. The development of the colleague peer group is not really a tendency that opposes aggressive individualism, since informal colleague groups as well as formally structured teams frequently compete with each other. As Maccoby and Jacklin state:

> Male competition in real-life settings frequently takes the form of groups competing against groups (as in team sports), an activity that involves

347

within-group cooperation as well as between-group competition, so that cooperative behavior is frequently not the antithesis of competitiveness.[2]

Except where the occupation is almost exclusively female, women have been excluded from most individual and team competition. The major role of women at work has been to be either docile, silent handmaidens or one of the prizes of success. As handmaidens, women keep the operation going smoothly for men;[3] as sexual prizes, they enhance and validate the successfulness of men.[4] In this article, I examine this systematic exclusion of women from the peer groups that dominate all but the almost totally female occupations and professions in American society.

A BAND OF BROTHERS

In most occupations, the organization of work is supposed to be based either on notions of bureaucratic rationality and efficiency or on universalistic professional standards of competence. However, the shared norms of informal work groups are equally, if not more, significant in determining job performance. These informal shared norms determine what is proper and improper behavior in many areas of work, such as rate of production, attitudes toward clients or customers, demeanor toward superiors and inferiors, dress, and major and minor rule violations. The norms are rooted in trust in the members of one's group, an exchange of favors among peers, and loyalty to those who bestow sponsorship and patronage. Thus, in bureaucratic organizations, the formal organization of work is strongly influenced by entrenched peer work groups and empire builders with their loyal followers; in professional organizations, careers are shaped through the patronage and standards of exclusive inner circles; and in blue-collar work, the peer group determines which of management's rules are to be obeyed and which ignored.

While universalistic standards imply an acceptance of any and all who are qualified to do the work, the informal norms serve as overt or subtle bases for inclusion of novices in the inner circles of work life or their exclusion. Those who are excluded are felt to be not quite trustworthy — it is felt that they will be unreliable as colleagues or work partners. As Hughes has said, "The colleague group is ideally a brotherhood; to have within it people who cannot, given one another's attitudes, be accepted as brothers is very uncomfortable."[5]

Those who are excluded from informal work groups are at a disadvantage in filling the true requirements of their jobs, since important aspects of the work experience are not shared with them. Additionally, they are not sponsored for promotion, and, should they gain a formal position of power, they discover it is extremely difficult to find loyal subordinates or exert their authority.[6] Therefore, they rarely rise to truly high levels of power and prestige within their work organizations. As a result, they have fewer resources to offer their colleagues, which further perpetuates their exclusion from the colleague peer groups.[7] To cite Hughes again, the first of their kind to attain a certain status are forever marginal because they are not invited to participate in "the informal brotherhood in which experiences are exchanged, competence built up, and the formal code elaborated and enforced."[8]

Davis, in his essay on the problems the visibly disabled have in group situations, discusses how the handicap becomes the focal point of the interaction, excluding the true focus.[9] Embarrassment is barely contained, stereotypical characteristics are attributed to the deviant, and the "normals" are not sure what can and cannot be expected of the different one. As a result, the deviant is never fully included as a normal participant. Rather, as Davis says, "The interaction is kept starved at a bare subsistence level of sociability. As with the poor relation at the wedding party . . . sufficient that he is here, he should not expect to dance with the bride."[10] For women breaking into male occupations, who also have a visible handicap, the line would go: Sufficient we gave her a job, she shouldn't expect to go out to lunch with the boys.[11]

For the woman at work, it is important to know why it is so easy for men to find reasons to exclude women from their inner circles and work peer groups, in what ways this exclusion does or does not resemble the exclusion of some men, and how women can counteract this process.

REASONS FOR LACK OF TRUST OF WOMEN BY MALE COLLEAGUES

Like Trusts Like

Men and women in America are brought up in different cultural worlds. American boys are raised in a world filled with machinery, sports, and superheroes, with the goal of successful conquest; American girls are raised in a world filled with doll babies and dollhouses, clothes, cosmetics, and the goal of successful marriage. They may even be brought up in different *moral* worlds — most American males learn the ideal is to curse, drink, smoke, gamble, and sleep around; most American females learn the ideal is to act virtuously and interest themselves in higher things, such as art, music, dance, literature, religion, and the social welfare of the downtrodden. So, in adulthood, we find men making policy, enforcing work norms, and deciding on sponsorship in smoke-filled rooms, over the three-martini lunch, at poker games, and at parties with prostitutes. As brother breakers of the moral code, men learn to look the other way, and this enforces their trust in one another.[12]

Examples of similar colleague protectiveness can be found in other countries. In Japan, for instance, the all-male after-work bar is the only place a man can go to unburden himself, knowing his colleagues will console him. According to Shaplen, "they protect him and side with him, whether he is right or wrong, in his personal and sometimes his professional affairs."[13] Other examples that come to mind are the working-class pubs and saloons of the British and Irish, and the exclusive clubs of the English upper class, where the members belong to similar occupations or have gone to the same school. Jan Morris can provide some interesting examples of male cohesiveness. Once a male member of a close-knit, homogeneous army unit, she has undergone a sex-change operation and is living as a female.

> Sometimes nowadays I hear a party of men sharing a joke or an experience which, though not necessarily prurient, they would not think of sharing with a woman; and I think to myself not without a wry nostalgia that once long ago, in the tented mess of the 9th Queen's Royal Lancers, they would have unhesitatingly shared it with me.[14]

As upholders of the moral code and traditional moral entrepreneurs,[15] women are not to be trusted to look the other way unless they are the subordinates of men. Secretaries, file clerks, typists, and receptionists know that, if they publicize their boss's dirty secrets, they will be out of a job.[16] As Szymanski points out, because they have access to the details of corporate deals, women must be thoroughly subordinate and loyal.[17] Kanter calls the traditional secretary–manager relationship "patrimonial."[18]

Even when women are equals, their moral stance will set them apart from their colleagues. Thus, Mary Anne Krupsak, past lieutenant governor of New York State, described herself in her 1974 election campaign as "not just one of the boys"—an emphasis on both her femaleness and her political purity. Another woman politician, New Jersey State Senator Alene S. Amond, had to file suit because she was barred from party caucuses after she reported to the press secret deliberations that fostered her fellow legislators' interests at the expense of their constituents.[19]

Similarly, men who come from a different cultural background or who are felt to have a different moral code have frequently been excluded from inner circles by those men already entrenched in a particular occupation or profession.[20] The police provide an excellent example of peer-group loyalty based on shared norms of sometimes doubtful morality. According to Stoddard, the police "code" of semilegal and illegal practices is taught to new recruits in informal interaction.[21] At the same time, the "old hands" carefully test the discretion and loyalty of the newcomers to see if they can be trusted

> All "code" practitioners have the responsibility of screening new recruits at various times to determine whether they are "alright guys," and to teach by example and mutual involvement the limitations of "code" practices. If the recruit accepts such training, he is welcomed into the group and given the rights and privileges commensurate with this new status. If he does not, he is classified as a "goof" and avoided by all the rest.[22]

At present, according to Tyree and Treas, women more frequently than men are found in jobs where they do not share the social background of their peers.[23] Whether the inclusion of women in colleague groups will lead to different attitudes and practices at work or whether they will gradually assimilate the norms of male old hands probably depends on their numbers, the homogeneity of their other social characteristics, and the extent to which they form an in-group of their own.[24]

Sex Games

351

Women in the
Informal
Organization of
Work

The second reason women are felt to be disruptive of male inner circles is sex. (The same attitude is held about homosexuals.) When sexual relations are a possibility, the comfortable intimacy of colleague relations is disrupted by the threat of seductions, pursuits, rivalries, jealousies, and the private intimacy of the couple.[25]

The prime loyalty of the couple is to each other, not to the group. They can talk intimately about the others and share opinions. They themselves in turn are treated not as individuals but as a team. They are liked or disliked in tandem. They cannot dispense favors as individuals, or enter another inner circle as an individual, because the others will mentally include the partner in their calculations of trust and loyalty. Thus, the loyalties and enmities of one usually become the loyalties and enmities of the other. Even if they emphasize their individuality, unless they work in widely separated spheres, they may find it easier to operate openly as a team.

Whether membership in a male/female team is advantageous to women is questionable. Epstein thinks that, because of incipient jealousy on the part of spouses, women are not likely to be chosen by men as protégés.[26] If they are chosen, she feels that they are not likely to be designated as successors who can attain individual recognition; rather, they are likely to become identified with a particular person and paid off in affection rather than in promotion, salary, or coauthorship.[27] Wilkie and Allen found, however, that while male/female pairs were less likely to rotate the order of names on papers than single-sex pairs, the man was not significantly more likely than the woman to be the senior author.[28] As they put it, "Perhaps traditional roles, which characteristically define, if not the man as the principal, at least one of the pair as the principal, play some part in hampering the development of equal collaboration between professionals of different sexes."[29]

The growing casualness about sex relations in general may soon permit long- and short-term coupling to be compatible with colleague cohesiveness. We may soon see the day when going to bed with a fellow worker will be no more remarked on, should it become known, than going out to lunch. But in order for that to happen, the norms will have to be such that male/female relations do not necessarily imply a special social relationship. In short, women will have to be invited out to lunch in the first place.

Untrustworthy Mothers

The last reason for men's lack of trust in women as colleagues is peculiar only to women, since it concerns their role as mothers. A very long time ago, working women were usually unmarried, childless, or beyond childbearing age.[30] They were thus considered free of the possibility of getting inconveniently pregnant and disrupting the work team. Later, married women left work immediately on becoming pregnant, or, if they were "career women" who planned to continue working, they carefully limited and timed their pregnancies to be least disruptive of work schedules.

Today, such timing is even easier, since a contraceptive failure can be corrected by a legal abortion at an early date. However, while women may be relied on to use contraception fairly efficiently, will they be willing to have an abortion to interrupt an ill-timed pregnancy? Men may feel (or want to believe) that women are not that "cold-blooded,"[31] even though Guttmacher[32] and Rosen and Martindale[33] found that women with feminist orientations are quite willing to have abortions should an accidental pregnancy interfere with career goals.

Women are not expected to be able to put their work before their child's welfare. Yet they are pressured to be available during vacations, and when a child is ill, emotionally troubled, or mentally retarded, to an extent that men are not. Duberman suggests that women do not want to relinquish or truly share their household responsibilities because it is part of their pride in being a woman to be able both to work and to take care of their families.[34] She cites one professional woman who felt that by being good at *all* her jobs— teaching, mothering, and housewifery—she showed up men, who were successful in only their occupational role.

However, by refusing to give up their prime directive, women place themselves in a position of being not quite reliable colleagues to men, who doubt they can do it all—or who want to make sure they do *not* do it all. As Coser and Rokoff have shown, as long as women are the responsible parents, their loyalties to their families will be considered potentially disruptive of colleague relationships.[35]

PRIMARY LOYALTIES: MALE AND FEMALE

The question of primary loyalty goes to the heart of the problem of women and the informal organization of work. If there is a conflict, where should a working woman's loyalties lie—with her colleagues or her love partner? With her work team or her family? With her professional equals or with all women employees?

The traditional sexual division of labor has kept most colleague groups unisex, eliminating to a great extent the disruptive possibilities of sexual relations among colleagues. Formerly, it was a common norm that sexual couples did not work in the same place, so that the open admission of a love relationship between coworkers meant that one person left—usually the one who was lower in status. Thus, the conflict between loyalty to the love partner and loyalty to colleagues was eliminated by written or unwritten antinepotism rules.

Up to now, male colleague loyalties have been part of their main role of economic provider and have enhanced their possibilities of individual success, while female colleague loyalties in industrial society have been secondary to their main role of mother-wife. Is there a way that women can develop colleague loyalties that permit them to succeed as individuals and do not exacerbate interpersonal conflicts? I suggest that there is. Women must develop or strengthen inner circles of their own within male-dominated occupations and professions.

CREATING A BAND OF SISTERS

353

Women in the
Informal
Organization of
Work

The present composition of inner circles cannot be combated by strict credentialism. The application of universalistic standards of training and experience to the formerly excluded will only perpetuate their exclusion, since the inner-circle principle starts in training and educational institutions. Since it is a fact of work life that colleagues band together both to shape their work roles and for patronage, sponsorship, and mutual help up the ladder, the formerly excluded must form inner circles of their own and expand their power through their own selective recruitment and sponsorship. Groups of women students in medical and law schools have already successfully expanded the recruitment of women and also changed modes of teaching and curricula to meet their own needs.[36] In the academic world and in the professions, women have used women's caucuses in lieu of individual patrons to find jobs for available women and women for available jobs.[37]

Given the low number of women likely to be found in most male-dominated occupations, women must cast a wide net to form a band of sisters. They must cut across status hierarchies or extend their contacts outside their own particular organizations. Even if their day-to-day commitment is to their immediate workplace and colleague groups, the ultimate commitment of women who want to advance the cause of women must be to other competent, able women.

This process of women developing loyalty to women may become the "new credentialism" of the "insider," as Merton[38] claims, but I believe it is a political necessity at present.[39] Indeed, it seems to have been a political necessity since 1840, when Margaret Fuller advocated that rather than joining with men, women should themselves take up weapons and mutually help one another.[40]

NOTES

1. Ian I. Mitroff, "Norms and Counter-norms in a Select Group of the Apollo Moon Scientists: A Case Study of the Ambivalence of Scientists," *American Sociological Review* 39 (1974), 579–95.

2. Eleanor Emmons Maccoby and Carol Nagy Jacklin, *The Psychology of Sex Differences* (Stanford, Calif.: Stanford University Press, 1974), 274.

3. Albert Szymanski, "Race, Sex, and the U.S. Working Class," *Social Problems* 21 (1974), 724; and Rosabeth Moss Kanter, *Men and Women of the Corporation* (New York: Basic, 1977), 69–103.

4. Robert Seidenberg, *Corporate Wives—Corporate Casualties?* (Garden City, N.Y.: Anchor, 1975), 143, 147.

5. Everett Cherrington Hughes, "Dilemmas and Contradictions of Status," in Lewis A. Coser and Bernard Rosenberg, eds., *Sociological Theory* (New York: Macmillan, 1969), 362.

6. Rosabeth Moss Kanter, "Women and the Structure of Organizations: Explorations in Theory and Behavior," in Marcia Milman and Rosabeth Moss Kanter, eds., *Another Voice: Feminist Perspectives on Social Life and Social Science* (Garden City, N.Y.: Anchor, 1975), 60–63.

7. Jean Lipman-Blumen, "Toward a Homosocial Theory of Sex Roles: An Explanation of the Sex Segregation of Social Institutions," *Signs* 1 (spring 1976 supplement), 15–31.

8. Hughes, 360.

9. Fred Davis, *Illness, Interaction, and the Self* (Belmont, Calif.: Wadsworth, 1972), 130–49.

10. Ibid., 140.

11. For analyses of the subsequent effects of tokenism, see Rosabeth Moss Kanter, "Some Effects of Proportions on Group Life: Skewed Sex Ratios and Responses to Token Women," *American Journal of Sociology* 82 (1977), 965–90; and Judith Long Laws, "The Psychology of Tokenism: An Analysis," *Sex Roles* 1 (1975), 51–67.

12. Kanter, *Men and Women of the Corporation*, 49–67. She argues that it is the "uncertainty quotient" in managerial decision making that necessitates trust and therefore social homogeneity among corporation managers.

13. Robert Shaplen, "A Reporter at Large: From MacArthur to Miki—III," *New Yorker*, Aug. 18, 1975, 38–65.

14. Jan Morris, *Conundrum* (New York: New American Library, 1974), 34.

15. Herman P. Lantz, Jane Keyes, and Martin Schultz, "The American Family in the Preindustrial Period: From Base Lines in History to Change," *American Sociological Review* 40 (1975), 21–36.

16. B. J. Phillips, "The Secretary's Dilemma," *Ms.* 3 (1975), 66–67, 120.

17. Szymanski, "Race, Sex, and the U.S. Working Class," 724.

18. Kanter, *Men and Women of the Corporation*, 69–103.

19. Donald Janson, "28 New Jersey Senators Ordered to Trial for Closing Caucus to Women Colleagues," *New York Times*, Feb. 19, 1975, 1, 39. See also Kristen Amundsen, *A New Look at the Silenced Majority* (Englewood Cliffs, N.J.: Prentice-Hall, 1977), 67–68.

20. David N. Solomon, "Ethnic and Class Differences among Hospitals as Contingencies in Medical Careers," *American Journal of Sociology* 61 (1961), 463–71.

21. Ellwyn Stoddard, "The Informal 'Code' of Police Deviancy: A Group Approach to 'Blue-Coat' Crime," in Clifton D. Bryant, ed., *Deviant Behavior: Occupational and Organizational Bases* (Chicago: Rand McNally, 1974), 218–38.

22. Ibid., 229.

23. Andrea Tyree and Judith Treas, "The Occupational and Marital Mobility of Women," *American Sociological Review* 39 (1974), 293–302.

24. Kanter, "Some Effects of Proportions on Group Life"; and Judith Lorber, "Women and Medical Sociology: Invisible Professionals and Ubiquitous Patients," in Marcia Millman and Rosabeth M. Kanter, eds., *Another Voice: Feminist Perspectives on Social Life and Social Science* (Garden City, N.Y.: Anchor, 1975), 75–105.

25. Donald Roy, "Sex in the Factory: Informal Heterosexual Relations between Supervisors and Work Groups," in Clifton D. Bryant, ed., *Deviant Behavior: Occupational and Organizational Bases* (Chicago: Rand McNally, 1974).

26. Cynthia Fuchs Epstein, *Women's Place* (Berkeley: University of California Press, 1971), 169; and Epstein, "Bringing Women In: Rewards, Punishments, and the Structure of Achievement," in Ruth B. Kundsin, ed., *Women and Success: The Anatomy of Achievement* (New York: Morrow, 1974), 13–21.

27. Cynthia Fuchs Epstein, "Ambiguity as Social Control: Consequences for the Integration of Women in Professional Elites," in Phyllis L. Steward and Muriel G. Cantor, eds., *Varieties of Work Experience: The Social Control of Occupational Groups and Roles* (Cambridge, Mass.: Schenckman, 1974), 32.

28. Jane Riblett Wilkie and Irving Lewis Allen, "Women Sociologists and Co-Authorship with Men," *American Sociologist* 10 (1975), 19–24.

29. Ibid., 24.

30. Valerie Kincade Oppenheimer, "Demographic Influence on Female Employment and the Status of Women," *American Journal of Sociology* 78 (1973), 946–61.

31. For limited recent data on male attitudes, see Bernard M. Bass, Judith Krusell, and Ralph A. Alexander, "Male Managers' Attitudes toward Working Women," in Linda S. Fidell and John

DeLamater, eds., *Women in the Professions: What's All the Fuss About?* (Beverly Hills, Calif.: Sage Publications, 1971), 63–78; and Kanter, *Men and Women of the Corporation*, 106–7.

32. Sally Guttmacher and Dolores Kreisman, "Women's Work, Woman's Role, and Delay in Securing an Abortion" (Paper presented at annual meeting of the American Public Health Association, Chicago, 1975).

33. R. A. Hudson Rosen and Lois J. Martindale, "Abortion as 'Deviance': Traditional Female Roles vs. the Feminist Perspective" (Paper presented at the American Sociological Association annual meeting, San Francisco, 1975).

34. Lucile Duberman, *Gender and Sex in Society* (New York: Praeger, 1975), 128.

35. Rose Laub Coser and Gerald Rokoff, "Women in the Occupational World: Social Disruption and Conflict," *Social Problems* 18 (1971), 535–54.

36. Margaret A. Campbell, *Why Would a Girl Go into Medicine? Medical Education in the United States: A Guide for Women* (Old Westbury, N.Y.: Feminist Press, 1973); and Elaine Hilberman et al., "Support Groups for Women in Medical School: A First-Year Program," *Journal of Medical Education* 50 (1975), 867–75.

37. Ruth M. Oltman, "Women in the Professional Caucuses," in Fidell and DeLamater, eds., *Women in the Professions,* 123–44.

38. Robert K. Merton, "Insiders and Outsiders: A Chapter in the Sociology of Knowledge," *American Journal of Sociology* 78 (1972), 9–47.

39. For similar sentiments, see Arlie Hochschild, "Making It: Marginality and Obstacles to Minority Consciousness," in Kundsin, ed., *Women and Success,* 194–99; and Cynthia Secor, "Androgyny: An Early Reappraisal," *Women's Studies* 2 (1974), 161–69.

40. Secor, "Androgyny," 169.

Women's Work Is Never Done: The Division of Domestic Labor

SHELLEY COVERMAN

Women's roles have undergone significant changes in the twentieth century, but one dimension remains the same: Women still do the housework. Wives devote two to four times as many hours as husbands to domestic labor. They perform about three-quarters of all the household chores, regardless of wives' employment status, or couples' education, income, or sex-role ideology. The one clear conclusion is that employed wives do less domestic work than do nonemployed wives, but their husbands do not take on enough of the home workloads to change the division of labor appreciably. As we will see, this inequitable division of labor has negative consequences for wives' well-being and career achievements, and for those of other family members as well.

Domestic work both resembles and differs from paid work. Although there is some room for creativity and satisfaction (e.g., playing with children, cooking, decorating), most people find the major portion of the work boring and undesirable (Oakley, 1981). But unlike paid jobs that are routine, menial, and boring, domestic work is unending and uncontrollable. One can not predict when the washing machine will break down, or when a child will get ill or throw his or her dinner on the kitchen floor. Moreover, housework has little prestige. Nonetheless, because it is essential to daily functioning, the allocation of household chores often is a subject of difficult negotiation and conflict among household members.

Until recently, the devalution of housework was reflected in the lack of social-scientific research on the topic (Oakley, 1975). However, a growing number of scholars have begun examining various aspects of the division of domestic labor. In this chapter, we review these studies in order to answer the following questions: (1) Who does what in the household and has this changed over time? (2) Can we explain how labor is divided in the home?

and (3) What are the consequences to family members of the unequal division of domestic labor? Before addressing these questions directly, we must first examine how researchers define and measure domestic labor.

METHODOLOGICAL ISSUES

The conclusions of a study may vary considerably depending on how the researcher defines and measures domestic labor (Warner, 1986). Indeed, some of the inconsistencies in the findings on domestic work that we discuss later could be attributed to divergent definitions and measurement of that concept. For this reason, it is important to review some of the key methodological issues that have characterized research on household labor.

Defining Domestic Labor

The definition of domestic labor includes four kinds of activities. *Housework* refers to both male- and female-typed tasks performed inside and outside the household (e.g., cooking, laundry, shopping, vacuuming, making beds, repairs, yardwork, paying bills, and car maintenance). *Child care* includes teaching, playing with, and taking care of children. A less tangible type of activity is *support work,* which is maintaining the emotional well-being of family members. The last type is *status production* (Papanek, 1979), which encompasses activities such as entertaining and charitable work that require a spouse's in-home time, energy, and organizational skills and that promote the other spouse's job status. Historically, wives have engaged in status-production activities more often than have husbands.

Measuring Domestic Labor

Most of what we know about the division of domestic work derives primarily from surveys of married people. Hence, most of the following discussion will concern husbands and wives. Researchers have measured both the *time* spent, and the number or proportion of housework and child-care *tasks* performed by household members. Because support work and status production are hard to measure, these activities rarely are included. Thus, most studies underestimate the actual amount of domestic labor.

There are three different ways in which researchers can measure domestic labor. The *respondent summary estimate* (Pleck, 1985) asks each person to estimate the time spent in housework or child care during a particular time period (usually one day or one week). The *time diary* or *time budget* approach asks respondents to record in detail all activities they perform during a twenty-four-hour period and to give the activities' starting and ending times. Although time diaries are probably the most accurate method for collecting information on how people spend their time (Robinson, 1985), they also are expensive and difficult to collect (Pleck, 1985). The *relative distribution method* asks respondents who usually performs or is responsible for each task (self, shared equally, or partner) (Spitze, 1986; Warner, 1986). Some studies include children's contribution as well (Berk and Berk, 1978). It is also possible for researchers to derive a relative or proportional measure by calculating each spouse's proportion of work from time diaries or respondent summary estimates (Barnett and Baruch, 1987).

Table 1 shows the average number of hours spent in domestic labor as determined by eight different studies. Table 2 lists the proportion of domestic tasks as determined by five studies.

WHO DOES WHAT AND HAS IT CHANGED?

Two general patterns can be deduced from the data reported in Tables 1 and 2. First, wives spend from two to four times as much time in domestic labor as do husbands, even when they are employed (Table 1), and they perform about three to four times as many tasks (Table 2). Wives perform about 75 percent of all domestic tasks. Second, employed wives spend substantially less time in domestic work than do nonemployed wives. Full-time housewives spend over fifty hours per week in housework and child care, whereas employed wives average about twenty-six to thirty-three hours per week.

Not surprisingly, when we examine which spouse does which task, we find that couples still divide the labor along traditional lines. Women do female-typed tasks (e.g., indoor cleaning, cooking, laundry, child care) and men do male-typed tasks (e.g., repairs, outdoor tasks). Table 3 lists mean hours per week spent in selected activities, with data from the 1975–1976 *Study of Time Use* (Hill, 1985). Most tasks are female-typed. Furthermore, these tend to be daily tasks (e.g., cooking, washing dishes, laundry, baby care), whereas male activities are more intermittent (e.g., mowing the lawn,

T A B L E 1
Hours Per Week Spent in Domestic Labor (housework and child care)

Study	Year data collected	Employed wives	Nonemployed wives	All wives	Husbands
Walker and Woods	1967–68	33.6	56.7	—	11.2
Sanik[a]	1977	—	—	51.8	11.9
Meissner et al.	1971	16.1	32.2	33.6	4.2
Geerken and Gove[b]	1974–75	28.6	51.9	—	11.2
PSID (Davis)[b,c]	1976	29.3	36.8	32.6	5.0
QES[b]	1977	47.1[d]	—	—	25.1[d]
STU	1975–76	26.0[e]	51.0[e]	33.3[d]	11.3[d]
STU	1981	22.8[f]	—	29.3[g]	13.4[f]

[a] Replication of Walker and Woods (1976).
[b] Response-summary estimates; all other estimates are derived from time diaries.
[c] Housework only.
[d] Estimated by the author.
[e] Estimated by Cain (1984).
[f] Estimated by Shelton and Firestone (1986).
[g] Estimated by Juster (1985).

—Not Estimated.

TABLE 2
Division of Domestic Tasks[a]

Study	Year data collected	Wives' proportion	Husbands' proportion	Tasks included
NLS (Spitze)	1974, 1976	.75 (young women) .73 (mature women) .70 (full-time workers)	—	Housework and child care
Berk and Berk	1976	.84	.21	Housework only
Barnett and Baruch	1980–81	—	.16	Feminine tasks only
Atkinson and Huston	1981	.75	—	Feminine tasks only
PSID (Berardo et al.)	1976	.79	.14	Housework only

[a] Proportions do not add up to 1.0 because of various measurement contingencies (e.g., children's proportions were included, husbands' proportions were not).

— Not estimated.

car repairs, painting the house) or are associated with more leisurely activities (e.g., barbecuing, taking the kids on an outing).

Has the Division of Labor Changed?

We often hear that men's and women's gender roles are "converging." Supposedly, women are taking on more of the male breadwinner role, while men are doing more household work. It is true that women's labor-force participation has increased substantially, but it is not clear that this has had any effect on the division of labor in the home. When Vanek (1974) compared time-budget studies from the 1920s to those from the 1960s, she found that nonemployed women in 1924 spent about fifty-two hours per week doing housework, whereas, in the 1960s, nonemployed women spent fifty-five hours per week doing housework.

As Vanek notes, this constancy in housework time is remarkable, given the changes in household technology that have occurred. For example, we would expect that it would take much less time to do laundry in the 1960s than in the 1920s, given hot and cold running water in homes, washing machines and dryers, permanent-press fabrics, and a variety of laundry products. Yet, Vanek found that the amount of time spent doing laundry increased, probably because people now have more clothes and wash them more often. It may also be the case that households in the 1920s, including working-class families, were more likely to send laundry out to be cleaned because facilities at home were inadequate. The general invariance in house-

T A B L E 3

Weighted Mean Hours Per Week Spent in Domestic Activities by Sex: Study of Time Use, 1975–1976

		Men (N = 410)	Women (N = 561)
Household activities			
Meal preparation		1.57	7.25
Meal cleanup		0.33	2.30
Indoor cleanup		0.85	5.03
Outdoor cleanup		1.59	0.56
Laundry		0.13	2.44
Repairs/maintenance		2.14	0.68
Gardening/pet care		0.94	1.00
Other household		0.92	0.72
	Subtotal:	8.47	19.98
Child care			
Baby care		0.24	0.90
Child care		0.24	0.99
Helping/teaching		0.07	0.15
Reading/talking		0.07	0.30
Indoor playing		0.13	0.18
Outdoor playing		0.06	0.12
Medical care — child		0.01	0.09
Babysitting/other		0.14	0.64
Travel — child care		0.23	0.50
	Subtotal:	1.19	3.87
Obtaining goods and services			
Everyday shopping		1.45	2.78
Durable/house shop		0.19	0.08
Personal care services		0.06	0.35
Medical appointments		0.15	0.37
Government/financial services		0.15	0.19
Repair services		0.11	0.17
Other services		0.11	0.13
Errands		0.04	0.06
Travel — goods/services		1.60	2.14
	Subtotal:	3.86	6.27
	TOTAL:	13.52	30.12

SOURCE: Hill (1985).

work time also could be attributed to today's larger housing units, higher standards of cleanliness, and the time required to purchase and maintain household appliances. Vanek also attributes this constancy to Parkinson's law; that is, activities expand to fill the time available.

Subsequent researchers have both supported (Strasser, 1982) and refuted (Cain, 1984) Vanek's claims. Four studies that have compared data collected between 1965 and 1981 find declines in both employed and nonemployed women's housework time. Respondent summary estimates from the *Panel Study of Income Dynamics* (PSID) (Davis, 1982) indicated that wives' housework time went from 36.8 hours in 1972 to 32.6 hours per week in 1976. Time-diary estimates from the *Study of Time Use* (STU) for 1965 and 1975 showed a decline of 6.6 hours (Robinson, 1980). However, all but 2.5 hours could be attributed to wives' higher labor-force participation and fewer children. Shelton and Welsh (1987) compared the 1975 STU estimates with similar data collected in 1981. They found that women reduced their housework time regardless of employment status, and that full-time homemakers decreased their time the most (by about 2 hours per week)! Analyzing the same data, Juster (1985) found a decline of 1.5 hours per week in housework and child-care combined (from 30.78 to 29.28). These small reductions in women's housework time do not change the fact that married women, including those who are employed, still are responsible for the majority of work done in the home.

Studies of change in men's domestic work are too recent to suggest any long-term trends. Several recent studies have concluded that men are increasing their involvement in domestic labor, even though the data they examine do not support such a conclusion. For example, although Stafford (1980) concludes that men have increased their housework slightly, the analyses he reports do not indicate any significant change. Only two studies to date have found some evidence of a slight increase. Davis (1982) found an increment in men's housework from 2.4 hours per week in 1972 to 5.0 hours in 1976. Juster's (1985) analysis showed that husbands increased their weekly housework *and* child-care time from 13.4 hours in 1975 to 14.7 hours in 1981.[1] Other studies have found no evidence of an increase in men's time spent in housework and child care (Duncan et al., 1973; Sanik, 1981; Coverman and Sheley, 1986).

Some researchers argue that husbands' *proportion* or share of work in the household is increasing because their wives' *amount* is decreasing. For example, if a husband spent eleven hours per week doing domestic work in 1975 and 1980, and his wife spent thirty-five hours per week in 1975 and thirty hours in 1980, his *proportion* of domestic work time would have increased from 24 percent (11/46) in 1975 to 27 percent (11/41) in 1980, even though the *amount* of domestic work he performed had not changed.

Two other important research questions are whether husbands of employed wives, and whether husbands with children, do more housework. Most, but not all, studies have found that men with employed wives are more involved in household tasks. For example, among one group of respondents, husbands of employed wives spent about twenty-six more minutes per day doing domestic labor than did husbands of nonemployed wives (Coverman, 1985). This difference, however, is too small to suggest any real change in the division of labor. Results of analyses of the effect of children on domestic-work allocation are somewhat ambiguous: Some studies find that the number of children is positively correlated with men's domestic hours (Farkas, 1976; Coverman, 1985), whereas others find a much weaker effect (Miller and Garrison, 1982; Hiller and Philliber, 1986). Some of the ambiguity of the effects of this variable might be attributable to the fact that children affect participation in housework and child-care differently. Coverman and Sheley (1986) found that the number and ages of children did not significantly affect the time husbands spent in housework, but these factors strongly influenced husbands' child-care time—men with preschool children did more child care than did men with older children. Corroboration of these results appears in Berk and Berk's (1979) finding that the primary adjustment in the division of labor once children enter the picture is that fathers take on some child care (usually playing) in the evening after dinner, when the wife is doing the dishes.

We can conclude that neither increased technology nor wives' increased labor-force participation has brought any real change to the division of domestic labor. Men are doing at most one or two more hours domestic work per week than previously, and they spend this time playing with their children (Pleck and Lang, 1978; Berk and Berk, 1979). There is little evidence that men are increasing their performance of female-typed household tasks. Wives still do the great majority of housework and child care.

EXPLANATORY FRAMEWORKS

Several theoretical perspectives attempt to explain the division of household labor by focusing on different variables as important determinants of the organization of work in the home. These theories are the relative power–relative resources, ideology, class and race, and demand–response capability theories. The last theory appears to fare the best, although none of these theories provides a definitive answer.

Relative Power–Relative Resources

The relative-power perspective stems from a sociological power framework (Blood and Wolfe, 1960) and the relative-resources hypothesis is derived from microeconomics (England and Farkas, 1986). Both perspectives hypothesize that the most powerful partner in a relationship, or the spouse with the most resources, will perform the least domestic work (Coverman, 1985). Researchers use variables such as education, earnings, and occupational position as indicators of power or resources in the household. Implicit in this perspective is the notion that it is one spouse's power (or resource) *in relation to that of the other* that predicts how much housework each partner will do. Thus, to measure *relative* power of a husband and wife, we use the ratio of wife's to husband's earnings (or education, or occupational position) (Farkas, 1976) or the difference between them (Ross, 1987).

The results are mixed. The studies that have used *ratio* measures of relative wife–husband power or resources (e.g., education, earnings, occupational position) have found that these variables exert little influence on the organization of domestic work (Farkas, 1976; Coverman, 1985; Spitze, 1986). However, a recent study that measured husband's earnings minus wife's earnings (Ross, 1987) found that, the more the husband's earnings exceed his wife's, the less housework the husband does. Ross' study is the first to lend support to the relative-resources hypothesis as an explanation of household-labor allocation.

Another perspective maintains that a person's attitudes and ideology about women's and men's proper roles determine how much household work she or he will perform. Although there is a fair amount of evidence suggesting that a liberal sex-role ideology increases men's housework and child care and decreases women's (Perrucci et al., 1978; Huber and Spitze, 1983; Hiller and Philliber, 1986; Ross, 1987), there also is evidence that suggests that such ideology exerts little or no effect (Rubin, 1976; Atkinson and Huston, 1984; Coverman, 1985).

Class and Race

Although we know that there are class differences in sex-role *attitudes* (Rubin, 1976; Thornton et al., 1983), it is not at all clear that there are corresponding class differences in sex-role *behavior*. Class position has been measured by socioeconomic characteristics, such as education, occupation, or earnings, or by Marxist categories that indicate whether a person owns or controls the means of production. Whatever measure is used, the results follow no discernable pattern. For example, Berk and Berk (1978) and Beer (1983) found that being a professional or manager increased men's domestic participation, whereas other analyses report no effect (Perrucci et al., 1978; Coverman and Sheley, 1986). Findings from studies that used other indicators of social class, such as education and earnings, are just as inconsistent (for reviews of this research, see Miller and Garrison, 1982; Pleck, 1983; and Coverman, 1985).

The evidence on differences between blacks and whites is similarly inconsistent. Several studies have found that black husbands do more work in the home than do comparable white husbands (Miller and Garrison, 1982; Ross, 1987). However, others have failed to find differences in the division of labor in the homes of whites and blacks (Spitze, 1986; Coverman and Sheley, 1986).

Demand–Response Capability

The demand–response capability framework has also been called "time availability" (Stafford et al., 1977; Ross, 1987) or the "situational view" (England and Farkas, 1986). This approach assumes that the amount of domestic labor spouses perform depends on *demands* on spouses to do household tasks and on spouse's *capacity to respond* to such demands (Coverman, 1985). Demand factors include spouse's (usually wife's) employment status and number of children. Indicators of response capability include number of hours in paid work, flexibility of job schedule, and ability to purchase substitutes to perform housework or child care. Essentially, this perspective argues that husbands participate in domestic activities only when circumstances demand it (e.g., their wives are working when the children need care) and when and if their work schedules permit it.

The studies show that employed wives perform significantly less domestic work than do nonemployed wives, and that their husbands may do a little more (Pleck, 1983; Ross, 1987). There has been little investigation of the effect of flexible work schedules, but what there is suggests that these have no effect (Bohen and Viveros-Long, 1981; Barnett and Baruch, 1987). A fairly consistent finding, however, is that, the more time both men and women spend on the job, the less time either spends in domestic labor (Pleck, 1985; but see Barnett and Baruch, 1987, for opposite findings). As noted earlier, it appears that children increase men's child-care time, if not their contribution to the housework. The evidence appears to provide the most support for the perspective of demand–response capability, although there are some inconsistent findings here as well.

CONSEQUENCES OF THE UNEQUAL DIVISION OF DOMESTIC LABOR

The unequal division of domestic labor affects family members both economically and psychologically. Studies of economic consequences suggest a negative relationship between domestic involvement and economic attainment, although the direction of causality is not always clear (e.g., does spending a lot of time doing housework lead to spending less time on the job, or is the reverse true?). The fact that women are socialized to be primarily responsible for housework and child care influences their occupational choices in the direction of female-typed jobs (Marini and Brinton, 1984), which pay less. It also leads to a "looser attachment" to the labor force, with more frequent part-time, temporary, or intermittent labor-force participation (Rosenfeld, 1980; Coverman, 1983). Further, employers often discriminate against women for some jobs on the (unproven) assumption that the women's family responsibilities will impinge on their productivity on the job (England and Farkas, 1986). Because family responsibilities do not affect men's labor-force participation in this way, men are not forced, as many women are, to make a choice between work and family involvement.

Direct tests of the effect of domestic activities on labor-force outcomes also demonstrate a negative relationship. Studies indicate that, controlling for qualifications and other relevant criteria, the more time husbands and wives spend in housework and child care, the lower their earnings (Coverman, 1983; Hersch, 1985; Shelton and Firestone, in press). Some researchers speculate that this relationship may be reciprocal (i.e., a high income also may lead one to spend less time in domestic work), but the evidence for this theory is inconclusive (Coverman, 1983). Since we know that wives spend much more time than do husbands in domestic work, this research suggests that the time wives spend in domestic work is one of the factors that contributes to their lower earnings, relative to husbands. In sum, the unequal division of domestic labor decreases women's economic attainment. Stated another way, sex inequality in the household reinforces sex inequality in the labor force.

What about the psychological implications of the unequal division of labor? One of the most consistent findings is that women exhibit higher rates of psychological disorder than do men (Reskin and Coverman, 1985; Thoits, 1986). In the early 1970s, this sex difference often was attributed to the different levels of satisfaction and rewards women and men derived from their respective roles, on the assumption that the unsatisfactory nature of the "housewife" role was detrimental to women's health (Gove and Tudor, 1973).

This sex difference in psychological health has persisted into the 1980s, and the more recent research in this area has changed its focus as more women are employed and fewer women are housewives. Today, the most likely explanation of women's greater distress is that it stems from simultaneously fulfilling too many roles (e.g., parent, spouse, paid worker, homemaker).

Multiple role identities can either enhance or impair psychological functioning, depending on the particular constellation of roles held (Thoits, 1986; Baruch et al., 1987). Evidence on the direct effect of domestic work on distress is somewhat mixed. Some researchers find that housework overload increases the likelihood of depression in employed wives (Pearlin, 1975); others find no effect (Pleck, 1985). The effect of children on women's psychological distress is consistently detrimental (Reskin and Coverman, 1985). Although employment does increase a woman's sense of well-being (Kessler and McRae, 1982), women employed full-time who have preschool children and who either are single heads of households or have husbands with low or no incomes suffer more stress than do nonemployed women. This is corroborated by the findings that, the more help women receive with domestic tasks from husbands, the better their psychological health (Kessler and McRae, 1982; Pleck, 1985). We can conclude that the more work women have to do in fulfilling their various roles, and the less help they receive from family members or other sources, the more likely they are to suffer psychological distress.

Families in general also are affected by the unequal division of domestic labor. People are using more convenience foods, fast-food restaurants, and the like, and are decreasing their standards of household maintenance and cleanliness. Indeed, the most significant difference between one– and two–wage-earner households is that less housework gets done in the latter. Does this imply that men are not affected? Not at all. Men who must spend long hours on their jobs often miss some of the emotional benefits (as well as the less desirable domestic tasks) associated with family involvement. Children also suffer from limited interaction with their fathers (Biller, 1974). As women are increasingly employed, children's time with both parents is limited, and there are insufficient societal substitutes available for child care (e.g., after-school programs or child care for preschool children).

These problems underscore the need for social change to alleviate them. One beneficial change would be men's increased participation in housework and child care. Further, new work and family policies—such as greater availability of flexible work schedules, parental leaves, affordable and high-quality child-care facilities, job sharing, and other alternatives—would facilitate both men and women combining their home and work roles (Bureau of National Affairs, 1986).

NOTES

1. Juster cautions the reader, however, that the 1981 data may not be generalizeable to the population in general because sample attrition from 1975 to 1981 resulted in some disproportionate loss of nonwhite, low–education-level, and low-income respondents.

REFERENCES

Atkinson, Jean and Ted L. Huston. 1984. "Sex role orientation and division of labor early in marriage." *Journal of Personality and Social Psychology* 46(2):330–345.

Barnett, Rosalind C. and Grace K. Baruch. 1987. "Determinants of fathers' participation in family work." *Journal of Marriage and the Family* 49(Feb.):29–40.

Baruch, Grace K., Lois Biener, and Rosalind C. Barnett. 1987. "Women and gender in research on work and family stress." *American Psychologist* 42(Feb.):130–136.

Beer, W. R. 1983. *Househusbands: Men and Housework in American Families.* New York: Praeger.

Berardo, D. H., C. L. Shehan, and G. R. Leslie. 1987. "A residue of tradition: Jobs, careers, and spouses' time in housework." *Journal of Marriage and the Family* 49(May):381–390.

Berk, R. and S. Berk. 1978. "A simultaneous equation model for the division of household labor." *Sociological Methods and Research* 6 (May):431–465.

Berk, Sarah F. 1987. "Women's unpaid labor: Home and community." Pp. 287–302 in A. Stromberg and S. Harkess (eds.), *Women Working,* 2nd ed. Palo Alto, CA: Mayfield.

Biller, Henry B. 1974. *Paternal Deprivation.* Lexington, MA: D.C. Heath.

Blood, R. and D. Wolfe. 1960. *Husbands and Wives.* New York: Free Press.

Bohen, H. H. and A. Viveros-Long. 1981. *Balancing Jobs and Family Life: Do Flexible Work Schedules Help?* Philadelphia: Temple University Press.

Bureau of National Affairs. 1986. *Work and Family: A Changing Dynamic.* Washington, D.C.: Bureau of National Affairs.

Cain, Glen G. 1984. "Women and work: Trends in time spent in housework." Discussion Paper No. 747-84, Institute for Research on Poverty.

Coverman, Shelley. 1983. "Gender, domestic labor time, and wage inequality." *American Sociological Review* 48:623–637.

Coverman, Shelley. 1985. "Explaining husbands' participation in domestic labor." *Sociological Quarterly* 26:81–97.

Coverman, Shelley and Joseph F. Sheley. 1986. "Change in men's housework and child-care time, 1965–1975." *Journal of Marriage and the Family* 48(May):413–422.

Davis, Margaret R. 1982. *Families in a Working World: The Impact of Organizations on Domestic Life.* New York: Praeger.

Duncan, Otis, H. Schuman, and B. Duncan. 1973. *Social Change in a Metropolitan Community.* New York: Russell Sage.

England, Paula and George Farkas. 1986. *Households, Employment, and Gender: A Social, Economic and Demographic View.* New York: Aldine.

Farkas, G. 1976. "Education, wage rates, and the division of labor between husband and wife." *Journal of Marriage and the Family* 39(Aug.):473–483.

Gove, Walter R. and Jeannette Tudor. 1973. "Adult sex roles and mental illness." *American Journal of Sociology* 78(Jan.):812–835.

Hersch, Joni. 1985. "Effect of housework on earnings of husbands and wives: Evidence from full-time piece rate workers." *Social Science Quarterly* 66(Mar.):210–217.

Hill, Martha S. 1985. "Patterns of time use." Pp. 133–176 in F. Thomas Juster and Frank P.

Stafford (eds.), *Time, Goods, and Well-Being.* Ann Arbor, MI: Institute for Social Research, University of Michigan.

Hiller, Dana V. and William W. Philliber. 1986. ''The division of labor in contemporary marriage: Expectations, perceptions, and performance.'' *Social Problems* 33(Feb.):191–201.

Huber, J. and G. Spitze. 1983. *Sex Stratification: Children, Housework, and Jobs.* New York: Academic Press.

Juster, F. Thomas. 1985. ''A note on recent changes in time use.'' Pp. 314–332 in F. Thomas Juster and Frank P. Stafford (eds.), *Time, Goods, and Well-Being.* Ann Arbor, MI: Institute for Social Research, University of Michigan.

Kessler, Ron and James McRae. 1982. ''The effect of wives' employment on the mental health of married men and women.'' *American Sociological Review* 47(Apr.):216–227.

Marini, Margaret Mooney and Mary C. Brinton. 1984. ''Sex typing in occupational socialization.'' Pp. 192–232 in Barbara F. Reskin (ed.), *Sex Segregation in the Workplace.* Washington, D.C.: National Academy Press.

Meissner, Martin, E. W. Humphreys, S. M. Meis, and W. J. Scheu. 1975. ''No exit for wives: Sexual division of labour and the cumulation of household demands.'' *Canadian Review of Sociology and Anthropology* 12:424–439.

Miller, Joanne and Howard H. Garrison. 1982. ''Sex roles: The division of labor at home and in the workplace.'' *Annual Review of Sociology* 8:237–262.

Oakley, Ann. 1975. *The Sociology of Housework.* New York: Pantheon Books.

Oakley, Ann. 1981. *Subject Women.* New York: Pantheon Books.

Papanek, Hanna. 1979. ''Family status production: The 'work' and 'non-work' of women.'' *Signs* 4(4):775–81.

Pearlin, Leonard I. 1975. ''Sex roles and depression.'' In N. Datan and L. Ginsberg (eds.), *Life-Span Developmental Psychology.* New York: Academic Press.

Perrucci, C. C., H. R. Pottes, and D. C. Rhoads. 1978. ''Determinants of male family-role performance.'' *Psychology of Women Quarterly* 3 (Fall):53–66.

Pleck, Joseph H. 1983. ''Husbands' paid work and family roles: Current research issues.'' Pp. 251–333 in Helen Z. Lopata and Joseph H. Pleck (eds.), *Research in the Interweave of Social roles (Vol. 3): Jobs and Families.* Greenwich, CT: JAI Press.

Pleck, Joseph H. 1985. *Working Wives/Working Husbands.* Beverly Hills, CA: Sage.

Pleck, Joseph H. and L. Lang. 1978. *Men's Family Role: Its Nature and Consequences.* Wellesley, MA: Wellesley College Center for Research on Women.

Quinn, R. and G. Staines. 1979. *Quality of Employment Survey, 1977: Cross-Section.* Ann Arbor, MI: Inter-University Consortium for Political and Social Research.

Reskin, Barbara F. and Shelley Coverman. 1985. ''Sex and race interactions in the determinants of psychophysical distress: A reappraisal of the sex-role hypothesis.'' *Social Forces* 63 (June):1038–1059.

Robinson, John P. 1980. ''Housework technology and household work.'' Pp. 53–68 in S. F. Berk (ed.), *Women and Household Labor.* Beverly Hills, CA: Sage.

Robinson, John P. 1985. ''The validity and reliability of diaries versus alternative time use measures.'' Pp. 33–62 in F. Thomas Juster and Frank P. Stafford (eds.), *Time, Goods, and Well-Being.* Ann Arbor, MI: Institute for Social Research, University of Michigan.

Rosenfeld, Rachel A. 1980. ''Race and sex differences in career dynamics.'' *American Sociological Review* 45(Aug.):583–609.

Ross, Catherine E. 1987. ''The division of labor at home.'' *Social Forces* 65(Mar.):816–833.

Rubin, L. B. 1976. *Worlds of Pain: Life in the Working-Class Family.* New York: Basic Books.

Sanik, Margaret Mietus. 1981. ''Division of household work: A decade comparison, 1967–1977.'' *Home Economics Research Journal* 10:175–180.

368   Shelton, Beth Anne and Juanita Firestone. In press. "The impact of household labor time on the gender gap in earnings." *Gender and Society*.

Shelton, Beth Anne and Sandy Welsh. 1987. "Changes in women's housework and childcare time, 1975–81." Unpublished ms., Department of Sociology, SUNY-Buffalo.

Spitze, Glenna. 1986. "The division of task responsibility in U.S. households: Longitudinal adjustments to change." *Social Forces* 64(Mar.):689–701.

Stafford, Frank P. 1980. "Women's use of time converging with men's." *Monthly Labor Review* 103(Dec.):57–59.

Stafford, R., E. Backman, and P. Dibona. 1977. "The division of labor among cohabiting and married couples." *Journal of Marriage and the Family* 39(Feb.):43–54.

Strasser, Susan. 1982. *Never Done: A History of American Housework*. New York: Pantheon.

Thoits, Peggy A. 1986. "Multiple identities: Examining gender and marital status differences in distress." *American Sociological Review* 51(Apr.):259–272.

Thornton, A., D. F. Alwin, and D. Camburn. 1983. "Causes and consequences of sex-role attitudes and attitude change." *American Sociological Review* 48(Apr.):211–217.

Vanek, J. 1974. "Time spent in housework." *Scientific American* 231(Nov.):116–120.

Walker, K. and M. Woods. 1976. *Time Use: A Measure of Household Production of Family Goods and Services*. Washington, D.C.: American Home Economics Association.

Warner, Rebecca. 1986. "Alternative strategies for measuring household division of labor." *Journal of Family Issues* 7(June):179–195.

Part Five

Institutions of Social Control

The Legal Revolution

JO FREEMAN

In the 1960s and 1970s, there was a revolution in public policy toward women. Beginning with passage of the Equal Pay Act in 1963 and the prohibition against sex discrimination in employment in 1964, Congress added numerous laws to the books that altered the thrust of public policy toward women from one of protectionism to one of equal opportunity. While implementation leaves much to be desired, and equal opportunity by itself will not eradicate women's secondary position in society, the importance of this fundamental change should not be underestimated.

Parallel to this development, the Supreme Court fundamentally altered its interpretation of women's position in society. Until 1971, the judicial approach to woman was that her rights and responsibilities, opportunities and obligations, were essentially determined by her position in the family — her role as a wife and mother. Women were viewed first and foremost as members of a dependent class whose individual rights were subservient to their class position. From this perspective, virtually all laws that classified by sex were constitutional. Today, most such laws have been found unconstitutional. The remaining laws and practices that treat the sexes differently are subject to more searching scrutiny than in the past, and the Court is particularly disapproving of rationalizations for them that encourage dependency.

THE TRADITION OF INSTITUTIONALIZED DEPENDENCE

Until the 1930s, the primary locus of governmental authority was in the states, not in the federal government. Most of the laws that heavily affected people's lives were state laws. Although laws passed by Congress take precedence when there is a conflict, it is only in the last fifty years that the Supreme Court has interpreted the Constitution to allow an expansion of federal authority, and there are still many policy arenas that are reserved to the states. The state legislature is not the only source of state law. This country inherited from Great Britain a large body of "common law," which was essentially the collective wisdom of individual judges deciding individual cases over hundreds of years, as collected and commented on by several great British jurists. This common law has remained operative in every state and in any policy arena in which a state legislature has not passed a superceding statute. Although all new law is now supposed to be statutory in origin, the power of individual judges to interpret statutes as well as to reinterpret the original common law, and their willingness to adapt both to changing circumstances, has created an American common law in each state.

Family Law

Under the English common law, a woman lost her legal identity upon marriage; it *merged* into that of her husband under the feudal doctrine of *coverture*. The result was succinctly stated by Justice Black in 1966 as resting "on the old common-law fiction that the husband and wife are one . . . [and] that . . . one is the husband."[1] The consequences were described by Edward Mansfield when he wrote the first major American analysis of *The Legal Rights, Liabilities and Duties of Women* in 1845.

> It appears that the husband's control over the person of his wife is so complete that he may claim her society altogether; that he may reclaim her if she goes away or is detained by others; that he may use constraint upon her liberty to prevent her going away, or to prevent improper conduct; that he may maintain suits for injuries to her person; that she cannot sue alone; and that she cannot execute a deed or valid conveyance without the concurrence of her husband. In most respects she loses the power of personal independence, and altogether that of separate action in legal matters.[2]

At common law, these marital disabilities were offset by spousal obligations. The fundamental basis of the marital relationship was that husbands and wives had reciprocal—not equal—rights. The husband had to support the wife and children, and the wife had to render services as a companion, homemaker, and mother in return. This doctrine did not mean a wife could sue a husband for greater support, since by definition she did not have a separate legal existence. Nor did it give her a right to an allowance, wages, or income of any sort. But it did permit wives to obtain "necessaries" from merchants on their husbands' account. Even after the all the states passed Married Woman's Property Acts in the nineteenth century, permitting wives to retain control of their separate property, husbands were still obligated to pay their wives' debts when these were incurred for family necessities.[3] This spousal obligation continued after death or divorce. On marriage, a wife obtained a *dower* right to the use, for her natural life, of one-third of the husband's property after his death, regardless of any will to the contrary. She retained that right even if he sold the property before he died, unless she specifically relinquished it to the purchaser. If the marriage should end in divorce, she was entitled to continued support (although not to the custody or guardianship of the children) unless she was at fault for the demise of the relationship.

Eight states that were originally controlled by France or Spain did not inherit the English common law, and thus followed somewhat different rules.[4] Under their *community-property* systems, each spouse is considered owner of half of the earnings of the other, and all property acquired during marriage (other than gifts and inheritances) is jointly owned by both spouses, regardless of who paid for it or in whose name it is. However, the result was often the same, because the husband was considered to be the head of the household and as such could manage and dispose of the community property as he wished.

In 1979, Louisiana became the last state to give both spouses the legal right to manage the community property. The case that led to this change is a good example of how little protection joint ownership really gave to a wife. Louisiana's "head and master" law permitted a husband the unilateral right to dispose of jointly owned community property without his wife's knowledge or consent. In 1974, Joan Feenstra had her husband incarcerated for molesting their minor daughter. To pay the attorney who represented him in this action, he executed a mortgage on their home. Louisiana law did not require the husband to get his wife's permission to do this, or even to inform her of his action, although the house had been paid for solely out of her earnings. After the charges were dropped, a legal separation was obtained, and the husband had left the state, the attorney foreclosed on the mortgage, and Joan Feenstra challenged the constitutionality of the statute in federal court. During legal proceedings, Louisiana changed the law to permit equal control, but only prospectively. However, the Supreme Court declared that the original statute had been unconstitutional and invalidated the mortgage.[5]

The passage by the states of Married Woman's Property Acts throughout the nineteenth century eventually removed the worst of women's legal disabilities. What was left prior to the contemporary feminist movement—which began in the mid-sixties—was something of a patchwork quilt, in which common-law dictates and statutory changes varied from state to state. In most states, married women did not have the legal right to retain their own name or to maintain a separate domicile. Husbands remained liable for support of their families, but a wife was responsible if the husband had no property and was unable to support them, or himself. Parental preference in guardianship and custody of children gradually shifted to the standard of what was in the best interests of the child, although several states provided that, all else being equal, the mother should be preferred if the child was of tender years, and the father should be preferred if the child was old enough to require education or preparation for adult life. Some states gave husbands a right equivalent to that of "dower," in effect requiring his permission before a wife could sell her separate property, just as hers was necessary for him to convey his completely. Half of the community-property states provided that a wife could control her own earnings. In virtually all states, wives could contract and sue independently of their husbands, although some states still required the husband's permission for a married woman to participate in an independent business, and a few denied wives the legal capacity to become a surety or a guarantor.[6] Indeed, in the 1920s, Miriam Ferguson, elected governor of Texas after her husband had been impeached, had to secure a court order relieving her of her marital disabilities so there would be no doubt about the legality of her acts as governor.[7] And in the 1960s, a married Texas woman successfully defended against the United States government's efforts to collect a judgment against her for an unpaid Small Business Administration loan on the grounds that her disability to bind her separate estate by contract had not been removed by court decree, as required by Texas law.[8]

Protective Labor Legislation

Protective labor legislation refers to numerous state laws that restricted the number of hours women could work and the amount of weight they could lift, occasionally provided for special privileges such as rest periods, and often excluded them entirely from night work or certain occupations. The first effective law, enacted in Massachusetts in 1874, limited the employment of women and children to ten hours per day. By 1900, fourteen states had such laws, and by the mid-sixties every state had some form of protective labor legislation.[9] There were two forces behind the drive for this legislation. One was organized labor, which saw women workers as competitors. Their policy was explicitly stated by President Strasser of the International Cigar Makers Union in 1879: "We cannot drive the females out of the trade, but we can restrict this daily quota of labor through factory laws."[10] The other was social reformers, who found the Supreme Court unreceptive to protective laws that applied to both sexes.

In 1905, the Supreme Court declared unconstitutional a New York law that prohibited bakers from working longer than ten hours per day or sixty hours per week. The Court found in *Lochner v. New York* that "the limitation necessarily interferes with the right of contract between the employer and employee . . . [which] is part of the liberty of the individual protected by the Fourteenth Amendment."[11] Three years later, it upheld an Oregon law that restricted the employment of women in factories, laundries, or other "mechanical establishments" to ten hours per day on the ground that women's

> physical structure and a proper discharge of her maternal functions — having in view not merely her own health but the well-being of the race — justify legislation to protect her. . . . The limitations which this statute places upon her contractural powers . . . are not imposed solely for her benefit, but also largely for the benefit of all. . . . The reason . . . rests in the inherent difference between the two sexes, and in the different functions in life which they perform.[12]

With this precedent, the drive for protective legislation became distorted into a push for laws that applied to women only on the principle that half a loaf was better than none. Reformers eventually persuaded the Supreme Court that maximum hours and other forms of protective labor legislation were valid health measures for men as well as women,[13] but the opposition of organized labor to protective legislation for men focused reformers' efforts on securing it for women. The 1938 Fair Labor Standards Act eventually provided federal protection for both sexes, but by the mid-sixties most states had numerous sex-specific laws governing the conditions under which women could work. The effect of these laws on women was controversial when they were passed, and continued so long after they were in place. Those who supported them, particularly the Women's Bureau of the Department of Labor, claimed they effectively reduced the economic exploitation of women. Those who opposed them, including the National Woman's Party and the National Federation of Business and Professional Women, argued that they kept women out of jobs requiring night work, and from promotions into positions requiring overtime or lifting of more than the prescribed weights. In fact, during War World II, protective labor laws were suspended to allow women to work in war industries, and were reimposed after the war, when women were forced to leave these jobs.[14]

Civil and Political Rights

It is a common myth that, when the Nineteenth Amendment extended suffrage to women on the same basis as men in 1920, all other civil and political rights automatically followed. In reality, few followed easily; most required continued struggle. In the first few years after Suffrage, there were even attempts to keep women from running for public office on the grounds that the right to vote did not bring with it the right to be voted on. One of the first uses to which women put their new right to vote was to change federal law to give women equal rights to citizenship with men. Although the English common law allowed married women to retain their citizenship when they married foreign nationals, in the nineteenth century both Britain and the United States adopted the idea that a married woman's nationality should be that of her husband. In 1907, the United States made this principle automatic regardless of where the couple lived or whether the husband intended to become a U.S. citizen. The first decade of the twentieth century was a period of heavy immigration, and the consequences of this law to native-born American women who married immigrants were quite onerous. Many states prohibited aliens from inheriting or buying real property, or closed them out of some professions (e.g., law, medicine, teaching). During World War I, many American women married to foreign nationals found themselves classified as enemy aliens and had their property confiscated. Feminists achieved one of their first legislative successes in 1922, when Congress passed an act separating a married woman's citizenship from that of her husband. However, this bill did not create equal citizenship rights, or completely rectify major injustices. For example, in 1928, Ruth Bryan Owen's election to Congress was challenged by her opponent on the grounds that she had not met the constitutional requirement of seven years of citizenship. Owen, daughter of frequent Democratic Presidential candidate William Jennings Bryan, had lost her citizenship in 1910 when she married a British army officer. The 1922 act did not automatically restore her citizenship, but only gave her the right to be renaturalized. The requirements were so burdensome that she had not been renaturalized until 1925. This injustice, and continual lobbying by women's organizations, prompted several revisions in the law until citizenship rights were finally equalized in the thirties.[15]

The longest battle was over jury service, which feminists believed was an important indicia of citizenship, even though potential jurors are often less than enthusiastic about being called to serve. Traditionally, under the common law, juries had been composed exclusively of men, except in certain situations involving a pregnant woman. In this country, the First Judiciary Act of 1789 mandated that federal jurors should have the same qualifications as those of the state in which the federal court was sitting, and no state permitted women to sit as jurors until Utah did so in 1898. Only twelve states conferred jury duty with enfranchisement. In the rest, many decades of trench warfare in the legislatures were necessary just to achieve the right to be in the jury pool; equal obligation to serve was the exception. It was not until the Civil Rights Act of 1957 that all citizens were qualified to sit on federal juries, regardless of state law. At that time, three states still completely excluded women (Alabama, Mississippi, South Carolina), and in only twenty-one were women eligible on the same basis as men were. In eighteen states and the District of Columbia, women were exempted based solely on their sex; in eight states, the exemption was limited to women with family responsibilities.[16]

Women have often found employment opportunities in the state and federal civil service that they did not find in the private sector, but they have also found these opportunities limited by law and by official rulings. In 1919, all federal civil-service examinations were finally opened to women, but each department head could specify the sex of those he wished to hire for any position. This was not changed until 1962. Ironically, the right to specify sex was *not* opposed by most women in government. Civil service rules gave veterans preference over nonveterans, and since few women were veterans, many were concerned that they would not be hired for even the lowest-level clerical jobs if sex could not be specified. However, they were all opposed to laws and administrative rulings that prohibited both spouses from holding government jobs; even when the rulings did not explicitly state that the wife would be the spouse to lose her job, that was the practice. The first attempt to remove married women from the federal civil service was made in 1921. This effort failed, but a similar one was finally successful in 1932. Since federal employees included school teachers in the District of Columbia and military draftees, a teacher married to an Army private could find herself dependent solely on his income. Many other states followed suit during the Depression, in the belief that hard times required that jobs be distributed as widely as possible. One job per family was the demand; removal of women was the outcome. Teachers were the hardest hit; by 1931 most school systems would not hire married women and would not retain women when they married. Although the federal law was repealed in 1937 and pressure on married women eased with World War II, when these women were needed in the labor force, state laws limiting their employment in government positions still existed as late as the fifties.[17]

For many decades, the courts made it clear that the traditional concern of public policy with women's family role went far beyond her legal rights and obligations within the marital relationship. Indeed, her family role formed the basis of her legal existence. The earliest case challenging a discriminatory law to reach the Supreme Court was instigated by Myra Bradwell, who objected to Illinois' refusal to admit women to the practice of law. She, and other women, looked to the newly ratified Fourteenth Amendment as an opportunity to remove some onerous legal barriers. In 1873, the Supreme Court rejected her argument that admission to the bar was a privilege and immunity of citizenship that could not be abridged by the states. Most telling was a concurring opinion by three justices, which explained that:

> The natural and proper timidity and delicacy which belongs to the female sex evidently unfits it for many of the occupations of civil life. The constitution of the family organization, which is founded in the divine ordinance, as well as in the nature of things, indicates the domestic sphere as that which properly belongs to the domain and functions of womanhood. The harmony, not to say identity, of interests and views, which belong, or should belong, to the family institution is repugnant to the idea of a woman adopting a distinct and independent career from that of her husband. . . .
>
> It is true that many women are unmarried and not affected by any of the duties, complications, and incapacities arising out of the married state, but these are exceptions to the general rule. The paramount destiny and mission of woman are to fulfill the noble and benign offices of wife and mother. This is the law of the Creator, and the rules of civil society must be adapted to the general constitution of things, and cannot be based upon exceptional cases.[18]

This rationale continued for almost a century. As late as 1961, Court decisions have reflected a refusal to see women as individual people in preference to their identity as members of a class with a specific social role. That year, a unanimous Court rejected a request by a Florida woman to overturn her conviction by an all-male jury for murdering her husband with a baseball bat during a "marital upheaval." Florida did not completely exclude women from jury service, but it was one of seventeen states that exempted women solely on the basis of their sex. This exemption took the form of assuming women did not wish to serve unless they registered a desire to do so with the court clerk, an assumption not made for men. Consequently, when Gwendolyn Hoyt's trial took place in 1957, only 220 women out of 46,000 eligible registered female voters had volunteered, and only ten of these were among the 10,000 people on the jury list constructed by the court clerk. The Court rejected her argument that "women jurors would have been more understanding or compassionate than men in assessing the quality of [her] act and her defense of 'temporary insanity'." Instead it ruled that

> the right to an impartially selected jury . . . does not entitle one . . . to a jury tailored to the circumstances of the particular case. . . . It

requires only that the jury be indiscriminately drawn from among those eligible in the community for jury service, untrammeled by any arbitrary and systematic exclusions. . . .

. . . Despite the enlightened emancipation of women from the restrictions and protections of bygone years, and their entry into many parts of community life formerly considered to be reserved to men, woman is still regarded as the center of home and family life. We cannot say that it is constitutionally impermissible for a State, acting in pursuit of the general welfare, to conclude that a woman should be relieved from the civic duty of jury service unless she herself determines that such service is consistent with her own special responsibilities.

. . .

This case in no way resembles those involving race or color in which the circumstances shown were found by this court to compel a conclusion of purposeful discriminatory exclusions from jury service. (cites omitted) There is present here neither the unfortunate atmosphere of ethnic or racial prejudices which underlay the situations depicted in those cases, nor the long course of discriminatory administrative practice which the statistical showing in each of them evinced.[19]

The Fourtenth Amendment

To understand the logic of the Court and to appreciate the significant change in orientation that the Supreme Court began in 1971, one has to understand the structure of legal analysis that has developed around the Fourteenth Amendment. The most far-reaching of the Civil War Amendments, the simple language of Section I imposed restrictions on state action that had previously been imposed on only the federal government. These were that

No state shall make or enforce any law which shall abridge the privileges or immunities of citizens of the United States; nor shall any State deprive any person of life, liberty, or property, without due process of law; nor deny to any person within its jurisdiction the equal protection of the laws.

The Supreme Court ruled very early that the "privileges and immunities" clause did not convey any rights that had not previously existed, and thus shut that avenue of legal development.[20] The due-process clause was for many decades used to undermine state economic regulations, such as those found unconstitutional in *Lochner* and *Adkins*, as well as most of the New Deal legislation prior to 1937. Consequently, the quest for equality has focused on the "equal-protection" clause. Until 1971, this quest was a futile one for women. Initially, the courts ruled that race and only race was in the minds of the legislators when the Fourteenth Amendment was passed. "We doubt very much whether any action of a state not directed by way of discrimination against negroes as a class or on account of their race will ever be held to come within the purview of this provision."[21] The prohibition on racial discrimination was soon expanded to include national origin[22] and alienage.[23] However, what is prohibited is not *all* legal discrimination, but only *invidious* discrimination. If a *compelling* state interest can be shown, distinct laws or state practices — such as those necessary to integrate school districts

—based on race or nationality are permitted. The essence of this approach is that certain classifications are "suspect" and thus are subject to "strict scrutiny" by the courts. Unless there is a "compelling state interest," they will be struck down. Classifications that are not suspect are not subject to the same searching inquiry. The state need only show that there is a rational basis for their existence, and the court will defer to the legislature.

In practice, classifications that are subject to strict scrutiny are almost always invalidated as unconstitutional. Classifications for which only a rational basis need be shown have almost always survived. The courts have shown great deference to the state legislatures and have gone out of their way to construct rationalizations for legal distinctions that to the untrained eye might seem to have only the flimsiest of reasons.[24] The consequence has been a "two-tier" system in which the level of analysis applied, rather than the reason for the classification, determines the outcome. The "strict scrutiny" test is usually fatal, whereas the "rational basis" test is usually meaningless. Thus, to eliminate a legal classification, one has to convince the courts that it should be subject to strict scrutiny.

The Turning Point: *Reed* and *Frontiero*

Only ten years after *Hoyt*, the Supreme Court changed its view. The turning point came in 1971, when the Court unanimously held unconstitutional an Idaho statute giving preference to males in the appointment of administrators of estates. In *Reed v. Reed*[25] the Court found the "administrative convenience" explanation of the preference for males to have no rational basis. Although unexpected, this development was not unforeseeable. During the previous few years, the Court had been adding a bit of bite to the rational basis test by looking more closely at state rationalizations as they applied to *some* statuses or *some* interests that did not trigger strict scrutiny.[26] During the previous two years the emerging women's movement had become publicly prominent, and the Equal Rights Amendment had been battling its way through Congress.[27] A still stronger position was taken 17 months later, when Air Force Lieutenant Sharon Frontiero challenged a statute that provided dependency allowances for males in the uniformed services without proof of actual economic dependency, but permitted them for females only if they could show they paid one-half of their husband's living costs. Eight members of the Court found the statute unconstitutional, but they split as to the reason. Four applied strict scrutiny, using language very different from that of previous cases.

> There can be no doubt that our Nation has had a long and unfortunate history of sex discrimination. Traditionally, such discrimination was rationalized by an attitude of "romantic paternalism" which, in practical effect, put women not on a pedestal, but in a cage.
>   . . .
> Moreover, since sex, like race and national origin, is an immutable characteristic determined solely by the accident of birth, the imposition of special disabilities upon the members of a particular sex because of

their sex would seem to violate "the basic concept of our system that legal burdens should bear some relationship to individual responsibility. . . . " *Weber v. Aetna Casualty & Surety Co.,* 406 U.S. 164, 175 (1972). And what differentiates sex from such nonsuspect statuses as intelligence or physical disability, and aligns it with the recognized suspect criteria, is that the sex characteristic frequently bears no relation to ability to perform or contribute to society. As a result, statutory distinctions between the sexes often have the effect of invidiously relegating the entire class of females to inferior legal status without regard to the actual capabilities of its individual members.[28]

Three justices found the statute unconstitutional on the authority of *Reed* — that administrative convenience was not a rational basis — while deliberately avoiding the characterization of sex as a suspect classification.[29] They gave as the compelling reason for such avoidance the fact that

the Equal Rights Amendment, which if adopted will resolve the substance of this precise question, has been approved by the Congress and submitted for ratification by the States. If this Amendment is duly adopted, it will represent the will of the people accomplished in the manner prescibed by the Constitution. By acting prematurely and unnecessarily. . . . the Court has assumed a decisional responsibility at the very time when state legislatures, functioning within the traditional democratic process, are debating the proposed Amendment. It seems . . . that this reaching out to pre-empt by judicial action a major political decision which is currently in process of resolution does not reflect appropriate respect for duly prescribed legislative processes.[30]

Intermediate Scrutiny

In cases after *Reed* and *Frontiero,* the Court applied a "strict rational-basis" standard with greater and greater scrutiny, until in 1976 a new standard, subsequently referred to as one of "intermediate scrutiny," was articulated. On the surface, *Craig v. Boren* did not appear to be a potentially momentous case. It concerned an Oklahoma law that prohibited the selling of "3.2" beer to men under twenty-one, but allowed its sale to women over eighteen. The state's rationale for this law was that more than ten times as many males as females between eighteen and twenty-one were arrested for drunk driving. The Court found the law unconstitutional, holding that "classifications by gender must serve important governmental objectives and must be substantially related to achievement of those objectives." It was not satisfied that "sex represents a legitimate, accurate proxy for the regulation of drinking and driving."[31]

After *Craig,* the Court no longer wrote plurality opinions in which some justices supported use of strict scrutiny in gender cases and others concurred or dissented on a different basis. Instead the "heightened scrutiny" of the new intermediate standard was applied consistently, although not unanimously, usually but not always to strike down laws that made distinctions by sex. Yet, even before *Craig,* the language of the post-*Reed* decisions reflected an approach by the Court to women's status very different from that taken in previous cases. No longer was a woman's family status the determinant of her legal status. Instead, the very articulation by a state of the desirability of economic dependency or of women's unique responsibility for family obligations to justify a sex-discriminatory law was viewed as irrational. Two cases decided in the spring of 1975 illustrate this profound transformation from the assumptions of *Hoyt* and earlier cases.

Weinberger v. Wiesenfeld challenged a provision of the Social Security Act that provided benefits for the surviving widow and minor children of a working man covered by the Act, but for only the minor children of a covered woman. The unanimous opinion of the Court pointed out that

> Since the Constitution forbids . . . gender-based differentiation premised upon assumptions as to dependency . . . [it] also forbids the gender-based differentiation that results in the efforts of female workers required to pay social security taxes producing less protection for their families than is produced by the efforts of men.

The Court further recognized the father's as well as the mother's responsibility for child care.

> It is no less important for a child to be cared for by its sole surviving parent when the parent is male rather than female. And a father, no less than a mother, has a constitutionally protected right to the "companionship, care, custody, and management" of "the children he has sired and raised."[32]

A month later, the Court went further in *Stanton v. Stanton,* a Utah case in which a divorced father ceased paying child support for his daughter when she reached age eighteen, but continued that for his son on the grounds that in Utah girls were no longer minors after they reached age eighteen, but boys were minors until age twenty-one. The Court found that

> No longer is the female destined solely for the home and the rearing of the family, and only the male for the marketplace and the world of ideas. . . . If the female is not to be supported so long as the male, she hardly can be expected to attend school as long as he does, and bringing her education to an end earlier coincides with the role-typing society has long imposed.[33]

The Supreme Court has continued to strike down state statutes that reinforced role-typing and economic dependency, or that rested on "archaic and overbroad generalizations." In doing so, it has invalidated statutes that provided Social Security benefits payable to widows but not to widowers,[34] that provided alimony for wives but not for husbands,[35] that permitted an unwed mother but not the father to block adoption of illegitimate children,[36] that paid welfare benefits to families with unemployed fathers but not to those with unemployed mothers,[37] and that gave worker's compensation death benefits to widows, but to widowers only if they could prove economic dependency.[38]

Revising Old Rulings

This change in perspective brought a new look at old decisions and took the court to some new conclusions. In 1975, *Taylor v. Louisiana* gave it an opportunity to review a statute limiting women's jury service that was virtually identical to the one it had upheld in *Hoyt* in 1961. At that time, although no state completely excluded women, and even Florida had revised its law, women were still eligible for special exemptions in many states.[39] Taylor had been sentenced to death for aggravated kidnapping, but even before he was tried he claimed denial of his Sixth Amendment right to a fair trial by "a representative segment of the community." This time the Court agreed. While it did not specifically overrule *Hoyt,* it did say *Hoyt* was out of date. Substantiating its position with a lengthy footnote on women's labor-force participation, the Court concluded, "If it was ever the case that women were unqualified to sit on juries or were so situated that none of them should be required to perform jury service, that time has long since passed."[40]

In 1982, the Court also ruled for the third time in twelve years on the issue of whether sex-segregated schools were violative of the Constitution, and for the first time, in a very limited context, it held that they were. This change illustrates how far the Court has come in what, for legal doctrine, is a very short period of time. Mississippi University for Women (MUW) had established a Nursing School in 1970. Like the rest of its programs, this one was restricted to women only. Men could audit classes, and could participate as though they were students, but they could not matriculate. A male registered nurse who lived in the town in which MUW was located wanted to earn a bachelor's degree in nursing but did not want to move to attend one of the other two schools in Mississippi that offered that degree and were coeducational. In a 5 to 4 decision written by the newest member of the Court, Justice Sandra Day O'Connor, the Court held that "MUW's policy of excluding males from admission . . . tends to perpetuate the stereotyped view of nursing as an exclusively woman's job," and thus is not consistent with the state's claimed justification that the single-sex admissions policy "compensates for discrimination against women and, therefore, constitutes educational affirmative action." Instead the Court found that the "policy of permitting men to attend classes as auditors fatally undermines its claim that women, at least those in the School of Nursing, are adversely affected by the presence of men."[41]

The Court had found differently only twelve years previously when it affirmed without a written opinion the ruling of a District judge that men could not attend South Carolina's female-only state college.[42] The lower court had relied on the rational basis test — eight months before *Reed.* Midway between these two cases, a more ambivalent Court had split 4 to 4 (Justice Rehnquist did not participate) on whether or not Philadelphia could maintain sexually segregated public high schools. Although the city had many co-ed schools, it had only two college preparatory high schools for academically superior students — one for boys and one for girls. Susan Vorchheimer did not want to be forced to choose between a co-ed environment and an academically enriched one. However, the schools were similar in their offerings except for a better science curriculum at that for boys, and Vorchheimer did not maintain that she wanted to attend the boys' high school to avail herself of science courses. The district court found that the School Board could not substantiate "separate but equal" schools, but the circuit court found otherwise. Placing great weight on Vorchheimer's failure to allege any educational deprivation, and the fact that attendance at the superior schools was voluntary, it completely ignored the "intangible factors" on which the Supreme Court had relied in dismantling racially segregated schools. "If there are benefits or detriments inherent in the system, they fall on both sexes in equal measure." By dividing equally on appeal, the Supreme Court left the decision in force but without the precedential value of an affirmation.[43]

Current Rationales for Sex-Discriminatory Laws

In upholding sex-segregated schools, the circuit court in *Vorchheimer* had relied on the Supreme Court decision in *Kahn v. Shevin*. This case established one of the two rationales on which sex-discriminatory statutes have continued to be upheld: that women benefit. Decided in 1974, before *Craig* but after *Frontiero,* it upheld a Florida statute giving widows, but not widowers, a $500 property-tax exemption. The majority ruled that the state law was "reasonably designed to further the state policy of cushioning the financial impact of spousal loss upon the sex for which that loss imposes a disproportionately heavy burden,"[44] without questioning whether there might be some more appropriate indicator than sex of financial incapacity. Even after *Craig* established a more stringent standard than reasonableness, the Court continued to look favorably on statutes that it thought operated "to compensate women for past economic discrimination." *Califano v. Webster* upheld a Social Security provision that, prior to 1972, permitted women to eliminate more low-earning years from the calculation of their retirement benefits than men were permitted to eliminate because it "works directly to remedy some part of the effect of past discrimination."[45]

Schlesinger v. Ballard introduced the second rationale, that men and women are not "similarly situated." Federal statutes that provided more time for female than for male naval officers to attain promotion before mandatory discharge were upheld as being consistent with the goal of providing women equitable career-advancement opportunities. The Court found that, because women were restricted from combat and most sea duty, it would take longer for them to compile favorable service records than it would for men. Therefore, "the different treatment of men and women naval officers . . . reflects, not archaic and overbroad generalizations, but, instead the demonstrable fact that [they] are *not* similarly situated with respect to opportunities for professional service."[46] This explanation was also relied on to uphold a California statute that made statutory rape a crime that only males could commit against females. The state Supreme Court had already subjected the classification to "strict scrutiny" and found a "compelling state interest" in preventing teenage pregnancies. Applying the lesser standard of "important governmental objectives," the Supreme Court came to the same conclusion, but only by ignoring the dissent's objection that a sex-specific statute was not "substantially related" to the stated goal as long as a gender-neutral one could achieve the same result.[47]

Draft Registration

This line of cases led inexorably to *Rostker v. Goldberg,* which contested the requirement that males but not females register for a potential draft. Draft registration had been discontinued in 1975, but was reactivated by President Carter in 1980 as part of his response to the Soviet invasion of Afghanistan. In his request to Congress for funds for this purpose, Carter also asked that the statute be amended to permit registration and conscription of females as well. After extensive debate, Congress left the statute intact. This activated a lawsuit that had begun in 1971 but been dormant for many years. Three days before draft registration was to begin, a lower federal court found the Act unconstitutional and enjoined the government from further registration. Relying on the intermediate scrutiny test of *Craig,* the court concluded that "military opinion, backed by extensive study, is that the availability of women registrants would materially increase flexibility, not hamper it."[48] The injunction was lifted and registration continued while the Supreme Court pondered the effect of its new approach to gender cases on the oldest bastion of the male establishment. In this effort, the Court was caught between the conflicting demands of two institutions to which it had traditionally deferred—the Congress and the military. The Court has always accorded great weight to the decisions of Congress, which had restricted registration to men. It has also deferred to judgments by the executive departments in the area of military affairs, and the military had testified before Congress that women should be registered (although not drafted). However, the Court noted that Congress' thorough consideration of the issue clearly established that its decision to exempt women was not the "accidental byproduct of a traditional way of thinking about females." It concluded that the "purpose of registration . . . was to prepare for a draft of *combat* troops" and that "women as a group, . . . unlike men as a group, are not eligible for combat." Because men and women were not "similarly situated" with regards to military service, it was not unconstitutional to distinguish between them. "The Constitution requires that Congress treat similarly situated persons similarly, not that it engage in gestures of superficial equality."[49]

On the surface, it might seem desirable for the Court to require equality where men and women are similarly situated, but to make exceptions apparently in women's favor where they are not. However, since there are very few circumstances in which men and women are similarly situated, this line of thought could easily lead to a return of the inequitable protectionism of the *Muller* era. The different standards that that case legitimated for men and women provided only limited benefits. In the long run, women were protected from better jobs, overtime, and the opportunity to compete with men rather than to be dependent on them.

An example of the consequences of protecting women from military service is to be found in *Personnel Administrator of Massachusetts v. Feeney.* While the federal government and almost all states give veterans preference for civil service jobs, Massachusetts is one of the few that gives them an absolute preference. After job candidates' scores have been computed on the basis of an examination and of an assessment of training and experience, those who pass are ranked. However, all passing veterans are ranked ahead of all nonveterans.[50] Consequently, nonveteran Helen Feeney had never been able to secure one of the many civil-service jobs for which she took examinations over a twelve-year period, even though she scored very high. She held a lower-level civil-service job during this period that was abolished in 1975, prompting her lawsuit. A lower federal court held the statute unconstitutional on the grounds that, while it was not intended to discriminate against women, since only 1.8 percent of the veterans in Massachusetts were female, the exclusionary impact was so severe that the state should be required to find a less extreme form of rewarding veterans. The Supreme Court found otherwise. Ignoring the fact that until recently women were restricted to only 2 percent of the armed forces, the Court nonetheless said that a neutral law with an adverse impact is unconstitutional only if discriminatory intent can be shown. It rejected the argument that the exclusion of women was such an inevitable and foreseeable consequence that the Massachusetts legislature must be held responsible for intending it even if that were not the primary objective. Instead the Court said that "the law remains what it purports to be: a preference for veterans of either sex over nonveterans of either sex, not for men over women."[51]

The Court has held in three other cases that gender-neutral distinctions that nonetheless had a discriminatory impact were not unconstitutional. *Geduldig v. Aiello* upheld the exclusion of pregnancy from coverage under the California disability insurance system. The Court said that the "program does not exclude anyone from benefit eligibility because of gender but merely removes one physical condition—pregnancy—from the list of compensable disabilities. While it is true that only women can become pregnant, it does not follow that every legislative classification concerning pregnancy is a sex-based classification. . . . "[52] *Parham v. Hughes* concerned a Georgia statute that permitted mothers but not fathers of illegitimate children to sue for the wrongful death of a child. Since fathers who subsequently legitimated their children could also sue, the court found that the actual distinction in the law was not one of gender but one between fathers who did and did not legitimate their children.[53] Similar reasoning was followed in *Lehr v. Robertson,* in which an illegitimate father objected to an adoption without his consent.[54] In these cases, findings that the distinction was not gender-based led the court to apply the rational basis test, and to conclude that the statute was reasonable.

LOWER FEDERAL AND STATE CASES

Not all cases challenging gender-based laws reach the Supreme Court. Since *Reed*, there have been hundreds of cases that were resolved by lower or state courts. In most cases, the federal courts, following the lead of the Supreme Court, have held gender-based distinctions to be invalid. Sometimes, they have not done so, and the case has not been appealed to the Supreme Court or has been denied review. When this happens, the geographical area over which that court has jurisdiction must abide by the decision, but courts elsewhere are free to formulate their own (although they are often influenced by other courts). Some courts have held to be constitutional laws that forbid a person of one sex to massage a person of another, B girls (but not boys) to solicit patrons for drinks, women (but not men) to work as topless dancers, and mothers to sign the driver's license applications of minors if the father is alive and has custody. A Maryland law that made it more difficult for husbands than for wives to prove libel if accused of extramarital sexual activity was also upheld. Laws that have been held to be unconstitutional include those that denied a wife the right to sue a third party for loss of her injured husband's consortium, that prohibited some bars from serving beverages to women, that established different ages for males and females to be tried in juvenile court or different sentences for convicts, and that required that the prefix "Miss" or "Mrs." appear before a woman's name on her voter-registration affadavit.[55]

When state courts have had to rule on gender-based laws or other state actions, they have generally looked to the Supreme Court and its current equal protection analysis, even when state equal rights amendments might have provided a different standard. Since 1968, fifteen states have added some form of equal-rights provision to their state constitutions or have included it in a general constitutional revision. Eight use language similar to that of the proposed federal amendment. Most of the others have clauses patterned after the equal-protection clause of the Fourteenth Amendment, with sex included as a category. The ERA states are Alaska, Colorado, Connecticut, Hawaii, Illinois, Louisiana, Maryland, Massachusetts, Montana, New Hampshire, New Mexico, Pennsylvania, Texas, Virginia, and Washington. Utah and Wyoming included similar provisions in their original constitutions when they became states in 1896 and 1890, respectively. The judicial decisions are highly varied. Washington and Pennsylvania courts have taken an even stricter approach than has the Supreme Court, striking down virtually all gender-based statutes, including ones that excluded women from contact sports dominated by men.[56] Several state supreme courts have avoided interpreting their equal rights amendments by deciding cases on other grounds or by refusing to review them at all. Utah, Louisiana, and Virginia have followed a traditional rational basis standard and have found virtually all sex-based laws to be reasonable. Several states have applied the strict scrutiny standard,[57] and others have relied on lesser standards (usually derived from the latest Supreme Court language) or have not articulated a specific standard. Thus, laws that have been held violative of an equal-rights amendment in some states have been upheld in others. Even in states where the highest court has held sex to be a suspect class, such as Illinois, lower state courts have applied the rule inconsistently, with the result that statutes invalidated in one jurisdiction are upheld in another.[58]

Of those states that do not have equal rights amendments, only California and Oregon have declared sex to be a suspect class, and California did so a few months before *Reed.*[59] Oregon did not even rely on the federal Constitution; in 1982, the state Supreme Court interpreted a long-standing state constitutional prohibition against granting any citizen or class of citizens special privileges to invalidate legal classifications by sex.[60] Several others have followed the Supreme Court in finding many sex-based statutes to be unreasonable. Yet even these states have found statutes to be rationally related to reasonable goals such as those permitting wives to share in their husband's property after divorce but not vice versa[61] and those prohibiting girls from having paper routes before age eighteen.[62]

Some issues, such as maternal preference in custody cases, have provoked extremely varied responses. The Utah supreme court found it "wise" that children should be in the care of their mother. Maryland permits the use of maternal preference as a tiebreaker. But in New York, where voters rejected a state ERA, a court held that the maternal preference rule violated the Fourteenth Amendment.[63]

Although courts acting under a state equal rights amendment are not limited to standard equal-protection analysis, few have chosen to break new paths. Those in states with equal rights amendments are likely to apply a stricter standard than are those in states without one, but most tend to follow the lead of the Supreme Court. Judges also respond to legislative history, the political culture of their own geographic area, current public debate, and their perception of the customs and mores about proper sex roles. In effect, courts are not institutions removed from society, responding only to legislative dictate and abstract legal analysis. Nor is the law static; instead, it is a tool, viable only when it is used actively. The changes in judicial attitude of the last few years have not occurred in a vacuum. They have been as much a response to the women's liberation movement as the many legislative changes have been.

LEGISLATIVE GAINS

The legislative changes in public policy have been as vast as the judicial changes, but they began earlier. The first federal law to improve women's economic position was the 1963 Equal Pay Act. First proposed in 1868 at the National Labor Union Convention, the Act did not become a national issue until World War I. During the war, women held jobs previously held by men, creating concern that they would depress the wage rates and that men would be forced to work at the lower rates after the war. Montana and Michigan enacted the first state equal-pay laws in 1919, but it was not until after World War II that a major bill covering 61 percent of the labor force was placed before Congress, and another fifteen years went by before it was passed.[64]

Title VII and the EEOC

When Congress debated the 1964 Civil Rights Act, one of the most controversial sections in it was Title VII, which prohibited discrimination in employment. At the urging of the National Woman's Party, Representative Howard W. Smith of Virginia, an ERA supporter but a civil-rights opponent, proposed a floor amendment to add "sex" to "race, religion, color and national origin." While this provision was strongly supported by the women of the House, most of the House liberals opposed it, as did the Women's Bureau of the Labor Department. They were concerned that this additional responsibility would dilute enforcement efforts for minorities. Nonetheless, neither side felt strongly enough about it to spend more than a few hours in debate, and little of this was serious.[65] The Equal Employment Opportunity Commission (EEOC), created to enforce Title VII, responded to this mandate by ignoring the sex provision. This led several people within the EEOC, and many outside it, to think that it was necessary to create an organized group supporting women's rights to put pressure on the government. As government employees, they could not organize such a group, but they spoke privately with those whom they thought could do so, including Betty Friedan and many members of the state Commissions on the Status of Women. Partially as a result of their efforts, the National Organization for Women (NOW) was formed in 1966; it directed a good portion of its initial energies at changing the guidelines of the EEOC.[66]

Initially, the EEOC supported protective labor laws, largely because organized labor had fought for them for years and had argued that they were a necessary protection for women. Despite this lack of support, many blue-collar women who believed their denial of job opportunities was justified by employers on the basis of state protective laws saw Title VII as an opportunity to take their cases to court. The court decisions were repeatedly in their favor. Within a few years, virtually all such laws were rendered void, or were subsequently applied to men as well. These court rulings — none of which reached the Supreme Court — not only forced the EEOC to change its rules, but also paved the way for passage of the Equal Rights Amendment (ERA). The primary opposition to the ERA had always been from those who feared it would eradicate protective labor laws. By 1970, this issue was moot. Thus, by the time the emerging new feminist movement was turning its attention to the ERA, its only major opposition was fading from the field. After a two-year battle led by Martha Griffiths in the House, involving a potpourri of feminist, women's, establishment, and liberal organizations, the ERA was sent to the states for ratification on March 22, 1972.[67]

Although the ERA was not ratified, the two-year battle had beneficial side effects. It created a recognition in Congress that there was a serious constituent interest in women's rights, and established liaisons between feminist organizations and congressional staff. With this impetus, the same Congress that sent the ERA to the states passed a bumper crop of women's rights legislation — considerably more than all relevant legislation previously passed in the history of this country. In addition to the ERA, there were laws that (1) expanded the coverage of Title VII and the enforcement powers of the EEOC; (2) prohibited sex discrimination in all federally aided education programs (Title IX); (3) added sex discrimination to the jurisdiction of the U.S. Commission on Civil Rights; (4) prohibited sex discrimination in state programs funded by federal revenue sharing; (5) provided free day care for children of poor families and a sliding fee scale for higher-income families, which was vetoed by President Nixon; (6) provided for a child-care tax deduction for some parents; and (7) added prohibitions against sex discrimination to a plethora of federally funded programs, including health training, Appalachian redevelopment, and water pollution.

Subsequent Congresses have not passed as many major laws in this area, but they have been active. Their actions include passage of the Equal Credit Opportunity Act; passage of the Women's Educational Equity Act, which provides grants to design programs and activities to eliminate stereotyping and to achieve educational equity; creation of the National Center for the Control and Prevention of Rape; an amendment to the Foreign Assistance Act requiring particular attention be given to programs; initiation of projects and activities that tend to integrate women into the national economies of foreign countries; prohibitions of discrimination in the sale, rental, or financing of housing; passage of an amendment to Title VII to include pregnancy in employment disability insurance coverage; admission of women to the military academies; and addition of still more antidiscrimination provisions to federally funded programs.

The states have also been active arenas in the last fifteen years. Laws have been passed in most states prohibiting sex discrimination in employment, housing, and credit, and in some states prohibiting discrimination in insurance, education, and public accommodations. Most states now have no-fault divorce provisions; all but four have equal custody and support laws (two others have equal custody but provide support for only the wife). The changes have been partially a result of pressure from feminist and other public-interest groups and partially in response to changes in federal legislation and Supreme Court decisions. Many states have followed the lead of the federal government in conducting studies to identify gender-based distinctions in their laws and to recommend changes. Most of these studies were carried out in response to efforts to adopt a state equal rights amendment or to ratify the federal amendment.

THE CHALLENGES AHEAD

Although the successes of feminist groups in achieving legislative changes are notable, there are also some outstanding failures. The most prominent is the failure to stop the antiabortion movement from curtailing women's constitutional right to abortions. The most unnoticed is the failure to make child care a national issue. After presidential vetoes by Nixon and Ford, all Carter had to do was to have a member of his administration testify against a proposed bill in 1979 to kill that bill in the Senate committee. In the last several years, there has been a burgeoning interest in child care due to the enormous increase in the number of mothers of small children in the labor force and the realization that lack of child care is an impediment to getting women off welfare. But this interest has not been led by feminist organizations; indeed, much of it has originated with conservatives. Feminist groups also failed, largely by not trying, to retain a provision to lessen veterans' preference in the 1978 Civil Service Reorganization Act. Their attention that year was devoted solely to extending the deadline to ratify the ERA.

This issue aside, the failures are largely on issues that touch on the family.[68] They point to what will be the biggest challenge to developing future public policy affecting women: breaking the tradition that a woman's obligations and opportunities are and should be primarily defined by her family circumstances. Although most of the legislation, as well as administrative and court rulings, of the last two decades have ignored women's family status, they were able to do so because the particular issues were economic ones, and in a time of an expanding economy and expanding welfare roles, it seemed expeditious—even conservative—to enhance a woman's right to support herself. But there is still a fundamental assumption that the principle economic unit is the two-parent family, only *one* of whom is the primary wage earner, with the other being a dependent.

It is this assumption that feminist theory and feminist policy proposals need to challenge. Feminist proposals must recognize that all adults should have responsibility for the support of themselves and their children, regardless of their individual living situation, and that all are entitled to policies that will facilitate carrying out this responsibility regardless of sex, or marital or parental status. Acceptance of this idea would require an entire reconception of women's role in the labor force, of what is a family, and of what our social obligations to the family are. It would also involve the recognition that one cannot have primary responsibility both to a career and to a family, and that rather than divide such responsibilities by sex, as is done now, we should make modifications in both so that women and men can participate equally in both.

The current attitude toward the employment of women can best be characterized as supporting "equal employment opportunity." This view asserts that women who are like men should receive the same treatment as do men. Although much improved over earlier views, it accepts as standard the traditional male lifestyle, and that standard in turn assumes that one's primary responsibility should and can be one's job, because one has a spouse (or spouse surrogate) whose primary responsibility is the maintenance of house and family obligations. Women whose personal lifestyle and resources permit them to fit these assumptions could, in the absence of sex discrimination, succeed equally with men.

But most women cannot do so, however, because our traditional conception of the family, and of woman's role within the family, make this impossible. Despite the fact that less than 10 percent of all adults live in units composed of children plus two adults, only one of whom is income producing, our entire social and economic organization assumes this unit as the norm and maintains that it is socially desirable for one class of adults to be economically dependent on another. Consequently, couples who equalize family responsibilities, or singles who take on them all, pay a price for deviancy. And women who spend the greater part of their lives as dependent spouses only to find their "career" ended by death or divorce pay a price for conformity. The fact that a majority of the population is paying these prices is compelling some reforms, but what is necessary is a total reorganization.

This reorganization must abolish institutionalized sex-role differences and the concept of adult dependency. It must recognize the individual as the principle economic unit, regardless of in what combinations individuals do or do not choose to live, and must provide the necessary services for individuals to support themselves and help to support their children. In pursuit of these goals, programs and policies need to make participation by everyone in the labor force to the full extent of their abilities both a right and an obligation. They should also encourage and facilitate the equal assumption of family responsibilities without regard to sex, as well as develop ways to reduce conflict between the conduct of one's professional and private lives. Although transition policies are necessary to mitigate the consequences of adult dependency, the goal should be abolition of the sexual division of labor. These policies should not permanently transfer dependency from "breadwinners" (male earners) to society in general, nor should they encourage dependency for a major portion of a person's life by extolling dependency's benefits and minimizing its costs. Instead, transitional policies should educate women to the reality that they are ultimately responsible for their own economic well-being, but are entitled to the opportunities to achieve it.

Needless to say, the consequences of revising our policies to focus on the individual rather than on the family as the basic economic unit, deliberately to eradicate the sexual division of labor in both the family and the work force, to establish equal participation in the labor force as a right as well as an obligation, and to institutionalize the support services necessary to achieve these goals, would not be felt by only women. Such policy changes would reverberate throughout our entire economic and social structure. Thus, we should not anticipate their achievement in the near future. But we will not be able to anticipate their achievement at all until the ideas are raised and the need for change understood. To do this, the feminist movement needs to return to its origins, and to begin the process of questioning and consciousness raising all over again.

NOTES

1. *United States v. Yazell,* 382 U.S. 341, 361 (1966) (Black, J., dissenting).

2. Edward Mansfield, *The Legal Rights, Liabilities and Duties of Women,* Salem, Mass.: Jewett and Co., 1845, p. 273.

3. 41 *American Jurisprudence Second,* "Husband and Wife" § 348. A husband was not chargeable for any debts other than necessities. There are many state court decisions on what constitutes a necessity, and what proof must be offered that a husband failed to supply it.

4. They are California, Idaho, Texas, Washington, Arizona, Louisiana, Nevada, and New Mexico.

5. *Kirchberg v. Feenstra,* 450 U.S. 455 (1981).

6. Since these laws have changed over time, there is no single source. The *Handbook on Women Workers,* published by the Women's Bureau of the Department of Labor every few years since its inception in 1920, usually has a section on state laws. In the early sixties, State Commissions on the Status of Women compiled the laws of their states. Leo Kanowitz summarized the status of *Women and the Law: The Unfinished Revolution,* Albuquerque: University of New Mexico Press, 1969, as it existed in the mid-sixties. And various legal reference works, such as *American Jurisprudence Second,* regularly compile and annotate state court decisions on different aspects of the law, including those affecting women.

7. *Equal Rights,* Nov. 8, 1924, p. 307; Jan. 31, 1925, p. 403.

8. *United States v. Yazell,* 382 U.S. 341 (1966).

9. Elizabeth Baker, *Technology and Women's Work,* New York: Columbia University Press, 1964, pp. 91–96.

10. Quoted in Alice Henry, *The Trade Union Woman,* New York: Appleton and Co., 1915, p. 24.

11. *Lochner v. New York,* 198 U.S. 45, 53 (1905).

12. *Muller v. Oregon,* 208 U.S. 412, 422 (1908).

13. *Bunting v. Oregon,* 243 U.S. 426 (1917). An exception was minimum wage legislation, which the Supreme Court would not uphold for either men or women until Justice Roberts's dramatic reversal of his opposition to Roosevelt's New Deal legislation in 1937 shifted the direction of the 5 to 4 decisions. Compare *Adkins v. Children's Hospital,* 261 U.S 525 (1923) with *West Coast Hotel Co. v. Parrish,* 300 U.S. 379 (1937).

14. Baker, pp. 401–4.

15. J. Stanley Lemons, *The Woman Citizen: Social Feminism in the 1920s,* Urbana, Ill.: University of Illinois Press, 1973, pp. 63–8, 235–6. The House Committee on Elections responded favorably to Owen's eloquent appeal and condemnation of the limitations of the 1922 Cable Act. It recommended she be seated, and the House concurred.

16. The common-law doctrine was appropriately called "propter defectum sexus" or a "defect of sex." Lemons, pp. 69–73. The *Handbook of Women Workers* also lists the statutes on jury service. Federal law is at 28 U.S.C. § 1861.

17. Lemons, p. 79. Susan Ware, *Holding Their Own: American Women in the 1930s,* Boston: Twayne, 1982, p. 28. Lois Scharf, *To Work and to Wed: Female Employment, Feminism, and the Great Depression,* Westport, Conn.: Greenwood Press, 1980, Chapter 4.

18. *Bradwell v. Illinois,* 83 U.S. (16 Wall.) 130, 141–142 (1873), (J. Bradley, concurring). See also *Ex parte Lockwood,* 154 U.S. 116 (1893).

19. *Hoyt v. Florida,* 368 U.S. 57, 59. 61, 62, 68 (1961).

20. *Slaughter House Cases,* 83 U.S. (16 Wall.) 36 (1872).

21. Ibid.

22. *Yick Wo v. Hopkins,* 118 U.S. 356 (1886).

23. *Truax v. Raich,* 239 U.S. 33 (1915).

24. Laurence H. Tribe, *American Constitutional Law,* New York: The Foundation Press, 1978, pp. 994–1002. "Strict scrutiny" is also employed where fundamental rights, such as voting, travel, procreation, criminal appeals or those protected by the First Amendment, are involved.

25. *Reed v. Reed,* 368 U.S. 57 (1971).

26. Tribe, p. 1082.

27. Jo Freeman, *The Politics of Women's Liberation,* New York: McKay, 1975, pp. 147–148, 213–220.

28. *Frontiero v. Richardson,* 411 U.S. 677, 684, 686–687 (1973). This opinion was subscribed to by Justices Brennan, Douglas, White, and Marshall.

29. The three were Powell, Burger, and Blackmun. Justice Stewart concurred without joining either opinion, and Justice Rehnquist dissented for the reasons stated in the district court opinion, *Frontiero v. Laird,* 341 F.Supp. 201 (1972), that administrative convenience was a rational basis. If Stewart had joined the four justices who wrote the plurality opinion, sex would have become a "suspect" classification. This would have changed many subsequent judicial decisions, particularly by state and lower federal courts, and perhaps made the state and federal ERAs *legally* unnecessary.

30. *Frontiero v. Richardson,* 411 U.S. 677, 692 (1973).

31. *Craig v. Boren,* 429 U.S. 190, 197, 204 (1976).

32. *Weinberger v. Wiesenfeld,* 420 U.S. 636, 645, 652 (1975).

33. *Stanton v. Stanton,* 421 U.S. 7, 14–15 (1975).

34. *Califano v. Goldfarb,* 430 U.S. 199 (1977).

35. *Orr v. Orr,* 440 U.S. 268 (1979).

36. *Caban v. Mohammed,* 441 U.S. 380 (1979).

37. *Califano v. Westcott,* 443 U.S. 76 (1979).

38. *Wengler v. Druggists Mutual Insurance Company,* 446 U.S. 142 (1980).

39. In 1966 a three-judge federal district court found Alabama's total exclusion unconstitutional under the Fourteenth Amendment, *White v. Crook*, 251 F.Supp. 401 (M.D. Ala. 1966), and the Supreme Court of Mississippi ruled that "the legislature has the right to exclude women so they may continue their service as mothers, wives and homemakers, and also to protect them . . . from the filth, obscenity and noxious atmosphere that so often pervades a courtroom during a jury trial." *State v. Hall*, 187 So.2d. 861, 863 (Miss.), appeal dismissed 385 U.S. 98, 87 S.Ct. 331, 17 L.Ed.2d 196 (1966). Mississippi's law was changed by the legislature in 1968, and South Carolina's by a voter referendum in 1967. According to the 1975 *Handbook on Women Workers*, at that time six states exempted women solely on the basis of sex, and ten allowed only women to be excused due to family responsibilities; p. 366.

40. *Taylor v. Louisiana*, 419 U.S. 522, 537 (1975). Seven justices joined in the opinion. Burger concurred and Rehnquist dissented. Because the decision rested on the Sixth Amendment establishing the rights of criminal defendants, the states could still exclude or limit women's participation on civil juries. However, both criminal and civil juries are drawn from the same pool, so the practical effect of *Taylor* was to remove all sex specific restrictions on all juries.

41. *Mississippi University for Women et al. v. Joe Hogan*, 458 U.S. 718. 73 L.Ed.2d 1090, 1100, 1101–1102. 102 S.Ct. 331 (1982). However, since Congress in Title IX of the 1972 Educational Amendments Act had specifically authorized the continuance of single-sex public undergraduate institutions which "traditionally and continually from its establishment has had a policy of admitting only students of one sex," 20 U.S.C. § 1681(a), this ruling probably applies only to the School of Nursing and not to the entire University.

42. *Williams v. McNair*, 401 U.S. 951 (1971) affirming 316 F.Supp. 134 (D.S.C. 1970).

43. *Vorchheimer v. School District of Philadelphia*, 430 U.S. 703 (1977), 532 F. 2d 880, 886, (3rd Cir. 1976), overturning 400 F. Supp. 326 (E.D.Pa. 1975).

44. *Kahn v. Shevin*, 416 U.S. 351, 355 (1974).

45. *Califano v. Webster*, 430 U.S. 313, 318 (1977). Ruth Bader Ginsburg argues that this case is very different from *Kahn* in that the "Court's majority opinion . . . carefully distinguishes knee-jerk categorization by sex from legislation deliberately enacted to compensate for discriminatory conditions encountered by a group not dominant in society. . . . *Webster* thus attempts to preserve and to bolster a general rule of equal treatment while leaving a corridor for genuinely compensatory classification." She believes that this kind of "affirmative action" should be Constitutional. "Some Thoughts on Benign Classification in the Context of Sex," 10 *Connecticut Law Review* 822–23 (1978). While a professor at the Columbia University Law School and General Counsel to the American Civil Liberties Union, Ginsburg was the principal author of the brief in *Reed* and argued before the Supreme Court in *Goldfarb, Wiesenfeld, Kahn*, and *Frontiero*. She is currently a judge on the U.S. Court of Appeals for the District of Columbia.

46. *Schlesinger v. Ballard*, 419 U.S. 498, 508 (1975).

47. *Michael M. v. Superior Court of Sonoma County*, 450 U.S. 464, 472, (1981). Most states have gender-neutral statutory rape laws. Prior to this case three Circuit courts had struck down gender-based statutory rape laws, and the Supreme Court had declined a request to review one of them. See *Navedo v. Preisser*, 630 F.2d 636 (8th Cir. 1980), *U.S. v. Hicks*, 625 F.2d 216 (9th Cir. 1980), *Meloon v. Helgemoe*, 564 F.2d 602 (1st Cir. 1977), *cert. denied* 436 U.S. 950 (1978).

48. *Rostker v. Goldberg*, 509 F.Supp. 586, 603 (E.D. Pa. 1980).

49. *Rostker v. Goldberg*, 453 U.S. 57, 74, 76, 79 (1981). Women are restricted from combat in the Navy and Air Force by statute, 10 U.S.C. § 6015 and § 8549, and in the Army and Marine Corps by internal policy.

50. The benefits to veterans of this affirmative-action program can be seen in statistics on the Federal Civil Service, which only gives a point preference in computing scores. In 1979, women were 41 percent of those who passed the entry-level Professional and Administrative Exam, but only 27 percent of those who were hired. Veterans were 20 percent of those who passed, but 34 percent of those hired. Women were 41 percent of the civilian labor force, but only 30 percent of the civil service. Veterans were 25 percent of the labor force, but held 48 percent of all federal civil service jobs. Since many veterans are career military officers, retired after only 20 years with excellent pensions, training, and experience, they held 65 percent of the three highest grades in the civil service, while women held only 3.2 percent. Jo Freeman, "Women and

Public Policy, An Overview," *Women, Power and Policy,* ed. Ellen Boneparth, New York: Pergamon, 1982, p. 61.

51. *Personnel Administrator of Massachusetts v. Feeney,* 442 U.S. 256, 280 (1979), overturning 451 F.Supp. 143 (Mass. 1978).

52. *Geduldig v. Aiello,* 417 U.S. 484, 496 n20, (1974). However, the Seventh Circuit found unconstitutional a provision in the unemployment compensation law, which denied coverage to pregnant women who were willing and able to work. *International Union v. Indiana Employment Security Board, 600 F.2d.* 118 (7th Cir. 1979).

53. *Parham v. Hughes,* 441 U.S. 347 (1979).

54. *Lehr v. Robertson,* 463 U.S. 248 (1983).

55. These cases and others are reviewed by Daniel A. Per-Lee, "Validity, Under Equal Protection Clause of Fourteenth Amendment, of Gender-Based Classifications Arising by Operation of State Law — Federal Cases," 60 *Lawyer's Edition Second* 1188 (1979).

56. However, even Washington upheld the denial of a marriage license to two males on the grounds that both sexes were affected equally by the requirement that legal marriages be heterosexual. *Singer v. Hara,* 11 Wash. App. 247, 522 P.2d 1187 (1974). It also supported statutes requiring election of an equal number of men and women to Democratic party committees as a rational means to achieve desired equality. *Marchioro v. Chaney,* 90 Wash. 2d. 298, 582 P.2d. 487 (1978).

57. But this has not prevented them from upholding school regulations restricting the length of boys' but not girls' hair, *Mercer v. The Board of Trustees,* 538 S.W.2d. 201 (Tex. Civ. App. 1976), or prison regulations that required women visitors to male prisons to wear brassieres, *Holdman v. Olim,* 581 P.2d. 1164 (Hawaii 1978).

58. Comment, "Equal Rights Provisions: The Experience Under State Constitutions," 65 *California Law Review* 1086–1112 (1977); Paul M. Kurtz, "The State Equal Rights Amendments and Their Impact on Domestic Relations Law," 11 *Family Law Quarterly,* 101–150 (1977); Dawn Marie Driscoll and Barbara J. Rouse, "Through a Glass Darkly: A Look at State Equal Rights Amendments," 12 *Suffolk University Law Review* 1282–1311 (1978); Philip E. Hassman, "Construction and Application of State Equal Rights Amendments Forbidding Determination of Rights Based on Sex," 90 *American Law Reports Third* 158–216, (1979).

59. *Sail'er Inn v. Kirby,* 5 Cal. 3rd 1, 485 P.2d 529, 95 Cal. Rptr.. 329 (1971), invalidated a state statute prohibiting women from tending bar.

60. *Hewett v. State Accident Insurance Fund Corporation.* 294 Or. 33, 653 P.2d 970 (1982).

61. *M. v. M.,* 321 A.2d. 115 (Del. Sup. Ct. 1974).

62. *Warshafsky v. Journal Co.,* 63 Wis.2d. 130, 216 N.W.2d. 197 (Wis. 1974).

63. Compare *Cox v. Cox,* 532 P.2d. 994 (Utah 1975); *Cooke v. Cooke,* 21 Md. App. 376, 319 A.2d. 841 (Md. 1974); *State ex. rel. Watts v. Watts,* 77 Misc.2d. 178, 350 N.Y.S.2d. 285 (N.Y. Fam. Ct. 1973).

64. Jo Freeman, *The Politics of Women's Liberation,* (New York: David McKay, 1975) pp. 174–177.

65. Carl M. Brauer "Women Activists, Southern Conservatives, and the Prohibition of Sex Discrimination in Title VII of the 1964 Civil Rights Act," *The Journal of Southern History,* Feb. 1983, p. 37. 110 *Congressional Record,* February 8, 1964, pp. 2577–84.

66. Freeman, 1975, p. 54.

67. The actual transition from protective labor laws to equal employment opportunity took longer and was more complex, and a few such laws still remain on the books. See U.S. Dept. of Labor, Women's Bureau, *State Labor Laws in Transition: From Protection to Equal Status for Women,* 1976, and compare it with *Time of Change: 1983 Handbook on Women Workers,* Bulletin 298, Washington, D.C.: U.S. Government Printing Office, Chapter 7.

68. Joyce Gelb and Marian Lief Palley argue that success is more likely when the issue is perceived as effecting role equity — extending to women rights enjoyed by other groups — rather than role change. *Women and Public Policies,* 2d ed, (Princeton, N.J., Princeton University Press, 1987), p. 5.

Out of Order: A Critical Perspective on Women in Religion

MARTHA J. REINEKE

Religion expresses and shapes the ideals, hopes, and needs of humankind. When humans wish to distinguish those ideas and experiences that are of utmost seriousness and value in their lives from those that are of secondary importance, they find in religious beliefs and practices answers to their questions of "ultimate concern."[1] Religion classifies and organizes such key aspects of experience as sexuality, birth, death, power, and violence. It grounds a people's deepest convictions and provides a basis for decisions based on a knowledge of good and evil, right and wrong. Religion, more than any other institution, "patrols the borders" that separate order from disorder in society, dispensing information, protection, and judgments. Interestingly, when religion attends to meaning and order, chaos and disorder, the human body is among its most common reference points. Why the body?

In her ground-breaking study of religion, *Purity and Danger: An Analysis of the Concepts of Pollution and Taboo,* anthropologist Mary Douglas notes that "the more personal and intimate the source of ritual symbolism, the more telling its message. The more the symbol is drawn from a common fund of human experience, the more wide and certain its reception."[2] Religion, engaged in mental "fence making," appeals to the human body, rather than to actual door posts, fence rows, and stone walls for images of order and meaning because the body is the most intimate and certain of boundaries.[3]

Significantly, religion does not symbolically account for order and proscribe disorder in the world by appeal to generic human bodies. Rather, religion most often demarcates order from disorder by appeal to the *female* body. The female body, site of processes men have perceived historically as mysterious and potentially dangerous, offers a most graphic symbolism of issues of ultimate concern. Women carry potential for order and meaning

---

(life) and disorder or chaos (death) in their very bodies: menstruation (potential for life), reproduction (successful or miscarried creation), and aging (movement toward death) all testify to the triumphs and tragedies of existence. That religion, wanting to protect society from dangers that lurk on the margins of society, threatening disorder, acts most often against women is no wonder. Women, who symbolize with their bodies the powers and dangers to be contested, are also those humans least likely to have the power to protest the literal inscription of societal meaning on their bodies. Moreover, gender differences in women's and men's experience of religion can be traced to the role religion plays in advancing order and gaining control over the forces of disorder by controlling women and their bodies: Power asserted over women is power asserted over the very powers of creation.

How does this happen? In this essay, I want to examine how those religious myths, rituals, and sacred symbols that are focused on the human body are among the primary vehicles for (1) socializing women to gender roles, (2) assigning women to subservient positions within a gendered caste system, and (3) controlling women's sexuality through use of power. I will also, in assessing a "verdict" on religion that will be sensitive to women's current concerns about sexism, point to instances in which women have experienced religion in nonoppressive ways. By way of contrast, such examples offer important insights for women scholars about the possible role for religion in the creation of nonsexist societies.

RELIGION AND THE PRESCRIPTION OF GENDER ROLES

Maleness and femaleness are culturally established, and religion is a primary vehicle for this socialization process. Classification systems that specify appropriate female behavior and distinguish it from that of males establish and enforce order in society. A good example is found in the religion of Hinduism.

Hinduism, the religion of India, is preoccupied with questions of order and disorder. Hindus believe that humans are locked into a cycle of suffering and disorder that persists across numerous lifetimes. This endless cycle of rebirth, which Americans sometimes call "reincarnation," is more properly called *samsara*. *Samsara* is countered by religious wisdom. Hindus, united in their desire to achieve an ordered unity of existence that they call *moksha*—liberation or salvation from *samsara*—differ from one another only in the variety of ways they seek *moksha*. The caste system, an elaborate hereditary division of labor among persons, places Hindus at different points along a common journey to *moksha*. Each person is born into one of four major castes: *brāhman* (priests), *kshatriya* (warriors), *vaiśya* (artisans and merchants), or *śūdra* (peasants). Upward mobility within one's own life is not possible: One's current life is the just product of one's previous lives. However, across a series of lifetimes, liberation is possible. Fit for the particular degree of freedom offered by one's present caste and gender, each Hindu makes his or her own way through *samsara*, toward *moksha*. For the priests, for example, wisdom that liberates is a product of meditation on the unity of all things in Brahman: Cosmic Principle or Ultimate Reality. For others—peasants, for example—*moksha* is a bliss attained in devotion to a god or a goddess. Sacrifices to the god or goddess, celebrations, and festivals free the devotee from enslavement in the prison of *samsara* and bring the devotee close to that god and to *moksha*.[4]

Women in Hinduism are traditionally socialized to find the fulfillment of their lives and their purpose in being good wives and the mothers of sons. A good wife treats her husband as a god.[5] She embodies the virtues of self-sacrifice, submission, and patience. Her role in life is to facilitate her husband's spiritual journey to *moksha*. Because, according to Hinduism, a woman is defined solely in relation to her husband, an unmarried woman or a widow is a nonentity in Indian life. She falls outside the parameters of the classification system that describes appropriate female behavior. Consequently, the unmarried woman or widow poses a threat to societal order.

One consequence of this narrow definition of womanhood is the continuing practice of child marriages. Although the legal age of marriage is eighteen years, the most common age of females at the time of marriage, according to the most recent information, is nine.[6] To the extent that such early marriages are consummated and result in pregnancy, serious health problems may result. Another problem women face traditionally in India is widowhood. Because a husband's *karma* or spiritual status is intimately linked with his wife's, a widow enhances her husband's prospects for a higher rebirth or for *moksha* by either pursuing an ascetic life—begging for food, sleeping on the ground without shelter—or by joining her husband on his funeral pyre and dying with him. Although this latter custom has been outlawed, it continues in the form of "kitchen accidents." As a result of the often intolerable living conditions for widows, in the past three years some women have marched in New Delhi advocating the reinstatement of *sati,* or widow-burning.[7]

The experiences of women within Hinduism clearly illustrate the demarcation of order from disorder in Indian society through the inscription of order on female bodies. Hindu views of women mirror broad societal concerns about powers and dangers that lead Hindus who want to understand and control these powers and dangers to focus on the human body in general and on the female body in particular.

The human body provides the model for cultural order: The highest castes are associated with the human mind (meditation and knowledge); the lowest castes are associated with bodily waste (washers, barbers, sweepers). Crucial to the caste system is the control of order in the society by surveillance of body "borders." Disorder, in the form of pollution, lurks everywhere. For this reason, the society is particularly preoccupied with body orifices, which represent social exits and entrances.[8]

Bodily pollution threatens most at two points: material sustenance and reproduction. To share food is to share in the nature of another.[9] Yet, because food is produced through the combined efforts of persons of several castes—blacksmiths, carpenters, ropemakers, peasants—it is threatened by massive impurities. To counter impurity, elaborate precautions must be taken. Some food is, by definition, impure for the higher castes. Other food, potentially impure, is cleansed through rituals of preparation that constitute a symbolic break with the threat of disorder.[10]

More than those regarding food, concerns about women's roles in reproduction and about possible threats to hereditary purity constitute a central focus of Hinduism. Because cultural purity, which is the litmus test for cultural order, is transmitted biologically, Hinduism is to a great extent preoccupied with the protection and control of women's bodily orifices.[11] Children take their caste from their mother; hence, a woman who has sexual relations with a lower-caste man pollutes herself, endangers her future children, and subjects society as a whole to danger. For this reason, the chastity of unmarried female children is of great concern. Marriage prior to first menstruation is encouraged because the more likely virginity of the child-bride decreases the threat of pollution. The pressure is highest on Brahman (upper-caste) female children, for the threat of pollution from lower castes is greatest for them.

The caste system prescribes a hierarchy of order based on gender, which is no less significant than that based on the division of labor. Caste hierarchy, "writ large" in the world, is duplicated on a smaller scale within the family. There, when a woman treats her husband as a god, she duplicates the essence of the social hierarchy: Those who are lower in life offer themselves to the higher.[12] The ethics of self-sacrifice structure order at every point. For this reason, each woman adopts a life of extreme asceticism (self-denial) and service to her husband. She is taught that a woman's strength lies in her submission to her husband and is marked by service, chastity, and devotion. So significant is this lesson that even the stories of the gods and goddesses confirm its truth: A woman's feminine behavior constitutes the pillar of stability that supports even the cosmos.[13]

For humans, death constitutes a fundamental threat to societal stability, one that religions attempt to counter with rituals enacted on behalf of order. In Hinduism, not all persons can be insulated from the experience of death, but a man acquires through marriage a kind of "insurance" against the brute reality of death: He who attends properly to the requirements of a "good marriage" (i.e., a marriage that produces a son and a grandson) advances toward *moksha*. Moreover, a man's spiritual status can also be advanced by his wife's actions: Her devotion and sacrifices will enhance his prospects in his next life. A widow, assuming responsibility for her husband's death, feels guilt because she has failed as a result of lack of devotion or adequate sacrifice to ensure her husband's longevity.[14] The fundamental failure of human life — that we do not live forever — thus is made understandable (i.e., reasonable, orderly) when a woman takes responsibility for it, through ritual. Traditionally, that responsibility is exacted from a woman by widow-sacrifice: *sati*.[15] Less traditionally, and more commonly today, a widow lives on the margins of society. Greater asceticism is demanded from her than from a married woman. The widow shaves her head, lest her attractiveness create opportunities for sexual encounters that will bring impurities into the family. Eating as little as possible, demanding no shelter or material provisions, the widow will continue to live sacrificially, on the margins of life, on the verge of death.

The hierarchy of male and female lives is one aspect of a caste system in India. Another kind of caste system, founded on a less systematic, but no less powerful, subordination of women to men, exists in cultures influenced by three religions that originated in the Near (Middle) East: Judaism, Christianity, and Islam.

These three religions share in common the tenets of "ethical monotheism." All worship only one God and share an historical tradition about this God, who communicates with humans through prophets. Judaism, the oldest of the three, and Christianity have a common scripture, which records the relationship between God and humans: the Hebrew Bible is the Christian Old Testament.[16] In the Moslem scriptures—the Qur'an—the prophet Muhammad proclaims the fundamental belief in one God and recounts revelations about religious forebears (e.g., Moses, Abraham, Isaac, Mary, Jesus) known also to Christians and Jews.

Judaism, Christianity, and Islam also share a common concern for ethical behavior. Indeed, all three religions link the words "response" and "responsibility:" One who hears the word of God and *responds* is one who acts with *responsibility* to counter injustice and to create a more just world. Meaning and order are established in the world, and sin and disorder are challenged successfully to the extent that humans hear the word of God and are inspired to action.

Linked by a common focus on ethical behavior and the one God, Jews, Christians, and Moslems are distinguished from one another in their understandings of the word of God spoken to them. For Judaism, the definitive word of God is located in the Law (Torah). The Law constitutes a covenant (contract) between God and the people. Humans respond to God correctly when they keep the Law, for the basis of order and meaning in human existence is located there.

For Christianity, the word of God is decisively present in the life and teachings of Jesus. That Christianity is alone among the Western religions in divinizing its prophet accentuates the Christian claim that Jesus *is* God's presence and truth: He is the way, the truth, and the life. Meaning and order in human existence flow from Jesus, for in him "all things hold together" (Colossians 1:17).

Islam, the newest of the three religions that originated in the Near East, is distinguished from both Judaism and Christianity in its understanding of the word of God. According to Islam, because Judaism has increasingly misunderstood and distorted the authentic word of God spoken through Moses and recorded in the Torah, the word of God must be delivered to humans again. For Islam, the status of the word of God in Judaism is much like the status of a sentence at the end of the children's game of "telephone:" at its origin, the Torah spoke truth, but in Muhammed's day, the message had been so altered by various interpreters of Torah that its original meaning had been lost. The game had to be called off and a new speaker (Muhammed) summoned to express God's word clearly in the Qur'an, so that humans could again serve God.

According to Islam, Christian beliefs are also in error. Christians wrongly dilute the rigor of monotheism when they treat the prophet Jesus as a divine being, the Son of God. Were Christians to attend rightly to the *message* of God, rather than to the *messenger*, they would be on the correct path of faith, a path that culminates, not with any incarnate messenger of the one God, but with the direct revelation in the Qur'an of God's word.

We can detect caste differences ascribed to gender in Judaism, Christianity, and Islam. A caste system is visible wherever we can locate ''a social arrangement in which access to power and socioeconomic benefits are fixed, typically from birth, according to certain ascribed characteristics of the individual.''[17] Symbols, myths, and rituals are primary vehicles for the teaching of caste differences that are ascribed to gender. The morning prayer of male Orthodox Jews makes this explicit. It includes the phrase, ''Praised are you, O Lord our God, King of the Universe, who has not created me a woman.''[18] Creation stories often assign to women the responsibility for the presence of evil or troubles in the present world. In these myths, women's presumed characteristics of sexual allure, curiosity, and gullibility are often blamed for humankind's problems, primarily humankind's inattention to God's Law and word.

For example, folk Judaism attributes to Lilith, Adam's first wife, who refused to obey him and fled from him, all kinds of evils and dangers to family life. In this Jewish tradition, Lilith is contrasted with Eve who, as the second, and obedient, wife, was taken from Adam's side.[19] In Christianity, no Lilith tradition functions to consign evil to a runaway wife. Instead, Christian theology places the responsibility for evil squarely on Eve's shoulders. She caused humankind's fall away from obedience to God's word into sin. The early Christian theologian, Tertullian, for example, writes about Eve:

> You are the Devil's gateway. You are the unsealer of that forbidden tree. You are the first deserter of the divine law. You are she who persuaded him whom the Devil was not valiant enough to attack. You destroyed so easily God's image man. On account of your desert, that is death, even the Son of God had to die.[20]

To the extent that the Christian theologian depicts all women as Eve's daughters, women are responsible, as a caste, for evil in the world and for all of its consequences.

In other instances of Christian theology, the story of the Fall of humans into sin is interpreted, not in a way that blames woman (Eve) for evil in the world, but rather in a way that justifies and legitimates a gendered hierarchy. Women must be subordinate to man, but not so that she may be punished; rather, because the social order of the world has been transformed by human sin, woman's subordination to man is required for a return to order and obedience.

The Christian theologian Luther, for example, believes that in original creation Eve was the equal of Adam. Yet, through the Fall into sin, Eve, and all women after her, became inferior. For Luther, her subjugation is an expression of divine justice that reorders the affairs of the world to counter humans' earlier Fall away from God into disobedience and disorder:

This punishment too springs from original sin; and the woman bears it just as unwillingly as she bears those pains and inconveniences which have been placed upon her flesh. The rule remains with the husband, and the wife is compelled to obey him by God's command. He rules the home and the stage, wages war, defends his possessions, tills the soil, builds, plants, etc. The woman, on the other hand, is like a nail driven into the wall. She sits at home . . . the wife should stay at home and look after the affairs of the household as one who has been deprived of the ability of administering those affairs that are outside and concern the state. . . . In this way Eve is punished.[21]

The judgments that Luther wants to make about the origins of sin and about the painful and disruptive consequences of evil in the world are made in view of that most powerful of human symbols: the human body. Specifically, Eve's body, source of willful disobedience, both symbolizes the plight of humanity and points to the source of redemption. Redemption is possible for all humanity only if women bear the pain placed on their flesh, a pain that, in circumscribing their cultural position, effects the punishment necessary for humans to be returned to orderly relationship with one another and with God.

In statements of Jewish belief, located in important Jewish teachings called the Talmud, attitudes toward women also demonstrate the significance of caste hierarchy to societal order. Writings by the Pharisees and Flavius Josephus, for example, emphasize the inferiority of women to men. Women are "overcome by a spirit of fornication" and "plot in their hearts against men."[22] In both the *Book of Jubilees* and *The Testaments of the Twelve Patriarchs,* composed between 109 and 106 B.C.E., the danger of fornication with women (a danger to Judaism from within) is linked to the danger of foreign cultures (a danger to Judaism from without).[23] That all women are overcome with lust and harbor a predisposition for evil deeds becomes linked in the authors' minds with impending seduction of the Jews by foreign cultures. Women's bodies symbolize the powers and dangers to be contested if the covenant with God is to be kept.

In the Diaspora exile after 70 C.E., which occurred as a result of conquest by the Roman Empire, misogynistic tendencies are extended, in part, as a result of the ever greater challenges to Jewish identity in the face of the dispersion of the Jewish people beyond the borders of Palestine. That the wild and unruly sexuality of women requires strict subordination of women, as a caste, to men, underscores the need for greater order in the Jewish Diaspora.[24] Talmudic prescriptions for order and identity, "writ large," repeat earlier inscriptions of a moral code on women's bodies: Just as individual women must be discouraged from fornication, so also must Israel not play the harlot.

When compared with Judaism and Christianity, Islam most explicitly argues that social order depends on the careful attention to caste differences based on gender. Order in society is based on the separation of men's and women's lives into separate spheres. Men find their place in the public sphere and worship in the mosque; women find their place in the private sphere — the home — where they also pray. If a woman finds that she must leave the seclusion of the home to enter the public sphere, although such an act is discouraged in traditional Islam, she should be veiled from head to toe, so that no part of her body is displayed.[25]

The Islamic attribution of societal disorder to disobedient women is clearly visible in the Islamic imagery of Paradise: Paradise is "the Garden." It is a beautiful place with fountains, pastures, cool pavilions, fruits, and *hur:* lovely virgins. In the Garden, every male will have not only his wife but also seventy *hur.* The *hur* are never sick, never menstruate, and are never bad-tempered. Each time a man returns to a *hur,* he will find her virginity once again intact. Both daily human existence and imagery of the Judgment scene contrast dramatically with the Garden. In daily existence, women are sometimes sick and grumpy, they do menstruate, and their purity, after a single act of intercourse, is forever in doubt. In the Judgment scene, through which order is served and sinners are punished, the fantasy of Paradise is reversed: the sinful and disordered world condemned in the Judgment is a world in which women are in charge of men.[26]

Through use of such imagery, women are taught to conform to a caste role. They learn that good women are like the women of the Garden; bad women are like the women of the Judgment scene. Unfortunately, they also learn that women inevitably fall short of the required purity because they do menstruate and because, unlike the perpetually virginal *hur,* their virginity ends with the first act of intercourse. This sad truth, confirmed daily by women's bodies, serves in Islam both to justify men's wariness of women and to establish men's right to demand obedience of women, lest women's tendency toward immoral behavior throw the world into even greater disorder.

Of course, Judaism, Christianity, and Islam are not alone in ascribing order in society to women's obedience, and decay to their disobedience. Hinduism's goddess tradition provides another mythic explanation of gender differentiation. Hindu religious myths tell us that an independent or autonomous goddess is dangerous, and is prone to destructive use of her powers. Hence, Hindu goddesses are paired with male consorts—gods—by whom they are tamed and through whom their ambiguous powers are controlled.[27] To human women, goddesses represent the feminine ideal. They are chaste, virtuous, and obedient to their husbands. To depart from this ideal, by preserving one's autonomy through not marrying, is to flirt with danger. Just as demonic powers visit the independent goddess (e.g., Kali), so also will they visit independent human females. Dangers, large and small, are countered only as females—both divine and human—are obedient in their roles as wives. This symbolic message extends to a third area of primary linkage between religion and gender ideologies: power and sexuality.

POWER AND SEXUALITY

Religion—in ritual, word, and act—creates borders that separate societal order from disorder and protects these borders against threats from outside. To specify the boundaries of order, religion appeals to body symbolism, believing that a power asserted over the body is a power asserted in the social sphere and that a threat issued against the social body is a threat registered also by the human body. Religion acts to reinforce social order by controlling bodies and addresses fears about social disorder by appeal to fear of sexuality. Because the female body has been perceived historically as a source of dangerous power to be purified, controlled, and occasionally destroyed by men, women's bodies are the preferred focus in religious rituals and writings that aim to counter the forces of disorder.

One strong example of this thesis is visible in the Middle East between 800 and 500 B.C.E., when the Israelites moved into Canaan. The Canaanite society was agricultural and sedentary, and a large focus of Canaanite religious practice was symbols of fertility. Although the Canaanite society was not matriarchal in organization, power was diffused among both men and women.[28] Women took a primary role in the religious practices — assuming leadership in many temple rites devoted to gods and goddesses and celebrating fertility of land and people.[29] With the entrance of the Israelites into Canaan, military conflict was matched by cultural confrontation, for the Israelites were a strongly patriarchal, tribal society. Israelite leaders used religious rituals and beliefs — often focused on the female body — to distinguish ordered, approved beliefs and behaviors in Israel from those disruptive of order. Women, once major participants in temple rites and primary symbols of the celebrated sexuality of males and females, came to represent powers of fertility to be feared. Menstruating women were forbidden to enter the temple sites, now devoted to worship of the one God, Yahweh. After the birth of a child, women were forbidden to enter the temple for forty days in the case of a male child, for eighty in the case of a female child.[30] Rituals with water, enacted by the Canaanites to celebrate the life-giving powers of water, were transformed by the Israelites into rituals of purification. Much of the focus was purification from female pollution. Religion enabled the Israelites to transpose the Canaanite society's threat to Israelite identity and order to the female body. In turn, the Israelites could assert their power over the Canaanites by asserting control over women's bodies. If the female body — key site of mysterious, and potentially disorderly or polluting, processes — could be controlled and purified, then so could Israel. In each instance, a fundamental commitment to societal order was served.

Interestingly, one of the more significant dynamics between social order and sexuality is visible also in the religion of the people of Israel, as recorded in the writings of the prophets (e.g., Isaiah, Ezekiel), which both Jews and Christians include among their sacred writings. The prophets wrote during a time in which the ancient Israelites continue to define themselves as a monotheistic culture over against the polytheism of their neighbors. At times, the Israelites feel threatened by their neighbors, not only because the neighbors confront the Israelites with opposing, and potentially attractive, religious beliefs, but also because they pose a genuine military threat to the continued existence of Israel. Reacting to outside powers, the prophets, summoning the energies of the people against the outside threat, use language that correlates power and sexuality.[31] Isaiah, for example, inveighs against the moral decay of Israel, calling for a time when "the Lord shall have washed away the filth of the daughters of Zion" (Isa. 3: 16–26, 4:

1–4). Ezekiel accuses Israel of playing the whore. God speaks through him to Israel in those terms:

> I will gather all your lovers, with whom you took pleasure . . . and I will judge you as women who break wedlock and shed blood are judged, and bring upon you the blood of wrath and jealousy. . . . they shall strip you of your clothes and take your fair jewels, and leave you naked and bare. They shall bring up a host against you, and they shall stone you and cut you to pieces with their swords. (Ezek. 16: 37–40)

If we take anthropologist Mary Douglas' arguments seriously, the prophets' correlation of threats to power with sexuality is not merely coincidental. When societies perceive that their borders are threatened, they often try to redraw the boundaries of social order. Their "drawing exercises" often appeal to that most dominant of border images, the human body, and to that most mysterious and potentially threatening of bodies, the female body. To redefine appropriate sexuality and to distinguish it from "dirty" sexuality is to "clean house" in a larger sense: A society with sexual order is a society with political order as well.

Chinese religion offers an important variation on the negative theme of female sexuality. Religion in China, traditionally varied and diverse, includes Buddhism. The teachings of the Buddha direct a person in meditation toward enlightenment, which, not unlike Hinduism, frees one from the chains of an endless cycle of rebirth (*samsara*) and delivers one into the peace of *nirvana*. Mahayana Buddhism, a form of Buddhism found in China, teaches that the way to enlightenment may be difficult. Therefore, assistance is available from *bodhisattvas*—enlightened ones who labor on behalf of another's enlightenment. The *bodhisattvas* are often imaged as gods and goddesses who reside in various celestial Buddha-lands or Paradises. Their powers may be summoned on behalf of one's quest for enlightenment through devotion and ritual.

In China, a tradition of female, and not only male, *bodhisattvas* is melded with traditions of folk religion. "Folk religion" encompasses a variety of cultural expressions of religion in China. One does not "join" a folk religion; one becomes part of it by virtue of one's very existence in China. Central to these folk expressions of religion, the communist revolution notwithstanding, is ancestor veneration. For the Chinese, order in the present society is founded on the honoring of past order. Moreover, because those who lived in the past were more attuned to the fundamental order of existence, it is best, the Chinese believe, to give careful attention to the ancestors. Ritual evocation of the ancestors and their wisdom therefore constitutes a central aspect of Chinese culture. From daily activities such as farming, to medicine, to the opera, traditional Chinese life revolves around practices that display attentiveness to the ancestors. Ancestors who are significant, not only to an individual family, but also to a larger community, are referred to as gods and goddesses.

Thus, we can see that a strong goddess tradition stems from both Buddhism and folk religion in China. In this tradition, goddesses such as Kuan-Yin and Ma Tsu are portrayed in unambiguously positive language. Kuan-Yin, Goddess of Mercy, is often the principle deity in Buddhist temples. Ma

Tsu, whose origins are located in folk religion, is a central figure for worship and the overseer of the fishing industry in Taiwan. Interestingly, while the goddesses exemplify wholly positive characteristics of care and compassion, they do so in sharp contrast to human females. Two messages dominate socialization of human females through religious ideologies. First, human females bear the marks of pollution through menstruation, sexual intercourse, and childbirth. Second, the greatest tragedy in a woman's life is to remain childless. Female identity is formed by childbearing, but that power is interpreted negatively as pollution, so as to circumscribe it. The goddesses, who become deities subsequent to earthly tragedies that prevent them from fulfilling their proper roles in earthly life as human wives and mothers, escape the marks of pollution and for that very reason attain their genuine and larger power as deities. In a sense then, while goddesses are identified as members of the human female gender, they also violate cultural definitions of the female gender and cultural restrictions on female power. That violation is conservatively interpreted within Chinese culture so as to exclude human females from identifying with the goddesses. Pollution ideologies and negative views of female sexuality and power are preserved, rather than challenged, by goddess mythology.[32]

The fear of sexuality is prevalent in Christianity as well. Mary, the Mother of Jesus, has strong parallels with the compassionate goddesses of Chinese religion. She is distinguished, in her virginity, from all other women. In her purity she is the "new Eve," as contrasted with the sinful sexuality of the first Eve. Although the Bible documents that Mary and Joseph had other children after Jesus, Church theology in later times conveniently ignores this, emphasizing Mary's complete break with sexuality and reproduction. Mary is always, and perpetually, a virgin.[33] As such, she can represent the virginity of the Christian church; i.e., its order and purity in relation to assaults from non-Christian influences.

Historically, whenever specific Christian groups have felt external pressures threatening their existence, Christian theologies, highlighting the dangers of sexuality, have reasserted the values of sexual asceticism and celibacy. For example, in the earliest years of Christianity, when it was a tiny and fragile religion, the Apostle Paul advocated celibacy. He recommended marriage only as a last resort (1 Corinthians 7: 6–9). Later, Jerome articulated a quantitative measure of the value of perpetual virginity: Marriage brings but a thirtyfold yield of virtue, widowhood sixtyfold, and virginity a hundredfold.[34] When the fragility of Christian communities is revisited later in the history of Christianity—for example, in the utopian experiment of the Shakers—asceticism and requisite celibacy become requirements of the Christian life.[35] The body comes to symbolize the necessity of impermeable, virgin walls of the new society.[36]

To be sure, celibacy and sexual asceticism often have been recommended for both men and women in the Christian religion. However, the dynamics are not the same for both genders; rather, the woman "plays the heavy." It is from the dangers of *her* sexuality that both man and woman are to be saved, if they adopt the celibate life or practice sexual asceticism.

That religious sanctions can be used to enforce gender roles and specified forms of approved sexuality is nowhere more clearly visible than in that darkest chapter of the history of Christianity, when persecution of witches focused primarily on women. Women who deviated from religiously established norms for females—women of independent financial means, usually widows, women practitioners of folk medicine, poor women, and women who were single or who otherwise did not have the protection of propertied men—were the most likely victims. Although the issue was female power, the language of the witchcraft trials focused on the sexual behavior of the women accused of witchcraft. Trial records exhibit an exaggerated fear of female sexuality. Recent scholarly estimates suggest that several hundred thousand witches were killed between 1440 and 1770. There has not been a parallel persecution of men as men, although men have been persecuted in greater numbers as members of other minorities, primarily as Jews.[37]

Significantly, the witchcraft craze occurred during the Renaissance, a time of great cultural change and of challenges to traditional economic and political authority. As is so often the case, threats to power in a broad sense were responded to not only on a large social scale, but also on a smaller scale: Women who had no decisive political power of their own were the most vulnerable to charges of witchcraft.

Christian theology's negative view of female sexuality illustrates that dominant religious images of women in Christianity are built on dualistic images of the human being. Women are universally devalued, based on the assumption of a hierarchy of culture over nature. As a realm of culture and reason is contrasted by Christian theologians with a realm of nature and emotion, women, because of their reproductive processes, are identified with nature and men are identified with culture and reason. Christian theology, identifying men with the cultural norm, measures women against that norm and finds them wanting. Men define culture and oppose themselves to women, whom they find inferior and beneath them. Associating women not only with nature, but also with sexual passion, lack of reason, domestic activities, and reproduction, men propose to dominate and control women, just as they are mandated, by Scriptures (Genesis 1: 28) to subdue and dominate the earth.

Female sexuality, interpreted according to this dualistic scenario, is highly problematic: The irrational, and potentially chaotic, sexuality of women is either controlled, in service to a Christian culture, or is dangerously out of control and is evil. Measured against the cultural and religious norm, female sexuality, in its evil mode, is that of the tempter, seducer, or polluter and, in its approved mode, is that of virgin, chaste bride, or mother. Although, according to Christian theology, both male and female are created in the image of God, Christian theologians, to the extent that they think dualistically, have placed women closer to the realm of nature, and hence to sexuality and death, than they have placed men.[38] Although human males obviously have bodies, in Christian theology they are "essentially" beings of reason and spirit; in contrast, women are "essentially" linked to nature and partake of the order of reason and spirit only secondarily. Moreover, even as men can bring their bodies under their conscious control in order to dominate both their bodies and their surroundings, women, according to the dualistic scenario, are subject to their bodies. If women are not ruled by men, they are ruled by their passions, and evil or chaos abounds. Hence, religiously approved roles for women, defined and legitimated by Scripture and tradition, are narrowly limited to those clearly controlled by men (e.g., wife, daughter) or distinguished from nature and reproduction (e.g., the Virgin Mary or the celibate nun).

Exclusively masculine imagery for the deity in the Christian religion teaches the lessons of dualism: Those who find themselves in the realm of culture are closer to God. In a Vatican declaration of 1976 against women's ordination, this dualistic vision was reconfirmed. The Roman Catholic Church hierarchy concluded that women cannot be priests because "there must be a physical resemblance between the priest and Christ."[39] The possession of male genitalia becomes the essential prerequisite for representing Christ, who in his maleness is the disclosure in earthly culture of the male God. The celibacy of the priest, confirming the celibacy of Jesus, links both to a realm distant from that of nature, embodiment, reproduction, and women.

Dualistic presuppositions even underlie the Christian Trinity: the three-part division of the deity speaks of a Father, Son, and Holy Spirit—but includes no Mother. The concept of the Trinity is a product of Christian reflection on God's relationship to the world and to humankind. Early Christian theologians wanted to preserve the unity of God (e.g., God's absolute power and knowledge) independent of the world and humankind. But they also wanted to acknowledge God's presence and power in the world and in individual human lives. The concept of the Trinity affirms both: Even as the unity of the Godhead is maintained, God enters the world in the form of the Son and transforms the world because humans are empowered by the Spirit for new life.[40]

That female imagery is absent from the Trinity is a result of dualistic presuppositions shared by the theologians who shaped the concept of the Trinity over a period of years. The Spirit, the third member of the Trinity, was modeled on the Jewish concept of Wisdom, traditionally personified as female. In Jewish thought, Wisdom—a wise and beautiful woman—reveals God to humans and brings God's transforming possibilities to them. Remnants of the Jewish Wisdom tradition remain in early Christianity;[41] Luke, for example, mentions that the Wisdom (*Sophia*) of God sends prophets and apostles to humankind (Luke 12: 49–50). Syriac Christianity (third century) maintained the feminine imagery of Wisdom when it translated Wisdom into the concept of the Holy Spirit. Including odes to a female Spirit among their hymns, Syriac Christians spoke of the spirit as the womb of rebirth and announced that they were nurtured on the milk of the Spirit.[42] Even so, Christian theologians, for the most part, excluded female imagery from their reflections about the Spirit, enforcing that dualistic presupposition that equates the male with God, the female with all that deviates or is separated from the divine. Thus, over a period of centuries, Christians lost all memories of the female Spirit–Wisdom celebrated by their Jewish forebears and the early Syriac Christians. According to later Christianity, female-associated images belonged to the realm of nature, not to that of God. Exclusively masculine imagery for the Trinitarian relationship between God and the world prevailed.

In this essay, I have shown that religion, that institution in society most likely to prescribe and defend the foundations of the social order, has regularly demarcated order from disorder by appeal to the female body. That women's bodies, more mysterious than men's, have been appropriated by religion, when it has wanted to circumscribe order and to find protection against the powers and dangers of chaos, has had onerous consequences for women. Granted that the female body has been religion's symbolism of choice, does that mean that religion has always oppressed women or are there exceptions to patterns of oppression described in this essay?

Although the record is meager, a fact perhaps attributable to the predominance of men as recorders of history, we know that in some instances women, subverting both men's prescriptions for their orderly behavior and men's descriptions of their potential for disorderly behavior, have gained a measure of freedom. Instances of liberating behavior by women, associated with religious belief, fall into three categories.

First, some women have been able to interpret the religious demands on them in such a way as to countermand men's prescriptions for their behavior. Hindu women poet-saints, among whom we find Mahadeviyakka (1106–1167 C.E.) and Lallesvari (fourteenth century C.E.), are a most dramatic example of this instance of patriarchal subversion. Both strove to live according to the *Bhagavad-gita,* a key devotional text in Hinduism. The *Bhagavad-gita,* according to the traditional interpretation, teaches that devotion (*bhakti*) to a god is not incompatible with the social obligations (*dharma*) one inherits by virtue of gender and caste, because performance of one's social role *is* an act of devotion to that god. But Mahadeviyakka's and Lallesvari's elaborations on this teaching offered a different interpretation. Both wrote that, if a woman's devotion to a god demands her complete attention, she may be exempted from her *dharma*—her inherited role as a wife and mother subservient to her husband, for *bhakti* has a higher value than *dharma.* Although in no way a conventional reading of the *Bhagavad-gita,* this "proto-feminist" interpretation provided these women with grounds for evading traditional women's roles. Their poetry describes their struggle to reconcile *dharma* and *bhakti,* highlights the resolution of the struggle in favor of renunciation of their marriages to human men in order to engage in an all-consuming devotion to a god, and conveys their intimate and erotic passion for their new, divine husband. Preserved to this day, the honored poetry of these women constitutes a remarkable record of emancipation.[43]

Appealing to a second strategy subversive of patriarchy, some women have exchanged the traditional female role, and its requirements, for that of an "honorary male." Both Buddhist and Christian nuns exemplify this possibility for liberation. In China, for example, biographies that date from 516 C.E. describe nuns who adopted an ascetic lifestyle that included the celibacy necessary for honorary-male status. In marked contrast to their lay counterparts, these Buddhist nuns are praised for their own worth, without regard to the quality of their relationships to husbands or sons, the traditional standard of valuation for Chinese women. Noted for their literary skill and erudition, these nuns are known to have lectured to other nuns and to large congregations of laypeople about the Buddha's teachings.[44]

A similar history of emancipated women can be traced in the early years of Christianity. Christian writings, dating from the same time period as the New Testament but not located in the Bible, record the leadership of celibate women — widows or virgins — in the Christian communities.[45] Among these early Christian groups, the titles "widow" and "virgin" referred to women's spiritual status, rather than to their marital or physiological status: They signified women's complete devotion and commitment to Christ, in exclusion of marriage or remarriage to any man. For example, "the virgin Thecla," commissioned in ministry by the Apostle Paul, left home on the eve of her wedding to follow Paul. Her ministry became noted throughout Asia Minor.[46] Women in the first two centuries of the Christian era who committed themselves to service to Christ, like Thecla, could pursue vocations with considerable authority and autonomy. Even so, that they became equals in ministry with men only by becoming honorary males is graphically illustrated in stories about Thecla that note her rejection of marriage and her assumption of a male style of dress.

In later centuries, Christian women who accepted the celibate lifestyle lived together in monasteries. Granted considerable autonomy from domination by men, nuns rose to positions of authority not otherwise possible for women. Some abbesses were even accorded the right to authorize priests to serve in areas over which the abbesses had established ecclesiastical control.[47] Like their Buddhist counterparts, nuns experienced remarkable levels of freedom, both from the obligations traditionally imposed on women in their society and for the pursuit of vocational goals such as higher education; philosophical treatises, theological writings, plays, and poetry are attributed to them.[48]

In seeking a means of liberation from the constraints placed on women by patriarchy, some women have explored a third option: They have adorned the sphere to which they are allotted by patriarchy such that, although the parameters of that sphere have not been "recarved," in violation of patriarchal authority, the sphere has acquired, nevertheless, trappings of freedom. Women in Judaism and Islam, consigned to the home, have represented this possibility most often. For example, Moslem women, excluded from participation in religion at the mosque, sometimes have developed a ritual life that functions independently of men. In some rural areas of Iran, for example, women perform rituals that summon powers inherent in plants and minerals in order to overcome problems such as sickness or economic hardship. Within their own sphere, these women have authority in relation to other women, based on their abilities to summon powers on behalf of health and economic prosperity.[49] In certain sectors of Judaism, ambivalence toward the role of women has been balanced by an appreciation for women's leadership within the home. In their roles as leaders of religious life in the home, just as men are leaders of religious life in the outside world, some Jewish women may have approached the ideal of the "separate, but equal" sphere.[50]

Regrettably, despite their promise, all three categories that exemplify instances of liberating behavior for women in religion historically have had serious shortcomings. The subversion of religious teachings, exemplified by the Hindu women-saints, was successful, but only because these women's extreme devotion, so articulately expressed, was exceptional. As a distinct minority, these female poet-saints posed no substantive threat to the social order. Were Hindu women to have engaged in behavior such as theirs on a massive scale, it is likely that patriarchal authority would have been summoned against them.

Like the poet-saints, women who assumed the roles of honorary males were exceptions to the majority of women. Again, like the poet-saints, the price of freedom — celibacy — was high. That women were exempted from negative attributions of sexuality when they denied their sexuality and lived as celibate, honorary men could not constitute freedom from patriarchy, for these women gained freedom only because they accepted men's initial verdict about women: Women harbor life-threatening powers of chaos and evil in their mysterious bodies, which can be countered only if they live celibate, cloistered lives. Moreover, to the extent that the role of honorary male did provide women with substantive power, the patriarchs moved swiftly to suppress it.

Denied continued economic support, Buddhist nuns gradually faded into social, economic, and intellectual obscurity.[51] As larger numbers of women in the early Christian communities modeled themselves on women such as Thecla, their quest for autonomy was thwarted and their movement repressed. Indeed, I Timothy in the New Testament was written apparently to counter the growing independence of Christian women. With its recommendation for women to keep silent (I Timothy 2: 11) and its suggestion that churches support only "real" widows (I Timothy 5: 3 – 16), I Timothy depicts a concerted effort to discourage young, never-married women and widows still in their child-bearing years from pursuing vocations devoted to Christ.[52] So also did nuns in later centuries find their freedom constrained. In the late Medieval era, centers of learning were transferred from the monasteries to the new universities, from which women were excluded. Convents were supervised by male bishops, and nuns' behavior was regulated by the requirement of regular confession before male priests. Nuns were strictly cloistered, and new religious orders, such as the Jesuits, did not include female branches.[53] A period of women's independence and autonomy was followed by a dramatic reassertion of patriarchal authority.

As for the third option elected by women in search of freedom, the autonomy of the home sphere, while making possible some freedom for women, has not been without its serious drawbacks: Women who may have wished to participate in the public sphere, in order to pursue educations and careers, have been necessarily excluded from achievement of these aims. An absence of choice, rather than true freedom, has prevailed.

The three avenues to emancipation that we have examined share in common a fundamental conservatism: not disavowing the basic structure of patriarchy, they liberate women only because they promise subversion from within. Their failure to offer genuine possibilities for liberation suggests that women today must focus their critical attention on religion, not only when it is obviously acting as an institution of social control to oppress women—as described in the first part of this essay—but also when it is not obviously oppressive. Women must be wary, and not only because we have seen that women can opt for a liberating lifestyle only to the extent that their chosen role does not truly challenge patriarchal authority. Because the roles women elect, although apparently subversive, may be but contemporary versions of "the exceptional woman," "the honorary male," or "the guardian of the hearth," women must be prepared to be critical of roles that, on the surface, look emancipating. Each of those roles historically has extracted its price, offering liberation to only that minority of women willing to deny their sexuality, to forfeit motherhood, or to confine their expressions of freedom to the sphere of the home. To the extent that women today are not reconciled to making these sacrifices, they must summon their creative energies to envision lifestyles and roles that will enable them to tell a happier tale about women in religion.

NOTES

1. Paul Tillich, *Systematic Theology*, Vol. 1, (Chicago: University of Chicago Press, 1967), pp. 11–13.

2. Mary Douglas, *Purity and Danger: An Analysis of the Concepts of Pollution and Taboo* (Boston: Ark Paperbacks, Routledge & Kegan Paul, 1985), p. 114.

3. Ibid., p. 115.

4. Thomas J. Hopkins, *The Hindu Religious Tradition* (Belmont, CA: Wadsworth Publishing Co., 1971).

5. Katherine Young, "Hinduism," in *Women in World Religions*, ed. Arvind Sharma (Albany: State University of New York Press, 1987), pp. 59–105; pp. 73–74.

6. Joni Seager and Ann Olson, *Women in the World: An International Atlas* (New York: Simon & Schuster, 1986), p. 3.

7. Juthica Stangl, "India: A Widow's Devastating Choice," *Ms. Magazine*, September 1984, pp. 37–39.

8. Douglas, *Purity and Danger*, p. 123.

9. Ibid., p. 126.

10. Ibid., p. 127.

11. Ibid., pp. 125–26.

12. Young, "Hinduism," p. 75.

13. Ibid., pp. 78–79.

14. Ibid., pp. 84–85.

15. Ibid., p. 83. The word for good (i.e., obedient, self-denying) woman—*satī*—is identical, but for the diacritical mark, with the act of widow sacrifice: *satī* (p. 257, note 2).

16. The Hebrew Bible consists of the Torah (Genesis, Exodus, Leviticus, Numbers, and Deuteronomy), the Prophets (Joshua, Judges, 1 and 2 Samuel, 1 and 2 Kings, Isaiah, Jeremiah, Ezekiel, Josea, Joel, Amos, Obadiah, Jonah, Micah, Nahum, Habakkuk, Zephaniah, Haggai, Zechariah, and Malachi), and the Writings (Psalms, Proverbs, Job, Song of Solomon, Ruth, Lamentations, Ecclesiastes, Esther, David, Ezra, Nehemiah, and 1 and 2 Chronicles).

17. Meredith McGuire, *Religion: The Social Context*, 2nd ed. (Belmont, CA: Wadsworth Publishing Co., 1987), pp. 98–99. McGuire rightly notes that caste status confers necessary but not

412   sufficient advantages to men's chances for recognition, power, and prestige: "Not all men obtain these privileges in the social system, but maleness is virtually a prerequisite. Some men suffer exploitation and discrimination, but not because of their gender. Religiously legitimated caste distinctions thus do not empower all men; they do, however, disempower all women by virtue of their gender identity" (Ibid.).

18. Ibid.

19. Rosemary Ruether, *Sexism and God-Talk: Toward a Feminist Theology* (Boston: Beacon Press, 1983), p. 168.

20. Ibid., p. 167.

21. Martin Luther, *Lectures on Genesis*, Gen. 3:16, in *Luther's Works*, Vol. 1, ed. Jaroslav Pelikan (St. Louis: Concordia Publishing House, 1958), pp. 202–203. As cited in Ruether, *Sexism*, p. 97.

22. Denise Carmody, "Judaism," in *Women in World Religions*, pp. 183–207; p. 193.

23. Ibid., p. 194.

24. Ibid.

25. Jane I. Smith, "Islam," in *Women in World Religions*, pp. 235–51; pp. 240–41.

26. Jane I. Smith and Yvonne Haddad, "Women in the Afterlife: The Islamic View as Seen from the Qur'an and Tradition," *Journal of the American Academy of Religion* 43:39–50, 1975; cited in Denise L. Carmody and John T. Carmody, *Ways to the Center: An Introduction to World Religions*, 2nd ed. (Belmont, CA: Wadsworth Publishing Co., 1984), pp. 333; 390, note 77.

27. Richard Brubaker, "The Untamed Goddesses of Village India," in *The Book of the Goddess: Past and Present*, ed. C. Olson (New York: Crossroad Press, 1983), pp. 145–161, pp. 158–59.

28. Judith Ochshorn, *The Female Experience and the Nature of the Divine* (Bloomington, IN: Indiana University Press, 1981), pp. 24–34, 57–58, 89–90.

29. Ibid., p. 37.

30. Roslyn Lacks, *Women and Judaism* (Garden City, NY: Doubleday & Company, 1980), pp. 152–53.

31. Ochshorn, *The Female Experience*, pp. 161–63.

32. P. Steven Sangren, "Female Gender in Chinese Religious Symbols: Kuan Yin, Ma Tsu, and the 'Eternal Mother,'" *Signs: Journal of Women in Culture and Society* 9 (11): 4–25, 1983.

33. Ruether, *Sexism and God-Talk*, p. 150.

34. Ibid., p. 143.

35. Ibid., p. 196.

36. Douglas, *Purity and Danger*, p. 158.

37. McGuire, *Religion: The Social Context*, p. 107.

38. Ruether, *Sexism and God-Talk*, pp. 72–75. Ruether attributes her analysis to Sherry Ortner, "Is Female to Male as Nature Is to Culture?" in *Woman, Culture and Society*, ed. M. Z. Rosaldo and L. Lamphere (Stanford, CA: Stanford University Press, 1974), pp. 67–87.

39. "Declaration on the Question of Admission of Women to the Ministerial Priesthood," Section 27, Vatican City, 15 October, 1976, as cited in Ruether, *Sexism and God-Talk*, p. 275, note 10.

40. Rosemary Ruether, *Womanguides: Readings Toward a Feminist Theology* (Boston: Beacon Press, 1985), pp. 21–22.

41. Elizabeth Fiorenza, *In Memory of Her: A Feminist Theological Reconstruction of Christian Origins* (New York: Crossroad Press, 1983), pp. 132–36.

42. Ruether, *Womanguides*, pp. 24, 29–31.

43. David Kinsley, "Devotion as an Alternative to Marriage in the Lives of Some Hindu Women Devotees," in *Journal of Asian and African Studies* XV (1–2): 83–93, 1980.

44. Nancy Schuster Barnes, "Buddhism," in *Women in World Religions*, pp. 105–135; pp. 123–25.

45. Dennis MacDonald, *The Legend and the Apostle* (Philadelphia: Westminster Press, 1983) is a book about one of these accounts, *The Acts of Paul and Thecla.*

46. Ibid., pp. 90–96.

47. Rosemary Ruether, "Christianity," in *Women in World Religions,* pp. 207–235; p. 219.

48. Ibid.

49. Erika Friedl, "Islam and Tribal Women in a Village in Iran," in *Unspoken Worlds: Women's Religious Lives in Non-Western Cultures,* eds. Nancy Falk and Rita Gross, (San Francisco: Harper & Row, 1980), pp. 159–74; pp. 163–64.

50. Lacks, *Women and Judaism,* p. 124.

51. Barnes, "Buddhism," pp. 131–32.

52. MacDonald, *The Legend and the Apostle,* pp. 54–78.

53. Ruether, "Christianity," p. 219.

The Experiences of Minority Women in the United States: Intersections of Race, Gender, and Class

ELIZABETH M. ALMQUIST

Minority women confront all the issues and problems that white women face. They know the joys and sorrows of children, housework, jobs, and relationships with men and other women. They experience the pain and trauma associated with rape, sexual harassment, exclusion, discrimination, and every other kind of mistreatment of women. Minority women share many of the same feminist goals that majority women seek and are increasingly aware that their smaller paychecks and constricted job opportunities reflect gender discrimination as much as race discrimination. Despite all these commonalities, minority women are likely to interpret their experiences within a different framework than white women do, to assign different priorities to feminist goals, and to view white women with some suspicion and feelings of apartness.

Race (or ethnicity) and race discrimination erect enormous barriers between minority and white women, and among various groups of minority women. There are a number of different minority groups in the United States. Within each group, women's identity and experiences are further subdivided by differences in age, marital status, social class, and the like. To expose some of the barriers that have divided different groups of women, I first describe the unique historical experiences of Native American, black, Hispanic, and Asian women.

THE FORCES THAT DIVIDE: RACIAL DIVISIONS IN THE UNITED STATES

Historically, the major racial groups were geographically distant from one another, with blacks concentrated in the Southeast, Mexican-Americans—as the largest Hispanic group—in the Southwest, and Asians on the west coast. Only Native Americans were dispersed throughout the North American continent. Historically as well, the white majority used the different groups to fill different economic functions. Social definitions of race, ethnicity, and color were imposed on top of geographic distances and economic divisions. Therefore, women from the different groups lived apart from one another.

Despite all the differences among groups, we find some surprising similarities. Women played crucial productive, family, and community roles, working very hard and seeing themselves as partners with their husbands and brothers. Contact with whites disrupted family life in every instance, and women were too often defined as sexual property. So the history of minority women involved continuous struggles to survive and to protect entire groups against the onslaughts of the white majority. Today, we find further similarities among different groups of women: increasing similarities in the family situations and worklives, increasing activism in both minority group and feminist movements, increasing efforts to understand and transcend barriers of race, gender, and class.

The following sections provide only brief glimpses of the larger minority groups, with an eye toward locating them within social time and space. None of the information is as complete or as detailed as I would like, because some groups are too small or are too recent arrivals to be given separate coverage by the U.S. Bureau of the Census, because the data on minority groups is limited (See Table 1), and because social scientists and historians have not paid much attention to women within these groups.

Native American Women: The Invisible Minority

Before the coming of the white man, Native American[1] women played crucial productive and social roles in hundreds of diverse and separate groups. The European invaders neither noticed nor appreciated differences among tribal cultures. They swept across the North American continent, killing native people either deliberately or accidentally by spreading diphtheria, whooping cough, and other diseases to which native people had no immunities. Native Americans who survived were herded onto reservations that were perceived as having few natural resources, and the much-hated Bureau of Indian Affairs was established to protect and control these groups. In the process, most groups lost their traditional means of earning a living, significant social and family distinctions among the tribes were obliterated,[2] Native Americans were denied the right to vote, and only a few were allowed to obtain a formal education. These policies and practices combined to ensure that Native Americans would be largely confined to rural areas where

T A B L E 1
Characteristics of Minority Groups[a]

Minority group	Native American	Black	Mexican-American	Puerto Rican	Cuban	Chinese	Japanese	Filipino	Korean	Asian Indian	Vietnamese
Total population[b]	1,479	26,092	8,679	2,005	806	812	716	782	357	387	245
Foreign born (percent)	2.5	2.8	26.0	51.0	77.9	63.3	28.4	64.7	81.9	70.4	90.5
Households headed by women (percent)	26.1	41.1	18.1	39.5	16.2	11.1	14.2	14.8	13.5	8.7	17.0
Cumulative fertility[c]	3450	3184	3646	3202	2033	2233	1872	2216	2045	2197	3391
Median family income	$13,678	12,627	14,765	10,734	18,245	22,599	27,354	23,687	20,459	24,993	12,840
Families in poverty (percent)	24	26	21	35	12	11	4	6	13	7	35
High-school graduates											
Women (percent)	54	52	36	39	53	67	80	75	70	72	54
Men (percent)	57	51	39	41	58	75	84	73	90	89	71
Ratio	.95	1.02	.92	.95	.91	.89	.95	1.03	.78	.81	.76
Labor-force participation (percent)											
Women	48	53	49	40	55	58	59	68	55	47	49
Men	70	67	80	71	78	74	79	78	78	84	65
Professionals (percent)											
Women	14.5	15.2	8.4	10.9	11.5	20.4	17.8	27.1	14.2	34.1	11.6
Men	9.8	7.9	5.5	7.0	12.3	30.3	22.0	19.1	23.6	49.7	20.6
Managers (percent)											
Women	6.5	4.7	4.2	4.6	6.5	10.4	8.3	6.4	5.7	6.4	4.3
Men	7.8	5.7	5.1	6.3	12.9	15.0	17.0	9.3	14.5	14.9	4.7

[a]SOURCE: United States Bureau of the Census. 1983. *Characteristics of the Population, 1980. Chapter C. General Social and Economic Characteristics, U.S. Summary.* PC80-1-C1.
[b]Total population in thousands.
[c]Number of children ever born per 1,000 women aged fifteen to forty-five.

jobs are few and far between, that they would have few opportunities to influence political affairs, and that they would become the most invisible of minority groups.

These policies and practices significantly reduced Native American women's status by destroying their traditional patterns of contributing greatly to the group's basic subsistence. The examples are numerous. In the horticultural groups, farming provided the main source of food, and hunting was supplementary. Women did much of the farming, and in some of these societies such as the Choctaw and Iroquois,[3] women controlled their own labor, controlled the food and other products of their labor, and played major roles in tribal decision making. Traditionally, land was "owned" by the entire group or by large extended families. Christian missionaries were appalled when they saw women doing agricultural work and thought that men did not care about providing for their families. In cooperation with the federal government, policies were introduced that made individual men the property holders and reduced women's participation in food production.

Women also played very important roles in food production in foraging societies, including the buffalo-hunting tribes of the Great Plains. Women were responsible for preserving and cooking the meat, for making clothes and shelters from the hides, and for supplementing the meat by gathering many kinds of wild plant foods. In other hunting and gathering societies, meat was less important and women's foraging for plant foods was even more important. All the groups that relied on hunting and gathering lost their traditional sources of food, and were expected to learn to farm according to "white" methods, which always included only secondary roles for women.

In some herding societies, such as the Navajo, women traditionally tended the sheep and wove blankets from the wool. Beginning in the 1930s, government policy parceled out land to men only and limited the number of sheep that a family could own. Women lost their major source of wealth, and their sense of security and bargaining power within the family was taken away.[4] Seeking work in town was frowned on for women, and they could choose only restaurant work, seasonal agricultural employment, or domestic service. Men left the reservation to find jobs, and divorce and desertion rates skyrocketed. Women's difficulties were compounded because women lost their traditional culture but did not perceive Anglo (white)[5] culture as worthy of being emulated.[6] Shirley Hill Witt[7] suggests that the loss of meaningful roles for women is a factor promoting the high birth rate among the Navajo.

Today, Native American women juggle numerous responsibilities with limited resources. Poverty and unemployment pervade the reservation areas. Native American women have relatively low labor-force participation rates outside the home (see Table 1), in part because of heavy family responsibilities and the lack of jobs in rural areas. Inside the home, women contribute substantially to family subsistence by raising gardens, tending sheep and cattle, making clothing and household objects, or making and selling souvenir items. Many women spend a great deal of time working on behalf of the Pan-Indian movement, which is concerned with maintaining or regaining traditional tribal culture, including language, customs, dress, religion, and ceremonies. In choosing to be the keepers of the culture,[8] women make a lifelong commitment.

The Native American movement is designed to maximize Native American self-determination. Federal control over Native American affairs is exercised through the Bureau of Indian Affairs (BIA). Technically, the tribes own their reservation lands and the natural resources these lands contain. But contracts with the oil, uranium, and coal mining companies must be negotiated through the BIA, and Native Americans rightfully believe they are being cheated in the process. The large companies, the federal government, and tourists encroach on native lands, destroying the beautiful mother earth, turning farmland and sacred shrines into mines or tourist facilities, and relocating thousands of Native Americans away from their ancestral homes. To confront these massive changes requires running a gauntlet of twisted legal and bureaucratic procedures. The Native American movement is not concerned with achieving material gains but with educating doctors, lawyers, and other professionals to regain some control. Women are active participants, readily taking leadership roles and often forming the majority of protest marchers.[9] On a day-to-day basis, they work to maintain movement organizations, to educate the people in both traditional and "white" lifeways, to provide health care, and to reduce alcoholism, suicide, and violence.

Over half of the nearly 2 million Native Americans now reside in cities and towns. The city is a cold and lonely place. Native Americans socialize mainly with other Native Americans, avoiding contact with whites who are antagonistic toward them. A large number return to their rural homes periodically to renew contacts with family and friends.

Shirley Fiske[10] suggests that Native American women are less prepared for life in the city than are Native American men. These women more often grew up only on the reservation, less often went away to boarding school, and less often served in the military. Caught between native and white lifeways, Fiske argues, Native American women specifically choose to remain bicultural in orientation. This means accepting enough Anglo culture to get a job, to communicate with employers and with the children's teachers, to establish residence and to vote, and to negotiate the intricacies of federal bureaucracies. It also means rejecting the materialistic values of Anglo culture and retaining an emphasis on native values, such as sharing material goods, being noncompetitive, avoiding manipulation of other people, and not criticizing them.[11] This communal orientation works well in establishing shared bonds with other Native Americans, and it helps to ease the burdens and tensions of life in the often-hostile white city. Women get along by being politely formal toward whites and reserving warmth and emotional responsiveness for family and friends. Most Native American women are first- or second-generation urban residents. They are making life choices now that will affect all future generations.

African American Women: The Largest Minority

My mother used to say that the black woman is the white man's mule and the white woman is his dog. Now, she said that to say this: we do the heavy work and get beat whether we do it well or not. But the white woman is closer to the master and he pats them on the head and lets them sleep in the house, but he ain't gon' treat neither one like he was dealing with a person. Nancy White[12]

African women were brought to the United States to work, to produce, and to reproduce. At first male slaves had been preferred for work in the fields and in the skilled jobs demanded by the expanding agricultural economy. When the United States committed itself to ending the slave trade, large numbers of black women were imported to increase the slave population. Thus, there was an early definition of black women as sexual property, a definition that was enlarged because slave women had no power to prevent sexual assaults by white men. In their ignorance, many white men came to believe that black women actually enjoyed their sexual assaults. Slave women performed multiple roles. They worked as both field hands and domestic servants; they were required to have children, sometimes through forced breeding with selected male slaves; and they cared for their families and children in the slave quarters after all their other work was finished.[13] Women were sometimes given a few days off after childbirth to nurse their children, but this was not done in recognition of their needs for rest and recovery. Instead, the slave owner was protecting his or her investment in human chattel.

After slavery, black women continued to work as domestic servants or as hired labor in the fields owned by their former masters. Two world wars lured thousands of blacks to the North, with promises of work in defense-related industries.[14] For women, the change of venue meant little in the way of real employment gains. They continued to work as maids and babysitters in white homes, and as cooks, dishwashers, and janitors in hotels, restaurants, and office buildings. The few women who were able to obtain a college education concentrated heavily in teaching because they could find jobs in segregated schools. It was long after World War II before enough school doors were open to allow black women to move out of domestic and service work and into professional and clerical occupations. In the last two decades, black women have scored impressive increases in educational attainment and strong gains in professional fields previously dominated by white women. Despite this, no group has shattered white male control over the elite professions that offer the highest pay and the most prestige.[15] Further, black women, like all other groups of women, are still notably absent from managerial occupations, from the skilled crafts, and from factory supervisory work. Employers are especially unwilling to place women of color in positions where these women would supervise or work alongside of white men.

Black women have had exceptionally high rates of paid employment. Sheer necessity compels many to work, because high unemployment rates create economic insecurity for all blacks and because the sex ratio (number of men per 100 women) among blacks in the South and East has been very low.[16] Historically, male scarcity was created when black men moved out of the South more rapidly than did black women, suffered heavy casualty rates as front-line troops in various wars, and experienced high death rates from poor health and poor health care. Contemporary conditions recreate male scarcity. Poverty and discrimination take a heavy toll in apathy, alcoholism, drug abuse, crime, poor health, early deaths, unemployment, and low wages. Coupled with longer prison sentences and more frequent enactment of the death penalty for blacks compared to whites, these factors result in proportionately fewer black than white men to marry and to fill breadwinner roles.

After slavery, whites imposed a different system of social control, including segregated housing, workplaces, and schools. They tried to impose a stronger set of stereotypes, portraying black women as docile, obedient creatures who existed to serve the interests of whites and alternately as emasculating matriarchs who dominated black men. Race discrimination created a shortage of black men, and those men who were available had low earnings. Race and gender discrimination kept black women's own earnings even lower.

Black women coped with oppression in myriad ways,[17] and their coping strategies continue in the present day. They frequently form extended households, with three generations living together and pooling resources. Black relatives and friends seem more willing than white ones to adopt informally children whose mothers are experiencing financial or emotional distress. The mothers see informal adoption as a much better alternative than formal adoption, because they do not have to relinquish custody and the children are placed with people whom the mothers know and trust.[18] These customs may have originated as a response to the uncertainties of family life during the time immediately following slavery, or they may be seen as adaptive patterns that are continuously made necessary by current conditions. In either case, black women have had to be very resourceful to survive. Yet they are stereotyped and ridiculed by outsiders because their assertiveness is a threat to the status quo.[19]

During slavery, free black women fought for its abolition. After slavery, many black women fought for suffrage, organized clubs to extend their own education, sought better schooling for their children, and formed groups to help the sick and impoverished.[20] The last few decades have brought new varieties of activism. Just as Native American women formed a critical mass to carry out the Native American movement, so black women organized through the churches and provided a solid foundation for the Civil Rights movement.[21] During the 1960s and 1970s, they organized and led the National Welfare Rights Organization.[22]

During those decades as well, the Black Power movement brought a variety of cross-currents and conflicting pressures. Above all else, that movement sought to reassert the masculinity of black men. Thus, black women who practiced birth control and sought abortion rights were denounced as contributing to black genocide. Advocates of increased education and better jobs for black women were put down as threats to black men's self-esteem, which was already undermined by racism.[23] Black women were becoming increasingly feminist in attitude, but they saw organized feminism as unreceptive to their interests.[24] Consequently, they formed their own feminist organizations, including the Combahee River Collective.[25]

Today, there is a flowering of scholarship on black women. Black women scholars are producing a variety of insightful analyses of their own position and of the entire society. These writings assert the need for black women to define themselves and their priorities; to refuse any simplistic explanations of the conditions in which they live;[26] to combine with other groups to achieve specific changes that are mutually beneficial; and to recognize that race, class, and gender oppression are inseparable.[27]

Mexican-American Women

Anglo women sensitive to Chicanas as members of a minority must guard against a very basic conceptual mistake. All minorities are not alike. To understand the black woman is not to understand the Chicana. To espouse the cause of minority women, Anglos must recognize our distinctiveness as separate ethnic groups. Conseuelo Nieto[28]

Mexican-American women comprise the largest and oldest Spanish-origin group. Contrary to stereotype, a large but unknown number are the descendants of Spanish and Spanish–Native American ancestors who lived in the Southwest long before Mexico ceded that territory to the United States. Only some are illegal aliens or recent migrants. Throughout this century, turbulent economic and political conditions in Mexico have constantly encouraged Mexicans to cross the Rio Grande River—a border that they regard as artificial. Therefore, many Mexican-Americans have dwelt in the United States for several generations.

The Spanish conquistadores arrived in the New World largely without women. The first Mexicans were created by the union of Spanish men and Native American women. The Spaniards bartered trade goods for women, or captured the women by force. In at least one incident, native women were baptized as Catholics before they were systematically raped by the Spanish soldiers.[29]

The Spaniards looked down on the indigenous women, both because these women were natives and because they were women. They treated them as sexual, domestic, and laboring servants. Indigenous men began to emulate the Spaniards. Women were to be taken by conquest, treated as property, and used to bolster the men's status as property holders.

The Catholic church helped to institutionalize a very unequal relationship between women and men. The Spaniards had discovered that they could control Native American women servants and keep them laboring in the *encomienda*[30] system by teaching them to venerate the Virgin Mary. The *Marianisma* ideal taught women to be silent, to endure pain and sorrow, and to think in fatalist terms. Good women were identified as virgins, saintly mothers, and martyrs. To follow Mary, women had to be submissive, altruistic, and self-denying. The only alternative was to follow in the footsteps of the self-serving temptress, Eve. These ideals were incorporated into the culture of the new nation of Mexico, part of which was taken over by the United States.

The dichotomy between woman as Mary and woman as Eve continues today in somewhat modified form. Real people do not fit either category, but they are pressured to do so. Women worry about deviating from the Marianisma ideal, because even minor deviations cast the woman as the negative Eve. A good mother is one who unconditionally loves her children and places their needs before her own. "Women accept this definition of themselves because of some security that comes with the role, but this acceptance lends itself to a subtle pernicious undermining of women's self-esteem."[31]

The Marianisma concept for women complements the machismo concept for men. In the popular image, a macho male is a virile person who conquers and exploits women sexually. But "machismo also consists of manliness in a broader sense than just sexual prowess. It includes the elements of courage, honor, and respect for others, as well as the notion of providing fully for one's family."[32] Machismo supports the pattern of male dominance. Together, these cultural ideals promote large families among Mexican-Americans. Children are evidence of the husband's machismo, while the Marianisma ideal stresses that "bearing and rearing children are the woman's most important function, symbolizing her maturity."[33]

Betty Garcia-Bahne[34] argues that Anglo exploitation and domination contributed to the large families and distinct marital role structures of Mexican-Americans. When Mexico ceded the Southwest Territory in 1848, Anglos poured into the territory, displacing Spanish-Mexican landowners and turning peasants into a semicolonized labor force to build the infrastructure for the developing capitalist industry.

Mexican-Americans struggled to survive. They could not rely on Anglo courts for justice or on Anglo capitalists for steady work and adequate pay. They had to rely on themselves and their extended families for support and assistance. Garcia-Bahne suggests that the Mexican-American worker faced a tough, competitive, and authoritarian situation on the job, and tended to reproduce this relationship in his family. He had little reason to be certain that he could continue to fill the breadwinner role; the low wages that he did earn undermined his manliness. For these reasons, he demanded extra obeisance and respect from his wife.

Because of their relatively continuous immigration from Mexico, Mexican-American women and men workers were regarded as a supply of cheap, exploitable, and dispensable labor. In the huge agribusinesses, in the fields and the canneries, entire families worked together, because the work was seasonal and the wages of all members were required to support the family. Women and girls worked under the watchful eye of husbands and fathers, who made certain that they did not violate traditional norms of behavior and were protected from unwelcome sexual advances.[35] As industrialization developed, Mexican-Americans were increasingly employed as factory operatives. Women especially were preferred for sewing jobs in garment factories. By the 1930s, about one-half of employed Chicanas were in domestic- and personal-service work, one-fifth were agricultural laborers, and another one-fifth were employed in manufacturing.[36]

Recent interpretations and evidence[37] dispute Garcia-Bahne's interpretation of male dominance in the family. These views depict Mexican-American women in firm partnership with men, strengthening the family and facing adversity together. Today, Mexican-American women display equalitarian attitudes and resent any attempts to divide women from men.

In recent years, Mexican-Americans have dispersed somewhat around the country, becoming highly urbanized and well educated. Mexican-American women's rates of labor force participation increasingly resemble those of Anglos. Unfortunately, these women have not been able to exchange their educational qualifications for jobs and salaries at the same level that Anglos have. This is particularly apparent among high-school graduates, where the occupational prestige of Mexican-Americans lags far behind that of the majority group.[38] Mary Romero[39] found that Mexican-American women and men still confront stereotypes and barriers that prevent full occupational assimilation. Mexican-American women are still more heavily concentrated in blue-collar and lower white-collar occupations than are Anglo women, and they have particularly been excluded from higher-status professional and managerial work. Affirmative-action legislation has had only minimal impact on these patterns.

For the last several decades, Mexican-Americans have been increasingly active in a variety of social movements to enhance their political, educational, and economic opportunities. These activities spawned an awareness of sexism and often served as the springboard for feminist organizing. With roots in the working-class union movement as well, the Chicana feminist movement includes a growing number of local and regional associations that publish newsletters, encourage labor activities and strikes, work to secure better health care, and support women candidates for public office. Superficially, many of these activities resemble those of Anglo feminists. Terry Mason[40] points out, however, that the Chicana feminist movement differs, in that it depicts at least some aspects of traditional women's roles (being a wife and mother) in a positive light. Mason suggests that Chicanas dislike Anglo feminists who appear to condemn all aspects of traditional femininity. The Chicana movement does not portray an overriding opposition between women and men; men are not pictured as the enemy or blamed for the limitations placed on women.

The Mexican-American population is quite diverse, with large segments highly acculturated to Anglo middle-class patterns and other segments relatively aloof from them. In the face of this diversity, there is a strong need to stress Chicano unity to mobilize the population in pursuit of human-rights goals. Many Mexican-Americans see themselves as a colonized population. Maxine Baca Zinn[41] argues that the main strategy for achieving decolonization and for forming the New La Raza is to use the family as the basic organizational unit of the movement. In this "political familism," machismo is being redefined to mean active striving for the good of the Mexican-American people. All members, young and old, men and women, are urged to contribute to the movement. Women are valued for their contributions to the family as well as for their activities outside the home. Chicana feminism places little stress on liberation for women alone; it emphasizes instead the benefits that can be obtained for Chicanos as a group.

Puerto Rican Women on the Mainland

[My mother] once told me her idea of hell was to be a single mother of two children under five in the South Bronx. I'm afraid of ever knowing what she meant. Aurora Levins Morales[42]

Puerto Ricans have been citizens of the United States since 1917, a condition that facilitates frequent movement back and forth between the island and the mainland. Puerto Rico is an island colony belonging to the United States, with a poorly developed economy.[43] Migrants to the mainland tend to be from rural areas and to lack advanced education or job skills specifically applicable in an urban setting. Still, Puerto Ricans perceive the mainland as offering a wealth of opportunities, and they choose to concentrate in the New York City area. Puerto Ricans who move to other cities receive better jobs and pay than do those in New York,[44] but that city remains the major point of arrival and of departure for the journey home.

Many factors contribute to the decision to return to the island: a Puerto Rican's lack of English language skills, hostility expressed toward dark-skinned people, and the Anglo emphasis on competition and material gain. Puerto Rican values stress generosity, personalism, and spiritual rather than material matters. These conflict with the emphasis on efficiency and rationality of the Anglo-Protestant culture Puerto Ricans encounter.[45] In addition, friends and family, sometimes even young children, are back home on the island. Migrants know that they can return to people who care about them.

Women experience migration, transience, and discrimination in ways that are personally disruptive and that make family life difficult. More women than men return to Puerto Rico. Some are women who have lost their jobs, older women whose children are grown, or women whose marriages have dissolved. As Lourdes Miranda King points out,

> It is not unusual to find women working in the United States whose children are cared for by grandmothers or other relatives in Puerto Rico, or to find wives and children living in Puerto Rico while their husbands find work in the mainland, or to find working wives in Puerto Rico "pioneering the resettlement" of husband and children—different patterns yet with the same divisive effect on families. The woman is thrust into the role of sole supporter, creating the new immigrant woman and incidentally destroying the myth of the passive female.[46]

It is impossible to understand the lives of Puerto Rican women on the mainland without examining their lives on the island. Quite briefly, island culture is a mixture of Spanish, African, and Native American antecedents, resulting in a blend that is uniquely Puerto Rican. The culture emphasizes macho values for men, virginity and honor for women. Girls experience many more restrictions in dress, conduct, movement, and language use than do boys. A girl is not permitted to be openly aggressive and must channel her ambitions into narrowly defined areas—marriage, some schooling, and a limited range of jobs. These include the helping professions—nursing and teaching—if she is well educated, and service work and manufacturing jobs if she is not.[47] Marriages are not particularly equalitarian. Marya Munoz Vasquez points out that men will do housework only if the windows are closed and the curtains drawn. "If someone learned that the husband was helping his wife or catering to her wishes, he would be described as *sentado en el baul* (the implication is that his wife dominates him)."[48] Wives defer to husbands by consulting them about everyday decisions. Men strive to maintain a public image of being dominant and macho even if their personal values are at variance with the social norm. The emotional distance between husband and wife and the unbalanced power structure contribute to women's deep psychological investment in their children.

Puerto Rican women carry these expectations with them to the mainland, where the latter are often shattered. In New York, there is not always a husband to consult, women need to act independently, and children born outside marriage are more heavily stigmatized. Puerto Rican women find their mainland-reared children more boisterous, harder to control, and more detached.[49] Jobs are difficult to find. The stereotype is that women have an easier time finding work than men do. In fact, women's employment status has declined more than men's has because of the recent deterioration of the industrial economy in the Northeast.[50] Nonetheless, belief in women's greater economic success persists, echoing the false rhetoric that black women encounter.

Puerto Ricans share some similarities with other minority groups. The pattern of moving back and forth between Puerto Rico and the mainland and of being first-generation urbanites resembles Native Americans' movement between the reservation and the city. The Spanish heritage and strict emphasis on traditional gender roles is shared with Mexican- and Cuban-Americans. Economically (e.g., in per capita income), Puerto Ricans are slightly above Native Americans and blacks and slightly below Mexican- and Cuban-Americans. Finally, Puerto Ricans on the mainland are beginning to organize to demand the rights and services accorded other U.S. citizens. Women are active in this movement. While some Puerto Rican women think that men should take leadership roles and receive extra respect for doing so, other women are becoming sufficiently radicalized to begin to press for women's rights as well.[51]

Cuban Women in the United States

Cuban immigrants began arriving in the United States soon after the fall of the Batista government and Castro's rise to power. The first groups were people who had been prominent in the Batista regime, from well-educated affluent families. Castro's policy is to allow almost everyone who wishes to leave Cuba to do so. More recent migrants have been less well educated. The special programs that were instituted to settle Cuban refugees outside the Miami area have been all but abandoned now, so that a large proportion remain where they first entered the country.[52]

The early Cuban women immigrants had been well educated but were not oriented toward working for pay. The tradition of *vergenza* (female dignity and honor) prevailed in Cuba. Women from the middle and upper classes were expected to be bright and energetic but not to traffic too frequently in men's affairs of business and politics. These women were accustomed to having domestic servants to do housework and to care for their children.[53]

The transition to the United States was abrupt and disorganizing. Many wives came with their children to face an uncertain future in this country. The early immigrants believed that their stay here would be temporary and that they would soon return to Cuba. Later immigrants did not share this illusion, as the Castro government showed no signs of failing. Regardless of marital status, the era in which they immigrated, or their level of preparation, many Cuban women were thrust into the labor force. Lacking English language skills, they were unlikely to find secretarial and clerical jobs; and lacking the specific credentials, even highly educated women were unable to enter teaching, medicine, and law. Most found jobs only as factory operatives and in domestic service, as did their husbands and brothers, but many men were eventually able to acquire credentials and to resume professional careers.[54]

The ranks of Cuban women are constantly replenished by recent immigrants.[55] Working may be a relatively permanent adaptation for Cuban women in the United States, and the occupational patterns of these women increasingly resemble those of Anglo women. Myra Marx Ferree[56] emphasizes that many of the first immigrant groups worked only to regain the socioeconomic status their families lost in moving to this country. She found few differences between working and nonworking Cuban women in Florida. Working women were more interested in issues of pay and working hours, but they expected to continue to do most of the household work. Women's attitudes toward family and gender roles were determined more by the age at which they entered this country than by their labor-force status. Women who came as children, or who were born here, were less likely to accept restrictions on women's roles than were women who migrated as adults. The younger women looked forward to more equalitarian family roles than those their mothers and grandmothers had experienced.

Asian-American Women

There are several distinct groups of Asian-American women. In the nineteenth century, most Chinese and Japanese immigrants were male sojourners intent on making money and returning to their native lands. Few prospered in the mines, railroads, and canneries of the west coast, and some returned empty-handed. Asian men on the west coast had to compete with white migrants for jobs and resources. Consequently, prejudices and stereotypes were formed, and sometimes open hostilities erupted. The Chinese Exclusion Acts and other restrictive legislation affected the numbers of Asian women entering the country and the subsequent formation of families.[57] The Japanese were more likely to bring wives with them than were the Chinese; nonetheless some, like the Chinese, sent back to their homeland for "picture brides."[58]

Because of the character of immigration legislation and the patterns of immigration, there was an unbalanced sex ratio among Asian groups. The figures are startling. In California in 1920, there were 529 Chinese men and 171 Japanese men for every 100 women of their respective nationalities.[59] The presence of so many single men created a need for services typically performed in families. A sizable segment of the population, especially among the Chinese, ran boardinghouses, laundries, and restaurants. Chinese women were imported and were forced to serve as prostitutes. The demand for their services was high among the single men who had no other form of sexual outlet. The wages of prostitutes, camp cooks, and laundry workers were low, however, because the wages of the men they served were low.[60]

Japanese women were able to come to the United States and to establish families before the restrictive Immigration Act of 1924. Some were able to buy land and to establish truck farms on the west coast. Japanese women worked side by side with their husbands in the fields throughout the long day and returned to the household at night to do all the housework. Men did not participate in housework and child care. Japanese women were expected to sacrifice their own well-being so that the family could gain a foothold in the new land. They were to defer to their husbands, even to go hungry so that men could eat when food was scarce.[61] The more prosperous the Japanese became, the more resentment other groups directed toward them. Anti-Japanese sentiment climaxed during World War II, when people of Japanese ancestry were forced to move to relocation camps in the interior. After the war, there were very few new Japanese immigrants of either sex.

In contrast, Chinese women did not arrive in great numbers until after World War II, when they came as the wives of returning servicemen, both Anglos and Chinese-Americans.[62] Contemporary immigrants of Chinese ancestry come from many different Asian countries; they are often students who elect to stay in the United States. The Chinese-American population has increased dramatically, and the sex ratio has evened out.

Filipino men began migrating to the United States in large numbers after World War II. Among recent Filipino immigrants, increasing numbers have been women, but Filipinos still have the largest excess of men of any Asian group.[63] Filipino women exemplify the effect of immigration policies on a group's composition. Since 1952, immigration policies have given first preference to the children and spouses of people who are already citizens of the United States, second preference to highly skilled professionals, and third preference to workers in skilled or unskilled occupations for which laborers are needed.[64] Filipino women typically migrate after receiving extensive specialized education for medical careers. Filipinos are far more likely than are members of any other group, including Anglos, to be doctors, nurses, or medical technologists. Specialization in medicine has given Filipino women an opportunity to come to this country and an avenue for assimilation as well.

In part because of immigration policy, and in part because of extensive upward mobility among Asians, there are very sharp differences between older and younger generations of Asian women.[65] Older women are factory workers—often seamstresses—or they are in service jobs as restaurant workers, hairdressers, nurses' aides, and the like. Younger Asian women resemble Anglo women in occupational distribution, with high proportions doing secretarial and clerical work. Younger Asian women have been well educated, but they encounter artificial ceilings on their professional achievements, and face stop signs along the road to managerial posts.

Generational differences in education and jobs are accompanied by strong differences in values and lifestyles. Japanese parents worry about their children remaining faithful to traditional religious beliefs and are especially concerned about their daughters marrying Anglos.[66] Older Asians hold traditional values for their children. Members of both sexes, but girls particularly, are supposed to be modest, unassuming, and strongly oriented toward family. This means that younger women who espouse feminist values, who place individual desires over family needs, or who merely pursue a chosen career actively are in danger of coming into conflict with their parents. There is little social support for the independent, self-achieving woman.

The traditional Chinese family had roles rigidly prescribed on the basis of sex and age. The father—"the terrible old one"—was a patriarch with supreme authority. Wives and daughters were expected to serve the male head of the family and to produce male heirs. Education was not necessary for women; in fact, it might endanger feminine virtues of modesty, inconspicuousness, patience, gentleness, and sensitivity to others. This stark picture of family roles was the ideal model in traditional China.[67] Young Chinese-American women are likely to have foreign-born parents and grandparents and to experience conflict with them over proper demeanor, dress, regard for elders, dating, mate selection, and career choice. Although Lucy Huang suggests that younger Chinese respond to their parents with resignation (and not rebellion),[68] other adaptations can occur as well. These women face a primary conflict between the assertiveness and activism needed to succeed in a chosen career and the reserve and modesty demanded by Chinese culture.

In the popular and scholarly literature, Asian Americans are depicted as a "model" minority: polite, deferential, hard-working, achievement-oriented, and economically well placed.[69] Indeed, Asians have had to be many of these things to survive against hostile stereotypes and repeated harassment. Their struggles have enabled each successive generation to attain more education and higher-status occupations than the previous one. Despite their upward movement, Asian Americans have had difficulty entering management careers in white-owned businesses, and they do not receive the same rates of pay within occupations as whites do.[70]

In the last two decades, Asian American groups organized to protest negative stereotyping, to counteract employment discrimination, and to reclaim Asian identity. Whites are puzzled by these efforts, because they do not know the history of Asians in this country and they fail to recognize the depths of hostility and humiliation that Asians have experienced.[71]

Esther Ngan-Ling Chow[72] describes women's participation in Asian-American movements designed to eliminate racism, to improve the well-being of deprived Asians, and to foster pride in Asian cultural heritage. Because Asians have been segregated from whites, women's strongest ties are to their specific Asian group. They have felt somewhat aloof or estranged from the feminist movement. Recent events encourage women to become more radical in pursuit of women's interests. These include the hostility of Asian men toward independent women; the vicious stereotyping applied specifically to Asian women by whites; and the mistreatment, desertion, and physical abuse of Asian women by Anglo husbands. Asian feminism is tempered by concern over the well-being of impoverished Asians and the need to identify as Asians in a race-conscious society. Hence, similar to blacks and Mexican-Americans, Asian feminists place more emphasis on jobs and health, and give lower priority to abortion rights or political office-holding for women.[73]

So little has been written about other groups of Asian-American women that I hesitate to mention them in this context. There are several hundred thousand Vietnamese, Laotians, and Cambodians residing in this country. Only the Vietnamese are identified separately in publications from the 1980 U.S. Census. As recent refugees, their fate in this country is an open question.

Two other groups are identified in the Census — Koreans and Asian Indians (people from India). Most have migrated in the past twenty years. Unlike the refugee groups, Koreans and Asian Indians are typically very highly educated and possess financial resources that are sufficient to place them in high status positions. Indeed, the proportions of men in the groups who are professionals and managers exceed the proportions of Anglo men who reach these lofty occupational levels. The occupational patterns of Korean and Asian Indian women are not so exalted; they resemble those of Anglo women. Interestingly, the degree of inequality between women and men in the attainment of managerial and professional occupations was higher among Koreans and Asian Indians than among the other nine groups for which current data are available.[74]

GENDER AND JOBS: A SCHOLARLY VIEW

Gender inequality refers to differences between women and men in access to rewards, resources, positions, rights, and privileges, and it varies a great deal among the eleven groups. I measured gender inequality in the attainment of professional and technical occupations by comparing women's share of the total professional positions held by each group with women's share of the total labor force in each group. The resulting value — women's adjusted share — has a plus sign when women's share of the professional positions exceeds their share of the total labor force and indicates that women are overrepresented, compared to men, in that job category for that group. The resulting value has a minus sign when women are underrepresented, compared to men, in that job category. Similar procedures were carried out for the job category "managers, executives, and administrators." (See Table 2.)

Do the positive signs for professional occupations for Native Americans, blacks, and other groups in Table 2 indicate that women have exceeded men in job attainment? No. The professional category includes a very large number of different specific occupations that vary enormously in the power, pay, and prestige attached to them. Minority women are more heavily concentrated in the lower-paying, less prestigious occupations than are minority men. The managerial jobs also differ greatly and follow the rule that

TABLE 2
Gender Inequality in Minority Groups, 1980

Minority group	Women's share of		Gender inequality		Women's share of		Gender inequality	
	Professional positions (percent)	Labor force (percent)	Adjusted share	Rank	Managerial positions (percent)	Labor force (percent)	Adjusted share	Rank
Native American	53.5	43.5	+10.0%	(8)	39.1	43.5	− 4.4%	(9)
Black	65.7	49.9	+15.8	(11)	45.0	49.9	− 4.9	(8)
Mexican American	47.8	37.5	+10.3	(9)	33.3	37.5	− 4.2	(10)
Puerto Rican	49.9	39.2	+10.7	(10)	32.2	39.2	− 7.0	(7)
Cuban	42.7	44.3	− 1.6	(6)	28.5	44.3	−15.8	(4)
Chinese	34.3	43.7	− 9.4	(3)	35.0	43.7	− 8.7	(6)
Japanese	42.7	48.0	− 5.3	(5)	31.1	48.0	−16.9	(2)
Filipino	61.4	52.9	+ 8.5	(7)	43.5	52.9	− 9.4	(5)
Korean	39.6	52.3	−12.7	(2)	30.0	52.3	−22.3	(1)
Asian Indian	26.9	34.9	− 8.0	(8)	18.6	34.9	−16.3	(3)
Vietnamese	28.6	41.6	−13.0	(1)	39.1	41.6	− 2.5	(11)

SOURCE: U.S. Bureau of the Census (1983).

the higher the prestige, pay, or authority of an occupation, the fewer the women found in it. Because of the within-category variability, the figures in Table 2 provide only estimates of the specific amount of inequality between women and men in the attainment of high-status occupations.

The minority groups were rank ordered according to the degree of gender inequality in each of the two job categories. A 1 was assigned to the group with the greatest amount of inequality; an 11 was assigned to the group with the least inequality. Table 3 uses rank-order correlation to show how gender inequality in jobs is related to a series of minority group characteristics. A positive sign indicates that characteristic is associated with greater gender inequality in jobs; a negative sign indicates that variable or characteristic is associated with lesser gender inequality in jobs *across all groups.* The larger the numerical value of the correlation, the stronger the link between a variable and the degree of gender inequality.

The various minority-group characteristics are grouped into three rough

T A B L E 3
Determinants of Gender Inequality in Professional and Managerial Occupations

	Rank order correlations with gender inequality	
Independent variables	Professional positions	Managerial positions
Gender-related variables		
Sex ratio	−.154	−.545
Men's advantage in education	+.891	+.318
Marital status of women		
Single, never married	−.409	−.809
Currently married	+.709	+.627
Currently divorced	−.725	−.116
Cumulative fertility	−.373	−.918
Percent women in labor force	+.209	+.418
Race and ethnic group characteristics		
Population size	−.891	−.436
Percent foreign born	+.773	+.327
Class of worker/type of employment		
Private wage and salary workers	+.218	−.218
Government employees	−.575	−.170
Self-employed	+.500	+.709
Unpaid family workers	+.784	+.543
Social class/economic resources		
Median family income	+.473	+.709
Percent below poverty level	−.236	−.727
Percent college graduates	+.672	+.709
Percent unemployed	−.673	−.727

categories: a set of variables related to gender and fertility within each group (gender); a set that reflects the unique historical and contemporary circumstances related to racial and ethnic membership (race); and a set that reflects the socioeconomic status of minority groups (class). Several variables in each set are connected to the level of gender inequality.

Considering the gender-related characteristics, the groups with the *lowest* levels of inequality between women and men are those with relatively few men; those in which men have only a slight advantage over women in school years completed; those with larger proportions of women who have never married or are currently divorced, or who have large numbers of children; and those with somewhat fewer numbers of women employed. These low-inequality groups include Native Americans, blacks, Mexican-Americans and Puerto Ricans.

Minority-group characteristics are also linked to gender inequality. Groups with high proportions of recent immigrants, that are small in size, and that engage in considerable self-employment exhibit the *highest* levels of inequality. These include the Chinese, Asian Indians, Koreans, and, to a lesser extent, Japanese and Cubans. These are groups in which men have an enormous educational advantage over women, which shows up in much higher proportions of men attaining high-status positions. In these groups as well, men become the self-employed doctors, lawyers, counsellors, and accountants in private practice, and the managers of the family business. Women, on the other hand, become secretaries or receptionists in their husband's offices or unpaid service workers in the family grocery store, motel, or repair shop.

Groups with large populations—blacks, Native Americans, and Mexican-Americans—have low levels of gender inequality. This is because the larger the group, the greater the economic discrimination against it, and the fewer the resources possessed by it. The third panel of Table 3 shows clearly that social class affects gender inequality in jobs. For every variable considered, groups with more resources and advantages exhibit great inequality between women and men; those with fewer resources exhibit a good deal less inequality in occupations.

These findings, coupled with the correlations (not shown) among the several independent variables, suggest several conclusions:

1. *Gender, race, and class intertwine in numerous ways.* For instance, large racial and ethnic groups are typically indigenous groups who experience greater discrimination and acquire limited economic resources. Smaller immigrant groups have higher class standing; they shun government employment and provide men with greater educational advantages over women. The higher the overall level of educational attainment of a group, the greater the disparity between women and men in school years completed. Because of the small number of minority groups, I had to examine the effects of each variable on gender inequality in jobs separately, when in reality their effects are overlapping and interactive.

2. *Employers, both public and private, play a part in producing varying levels of gender inequality in jobs.* They choose which groups to employ and they

assign men and women to different job levels, with commensurate differences in prestige, pay, and opportunities for advancement.

3. *The actual level of gender inequality in jobs reflects the opportunities and achievements of men as much as it does those of women.* Across minority groups, there are greater differences among men in the absolute level of occupational achievement than there are among women. (See Table 1 for the percent of men and of women in each occupational category.) Men are exceptionally advantaged in some groups (e.g., Asian Indians) and exceptionally disadvantaged in others (e.g., Mexican-Americans, blacks), but the percent of women who are in professional and managerial jobs varies within a much more limited range. This finding implies that people in general and employers in particular make distinctions among different groups of men, but tend to lump women together in an undifferentiated mass.

4. *Contrary to predictions,[75] groups with the greatest economic resources (higher social class) exhibit the greatest disparities between women and men, whereas groups with the fewest economic resources exhibit the smallest disparities between women and men in occupational achievement.* This finding provides very strong evidence of the substantial effect of social class on disparities between women and men.

I interpret the connection between higher social class and gender inequality in the following way.[76] In all groups, men and women share equally the goods and resources necessary for basic survival (food, clothing, shelter), but men tend to control surplus goods and resources and to use these surpluses to enhance their advantaged position. Men's control over surplus goods and resources is reflected in the higher and more specialized education obtained for sons rather than for daughters and in the priority assigned to husbands' over wives' careers.

In this view, men have greater privileges than do women in all groups, but men's privileges are greatest in the groups with highest social class standing. Minority groups with the lowest levels of education, jobs, and income in American society have the fewest surplus resources. Women contribute a large share of the family income, and are respected accordingly. The limited resources must be used for survival needs and are shared equally. Neither sons nor daughters are able to attain much advanced schooling, and the level of gender inequality in occupations remains relatively low.

By contrast, minority groups with higher levels of education, jobs, and income display more male dominance, especially over the surplus. Sons and daughters are equally highly likely to be sent to college, but sons are encouraged to complete graduate-level professional, technical, or business training. The specialized credentials of the sons translate into more high-status professional and managerial jobs than daughters are able to attain. Because of their greater income, husbands in the more advantaged groups can command more support, personal care taking, and services from their wives than can men in the less advantaged groups. These men may be more consciously egalitarian in attitudes than are men in lower-level jobs; nonetheless, they have the power to exert more authority in household affairs.[77]

There are many ways of viewing reality. In this section, I try to echo the themes and concerns expressed primarily by the minority women whose views are recorded in the book *This Bridge Called My Back: Writings by Radical Women of Color.*[78] These authors and scholars and leaders do not represent all the different communities of minority women. Yet their voices ring loud and true as they speak frankly of how they interpret the constraints imposed on their lives by the forces of race, class, gender, and sometimes homophobia, and describe their visions of the better world they hope to build.

Growing Up: Dual Identities

Many themes are interwoven throughout the book, and throughout other writings by women of color.[79] We can usefully begin with the earliest memories of these women, which are frequently of racist experiences involving denial or denigration of their identity as a minority-group member. Aurora Morales[80] remembers going from place to place in New York with her mother pretending to be an Italian, hiding their Puerto Rican identity, in order to rent an apartment. Barbara Cameron's[81] childhood was marred by many incidents of white terrorism; she watched as Anglos senselessly gunned down Native Americans who were her friends and relatives. The experience of even a little violence, whether based on ethnicity or not, engenders feelings of helplessness. As Naomi Littlebear writes, "I need to feel control of my own life—violence has on some level rendered me helpless and given me a deep fear of being powerless."[82] It was many years later before Littlebear could state with equanimity, "I've been through so much pain that I've popped out the other side."[83]

Growing up and establishing a satisfactory sense of self is often traumatic for any youngster. But whites in American society do not have to contend with the issue of racial identity. Their whiteness is a given, an established fact that is comfortable and never questioned. This is not the case for people of color, whose identities are dual in nature. On one side are the pressures to identify as an American, to try to achieve a taken-for-granted identity as an ordinary citizen. People of color must identify with general American or Anglo culture just to survive. From an ethnic perspective, however, Anglos and Anglo culture are not very desirable. For a Puerto Rican woman, Anglos may be perceived as too harsh, constrained, limited, and uptight. A Japanese woman might see the same people as too loose, unrestrained, and noisy. The only point on which the two might agree is that Anglos are uncommonly selfish.

At the same time that people of color must outwardly identify with and accept Anglo culture, they must carefully portray themselves within the minority community as a true member of their own group. Aurora Morales describes the intricate juggling of identity: "Where I grew up, I fought battles to prove I was Puerto Rican with the kids who called me 'Americanita' but I stayed on the safe side of that line: Carribean island, not Portah

Rican; exotic tropical blossom, not spic—living halfway in the skin and separating myself from the dark, bad city kids in Nueva York."[84]

Language and Culture

Growing up in a distinctive ethnic community means learning two different cultures and two very different modes of speaking. Language is more than a series of words and sounds put together to establish sentences. Language includes subtle inflections, symbols, and nuances. Language is an instrument without which culture would not survive, and it conveys a whole world of meaning. One's native language—whether it is standard American English or black English, Tex-Mex or Puerto Rican Spanish—reminds one of home, family, and community. Even the women of color who are most acculturated to Anglo culture yearn to return to their own origins via language, to hear the words spoken by their loved ones in the rhythms they have known since childhood.

As professionals or executives, acculturated women are successful in the Anglo-dominated career world; they appear to move easily in what is, for them, a foreign existence. These women are often asked to be spokespersons for their group, to describe their own culture for Anglo outsiders. They believe that such token roles are traps. If they speak from their hearts and describe the crushing experiences of racism, the Anglo audience will feel guilt; if they describe what they really want—a sense of autonomy within a community built around their own values—the Anglos will feel threatened.[85] A hostile audience is not an inviting prospect. Equally daunting is the probability of being dismissed as not typical of the group, or of finding the work a complete waste of time:

> When Third World women are asked to speak representing our racial or ethnic group, we are expected to move, charm, or entertain, but not to educate in ways that are threatening to our audiences. We speak to audiences that sift out those parts of our speech (if what we say does not fit the image they have of us), come up to shake our hands with "That was lovely my dear, just lovely," and go home with the same mind set they come in with.[86]

Minority women perceive that portraying their own lives to outsiders is an impossible task. Even when they try, they have to do so in their *second* language.[87]

Growing Up Female

People of color endure growing-up experiences that are confounded by the issue of gender. All cultures prescribe different roles for women and men. Gender roles often contain internal contradictions.

Women's prescribed gender roles are particularly fraught with dualisms in regard to sexuality. To be successful as a woman means being able to attract and keep a man. Thus, just like many Anglo women, minority women have to negotiate the tricky labyrinth of displaying a "come hither" attitude to men but stopping those men before they get too close; of exuding an alluring sensuality for all men but reserving actual intercourse for the one and only special man; and sometimes of using sexuality to entice men while having been taught that they will not enjoy actual intercourse at all.[88]

These hide-and-seek games concerning sexuality are as familiar to white women as they are to women of color. Yet women of color experience some additional twists on the dating–rating–mating contests. For instance, it may be even more difficult for a minority woman than for her white counterpart to accept her sexuality as a lesbian and to identify herself publicly as gay. This is so because of the special concern of minority groups to at least appear to conform to Anglo culture, and the very great efforts expended by minority group members to stamp out any signs of nonconformity.[89]

Heterosexual minority women face the quandary of becoming attached to white men much more frequently than Anglo women consider linking up with minority men. In some respects, white men are very attractive to minority women. They carry the comfort of full-fledged acceptance in white-dominated society, and frequently they have the glamor of more money and resources than minority men. Yet the man's very whiteness erects a barrier. His own growing-up experiences may render him incapable of understanding the minority woman. Furthermore, men of all groups come to view women as sexual property, i.e., as nonpersons whom the man may possess, treat, and dispose of as he sees fit. Given that the dominant group has been accustomed to seeing minority groups as instruments for reaching their own ends, as slaves, or as inferior persons, how tempting it must be for the white man to regard minority women especially as sexual property, as unfit for marriage, or as having no need or right to be treated decently.

Suppose that, in spite of all this, a minority woman chooses to align herself with a white man. Then minority men feel betrayed because they believe the white man has not only emasculated the black man, the Hispanic man, the Asian man, the Native American man, or whomever, but also the white man has stolen his sexual property.

And what of minority women's relationships with minority men? Anglo culture virtually equates masculinity with money, whiteness, and sexual prowess. Many minority persons of both sexes believe that Anglos have conspired to rob minority men of each of these. Therefore, minority women feel especially concerned to support men's egos and to help men build a strong sense of masculinity.[90]

Gender roles reach far beyond issues of love and sex. Gender-type proscriptions and prescriptions pervade every nook and cranny of human life.[91] In all cultures, women are viewed as less valuable and less powerful than men. Growing up for all girls means coming to terms with these negative views and stereotypes.

Typically, the mother is charged with teaching these lessons to her daughter. Gloria Anzaldua describes the multiple contradictions she learned from her widowed mother:

Though she loved me she would only show it covertly—in the tone of her voice, in a look. Not so with my brothers—there it was visible for all the world to see. They were male and surrogate husbands, legitimate receivers of her power. Her allegiance was and is to her male children, not to the female.

Seeing my mother turn to my brothers for protection, for guidance —a mock act. She and I both knew she wouldn't be getting any from them. Like most men they didn't have it to give, instead needed to get it from women. . . .

Yet she could not discount me. "Machona—india ladina" (masculine—wild Indian), she would call me because I did not act like a nice little Chicanita is supposed to act: later, in the same breath she would praise and blame me, often for the same thing—being a tomboy and wearing boots, being unafraid of snakes or knives, showing my contempt for women's roles, leaving home to go to college, not settling down and getting married, being a politica, siding with the Farm-workers. Yet, while she would try to correct my more aggressive moods, my mother was secretly proud of my "waywardness." (Something she will never admit.) Proud that I'd worked myself through school. Secretly proud of my paintings, of my writing, though all the while complaining because I made no money out of it.[92]

Divisions within the Minority Community

Generational differences erect barriers among women. The speed of social change in this country guarantees that contemporary women will inhabit a world that is different from that of their mothers. And mothers and daughters can inhabit different worlds *at the same time* within this country. The possibilities are endless: mother came to this country as a foreign immigrant to the west coast while daughter grew up as an American citizen in the interior; or mother battles the legacy of slavery in the rural South while daughter copes with sexism and racism in the urban North; or mother lives on the Lakota Sioux Indian Reservation while daughter lives and works in the dry heat of Los Angeles; "or" (but probably "and") mother scrubs floors, waits on white people, and struggles with poverty so that daughter might go to college and have a professional career.

But it is not just the separate worlds that divide mother and daughter; it is the separate thinking as well. The mothers taught daughters to survive in a racist, classist, sexist, and homophobic society, for which the daughters are eternally grateful. The mothers also counseled patience, tolerance, occa-sional deceit, and suppression of anger—for to recognize the injustices would make a difficult situation intolerably worse. Yet the daughters are coming to a full realization of their own anger at the injustice that they suffer, that their mothers and fathers endured, and that their brothers speak against, although often for men only. The daughters can no longer accept stereotyped and negative definitions of themselves based on either race or gender. They perceive that their mothers did accept those hatreds in order to survive, that their mothers do not understand their own thinking about injustice, and that their mothers are afraid that the daughters will be disillu-sioned or harmed by the views they have chosen.[93] The mothers perceive their daughters' lives as rejections of their own. To reach across these barriers, to heal and soften the divisions between mother and daughter, is a top priority for minority women.

A minor theme in the personal writings of minority women concerns the barriers between sisters, i.e., between them and other women within their own group. Minority women are painfully aware that whites and men control the bulk of the resources and most of the power in all situations in American society. As minority women, they control little of either. They understand that it is frequently advantageous and often critical to ally themselves with the powerful others (whites or men). Minority women struggle against this system of power and, privately at least, provide plenty of support for one another. How painful it is, then, to find that the same women who supported them in private, sometimes go over to the other side in public where the support would really count.

Another minor theme concerns relationships with brothers (men in the same group). Minority feminism frequently originated from participation in minority-group movements, where women gained in courage to strike out against racial oppression and developed a strong sense of the injustice of sexism. Yet to pursue feminism is to invite rejection from minority men. Merle Woo describes the complex web of gender and race:

> Some of the male writers in the Asian American community seem never to support us. They always expect us to support them. . . . We almost always do. Anti–Yellow men? Are they kidding? We go to their readings, buy and read and comment on their books, and try to keep up a dialogue. And they accuse us of betrayal, are resentful because we do readings together as Women, and so often do not come to our performances. And all the while we hurt because we are rejected by our brothers. . . . These men of color . . . fight the racism in white society, but they have bought the white male definition of "masculinity". . . .
>
> Some Asian men don't seem to understand that by supporting Third World women and fighting sexism, they are helping themselves as well. I understand all too clearly how dehumanized Dad was in this country. To be a Chinese man in America is to be a victim of both racism and sexism. He was made to feel he was without strength, identity, and purpose. He was made to feel soft and weak, whose only job was to serve whites. Yes, Ma, at one time I was ashamed of him because I thought he was "womanly.". . . I didn't know that he spent a year and a half on Angel Island; that we could never have our right names; that he lived in constant fear of being deported; that, like you, he worked two full-time jobs most of his life; that he was mocked and ridiculed because he speaks "broken English." And Ma, I was so ashamed (of his being humiliated by whites) when I was only six years old that I never held his hand again.[94]

Attitudes toward White Women

To grow up as a minority group member is to learn self-hatred through the vicious racism in American society. Minority women struggle to replace self-hatred with love, respect, and esteem for themselves, for their parents, and for other members of their own group. They also acknowledge their feelings toward other minority groups: Several authors in *This Bridge Called My Back* point out that they could not help but learn to be racist in a society that uses racism "both to create false differences among us and to mask very, very significant ones—cultural, economic, political."[95] In discussing the racist images she derived from television, books, movies, and magazines, Barbara Cameron says "We are all continually pumped with gross and inaccurate images of everyone else and we all pump it out."[96] To transcend such false images requires performing painful self-analysis,[97] recognizing the differences in historical experience among different groups of women, allowing each group time and space to separate and come to terms with their own lives and experiences, and finally uniting across the barriers of race, class, and sexual preference.[98]

At this stage of feminist consciousness among minority women, identifying with other women of color is difficult, identifying with white women is doubly so. Some of the worst instances of racism are suffered through the hands of white women. Even without those instances, perceptions of whites and feelings toward whites are greatly mixed. Each view is grounded in reality and is thought out with awareness of its implications.

Some women of color believe that white women can never know the full horror of brute racism or the grinding desperation of intense poverty.[99] In this view, racial divisions are so strong that white women can never relinquish the advantages they have by being white; in a crisis, they will inevitably support white men or the capitalist economic system that white men control. This perception coincides with having experienced the white feminist movement as "elitist, crudely insensitive, and condescending," and white women as "limited, bigoted, and myopic."[100]

Other minority women believe that it is wrong to judge white women on the basis of their race; in fact, that kind of racism is precisely what all women must work to eradicate. In this view, white women are racist because they have been linked with the white power structure and oppressed by white men.[101] This perception accompanies the hope that, through intense efforts, women of all groups can come to understand one another and the forces that divide them, and ultimately can work together to build a better society.

CONCLUSION: MINORITY WOMEN AND FEMINISM

This essay has ranged widely over the historical experiences of diverse groups, through a social science approach to understanding the creation of gender inequality in jobs, toward some of the ideas expressed by minority women themselves. Each approach offers a different perspective of the lives of minority women. Yet I believe each approach leads to the same findings and implications, and these have distinct consequences for the kind of feminism minority women choose.

The first finding is that, while there are many forces that divide, individual women do not and cannot compartmentalize their lives. They cannot neatly separate their experiences into distinct categories and label some "racial," some "gender," and some "social class." They are not members of minorities first and women second. Nor are they women first and members of minorities second. They are individuals who have incorporated a whole constellation of roles, characteristics, and experiences into their self-concepts. Yet gender and race are master statuses, channeling these women into certain roles and impinging on their lives at every turn.

Second, what is true for the individual is true for the society. The forces of race, gender, and class are inseparable. Where minority women have been feminist activists, their activities and viewpoints are affected by a deep concern for the well-being of their own ethnic group. Women have been exceptionally active in all types of minority-group movements as well. For many, their treatment as second-class citizens in minority movements crystallized their awareness of sexism, galvanizing them into action on that front. Yet the experience of racism makes them reluctant to form enduring links with white feminist groups, and the experience of sexism often puts them at loggerheads with minority males. The experience of class oppression may turn their immediate attention to crushing financial issues. Thus gender, race, and class intertwine, weaving patterns that both unite minority women with and separate them from other groups.

Third, minority women must be free to define themselves, their priorities, and their goals based on their own analysis of their condition in American society. In the near future, producing such an analysis requires some separatism, so that various individuals and groups may sort out their unique experiences, reclaim their own identities, and emerge with a fresh perspective on the many forces that shape American society.

Fourth, white women can know and understand the conditions of minority women, but it is their responsibility to find out. Minority women do not want the task of explaining themselves to anyone.

Finally, the white feminist movement can incorporate minority women, but for it to do so movement members must go far beyond merely expressing a desire to be inclusive. The movement must embrace all the issues that confront women, especially those of race and class. Barbara Smith put the matter very well:

> The reason racism is a feminist issue is easily explained by the inherent definition of feminism. Feminism is the political theory and practice to free all women: women of color, working-class women, poor women, physically challenged women, lesbians, old women, as well as white economically privileged heterosexual women. Anything less than this is not feminism, but merely female self-aggrandizement.[102]

NOTES

1. Native Americans prefer to be called by their own tribal names—Zuni, Hopi, Pueblo, etc.—but recognize that that is unlikely to happen. Therefore, they opt for "Native Americans" as a label. Few want to be called "Indians," because that is indeed a misnomer.

2. John Price, "North American Indian Families," in Charles H. Mindel and Robert W. Habenstein, eds., *Ethnic Families in America* (New York: Elsevier North-Holland, 1976), pp. 248–70.

3. Judith K. Brown, "Economic Organization and the Position of Women among the Iroquois," *Ethnohistory,* 17 (1970), pp. 151–63.

4. Laila Sheekry Hamamsy, "The Role of Women in a Changing Navajo Society," *American Anthropologist,* 59 (1957), pp. 101–11.

5. The term "Anglo" is widely used in the Southwest to distinguish whites from Mexican-Americans and from Native Americans. In this article, the terms "white," "Anglo," "majority," and "dominant group" are used synonymously. They refer to the great bulk of U.S. citizens who, despite their specific ethnic backgrounds, participate in and are products of the mainstream culture.

6. Joan Ablon, "Relocated American Indians in the San Francisco Bay Area: Social Interaction and Indian Identity," in Howard M. Bahr, Bruce A. Chadwick, and Robert C. Day, eds., *Native Americans Today: Sociological Perspectives* (New York: Harper and Row, 1972), pp. 412–27. See also James Downs, "The Cowboy and the Lady: Models as a Determinant of the Rate of Acculturation among the Pinon Navajo," in *Native Americans Today,* pp. 275–91.

7. Shirley Hill Witt, "Native Women Today: Sexism and the Indian Woman," in Sue Cox, ed., *Female Psychology: The Emerging Self* (Chicago: Science Research Associates, 1976), pp. 249–59.

8. Carol Cornelius Mohawk, "Native Women: Working for the Survival of Our People," *Akwesasne Notes* (Late Fall, 1982), pp. 4–5.

9. Rosemary Ackley Christensen, "Indian Women: A Literature Search through Historical and Personal Perspectives" (not dated, circa 1983), xeroxed publication of the Indian Education Department of the Minneapolis, Minnesota, public schools.

10. Shirley Fiske, "Rules of Address: Navajo Women in Los Angeles," *Journal of Anthropological Research,* 34 (1978), pp. 72–91.

11. Rosalie Wax and Robert Thomas, "The Enemies of the People," in *Native Americans Today,* pp. 177–92.

12. A woman interviewed by John L. Gwaltney in *Drylongso: A Self-portrait of Black America* (New York: Vintage, 1980). Quotation cited by Patricia Hill Collins in "Learning from the Outsider Within: The Sociological Significance of Black Feminist Thought," *Social Problems,* 33 (1986), pp. 514–532.

13. Frances M. Beal, "Slave of a Slave No More: Black Women in Struggle," *The Black Scholar,* 6 (1975), pp. 16–24.

14. Elizabeth F. Hood, "Black Women, White Women: Separate Paths to Liberation," *The Black Scholar,* 9 (1978), pp. 45–56.

15. Natalie J. Sokoloff, "Evaluating Gains and Losses by Black and White Women and Men in the Professions, 1960–1980," *Social Problems,* 35 (1988) pp. 36–53. See also Patricia A. Gwartney-Gibbs and Patricia A. Taylor, "Black Women Workers' Earnings Progress in Three Industrial Sectors," *Sage* 3 (1986), pp. 20–25; and Mary Romero, "Twice Protected? Assessing the Impact of Affirmative Action on Mexican-American Women," *Ethnicity and Public Policy,* 5 (1986), pp. 135–56.

16. Jacquelyne Jackson, "But Where Are the Men?" *The Black Scholar,* 3 (1971), pp. 30–41.

17. Elmer P. Martin and Joanne Mitchell Martin, "The Black Woman: Perspectives on Her Role in the Family," *Ethnicity and Public Policy,* 5 (1986), pp. 184–205.

18. Norma Carson, "The Role of Informal Adoption in the Liberation of Black Women" (Paper presented at the annual meeting of the Mid-South Sociological Association, Jackson, Miss., October, 1982).

19. Cheryl Townsend Gilkes, "From Slavery to Social Welfare: Racism and the Control of Black Women," in Amy Smerdlow and Helen Lessinger, eds., *Class, Race, and Sex: The Dynamics of Control* (Boston: G. K. Hall, 1981), pp. 288–300.

20. Martin and Martin, *op. cit.;* Hood, *op. cit.*

21. Aldon Morris, "The Black Southern Sit-In Movement: An Analysis of Internal Organization," *American Sociological Review,* 46 (1981), pp. 744–767.

22. Guida West, *The National Welfare Rights Movement: The Social Protest of Poor Women* (New York: Praeger, 1981).

23. Linda J. M. LaRue, "The Black Movement and Women's Liberation," in Cox, ed., *Female Psychology*, pp. 216–25.

24. Diane K. Lewis, "A Response to Inequality: Black Women, Racism, and Sexism," *Signs: Journal of Women in Culture and Society*, 3 (1977), pp. 339–61.

25. The Combahee River Collective, "A Black Feminist Statement," Gloria T. Hull, Patricia Bell Scott, and Barbara Smith, eds., *All the Women Are White, All the Blacks Are Men, But Some of Us Are Brave: Black Women's Studies* (Old Westbury, N.Y.: Feminist Press, 1982), pp. 13–22.

26. Barbara Cameron, "Entering the Lives of Others," in Cherrie Moraga and Gloria Anzaldua, eds., *This Bridge Called My Back: Writings by Radical Women of Color* (Watertown, Mass.: Persephone Press, 1981), p. 23.

27. Collins, *op. cit.*

28. Consuelo Nieto, "The Chicana and the Women's Rights Movement: A Perspective," *Civil Rights Digest*, 6 (1974), pp. 36–42.

29. Anna Nieto-Gomez, "Heritage of *La Hembra*," in Cox, ed., *Female Psychology*, pp. 226–34.

30. The *encomienda* was a plantationlike enterprise, controlled by a Spanish landlord. The native people worked there in a relationship to the Spanish master that was semifeudal and semislave.

31. Betty Garcia-Bahne, "*La Chicana* and the Chicano Family," in Rosaura Sanchez and Rosa Martinez Cruz, eds., *Essays on la Mujer* (Los Angeles: University of California, Chicano Studies Center Publications, 1977), p. 39.

32. David Alvirez and Frank D. Bean, "The Mexican-American Family," in Mindel and Habenstein, eds., *Ethnic Families in America* (New York: Elsevier North-Holland, 1976), pp. 270–89.

33. Leo Grebler, Joan W. Moore, and Ralph C. Guzman, *The Mexican-American People* (New York: Free Press, 1970), p. 366.

34. Garcia-Bahne, *op. cit.*

35. Nieto-Gomez, *op. cit.*

36. Romero, *op. cit.*, p. 138.

37. Margarita B. Melville, "Selective Acculturation of Female Mexican Migrants," in Margarita B. Melville, ed., *Twice a Minority: Mexican American Women* (St. Louis: C. V. Mosby Co., 1980), pp. 155–63; and Maxine Baca Zinn, "Political Familism: Toward Sex Role Equality in Chicano Families," *Atzlan*, 6 (1975), pp. 13–26.

38. Dudley L. Poston, Jr., and David Alvirez, "On the Cost of Being a Mexican-American Worker," *Social Science Quarterly*, 53 (1973), pp. 697–709. See also Laura E. Arroyo, "Industrial and Occupational Distribution of Chicana Workers," *Atzlan*, 4 (1974), pp. 343–82; and Romero, *op. cit.*

39. Romero, *op. cit.*

40. Terry Mason, "Symbolic Strategies for Change: A Discussion of the Chicana Women's Movement," in Melville, ed., *Twice a Minority*, pp. 95–108.

41. Zinn, *op. cit.*

42. Aurora Levins Morales, "And Even Fidel Can't Change That," in Moraga and Anzaldua, eds., *This Bridge Called My Back*, p. 53.

43. Michael Myerson, "Puerto Rico, Our Backyard Colony," in Francesco Cordasco and Eugene Bucchioni, eds., *The Puerto Rican Experience* (Totowa, N.J.: Rowman and Littlefield, 1973), pp. 114–24. See also Eva E. Sandis, "Characteristics of Puerto Rican Migrants to and from the United States," Cordasco and Bucchioni, *The Puerto Rican Experience*, pp. 127–49.

44. Lois Gray, "The Jobs Puerto Ricans Hold in New York City," *Monthly Labor Review*, 28 (1978), pp. 12–16.

45. Joseph P. Fitzpatrick, "The Puerto Rican Family," in Mindel and Habenstein, eds., *Ethnic Families in America*, pp. 192–217.

46. Lourdes Miranda King, "*Puertorriquenas* in the United States: The Impact of Double Discrimination," *Civil Rights Digest* (1974), p. 24.

47. Edward W. Christensen, "The Puerto Rican Woman: A Profile," in Edna Acosta-Belen, ed., *The Puerto Rican Woman* (New York: Praeger Publishers, 1979), pp. 51–63. See also Edna Acosta-Belen and Barbara R. Sjostrom, "The Educational and Professional Status of Puerto Rican Women," in *The Puerto Rican Woman,* pp. 64–74.

48. Marya Munoz Vasquez, "The Effects of Role Expectations on the Marital Status of Urban Puerto Rican Women," in Acosta-Belen, ed., *The Puerto Rican Woman,* p. 80.

49. Fitzpatrick, "The Puerto Rican Family."

50. Gray, *op. cit.*

51. King, *op. cit.*

52. Geoffrey Fox, "Cuban Workers in Exile," *Transaction,* 8 (1971), pp. 21–30.

53. Myra Marx Ferree, "Employment Without Liberation: Cuban Women in the United States," *Social Science Quarterly,* 60 (1978), pp. 35–50.

54. Elizabeth M. Almquist, *Minorities, Gender and Work,* (Lexington, Mass.: D.C. Heath, 1979).

55. Alexjandro Portes and Alex Stepick, "Unwelcome Immigrants: The Labor Market Experiences of 1980 (Mariel) Cuban and Haitian Refugees in South Florida," *American Sociological Review,* 50 (1985), pp. 493–514.

56. Myra Marx Ferree, *op. cit.*

57. Norris Hundley, Jr., *The Asian American: The Historical Experience* (Santa Barbara, Calif.: ABC-Clio, 1976).

58. Rose Hum Lee, "Chinese Americans," in Francis Brown and Joseph S. Roucedk, eds., *One America* (New York: Prentice-Hall, 1951), pp. 309–18; Harry L. Kitano, *Japanese Americans: Evolution of a Subculture* (Englewood Cliffs, N.J.: Prentice-Hall, 1976).

59. Monica Boyd, "Oriental Immigration: The Experience of the Chinese, Japanese, and Filipino Populations in the United States," *International Migration Review,* 5 (1971), pp. 48–80.

60. Lucie Cheng Hirata, "Free, Indentured, Enslaved: Chinese Prostitutes in Nineteenth Century America," *Signs: Journal of Women in Culture and Society,* 5 (1979), pp. 3–79.

61. Irene Fujitomi and Diane Wong, "The New Asian-American Woman," in Stanley Sue and Nathan Wagner, eds., *Asian Americans: Psychological Perspectives* (Palo Alto, Calif.: Science and Behavior Books, 1973).

62. Boyd, *op. cit.*

63. Ibid.

64. Elaine M. Murphy and Patricia Cancellier, *Immigration: Questions and Answers* (Washington, D.C.: Population Reference Bureau, 1982).

65. The Bureau of the Census has not published data by age for minority groups from the 1980 census. Some of this discussion relies on the 1970 census data described in Almquist, *Minorities, Gender and Work.*

66. R. Brooke Jacobsen, "Changes in the Chinese Family," *Social Science,* 51 (1976), pp. 26–31; Fujitomi and Wong, *op. cit.* For a fascinating fictional account of the relationships within families with one or more parents born abroad, see Maxine Hong Kingston, *China Men* (New York: Ballantine, 1980).

67. Lucy Jen Huang, "The Chinese American Family," in Mindel and Habenstein, eds., *Ethnic Families in America,* pp. 124–47.

68. Ibid.

69. Charles Hirschman and Morrison G. Wong, "The Extraordinary Educational Attainment of Asian-Americans: A Search for Historical Evidence and Explanations," *Social Forces,* 65 (1986), pp. 1–27; Victor Nee and Jimy Sanders, "The Road to Parity: Determinants of the Socioeconomic Attainments of Asian Americans," *Ethnic and Racial Studies,* 8 (1985), pp. 75–93.

70. Robert M. Jiobu, "Earnings Differentials between Whites and Ethnic Minorities: The Cases of Asian Americans, Blacks, and Chicanos," *Sociology and Social Research,* 61 (1976), pp. 24–38.

71. Mitsuye Yamada, "Invisibility Is an Unnatural Disaster: Reflections of an Asian American Woman," in Moraga and Anzaldua, eds., *This Bridge Called My Back,* pp. 35–40.

72. Esther Ngan-Ling Chow, "The Development of Feminist Consciousness Among Asian American Women," *Gender and Society,* 1 (1987), pp. 284–299. See also, Bok-Lim Kim, "Asian Wives of U.S. Servicemen: Women in Shadows," *Amerasia Journal,* 4 (1977), pp. 91–115; and Chalsa Loo and Paul Ong, "Slaying Demons with a Sewing Needle: Feminist Issues for China-town Women," *Berkeley Journal of Sociology,* 27 (1982), pp. 77–88.

73. Similar patterns distinguish blacks and whites. See, Elaine J. Hall and Myra Marx Ferree, "Race Differences in Abortion Attitudes," *Public Opinion Quarterly,* 50 (1986), pp. 193–207; and H. Edward Ransford and Jon Miller, "Race, Sex and Feminist Outlooks," *American Sociological Review,* 48 (1983), pp. 46–59.

74. Elizabeth M. Almquist, "Labor Market Gender Inequality in Minority Groups," *Gender and Society,* 1 (1987), pp. 400–14.

75. See Almquist, "Labor Market Gender Inequality in Minority Groups." The finding that greater gender inequality occurs in higher-social-class groups contradicts Betty Garcia-Bahne's hypothesis that working- and lower-class minority men would be more sexist than middle-class "successful" men in both attitudes and behavior (see Garcia-Bahne, *"La Chicana* and the Chicano Family").

76. Gerhard Lenski has proposed similar views about class stratification in whole societies. See *Power and Privilege: A Theory of Social Stratification* (New York: McGraw-Hill, 1966).

77. Janice M. Steil, "Marital Relationships and Mental Health: The Psychic Costs of Inequality," in Jo Freeman, ed., *Women: A Feminist Perspective,* Third Edition, (Palo Alto, Calif.: Mayfield, 1984), pp. 113–23.

78. As already indicated, *This Bridge Called My Back: Writings by Radical Women of Color,* was edited by Cherrie Moraga and Gloria Anzaldua, and was published in Watertown, Massachusetts by Persephone Press in 1981. Subsequent references to articles in this book refer to it simply as *"This Bridge."*

79. See Angela Davis, *Women, Race and Class* (New York: Random House, 1981); Paula Giddings, *When and Where I Enter: The Impact of Black Women on Race and Sex in America* (New York: Bantam, 1984); Margaret C. Simms and Julianne M. Malveaux, eds., *Slipping through the Cracks: The Status of Black Women,* (New Brunswick, N.J.: Transaction, 1986).

80. Morales, *op. cit.,* pp. 53–57.

81. Barbara Cameron, "Gee, You Don't Seem Like an Indian from the Reservation," *This Bridge,* pp. 46–52.

82. Naomi Littlebear, "Earth-Lover, Survivor, Musician," *This Bridge,* p. 158.

83. Ibid.

84. Morales, *op. cit.,* p. 53.

85. Doris Davenport, "The Pathology of Racism: A Conversation with Third World Wimmin," *This Bridge,* pp. 85–91.

86. Mitsuye Yamada, "Asian Pacific American Women and Feminism," *This Bridge,* p. 71.

87. Barbara Smith and Beverly Smith, "Across the Kitchen Table: A Sister to Sister Dialogue," *This Bridge,* pp. 113–27.

88. Morales, *op. cit.,* p. 56.

89. Morraga, *"La Guera," This Bridge,* pp. 27–34.

90. The authors in *This Bridge* actually say very little about the need to build or restore the threatened masculinity of minority men. I suspect radical and lesbian women have moved beyond this issue in the 1980s.

91. Laurel Richardson, *The Dynamics of Sex and Gender,* Third Edition, (New York: Harper and Row, 1988).

92. Gloria Anzaldua, *"La Prieta," This Bridge,* p. 201.

93. Yamada, *op. cit.,* describes the painful process of coming to grips with her identity as an Asian woman.

94. Merle Woo, "An Open Letter to Ma," *This Bridge,* p. 145.

95. Mirtha Quintanales, "I Paid Very Hard for My Immigrant Ignorance," *This Bridge,* p. 153.

96. Cameron, *op. cit.,* p. 49.

97. Quintanales, *op. cit.,* p. 154.

98. Smith and Smith, *op. cit.,* p. 126.

99. Ibid., p. 113.

100. Davenport, *op. cit.,* p. 86.

101. Smith and Smith, *op. cit.*

102. Quoted at the beginning of the section "Entering the Lives of Others: Theory in the Flesh," in *This Bridge,* p. 23.

What Price Independence? Social Reactions to Lesbians, Spinsters, Widows, and Nuns

ROSE WEITZ

For seven days in 1981, nineteen-year-old Stephanie Riethmiller was held captive by two men and a woman in a secluded Alabama cabin. During that time, according to Riethmiller, her captors constantly harangued her on the sinfulness of homosexuality, and one captor raped her nightly. Riethmiller's parents, who feared that their daughter was involved in a lesbian relationship with her roommate, had paid $8,000 for this "deprogramming"; her mother remained in the next room throughout her captivity. When the kidnappers were brought to trial, the jury, in the opinion of the judge, "permit[ted] their moral evaluations to enter into their legal conclusions" and failed to bring in a guilty verdict (Raskin 1982, 19).

As the Riethmiller case shows, the individual who identifies herself as a lesbian — or who is so labeled by others — may face severe social, economic, and legal sanctions. Along with communists, the diseased, and the insane, persons who openly acknowledge their homosexuality may be denied admission to the United States. In most U.S. jurisdictions, discrimination against homosexuals in housing, employment, child custody, and other areas of life is legal, while homosexual behavior is illegal. Gay persons are not covered under any of the national Civil Rights Acts, and most court decisions have held that they are not covered under the equal-protection clause of the United States Constitution. Moreover, in 1986 the U.S. Supreme Court ruled in *Bowers v. Hardwick* that state antisodomy laws are legal. (For an excellent, inclusive analysis of the legal status of homosexuality, see Achtenberg 1985.)

These legal restrictions reflect generally held social attitudes. National surveys in recent years have found that slightly more than half (51 percent) of American adults believe homosexuality should not be considered an acceptable lifestyle (*Gallup Report* 1982). A similar proportion (55 percent) believe homosexual relationships between consenting adults should not be legal—an increase of 12 percent since 1977 (*Gallup Report* 1987).

CROSS-CULTURAL AND HISTORICAL VIEWS OF LESBIANISM

To most Americans, stigmatization and punishment of lesbianism seem perfectly natural. Yet such has not always been the case. In fact, a study of attitudes toward homosexuality in seventy-six cultures around the world found that in 64 percent of those cultures "homosexual activities of one sort or another are considered normal and socially acceptable for certain members of the community" (Ford and Beach 1951, 130).

In the western world, male homosexuality, which had been an accepted part of Greek and Roman culture, was increasingly rejected by society as the power of the Christian church grew (Barrett 1979). Yet lesbianism generally remained unrecognized legally and socially until the beginning of the modern age. Instead, beginning with the Renaissance, intimate "romantic friendships" between women were a common part of life, at least among the middle and upper classes (Faderman 1981).[1]

> Women who were romantic friends were everything to each other. They lived to be together. They thought of each other constantly. They made each other deliriously happy or horribly miserable by the increase or abatement of their proffered love. They were jealous of other female friends (and certainly of male friends) who impinged on their beloved's time or threatened to carry away a portion of her affections. They vowed that if it were at all possible they would someday live together, or at least die together, and they declared that both eventualities would be their greatest happiness. They embraced and kissed and walked hand in hand, and some even held each other all night in sleep. But unless they were transvestites or considered "unwomanly" in some male's conception, there was little chance that their relationships would be considered lesbian. [Faderman 1981, 84.]

We cannot know whether most romantic friends expressed their love for women genitally, and we do know that most were married to men (at least in part for economic survival). A reading of letters and journals from this period leaves no doubt, however, of the erotic and emotional intensity of these relationships between women and little doubt that in another era the relationships would have been expressed sexually (Smith-Rosenberg 1975; Faderman 1981). Yet belief in the purity of these relationships lingered even into the twentieth century. For example, when the British Parliament attempted in 1885 to add mention of lesbianism to its criminal code, Queen Victoria refused to sign the bill, on the ground that such behavior did not exist (Ettorre 1980).

Given that lesbianism has not always elicited negative social reactions, the current intolerance of it cannot derive from some universal biological or ethical law. What, then, causes these negative social reactions? I suggest in this article that at least part of the answer lies in the threat that lesbianism presents to the power of males in society. Furthermore, I suggest that whenever men fear women's sexual or economic independence, all unmarried women face an increased risk of stigmatization and punishment. The experience of such diverse groups as lesbians, medieval nuns, and Hindu widows shows the interrelated social fates of all women not under the direct control of men.

LESBIANS AND THE THREAT TO MALE POWER

Western culture teaches that women are the weaker sex, that they cannot flourish — or perhaps even survive — without the protection of men. Women are taught that they cannot live happy and fulfilled lives without a Prince Charming, who is superior to them in all ways. In the struggle to find and keep their men, women learn to view one another as untrustworthy competitors. They subordinate the development of their own psychological, physical, and professional strengths to the task of finding male protectors who will make up for their shortcomings. In this way, Western culture keeps women from developing bonds with one another, while it maintains their dependence on men.

Lesbians[2] throw a large wrench into the works of this cultural system. In a society that denigrates women, lesbians value women enough to spend their lives with women rather than with men. Lesbians therefore do not and cannot rely on the protection of men. Knowing that they will not have that protection, lesbians are forced to develop their own resources. The very survival of lesbians therefore suggests the potential strength of all women and their ability to transcend their traditional roles. At the same time, since lesbians do not have even the illusion of male protection that marriage provides, and since they are likely to see their fate as tied to other women rather than to individual men, lesbians may be more likely than heterosexual women to believe in the necessity of fighting for women's rights; the heavy involvement of lesbians in the feminist movement seems to support this thesis (Abbott and Love 1972).

Lesbians also threaten the dominant cultural system by presenting, or at least appearing to present, an alternative to the typical inequality of heterosexual relationships. Partners attempting to equalize power in a heterosexual relationship must first neutralize deeply ingrained traditional sex roles. Since lesbian relationships generally contain no built-in assumption of the superiority of one partner,[3] developing an egalitarian relationship may be easier. Lesbian relationships suggest both that a love between equals is possible and that an alternative way of obtaining such a love may exist. Regardless of the actual likelihood of achieving equality in a lesbian relationship, the threat to the system remains, as long as lesbian relationships are believed to be more egalitarian. This threat increases significantly when, as in the past few years, lesbians express pride in and satisfaction with their lifestyle.

If lesbianism incurs social wrath because of the threat it presents to existing sexist social arrangements, then we should find that lesbianism is most negatively viewed by persons who hold sexist beliefs. Evidence from various studies (summarized in Weinberger and Millham 1979) supports this hypothesis. Homophobia (i.e., fear and hatred of homosexuals) appears strongly correlated with support for traditional sex roles. Survey data suggest that support for traditional sex roles explains homophobia better than do negative or conservative attitudes toward sex in general (MacDonald et al. 1973; MacDonald and Games 1974).

Historical data on when and under what circumstances lesbianism became stigmatized also support the contention of a link between that stigma and the threat lesbianism poses to male power. As described in the previous section, romantic friendships between women were common in both Europe and America from the Renaissance through the late nineteenth century. The women involved were generally accepted or at least tolerated by society even in the few cases where their relationships were openly sexual. That acceptance ceased, however, if either of the women attempted to usurp male privilege in some way — by wearing men's clothing, using a dildo, or passing as a man. Only in these circumstances were pre–modern-era lesbians likely to suffer social sanctions. In looking at both historical records and fiction from the thirteenth through the nineteenth centuries, Faderman (1981) found that women were, at most, lightly punished for lesbianism unless they wore male clothing.[4] She therefore concludes that "at the base it was not the sexual aspects of lesbianism as much as the attempted usurpation of male prerogative by women who behaved like men that many societies appeared to find most disturbing" (Faderman 1981, 17).

As long as the women involved did not attempt to obtain male privileges, romantic friends ran little risk of censure before the late nineteenth century. The factors behind the shift in attitude that occurred at that time again suggest the importance of the threat that lesbianism seemed to pose to male power.

Before the twentieth century, only a small number of independently wealthy women (such as the Ladies of Llangollen [Mavor 1973]) were able to establish their own households and live out their lives with their female companions (Faderman 1981). By the second half of the nineteenth century, however, the combined effects of the Civil War in this country and of male migration away from rural areas in both the United States and Europe had created a surplus of unmarried women in many communities. At the same time, the growth of the feminist movement had led to increased educational opportunities for women. These factors, coupled with the growth of industrialization, opened the possibility of employment and an independent existence to significant numbers of women.

Once female independence became a real economic possibility, it became a serious concern to those intent on maintaining the sexual status quo. Relationships between women, which previously had seemed harmless, now took on a new and threatening appearance. Only at this point do new theories emerge that reject the Victorian image of the passionless woman (Cott 1978), acknowledge females as sexual beings, and define lesbianism as pathological.

Stereotypes of lesbianism, first developed in the early twentieth century, reduce the threat to existing social arrangements by defusing the power of lesbianism as a viable alternative lifestyle. According to these stereotypes, all lesbians are either butches or femmes, and their relationships merely mimic heterosexual relationships. Lesbianism, therefore, seems to offer no advantages over heterosexuality.

Cultural stereotypes defuse lesbian sexuality by alternately denying and exaggerating it. These stereotypes hold that women become lesbians because of either their inability to find a man or their hatred of men. Such stereotypes deny that lesbianism may be a positive choice, while suggesting that lesbianism can be "cured" by the right man. The supposed futility of lesbian sexuality was summed up by best-selling author Dr. David Reuben in the phrase, "one vagina plus another vagina still equals zero" (1969, 217). (Reuben further invalidated lesbianism by locating his entire discussion of the subject within his chapter on prostitution; male homosexuality was "honored" with its own chapter.) In other cultural arenas, lesbians and lesbianism are defined in purely sexual terms, stripped of all romantic, social, or political content. In this incarnation, lesbianism can be subverted into a vehicle for male sexual pleasure; in the world of pornographic films, men frequently construct lesbian scenes to play out their own sexual fantasies.

In sum, strong evidence suggests that the negative social reactions to lesbianism reflect male fears of female independence, and that social sanctions and cultural stereotypes serve to lessen the threat that these independent women pose to male power.

If this hypothesis is true, then it should also hold for other groups of women not under direct male control. Next, I briefly discuss how, historically, negative social reactions to such women seem most likely to develop whenever men fear women's sexual or economic independence.

SPINSTERS, WIDOWS, AND WOMEN RELIGIOUS

The inquisition against witches that occurred from the fifteenth through the seventeenth centuries represents the most extreme response in the Western world to the threat posed by independent women. The vast majority of the persons executed for witchcraft were women; estimates of the number killed range from under 100,000 to several million (Daly 1978). Accusations of witchcraft typically involved charges that the women healed sickness, engaged in prohibited sexual practices, or controlled reproduction (Ehrenreich and English 1973). Such activities threatened the power of the church by giving individuals (especially women) greater control over their own lives, reducing their dependence on the church for divine intervention while inhibiting the natural increase of the Catholic population.

The witchcraft trials occurred in a society undergoing the first throes of industrialization and urbanization (Nelson 1979). The weakening of the rural extended family forced many women to look for employment outside the home. These unattached women proved especially vulnerable to accusations of witchcraft (Nelson 1979; Daly 1978). As Mary Daly points out, "The targets of attack in the witchcraze were not women defined by assimilation into the patriarchal family. Rather, the witchcraze focused predominantly upon women who had rejected marriage (Spinsters) and some who had survived it (widows)" (1978, 184).

Contemporary theological beliefs regarding female sexuality magnified the perceived economic and social threat posed by unmarried women. The medieval church viewed all aspects of female sexuality with distrust; unless a woman was virginal or proven chaste, she was believed to be ruled by her sexual desires (Ehrenreich and English 1973). Catholic doctrine blamed Eve's licentiousness for the fall from grace in the Garden of Eden. According to the most popular medieval "manual" for witchhunters, the *Malleus Maleficarum,* most witches were women because "all witchcraft comes from carnal lust, which is in women insatiable" (Kramer and Sprenger 1971, 120). Given this theology, any woman not under the direct sexual control of a man would appear suspect, if not outright dangerous.

For most women living before the nineteenth century who wished to or were forced to remain unmarried, entering the religious life was the only socially acceptable option.[5] During the Middle Ages, a woman could either become a nun or join one of the "secular convents" known as *Beguines* (Nelson 1979; Boulding 1976). Beguines arose to serve the population of surplus unmarried women that had developed in the early European cities. Residents of Beguines took a vow of chastity and obedience while living there, but they could marry thereafter. They spent their days in work and prayer.

Beguines threatened the monopolies of both the guilds and the church. The guilds feared the economic competition of these organized skilled women workers, while the church feared their social and religious independence (Nelson 1979); the Beguines' uncloistered life seemed likely to lead women into sin, while the lack of perpetual vows freed them from direct church supervision. For these reasons, the church in the fourteenth century ordered the Beguine houses dissolved, although some have continued nonetheless to the present day. Residents were urged either to marry or to become nuns (Boulding 1976).

The history of convents similarly illustrates the church's distrust of independent women (Eckenstein 1963). In the early medieval period, many nuns lived with their families. Some nuns showed their religious vocation through the wearing of a veil, while others wore no distinctive dress. Convents served as centers of learning for women, providing educational opportunities not available elsewhere. During this period, many "double monasteries" flourished, in which male and female residents lived together and shared decision-making authority.

Given medieval ideas regarding the spiritual weakness and inherent carnality of women, the independence of early medieval nuns could not be allowed to last long. The developing laws of feudalism increasingly restricted the right of women to own land, so that, by the Renaissance, women faced increasing difficulties in attempting to found or to endow convents, while friars began to take over the management of existing convents (Eckenstein 1963). The church gradually closed all double monasteries, pressuring nuns to enter cloisters and to wear religious habits. Education for nuns increasingly seemed unnecessary or even dangerous. For this reason, by the six-teenth century, church authorities had significantly decreased the educa-tional opportunities available in most convents, although some convents did manage to preserve their intellectual traditions. Once Latin ceased to be taught to them, nuns were effectively excluded from all major church decisions.

As Protestant ideas began to infiltrate Europe, the status of unmarried women declined. One of the few areas in which Catholics and early Protes-tants agreed was the danger presented by independent women. Responding to flagrant sexual offenses in medieval monasteries, Protestants concluded that few men—let alone women, given their basically carnal nature—could maintain a celibate life. They therefore viewed "the religious profession [as] a thing of evil and temptation in which it was not possible to keep holy" (Charitas Perckheimer, quoted in Eckenstein 1963, 467). To Protestants, "marriage was the most acceptable state before God and . . . a woman has no claim to consideration except in her capacity as wife and mother" (Eck-enstein 1963, 433). These beliefs, coupled with the political aims of Protes-tant rulers, culminated in the forced dissolution of convents and monasteries in many parts of Europe. In Protestant Europe, women were left without a socially acceptable alternative to marriage, while, in Catholic Europe, nuns had been stripped of their autonomy.

The belief in female carnality continued until the nineteenth century. At that point, while lower-class women were still considered sexually wanton by their social betters, prescriptive literature began to paint an image of upper-class women as passionless (Cott 1978). In this situation, unmarried lower-class women continued to suffer severe social sanctions as real or suspected prostitutes. Unmarried upper-class women continued to be stigma-tized as unnatural, since they were not fulfilling their allotted role as wives and mothers. These upper-class women did not seem particularly threaten-ing, however, since they were assumed, at least in public discourse, to be asexual beings. As a result, social sanctions against them diminished sharply, not to emerge again until women's new-found economic independence significantly changed the social context of romantic friendships among women.

In this historical overview, I have so far discussed only events in the Western world. In the West, widows probably evoke less of a sense of threat than do other unmarried women, since widows do not generally seem to have chosen their fate. It is instructive to compare the fate of Hindu widows, who are believed to have caused their husbands' deaths by sins they com-mitted in this or a previous life (Daly 1978; Stein 1978).

Since a Hindu woman's status is determined by her relationship to a man, and since Hindu custom forbids remarriage, widows literally have no place in that society. A widow is a superfluous economic burden on her family. She is also viewed as a potential source of dishonor, since Hindus believe that "women are by nature sexually unreliable and incapable of leading chaste lives without a husband to control them" (Stein 1978, 255). For the benefit of her family and for her own happiness in future lives, a widow was in the past expected to commit suttee—to throw herself alive onto her husband's burning funeral pyre.[6] The horror of suttee was multiplied by the practice of polygamy and by the practice of marrying young girls to grown men, which resulted in the widowing of many young girls before they even reached puberty (Stein 1978; Daly 1978). Suttee, child marriage, and polygamy are illegal under the current government, but they do still occur.

As her only alternative to suttee, a widow was allowed to adopt a life of such poverty and austerity that she rarely survived for long. Her life was made even more miserable by the fact that only faithful wives were permitted to commit suttee. The refusal to commit suttee might therefore be regarded as an admission of infidelity. If a woman declined to immolate herself, her relatives might force her to do so, to protect both her honor and the honor of her family.

STIGMATIZATION OF MALE HOMOSEXUALS

Reflecting the basic concerns of this book, this article has discussed male homosexuality only in passing. Nevertheless, we cannot ignore that the sanctions against male homosexuality appear even stronger than those against lesbianism. Why might this be so? First, I would argue that anything women do is considered relatively trivial—be it housework, mothering, or lesbianism. Second, whereas lesbians threaten the status quo by refusing to accept their inferior position as women, gay males may threaten it even more by appearing to reject their privileged status as men. Prevailing cultural mythology holds that lesbians want to be males. In a paradoxical way, therefore, lesbians may be perceived as upholding "male" values. Male homosexuality, on the other hand, is regarded as a rejection of masculine values; gay males are regarded as feminized "sissies" and "queens." Thus, male homosexuality, with its implied rejection of male privilege, may seem even more incomprehensible and threatening than lesbianism. Finally, research indicates that people in general are more fearful and intolerant of homosexuals of their own sex than of homosexuals belonging to the opposite sex (Weinberger and Millham 1979). The greater stigmatization of male than female homosexuality may therefore simply reflect the greater ability of males to enforce their prejudices.

CONCLUSIONS

The stigmatization of independent women—whether spinster, widow, nun, or lesbian—is neither automatic nor natural. Rather, it seems to derive from a particular social constellation in which men fear women's sexual and economic independence. Sociological theory explains how stigmatizing individuals as deviant may serve certain purposes for the dominant community, regardless of the accuracy of the accusations leveled (Erikson 1962). First, particularly when social norms are changing rapidly, labeling and punishing certain behaviors as deviant emphasizes the new or continued unacceptability of those behaviors. The stigmatization of "romantic friendships" in the early twentieth century, for example, forced all members of society to recognize that social norms had changed and that such relationships would no longer be tolerated. Second, stigmatizing certain groups as deviant may increase solidarity within the dominant group, as the dominant group unites against its common enemy. Third, stigmatizing as deviant the individuals who challenge traditional ideas may reduce the threat of social change, if those individuals either lose credibility or are removed from the community altogether.

These principles apply to the stigmatization of independent women, from the labeling of nontraditional women as witches in medieval society to the condemnation of lesbians in contemporary society. Medieval inquisitors used the label *witch* to reinforce the normative boundaries of their community, to unite that community against the perceived source of its problems, and to eliminate completely women who seemed to threaten the social order. Currently, the word *lesbian* is used not only to describe women who love other women but also to censure women who overstep the bounds of the traditional female role and to teach all women that such behavior will not be tolerated. Feminists, women athletes, professional women, and others risk being labeled lesbian for their actions and beliefs. Awareness of the potential social consequences of that label exerts significant pressure on all women to remain in their traditional roles.

Antifeminist forces have used the lesbian label to denigrate all feminists, to incite community wrath against them, and to dismiss their political claims. In 1969 and 1970, some feminists responded to this social pressure by purging lesbians from their midst and proclaiming their moral purity (Abbott and Love 1972). This tactic proved extremely self-destructive, as movement organizations collapsed in bitterness and dissension. In addition, eliminating lesbian members had little effect, since lesbian-baiting by antifeminists was equally damaging to the movement, whether or not it was accurate.

By late 1970, many feminists had realized that trying to remove lesbians from their organizations was both self-destructive and ineffective. In response to this knowledge, various feminist organizations went on record acknowledging sexual preference as a feminist and a civil rights issue and supporting the rights of lesbians (Abbott and Love 1972). In a press conference held in December 1970, various women's liberation activists stated:

> Women's Liberation and Homosexual Liberation are both struggling toward a common goal: a society free from defining and categorizing people by virtue of gender and/or sexual preference. "Lesbian" is a label used as a psychic weapon to keep women locked into their male-defined "feminine role." The essence of that role is that a woman is defined in terms of her relationship to men. A woman is called a Lesbian when she functions autonomously. Women's autonomy is what Women's Liberation is all about. [quoted in Abbott and Love 1972, 124.]

A leaflet distributed the same month by the New York branch of the National Organization for Women acknowledged that, when charges of lesbianism are made, "it is not one woman's sexual preference that is under attack — it is the freedom of all women to openly state values that fundamentally challenge the basic structure of patriarchy" (quoted in Abbott and Love 1972, 122).

It seems, then, that the fates of feminists and lesbians are inextricably intertwined. Unless and until women's independence is accepted, lesbians will be stigmatized, and unless and until the stigma attached to lesbianism diminishes, the lesbian label will be used as a weapon against those who work for women's independence.

NOTES

1. We have few first-hand data about the intimate lives of lower-class women. Few poorer women could write, and, even if they could and did record their lives, their letters and journals were rarely preserved.

2. I am using the terms *lesbian* and *heterosexual* as nouns simply to ease the flow of the writing. This article focuses on stigmatization, not on some intrinsic quality of individuals. Hence, in this article, *lesbian* and *heterosexual* refer to persons who adopt a particular lifestyle or who are labeled as doing so by significant others. These terms reflect shared social fates, not some essential, inflexible aspect of the individual.

3. Although there is no way to ascertain exactly what proportion of lesbian couples adopted butch–femme relationships in the past, recent studies suggest that such relationships have all but disappeared, especially among younger and more feminist lesbians (Tanner, 1978; Wolf, 1979; Peplau and Gordon, 1983; Harry, 1984; Lynch and Reilly, 1985/86).

4. The crime for which Joan of Arc was eventually condemned was not witchcraft but the heretical act of wearing male clothing.

5. However, it should be realized that convent life was not always a chosen refuge. Just as a father could marry his daughter to whatever man he chose, so too could he "marry" his daughter to the church.

6. Suttee was most common among the upper castes (where a widow meant an extra mouth, but not an extra pair of hands), but it occurred throughout Hindu society (Stein 1978).

REFERENCES

Abbott, Sidney, and Barbara Love. *Sappho Was a Right-on Woman: A Liberated View of Lesbianism.* New York: Stein and Day Publishers, 1972.

Achtenberg, Roberta (ed.). *Sexual Orientation and the Law.* New York: Clark Boardman Co., 1985.

Barrett, Ellen M. "Legal Homophobia and the Christian Church." *Hastings Law Journal* 30(4): 1019–27, 1979.

Boulding, Elise. *The Underside of History.* Boulder, Colo.: Westview Press, 1976.

Bowers v. Hardwick, 498 U.S. 186, 92, L.Ed. 2d 140, 106 S.Ct. 2841 (1986).

Cott, Nancy. "Passionlessness: An Interpretation of Victorian Sexual Ideology, 1790–1850." *Signs: Journal of Women in Culture and Society* 4(2): 219–36, 1978.

Daly, Mary. *Gyn/ecology: The Metaethics of Radical Feminism.* Boston: Beacon Press, 1978.

Eckenstein, Lina. *Women under Monasticism.* New York: Russell and Russell, 1963.

Ehrenreich, Barbara, and Deirdre English. *Witches, Midwives and Nurses: A History of Women Healers.* Old Westbury, N.Y.: Feminist Press, 1973.

Erikson, Kai T. "Notes on the Sociology of Deviance." *Social Problems* 9(spring): 307–14, 1962.

Ettorre, E. M. *Lesbians, Women and Society*. London: Routledge and Kegan Paul, 1980.

Faderman, Lillian. *Surpassing the Love of Men: Romantic Friendship and Love between Women from the Renaissance to the Present*. New York: William Morrow and Co., 1981.

Ford, Clellan S., and Frank A. Beach. *Patterns of Sexual Behavior*. New York: Harper and Row, 1951.

Gallup Report. "Backlash against Gays Appears to Be Leveling Off." 258:12–18, 1987.

Gallup Report. "Little Change in Americans' Attitudes towards Gays." 205:3–19, 1982.

Glenn, Norval D., and Charles N. Weaver. "Attitudes towards Premarital, Extramarital and Homosexual Relationships in the United States in the 1970s." *Journal of Sex Research* 15(2): 108–17, 1979.

Harry, Joseph. *Gay Couples*. New York: Praeger, 1984.

Kramer, H., and J. Sprenger. *Malleus Maleficarum*. Translated by Montague Summers. New York: Dover Publications, 1971.

Lynch, Jean M., and Mary E. Reilly. "Role Relationships: Lesbian Perspectives." *Journal of Homosexuality*. 12(2): 53–69, 1985/86.

MacDonald, A. P., and R. G. Games. "Some Characteristics of Those Who Hold Positive and Negative Attitudes towards Homosexuals." *Journal of Homosexuality* 1(1): 9–28, 1974.

MacDonald, A. P., J. Huggins, S. Young, and R. A. Swanson. "Attitudes towards Homosexuality: Preservation of Sex Morality or the Double Standard." *Journal of Consulting and Clinical Psychology* 40(1): 161, 1973.

Mavor, Elizabeth. *The Ladies of Llangollen: A Study of Romantic Friendship*. New York: Penguin Books, 1973.

Nelson, Mary. "Why Witches Were Women." In Jo Freeman (ed.), *Women: A Feminist Perspective*, 2d ed. Palo Alto, Calif.: Mayfield Publishing Co., 1979, 451–68.

Peplau, Letitia A., and Stephen L. Gordon. "The Intimate Relationships of Lesbians and Gay Men." In Elizabeth R. Allgeier and Naomi B. McCormick (eds.), *Changing Boundaries: Gender Roles and Sexual Behavior*. Palo Alto, Calif.: Mayfield, 1983, 226–44.

Raskin, Richard. "The 'Deprogramming' of Stephanie Reithmiller," *Ms.*, Sept. 1982, 19.

Reuben, David. *Everything You Always Wanted to Know about Sex But Were Afraid to Ask*. New York: David McKay Co., 1969.

Rivera, Rhonda R. "Our Straight-laced Judges: The Legal Position of Homosexual Persons in the United States." *Hastings Law Journal* 30(4): 799–956, 1979.

Smith-Rosenberg, Carroll. "The Female World of Love and Ritual: Relations between Women in Nineteenth Century America." *Signs: Journal of Women in Culture and Society* 1(1): 1–29, 1975.

Stein, Dorothy K. "Women to Burn: Suttee as a Normative Institution." *Signs: Journal of Women in Culture and Society* 4(2): 253–68, 1978.

Tanner, Donna M. *The Lesbian Couple*. Lexington, Mass.: D.C. Heath and Co., 1978.

Weinberger, Linda E., and Jim Millham. "Attitudinal Homophobia and Support of Traditional Sex Roles." *Journal of Homosexuality* 4(3): 237–45, 1979.

Wolf, Deborah Goleman. *The Lesbian Community*. Berkeley: University of California Press, 1979.

The Sexual Politics of Interpersonal Behavior

NANCY HENLEY AND
JO FREEMAN

       Social interaction is the battlefield on which the daily war between the sexes is fought. It is here that women are constantly reminded what their "place" is and here that they are put back in their place, should they venture out. Thus, social interaction serves as the locus of the most common means of social control employed against women. By being continually reminded of their inferior status in their interactions with others, and continually compelled to acknowledge that status in their own patterns of behavior, women may internalize society's definition of them as inferior so thoroughly that they are often unaware of what their status is. Inferiority becomes habitual, and the inferior place assumes the familiarity —and even desirability— of home.

       Different sorts of cues in social interaction aid this enforcement of one's social definition, particularly the verbal message, the nonverbal message transmitted within a social relationship, and the nonverbal message transmitted by the environment. Our educational system emphasizes the verbal message but teaches us next to nothing about how we interpret and react to the nonverbal one. Just how important nonverbal messages are, however, is shown by the finding of Argyle et al.[1] that nonverbal cues have over four times the impact of verbal ones when verbal and nonverbal cues are used together. Even more important for women, Argyle found that female subjects were more responsive to nonverbal cues (compared with verbal ones) than male subjects. This finding has been confirmed in the extensive research of Rosenthal and his colleagues:[2] in studies of subjects of all ages and from a variety of occupations and cultures, they found consistently greater sensitivity to nonverbal communication among females than among males. If women are to understand how the subtle forces of social control work in their lives, they must learn as much as possible about how nonverbal cues affect people and particularly how they perpetuate the power and superior status enjoyed by men.

THE WORLD OF EVERYDAY EXPERIENCE

Even if a woman encounters no one else directly in her day, visual status reminders permeate her environment. As she moves through the day, she absorbs many variations of the same status theme, whether or not she is aware of it. Male bosses dictate while female secretaries bend over their steno pads. Male doctors operate while female nurses assist. At lunchtime, restaurants are populated with female table servers who wait on men. Magazine and billboard ads remind the woman that home maintenance and child care are her foremost responsibilities and that being a sex object for male voyeurs is her greatest asset. If she is married, her mail reminds her that she is a mere "Mrs." appended to her husband's name. When she is introduced to others or fills out a written form, the first thing she must do is divulge her marital status, acknowledging the social rule that the most important information anyone can know about her is her legal relationship to a man. Her spatial subordination is shown in ways parallel to that of other animal and human subordinates: Women's "territory" (office space at work, individual rooms, or space at home) tends to be less extensive and less desirable (e.g., not having office windows) than is men's. Women are not as free to move in others' territory or "open" territory (e.g., city streets) as are men.

Advertisements form a large part of our visual world, and the messages of advertisements are subtle but compelling in suggesting that the way the sexes are shown in them is the usual and appropriate arrangement. Sociologist Erving Goffman[3] describes six themes involving gender distinctions in advertising pictures: *relative size,* especially height, used to symbolize the greater importance of men than of women; *feminine touch* that is delicate, not truly grasping; *function ranking,* in which males direct and guide action while females are directed or watch; *the family,* in which fathers are linked with boys (and are distant) and mothers are linked with girls and girlhood; the *ritualization of subordination,* in which women, by lower spatial position, canting postures of the head and body, smiles, and clowning, display subordinate status to men; and *licensed withdrawal,* in which women are shown as relatively less oriented to the situation (often flooded with emotion or distracted by trivia) and are dependent on men. Goffman draws a parallel between the ritual of our everyday interaction and the hyperritualization of advertising: our "natural expressions" are commercials too, performed to sell a view of the world and of female – male (as well as other) relationships.

ASYMMETRY IN SOCIAL INTERACTION

Environmental cues set the stage on which the power relationships of the sexes are acted out and the assigned status of each sex is reinforced.[4] Although studies have been made of the several means by which status inequalities are communicated in interpersonal behavior, these studies do not usually deal with power relationships between men and women. Goffman has pointed to many characteristics associated with status:

> Between status equals we may expect to find interaction guided by symmetrical familiarity. Between superordinate and subordinate we may expect to find asymmetrical relations, the superordinate having the right to exercise certain familiarities which the subordinate is not allowed to reciprocate. Thus, in the research hospital, doctors tended to call nurses by their first names, while nurses responded with "polite" or "formal" address. Similarly, in American business organizations the boss may thoughtfully ask the elevator man how his children are, but this entrance into another's life may be blocked to the elevator man, who can appreciate the concern but not return it. Perhaps the clearest form of this is found in the psychiatrist–patient relation, where the psychiatrist has a right to touch on aspects of the patient's life that the patient might not even allow himself to touch upon, while of course this privilege is not reciprocated.
>
> Rules of demeanor, like rules of deference, can be symmetrical or asymmetrical. Between social equals, symmetrical rules of demeanor seem often to be prescribed. Between unequals many variations can be found. For example, at staff meetings on the psychiatric units of the hospital, medical doctors had the privilege of swearing, changing the topic of conversation, and sitting in undignified positions; attendants, on the other hand, had the right to attend staff meetings and to ask questions during them . . . but were implicitly expected to conduct themselves with greater circumspection than was required of doctors. . . . Similarly, doctors had the right to saunter into the nurses' station, lounge on the station's dispensing counter, and engage in joking with the nurses; other ranks participated in this informal interaction with doctors, but only after doctors had initiated it.[5]

A status variable that illustrates rules of symmetry and asymmetry is the use of terms of address, widely studied by Brown and others.[6] In languages that have both familiar and polite forms of the second person singular ("you"), asymmetrical use of the two forms invariably indicates a status difference, and it always follows the same pattern. The person using the familiar form is always the superior to the person using the polite form. In English, the only major European language not to have dual forms of address, status differences are similarly indicated by the right of first-naming (addressing a person by his or her given name rather than surname): The status superior can first-name the inferior in situations in which the inferior must use the superior's title and last name. An inferior who breaks this rule by inappropriately using a superior's first name is considered insolent.[7]

According to Brown, the pattern evident in the use of forms of address applies to a very wide range of interpersonal behavior and invariably has two other components: (1) whatever form is used by a superior in situations of status inequality can be used reciprocally by intimates, and whatever form is used by an inferior is the socially prescribed usage for nonintimates; (2) initiation or increase of intimacy is the right of the superior. To use the example of naming again to illustrate the first component, friends use first names with each other, whereas strangers use titles and last names (although "instant" intimacy is considered proper in some cultures, such as our own, among status equals in informal settings). As an example of the second component, status superiors, such as professors, specifically tell status inferiors, such as students, when they may use the first name, and often rebuff the inferiors if they assume such a right without invitation.

The relevance of these patterns to status differences between the sexes is readily seen. The social rules say that all moves to greater intimacy are a male prerogative: It is boys who are supposed to call girls for dates, men who are supposed to propose marriage to women, and males who are supposed to initiate sexual activity with females. Females who make "advances" are considered improper, forward, aggressive, brassy, or otherwise "unladylike." By initiating intimacy, they have stepped out of their place and usurped a status prerogative. The value of such a prerogative is that it is a form of power. In interactions between the sexes, as in other human interactions, the one who has the right to initiate greater intimacy has more control over the relationship. Superior status brings with it not only greater prestige and greater privilege but also greater power.

DEMEANOR, POSTURE, AND DRESS

The advantages of superior status are exemplified in many of the means of communicating status. Like the doctors in Goffman's research hospital, men are allowed such privileges as swearing and sitting in undignified positions, but women are denied them. Although the male privilege of swearing is curtailed in mixed company, the body movement permitted to women may be circumscribed even in all-female groups. It is considered "unladylike" for a woman to use her body too forcefully, to sprawl, to stand with her legs widely spread, to sit with her feet up, or to cross the ankle of one leg over the knee of the other. Many of these positions are ones of strength or dominance.

Henley[8] has reviewed the research evidence for sex differences in nonverbal behavior, linking it with evidence for differences due to power, status, or dominance. She concludes that the symbols and gestures used by males tend to be those of power and dominance, while the gestures of females tend to be those of subordination and submission. Wex[9] reached similar conclusions through her examination of the public postures of women and men photographed in Germany.[10] The more "feminine" a woman's clothes, the more circumscribed the use of her body. Depending on her clothes, she may be expected to sit with her knees together, not to sit cross-legged, or not even to bend over. Although these taboos seem to have lessened in recent years, how much so is unknown, and there are recurring social pressures for a "return to femininity," while etiquette arbiters assert that women must retain feminine posture no matter what their clothing.

Prior to the 1920s, women's clothes were designed to be confining and cumbersome. The dress-reform movement, which disposed of corsets and long skirts, was considered by many to have more significance for female emancipation than women's suffrage.[11] Today women's clothes are often designed to be revealing of their bodies, but women are expected to restrict their body movements to avoid revealing too much. Furthermore, because women's clothes are contrived to cling and reveal women's physical features, rather than to be loose as men's are, women must resort to purses instead of pockets to carry their belongings. These "conveniences" (purses) have become, in a time of unisex clothing and hairstyles and other blurred sex distinctions, one of the surest signs of sex, and thus have developed the character of a stigma, a sign of women's shame—for example, when they are used by comics to ridicule both women and transvestites.

ACCESS TO A PERSON'S SELF AND BODY

Women in our society are expected to reveal not only more of their bodies than men but also more of their minds and souls. Whereas men are expected to be stolid and impassive and not to disclose their feelings beyond certain limits, women are expected to express their feelings fully. Female socialization encourages generally greater expression of emotion than does male socialization (although expression of anger is more sanctioned for men than for women). Both socialization and expectations of others (social norms) are probably implicated in the frequent research finding that females are more self-disclosing to others than males are.[12] Self-disclosure involves both expression of emotion and revelation of other personal and intimate information. Not only do we expect women to be more self-disclosing than men, but we see negative implications when women are not self-disclosing, or when men are: A psychological study found that men who were very self-disclosing, and women who were *not* very self-disclosing, were considered by others to be more psychologically maladjusted than were nondisclosing men and disclosing women.[13] Such self-disclosure gives away knowledge about oneself, putting women at an immediate disadvantage relative to men: knowledge, as is often noted, is power.

The inverse relationship between disclosure and power has been reported in Goffman's earlier cited observations in a research hospital and in other studies. Slobin, Miller, and Porter[14] stated that individuals in a business organization are "more self-disclosing to their immediate superior than to their immediate subordinates." Self-disclosure is a means of enhancing another's power. When one person has greater access to information about another person, he or she has a resource the other person does not have. Thus, not only does power give status, but also status gives power. And those possessing neither must contribute to the power and status of others continuously.

Another factor adding to women's vulnerability is that they are socialized to *care* more than men—especially about personal relationships. This puts them at a disadvantage, as Ross articulated in what he called the Law of Personal Exploitation: "In any sentimental relation the one who cares less can exploit the one who cares more."[15] The same idea was stated more broadly by Waller and Hill as the Principle of Least Interest: "That person is able to dictate the conditions of association whose interest in the continuation of the affair is least."[16] In other words, women's caring, like their openness, gives them less power in a relationship.

One way to indicate acceptance of one's place and deference to those of superior status is to follow the rules of "personal space." Sommer has observed that dominant animals and human beings have a larger envelope of inviolability surrounding them—i.e., they are approached less closely—than those of lower status.[17] Willis made a study of the initial speaking distance set by an approaching person as a function of the speakers' relationship.[18] His finding that women were approached more closely than men—i.e., their personal space was smaller or more likely to be breached—is consistent with women's lower status. Likewise, women tend to yield space (step out of the way) when approached by men or in passing them, rather than men yielding, just as subordinate animals yield to dominant ones. And women's time, like their space, can be invaded readily.[19]

TOUCHING

Touching is one of the closer invasions of one's personal space, and in our low-contact culture it implies privileged access to another person. People who accidentally touch other people generally take great pains to apologize; people forced into close proximity, for example, in a crowded elevator, often go to extreme lengths to avoid touching. Even the figurative meanings of the word convey a notion of access to privileged areas—e.g., to one's emotions (one is touched by a sad story), or to one's purse (one is touched for ten dollars). In addition, the act of touching can be a subtle physical threat.

Remembering the patterns that Brown found in terms of address, it is enlightening to consider the interactions between pairs of persons of different status, and to picture who would be more likely to touch the other (put an arm around the shoulder or a hand on the back, tap the chest, hold the arm, or the like): teacher and student; master and servant; police officer and accused; doctor and patient; minister and parishioner; adviser and advisee; supervisor and worker; business executive and secretary. Again, we see that the form used by the status superior—touching—is the form used between intimates of equal status. It is considered presumptuous for a person of low status to initiate touch, like first-naming, with a person of higher status.

Some earlier observational and self-report studies indicated that females were touched more than males were, both as children (from six months on) and as adults.[20] Henley specifically tested the hypothesis that touching is associated with status.[21] In observations of incidents of touch in public urban places, higher-status persons did touch lower-status persons significantly more. In particular, men touched women more, even when all other variables were held constant. In a more comprehensive observational study and review of the evidence, Major reported findings similar to Henley's.[22] Henley also observed greater touching by higher-status persons (including males) in the popular culture media. She reported on a questionnaire study in which both females and males indicated greater expectations of being touched by higher-status persons, and of touching lower-status and female persons, than vice versa.[23]

One study using judgments of female–male pairs in magazine photographs further confirmed the dominance connotations of touch; the researchers found that being touched reduced the perceived dominance of the person touched (although it did not increase the toucher's perceived dominance).[24] In another observational study in public places, researchers found that when mixed-sex couples walked together in public, the female was most often on the side of the male's dominant hand; that is, she was on his right if he was right-handed and on his left if he was left-handed. These researchers speculated that such "strong-arming" reflected male dominance and would allow more convenient male touching of the female.[25]

This touching asymmetry becomes most ambiguous and problematic in heterosexual situations when females may protest males' touch as presumptuous, only to be told they are too "uptight." Female office, restaurant, and factory workers and students are quite used to being touched by their male superordinates, but they are expected not to "misinterpret" such gestures as sexual advances. However, women who touch men may be interpreted as conveying sexual intent, as they have often found out when their intentions were quite otherwise. Such different interpretations are consistent with the status patterns found earlier. If touching indicates either power or intimacy, and women are deemed by men to be status inferiors, touching by women will be perceived as a gesture of intimacy, since power is not an acceptable interpretation.

GAZE AND DOMINANCE

The most studied nonverbal communication among humans is probably eye contact, and here too we observe a sex difference. Researchers have found repeatedly that women look more at another person in a dyad than men do.[26] Exline, Gray, and Schuette suggest that "willingness to engage in mutual visual interaction is more characteristic of those who are oriented towards inclusive and affectionate interpersonal relations,"[27] but Rubin concludes that while "gazing may serve as a vehicle of emotional expression for women, [it] in addition may allow women to obtain cues from their male partners concerning the appropriateness of their behavior."[28] This interpretation is supported by the data of Efran and Broughton, which show that male subjects too "maintain more eye contact with individuals toward whom they have developed higher expectancies for social approval."[29]

Looking, then, may be indicative of some dependency and subordination. However, looking can also be an aggressive and dominant gesture, when it becomes a stare. Dovidio and Ellyson write, "In humans as in other primates, the stare widely conveys messages of interpersonal dominance and control. Research conducted over the past 60 years suggests that, in general, staring at another person is a dominance gesture while breaking eye contact or not looking is a sign of submission."[30] How can the same gesture — looking at another — indicate both dominance and deference? Henley suggests that women may watch men when they are not being looked at, but lower or avert their gaze when a man looks at them, as submissive animals do when a dominant animal looks their way.[31]

Also, as Dovidio and Ellyson point out, the meaning of gaze depends on the context, and on the patterning of looking with other behaviors, most notably with speaking. A series of experiments by Ellyson, Dovidio, and their colleagues has developed a measure of "visual dominance": the ratio of [looking at another while speaking] to [looking at another while listening]. In peer interaction, we tend to look while listening more than we look while speaking; however, visually dominant people, both men and women, have a greater proportion of look/speak to look/listen than do nondominant people. People with higher status, expert power, or an orientation to interpersonal control all showed higher visual dominance ratios than did people without those characteristics. Gender also affects visual dominance behavior: In an experiment with mixed-sex pairs, both female and male experts showed greater visual dominance in interaction with nonexperts; when there was no differential expertise, men still showed greater visual dominance than did women.[32] Like other tiny habits of which we are scarcely aware, women's "modest" eye lowering can signal submission or subordinate position even when that message is not intended.

VERBAL CUES TO DOMINANCE

Gestures of dominance and submission can be verbal as well as nonverbal. Subtle verbal cues—especially paralinguistic features, such as emphasis, inflection, pitch, and noncontent sounds—are often classified with nonverbal ones in the study of interpersonal interaction, because they have similar regulating functions aside from the traditional verbal content. Other features of verbal interaction, such as frequency and length of utterance, turn-taking patterns, interrupting, and allowing interruption, also help to regulate interaction and to establish dominance.

Sheer verbalization itself can be a form of dominance, rendering someone quite literally speechless by preventing that person from "getting a word in edgewise." Contrary to popular myth, men talk more than women, in both single-sex and mixed-sex groups. Within a group, a major means of asserting dominance is to interrupt. Those who want to dominate others interrupt more; those speaking will not permit themselves to be interrupted by their inferiors, but they will give way to those they consider their superiors.[33] It is not surprising, therefore, that Zimmerman and West found, in a sample of eleven natural conversations between women and men, that forty-six of the forty-eight interruptions were by males; other research on interruption consistently finds men interrupting more than women.[34]

In verbal communication, we find a pattern of differences between the sexes similar to that seen in nonverbal communication. It was observed earlier in this article that men have the privilege of swearing and hence have access to a vocabulary not customarily available to women. On the surface, this seems to be an innocuous limitation, but it is significant because of the psychological function of swearing: Swearing is one of the most harmless and effective ways of expressing anger. The common alternatives are to express one's feelings with physical violence or to suppress them and by so doing turn the anger in on oneself. The former is prohibited to both sexes (to different degrees), but the latter is decidedly encouraged in women.

Swearing is perhaps the most obvious sex difference in language usage. Of course, sex differences are also to be found in phonological, semantic, and grammatical aspects of language as well as in word use.[35] Austin, for example, has commented that "in our culture little boys tend to be nasal . . . and little girls, oral," but that in the "final stages" of courtship the voices of both men and women are low and nasal.[36] The pattern cited by Brown,[37] in which the form appropriately used by status superiors is used between status equals in intimate situations, is again visible: In the intimate situation, the female adopts the vocal style of the male.

In situations in which intimacy is not a possible interpretation, it is not power but abnormality that is the usual interpretation. Female voices are expected to be soft and quiet—even when men are using loud voices. Women who do not fit this stereotype are often called *loud*—a word commonly applied derogatorily to other minority groups or out-groups.[38] One of the most popular derogatory terms for women is *shrill*, which, after all, simply means loud (applied to an out-group) and high-pitched (female).

GESTURES OF SUBMISSION

Henley and LaFrance suggest that the nonverbal asymmetry of male and female is paralleled by the asymmetry of racial/ethnic/cultural dominance.[39] In any situation in which one group is seen as inferior to another, they predict, that group will be more *submissive,* more *readable* (nonverbally expressive), more *sensitive* (accurate in decoding another's nonverbal expressions), and more *accommodating* (adapting to another's nonverbal behaviors). How true this is for racially and ethnically oppressed groups remains to be shown; in this review, however, we have seen that these characteristics are among the nonverbal behaviors of females. Recent research by Snodgrass supports the contention that decoding sensitivity is associated with dominance and authority, rather than with gender per se.[40]

Other verbal characteristics of persons in inferior status positions are the tendencies to hesitate and apologize, often offered as submissive gestures in the face of threats or potential threats. If staring directly, pointing, and touching can be subtle nonverbal threats, the corresponding gestures of submission seem to be lowering the eyes from another's gaze, falling silent (or not beginning to speak at all) when interrupted or pointed at, and cuddling to the touch. Many of these nonverbal gestures of submission are very familiar. They are the traits our society assigns as desirable characteristics of females. Girls who have properly learned to be "feminine" have learned to lower their eyes, to remain silent, to back down, and to cuddle at the appropriate times. There is even a word for this syndrome that is applied only to females: *coy.*

Sexual interaction is expressed through nonverbal communication: the caress, the gaze, coming close to each other, the warm smile, smelling the other, provocative postures and inviting gestures; much sexual contact, unlike other forms of human interaction, is *purely* nonverbal. Sexual interaction, like all interaction, is conditioned by the social context in which it takes place. One particularly compelling aspect of that social context is that males have more power, prestige, and status than do females, a fact that cannot but affect heterosexual interaction. If even casual relationships between females and males are caught up in the social system in which males wield power over females, how much more does this power system affect the sexual relationship, which we consider the ultimate intimacy? In addition, in both heterosexual and homosexual interactions, relationships are affected by other power and status dimensions, such as work status, wealth, race, age, and interpersonal dominance. This power too is often expressed nonverbally.

Unfortunately, little has been written on nonverbal behavior, power, and sexuality examined simultaneously. However, the research and ideas presented earlier in this article may be applied to the sexual sphere. First, much can be said about a sexual relationship after observing the mutuality or nonmutuality of various gestures. For example, we may already believe that the person who is more dominant in the relationship is the one who takes a superior position in intercourse, the one around whose pleasure sexual activity is structured, and the one upon whose climax it is terminated. Beyond that, when gestures are not mutual (or not balanced over time), one person may dominate by initiating touching, hand-holding, and kissing; maintaining gaze; putting an arm around the other's back when sitting; initiating moves to greater intimacy in the course of a relationship or a single encounter; exerting more influence over the couple's spacing, postures, and walking pace; getting to hold hands with the preferred or dominant hand; having the hand in front when walking holding hands; and terminating as well as initiating hand-holding and kissing. Subordination may be expressed by the person who shows more emotional expressivity, shows more facial and kinesic activity, is more self-disclosing, accommodates timing and action to the other, and exhibits the reciprocal behaviors of those described as dominant.

These questions of who touches, who initiates, and who terminates apply, of course, to both heterosexual and homosexual relationships. However, in the heterosexual relationship, we often have a good idea of what the answers will be; in fact, heterosexual custom has prescribed male leadership and dominance. But these are changing times, and many think that few aspects of our society are changing faster than are sexual relationships and female–male interactions. Many people today do not wish to have unequal sexual relationships or to express sexual inequality unconsciously. However, since we generally take body language for granted and do not attend to it much, it may be hard to change: nonverbal expressions may lag behind changes in attitudes, values, and ideas. Slowness in changing this communication may keep us trapped in old modes of expression and old modes of relationship. No matter how egalitarian we may believe our relationships or sexual interactions to be, they will have an edge of inequality and imbalance until we bring our nonverbal expressions into line with our verbal ones.

DIFFERING INTERPRETATIONS OF THE SAME BEHAVIOR

Status differences between the sexes mean that many of the same traits and actions are interpreted differently when displayed by each sex. A man's behavior toward a woman might be interpreted as an expression of either power or intimacy, depending on the situation. When the same behavior is engaged in by a woman and directed toward a man, it is more likely to be interpreted as a gesture of intimacy—and intimacy between the sexes is typically seen as sexual in nature. Recent research confirms that, when women display dominance gestures to men, they are rated higher on sexuality and lower in dominance than men are rated when making the same gestures to women.[41] Because our society's values say that women should not have power over men, women's nonverbal communication is rarely interpreted as an expression of power. If the situation precludes a sexual interpretation, women's assumption of the male prerogative may be dismissed as deviant (castrating, domineering, unfeminine, or the like). Women in supervisory positions thus often have a difficult time asserting their power nonverbally—gestures that are socially recognized as expressions of power when used by male supervisors may be denied or misinterpreted when used by women.

CHANGE

Knowledge of the significance of nonverbal communication can help us to understand not only others' gestures but also our own, giving us a basis for social and personal change. However, just because certain gestures associated with males are responded to as powerful, women need not automatically adopt them. Rather than accepting "masculine" values without question, individual women will want to consider what they wish to express and how, and they will determine whether to adopt particular gestures or to insist that their own be responded to appropriately. There has been growing pressure on women to alter their verbal and nonverbal behavior[42] to the words and movements of "power"—i.e., to those associated with men—often with little thought of the implications. It would be mistaken to assume that such gestures are automatically better and that it is only women who should change. Revealing emotions rather than remaining wooden-faced and unexpressive, for example, may be seen as weak when only one person in an interaction is doing it; but, in the long run, openness and expressivity—by all people—may be better for the individual, the interpersonal relationship, and the society. Women who wish to change their nonverbal behavior can monitor it in various situations to determine when it contradicts their intention or is otherwise a disservice, and only then change. They will wish to keep those behaviors that give them strength, whether those behaviors are traditionally associated with women or with men.

NOTES

1. M. Argyle, V. Salter, H. Nicholson, M. Williams, and P. Burgess, "The Communication of Interior and Superior Attitudes by Verbal and Non-Verbal Signals," *British Journal of Social and Clinical Psychology,* 9 (1970), 222–31.

2. R. Rosenthal, J. A. Hall, M. R. DiMatteo, P. L. Rogers, and D. Archer, *Sensitivity to Nonverbal Communication: The PONS Test* (Baltimore: Johns Hopkins University Press, 1979).

3. E. Goffman, *Gender Advertisements* (New York: Harper and Row, 1979).

4. The term *power* is used here to mean social power, the ability to influence the behavior of others based on access to and control of resources; *status* refers to acknowledged prestige rankings within the social group; *dominance* is used to refer to a psychological tendency (desire to dominate) and immediate pairwise influence (rather than general social value or influence).

5. E. Goffman, "The Nature of Deference and Demeanor," *American Anthropologist,* 58 (1956), 473–502; reprinted in E. Goffman, *Interaction Ritual* (Garden City, N.Y.: Anchor, 1967).

6. Several studies are described in R. Brown, *Social Psychology* (Glencoe, Ill.: Free Press, 1965), 51–100.

7. For discussion of these rules vis-à-vis women and men, see S. McConnell-Ginet, "Address Forms in Sexual Politics," in D. Butturff and E. L. Epstein (eds.), *Women's Language and Style* (Akron, Ohio: University of Akron Press, 1978).

8. N. M. Henley, *Body Politics: Power, Sex, and Nonverbal Communication* (Englewood Cliffs, N.J.: Prentice-Hall, 1977).

9. M. Wex, *Let's Take Back Our Space: "Female" and "Male" Body Language as a Result of Patriarchal Structures* (Hamburg: Frauenliteraturverlag Hermine Fees, 1979).

10. See also S. J. Frances, "Sex Differences in Nonverbal Behavior," *Sex Roles,* 5 (1979), 519–35; I. H. Frieze and S. J. Ramsey, "Nonverbal Maintenance of Traditional Sex Roles," *Journal of Social Issues,* 32, no. 3 (1976), 133–41; M. LaFrance and C. Mayo, "A Review of Nonverbal Behaviors of Women and Men," *Western Journal of Speech Communication,* 43 (1979), 96–107; C. Mayo and N. M. Henley (eds.), *Gender and Nonverbal Behavior* (New York: Springer-Verlag, 1981); S. Weitz, "Sex Differences in Nonverbal Communication," *Sex Roles,* 2 (1976), 175–84.

11. W. L. O'Neill, *Everyone Was Brave: The Rise and Fall of Feminism* (Chicago: Quadrangle, 1969), 270.

12. E. P. Gerdes, J. D. Gehling, and J. N. Rapp, "The Effects of Sex and Sex-Role Concept on Self-Disclosure," *Sex Roles,* 7 (1981), 989–98.

13. V. J. Derlega, B. Durham, B. Gockel, and D. Sholis, "Sex Differences in Self-Disclosure: Effects of Topic Content, Friendship, and Partner's Sex," *Sex Roles,* 7 (1981), 433–47.

14. D. I. Slobin, S. H. Miller, and L. W. Porter, "Forms of Address and Social Relations in a Business Organization," *Journal of Personality and Social Psychology,* 8 (1968), 289–93.

15. E. A. Ross, *Principles of Sociology* (New York: Century, 1921), 136.

16. W. W. Waller and R. Hill, *The Family: A Dynamic Interpretation* (New York: Dryden, 1951), 191.

17. R. Sommer, *Personal Space* (Englewood Cliffs, N.J.: Prentice-Hall, 1969), Chapter 2.

18. F. N. Willis, Jr., "Initial Speaking Distance as a Function of the Speakers' Relationship," *Psychonomic Science,* 5 (1966), 221–22.

19. Henley, *Body Politics,* Chapters 2 and 3.

20. Henley, *Body Politics,* Chapter 7.

21. N. M. Henley, "Status and Sex: Some Touching Observations," *Bulletin of the Psychonomic Society,* 2 (1973), 91–93.

22. B. Major, "Gender Patterns in Touching Behavior," in Mayo and Henley (eds.), *Gender and Nonverbal Behavior.*

23. Henley, *Body Politics,* Chapter 7.

24. D. L. Summerhaves and R. W. Suchner, "Power Implications of Touch in Male–Female Relationships," *Sex Roles,* 4 (1978), 103–10.

25. R. J. Borden and G. M. Homleid, "Handedness and Lateral Positioning in Heterosexual Couples: Are Men Still Strongarming Women?" *Sex Roles,* 4 (1978), 67–73.

26. R. Exline, "Explorations in the Process of Person Perception: Visual Interaction in Relation to Competition, Sex, and Need for Affiliation," *Journal of Personality,* 31 (1963), 1–20; R. Exline, D. Gray, and D. Schuette, "Visual Behavior in a Dyad as Affected by Interview Control and Sex of Respondent," *Journal of Personality and Social Psychology,* 1 (1965), 201–9; Z. Rubin, "Measurement of Romantic Love," *Journal of Personality and Social Psychology,* 16 (1970), 265–73; J. F. Dovidio and S. L. Ellyson, "Patterns of Visual Dominance Behavior in Humans," in S. L. Ellyson and J. F. Dovidio (eds.), *Power, Dominance, and Nonverbal Behavior* (New York: Springer-Verlag, 1985).

27. Exline, Gray, and Schuette, "Visual Behavior in a Dyad," 207.

28. Rubin, "Measurement of Romantic Love," 272.

29. J. S. Efran and A. Broughton, "Effect of Expectancies for Social Approval on Visual Behavior," *Journal of Personality and Social Psychology,* 4 (1966), 103.

30. Dovidio and Ellyson, "Patterns of Visual Dominance Behavior," 129.

31. Henley, *Body Politics,* Chapter 9.

32. Dovidio and Ellyson, "Patterns of Visual Dominance Behavior." See also B. W. Eakins and R. G. Eakins, *Sex Differences in Human Communication* (Boston: Houghton Mifflin, 1978), 69.

33. B. Eakins and G. Eakins, "Verbal Turn-taking and Exchanges in Faculty Dialogue," in B. L. Dubois and I. Crouch (eds.), *Papers in Southwest English IV: Proceedings of the Conference on the Sociology of the Languages of American Women* (San Antonio, Tex.: Trinity University Press, 1976).

34. D. Zimmerman and C. West, "Sex Roles, Interruptions and Silences in Conversation," in B. Thorne and N. Henley (eds.), *Language and Sex* (Rowley, Mass.: Newbury House, 1975). See also C. West and D. Zimmerman, "Small Insults: A Study of Interruptions in Cross-Sex Conversations between Unacquainted Persons," in B. Thorne, C. Kramarae, and N. Henley (eds.), *Language, Gender and Society* (Rowley, Mass.: Newbury House, 1983).

35. M. R. Key, *Male/Female Language* (Metuchen, N.J.: Scarecrow, 1975); see also C. Kramarae, *Women and Men Speaking* (Rowley, Mass.: Newbury House, 1981); Thorne, Kramarae, and Henley (eds.), *Language, Gender and Society;* R. Lakoff, *Language and Woman's Place* (New York: Harper and Row, 1975); S. McConnell-Ginet, R. Borker, and N. Furman (eds.), *Women and Language in Literature and Society* (New York: Praeger, 1980); and B. Thorne and N. Henley (eds.), *Language and Sex: Difference and Dominance* (Rowley, Mass.: Newbury House, 1975).

36. W. M. Austin, "Some Social Aspects of Paralanguage," *Canadian Journal of Linguistics,* 11 (1965), 34, 37.

37. Brown, *Social Psychology.*

38. Austin, "Some Social Aspects of Paralanguage," 38.

39. N. M. Henley and M. LaFrance, "Gender as Culture: Difference and Dominance in Nonverbal Behavior," in A. Wolfgang (ed.), *Nonverbal Behavior: Perspectives, Applications, Intercultural Insights* (Lewiston, N.Y.: C. J. Hogrefe, 1984).

40. S. E. Snodgrass, "Women's Intuition: The Effect of Subordinate Role upon Interpersonal Sensitivity," *Journal of Personality and Social Psychology,* 49 (1985), 146–55; S. E. Snodgrass and R. Rosenthal, "The Effect of Role on Interpersonal Sensitivity: Further Evidence." Paper presented at the Eastern Psychological Association Meeting, Arlington, VA, April 1987.

41. N. M. Henley and S. Harmon, "The Nonverbal Semantics of Power and Gender: A Perceptual Study," in S. L. Ellyson and J. F. Dovidio (eds.), *Power, Dominance, and Nonverbal Behavior* (New York: Springer-Verlag, 1985).

42. E.g., R. Lakoff, *Language and Woman's Place;* L. Z. Bloom, K. Coburn, and J. Pearlman, *The New Assertive Women* (New York: Dell, 1976).

Sexism and the English Language: The Linguistic Implications of Being a Woman

KAREN L. ADAMS AND NORMA C. WARE

To analyze sexism in the English language—what it looks like, and how it affects the way women think, feel, and act in our society[1]—we must look at two aspects of the relationship of language to society: reference and usage. First, how are female human beings referred to in English; what are the cultural attitudes these kinds of references suggest; and what are their implications for the ways women see themselves and their role in society? Second, what are characteristic speech habits of both women and men, and how do these speech habits affect the way women lead their lives? Then we can take up the question of change: What is being done to combat linguistic sexism, and what more could be done?

REFERRING TO WOMEN

One of the most intriguing characteristics of language is that it acts as a kind of social mirror, reflecting the organization and dynamics of the society of which it is a part. Because of this, we can learn a great deal about our society by looking at some of the words used in English to refer to women.

The Sexualization of Women

English words used to refer to women are often "sexually weighted." This is evident in some sex-specific pairs of nouns that are similar in meaning but in which the female form has taken on sexual overtones. A prime example is the set of terms *master* and *mistress*. Both of these words refer to someone who possesses or has power over someone or something else, as in "He is the master of his fate," or "She is the mistress of a great fortune." However, as Lakoff has pointed out, the word *mistress* has acquired a sexual connotation that its masculine counterpart has not.[2] Thus, we can use a sentence like "Jane is Tom's mistress" to report the fact that Jane and Tom are sleeping together and be understood perfectly, while to attempt to describe the same situation with the expression "Tom is Jane's master" is to invite communicational disaster. The latter sentence fails to express its intended meaning because the word *master* is devoid of sexual connotations.

This kind of asymmetrical relationship between what are ostensibly male–female equivalents is not restricted to a single example. In the pair *sir* and *madam,* the latter refers to the proprietor of a brothel as well as serving as a term of address. Even the words *man* and *woman* may be seen to conform to this pattern. The sexual overtones inherent in the word *woman* show through clearly in a sentence such as: "After six months at sea, the first thing Bill wanted to do on leave was to find a woman." Then there is the case of the male academician who objected to the title of a new course because it was "too suggestive"—the title was "Women in the Social Order."[3]

Another indication of the sexualization of women in English is that the language seems to have so many more ways of describing women in terms of their sexuality than it has for men. Schulz reports the findings of two investigators who, as part of a larger study of slang, managed to collect over 500 synonyms for *prostitute,* but only 65 for the masculine sexual term *whoremonger;*[4] and she herself "located roughly a thousand words and phrases describing women in sexually derogatory ways. There is nothing approaching this multitude for describing men."[5]

Schulz also points out that many once quite neutral terms relating to women have degenerated into terms that have sexual or negative connotations or both. She explains how the word *hussy,* for example, is derived from the Old English *huswif* (housewife), whose meaning was simply "female head of the household." A *spinster* was originally someone who operated a spinning wheel. A *broad* was simply a young woman, and *tart* and *biddy* were terms of endearment![6]

Linguists generally agree that, when a language has an elaborate vocabulary on a given topic, it means that this topic is of particular concern or importance to the society as a whole. What, then, can we conclude from the fact that English has so many terms describing women in specifically sexual ways? Is it that a woman's sexuality is considered the most salient aspect of her being, rivaling or even outweighing her humanity in importance? Furthermore, why are so many of these terms pejorative? Is it due to the well-known "sex is dirty" attitude that is characteristic of our culture? If this is true, notice where it leaves women—in the position of having the essence of their existence defined in terms of something that is considered unclean and distasteful. The implications of this are sobering at best.

The Trivialization of Women

A look at the kinds of people and things with which women tend to be grouped in the English language can also tell us a great deal about how our culture regards the female sex. Consider, for example, stock phrases such as *women and children first,* or *wine, women, and song.* Less proverbial but no less significant classifications have been offered by various prominent individuals in recent years. For instance, former Harvard President Nathan Pusey is reputed to have lamented the draining effect of the draft on male brainpower at the university with the words, "We shall be left with *the blind, the lame and the women.*"[7]

Examples like these are not difficult to find. The question is, what do these groupings imply about the kind of people women are considered to be? For us, at least, the implication is that women are immature (like children), frivolous (to be indulged in for entertainment purposes, like wine and song), and handicapped (like the blind and the lame). Singly or in combination, these presumed female attributes provide a convenient excuse for not taking women seriously; they serve to trivialize the female sex.

This trivialization effect appears elsewhere in the language as well; Lakoff has pointed out, for example, "that if, in a particular sentence, both *woman* and *lady* might be used, the use of the latter tends to trivialize the subject matter under discussion, often subtly ridiculing the woman involved." The expressions *lady atheist* (which appeared in the *San Francisco Chronicle,* January 31, 1972) and *lady sculptor,* with their connotation of eccentricity and frivolousness, are cited as cases in point.[8]

Similar in effect to the substitution of *lady* for *woman* is the common practice of referring to adult females as *girls.* Although it is probably true that the suggestion of youth is in some sense a desirable one in our youth-oriented culture, it is also true that the association carries certain decidedly negative connotations—irresponsibility, immaturity, "smallness" of body or mind, etc. What is associated with youth tends to lack stature, and therefore importance, almost by definition.

The parallel terms for men, *gentlemen* and *boys,* can have the same sort of trivializing effect, as in *gentleman scholar,* for example. However, the issue here is one of frequency. Males are referred to as *boys* or *gentlemen* much less often than females are called *girls* or *ladies.*[9]

Woman in Terms of Man

The English language also has a tendency to define women as a sort of male appendage. A woman's linguistic existence is in many cases expressed in essentially male terms, from a male point of view, or with male interests in mind. One example of this tendency is the fact that many of the nouns that refer to women performing various activities or roles are linguistically marked as derivatives of the basic (male) form. Thus, we have poet*ess* and act*ress,* songst*ress,* steward*ess,* usher*ette,* and major*ette,* not to mention proper names such as *Jeannette.* Only in matters of marriage and the few, female-dominated professions is the female form the primary one. Thus, we have widow*er, male* nurse, and *male* prostitute.

Another way in which English tends to classify women in essentially male terms is in social titles that make the declaration of a woman's marital status—i.e., her relationship to a man—obligatory. Until very recently, women had no choice but to reveal whether they were single or (ever) married every time they wanted to refer to themselves in the conventional title-plus-last-name manner. A woman was either *Miss* Somebody-or-other, or *Mrs.* Somebody-or-other.[10] Now, of course, one can be *Ms.* Somebody-or-other and supposedly avoid the whole issue. However, the use of *Ms.* is still often interpreted to mean "unmarried, and slightly ashamed of the fact." As one writer reports, "After four attempts to convince a travel agent that I was not 'Miss' or 'Mrs.' but 'Ms.,' she finally responded with 'Oh, I'm not married either, but it doesn't bother me.'"[11]

One of the more subtle ways in which the English language represents the female as a derivative, or subset, of the male is by means of the linguistic convention known as "generic man." In English, the same word that is used to refer to male human beings is also used in the generic sense to refer to all human beings: That word is, of course, *man*. English grammar books assure us that persons of both sexes are meant to be included in expressions such as *man the hunter, the man in the street, goodwill to men,* and *all men are created equal.* But is this really the case? If *man* is really generic, why is there something decidedly funny about the sentence, "My brother married a spaceman who works for NASA?"[12]

That generic man is not always quite what he appears to be is particularly well-illustrated by the following incident: At the end of one of the hour-long segments of Jacob Bronowski's highly acclaimed series, "The Ascent of Man," "the host of the series chatted for a few minutes with a guest anthropologist about what women were doing during this early period in the ascent of man."[13]

The same generic principle that makes *man* both male and female is supposed to apply to pronouns as well. We have all been taught that the third person singular pronoun *he* is both masculine and sex-indefinite. But again, if this is true, shouldn't the following statement sound perfectly natural: "No person may require another person to perform, participate in, or undergo an abortion against his will"?[14]

Recent research provides experimental evidence of the male bias in generic *man* and *he*. Two sociologists at Drake University asked college students to submit appropriate photographs for the various chapters of an introductory sociology textbook. One group of students was given a list of chapter titles, in which the generic term was not used (e.g., "Culture," "Family," "Urban Life," "Political Life," "Social Life"). Another group was given a list in which some of the titles had been changed to read "Urban Man," "Political Man," "Social Man," etc. Sixty-four percent of the students given the *man* titles submitted male-only pictures, whereas only 50 percent of the students given neutral labels submitted male-only pictures.[15]

Studies on generic *he* also offer clear evidence that, despite what the grammar books tell us, in actual use these generic terms do not apply equally to men and women. MacKay describes several studies showing that both men and women, with very high frequency, interpret the so-called generic *he* as incapable of referring to women.[16] Bem and Bem report on the practical consequences of this when high-school women responded to job advertisements containing generic *he* less often than to those containing *she*.[17]

All this is not to say, however, that generic terms are never interpreted generically. Grammar-book definitions and years of English composition classes have presumably had some impact, and sentences such as the following may well be taken as referring to both sexes:

1. Man the life boats!
2. Each student should pick up his paper upon entering the room.

The point is that this acceptance of the generic sense exacerbates, rather than solves, the problem. Because *man* and *he* are both generic and nongeneric, women find themselves caught in a linguistic contradiction of rather formidable proportions: They discover that they are being defined as both *man* and *not man* at the same time.[18] Precisely because the word is used to mean both male people and people in general, to the extent that women are included under the rubric of *man* and *he*, they lose their "linguistic identity" as women. By the same token, not to be included under that rubric amounts, linguistically speaking, to being defined out of the human race. The generic *man* convention sets up a linguistic structure whereby women can be portrayed in English *either* as women *or* as people, but not both.

Finally, we note that other words can be used in such a way as to exclude females from human groups. A television commentator was heard to say: "People won't give up power. They'll give up anything else first—money, home, wife, children—but not power."[19]

Implications and Consequences (or, So What?)

How does all this affect the way women live in the world? There are two views of the relationship of language to society and its effect on society. Some people maintain that the relationship between language and society is one of representation only, whereby language serves as a social mirror, reflecting the implicit values, attitudes, and prejudices of the society in which it is embedded but having no power to influence the perceptions or interactions of the people in that society. From this argument it follows that, while the picture the English language paints of women may be distasteful to us, that picture has no real effect on the way women think, the way they feel about themselves, or the way they lead their lives.

A considerable number of people disagree with this position, however. These people maintain that language not only reflects social values, attitudes, etc., but also reinforces them. In any language, it is easier to talk about some things than about others. Since many of the words that English offers for referring to women also have sexual connotations, it is easy to talk about women in a sexual way.

With the habit of talking about things in certain ways comes the habit of thinking about them in those ways. Thus, the language-based predisposition to talk about women in sexual terms makes it more likely that a speaker will think about them in those terms. It is in this sense, then, that language may be said to reinforce, as well as to reflect, prevailing social opinion.

One implication of this argument is that the ability of language to reinforce the status quo helps to perpetuate sexist attitudes and practices and to inhibit social change. Another implication is that, according to this theory, women are likely to come to "see themselves as the language sees them." If the tendency to talk about things in certain ways leads to the tendency to think about them in those ways, it follows that women speaking the English language will be encouraged to view themselves as sex objects, as trivial, as ambivalent about their status as complete human beings, etc.

The consequences of this relationship of language to society can be even more serious for minority women. Not only are sexist attitudes perpetuated through language, but so also are racist attitudes. Moreover, in bilingual communities, women may have to deal with additional stereotyping in another language. The result of this ability of language to reinforce negative attitudes and practices can be overwhelming in such cases.[20]

FEMALE AND MALE DIFFERENCES IN USAGE

Just as there are differences in the words that refer to women and men, so are there differences in the ways that women and men talk. In English, the same words, the same grammatical forms, and the same conversational strategies can be and are used by both women and men. However, the frequency of the usage of these words and strategies and the situations in which they are used differ depending on the speaker's and listener's sex.[21] The next sections describe examples of these differences and explain how they relate to control and dominance in verbal interaction.

Sex Roles and Speaking "Proper" English

In the society at large, the manner in which some people talk is more "prestigious" than the way others do. In the United States, as in other countries, it is generally the language of the urban, well-educated, and wealthier speakers that is held in higher esteem. These people's upper-middle class speech is the most acceptable and carries the label *standard English.* This standard language is taught in schools and is used by broadcasters and newspaper reporters.

Given the acknowledged existence of a standard language, one might expect speakers of English to strive equally to use the standard in an effort to sound more prestigious. However, one of the most consistent findings of studies on sex-based variations in English usage has been that women, no matter what their socioeconomic level, race,[22] or age, use more grammatically correct forms than do men, and pronounce words in more acceptable ways. This means that they succeed in sounding more like standard-English speakers than men do. In the case of bilingual communities, the effort to sound prestigious can mean that women use English more than they do the non-English language—Spanish, for example.[23]

Trudgill, in a study of Norwich English (a form of British English), found that there, too, women used prestigious speech forms more often than did men.[24] He also found that, when speakers were asked about their use of standard and nonstandard forms, differences between actual and perceived behavior appeared. It seems that speakers "perceive their own speech in terms of the norms at which they were aiming rather than the sound actually produced,"[25] so that there were always cases of overreporting and underreporting of actual usages. These instances were strongly correlated with sex differences, no matter what the class of the speaker. Women claimed that they used standard forms more frequently than they actually did, and men reported that they used them less frequently than they actually did. As Trudgill convincingly argues, the actual differences between female and male speech, combined with the differences in reporting, indicate that women and men identify with different role models of behavior and seek to talk like those models.

One explanation of the correctness of women's speech is presented by Thorne and Henley.[26] They point to research by Goffman[27] demonstrating that inferior status leads to careful and circumscribed behavior. They claim that women's usage of standard English is an example of this circumscribed behavior. A related argument is presented by Trudgill.[28] He characterizes women as "status conscious." Thus, he says, women act in ways that will improve their status. They seize on language as a way to do this, because often women's only readily available sources of prestige are those that have to do with appearance. However, it is questionable whether the use of correct speech truly has the effect of improving women's position in society. A final reason is that women's role in childrearing may lead them to view themselves as the teachers of the community standard.[29]

What of the male usage of less standard forms? Why does behaving like a man mean using lower-class speech? One explanation is that the prevalent socialization of males includes a male sex role of competitiveness, independence, and toughness, and working-class males are thought of as embodying these characteristics. Speaking the less acceptable or nonstandard language associated with working-class males then becomes a way for all males to be tough and independent.

Differences between women and men in the use of contentious language also relates to women's more circumscribed language behavior. Several studies have found that black girls know and may use forms of verbal dueling common in the black community, but that they use these forms with greater restraint or often not in the context of dueling.[30] Moreover, swearing, a way of shocking and antagonizing others as well as of releasing anger, is more frequent in the speech of males. Many of the terms used for swearing, such as *son of a bitch*, vilify women and, thus, show swearing to be a male domain. When women do swear, many tend to limit themselves to milder terms, such as *shit*, *hell*, and *damn*,[31] and most men and women consider swearing improper in female speech.

Weakness and Women's Speech

It is often claimed that women more frequently use certain language patterns that make their speech sound weak, tentative, and emotional. Examples are the use of fillers and hesitation markers, such as *ah*, *well*, and *um-m-m*; the use of hedges such as *sort of*, *I think*, *you know*, and *I guess*; the use of intensifiers, such as *really* and *very*; the use of tag questions at the ends of statements, such as "It's a nice day, *isn't it"*; and the use of certain models like *would* and *could* in nonpast contexts as in *Would you answer the phone?* However, studies attempting to verify these claims have resulted in inconsistent findings.

A study by Erickson, Lind, Johnson, and O'Barr[32] on the use of such forms in the testimony of courtroom witnesses verified that such patterns of speech are judged to be a sign of weakness and of a lack of competence and believability whether used by a male or by a female. But the study found that all these forms were used by men as well as by women, and some were used even more by men than by women.

Why did this study fail to demonstrate the predicted language pattern? In this case, the expert witnesses, female and male, used fewer of these forms than did the other witnesses. People who have high-status roles and who are familiar with the event are less likely to use such forms than are inexperienced witnesses.

In other cases, the forms in question carry different social and structural functions. In language, one form can be used to convey different effects. Dubois and Crouch[33] found in an academic discussion that men used tag questions more than women did. This had the effect of making a question sound more like an assertion and of making the speaker sound less uninformed, and thus conveyed an effect opposite of what Lakoff[34] had suggested—of weakening women's assertions. Preisler, in a study of women and men of different ages employed in different positions in the same British firm, found forms such as *I think,* which might be construed as tentative and weak in one context, to be part of a style for women managers of "careful deliberation and reflective weighing" in a task-oriented context.[35]

Other data from Preisler show that in general women used these "tentative" forms more than did men. Young clerical women employees in this British firm used the highest number of the language patterns he identified as weak and tentative. Men, on the other hand, were more likely to use imperative forms, such as, "Answer the phone." Other studies have found men and women using these same patterns with children.[36]

Women's voice quality or intonation is another attribute of women's speech that is associated with weakness. Intonation can be viewed as a musical scale, with a high point (a note), a low point (a note), and steps (notes) in between. Women's intonation range is wider than men's, sometimes giving what is interpreted as an emotional, and therefore weak, quality to the voice. This characterization comes about because large fluctuations in voice level can be used to convey emotion. Being emotional is a devalued behavior in our society. An additional difference in women's and men's intonation patterns is that women use more patterns that end at higher levels, as intonation patterns for questions do, thus giving a hesitant quality to their speech. Men rarely use these ending patterns.[37]

In this discussion on weakness and women's speech, it is important for us to be aware of a trap. Many people regard women as the weaker sex, so they assume that the language forms women use are weaker. However, we do not have a good idea of how forms function in different social contexts. Indeed, these forms that are labeled "weak" and "tentative" may and do function in many more positive ways than the labels assert. It is wrong to assume that these forms are in themselves always "weak" and "tentative." But we need to be aware that people may consider women's speech weak just because a woman is speaking, and to counteract this image we can monitor our speech for these "weak" forms and assert the positive aspects of these forms.

Differences in Conversational Strategies and Their Effect on Women

Another category of linguistic behavior that is relevant for understanding women's position in our society is conversational interaction. Sacks, Schegloff, and Jefferson[38] refer to conversation as a system that is "party administered" and "interactionally managed." This means that conversations are under the control of the individuals participating in them, and the interaction that arises is a consequence of the relationship among the speakers. Therefore, we would expect that the disparate statuses of females and males in our society show in these exchanges.

Interruptions. One characteristic of conversation is speaker-change or "turn taking." A speaker signals the finish of her or his turn in various ways: making eye contact, lowering the voice level, or calling on someone else to take over. The general strategy in conversations is for the listener to wait for one of these signals and then to start talking. However, there is another way to gain the floor—to interrupt.[39] This is considered impolite; however, as we found earlier, where proper speech behavior is concerned, women and men act differently.

Zimmerman and West, in a study of two-person conversations between twenty white, college-educated people twenty to thirty years old,[40] found that in same-sex conversations (ten female–female and ten male–male), interruptions were about the same and occurred in about 15 percent of the conversations. However, in mixed-sex conversations (eleven of them), this picture changed radically. Interruptions turned up in 99 percent of the conversations, and, except for two instances in one conversation, males were the interrupting parties. This extremely large difference in the frequency of interruptions in same-sex versus mixed-sex exchanges and the sex disparity of the interrupters suggest different motivation in the two cases. In same-sex exchanges, interruptions are idiosyncratic and may also be related to the parties' emotional involvement in the exchange. While these factors may affect interactions between the sexes as well, interruptions in mixed-sex exchanges also seem to be a systematic strategy to limit women's access to conversation. Moreover, this pattern is parallel to the interruptions found in adult–child interactions, where it is overwhelmingly the adult who interrupts the child.[41]

Selective Reinforcement. Women and men also handle the role of listener differently. A listener is expected to signal attentiveness in any of several ways: nodding the head, interjecting expressions such as *right, um-hmm,* or making more extensive verbal comments. Inadequate response from a listener can bring the exchange to a halt or at least make the speaker ask a question such as "Are you listening?"

Evidence that men listen differently from women is reported by Fishman[42] and Hirschman.[43] Both found that males use significantly fewer interjections such as *um-hmm* than do females, in both same-sex and mixed-sex verbal exchanges.[44] This lack of reinforcement by males can be seen as part of the competitive style of the male sex role. In conversations, this competitive style is manifested by attempts to dominate the exchange. One way of accomplishing this domination is to interrupt. Another way is to give only limited reinforcement. As Aries reports in her data on all-male, small-group interactions,[45] rather than encouraging one another, males concern themselves with establishing a hierarchy. They accomplish this by "brain picking" to see who knows the most, by telling jokes at one another's expense, and by telling stories about such physically threatening topics as castration and riots. It is easy to see how this difference in the use of reinforcers could make a woman, used to a supportive interaction style with other women, feel off-balance in mixed-sex interactions.

Another male strategy is to make a minimal or delayed response in an exchange. Speakers can infer from such a response that the listener thinks what they have to say is of little interest; they may then switch topics in an effort to engage the listener. In the data collected by Zimmerman and West, this was the effect in three of the ten mixed-sex exchanges.[46] These results suggest that males use the strategy at least partially as a way to control the topic by changing it to one on which they can talk freely.

Amount of Talk.   Another difference between women and men in conversations is the length of the turn at talking. We all know the stereotypes of the talkative woman and the strong, silent man. However, data from a variety of sources invalidate these stereotypes. Men often talk longer during their turns than women do. This substantially larger volume of speech can afford them a dominant position in an interaction.[47] For example, Aries found that in mixed-sex groups the men initiated 66 percent of the conversations, compared to 34 percent for women, and those who initiated talk were also the ones who took up more of the available time for talk and were considered leaders by the others. Men were also the recipients of more of the talk; the women in the groups oriented their remarks toward the men, rather than toward the other women, and drew the men out.[48] Indeed, the "talkative" woman may be one who talks as much or nearly as much as a man.[49]

CONCLUSION

A few years ago, the principal question being asked by those who recognized and objected to sexism in the English language was, can sexist language be changed? Is it in fact possible to legislate the changes necessary to wipe out language's sexist bias? This question is now well on its way to being answered affirmatively. In an attempt to eliminate sexist references to women, people have proposed many changes, and many of these are in use. Best known among them are the still-controversial *Ms.;* sex-indefinite substitutes such as sales*person,* mail *carrier,* spokes*person,* and *human*kind, for the ambiguous generic *man* constructions; and substitutes for generic *he,* such as extension of the use of *they* to the singular, the alternation of *she* or *he* with *he or she,* and the newly coined *s/he.*

Some of these proposed changes are already becoming institutionalized. Since the publication of the *American Heritage School Dictionary* in 1972 (the first of its kind to be made up of definitions and sample sentences premeditatedly nonsexist in nature), efforts to eliminate sexism from the country's reading matter have grown steadily in number and proportion. Major textbook publishers have distributed guidelines to their authors and editors, encouraging use of only nonsexist language in written material and providing specific examples of how to do this. Library catalogers are calling for the eradication of sexism in both the language and the concepts of card-cataloging systems, while various religious organizations are in the process of rewording the texts of materials used in their services.[50]

Along with these institutional efforts, the ongoing, day-to-day struggle of individual women to combat sexist language must be recognized. For example, more and more women are refusing to be called, or to call themselves, *girls.* These efforts are all the more praiseworthy because they are often undertaken with the knowledge that one result may be personal discomfort from ridicule.

The attack on the problems that women encounter in their use of language is also well under way at both institutional and personal levels. For example, assertiveness-training groups have as their goals (albeit often indirectly) changing the kinds of linguistic habits that we have described in this article. These groups are forming in all kinds of settings, from large corporations to informal workshops. In addition, an increasing number of articles in popular magazines and books describe sex differences in communication and assertive verbal behavior.[51] These publications often suggest how to break the patterns of male-dominated conversations and how to monitor the use of forms associated with "weak" and "hesitant" speech.

The fact that many such changes are under way, however, only gives rise to another, equally important question: Will the eradication of sexism in the English language help to eliminate this bias from other parts of society? The answer is yes. Language does, indeed, have the power to influence other parts of society; it can reinforce the status quo, or it can work to facilitate change. An awareness of sexist language is essential if we are to understand the traditional rules of interaction between women and men. Once we know these rules, we can work to modify them, to defy them, and to use them to our own advantage. Men and women can only benefit from the eradication of sexism in the English language.

NOTES

1. This article does not include information on the relationships between women and language in other societies, and what is true of English may not necessarily be true of other languages. Also, most of the data on usage that we describe are for white middle- and upper-class speakers, although when possible we have added data for minority women.

2. Robin Lakoff, *Language and Woman's Place* (New York: Harper and Row, 1975), 29. The extent to which the original meaning of *mistress* is still in use is open to question. Lakoff, for example, argues that the word is "practically restricted to its sexual sense." On the other hand, one of us maintains that she quite comfortably refers to herself as mistress of her pet dog and cat. Also Betty Lou Dubois and Isabel Crouch, in their article "The Question of Tag Questions in Women's Speech: They Don't Really Use More of Them, Do They?" *Language in Society*, 4 (1975), 289–94, criticize Lakoff's work and include the following quotes in which the word is used in a nonsexual sense: "It was not that she would make any demonstration; she just did not want to be looked at when she was not quite *mistress* of herself." (Italics added.) O. LaFarge, *Laughing Boy* (Boston: Houghton Mifflin, 1927, p 26; reprinted 1957). "The walls are full of pictures of famous people, from President Nixon to President Sadat of Egypt, all of them autographed to the *mistress* of the house—former movie star Shirley Temple Black." (Italics added.) P. J. Oppen-heimer, "Shirley Temple Black Talks about Her Times of Tears, Her Times of Triumph," *Family Weekly*, Nov. 1974, pp. 9–11.

3. Laurel Richardson Walum, *The Dynamics of Sex and Gender: A Sociological Perspective* (Chicago: Rand McNally College Publishing Co., 1977), 18. Walum also notes that the same word can have both sexual and nonsexual meanings, depending on whether it is used to refer to a male or to a female. She points out that "a male *tramp* is simply a hobo but a female *tramp* is a slut." Ibid.

4. A *whoremonger*, according to *Webster's Third New International Dictionary of the English Language Unabridged* (Springfield, Mass.: G. and C. Merriam Co., 1966), 2612, is an archaic term meaning "a man consorting with whores or given to lechery," and its synonyms are *whoremaster* and *fornicator.*

5. Muriel R. Schulz, "The Semantic Derogation of Women," in Barrie Thorne and Nancy Henley, eds., *Language and Sex: Difference and Dominance* (Rowley, Mass.: Newbury House Pub-lishers, 1975), 64–75.

6. Ibid., 66–68.

7. This example appears in Mary Ritchie Key, *Male/Female Language* (Metuchen, N.J.: Scarecrow Press, 1975), 82.

8. Lakoff, *Language and Woman's Place,* 23.

9. What is more likely to happen, we think, is that men will be referred to as *guys*, rather than *boys*—a term that seems distinctly less trivializing somehow. This could be one reason why young women seem so often to refer to one another as *guys* as well.

10. Even more striking in this regard is the fact that a woman is expected to take her husband's name upon marriage, so that she becomes not only *Mrs.* Somebody-or-other, but even *Mrs. John* Somebody-or-other. Related also is the familiar practice of referring to a married couple as "man and wife," now rapidly becoming obsolete.

11. Walum, *The Dynamics of Sex and Gender,* 19, note 2.

12. This example originally appeared in A. P. Nilsen, "Grammatical Gender and Its Relation-ship to the Equal Treatment of Males and Females in Children's Books" (Ph.D. dissertation, College of Education in the Graduate College, University of Iowa, Iowa City, 1973), 86–87. We discovered it in Casey Miller and Kate Swift, *Words and Women* (Garden City, N.Y.: Anchor Press/Doubleday, 1976), 29.

13. Miller and Swift, *Words and Women,* 20.

14. This example appears in Key, *Male/Female Language,* 89. It is interesting to note that *he* has not always been considered the correct third-person pronoun for referring to a single human being of indeterminate sex. Until about the eighteenth century, the correct choice of a pronoun for such a purpose was *they* or *he or she.* It was only when certain eighteenth-century grammar-ians decided that there was something inherently plural about *they*, and so prescribed a substi-tute for use in the singular, that our present generic *he* was born. Ann Bodine, "Androcentrism in Prescriptive Grammar: Singular 'They,' Sex-Indefinite 'He,' and 'He or She,'" *Language in Society*, 4 (Aug. 1975), 129–46.

15. Joseph W. Schneider and Sally W. Hacker, "Sex Role Imagery and Use of Generic 'Man' in

Introductory Texts: A Case in the Sociology of Sociology," *American Sociology* 8 (Feb. 1973), 12–18.

16. Donald G. MacKay, "Prescriptive Grammar and the Pronoun Problem," in Barrie Thorne, Cheris Kramarae and Nency Henley, eds., *Language, Gender and Society* (Rowley, Mass.: Newbury House Publishers, Inc., 1983), 38–53.

17. S. L. Bem and D. J. Bem, "Does Sex-Biased Job Advertising 'Aid and Abet' Sex Discrimination?" *Journal of Applied Social Psychology,* 3 (1973), 6–18.

18. Note that this same contradictory quality could also conceivably serve as a convenient way of covering up the exclusion of women. One can always claim to be using *man* in the generic sense, whether one actually is or not. Thus, the ambiguity inherent in the meaning and the usage of the word *man* effectively turns the term into yet another weapon in the arsenal of those who have an interest, for whatever reason, in keeping women in the social backwaters and out of the mainstream.

19. The late Frank McGee on the "Today Show," NBC-TV, June 19, 1972, quoted in Miller and Swift, *Words and Women,* 37.

20. For examples, see Patricia Bell Scott, "The English Language and Black Womanhood: A Low Blow at Self-Esteem," *Journal of Afro-American Issues,* 2 (1974), 218–24.

21. This article focuses on speech differences that vary according to sex, yet the way people talk is affected by numerous other considerations; for example, socioeconomic level—including education and occupation; the speaker's age; how well the speaker knows the listener; the topic discussed; the place of the conversation—such as a church or the speaker's own house; the method of communication—such as writing versus speaking; the speaker's personality; and the linguistic form used.

22. Examples of studies in which black women were found to use more standard forms than did black men include Roger D. Abrahams, "The Advantages of Black English." in Johanna DeStefano, ed., *Language, Society and Education: A Profile of Black English* (Worthington, Ohio: Charles A. Jones, 1973), 97–106; Frank Anshen, "Speech Variation among Negroes in a Small Southern Community" (Ph.D. dissertation, New York University, 1969); Walter Wolfram, *A Sociolinguistic Description of Detroit Negro Speech* (Washington, D.C.: Center for Applied Linguistics, 1969).

23. For studies about the preferred use of English over Spanish among some Hispanic women, see Victoria Patella and William Kuvlesky, "Situational Variation in Language Patterns of Mexican American Boys and Girls," *Social Science Quarterly,* 37 (1979), 855–64; Yoland Sole, "Sociocultural and Sociopsychological Factors in Differential Language Retentiveness by Sex," in Betty Lou Dubois and Isabel M. Crouch, eds., "American Minority Women in Sociolinguistic Perspective," *International Journal of the Sociology of Language,* 17 (1978), 29–44.

24. Peter Trudgill, "Sex, Covert Prestige and Linguistic Change in the Urban British English of Norwich," *Language in Society,* 1 (1972), 179–95, reprinted in Thorne and Henley, eds., *Language and Sex,* 88–104.

25. William Labov, *The Social Stratification of English in New York City* (Washington, D.C.: Center for Applied Linguistics, 1966), 455.

26. Barrie Thorne and Nancy Henley, "Difference and Dominance: An Overview of Language, Gender and Society," in Thorne and Henley, eds., *Language and Sex,* 17–18.

27. Erving Goffman, "The Nature of Deference and Demeanor," *American Anthropologist,* 58 (1956), 473–502, reprinted in Erving Goffman, *Interaction Ritual* (New York: Anchor Books, 1967), 47–95.

28. Trudgill, "Sex, Covert Prestige and Linguistic Change," 191–92.

29. Patricia Nichols, in "Networks and Hierarchies: Language and Social Stratification," in Cheris Kramarae, Muriel Schulz and William M. O'Barr, eds., *Language and Power* (Beverly Hills: Sage Publications, Inc., 1984), 23–42, argues that some of the greater degree of standardization in women's speech may be due not to gender identification, but rather to the fact that women are miscategorized according to their husband's socioeconomic status, when the women may be better educated and have better jobs than do their husbands. In addition, women may have more jobs in service positions or positions that expect and encourage the use of standard

English. Although this may be true, the over- and underreporting indicates that using standard forms is still an indication of appropriate sex-role behavior for women. The relationship of women's speech to their roles in a society is a topic discussed in Susan U. Philips, "Introduction: The Interaction of Social and Biological Processes in Women's and Men's Speech," in Susan U. Philips, Susan Steele, and Christine Tanz, eds., *Language, Gender and Sex in Comparative Perspective,* (Cambridge, Mass.: Cambridge University Press, 1987), 1–14.

30. Among such discussions are Edith Folb, *Runnin' Down Some Lines: The Language and Culture of Black Teenagers* (Cambridge, Mass.: Harvard University Press, 1980); Marjorie Harness Goodwin, "Directive–Response Speech Sequences in Girls' and Boys' Task Activities," in McConnell-Ginet, Borker and Furman, eds., *Women and Language in Literature and Society,* 157–73; Shirley Brice Heath, *Ways with Words: Language, Life, and Work in Communities and Classrooms* (Cambridge, Mass.: Cambridge University Press, 1983); and Claudia Mitchell-Kernan, "Signifying, Loud-Talking and Marking," in Thomas Kochman, ed., *Rappin' and Stylin' Out: Communication in Urban Black America* (Urbana: University of Illinois Press, 1972).

31. L. A. Bailey and L. A. Timm, "More on Women's—and Men's—Expletives," *Anthropological Linguistics,* 18, no. 9 (1976), 438–49.

32. B. Erickson, E. A. Lind, B. C. Johnson, and W. M. O'Barr, *Speech Style and Impression Formation in a Court Setting: The Effects of "Power" and "Powerless" Speech,* Law and Language Project Research Report no. 13 (Durham, N.C.: Duke University, 1977).

33. Dubois and Crouch, "The Question of Tag Questions."

34. Lakoff, *Language and Woman's Place,* 14–17.

35. Brent Preisler, "Linguistic Sex Roles in Conversation: Social Variation in the Expression of Tentativeness in English," in Joshua Fishman, ed., *Contributions to the Sociology of Language,* 45 (Berlin: Mouton de Gruyter, 1986), 289.

36. For example, Jean Berko Gleason, "Sex Differences in Parent–Child Interaction," in Philips, Steele, and Tanz, eds., *Language, Sex, and Gender in Comparative Perspective,* 189–99.

37. For further discussion of this notion, see Ruth Brend, "Male–Female Intonation Patterns in American English," in *Proceedings of the Seventh International Congress of Phonetic Sciences, 1971* (The Hague: Mouton, 1972), 866–69, reprinted in Thorne and Henley, eds., *Language and Sex,* 84–87.

38. Harvey Sacks, Emmanuel Schegloff, and Gail Jefferson, "A Simplest Systematics for the Organization of Turn-Taking in Conversation," *Language,* 50, no. 4 (1974), 696–735.

39. Interrupting is different from overlapping another's speech. Overlaps are instances in which the listener starts before the speaker has concluded, but the new speaker begins at or nearly at a signaled transition point. Interruptions do not occur at signaled transition points for speaker alternation and therefore are disruptions.

40. Donald Zimmerman and Candace West, "Sex Roles, Interruptions and Silences in Conversation," in Thorne and Henley, eds., *Language and Sex,* 105–29.

41. Candace West and Donald Zimmerman, "Women's Place in Everyday Talk: Reflections on Parent–Child Interaction," *Social Problems,* 24, no. 5 (June 1977), 521–29.

42. Pamela Fishman, "Interactional Shitwork," *Heresies,* 2 (May 1977), 99–101.

43. Lynette Hirschman, "Analysis of Support and Assertive Behavior in Conversations" (Paper presented at the summer meeting of the Linguistic Society of America, Amherst, Mass., July 1974).

44. It is interesting that, in mixed-sex exchanges, Hirschman found that both sexes use support forms less than they do when they are in same-sex situations. This is an indication that conversations do not flow as easily across sex boundaries.

45. Elizabeth Aries, "Interaction Patterns and Themes of Males, Females, and Mixed Groups," *Small Group Behavior,* 7, no. 1 (1976), 1–18.

46. Zimmerman and West, "Sex Roles, Interruptions and Silences," 124. The article refers to only ten mixed-sex exchanges here, although earlier it referred to eleven.

47. For an example of how men can use silence to dominate, see Jack W. Sattel, "Men,

Inexpressiveness, and Power,'' in Thorne, Kramarae, and Henley, *Language, Gender, and Society,* 119–24.

48. Aries, ''Interaction Patterns and Themes,'' 12–15.

49. For discussions on the effect of topic, participants, and setting on who dominates talk, see Philip Smith, ''Sex Markers in Speech,'' in K. R. Scherer and H. Giles, eds., *Social Markers in Speech,* (Cambridge: Cambridge University Press, 1979), 109–46; Carole Edelsky, ''Who's Got the Floor?'' *Language in Society,* 10 (Dec. 1981), 383–421.

50. Miller and Swift, *Words and Women,* 145–47.

51. Among such publications are Gloria Steinem, ''The Politics of Talking in Groups,'' *Ms.,* May 1981, 43; Lynn Bloom, Karen Coburn, and Joan Pearlman, *The New Assertive Woman* (New York: Delacorte Press, 1975); and B. W. Eakins and R. G. Eakins, *Sex Differences in Human Communication* (Boston: Houghton Mifflin Co., 1975).

Poverty Is a Woman's Problem

KATHLEEN SHORTRIDGE

The odds that people will be poor at some point in their lives are twice as great if they are female than if they are male. Almost two-thirds of the impoverished adults in the United States are women.[1] The female poor are composed of a number of different but overlapping groups: the working poor; the welfare poor; poor mothers with their poor children; poor blacks, browns, and other racial minorities; and the elderly poor. Women with a second disability, race as well as sex, are more likely to be poor than are other women. However, 54 percent of poor adult women are white and under age sixty-five. Thus, even without added disabilities, women have difficulty in obtaining an adequate income. This article addresses two questions: Who are the female poor, and why are they in poverty?

WHO ARE THE POOR WOMEN?

Figure 1 shows the distribution of the men, women, and children who are poor. Of the 18,649,000 females who live in poverty, approximately 34 percent are under the age of eighteen, and another 13 percent are elderly, over sixty-five. There are 9,868,000 working-age adult women under sixty-five who live in poverty. This represents 13.1 percent of the working-age adult women in the United States.

Most people have a general idea of who the poor are. Blacks and other racial minorities are likely to be poor. Children are disproportionately represented among the poor. People who are not employed, people on welfare, and workers in low-wage jobs are also poor. However, within each of these groups and in the society as a whole, most of the adult poor are women.

Race, Sex, and Poverty

The question of whether identifying women's poverty as an issue simply diverts attention from the severe poverty of blacks and other racial minori-

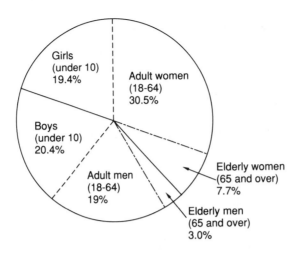

SOURCE: U.S. Bureau of the Census, *Money Income and Poverty Status of Families and Persons in the United States: 1986* (Advanced Data from the March 1987 Current Population Survey) Current Population Reports, Consumer Income Series P-60, no. 157, July 1987, Table 18.

F I G U R E 1 *Poverty Profile 1986: 32,370,000 Americans below the poverty line*

ties is a serious one. The fact is, however, that both variables, race and sex, contribute independently to the poverty equation. The black woman, with two strikes against her, is almost three times more likely to be poor as is a white woman. And an Hispanic woman is two and a half times more likely to be poor. Approximately 26.7 percent of the 12,366,000 poor adult women in the country are black and 12.3 percent are Hispanic.

Figure 2 indicates that blacks are somewhat more likely to be living in poverty than are people of Spanish origin (who might be black or white) and are far more likely to be living in poverty than are whites. Within each ethnic group, approximately two-thirds of the poor are women. In fact, the rate of female poverty among blacks is slightly higher than it is in the other groups; 68.0 percent of poor black adults are women, compared to 62.2 percent of poor white adults. Obtaining economic security for these women and their children is a pressing concern for the black community and the wider society.[2]

Age, Sex, and Poverty

The proportion of the poor who are women is greatest among the elderly—71.8 percent. Many women are widowed and lose their husbands' earnings and pensions. Many retire from their own jobs and reap the bitter harvest of a lifetime of low earnings—no retirement benefits, no savings. For women, the poverty rate is near its highest point for those in old age.

For men, the pattern is different. Although the poverty rate does rise for men over sixty and especially for those over sixty-five, this is not their time of greatest poverty, as Figure 3 indicates. For males, the period with the

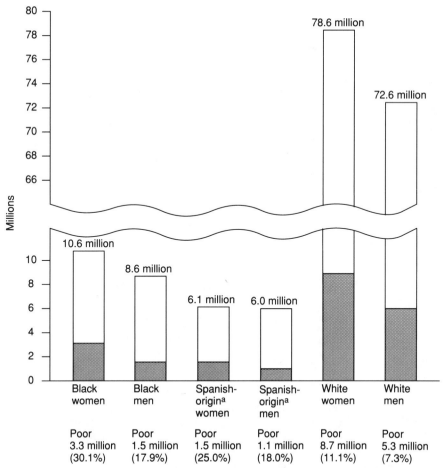

a"Spanish origin" includes both blacks and whites.

SOURCE: U.S. Bureau of the Census, *Money Income and Poverty Status of Families and Persons in the United States: 1986* (Advanced Data from the March 1987 Current Population Survey) Current Population Reports, Consumer Income Series P-60, no. 157, July 1987, Table 18.

F I G U R E 2 *Total adult population and poverty population by race and sex, 1986*

highest rate of poverty is childhood, the time when males are most likely to be dependent on the income of women.

Welfare, Sex, and Poverty

Is not poverty the problem that welfare programs, such as Aid to Families with Dependent Children (AFDC), were designed to cure? Well, yes and no. Welfare may ease, but it does not solve, the problem of poverty. No state in the country provides AFDC payments above the poverty level; payments range from 16 percent (Alabama) to 85 percent (California) of the poverty level. Between one-fourth and one-third of women on welfare also work, but

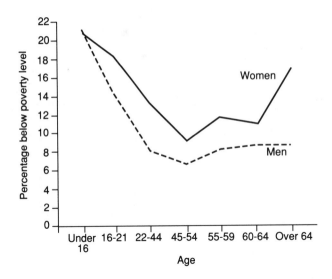

SOURCE: U.S. Department of Commerce, Bureau of the Census, "Characteristics of the Population below the Poverty Level: 1981," *Current Population Reports,* Consumer Income Series P-60, no. 138, Mar. 1983, Table 11.

F I G U R E 3 *Proportion below poverty level by age and sex*

they still do not receive enough income to raise themselves above the poverty level.[3]

As of 1985, there were 3,663,000 families receiving welfare, roughly 11 percent of the families with children under the age of eighteen. About 70 percent were female-headed families. Of these, 52 percent were headed by white women, 45 percent by black women, and 16 percent by Hispanic women.[4]

Low-Wage Work, Sex and Poverty

Employment is a classic solution to men's poverty, but women's work is different. Working women compose a significant portion of the female poor. In 1985, there were 54,495,000 adult working women, of whom 38,058,000 worked full-time; 7.9 percent of all working women and 5.6 percent of full-time working women lived in poverty. One third of all poor women worked at least part time in 1985.[5]

Female Heads of Households

Low income, stemming from inadequate wages, welfare payments, or retirement funds, is enough to keep many women hovering at the edge of poverty. But low income is only half of the poverty equation; the expense of supporting families is the other half.

The number of families in poverty decreased until 1975, but has been rising steadily since then. This is largely attributed to the 43 percent increase in the number of female-headed poverty-level families between 1975 and 1985. During the same period, the number of male-headed and married-couple families in poverty increased by only 24 percent.

There are over 10 million female-headed families. This category is the fastest growing family type in the United States. The number of households with children headed solely by women doubled in the 1970s. Of these, 45.4 percent were below the poverty level, including 38.7 percent of white female householders with children, 58.9 percent of black female householders, and 53.1 percent of Hispanic female householders. In contrast, only 8.9 percent of married-couple households and 17.1 percent of male-headed households with children are below the poverty line.

There is a bitter irony in the fact that one significant factor motivating female householders to gain greater financial security—their children—also greatly inhibits their ability to achieve such security. The incidence of poverty is four and a half times higher in families that include children; 53.8 percent of poor children live in female-headed households, and 53.6 percent of all children in female-headed households are poor.[6]

WHY ARE WOMEN POOR?

The profoundly disturbing reality of children raised in deprivation by women who are locked in poverty is not dealt with by our social system or economy. The classic solutions of husbands, welfare, or women's work are ineffective. These solutions are based on a myth of female dependence that has never reflected reality and is badly suited to current economic and family trends.

The myth of the dependent female assumes that virtually all women will be able to depend economically on men, and that therefore they do not need to be able to support themselves independently. This myth has led boys and girls to receive different sorts of education and training for adult life. The myth affects the occupational choices men and women make, and it results in discrimination against women in wages and in entry into lucrative fields.

The dependence myth, an attitude held by men and women alike, has never reflected reality for more than a small and relatively wealthy portion of the population. The fact is that women have always worked, and they have always been economically productive, whether they were married or not. In a rural, traditional society, the contribution of household labor was a significant portion of the family's productivity. Even during the 1950s, the heyday of the suburban "housewife," 30 percent of all women, and 50 percent of all black women, worked outside the home. Today, a woman can expect to spend thirty years of her life working outside the home.

The women's movement has challenged the dependence assumption vigorously over the last two decades, injecting more realism into women's occupational planning and eliminating some overt discrimination against women. Nonetheless, the assumption that women do not need the independent ability to support themselves that men do has remained a potent force, distorting the perceptions of women and contributing to their own poverty and to that of their families.

The reality is that men are not necessarily living up to their role in the female-dependence myth. For one thing, they die. There are 11 million widows in the United States today. Men also leave their wives. There are 8 million divorced women. One-fourth of both groups live in poverty.[7] There is a growing cadre of middle-class women who were plunged into poverty by the departure of their spouses. In 1985, only 3 percent of all divorced women received any alimony.[8] Many women who might have been perfectly happy to remain dependent spouses are not given the option.

Women as well as men leave marriages or other relationships that have become intolerable. The divorce rate has more than doubled since 1960, and it is still rising. Since women are almost invariably given custody of their children, the number of female-headed households doubled in the 1970s. There is no point in looking back to some "golden age" of married dependence for women.

Even if absent fathers are not supporting their former wives, do they not take some responsibility for supporting their children? Child support is meager under the best of circumstances and is essentially unavailable to the 2.8 million poor mothers with children present whose fathers are absent. Of all divorced mothers (approximately 3 million women in 1985), only 61.3 percent had an award from the court or an agreement to receive child support, and only 74 percent of these received any of it. Of mothers below the poverty level, only 40.4 percent were awarded child support, and 65.7 percent of these received at least some of it. The average amount received *for the entire year* was $2,215 for all mothers and $1,383 for poor mothers. At some level, these data make sense, of course, since the likelihood is that fathers are also very poor and have little to contribute to child support.[9]

In summary, exhusbands and absent fathers offer very little support to women and their families. The poorer the family is to begin with, the less likely it is that the father will be providing support.

SOLUTIONS TO WOMEN'S POVERTY

We have seen serious flaws in the dependence model for women. One theoretical alternative is independence. On a continuum ranging from economic dependence to economic independence, it has generally been assumed that women belonged at the dependence end of the scale, relying on men for economic support or, failing that, on welfare. If dependence did not work out, a woman was ill-equipped for attaining economic independence. Men, on the other hand, were expected to be economically independent and responsible for women.

Does independence seem to be working for men? Men are much less likely to be living in poverty than women. However, this fact masks some real flaws in the independence model. First, men really do not pull their own weight, as the scandalous record of absent fathers in paying child support makes clear. Second, economic support systems such as unemployment compensation are used heavily by men. Third, and most important, families with multiple earners, rather than sole male earners, are the strongest economically and are best able to weather hard times. (See Gerstel and Gross in this book.)

The value of an interdependent, multiple-earner model is especially apparent when unemployment strikes. Among married-couple families that experienced unemployment in 1987, in only 19.8 percent was no one in the family employed. Among female-headed households experiencing unemployment, 52.8 percent had no one else working and were very likely to be in poverty.[10]

Interdependence is an alternative to the extremes of dependence and independence. As this article has demonstrated, economic dependence has resulted in the widespread impoverishment of women. Economic independence, on the other hand, simply does not seem to be a realistic alternative for most, especially those who are uneducated, who have few job skills, or who have heavy family responsibilities.

Today, the notion of an interdependent economic unit is generally limited to married couples. However, such a unit could easily involve other family members, gay partners, unrelated adults, or several parents with children. Just as economic necessity is gradually changing the stereotype of marriage from one in which women are economically dependent on men to one in which the partners are economically interdependent, so economic stresses should be giving rise more generally to other forms of household organization based on economic interdependence.

The greatest obstacle to the creative development of alternative economically interdependent households may be social convention. Communes and cooperatives may seem to be limited to college students and radicals, and some leases do not permit occupancy by unrelated adults. Yet shared household arrangements are more rational than radical. When that is understood, economic and political pressure will carry along reluctant landlords.

The problems posed by entering into a relationship of interdependence that is not legally binding may also be a matter of concern. The poverty of women, however, is eloquent testimony to the limitations of the legal protections of marriage. Furthermore, some lawyers are dealing with the legal problems of alternative living arrangements and economic interdependence of unmarried persons through creatively drafted contracts and powers of attorney.

Despite the myths of dependence for women and independence for men, society's current response to economic stress is household organization based on economic interdependence of married couples. Developing other interdependent units is an important step toward elimination of the poverty, economic uncertainty, and crises that plague women today.

NOTES

1. The data in this article are generally drawn from U.S. Bureau of the Census, *Money Income and Poverty Status of Families and Persons in the United States: 1986* (Advanced Data from the March 1987 Current Population Survey) Tables 9, 18 and 19. *Current Population Reports,* Consumer Income

Series P-60, no. 157, July 1987. (When other sources are used, they are cited.) The term *poverty* and the notion of the *poverty line* or the *poverty level* follow the usage in that report. They are based on the definition developed by the Social Security Administration in 1964 and revised by a Federal Interagency Committee in 1969. The definition uses a series of income thresholds based on family size and composition; if a family income falls below the threshold, that family is characterized as being poor or below the poverty line. As an illustration, the average income threshold for a family of four was $11,203 in 1986.

2. "A Black Women's Movement," *Black Commentator,* ed. Patrice Johnson, spring 1981, 1.

3. Velma Burke "Welfare and Poverty Among Children" *Congressional Research Service Review,* July 1987, p. 5. The figures are for 1986 and include only the continental United States. Alaska paid a little over the poverty level.

4. U.S. Bureau of the Census, *Money Income of Households, Families and Persons in the United States: 1985* Series P-60, no. 156 *Current Population Reports* (Washington, D.C.: Government Printing Office, 1987), Tables 20 and 25.

5. U.S. Bureau of the Census, *Money Income and Poverty Status of Families and Persons in the United States: 1985* Series P-60, no. 158, *Current Population Reports,* Table 10.

6. Ibid., Tables 3 and 5.

7. Ibid., Table 8.

8. Lenore Weitzman, *The Divorce Revolution,* New York: Free Press, 1985, p. 323. Dr. Weitzman found, on the basis of a survey, that the husband's standard of living rose by 42 percent upon divorce, while the standard of living of the wife and children fell by 73 percent, on the average. While the husband had fewer dollars to spend than before the divorce, he was not constrained to spend them on the family. U.S. Bureau of the Census, "Child Support and Alimony: 1985 (Advanced Report)," *Current Population Reports,* Series P-23, no. 152, August 1987. Table I.

9. Ibid., Table E. Even the most carefully designed and vigorously administered child-support enforcement system will be only marginally successful at ensuring payment. See David L. Chambers, *Making Fathers Pay — the Enforcement of Child Support* (Chicago: University of Chicago Press, 1979).

Farewell to Alms: Women's Fare Under Welfare

DIANA M. PEARCE

Families headed by women have come to dominate the poor, and account for over 90 percent of the 3.8 million families receiving Aid to Families with Dependent Children (AFDC). In 1986, 11 percent of all children, and about half of children in one-parent families, received AFDC, often simply called "welfare." Unlike the popular image of the welfare mother, very few women receiving AFDC are permanent members of the welfare class. Nearly 60 percent of the current recipients started receiving welfare less than three years ago. (Unless otherwise stated, all data in this article are from *Background Material and Data on Programs within the Jurisdiction of the Committee on Ways and Means* 1988.) Moreover, few women are solely or even highly dependent on welfare as their source of income; according to a study of welfare recipients by Handler and Hollingsworth (1971), over half had worked during the past year, and over 90 percent were in paid employment at some time during their lives. Indeed, most women who turn to welfare do so because they find they cannot support themselves and even one child on their earnings alone.

Welfare policy today neither reflects the preponderance of women among the poor, nor meets these women's needs as working mothers. It is not even directed at providing more than minimal relief to children. The contemporary welfare system is still based on the "male pauper model" developed in the nineteenth century, and is oblivious to the feminization of poverty today. The result is that welfare policy not only is inappropriate — and hence is unsuccessful in eliminating women's poverty — but also is increasingly locking women into a life of poverty.

THE ORIGINS OF WELFARE PROGRAMS FOR WOMEN

Differentiating the "deserving" from the "undeserving" poor, or, in today's parlance, determining who is "truly needy," dominated welfare policy dur-

493

ing the last century. Widows were almost always among the deserving poor, as were women whose husbands were blind or disabled. Divorced or unmarried mothers were probably not considered deserving poor, but they were also relatively small in number. The undeserving poor were a group of people often termed *paupers*. *Pauper* was not synonymous with *poor*, but rather referred to those among the poor who, although able-bodied, had chosen a way of life outside the bounds of society, as vagrants, drunkards, or criminals: "Paupers were recognized by their extreme state of moral degeneracy, drunkenness, vice, corruption and criminality" (Handler and Hollingsworth 1971, 17). Most of those classified as paupers were men, although this was never stated explicitly.

Because of the threat to the social order posed by paupers, society expended much effort to limit the growth of pauperism. Pauperism was punished as if it were a crime. As late as 1934, fourteen states denied paupers the right to vote, and many states and localities required those receiving assistance to swear to their destitution by taking a "Pauper's Oath" (Brown 1940). Pauperism was also considered a contagious disease, and all members of the public, but especially the poor, were at risk. Like leprosy, pauperism was a disease much feared but little understood, and the approach taken was to isolate the carriers as much as possible; the form chosen was the poorhouse.

The myth persisted that most of the poor were able-bodied, and thus there were frequent campaigns to end all other aid and to put every poor person in the poorhouse, with obvious mixed results. Although records are not consistent, it is probably safe to say that on the average at least two-thirds of the inmates of poorhouses were not able-bodied (see Coll 1969). Instead, they included the sick, the mentally ill, the disabled, the aged, and children. By the end of the nineteenth century, various movements and organizations were seeking to remove these various groups of the "deserving poor" from the stigmatizing and demoralizing influence of the poorhouse. To this end, they began setting up specialized institutions; a number of famous hospitals and mental hospitals started as poorhouses.

Poor children presented a special problem. Although they clearly were not paupers, their *parents* might be, and they themselves might *become* paupers if left with their pauper parents. But separating children from their parents or removing the older ones from the streets and putting them in the poorhouses was not much better. There the children were subjected to the bad influence of the undeserving poor, and, like all the inmates, many found it difficult to leave the poorhouse, leading reformers to seek other solutions. The Child Saving Movement, as it was known, tried founding orphanages to which children from the slums and from the poorhouses were sent, to save them from pauperism. These orphanages, like those in a number of Third World countries today, contained many children who were there because their parents could not provide for them, not because they were orphans, or half-orphans (children with only one parent living).

The orphanage solution was fraught with problems, however: It was difficult to deal with older, street-wise children; younger ones "failed to thrive" (the death rate of infants at even the best institutions was very high);

and orphanages were very costly. Many reformers concluded that the best solution was to keep the family together. One of the prime movers for this course was Julius West, head of the Boy Scouts and an orphanage boy himself. Efforts by West and others culminated in the 1909 White House Conference on Children and Youth. It declared that, because "home life is the highest and finest product of civilization . . . , children should not be deprived of it except for urgent and compelling reasons," poverty not being one of them (quoted in Coll 1969, 77).

Although the private charities agreed with this statement in principle, they fought the development of public welfare programs that would provide support for families in their own homes. Nonetheless, it had become clear that the need was beyond their financial capacities. For example, in 1899, the New York Charity Organization Society was able to support fewer than one-third of the approximately 1,600 children referred to it for help; the others were sent to institutions, breaking up their families (Coll 1969). Spurred by revelations like these and inspired by the White House Conference, many states instituted programs to aid poor children in their homes; by 1913, twenty states had a Mother's Aid, Mother's Pension, or Aid to Dependent Children program, and by 1931 forty-five states had such a program (Bruno 1957).

During the first decades of this century, the poorhouses and orphanages gradually disappeared. Many poorhouses evolved into county homes for the aged or warehouselike mental institutions; others became hospitals, homes for the mentally retarded, or prisons for the criminally insane. The establishment of Mother's Aid programs on a large scale, coupled with the development of foster care and adoption by the new profession of social work, decreased the necessity for orphanages, and these institutions also gradually disappeared.

Support specifically designated for poor women who headed families was a byproduct of the concern for poor children. Unlike children, however, mothers were not automatically considered deserving poor; they might themselves be paupers or raise their children to become paupers. To avoid these pitfalls, a solution was developed by the nineteenth-century precursors to social workers, the Charity Organization Society's (COS) "friendly visitors." These volunteers were long on advice and short on aid (particularly cash). As described by a COS leader, Mrs. Lowell, the object was to provide the poor family with "one who shall go with them, not to carry alms, but sympathy, hope, courage, in short, brains and character" (quoted in Coll 1969, 55).

Although the responsibility for providing aid to mothers and their children was assumed by the government, the methods adopted were those used by private charity. Since the programs often included mothers who were single parents due to divorce and desertion, as well as widows, in virtually every program the mother had to be found to be "physically, mentally, and morally fit." Whether the mother provided a "suitable home" (that is, one worthy of aid for herself and her children) was determined in some cases by a juvenile judge (reflecting the "child saving" origins of these mother's aid programs), but in most cases by social workers or caseworkers. The criteria

used in the early decades of the twentieth century to make this determination varied from state to state:

> In Delaware, the mother had to "protect and foster" the child's religion
> and see that he or she attended school regularly.
>
> In Pennsylvania, the mother had to be a woman of "proved character
> and ability," whose husband was dead (in "its popular meaning," not
> just absent), and who did not keep men lodgers (for they might be a
> temptation to the mother or a demoralizing influence).
>
> In Kansas, the mother had to be "a provident woman of good moral
> character."
>
> In Minnesota, the mother could be required to learn English and to use it
> in her home.

In addition, intelligence tests and information from neighbors, clergy,
former employers, and relatives were used to determine whether a mother
was fit to raise her own children. If she was not, her children were taken
from her and were placed in foster homes or orphanages.

By providing aid in lieu of a husband's or father's income, the state was
acting financially as a husband, The mother, in turn, was expected to fulfill
the role of wife. A wifelike long-term dependence on the state for income
was considered desirable, to provide the family with a sense of financial
security and the children with a stay-at-home mother. For example, the
Minnesota law's stated purpose was

> to enable the State . . . to cooperate with responsible mothers in rear-
> ing future citizens, when such cooperation is necessary on account of
> relatively permanent conditions, in order to keep the mother and chil-
> dren together in the same household. . . . and secure to the children
> during their tender years her personal care and training. [1917 Minn.
> Laws, ch. 223, § 15, as amended.]

As expressed much later by Johnnie Tillman, the recipient head of the
National Welfare Rights Organization, welfare just replaces *a* man with *the*
man. The arrangement was thus a kind of pseudomarriage. In fact, early
twentieth-century legislators were quite explicit about this; as Pennsylvania's lawmakers explained:

> The father of a family is not only a breadwinner; his loss deprives
> the family of affection and discipline as well. . . . The lack is more than
> a material one and cannot be filled by money alone. Because the State
> felt this need of "fathering" its dependent children, the clause providing
> for the appointment of county boards of trustees was introduced. Their
> first duty is the proper administration of the funds; their second—
> equally important—is the supervision and guardianship of the mother
> and children. [1919 Pa. Laws no. 354.]

The mothers receiving this aid traded a high probability of poverty but
with some chance of self-sufficiency for economic dependence and a more
certain, albeit low, level of income.

In practice, of course, coverage was far from complete. Investigations showed that the actual implementation of state programs was spotty, with only about half of the counties nationwide actually providing any kind of program by the mid-1930s (Brown 1940). This finding, and the desire to set national standards, led the President's Committee on Economic Security in the thirties to propose an aid program that would go to all needy families. Congress enacted the Aid to Dependent Children program (later Aid to Families with Dependent Children) as one of the four programs under the Social Security Act of 1935, but limited it to single parents in need. Although nationwide in coverage, the program let state and local officials determine eligibility requirements and set benefit levels. This was crucial, for it permitted racial prejudice and local biases to enter into the determination of which mothers were "worthy" of aid and resulted in the disproportionate exclusion of racial minorities.

THE TRANSFORMATION OF WELFARE AND WOMEN'S POVERTY

Since the thirties, AFDC has become an important source of income for a large percentage of poor female-headed families. As a group, however, these families are no longer considered to be in the category of deserving poor. Poor women have become the twentieth-century equivalent of paupers, and AFDC has become an antipauperism program.

Three factors caused this double transformation of the poor and of welfare policy: (1) the broadening of eligibility rules (through federalization of the programs), (2) the increase of families headed by women who are divorced or unmarried rather than widowed, and (3) the increased labor-force participation of women.

By the late sixties, the liberalization of eligibility rules was such that virtually any single-parent family in need could receive AFDC. In almost half the states, two-parent families in need are also eligible. The turning point was a 1967 Alabama case, *King v. Smith* (392 U.S. 309 [1967]), in which the United States Supreme Court found that otherwise eligible needy children could not be denied aid due to their mothers' illicit cohabitation or the presence of illegitimate children. Only if a judge found that a home was so unsuitable that it required *removal* of the children could aid be withheld. Taking away the power to bar "unworthy" mothers from benefits broadened coverage, but it also created uncertainty in the public mind about whether AFDC mothers were, as a group, part of the deserving poor.

Even before this, the number of needy households headed by widows had begun to decrease, while the number headed by divorced, separated, or (more recently) never-married mothers began to rise. In 1940, 42 percent of all recipient mothers were widows, but by 1986, with longer male lifetimes and broadened Social Security coverage for widows, that proportion had dropped to 1.7 percent. The traditional view of marriage holds the wife responsible for its dissolution. Likewise, parenthood out of wedlock is frequently seen as stemming from choices made by the woman. In contrast, widows, like the sick and the blind, are considered to be in a situation that is not of their own making and thus to be deserving of charity. The shift from widows to ex-married or never-married mothers has therefore been a shift toward a group held responsible for their own poverty, at least in part, and not clearly deserving of charity.

The gradual federalization of eligibility standards also permitted many needy black (and later Hispanic) families to take advantage of AFDC. The delegation of power to the states to set eligibility standards had been virtual permission to discriminate on the basis of race, so that nonwhite participation at the beginning of the program had been very low. Less restrictive eligibility requirements and stronger federal control increased participation rates of eligible families, white as well as black. Although the majority of welfare recipients continue to be white, negative racial and cultural stereotypes persist, so that racism has reinforced the transformation of women into the undeserving poor.

Widows were not only not held responsible for causing their own poverty but also were not expected to alleviate that poverty through earning an income. Indeed, during the debate on the Social Security Act that established AFDC, mothers heading households alone were referred to as *unemployables.* But as women generally, and as mothers specifically, began to enter the paid labor force in ever larger numbers, including, most recently, mothers of very young children, it has become increasingly difficult to characterize single parents, whether widowed or not, as unemployables. Welfare policy in this area came full circle in 1967, when changes were made to encourage welfare mothers to work. Termed *work incentives,* the amendments allowed working welfare recipients to keep "thirty [dollars] and a third" of their earnings. (Earnings previously had been "taxed" 100 percent; that is, welfare benefits were reduced by one dollar for each dollar earned.)

By the 1960s, then, few welfare recipients were widows, and, however unfairly, welfare mothers were considered at least partially responsible for their single-parent status and their poverty. Moreover, however unfairly and unrealistically, they were assumed to be able to work their way out of poverty. Women in poverty gradually lost their status as a special class, with special programs and rules, and they became paupers, part of the undeserving poor. This led to a little-noticed but extremely important "sea change" in welfare policy and programs: Poor women came to resemble poor men, so the programs for women and those for men became indistinguishable. One indication of how profound the transformation was is the change in the questions asked when formulating welfare policy. Questions about how best to keep together families who had lost their male breadwinner, so that children could grow up with an at-home mother and with income security, were replaced with questions about what incentives would encourage or even force welfare mothers to seek paid work outside the home and to break out of "welfare dependence." In short, women in poverty have become part of the able-bodied poor or, in nineteenth-century terms, paupers. As paupers, they are presumed to be a threat to the social order when they are out of the paid labor force and assumed to be capable of working themselves out of poverty.

The poverty experienced by women is fundamentally different from that experienced by men. While women who are poor share many characteristics with poor men, such as little education, no skills, health problems, and/or minority status, their higher rates of poverty are due to two distinctly *female* causes: (1) women overwhelmingly bear the economic as well as the emotional burdens of raising children when the parents do not live together, and (2) women enter the labor market handicapped by their gender and thus earn considerably less than men.

Children

All too often, when a family with children breaks up, the man becomes single and the woman becomes a single parent (Pearce and McAdoo 1981). In 1985, only 36 percent of absent fathers — some estimates have been as low as 25 percent (Schulman 1981, citing a 1975 study) — actually provided child support, and the amount of annual support averaged only $2,215 per family, not per child. The proportion of separated mothers who receive support is 28 percent, and of those never married to the father is 11 percent (U.S. Bureau of the Census 1985, Table 1). This is no accident. Little pressure is put on fathers directly or through the court system to comply with child-support orders.

Nor is this loss replaced by public assistance. In only one state, Alaska, has the welfare payment reached the poverty line. The range in the other 49 states is from 46 percent to 97 percent of the poverty line — and from 1970 to 1987, the average payment fell over 30 percent after adjustment for inflation (Center for Budget and Policy Priorities [CBPP], 1988). In contrast, average income in real terms has risen about 1 percent for white families and has fallen about 5 percent for black families (Chapman 1982).

Not only has the economic burden of raising children fallen primarily on women, but also the costs of that burden have been increasing. The percentage of children in poverty has always been higher than that of all persons in families. For example, in 1970, the children's poverty rate was 15 percent, versus 13 percent for all persons. By 1986, however, the gap had widened: The percentage of children in poverty, 20 percent, was almost double the rate for all persons in families (11 percent). Within each racial/ethnic group, the presence of children under eighteen raises the chances of being poor much more for female-headed than for male-headed families (see Table 1).

Labor Market

Many women who head families seek to support themselves and their children. For women, however, the labor market provides a less certain route out of poverty than it does for men. While only about 5 percent of the families in which there was an employed male householder were in poverty in 1986, about 22 percent of all families headed by an employed female were

T A B L E 1
Poverty Rates of Families, by Racial/Ethnic Group and Gender of Householder and Presence of Children, 1986

	Poverty rate (percentage in poverty)			
	Families maintained by male householder and married-couple families		Families maintained by women alone	
Racial/ethnic group of householder	With no children	With children under 18	With no children	With children under 18
White	3.8	7.8	8.5	39.8
Black	10.8	13.1	17.8	58.0
Hispanic (includes both black and white)	8.8	20.3	18.5	59.7
Total	4.2	8.4	10.4	46.0

SOURCE: U.S. Bureau of the Census, *Money Income and Poverty Status of Families and Persons in the United States: 1986,* Current Population Reports, Series P-60, no. 157 (Washington, D.C.: U.S. Government Printing Office, 1987), Table 19.

poor (U.S. Bureau of the Census 1986). The reasons for this difference are many, including occupational segregation, expensive and scarce child care, sex discrimination, sexual harassment, and unequal returns on education. Women's greater part-time employment, however, is not a cause. As the data in Table 2 indicate, at each degree of labor-market involvement, black and Hispanic women experience higher rates of poverty than do all men, with only one significant exception (Hispanic men working part-time). It is not until women are working full-time, year-round that their poverty rates fall significantly. This is particularly true for black women. Even working full-time and year-round, black and Hispanic women had rates of poverty as high as those of white men *who did not work at all.*

Nonetheless, women who head households alone work part-time more often than men do; with their low wages and insecure jobs, welfare is often a necessary supplement to, but not a substitute for, their earnings. Few women are solely or even primarily dependent on welfare over long periods of time. One study of recipients found that AFDC averages only 69 percent of the income of those who were on welfare for at least four out of seven years and who had received over half of their income from welfare over that period. Moreover, these women constituted only 12 percent of all recipients in the study. More than twice as many, 26 percent, had also used welfare for a similar time period but it had constituted less than half of their income, averaging 37 percent of their total income over the seven years (Rein and Rainwater 1978). These and other studies document the seeming paradox that the *longer* a person is on welfare, the more likely the person is also to be *working,* either alternately or concurrently. The typical long-term welfare recipient is a woman who works, but whose skills, age, location, age and number of children, education, or health status limits her employment opportunities and thus her income from paid work.

500

Poverty Rates of Families, by Racial/Ethnic Group, Sex, and Work Experience of Household Head, 1986

	Poverty rate (percentage in poverty)							
	Male householder (male-only and husband–wife families)				Female householder (husband absent)			
Work experience of householder (1979)	Total	White	Black	Hispanic	Total	White	Black	Hispanic
Did not work	13	11	29	33	56	46	76	73
Worked part-year[a]	13	12	18	28	48	43	60	54
Worked full-year part-time	3	3	5	9	10	8	16	17
Worked full-year full-time	3	3	4	9	8	6	13	12

SOURCE: U.S. Bureau of the Census, *Money Income and Poverty Status of Families and Persons in the United States: 1986,* Current Population Reports, Series P-60, no. 157 (Washington, D.C.: U.S. Government Printing Office, 1987, Table 19).

[a]Includes both part-time and full-time.

THE MALE PAUPER MODEL OF WELFARE POLICY

The traditional analysis of the problem of poverty for the able-bodied poor has been quite simple: Their problem is joblessness, and the solution is to "give" them a job. Historically, application of this policy has sometimes been quite harsh, as when paupers were incarcerated in workhouses or were forcibly conscripted into the Army or Navy. At other times it has been less so, but always the programs have been guided by the principle that welfare should be not only less remunerative than the lowest-paying job but also so stigmatized and so inaccessible that it will be resorted to by only the most desperate.

Given the distinctive character of women's poverty, what effect has the application of the male pauper model had on women in poverty? In brief, the effects are that (1) welfare policy has been ineffective in leading women and their families out of poverty and into economic self-sufficiency, and (2) it appears to be increasingly locking women into a life of poverty (including but not limited to poverty through dependence on welfare). In short, the male pauper model is a failure when applied to women's poverty.

The simple formula "joblessness is the problem, jobs are the solution" does not work for women because their poverty is different from that of men. It is not the lack of jobs that leads women into poverty. Indeed, 90 percent of women on welfare have worked; when they turn to welfare, it is because they cannot support themselves solely on their earnings. For women, the combination of the economic burden of dependent children and gender handicap in the labor market makes jobs just one piece of the solution.

501

Treating women as though they are no different from able-bodied men who are poor has the long-run effect of locking women into poverty, or near poverty, whether or not they receive welfare assistance. Some of the ways in which this occurs are as follows:

1. The obsession with "put them to work" results in women taking jobs with income or benefits (particularly health insurance) that are insufficient for their families' needs.

2. Training available through the Work Incentive Program (WIN) or the Comprehensive Employment and Training Act (CETA) has too often been for traditionally female jobs (e.g., cafeteria worker) that pay poverty-level wages. Such "opportunities" thus reinforce the occupational segregation and ghettoization of women and the poverty that results.

3. Even in training programs, often no provision is made for child care, although half the mothers receiving welfare have a child under age six. For mothers of young children, the burden of both finding and paying for adequate child care is great enough to forestall their entering employment or training for many years.

In the short run, it is possible to force many women to take jobs. In the long run, however, some of these women will lose their jobs because they are in marginal, unstable industries, and some will leave their jobs because they need health benefits for themselves or their children that such jobs do not provide. Some will turn to welfare, and some will find other resources to fill their needs, but few will obtain adequate incomes.

BLACK WOMEN AND WELFARE

Black women heading families experience considerably higher rates of poverty than do white women or even black men. This reflects an important change in the last two decades; poverty rates for black male-headed families have dropped very rapidly, while those for black female-headed families have risen. In short, the burden of poverty in the black community has shifted to families that are headed by women; so that now black women maintain alone three-quarters of all poor black families (U.S. Bureau of the Census 1986, Table 3). As shown in Table 3, the proportion of persons in poverty who are in families maintained by women has risen for all groups (from 21 percent in 1960 to 48 percent in 1986), with the most dramatic shift occurring among black families. (The numbers for *persons* and for *families* in poverty differ slightly because of family size differences.)

Some observers believe this shift is polarizing the black community, not along class lines but rather along marital-status and gender lines. As Farley and Bianchi (1982, 20) found, the ratio of average per capita income in black female-headed families to that in husband–wife families had dropped in the last two decades from 0.63 to 0.47. That is, the average person (including children) in a black family headed solely by a woman now has an income

TABLE 3

Persons in Families in Poverty, by Race and Sex of Householder, 1960–1986

Year and racial/ethnic group of householder	Number of persons in families in poverty (in thousands)		Percentage of persons in families in poverty who are in families maintained by women alone
	All families	Families maintained by women alone	
1960			
Total	34,925	7,247	21
White	24,262	4,296	18
Black	9,112	2,416	26
Hispanic	—	—	—
1970			
Total	20,330	7,503	37
White	13,323	3,761	28
Black	6,683	3,656	55
Hispanic	2,252[a]	733[a]	32
1980			
Total	22,601	10,120	45
White	14,587	4,990	34
Black	7,190	4,984	69
Hispanic	3,143	1,319	42
1986			
Total	24,754	11,944	48
White	16,393	6,171	38
Black	7,401	5,473	74
Hispanic	4,469	1,921	43

SOURCE: U.S. Bureau of the Census, *Money Income and Poverty Status of Families and Persons in the United States: 1986*, Series P-60, no. 157 (Washington, D.C.: U.S. Department of Commerce, Aug. 1987), Table 16.

[a]Data are for 1972.

less than half that of the average person in a black husband–wife family.

The rising proportion of black families that are headed by women—above 43 percent by 1984—is sometimes cited as the reason that black families have not closed the income gap with white families (Green and Welniak, 1982). Although it is true that black husband–wife families, particularly when both spouses are working, have incomes that approach the level of similar white families, it should not be assumed that the two-parent households are the cause of high income levels. Conversely, it should not be assumed that one-parent households are the sole cause of poverty. Rather, it is apparent that the high rates of unemployment, underemployment, and poverty among young black men is an important cause of the formation and persistence of single-parent households by black women. Moreover, the black single mother is more likely to remain single longer and is less likely to marry or remarry than is the single white mother. The black mother is also less likely to receive child support, and when she does she receives less—just over half as much as the average white mother (Pearce and McAdoo 1981, 9). Although black women working full-time, year-round earn median wages that are 88 percent of those of similar white women, black women **503** who head households alone are less likely to be in the paid labor force—59 percent versus 64 percent of white women householders—and less than one-third of black women householders are working full-time year-round. Thus, their disadvantaged status in the labor market (a product of both gender and race), plus the economic burden of children and the lesser resources and greater poverty of the black community in general, cause black women to experience both more and greater poverty than do white women.

Although the welfare system cannot discriminate on the basis of race, there are a number of ways in which black women on welfare are especially disadvantaged. A disproportionate number of poor black women are in the South, particularly the rural South, where benefits are very low. Because food stamps are a federal program, while AFDC is locally administered (including the setting of benefit levels), the value of food stamps may be greater than that of the AFDC, although the latter is theoretically pegged at three times the amount necessary for a bare minimum diet. A third of Mississippi's welfare recipients live in free housing, either public housing that they are too poor to pay for or private housing so dilapidated that no one demands rent or mortgage payments for its use.

A NEW ERA IN OLD WINESKINS

The Reagan budget cuts in AFDC most severely affect those currently working. In about half the states, the average recipient who is also employed would actually be better off, considering average work expenses (such as car fare) and child-care costs, if she did not work at all. Many who received very small AFDC payments lose not only the AFDC benefit when they are cut from the rolls but also food stamps, Medicaid, and other benefits that are "tied" to AFDC.

It is difficult to avoid the conclusion that the system leaves mothers with only one route out of poverty—marriage. It is as though there were a new "less eligibility rule" operating for women. The original "less eligibility rule" provided that no one should receive from welfare more than he could earn at the lowest-paying job; it was designed to encourage men to go to work. The female "less eligibility rule" seems to be that no woman's life on welfare, or combination of work and welfare, should be better than she would have in the poorest marriage. (Ironically, this is the only aspect of welfare policy specifically aimed at women.) While this is obviously not an explicit rule, undeniably the welfare system rarely enables a woman to become economically independent, and welfare policymakers have expressed much concern to avoid policies that might promote the breakup of marriages, no matter how bad those marriages are.

One of the dilemmas facing social-welfare policymakers is that the goals of economic self-sufficiency and marital stability may well be inconsistent. Reviews of studies of AFDC and particularly of negative-income-tax experiments found that income guarantees, even at low levels, increased marital split rates (Bishop 1980; MacDonald and Sawhill 1978). Wrestling with this finding, Bishop chooses policy options on the assumption that "the political process has decided it is desirable, ceteris paribus, to minimize any marital destabilizing side-effects of government policy," even while he notes that this goal sometimes conflicts with other goals, including the one of "reducing the economic dependence of women" (1980, 324). He then goes on to propose wage supplements to the "working head" of the family, stating that "the husband's role as provider should be maintained" (p. 326).

Why has women's fare under welfare so consistently been impoverishment rather than freedom from want? Piven and Cloward (1971) have argued that the welfare system's raison d'être is the necessity of preserving social order; paupers who do not work but are not aged or ill are capable of revolution. "Regulating the poor" is thus a process of forcing the poor into the world of work, with its discipline and control, preferably in the profit economy but if necessary — for example, during the Depression — in public jobs programs. This does not, however, explain the drive to put *women* to work, for mothers are not historically seen as either the leaders or the troops of social revolutionary movements. One possible explanation is that women who do not need men or marriage for economic support are also threatening, in a different way, to the established social order, for they are outside the "discipline" of the institution of marriage.

Despite its efforts, public policy has not stemmed the steadily rising tide of households headed by women. Public policies can have and have had an impact on the poverty levels of those households, however, and this effect has not been a positive one. The feminization of poverty (Pearce 1978) has been further exacerbated, and the gender gap widened, by recent budget cuts and program changes. Liberalized divorce laws and lessened social restrictions on single parenting now permit women to be socially independent, but a discriminatory economic system prevents them from being economically independent. Women find themselves trapped between these opposing forces and frustrated by the conflicting messages coming from society's institutions. Although the welfare system bills itself as the safety net that backs up the failings of other economic and social systems, it hardly provides women with a way out of poverty. Indeed, since it has continued to apply a male pauper model precisely when the population in need has become increasingly female, its inappropriate programs reinforce rather than relieve women's poverty.

If one simply extrapolated the two trend lines, of more women-maintained families each year, and an increasing proportion of poor families being women-maintained families, by the year 2000, all of the poor will be in families maintained by women alone. Whether that happens will depend in large part on whether we make fundamental changes in welfare policy and programs. Without such changes, poverty will continue to be the common thread of women's fare under welfare.

REFERENCES

Bishop, H. 1980. "Jobs, Cash Transfers and Marital Instability: A Review and Synthesis of the Evidence." *Journal of Human Resources*, 15, no. 3, 301–34.

Brown, J. C. 1940. *Public Relief 1929–1939.* New York: Holt, Rinehart and Co.

Bruno, F. J. 1957. *Trends in Social Work: 1874–1976, a History Based on the Proceedings of the National Conference of Social Work*. New York: Columbia University Press.

Chapman, B. 1982. "Seduced and Abandoned." *Wall Street Journal*, Oct. 5.

Coll, B. O. 1969. *Perspectives in Public Welfare: A History*. Washington, D.C.: U.S. Department of Health, Education, and Welfare.

Editors of Marriage and Divorce Today. 1980. "Divorced Women: The Myth of Alimony, Property Settlements and Child Support." *Marriage and Divorce Today*, Nov. 24.

Farley, R., and S. M. Bianchi. 1982, "Social and Economic Polarization: Is It Occurring among Blacks?" Paper presented at the annual meeting of the American Sociological Association, San Francisco, Sept.

Green, G., and E. Welniak. 1982. "Changing Family Composition and Income Differentials." *Special Demographic Analyses*, no. CDS–80–7. Washington, D.C.: U.S. Bureau of the Census.

Handler, J. R., and E. J. Hollingsworth. 1971. *"The Deserving Poor": A Study of Welfare Administration*. Chicago: Markham Publishing Co.

Levitan, S. A. 1980. *Programs in Aid of the Poor for the 1980's*. 4th ed. Baltimore: Johns Hopkins University Press.

MacDonald, M., and I. Sawhill. 1978. "Welfare Policy and the Family." *Public Policy*, 26, no. 1 (winter), 89–119.

Nicol, H. 1975. "Preliminary Findings of Child Support Enforcement Research." Paper presented at the Fifteenth Annual Conference on Welfare Research Statistics, San Francisco, Feb.

Pearce, D. 1978. "The Feminization of Poverty: Women, Work and Welfare." *Urban and Social Change Review*, 11, no. 1, 2, 28–36.

Pearce, D., and H. McAdoo. 1981. *Women and Children: Alone and in Poverty*. Washington, D.C.: National Advisory Council on Economic Opportunity.

Piven, Frances Fox, and R. Cloward. 1971. *Regulating the Poor: The Functions of Public Welfare*. New York: Pantheon Books.

Rein, M., and L. Rainwater. 1978. "Patterns of Welfare Use." *Social Service Review* (Dec.) 511–34.

Schulman, J. 1981. "Poor Women and Family Law." *Clearinghouse Review*, 14, no. 9 (Feb.).

Shapiro, Isaac, and Robert Greenstein. 1988. *Holes in the Safety Nets: Poverty Programs and Policies in the States National Overview*. Washington, D.C.: Center on Budget and Policy Priorities.

U.S. Bureau of the Census, Current Population Reports, Series P-23, no. 152, *Child Support and Alimony: 1985 (Advance Data From March–April 1986 Current Population Surveys)*, U.S. Government Printing Office, Washington, D.C., 1987.

U.S. Bureau of the Census, Current Population Reports, Series P-20, no. 424, *Household and Family Characteristics: March 1987*, U.S. Government Printing Office, Washington, D.C., 1988.

U.S. Bureau of the Census, Current Population Reports, Series P-60, no. 157, *Money Income and Poverty Status of Families and Persons in the United States: 1986 (Advance Data from the March 1987 Current Population Survey)*, U.S. Government Printing Office, Washington, D.C., 1987.

U.S. Bureau of the Census, Current Population Reports, Series P-60, no. 160, *Poverty in the United States: 1986*, Washington, D.C.: U.S. Government Printing Office; 1988.

Women's Athletics and the Myth of Female Frailty

NANCY THEBERGE

Women's sport has historically been a setting marked by social and cultural struggle. Women have been discouraged or prevented from participating in sport by a complementary set of exclusionary practices and cultural ideals that viewed them as fragile and unsuited to strenuous physical activity. Throughout this century and especially since 1970, barriers to participation have weakened and cultural views of women athletes have been revised. Developments have not, however, led to unrestricted access or a renunciation of the myth of female frailty. As the account that follows shows, the history of women in sport is marked by a confusion of advances, barriers, setbacks, and slowed commitments. Women's sport remains an arena of struggle for control of both the institutions that regulate women's participation and the meaning of their sporting experience.

THE MYTH OF FEMALE FRAILTY AND WOMEN'S EARLY SPORT PARTICIPATION

The struggles waged in sport today are a legacy of the Victorian ideal of womanhood. This ideal held that women were morally and spiritually strong but physically and intellectually weak. Conventional wisdom supported by expert opinion held that for women strenuous activity, either physical or mental, was dangerous and irresponsible. By the middle of the century, these ideas had crystallized in an image of women as "weak, delicate and perpetually prone to illness."[1]

Challenges to the belief in female frailty appeared in the latter half of the nineteenth century. These challenges arose from several developments. Progress arising from the first wave of feminism that began in the 1850s eased some of the restrictions on women's social activities. Although sport had not been on the agenda of the early feminists, the gains women achieved in other areas paved the way for their entry into sport later in the century. The main beneficiaries of these gains were women from the upper classes who had both the time and the means to engage in recreational activities considered suitable to their position. These included riding, tennis, and golf.[2]

Another influence, which brought sport and physical activity to the middle classes, was the expansion of higher education for women in the latter half of the nineteenth century.[3] The debate over the wisdom and propriety of women's enrollment in colleges and universities included a discussion of the place of sport and physical education in the curricula of women's colleges. Proponents, primarily women physical educators, argued that mild forms of physical activity were a means to combat women's poor health and to foster their intellectual development. But the medical wisdom of the day saw both physical and intellectual exercise as dangerous to women's health. Women's smaller bodies, and their allegedly fragile structures and weak constitutions, were thought to make women unsuited for strenuous activity, including sports. Physical activity, it was argued, posed unacceptable risks to women's reproductive systems by causing uterine displacement.[4]

These claims were not supported by the limited scientific research. Nonetheless, prevailing views on women's moral responsibilities as wives and mothers compensated for the lack of evidence. Since sport apparently endangered women's reproductive capacities and developed traits unsuited to motherhood, it was argued that women had a moral obligation to refrain from such dangerous and irresponsible activity.[5]

Despite these arguments, throughout the first two decades of the twentieth century, women's participation in sport continued to increase. Two developments in the early twentieth century broadened the scope of participation beyond the middle and upper classes. The first was the beginning of organized sponsorship. In 1914, the Amateur Athletic Union (AAU), the governing body for amateur sports in the United States, voted to include women in its swimming programs. Women's competitions in track and field were added in 1922. Programs in both swimming and track and field were judged to be a success, and in 1923 the AAU approved participation by women in all sports under its jurisdiction.[6]

The second important development of the period was the beginning of industrial sponsorship of women's sports. Companies in a variety of industries, including manufacturing, banking, and insurance, provided athletic programs for employees. While the majority of these opportunities were for men, United States Labor Department surveys indicate that by the 1920s there were industrial programs for women in a number of sports, including baseball, basketball, volleyball, and track and field.[7]

The growth of industrial programs and organizational sponsorship paved the way for participation of American women in the Olympic Games. The first official representation occurred in 1920 in swimming and figure skating. Participation expanded to tennis and fencing in 1924 and track and field in 1928.[8] Between 1920 and 1932, American women were very successful in the Olympics. In 1932, led by the legendary Babe Didrickson, who won two golds and a silver medal, American women won all the women's track and field events save one (and this was won by a woman who competed for Poland but lived in the United States). American women also won all but one of the women's swimming events.[9]

The 1920s also saw the first commercial exploitation of women athletes and women's sport. This occurred in two ways. The first was the use of the female body to advertise and promote goods and services. A variety of nonathletic interests, including newspapers, real-estate firms, and advertising agencies, sold their products by using women athletes as an inducement in advertising. This practice provided a convenient way to circumvent restrictions on displaying sexually suggestive material. The presentation of the female body for commercial purposes was apparently acceptable when it was disguised as sport.[10]

The second form of commercial exploitation involved the marketing of women's athletics and athletic products. The 1920s were a period of expansion of commercial sport. This expansion mainly occurred in men's sport but also included women's activities. Included among the successful women's sports of the period were tennis, softball, and basketball. The marketability of these activities rested on selling the image of feminine athleticism. Helen Wills, the top woman tennis player of the era, was cited for upholding the "wonderful womanhood that uses sport to enhance its charm instead of to affect an artificial masculinity" and a well-known softball team was called "Slapsie Maxie's Curvaceous Cuties."[11]

DRAWING THE LINES: ADOPTION OF A MODIFIED MODEL OF WOMEN'S SPORT

The debate about women's sport took place at a time of expansion in men's sport, both professional and collegiate. Men's collegiate sport was also under attack for excessive violence and commercialism. Concern about these problems led to the formation in 1906 of the National Collegiate Athletic Association, the governing body of men's sport.[12] The problems in men's sport and concern about the increasing commercialization and competitive emphasis in women's sport provided the backdrop for the resolution of the debate about women's sport. Women in physical education approved of participation in physical activity and sport but rejected both competition and commercialism. In 1917, they formed the Committee on Women's Athletics (CWA) of the American Physical Education Association.[13] The growth of women's sport in preceding years had made clear the need for a coordinating body, and the CWA was mainly concerned with making, revising and interpreting rules.

In 1923, a second group was formed, the Women's Division of the National Amateur Athletic Federation (NAAF). The NAAF was established in 1922 to promote men's sport.[14] When in the same year the AAU voted to sponsor women's competitions in track and field, women physical educators became alarmed. They saw this development as furthering men's control over women's sport and leading it toward the competitive emphasis and resulting commercialism that existed in men's sport. In 1923, women physical educators formed the Women's Division of the NAAF to provide a forum for their position. The leadership of the Women's Division came from women active in the CWA, and the two groups shared the same philosophy and worked together. The philosophy of the Women's Division was effectively captured in their slogan: "A game for every girl and a girl in every game."[15]

The Women's Division worked throughout the 1920s to organize women's sport along a noncompetitive model of widespread participation in appropriate activities. In 1929, it petitioned the International Olympic Committee (IOC) to eliminate women's track and field from the Olympic Games. The Women's Division objected to women's participation in the Olympics because the Games were an elite competition that involved intensive training and investments of time and energy. These features contradicted the Women's Division's philosophy of widespread involvement in sport for the joy of participation. While these objections could have been applied to other sports, most notably swimming, the Division confined its petition to track and field. There were two likely reasons for this. First, events such as the discus and high jump, which involved overt displays of power and strength, presented the greatest affront to the image of feminine athleticism. The second likely reason for the focus on track and field was a class bias. Athletes in other sports, including swimming, usually came from the middle and upper classes. Track and field athletes usually came from working-class backgrounds. Moreover, they were often sponsored by industrial concerns, which were known for their commercial exploitation of women athletes.[16]

The petition to the IOC was unsuccessful and women's track and field remained in the Olympics. The Women's Division's failure in this effort indicated its limited influence on nonschool sports. The Women's Division was much more successful in implementing its ideas in its own sphere of influence, the schools and colleges.[17] This success was reflected in the adoption of a modified and restricted form of sport that was deemed suitable for women.

Perhaps the best known example of the modified model is women's basketball. Basketball was invented as a sport for men in 1892. Within a year, the game had been introduced to women at Smith College by the director of physical education, Senda Berenson. Berenson felt that basketball could be an enjoyable form of recreation for women if it were suitably adapted. She devised a number of rule changes that made the game slower and less physically demanding. One of these changes divided the court into zones and restricted players' movement across zones. In addition to making the game slower and less strenuous, this rule prohibited the best player from dominating the game. In this way, the revised version also avoided the elitism or star system encouraged in men's basketball.[18]

Women's basketball gained immediate acceptance and quickly became the most popular sport for college women. Berenson's rules were not widely adopted at the start, and in the first two decades of the century some games were played by men's rules and others according to women's rules. The lack of uniform rules may be explained by the organization of the sport at the time. Although a number of colleges played intercollegiate games, there was no system of competitions or championships and thus no strong demand for common rules.[19] This changed in the 1920s, when calls for an alternative model of women's sport grew stronger. In this decade, modified rules for women's basketball were widely adopted and intercollegiate competition was discouraged. With acceptance of a less strenuous and noncompetitive model of the sport, women's basketball was sharply differentiated from the men's game. This was the dominant version of the sport played by college women through the 1960s.[20]

Restrictions on the length of women's races were another example of limitations placed on women's activities. The introduction of track and field into the Olympics in 1928 included the 100-meter, 400-meter relay and 800-meter runs, the high jump, and discus. The 800-meter race was a particularly dramatic event. Of the eleven competitors who began the race, five failed to finish and several more appeared to be close to fainting at the finish. In their campaign to convince the IOC to eliminate women's track and field from the Olympics, the Women's Division of the NAAF cited the dangers of "overstrain" in Olympic track and field.[21] Although the IOC rejected the petition to eliminate women's track and field from the Olympics, it did drop the 800-meter race. This was significant, for the 800-meter race was a "long-distance" event.

Alternatives to the competitive emphasis in men's sports were established by introducing programs that stressed broad participation and deemphasized winning. A popular form of participation was the *play day,* which consisted of women from a number of schools coming together to play a variety of sports. Teams comprised players from different schools. This arrangement encouraged broad participation and reduced the competitive element of interschool competition. Play days were introduced in 1926 and by the 1930s had gained widespread acceptance. In 1930, a survey reported that 80 percent of colleges had women's play days; another survey in 1936 placed the figure at 70 percent.[22]

Another alternative to men's programs was the *telegraphic meet,* in which contestants participated in activities on their own campus according to agreed-on rules. Results were telegraphed to a designated official and later announced. This arrangement reduced the expense and effort of travel and thus encouraged widespread participation. As well, the absence of face-to-face competition minimized the emphasis on competition. Telegraphic meets were especially prominent in the 1930s in sports that lent themselves to this kind of participation, including archery, bowling, and riflery.[23]

In 1932, the Committee on Women's Athletics affiliated with the American Physical Education Association (APEA) and changed its name to the National Section on Women's Athletics (NSWA) of the APEA. In 1940, the NSWA absorbed the Women's Division of the NAAF in order to work more efficiently and effectively. In 1953, the NSWA was replaced by the National Section on Girls and Women in Sport; in 1957, it became the Division for Girls' and Women's Sports (DGWS) of the APEA, by now the American Alliance for Health, Physical Education and Recreation (AAHPER).[24] Throughout this period, women's sport leaders remained committed to the philosophy and model adopted in the 1930s. There were some exceptions of competitive programs, including a national collegiate golf tournament begun in 1941 and held annually except during World War II. But for the most part women's athletics in colleges and universities were dominated by the values and principles promoted by male physicians and adopted by women physical educators earlier in the century.

THE OLYMPICS: RETREAT FROM EARLY SUCCESSES

The fortunes of American women athletes in the Olympics took a downturn after the successes of 1932. In 1936 and from 1948 until 1960 (the Games were suspended during World War II), the performances of American women were largely disappointing. There were some exceptions. Patricia McCormick won two gold medals in diving (out of a total of two events) in both 1952 and 1956.[25]

This record reflects the power of the philosophy of women's sport adopted in schools and colleges during the 1930s and changing opportunities for women's participation. The anticompetitive philosophy of women physical educators meant that women who wished to compete at an elite level had to look outside the school system for their athletic development. In the 1920s, these opportunities were available in industrial programs. The successes of American women at the 1928 and 1932 Olympics were largely a result of these programs, as the majority of American Olympic women came from industry and very few came from the colleges.[26]

The downturn in American women's performances at the 1936 Olympics reflected industrial retrenchment during the Depression of the 1930s. During World War II, there was a short-lived revival of industrial programs, and women's leagues were a popular form of recreation and entertainment. When men returned from the war, women lost their jobs and support for industrial teams diminished.[27] With few opportunities to participate in sport outside the schools, and with acceptance of a nonelite and noncompetitive model of women's athletics in the education system, conditions for the development of women Olympic champions were hardly ideal.

THE MODIFIED MODEL AND THE MYTH OF FEMALE FRAILTY

The significance of the adoption of the modified model of women's sport is that it came to symbolize and reinforce the myth of female frailty that the growth of women's sport from 1890 through the 1930s had initially challenged. The debate had always been a struggle over the definition of and control over this activity. Arguments in the 1920s against duplicating the commercial and competitive excesses of men's sport reinforced nineteenth-century medical and social arguments against women's participation. To avoid the problems of men's sport, the model of women's sport that emerged in the 1930s acknowledged the ideal of female frailty and signified the "essential differences" between the sexes.

This model remained dominant through the 1960s. To be sure, women's sport and physical education was accepted in schools and colleges, and women athletes competed in the Olympics primarily in swimming and diving, track and field, gymnastics, skiing, and figure skating.[28] The other major women's sports during this period were tennis and golf. Until 1970, tennis was primarily an amateur sport, although women competed professionally in the 1920s and 1940s.[29] In golf, women competed as amateurs as early as 1895, and the Ladies Professional Golf Association was formed in 1950.[30]

Despite these opportunities, the organization of women's sport was dominated by the values and principles promoted by male physicians and adopted by women physical educators earlier in the century. Approval for women's participation was largely limited to sports considered feminine, competition in school sports was deemphasized, and competition in the Olympics was limited to less strenuous events. (The women's 800-meter race did not return to the Olympics until 1960.) Programs for girls and women were poorly funded and received little or no public support and attention. What interest there was in women's sport was excessively concerned with the femininity — or lack thereof — of women athletes. In all these respects, women's sport throughout this period remained a vehicle for reinforcing rather than challenging the myth of female frailty.

SOCIAL CHANGE IN WOMEN'S SPORT IN THE 1970s

Prompted by developments inside and outside of sport, women's athletics began to change in the 1970s. Outside of the sport arena, the 1960s was a period of social activism and concern for equality. An important aspect of this was the reemergence of feminism. The revived women's movement brought a challenge to traditional sex roles. The climate of social change of the 1960s and the influence of the feminist movement provided the backdrop for developments in women's sport in the 1970s.

Within sport, two events of the early 1970s had a major impact on women's participation. The first was the establishment of the Association for Intercollegiate Athletics for Women (AIAW) in 1972. Women's collegiate sport had always been governed by women working in a women's organization, first the Committee on Women's Athletics, then its successors, the National Section on Women's Athletics, the National Section on Girls and Women in Sport and the Division for Girls' and Women's Sports, (DGWS) of the AAHPER. Women's sport grew sufficiently in the 1950s and early 1960s that by the mid-1960s the need for a national organization to administer programs was acknowledged. In 1966, DGWS appointed a Commission on Intercollegiate Sports for Women to administer national championships. The first championships were offered in 1969. Following this, the need for an organization to coordinate and oversee the activities of university athletic programs was recognized; in 1972, the Commission was replaced with the AIAW.[31] In 1979, the AIAW separated from the AAHPER and became an autonomous governing body for women's intercollegiate sport with responsibilities similar to those exercised by the NCAA in men's sport.[32]

The second event was the passage of Title IX of the Educational Amendments Act in 1972. Title IX prohibited sex discrimination in educational institutions receiving federal funding—and this included virtually all institutions in the United States. Although Title IX did not single out sport as a target area, its obvious significance for sport was immediately apparent, since virtually all educational institutions had vastly unequal sport programs for males and females.

The years from 1972 to 1978 were marked by discussions between federal officials charged with enforcing Title IX and women's rights activists, educators, and athletic administrators. These negotiations were concerned with clarifying the meaning and application of Title IX. Final regulations required institutions to provide equality of opportunity for male and female students in their athletic programs but not equality *per se*. This meant that males and females must have equal selection of sports and levels of competition available to them and equal access to facilities, training, coaching, and scheduling of games and practices. The bill did not require sex integration of teams. It did provide that where an institution operates a team for members of one sex but not the other, the excluded sex must be allowed to try out for the team unless the sport involved is a contact sport.[33]

Once the regulations were in place, Title IX had a significant impact on the participation of females in school sport programs. In 1971, 7 percent of high-school athletes and 13 percent of collegiate athletes were female; in 1983, five years after institutions were required to be in compliance with the regulations, 35 percent of high-school and 31 percent of collegiate athletes were female.[34] The effects of the legislation were also evident in funding for athletic programs. In 1973, funding for women's collegiate programs totalled $4.2 million, or 3 percent of athletic-department budgets; in 1978, women's programs received $116 million, or 16 percent of total budgets.[35] Before 1972, no athletic scholarships were available to women; by 1984, more than 10,000 women's athletic scholarships were offered in U.S. colleges.[36]

Expanding opportunities in school sport have led to improved performances by American women in the Olympics. Improvement began in the 1960s, with successes both in swimming and diving and in track and field. It is significant that with the exception of Tennessee State University, a black college attended by a number of Olympic track stars,[37] neither sport was well organized in the schools. The role of university programs began to change in the 1970s, when the effects of the AIAW and Title IX began to be seen. By 1984, the importance of university programs was clear: More than 75 percent of women on the U.S. Olympic team had been university athletes.[38]

The growth of women's sport in educational institutions that followed the passage of Title IX set in motion a number of developments that have drastically altered the organization of women's sport. By 1979–1980, the AIAW had grown to 973 member institutions.[39] In 1980, the NCAA voted to offer national championships for women beginning in 1981–1982.[40] The NCAA justified this decision by arguing that Title IX required it to offer women's programs.[41] This move was the beginning of the end of AIAW. Faced with competition from the richer and more powerful men's organization, the AIAW could not survive. Two strategies the NCAA employed in this competition were particularly successful. The NCAA offered to pay travel and other expenses of teams competing in its national championships and encouraged television networks purchasing broadcast rights to the highly popular men's basketball games also to purchase rights to women's games.[42] After an unsuccessful legal battle to attempt to prevent the NCAA's incursion into women's sport, the AIAW ceased to exist in 1984.[43] Most women's athletic programs are now governed by the NCAA, where voting representatives are overwhelmingly male and women hold only 15 to 25 percent of positions on committees.[44] With these developments, control of women's collegiate sport passed from the hands of women working in a separate organization to those of men working in a male-dominated organization.

Loss of control also took place in individual institutions. Since the passage of Title IX, the proportion of women athletic administrators and coaches has declined in both high schools and universities. In 1973—1974, 79 percent of women's athletic programs were run by women; by 1985—1986, 85 percent of administrators in charge of women's programs were men.[45] As women's sport grew and drew a larger share of resources, many institutions merged men's and women's programs under one administrator, who almost always was a man. The visibility and importance attributed to men's sport ensured that the person judged to be most "qualified" to head a newly combined program would be the head of the men's program. The wealth of experience of heads of women's programs went largely unrecognized and unrewarded.

Explanations for the mergers of men's and women's programs are a matter of debate. Defenders view them as a well-intentioned effort to streamline athletic departments and argue that reorganization facilitated the growth of women's programs. One male athletic director recently observed that combining men's and women's athletic programs was "the single best thing we've done. It's an awful lot easier to lobby for athletes than to separately lobby for men and women."[46] Critics counter that justifications of mergers as efforts to improve the operations of departments mask the most important outcome of reorganization: removal of control of women's programs and of the accompanying budgets to the offices of male administrators.[47]

The takeover of administration of women's sport by men was accompanied by a similar move of men into coaching positions. This occurred because the increased status and funding prompted by Title IX made coaching women's programs more attractive and rewarding. As with administrators, the second-class status of women's sport put women coaches at a disadvantage in competitions with their male peers for the expanding number of positions in women's programs. In 1974, 81 percent of coaches of women's teams were women; in 1985–1986, only 51 percent were women.[48]

Changes following from Title IX have also had a profound influence on the values and organizing principles of women's sport. The guiding principle of the AIAW was an athlete-centered model of sport. The AIAW attempted to realize this principle through athlete representation on decision-making bodies, and through a bill of rights and guarantee of due process for athletes. In the NCAA, athletes are absent from the governing structure and decisions are often based on commercial interests rather than on the welfare of student athletes.[49]

The AIAW also attempted to avoid the problems arising from the commercialism and win-at-all-costs approach that had come to plague men's collegiate sport. The AIAW philosophy discouraged awarding athletic scholarships on the grounds they distorted the balance between academics and athletics and placed undue pressures on recipients. In 1973, the AIAW revised this position when threatened with a Title IX lawsuit by women athletes.[50] It also developed recruitment policies that differed markedly from the NCAA's practices. Under the NCAA, some high-school athletes are subjected to recruitment practices that can fairly be described as harassment. For superior athletes, this begins early in the high-school career and includes letters and telephone calls, as well as visits by coaches to the athletes' homes and by athletes to college campuses. Under the AIAW, recruitment was limited to the final year of high school. Off campus recruiting was limited to telephone calls and letters, and athletes were limited to one on-campus recruiting visit per institution.[51]

The years since the NCAA takeover of women's sport have seen the beginning of problems that can be traced to an emphasis on commercial and competitive success. In 1984, the NCAA announced the first reprimand of a women's program for recruiting violations and for provision of improper benefits to athletes.[52] In 1986, the first women's team was penalized, again for recruiting violations. The violation occurred in basketball, which has become the major women's sport in U.S. colleges. Penalties included restrictions on the coach's recruiting activities, disqualification of the team from participation in the national championship tournament, and suspension of the player who received the benefits, all for one year.[53] The title of an article in the *Chronicle of Higher Education* reviewing the incident effectively captures the changes that have taken place in women's basketball: "Big Jump in Money and Prestige Spurs Cheating in Women's Basketball, Coaches and Players Say." In commenting on the issue, a woman coach of one of the major women's teams in the country said, "I had hoped that people in women's athletics were more ethical than in men's sports, but it didn't turn out that way." Another woman coach remarked that while cheating occurred under the AIAW, the violations have increased under the NCAA. "The interest, money and prestige put pressure on a coach to win."[54]

RESISTANCE AND RETREAT IN THE 1980s

The takeover of women's sport by men and by the male model of sport is ironic because, since its passage, Title IX has been resisted by both male sport administrators and university officials. The NCAA correctly saw that the growth of women's sport would cost money and feared that this money would come from men's programs. It fought the application of Title IX to athletics both in the courts and by a vigorous lobbying effort of HEW and congressional officials.[55]

Resistance from university administrators also concerned the scope of the bill's application. Under the original guidelines issued by HEW, *all* programs and departments within an institution were subject to Title IX if *any* program or department received federal funds. Several court challenges were filed in which school districts and colleges argued that only specific programs and departments that received federal funds should come under the bill's jurisdiction. In a 1984 ruling in *Grove City College v. Bell,* the Supreme Court upheld the program-specific interpretation of Title IX. This revised interpretation effectively eliminated athletics from the bill's coverage, since few athletic departments receive federal funds directly.[56]

The effects of *Grove City* were felt immediately. Soon after the decision, the Department of Education's Office of Civil Rights dropped investigation of sixty-four Title IX complaints, including several complaints against university athletic departments.[57]

There also is evidence of erosion of gains achieved under Title IX. Schools have eliminated or cut women's athletic programs. In some cases, women's sports are clearly easy targets for cutbacks. More costly and favored men's programs are more secure. A case in point is recent developments at Southwest Texas State University. In 1986, citing financial cutbacks and lack of a competitive future, the university dropped women's gymnastics. In fact, the women's gymnastics program had one of the best competitive records of Southwest Texas State University teams and accounted for only a small portion ($47,000) of the $1.5 million annual athletic budget.[58] About half this budget went to men's football and basketball, which were less successful than women's gymnastics, and the remainder was divided among seven men's and women's teams. Similar stories of elimination or cuts in women's programs have been reported elsewhere.[59] The aftermath of *Grove City* has shown that, although women's sports never reached parity with men's, they are more than equal candidates for cuts in times of financial restraint.

THE OLYMPICS: AMBIVALENCE AMID EXPANSION

Unlike school sport programs, women's international sport has always been organized and administered by men. The first women were appointed to the International Olympic Committee in 1981. The major form of change affecting women in the Olympic Games has been a gradual increase in the number of women's events. In the 1988 Summer and Winter Games, 63 percent of events were open to men only, 31 percent to women only, and 6 percent to men and women competing together.[60] Although the gap between the number of men's and women's events is still considerable, it has been narrowing with each olympiad.

A review of the events that have been added indicates continuing ambivalence about the meaning of women's sport. The women's marathon, added in 1984, and the women's 10,000-meter race, added in 1988, are distance events. Other additions are multiple events that combine running, jumping, and throwing competitions. In 1964 the pentathlon was introduced; in 1984, it was replaced with the heptathlon. The challenge to the myth of female frailty indicated by the adoption of women's distance and multiple events marks progress for women in sport.

Other additions include team sports. Women's volleyball was introduced in the 1964 Games, women's basketball in 1976, and women's field hockey in 1980. The historical resistance to women's sport participation has been particularly strong in the case of team sports. Traditionally, sports in which it has been acceptable for women to compete internationally and professionally have been individual sports such as tennis, golf, skating, and swimming. The major exception in this regard would appear to be field hockey, which has been organized internationally since the 1930s. Until recently, however, women's field hockey has conformed to the model of restricted sport described earlier. Even at the international level, the structure of tournaments deemphasized competition and winning and focussed instead on the experience of participation.[61]

Resistance to women's participation in team sports has denied women one of the important forms of community and association that men have long enjoyed in such sports as football. Numerous autobiographical accounts have given testimony to the bonds men form through team sports. As well, the value of team sports in teaching boys to work together in pursuit of a common goal have often been cited as justification for inclusion of these sports in school and community athletic programs. The increased involvement of women in team sports is thus welcome for the opportunity it provides them to experience the benefits and pleasures of mutual association and cooperation.

Expansion of women's events in the Olympic Games has also included a number of traditionally "feminine" sports. Events introduced in the 1984 Games include synchronized swimming and rhythmic gymnastics. A related development has been the increasing popularity of artistic gymnastics (usually referred to simply as gymnastics). In recent Olympic Games, the "stars" among women competitors have been gymnasts, including Olga Korbut in 1972, Nadia Comanecci in 1976, and Mary Lou Retton in 1984. The current prominence of "feminine" sports exemplifies the mixed messages appearing in women's sports today. On the one hand, it must be acknowledged that world-class synchronized swimmers and gymnasts (like champions in other artistic sports) are highly accomplished athletes whose performances require remarkable skill and ability. Nonetheless, by their emphasis on beauty, form, and appearance, these sports provide symbolic confirmation of the special nature of women's sport. In this way, sports such as synchronized swimming and gymnastics reaffirm the stigma associated with women's sport participation.

THE STRUGGLE CONTINUES

The twentieth century has witnessed a story of struggle for control over the conditions and meaning of women's involvement in sport. The first wave of participation earlier in the century offered a challenge to the Victorian ideal of female frailty and to social control of women's bodies. This challenge was resisted, however, and the model of women's sport adopted in the 1930s accepted and confirmed the myth of female frailty. One of the significant ironies of events in this period is that, in school sport and physical education programs, women maintained institutional control but were dominated ideologically by the medical profession's power to define the limits of women's sporting experience.

Significant change has occurred in expansion of the number and variety of opportunities for women's sport participation, and in the level of women athletes' accomplishments. That women would compete in an Olympic marathon or in heavily publicized and promoted collegiate championships would have been unthinkable to leaders of women's sport in the 1930s. The model of restricted activity adopted in that period has been soundly rejected and the myth of female frailty has been exposed.

This progress has not occurred without cost. A significant loss was the removal of women from leadership positions in collegiate sport. Now more than ever before women lack control in their own sporting institutions. Moreover, the takeover of women's sport by the NCAA has meant that the athlete-centered model supported by the AIAW has been replaced by a competitive and commercial model that is beset by problems.

Progress was also threatened with the weakening of Title IX by the *Grove City* decision. In March 1988, however, Congress passed the Civil Rights Restoration Act, which restored the broad interpretation of Title IX. Supporters applauded the move as an important step that will, in the words of one woman sport administrator, "put the teeth back into Title IX."[62]

Historically, the exclusion of women from sport or their acceptance as unwelcome intruders provided powerful "confirmation" of their weakness and frailty. In a vicious circle of illogic and discrimination, women were excluded from sport, and their exclusion was interpreted as evidence of their weakness. Events of recent years have significantly changed these conditions. Women have gained unprecedented admission to the world of sport but on terms very different from the ideals envisioned by women's sport leaders both earlier in the century and more recently. The outcome of the struggles waged in women's sport has been partial integration into a male-controlled and male-defined institution.

NOTES

1. Lorna Duffin, "The Conspicuous Consumptive: Woman as an Invalid," in Sara Delamont and Lorna Duffin, eds. *The Nineteenth Century Woman* (London: Croom Helm, 1972), 26.

2. Paula Welch, "The Relationship of the Women's Rights Movement to Women's Sport and Physical Education in the United States 1848–1920," *Proteus*, 3, no. 1 (1986):34–40; Ellen Gerber, "Chronicle of Participation," in Ellen Gerber, Jan Felshin, Pearl Berlin and Waneen Wyrick, eds., *The American Woman in Sport* (Reading, Mass: Addison-Wesley, 1974), 23–30.

3. Gerber, "Chronicle of Participation," 49–54.

4. Gerber, "Chronicle of Participation," 14–17; Helen Lenskyj, *Out of Bounds: Women, Sport and Sexuality* (Toronto: Women's Press, 1986), 17–29. See also Carroll Smith-Rosenberg and Charles Rosenberg, "The Female Animal: Medical and Biological Views of Woman and Her Role in Nineteenth Century America," *Journal of American History*, 60, no. 2 (1973): 332–356.

5. Lenskyj, *Out of Bounds*, 29–55.

6. Gerber, "Chronicle of Participation," 38–39.

7. Ibid., 39–40.

8. Ibid., 139, 144. Although they did not achieve official status on Olympic teams until 1920, in 1900 and 1904 American women took part in athletic competitions associated with Olympic Games. See Gerber, "Chronicle of Participation," 138–139.

9. A complete record of Olympic results is contained in David Wallechinsky, *The Complete Book of the Olympics* (New York: Viking Penguin, 1988).

10. Stephanie Twin, Introduction to *Out of the Bleachers* (Old Westbury: New York, 1979), xxix–xxx; Betty Spears, "Prologue: The Myth," in Carole A. Oglesby, ed., *Women and Sport: From Myth to Reality,* (Philadelphia: Lea and Febiger, 1978), 11.

11. Twin, Introduction to *Out of the Bleachers,* xxix–xxx. The description of Helen Wills is cited in Twin, pp. xxix–xxx and was originally published in "Sketches from Helen: A Novel from Suzanne," *Literary Digest,* 89, no. 3 (1926): 66. See also Nancy Theriot, "Towards a New Sporting Ideal: The Women's Division of the National Amateur Athletic Federation," *Frontiers,* 3, no. 1 (1978): 2.

12. Betty Spears and Richard A. Swanson, *History of Sport and Physical Activity in the United States* (Dubuque, Iowa: Wm. C. Brown, 1978): 212–214.

13. Gerber, "Chronicle of Participation," 81.

14. Theriot, "Towards a New Sporting Ideal," 3.

15. Gerber, "Chronicle of Participation," 79–81; Theriot, "Towards a New Sporting Ideal," 1–7.

16. Gerber, "Chronicle of Participation," 145–153; see also Theriot, "Towards a New Sporting Ideals," 5.

17. Gerber, "Chronicle of Participation," 153; Theriot, "Towards a New Sporting Ideal," 4.

18. Ronald A. Smith, "The Rise of Basketball for Women in Colleges," *Canadian Journal of History of Sport and Physical Education,* 1, no. 2 (1970): 20–22.

19. Ibid., 22–23.

20. Ibid., 27–33.

21. Gerber, "Chronicle of Participation," 152.

22. Mabel Lee, "The Case for and against Intercollegiate Athletics for Women and the Situation Since 1923," *Research Quarterly,* 2 (1931): 117. The 1936 survey is cited in Gerber, "Chronicle of Participation," 66.

23. Gerber, "Chronicle of Participation," 65.

24. Ibid., 76–83.

25. Michael Levy, "3,000 Years in the Making: The Story of Women at the Summer Olympics," *Women's Sports,* July 1984, 35–36.

26. Gerber, "Chronicle of Participation," 40; see also John R. Tunis, "Women and the Sport Business," *Harpers Magazine,* 159 (July, 1929): 211–221.

27. Levy, "3,000 Years in the Making," 35.

28. Gerber, "Chronicle of Participation," 145.

29. Ibid., 125–130.

30. Ibid., 107–108.

31. Ibid., 81–85.

32. Bonnie Slatton, "AIAW: The Greening of American Athletics," in James H. Frey, ed., *The Governance of Intercollegiate Athletics* (West Point, N.Y.: Leisure Press, 1982): 152–153.

33. Patricia L. Geadelmann, "How Can I Determine if Equality Exists?" in Patricia L. Geadelmann, Christine Grant, Yvonne Slatton and N. Peggy Burke, eds., *Equality in Sport for Women* (Washington, D.C.: American Alliance for Health, Physical Education and Recreation): 38–42. Relevant sections of Title IX are also published in Spears and Swanson, *History of Sport and Physical Activity,* 284–86.

34. Susan Birrell, "The Woman Athlete's College Experience: Knowns and Unknowns," *Journal of Sport and Social Issues,* 11, no. ½ (1987): 83–84. The figures Birrell provides are as follows: in

1971, 3,666,917 boys and 294,015 girls participated in interscholastic athletics; in 1983–1984, 3,303,599 boys and 1,747,350 girls participated. In 1971, 172,447 males and 31,852 females competed in intercollegiate athletics; in 1983–1984, 188,594 males and 84,765 females competed.

35. Birrell, ''The Woman Athlete's College Experience,'' 84.

36. Charles S. Farrell, ''Many Women Link Anti–Sex-Bias Law to Outstanding Olympic Performances,'' *Chronicle of Higher Education,* August 29, 1984, 31–32.

37. Gerber, ''Chronicle of Participation,'' 153.

38. Farrell, ''Many Women Link Anti–Sex-Bias Law,'' 31.

39. Ann M. Seha, ''The Administrative Enforcement of Title IX in Intercollegiate Athletics,'' *Law and Inequality,* 2, no. 1 (1984): 129.

40. Randi Jean Greenberg, ''AIAW vs. NCAA: The Takeover and Implications,'' *Journal of the National Association of Women Deans, Administrators and Counsellors,* 47, no. 2 (1984): 29.

41. Linda Jean Carpenter, ''The Impact of Title IX on Women's Intercollegiate Sports,'' in Arthur T. Johnson and James H. Frey, eds, *Government and Sport: The Public Policy Issues* (Totowa, N.J.: Roman and Allenheld, 1985): 65.

42. Ibid.

43. Ibid.

44. Seha, ''The Administrative Enforcement of Title IX,'' 133.

45. Birrell, ''The Woman Athlete's College Experience,'' 86. Birrell's source in the 1973–1974 data was the AIAW. The 1986 data were taken from an unpublished study by R. Vivian Acosta and L.J. Carpenter, ''Women in Intercollegiate Sports: A Longitudinal Study–Nine Year Update'' (New York: Brooklyn College, 1986).

46. Courtney Leatherman, ''Female Athletes, Administrators Lobby for Bill to Counteract Effects of Grove City Ruling,'' *Chronicle of Higher Education,* July 22, 1987, 24.

47. Ibid; Carpenter, ''The Impact of Title IX,'' 65; Candace Lyle Hogan, ''What's in the Future for Women's Sports?'' *Women's Sports and Fitness,* June 1987, 43–47.

48. Birrell, ''The Woman Athlete's College Experience,'' 88. The 1974 data were published in Milton L. Holmen and Bonnie L. Parkhouse, ''Trends in the Selection of Coaches for Female Athletes: A Demographic Inquiry,'' *Research Quarterly for Exercise and Sport,* 52 no. 1 (1981): 9–18; the 1985–1986 data were taken from R. Vivan Acosta and Linda Jean Carpenter, ''Women in Intercollegiate Sport.''

49. Christine Grant, ''The Gender Gap in Sport: From Intercollegiate to Olympic Level,'' *Arena Review,* 8, no. 2 (1984): 40–43; Slatton, ''AIAW,'' 146–148.

50. R. Vivian Acosta and Linda Jean Carpenter, ''Women in Sport,'' in Donald Chu, Jeffrey O. Segrave, and Beverly Becker, eds., *Sport and Higher Education* (Champaign, Ill.: Human Kinetics Press, 1985), 319.

51. Greenberg, ''AIAW vs. NCAA,'' 32; Slatton, ''AIAW,'' 149.

52. ''NCAA Publicly Censures Alcorn State; First Action Against Women's Program,'' *Chronicle of Higher Education,* May 9, 1984, 27.

53. ''Women's Team Is Penalized,'' *New York Times,* Jan. 11, 1986, 43; ''Women's Basketball Team in Louisiana Penalized for Recruitment Violations,'' *Chronicle of Higher Education,* Jan 22, 1986, 29.

54. Charles S. Farrell, ''Big Jump in Money and Prestige Spurs Cheating in Women's Basketball, Coaches and Players Say,'' *Chronicle of Higher Education,* Jan. 29, 1986, 25.

55. Carpenter, ''The Impact of Title IX,'' 63–65; Seha, ''The Administrative Enforcement of Title IX,'' 130–133.

56. *Grove City College v. Bell* 465 U.S. 555 (1984); Carpenter, ''The Impact of Title IX,'' 68–73.

57. Ibid., 72–73; Leatherman, ''Female Athletes, Administrators Lobby,'' 24; Hogan, ''What's in the Future?,'' 44; Ellie McGrath, ''Let's Put Some Muscle Where it Really Counts,'' *Women's Sports and Fitness,* December 1986, 78.

58. Hogan, "What's in the Future?" 43–47.

59. Ibid.; McGrath, "Let's Put Some Muscle," 78.

60. In the 1988 Summer Olympics, 64 percent of events were open to men only, 30 percent of events were open to women only, and 6 percent of events were open to men and women. In the 1988 Winter Olympics, 61 percent of events were open to men only, 35 percent of events were open to women only, and 4 percent of events were open to men and women. A complete list of events is provided in Wallechinsky, *The Complete Book of the Olympics.*

61. Grant, "The Gender Gap in Sport," 34–38.

62. "Administrators Applaud Override." *USA Today,* March 23, 1988, C2. *Congressional Quarterly Weekly Report,* March 5, 1988, 563, and March 26, 1988, 774.

Women at West Point: Lessons for Token Women in Male-Dominated Occupations

JANICE D. YODER

What happens when a few women break the gender barrier and select careers dominated by and stereotypically associated with men? We have seen many of these barriers fall over the past decade or so. Women have made substantial gains in medical and law school, have run for political offices, and even have penetrated some skilled crafts. But, what happens to both the women and the organizations involved when gender boundaries are crossed? This paper will focus on the consequences of gender integration in one of the most traditionally masculine settings: the United States Military Academy at West Point.

In 1975, Congress mandated that the three military academies open their doors to women cadets. At that time, Project Athena was created to help facilitate women's entry into West Point. Although few organizations have been so exclusively male and so ceremoniously changed, what happened to the women at West Point offers lessons to both individuals and organizations grappling with gender integration.

Before describing what it was like for women cadets to be in the first coeducational class, we will first look at West Point itself, as it is a unique institution. Next, we will describe the changes that took place across the first four years of coeducation that contributed to some improvements in the status of women, in order to identify what both individuals and organizations can do to ease women's entry into nontraditional roles.

West Point blends much of what we are familiar with at civilian colleges with less familiar training for the military. Unlike a civilian school, the first day at West Point is July 1. After a day full of medical examinations, physical tests, hair cuts, uniform issuance, and some rudimentary training, cadets march in parade in front of parents and well-wishers. After these onlookers leave the post, life changes dramatically for the next five weeks of "Cadet Basic Training." Movie portrayals of boot camp are not far off; there is lots of physical exercise and a basic introduction to military life and requirements. About 10 percent of each class leaves the Academy before the summer ends.

When classes start, the parallels with civilian colleges become stronger, but with some glaring exceptions. For cadets, classes start at 7:30 A.M. and end in the mid-afternoon; then all cadets play a sport before dinner. After dinner, there is time only to study and to sleep before the 5:50 A.M. cannon shot that begins each day. It is a very regimented, full schedule. However, with the exception of a few classes (e.g., military history), courses are similar to those of civilians and students can major in a range of fields, although engineering is the most popular.

Finally, because tuition is free and a generous monthly allotment is provided for every cadet, cadets, unlike many civilian students, do not need a summer job. And, unlike civilians, cadets' summers are not spent away from school. After their freshman year, cadets engage in "Cadet Field Training," which is designed to introduce them to the various branches of the Army. After their sophomore year, they take part in "Troop Leader Training," which is designed to introduce them to life in the regular Army. And finally, during their last summer, after their junior year, cadets are assigned to conduct Cadet Basic and Field Training. Remember that the overriding mission of West Point is to train officers (i.e., leaders), and the conduct of these summer exercises provides hands-on experiences. After graduation, cadets owe the Army five years of service.

WOMEN AS TOKENS

In 1976, 119 women joined 1366 men as the first coeducational class to attend West Point. (These cadets graduated in 1980, so I will refer to them throughout as the class of 1980.) They entered an institution that had been designed exclusively by and for men and that exemplified masculinity. Furthermore, they did so as only a small proportion of their class (8 percent) and an even smaller proportion of the entire Academy (2 percent). In 1976, there were only two women for every 100 cadets.

Tokenism

Sociologists describe the situation these women faced as one of *tokenism*. Three factors define tokenism and each was operative at West Point. First, Rosabeth Moss Kanter (1977) describes tokens as any *underrepresented* group.

that constitutes less than 15 percent of the whole (members of the majority group are called "dominants"). Clearly, by this definition, women cadets are tokens and male cadets are dominants.

To this numerical definition, Judith Long Laws (1975) adds two requirements: external pressure and marginality. The admitting institution must have been under *external pressure* to admit the formerly excluded group. This is clearly true with the Academies; women were there simply because Congress mandated their matriculation. The Academies' determination to block integration is well documented, especially West Point's (see Stiehm, 1981).

Women's admission was marked by only minimal changes in training at the Academy, which, as we will see, contributed to women's continued marginal status there. *Marginality* refers to the failure of the dominant group to assimilate the newly admitted group into the status quo; hence, the newcomers always remain on the fringes of the organization. This marginality at the Academies was almost guaranteed by the law itself, which specified that only changes based on "proven physiological differences between men and women" were permissible (Public Law 94-106). Hence, all three components of tokenism are found for the first coeducational class at West Point.

Effects of Tokenism

Kanter (1977) closely observed a corporation with token numbers of women managers and documented three negative effects for women of being in a token occupational setting: visibility, contrast, and assimilation. Let us examine each of these in turn and discuss how each operated at West Point (see Yoder, Adams, & Prince [1983], and Adams & Yoder [1985] for the details of the following discussion).

Visibility. With only two women for each 100 cadets, women obviously stood out. Being in the spotlight has advantages, but when it is constant, it can be a liability. And, this is what happened to the highly visible token group of women at West Point.

One negative consequence is *pressure to perform well* at all times. We found both psychological and physiological evidence that women were experiencing greater performance pressures at West Point than were men. Using standard measures of psychological stress across the first summer of basic training, women showed significantly higher stress levels. Physiologically, over half the women reported disruptions of their regular menstrual cycles at this time, a change that cannot be fully explained by the physical activity of these physically fit women. The injury and illness rate for women cadets during basic training was almost five times that of men, and these figures probably underestimated women's actual incidences of injury. Our informal interviews revealed that many women failed to report injuries for fear that admission of weakness would jeopardize their acceptance as cadets.

A second negative consequence of visibility is fear by the dominant group that the tokens possess a *competitive edge*. In other words, men are fearful that the visibility of women cadets will highlight these women's achievements to the exclusion of men's. These fears among male cadets came to the foreground whenever men and women competed for scarce resources, such as preferred assignments for officers after graduation. As we also will see, these fears fueled concerns about the preferential treatment of women.

Contrast.   A second outcome of being a token is a contrast effect. When group members are essentially the same (for example, all men), individual differences among the members are readily seen. However, when a few different members are added to this group (for example, women), the tokens not only stand out (visibility), but the differences among the dominants fade. What stands out now is the overriding difference or contrast between women and men; other individual differences seem to blend into the background. This is the contrast effect.

One consequence of the contrast effect is uncertainty. Before women came to West Point, men were relatively certain about how to act and how to treat one another. Now that women were around, things changed. Male cadets asked themselves how they should act and how they should treat these new and different (contrasted) tokens. One way to resolve these uncertainties for dominants is simply to walk away from the issue—in other words, to *isolate* token group members.

Claims of preferential treatment became a mechanism whereby women were isolated at West Point. To see how this works, we must understand two aspects of cadets' lives: their leadership ratings and fraternization. The Academy is designed to train officers—that is, leaders. Needless to say, an important indicator of a cadet's success at the Academy is his or her *leadership rating*. A cadet's leadership rating encompasses evaluations from a variety of sources, including upperclass cadets and peers. *Fraternization* refers to biased treatment afforded a cadet because of a personal involvement. For many cadets, repeated association between a man and a woman was regarded as prima facie evidence of dating. Dating, in turn, reflects blatant fraternization, which could artificially inflate the leadership ratings given by one's partner. Although this may sound somewhat convoluted, the process is reminiscent of the "director's couch" and the often-heard claims that "she advanced on her back."

The effect for women was clear. To meet with a man repeatedly aroused suspicions of dating and ultimately, of preferential treatment. The solution also was clear; avoid any misperceptions by avoiding repeated contact. Our surveys indeed confirm that women felt isolated. When graduating cadets were asked whether they felt accepted by their peers as both persons and as cadets, women reported feeling less accepted on both counts than did men.

Isolation can exact the obvious personal toll on an individual and can have professional consequences. West Point is alive with informal social networks that pass helpful hints from one generation of cadets to the next. For example, my students told me that a real time-saving shortcut to spit-polished shoes is to use acrylic floor wax. To be cut off from such a rich source of useful information could only hurt these women cadets.

Assimilation. A second way to resolve the uncertainties generated by these new and contrasted female cadets is to assimilate them into stereotypic roles. Rather than dealing with cadet women as individuals, men can clear up uncertainties by assuming that each woman can be readily understood in terms of what is considered appropriate for women as a group—in other words, by *stereotyping*. A problem that this mechanism created for women cadets is that stereotypic feminine roles are often inconsistent with the demands of the role of cadet. Our observations confirmed this difficulty for some women at West Point.

Our observations of training programs suggested that women were often assigned to female-stereotyped tasks. For example, when the cadets were constructing a temporary bridge, which required a good bit of brawn, women were left to become passive observers of male activities. Since women were not expected to make significant physical contributions to these activities, they were relegated to peripheral roles. Since playing a peripheral role is not conducive to showing leadership ability, this treatment runs counter to a major training emphasis at West Point.

Similarly, women often found themselves in positions designed to protect them. Both our observations and survey responses from cadets themselves confirm this. When asked whether they ever felt protected because of their gender, almost half the women answered affirmatively, compared to less than 10 percent of the men. And again, being given protection is not compatible with assuming a leadership role.

Finally, when people are stereotypically treated as part of a larger class, discrimination can result. When graduating cadets were asked whether they ever felt victimized because of their gender, over half the women responded affirmatively, compared to less than 20 percent of the men. All this evidence convinced us that women indeed were being assimilated into roles stereotypically defined as feminine, and that these role prescriptions could conflict with the major training goals of the Academy's program of leadership development.

Ultimate Consequences

The first class of women at West Point clearly functioned according to what we know about tokenism. Their situation included the three ingredients necessary for token status: underrepresentative numbers (less than 15 percent of the whole), external pressure for admission, and marginality. Evidence for all three negative effects of being a token (visibility, contrast, and assimilation) was found at the Academy.

The ultimate consequence of this negative setting for women is that disproportionate numbers of women cadets dropped out of the Academy. Almost one-half of the 119 women in the first coed class left West Point prior to graduation. In contrast, the attrition rate for male cadets hovered consistently at about 36 percent. The attrition rates of women cadets remained significantly higher than those of men through the next four classes.

Attrition rates not only reflect the hardships encountered by individual cadets, but also create a potentially dangerous situation at the institutional level. Data on higher attrition rates among women can be used by policy-makers to justify a return to exclusionary practices. "We gave women a fair shot; they couldn't make it," becomes a seemingly defensible conclusion. However, if this conclusion is ever expressed, we can respond that women's "shot" may not have been fair and that further efforts to ensure their participation are warranted. It is to such efforts that we now will turn our attention.

REDUCING TOKENISM

As we will see later in this paper, some negative consequences of tokenism seem to appear whenever token numbers exist in a group. They do not simply disappear because time passes. Other factors must intervene to bring about positive change. In this section, we will explore some of these positive influences.

At West Point, although sexism and tokenism have not been totally eradicated, life definitely improved for women from 1976, when they first entered, to 1980, when they graduated. According to these first women, overt disparaging remarks and physical confrontations diminished across this four-year period (Priest, Grove, and Adams, 1980). In this section, we will explore three factors that may have contributed to this overall improvement: institutional changes, dominant-group members' attitudes, and the tokens themselves.

Institutional Policies

The institutional changes that occurred between 1976 and 1980 involved increasing numbers of women, organizational commitment, and standards of evaluation.

Numbers.   Kanter (1977) argues that 15 percent of the membership of a group is the critical point in determining how a group functions; when the proportion of tokens in a group is increased to this level, the dynamics of the group should change accordingly. In the first class, 8 percent of the students were women; during that year, however, only 2 percent of the full Academy were women. From 1976 to 1980, the overall composition of the Academy changed from 2 percent to 10 percent women. Although the group composition remained skewed, the increases in the number of women may have benefited female cadets. In other words, some of the positive changes we found across the first four years of gender integration may have resulted simply from the increased proportional representation of women. One possible solution to tokenism may be to alter the group's composition, increasing the numerical representation of the token members. However, if the composition remains skewed, this approach cannot be sufficient to end the problems associated with tokenism.

Organizational Commitment. A second positive influence at West Point was the strong organizational commitment to gender integration espoused by the top echelon. In 1975, when Congress debated the feasibility of admitting women to the Military Academies, representatives from West Point were staunch detractors of the proposal (Stiehm, 1981), and all personnel at West Point from officer/instructors to cadets were caught up in a heated debate. When the first women entered, they faced faculty and students in the three classes ahead of them riddled with objectors to their very presence.

Before the first class of women arrived at the Academy, Army officials made some key personnel changes in order to create a more supportive staff, including the replacement of the superintendent (akin to the president of a civilian university). This superintendent began each year by offering to transfer nonsupportive faculty. Although this seems like a minor step, military personnel are very sensitive to the norms established by high-ranking officers and behave accordingly. Similarly, researchers studying civilian racial integration of public schools found that citizens voiced fewer objections when busing programs were presented in strong tones implying that change was inevitable and that there was no room for dissent (Clark, 1953). Social psychologists have long known that, when change appears inevitable, people come to believe in the change by adopting positive attitudes toward it (Brehm, 1959; Pettigrew, 1961). Such continued institutional support by West Point officials at least reduced some of the more blatant attempts to harass and discriminate against women, thus creating an increasingly favorable atmosphere for women.

Standards of Evaluation. The final institutional area, standards of evaluation, is one suggested by our data, but not carried out by West Point. To make my point, let me give an illustrative example.

West Point is an institution steeped in tradition. It obviously was created by and for men exclusively. Nowhere is this more obvious than in its standards for physical training. For example, the obstacle and confidence courses are purposefully designed to be negotiated most easily by persons who are 5 feet 10 inches tall and about 145 pounds — the normative size of men, not women, in the age range of cadets (eighteen to twenty-six).

West Point is more than a university; it is a training ground for officers, and physical ability is very important for cadets. Research shows that those with strong physical ability also are rated more positively as leaders (Rice, Yoder, Adams, Priest, & Prince, 1984). However, the criteria for judging physical prowess are designed for a male physique. West Point's approach to this contradiction created a difficult problem for women (Yoder, 1983).

One obstacle on the traditional obstacle course completed by cadets requires that they scale an eight-foot wall as quickly as possible. The prescribed way to scale the wall is to run toward it, plant one's foot on it, push up so that one can get a grasp of the top of the wall, and pull one's dangling body up and over it.

The problem for women (and one that I heard repeatedly pronounced about women while I was at West Point) is that they have "inferior upper-body strength" relative to men. When most women approached this obstacle, they simply could not hoist themselves up and over the wall after achieving that fingertip grip. Many women failed the obstacle.

Academy planners tried to respond to this problem in an apparently nondiscriminatory way: they erected a platform next to the wall so that a cadet could get a better, higher grip on the top of the wall, making it easier to pull up one's body. Both women and men were free to use the platform at the cost of a time penalty.

Few men needed the platform, whereas most women did. Consequently, women felt inadequate; everyone knew and freely discussed their inadequate upper-body strength. And, the Academy had seemingly lowered its standards to accommodate women. No one won.

I was observing this obstacle one day, when a woman approached the wall in the old prescribed way, got her fingertips grip, and did an unusual thing: she walked her dangling legs up the wall until she was in a position where both her hands and feet were atop the wall. She then simply pulled up her sagging bottom and went over. She solved the problem by capitalizing on one of women's physical assets: lower-body strength.

She taught me a lot with her creative approach to this simple obstacle. I began to ask myself two related questions: (1) Is it necessary for cadets to scale walls in order for them to become good officers? and (2) If it is, how can standards be changed to exploit the positive characteristics of both men and women? Clearly, I could design a program of physical fitness that was impossible for most men and that was simple for women (e.g., various bending and stretching exercises that conform to women's greater flexibility), and it was no wonder that an institution designed for one gender exclusively did a similar thing. But, if physical training is important (and the first step is to think about whether it is), then how can it be accomplished in a way that benefits women and men by bringing out the best in both? These are questions that may not have been addressed at the Academy, and I believe they should be. In any event, they are questions that all institutions must ask if formerly excluded people are to have a fair shot at making it.

In summary, we have examined three institutional practices. Increases in the simple proportional representation of women must have eased some of the pressures for women cadets. Visible and consistently strong organizational supports for the inevitability of integration had a beneficial effect. The maintenance of standards and practices developed exclusively for men, however, failed to recognize the positive contributions that could be made by women and, in some instances, almost guaranteed that women would fail some tasks.

Changes in Dominants

When the first coed class arrived at West Point in 1976, as I mentioned, the three upper classes had been part of a heated debate about whether or not to admit women. Needless to say, the first women were not welcomed with open arms by many of their upperclass colleagues. But, over the first four years of integration, these all-male classes graduated, leaving behind a fully integrated Academy. As the presence of women became a commonplace fact of life at West Point, attitudes toward women among the male officers and cadets improved, creating a more positive atmosphere for the women.

Female and male cadets in the first three coed classes were asked to complete the Attitudes toward Women Scale (Spence and Helmreich, 1972), a standard psychological test designed to measure people's attitudes about the rights and roles of women in our current society. Each subsequent class of men reported more egalitarian attitudes—that is, less traditional beliefs about what is appropriate for women within our society (Yoder, Rice, Adams, Priest, & Prince, 1982). These increasingly positive attitudes among the dominant group also may have contributed to the more favorable outcomes experienced by women during the later phases of gender integration.

Interestingly, these changes in men's attitudes seem to reflect the impact of women's entry itself, rather than broader, societywide attitude changes. Using nationwide survey data, Cherlin and Walters (1981) found that sex-role attitudes improved in the general population from 1972 to 1975, then stabilized after 1975. The changes in men's attitudes at West Point took place between 1976 and 1979. This suggests that being part of the integration process itself may have positively influenced the attitudes of these men.

Commonly, we think of attitudes as predispositions that influence behavior. But social psychologists have long known that what people do can cause those people to reevaluate and change their attitudes (Deutsch & Collins, 1951; Festinger, 1957). In other words, if people are encouraged to engage in nonsexist behaviors, and freely do so, they may change their attitudes to be consistent with their new behavior. For men at West Point, those who participated in the newly integrated Academy—where, as we have seen, organizational leaders stressed egalitarian treatment—came to believe in what they were doing. Without making people feel forced to exhibit new behavior, we might concentrate on changing behaviors in order ultimately to change attitudes (see Aronson, 1969).

Support among Tokens

Previous studies of tokenism have examined small numbers of women acting in groups dominated by men. For example, Rosabeth Moss Kanter (1977) described work groups that included a handful of token female managers and Judith Long Laws (1975) looked at academic departments with one or two token women faculty members. The key point in these studies, as well as in our work at West Point, is that women were *proportionally* underrepresented. However, at West Point, this small percentage of women involved a sizable number of female cadets: 119 in the first class alone. One might expect greater solidarity to exist among some of these women cadets, since their numbers gave them ample opportunities to interact with and support one another.

Although West Point cadets fear fraternization (which can result from personal involvements), the Academy has long supported the development of professional mentoring relationships among cadets and between cadets and officers (Ellis & Moore, 1974). In fact, men at West Point dubbed their mentors "fairy godfathers." Given this atmosphere that supports mentoring and given the relatively large numbers of women cadets, we were surprised when our exit interviews of women cadets prior to their graduation indicated that senior women failed to mentor other women. This finding was confirmed by lowerclass women who reportedly wanted to develop sponsorial relationships with women in the first coeducational class but were seemingly shunned.

In trying to understand why senior women failed to mentor other women, we found that the literature on mentoring proposed two possibilities. The first is the "queen bee syndrome" (Staines, Tavris, & Jayaratne, 1974). The queen bee shuns her protege for self-interested reasons. She enjoys her special status as one of the few women in the work group, quells potential competition, and coopts membership in the dominant group. This position concludes that women's failure to mentor is rooted in their personalities as queen bees and that it is women's fault that they do not sponsor others.

A second possibility argues that senior women failed to mentor because their status as tokens discouraged mentoring. Our data are consistent with this explanation (Yoder, Adams, Grove, & Priest, 1985).

In their exit interviews, senior female cadets gave four reasons why they could not mentor others. First, their visibility as tokens and the resultant performance pressures left these women with little time and energy to devote to helping others. Just getting themselves through the stresses of being the first women cadets at West Point consumed all their energies. Second, the senior women expressed uncertainties about how to deal with subsequent classes of women. As tokens, their specialness was repeatedly touted; if indeed they were a unique class (being the first of their kind), how could they relate to later entrants? Uncertainties such as these, which again arise from their positions as tokens, discouraged women from relating to other, younger women.

Third, they described how the role of mentor felt inappropriate to them as women; rather, they regarded it as more fitting for men. Because women felt unaccepted by their male colleagues, one of the last things they wanted to do was to emphasize their gender. Some women thought that, if they kept company with other women, this would highlight their gender and would further isolate them from male cadets. These women desperately wanted to be accepted as cadets, not as *women* cadets. Therefore, they did everything from not wearing skirts as an option with their uniforms to avoiding being a part of a group of women.

But the most telling information about mentoring patterns was obtained from the all-female athletic teams at the Academy. In this setting, women reported that they mentored and were mentored by other women. Here, released from their token status, women were free to help other women and they did so. Advocates of a personality theory, such as the queen bee syndrome, would expect women to avoid mentoring in all situations. However, consistent with the tokenism explanation, when women were freed from the constraints of their token status, they mentored. Thus, a key point for those interested in promoting mentoring relationships among women is that tokenism inhibits this process.

BEYOND WEST POINT

Obviously, the experiences of the first women at West Point are in some ways unique. West Point itself is a singular organization, and few of us will ever have an opportunity to participate in the initial phases of gender integration. We are more likely to encounter tokenism in civilian organizations where women have participated as tokens over long periods of time. What lessons can we learn from the West Point experience and apply to these other settings? The primary lesson to emerge from West Point is that numbers are important.

Numbers Count

Whatever the setting, numbers do count. At West Point, we saw three negative consequences result from token numbers: visibility, contrast, and assimilation. Although the specifics of how these three effects are played out vary according to the organization in which they take place, they appear repeatedly.

After the class of 1980 graduated from West Point, the women left behind their roles in a newly integrated organization and assumed new token roles in a setting that was already integrated—the regular Army. Although they were no longer the first of their kind (women officers were nothing new), they continued to work in token numbers. And, as we might expect, they continued to experience difficulties (Yoder & Adams, 1984).

Following these women through questionnaires, interviews, and clinical observations, we found that they continued to experience stress, and they reported dissatisfactions whenever their work roles conflicted with others' gender expectations. For example, people expect leaders in our society to be men (Hollander & Yoder, 1980). We also know that women and men are rated negatively by others when they engage in sex-role–inappropriate behaviors (Cherry & Deaux, 1978). When women officers assumed the gender-inappropriate role of leader, a role that is not only appropriate but also necessary for officers, they were evaluated negatively and reported problems with their own adjustment. These women officers thought that their superiors gave them less career advisement, described a less favorable work atmosphere, and rated their relationships with superiors more negatively, as compared to their male counterparts. However, these women reported levels of career involvement and self-initiated career planning equal to those of men. Despite these women's strong career commitments, proportionally fewer women than men reenlisted in 1985.

Clearly, the stresses of tokenism extend beyond the initial phases of integration, even for the veterans of this phase. But, let us also take a brief look at settings other than the military. The original study to document evidence of visibility, contrast, and assimilation examined a corporate setting in which managerial women always worked in token numbers (Kanter, 1977). The same dynamics we observed at West Point occurred in the corporate setting. They also appeared in the public sector in a study of the federal bureaucracy (South, Bonjean, Markham, & Corder, 1982).

Even academia is not free from the effects of tokenism. Token women graduate students thought that others were less receptive to their presence, and the actual attitudes of male faculty members toward these token women were more negative than were those of faculty in departments with balanced or greater numbers of women (Holahan, 1979). One of the first papers to define tokenism (Laws, 1975) described the negative impact of token representation for women faculty, as did subsequent work by Young, Mackenzie, and Sherif (1980; 1982).

Tokenism can be found whenever group compositions are skewed. Tokenism, whatever its setting, is traumatic for the individual token. Case reports by tokens underscore the stresses suffered by tokens (Datan, 1980; Weisstein, 1977; Yoder, 1985). Two common reactions are a lowering of self-esteem and a desire to withdraw either by isolating oneself from the group or by leaving the position (Yoder, 1985). We already have seen the higher attrition rates for women at West Point and beyond.

A key to understanding and coping with tokenism is to recognize that what may appear to be flaws in individuals actually are the results of the situation in which tokens find themselves. We explored this idea when we looked at mentoring at West Point. When senior women failed to mentor other women, we could have blamed the upperclass women for behaving like "queen bees," rather than trying to understand how the situation of tokenism constrained their behavior. We concluded that the latter is a better explanation because, when these women were relieved of their token status, they mentored.

The tendency to accuse individuals is called "blaming the victim," and it occurs frequently (Ryan, 1976; 1981). But, we have seen that tokenism is, at least in part, the consequence of a situation where numbers are imbalanced. It is this situation that creates visibility, contrast, and assimilation effects. To blame tokens, not the situation, not only is inaccurate but also has two serious consequences. First, if the token internalizes this blame, she will suffer both the external effects of tokenism and self-disdain. This process may parallel what we know about other victims, such as victims of violence (Miller & Porter, 1983) and of sexual harassment (Jensen & Gutek, 1982). Second, blaming individuals can relieve the organization of its responsibility to change.

Long-Term Tokenism

Although women cadets are no longer a novelty at West Point, their numerical underrepresentation as tokens continues. As in most organizations with skewed compositions, cadets at West Point have settled into a steady state of tokenism. Unfortunately for us as investigators, West Point discontinued all research directed at women cadets in 1983, so we can only guess at what cadets' lives are like now. But our guess is an educated one. Since every other study of tokenism examined it as a steady state of affairs, we can surmise that visibility, contrast, and assimilation effects still occur at West Point with regularity.

Few of us will have the opportunity to break the gender barrier as did these women in West Point's first coed class. However, it is reasonably likely that some of us will encounter long-term tokenism. We have seen that numbers do count. What might we expect to find, given the West Point experience, if we joined as a token an organization with a skewed composition? And, more important, how can we as individuals cope effectively with our token status?

First, expect and prepare for stress. As we have seen, being a token is very stressful. Look for as many releases of stress as possible. In our follow-up surveys of women officers, those with the most supportive outside networks, such as were provided by spouses, were the most satisfied with their work. Spend the extra time and energy needed to build outside supports to help bolster you against the inside stresses.

Second, a mentor helps. Given the stresses faced by other token women, do not be put off if the mentor is not the ideal woman ahead of you on the organizational ladder. Be open to finding a mentor who works outside of your organization, but who has relevant experience to guide you professionally.

Third, learn to recognize visibility, contrast, and assimilation effects and view them accordingly. Studies such as this one and Kanter's (1977) can help you to identify each of these effects clearly, and doing so may help you to understand events that happen to you or to your colleagues. More important, understanding that these events are the consequence of the situation may help you to attribute them to tokenism rather than to a deficiency in yourself or to an insensitivity in another person. Learning not to blame the victim, especially when you *are* the victim, is another way to mitigate stress.

Finally, if possible, work to improve the gender balance of the group. The ultimate solution to tokenism is to eliminate it by balancing numbers. In the meantime, we know from West Point that we can seek to affect institutional policies, influence the behaviors and attitudes of dominants, and form networks among tokens.

REFERENCES

Adams, Jerome, & Janice Yoder. (1985). *Effective leadership for women and men.* Norwood, NJ: Ablex.

Aronson, Elliot. (1969). The theory of cognitive dissonance: A current perspective. In L. Berkowitz (ed.), *Advances in Experimental Social Psychology* (Vol. 4). New York: Academic Press.

Brehm, Jack. (1959). Increasing cognitive dissonance by a fait accompli. *Journal of Abnormal and Social Psychology*, 58, 379–382.

Cherlin, Andrew, & Pamela Walters. (1981). Trends in United States men's and women's sex-role attitudes: 1972–1978. *American Sociological Review* 46, 453–460.

Cherry, Frances, & Kay Deaux. (1978). Fear of success vs. fear of gender-inappropriate behavior. *Sex Roles, 4, 97–101.*

Clark, Kenneth. (1953). Desegregation: An appraisal of the evidence. *Journal of Social Issues, 9.*

Datan, Nancy. (1980). Days of our lives. *Journal of Mind and Behavior, 1, 63–71.*

Deutsch, Morton, & Mary Evans Collins. (1951). *Interracial housing: A psychological evaluation of a social experiment.* Minneapolis: University of Minnesota Press.

Ellis, Joseph, & Robert Moore. (1974). *School for soldiers.* New York: Oxford.

Festinger, Leon. (1957). *A theory of cognitive dissonance.* Evanston, IL: Row, Peterson.

Holahan, Carole K. (1979). Stress experienced by women doctoral students, need for support, and occupational sex-typing: An interactional view. *Sex Roles, 5, 425–436.*

Hollander, Edwin. P., & Janice Yoder. (1980). Some issues comparing men and women as leaders. *Journal of Basic and Applied Social Psychology, 1, 267–280.*

Jensen, I., & Barbara Gutek. (1982). Attributions and assignment of responsibility for sexual harassment. *Journal of Social Issues, 38, 121–136.*

Kanter, Rosabeth. (1977). *Men and women of the corporation.* New York: Basic Books.

Laws, Judith. (1975). The psychology of tokenism. *Sex Roles, 1, 51–67.*

Miller, Dale T., & C.A. Porter (1983). Self-blame in victims of violence. *Journal of Social Issues, 39, 139–152.*

Pettigrew, Thomas. (1961). Social psychology and desegregation research. *American Psychologist, 16, 105–112.*

Priest, Robert, Steven Grove, & Jerome Adams. (1980). Historical and institutional perspectives on women in Military Academy roles. Paper presented at the Meetings of the American Psychological Association, Montreal, September.

Rice, Robert, Janice Yoder, Jerome Adams, Robert Priest, & Howard Prince. (1984). Leadership ratings for male and female military cadets. *Sex Roles, 10, 885–902.*

Ryan, William. (1976). *Blaming the victim.* New York: Vintage.

Ryan, William. (1981). *Equality.* New York: Vintage.

South, Scott J., Charles M. Bonjean, William T. Markham, & J. Corder. (1982). Social structure and group interaction: Men and women of the federal bureaucracy. *American Journal of Sociology, 47, 587–599.*

Spence, Janet, & Robert Helmreich. (1972). The Attitudes toward Women Scale: An objective instrument to measure attitudes toward the rights and roles of women in contemporary society. *JSAS Catalog of Selected Documents in Psychology, 2, 66.*

Staines, Graham, Carol Tavris, & Toby Epstein Jayaratne. (1974, January). The queen bee syndrome. *Psychology Today, 55–58; 60.*

Stiehm, Judith. (1981). *Bring me men and women.* Berkeley: University of California Press.

Weisstein, Naomi. (1977). ''How can a little girl like you teach a great big class of men?'' the chairman said, and the other adventures of a woman in science. In S. Ruddick & P. Daniels (Eds.), *Working it out.* New York: Pantheon.

Yoder, Janice. (1983). Another look at women in the Army: A comment on Woelfel's article. *Sex Roles, 9, 285–288.*

Yoder, Janice. (1985). An academic woman as a token: A case study. *Journal of Social Issues, 41, 61–72.*

Yoder, Janice, & Jerome Adams. (1984). Women entering nontraditional roles: When work demands and sex roles conflict. *International Journal of Women's Studies, 7, 260–272.*

Yoder, Janice, Jerome Adams, Steven Grove, & Robert Priest. (1985). To teach is to learn: Overcoming tokenism with mentors. *Psychology of Women Quarterly, 9, 119–131.*

Yoder, Janice, Jerome Adams, & Howard Prince. (1983). The price of a token. *Journal of Political and Military Sociology, 11, 325–337.*

Yoder, Janice, Robert Rice, Jerome Adams, Robert Priest, & Howard Prince. (1982). Reliability of the Attitudes toward Women Scale (AWS) and Personal Attributes Questionnaire (PAQ). *Sex Roles*, 8, 651–658.

Young, Carlotta J., Doris L. Mackenzie, & Carolyn Sherif. (1980). In search of token women in academia. *Psychology of Women Quarterly*, 4, 508–525.

Young, Carlotta J., Doris L. Mackenzie, & Carolyn Sherif. (1982). "In search of token women in academia": Some definitions and clarifications. *Psychology of Women Quarterly*, 7, 166–169.

Part Six

Feminism

Feminist Organization and Activities from Suffrage to Women's Liberation

JO FREEMAN

The suffrage movement was not a united movement. It was a coalition of different people and organizations that worked together for a few intense years around the common goal of gaining the right for women to vote. Approximately 95 percent of the participants in the movement were organized under the umbrella of the National American Woman Suffrage Association (NAWSA). Throughout most of its history, this organization pursued the vote on a state-by-state basis. In 1916, NAWSA President Carrie Chapman Catt presented her "winning plan" to focus on a federal amendment while continuing with state work. She mobilized the coalition into high gear until success was achieved.

Her plan was stimulated by the challenge of Alice Paul, who had returned to the United States in 1913 after an apprenticeship in the British suffrage movement. There she had learned the value of publicity to be obtained by marches, civil disobedience, and hunger strikes. Paul persuaded NAWSA to let her organize a Congressional Committee to pursue a federal amendment, and, when she thought that support for her activities was insufficient, broke off to create a separate Congressional Union. One of Paul's strategies was to mobilize women in the states where women could vote. From her British experience, she adopted the idea of holding the party in power responsible for failing to pass the federal amendment. Since President Wilson was a Democrat, she organized enfranchised women to vote against *all* Democrats in 1914, including those Members of Congress who supported suffrage. In 1916, a separate National Woman's Party was created for this purpose, but Wilson was overwhelmingly reelected, carrying ten of the twelve states in which women could vote for president.

During World War I, NAWSA leaders worked both for suffrage and in support of the war effort. The Congressional Union worked only for suffrage. They flouted Wilson's slogan that the purpose of the war was "to make the world safe for democracy" by standing outside the White House with banners reading "How long must women wait for democracy?" The rate of state enfranchisement of women accelerated, and pressure on the President and Congress intensified. In January 1918, President Wilson declared his support for a federal amendment, and later that month the House passed the amendment without a single vote to spare. It was not until May 1919 that the Senate did likewise, and on August 26, 1920, the Nineteenth Amendment joined the Constitution.

NAWSA disbanded. Some of its members reorganized into a nonpartisan, nonsectarian League of Women Voters to provide women with political education and to work for a broad range of social reforms. Other members, including Catt, turned their energies to working for peace. Many more returned to the organizations from whence they had come, such as the Women's Trade Union League, the General Federation of Women's Clubs, and the National Consumer League. Still others founded new organizations, such as the National Federation of Business and Professional Women, and separate women's organizations within different occupations. Many returned to private life. The Congressional Union–National Woman's Party reorganized itself into a new National Woman's Party (NWP) and continued to work for women's equality with men.

THE NATIONAL WOMAN'S PARTY

Between the suffrage movement and the women's liberation movement, the paramount feminist issue was the Equal Rights Amendment (ERA). It was first proposed in 1921 by Alice Paul, who had decided that the next step was removal of all *legal* discrimination against women and that the most efficient way to do this was with another federal amendment. The ERA was aimed at the plethora of state laws and common-law rules that restricted women's jury service; limited their rights to control their own property, to contract, to sue, and to keep their own name and domicile if married; gave them inferior guardianship rights over their children; and generally stigmatized them as lesser citizens. It was vigorously opposed by progressive reformer Florence Kelley and her allies in the National Consumer League, the Women's Trade Union League, and the League of Women Voters, because Kelley feared it would also destroy the protective labor laws for which she had spent her life fighting.

The preponderance of these laws limited the hours women could work each day and each week, prohibited night work for women, and removed women from certain occupations altogether. Some states also required minimum wages for women only, although the Supreme Court declared this unconstitutional in 1923. Although many of these laws had passed before suffrage, Kelley and other progressives had joined the Suffrage Movement only after they became convinced that women must have the vote in order to pass more laws to improve the condition of working women. They were not about to see their decades of effort undermined by the utopian ideals of the militants.

The NWP was not initially hostile to protective labor laws; many members had fought for such laws in their home states. Early versions of the ERA exempted these laws from coverage. However, Kelley could not be convinced that *any* version would not be misinterpreted by the courts, and after much thought Paul and her colleagues decided that *any* exemption would become a universal exemption. Besides, Paul concluded, protective labor laws really hurt women more than they helped, because they encouraged employers to hire men. By the time the ERA was first introduced into Congress in December 1923, it had divided women's organizations into two warring camps, who fought each other to a stalemate for almost five decades.

The battle was more than a disagreement over what women wanted. Behind it was a fundamental disagreement over the meaning of *equality*. The NWP favored absolute equality of opportunity. Women would never achieve economic independence as long as laws treated them like children in need of protection. The reformers accepted fundamental differences in physiology and family role as incontrovertible. They noted that the female labor force was largely young, unmarried, and transitional. Labor unions did not want to organize women because the women were not permanent workers and did not earn enough to pay dues. Thus, collective bargaining did not offer the same protection for women workers that it potentially could for men. Only legislation could save women from gross exploitation by industrial capitalism.

Kelley called herself a socialist, although her allies in the women's organizations would not have used that term after it became tainted by the red scare of the twenties. Yet her view of women was solidly grounded in a conservative conception of the sexes. Whereas Kelley accepted the status quo, Paul was a feminist visionary; she saw what women could be, undistracted by their current reality. With rare and minor exceptions, she ignored any political issue other than removal of all legal barriers to women's equality and economic independence. During the twenties, she stifled any discussion within the NWP on the disenfranchisement of black women or the suppression of birth-control information. Despite her commitment to anticommunism, during the fifties she thwarted an attempt to broaden the base of the now miniscule NWP by including patriotic issues.

Hindered by declining numbers and influence, the NWP kept the feminist flame burning through some very hard times. The Depression led to an upsurge of extant public opinion against the employment of married women, or of any woman who had a male relative to support her. Such women were thought to be taking jobs away from men, who had families to support. The advent of the Roosevelt administration brought to power Kelley's disciples Frances Perkins and Molly Dewson, not to mention Eleanor Roosevelt, who, while a role model for activist women, thought the NWP "a perfectly useless organization." Their strong opposition to the ERA was based in part on their perception that it was primarily a class issue and not one of sexual equality. As social reformers, they argued that requiring equal rights under law would favor upper-class professional and executive women at the expense of working-class women who needed legal protection. While they acknowledged that there were many state laws that unfairly distinguished between men and women, they felt thought these should be eliminated state by state and law by law.

World War II saw a renewed interest in both the ERA and working women. Several organizations shifted their opinion from con to neutral to pro, following the lead of the National Federation of Business and Professional Women (BPW) in 1937, while many of the opposing organizations ceased to be active. The Republican Party first endorsed the ERA in 1940; the Democrats followed in 1944. The Senate voted on it for the first time in 1946. The ERA failed, and when it came up again in 1950, opponents were ready with a restrictive "rider" to exempt all laws for the protection and benefit of women. This rider was added on the Senate floor in both 1950 and 1953; after that, the ERA never left committee. In the meantime, the NWP went through two crippling internal disputes involving purges and lawsuits, and leadership of the opposition was taken over by the AFL-CIO and traditional liberal organizations such as the ACLU. The Women's Bureau of the Department of Labor, a leading opponent since the ERA's inception, briefly withdrew during the Eisenhower administration (Eisenhower was the only sitting president to endorse the ERA before 1972), but resumed its role with vigor when Kennedy appointed Esther Peterson as its director after he became President in 1961.

Peterson had two items on her agenda for women: passage of an Equal Pay Act and derailment of the ERA. The first was achieved in 1963. Her strategy for the second was the creation of a President's Commission on the Status of Women, which would propose a program of constructive action that would make the ERA unnecessary. Its final report urged "judicial clarification" of women's legal rights rather than a blanket declaration of legal equality, along with a lengthy list of other objectives. In the process of reaching these conclusions, the commission thoroughly documented women's second-class status. It was followed by the formation of a citizen's advisory council and fifty state commissions. Many of the people involved in these commissions, dissatisfied with the lack of progress made on their recommendations, became founders and early activists in new feminist organizations.

ORIGINS OF THE WOMEN'S LIBERATION MOVEMENT

When the women's liberation movement emerged in the 1960s, the ERA was a non-issue. It had even been dropped from the platforms of the political parties despite continual lobbying by the NWP. Founders of the new movement had no idea how much they owed to the lengthy battle over the ERA. Their focus was on the elimination of discriminatory practices and sexist attitudes, not on legal rights. Their role model was the Civil Rights movement, not the old Feminist movement.

The movement actually had two origins, from two different strata of society, with two different styles, orientations, values, and forms of organization. In many ways there were two separate movements. Although the composition of both branches was predominantly white, middle-class, and college-educated, initially the median age of the activists in what I call the older branch of the movement was about twenty years higher. The difference in age between the participants in the two branches reflected an important characteristic of society in the sixties known as the *generation gap*. Over time, the gap declined. Younger women joined older-branch organizations, and the women in the younger branch became older. Today, age is no longer a defining characteristic of different feminist groups (except for those organized into OWL—Older Women's Liberation).

The first new feminist organization was the National Organization for Women (NOW), which was founded in 1966. Its key progenitor and first president was Betty Friedan, who came to national prominence by publishing her best seller *The Feminine Mystique* in 1963. Many of NOW's founders and early participants were members or staff of the President's and State Commissions on the Status of Women. The Women's Bureau held annual conferences for Commission members, and it was at the third such conference that NOW was proposed. The immediate stimulus was the refusal of the Bureau to permit a resolution urging the Equal Employment Opportunity Commission (EEOC) to enforce the provision of the 1964 Civil Rights Act prohibiting sex discrimination in employment.

The addition of "sex" to a section of a major bill aimed at eradicating race discrimination had at the time seemed more of a diversionary tactic than one geared to improving the status of women. With little notice and no hearings, it had been added during the last week of floor debate by Rep. Howard W. Smith of Virginia, whose antagonism to civil rights was well known. What was not well known was that Smith had been a supporter of the ERA and the NWP for over twenty years, and had proposed the sex amendment at the latter's request. This was not the first time for this tactic. The NWP had a long-standing policy of demanding rights for women that were given to any other group. It had been lobbying for two decades to add "sex" to Executive Orders that prohibited discrimination on the basis of race by federal contractors. And it had successfully added sex amendments to two previous civil rights bills—in 1950 and 1956. These bills did not pass, but the 1964 bill did, creating a tool to attack sex discrimination that piggybacked on the civil rights struggle. Although the Women's Bureau had initially opposed the sex provision, it quickly changed its attitude. Its objection to the resolution by the conference it sponsored emanated less from concern about the EEOC than from concern that the NWP would demand such a resolution on the ERA.

The NWP's initial attitude toward NOW was not sisterly. It did not want its role as the preeminent feminist organization to be usurped, particularly by women who had an agenda broader than only the ERA. However, it knew an opportunity when it saw one. It infiltrated NOW as it had BPW and many other organizations, and in 1967 NOW endorsed the ERA. The debate was spirited but not acrimonious. Although labor-union women felt compelled to withdraw from NOW because their unions opposed the ERA, most participants were strong supporters. They were unaware of the decades of debate over protective labor legislation, and were very attuned to the importance of equality as a result of the Civil Rights movement. The latter had created a different frame of reference than that of the struggle to protect workers against industrial exploitation at the turn of the century.

Just as important, by 1967 the world was a very different place than it had been in the 1920s. Women were one-third of the labor force; the fastest growing segment was mothers of young children. The idea that working women were merely transitory was rapidly receding into the past. Despite the "back to the home" propaganda of the "feminine mystique" era of the 1940s and 1950s, women's participation in the labor force had risen steadily, while their position within it had declined. Opportunities to work, the trend toward smaller families, plus a change in preferred status symbols from a leisured wife at home to a second car and a color television set, helped to transform the female labor force from one of primarily single women under twenty-five, as it was in 1940, to one of married women and mothers over forty by 1950. Simultaneously, the job market became even more rigidly sex-segregated, except for traditionally female professional jobs such as teaching and social work, which were flooded by men. Women's share of professional and technical jobs declined by one-third, with a commensurate decline in women's relative income. The result of this was the creation of a class of well-educated, underemployed, and underpaid women. These women became the social base of the new movement.

Many of them joined NOW, but as with any social movement there was a mushroom effect, which resulted in numerous new organizations within a few years. In 1968, women who were unhappy with NOW's support of women's right to choose abortion left to form the Women's Equity Action League (WEAL) in order to focus on economic and educational issues. During the same year, Federally Employed Women (FEW) organized for equal opportunity within the government. In 1969, men and women who wanted to devote their energies to legalizing abortion founded the National Association to Repeal Abortion Laws. Between 1969 and 1971, women's caucuses formed in professional associations that did not already have separate women's organizations (from the suffrage and postsuffrage eras). In 1971, women who wanted to work within the political parties founded the National Women's Political Caucus.

In 1967 and 1968, unaware of and unknown to NOW or to the state commissions, the other branch of the movement was taking shape. While it did not begin on the campuses, its activators were on the younger side of the generation gap. Although few were students, all were under thirty and had received their political education as participants in or concerned observers of the social-action projects of the preceding decade. Many came directly from new left and civil rights organizations, where they had been shunted into traditional roles and faced with the contradiction of working in a freedom movement but not being very free. Others had attended various courses on women in the multitude of free universities springing up around the country during those years.

During 1967 and 1968, at least five groups formed spontaneously and independently in five different cities—Chicago, Toronto, Detroit, Seattle, and Gainesville, Florida. They arose at a very auspicious moment. The blacks had just kicked the whites out of the civil rights movement, student power had been discredited by Students for a Democratic Society (SDS), and the organized new left was on the wane. Only draft-resistance activities were on the rise, and this movement more than any other of its time exemplified the social inequities of the sexes. Men could resist the draft; women could only counsel resistance.

There had been individual temporary caucuses and conferences of women as early as 1964, when Stokely Carmichael of the Student Nonviolent Coordinating Committee (SNCC) made his infamous remark that "the only position for women in SNCC is prone." But it was not until 1967 that the groups developed a determined, if cautious, continuity and began to expand. In 1968, they held a national conference, attended by over 200 women from around this country and Canada on less than one month's notice. For the next few years, they expanded exponentially.

This expansion was more amoebic than organized, because the younger branch of the movement prided itself on its lack of organization. Eschewing structure and damning leadership, it carried the concept of "everyone doing her own thing" almost to its logical extreme. The thousands of sister chapters around the country were virtually independent of one another, linked only by journals, newsletters, and cross-country travelers. Some cities had a coordinating committee that tried to maintain communication among local groups and to channel newcomers into appropriate ones, but none of these committees had any power over the activities, let alone the ideas, of the groups it served.

One result of this style was a very broadly based, creative movement, to which individuals could relate as they desired, with no concern for orthodoxy or doctrine. Another result was political impotence. It was impossible for this branch of the movement to organize a nationwide action, even if there could have been agreement on issues. Fortunately, the older branch of the movement had the structure necessary to coordinate such actions and was usually the one to initiate them.

THE RAP GROUP

The most prevalent innovation of the younger branch was the development of the "rap group." Essentially an educational technique, it spread far beyond its origins and became a major organizational unit of the whole movement. From a sociological perspective, the rap group is probably the most valuable contribution by the women's liberation movement to the tools for social change. As such, it deserves some extended attention here.

The rap group serves two main functions. One is simply bringing women together in a situation of structured interaction. It has long been known that people can be kept down as long as they are kept divided from one another, relating more to their social superiors than to their social equals. It is when social development creates natural structures in which people can interact with one another and compare their common concerns that social movements take place. This is the function that the factory served for workers, the church for the southern Civil Rights movement, the campus for students, and the ghetto for urban blacks. Women were largely isolated in their individual homes, relating more to men than to one another. Natural structures for interaction are still largely lacking, although they have begun to develop. But the rap group provided an artificial structure that did much the same thing.

The second function of the rap group is as an actual mechanism for social change. It is a structure created specifically for the purpose of altering the participants' perceptions and conceptions of themselves and of society at large. The process is known as "consciousness raising" and is very simple. Women come together in groups of five to fifteen and talk to one another about their personal problems, personal experiences, personal feelings, and personal concerns. From this public sharing of experiences comes the realization that what each thought was individual is in fact common, that what each considered a personal problem has a social cause and probably a political solution. Women see how social structures and attitudes have limited their opportunities and molded them from birth. They ascertain the extent to which women have been denigrated in this society and how they have developed prejudices against themselves and other women.

This process of deeply personal attitude change makes the rap group a powerful tool. The need for any movement to develop "correct consciousness" has long been known. But usually this consciousness is not developed by means intrinsic to the structure of the movement and does not require such a profound resocialization of one's self-concept. This experience is both irreversible and contagious. Once women have gone through such a resocialization, their views of themselves and of the world are never the same again, even if they stop participating actively in the movement. Those who do drop out rarely do so without spreading feminist ideas among their own friends and colleagues. All who undergo consciousness raising feel compelled themselves to seek out other women with whom to share the experience.

There are several personal results from this process. The initial one is a decrease in self- and group-depreciation. Women come to see themselves and other women as essentially worthwhile and interesting. With this realization, the myth of the individual solution explodes. Women come to believe that, if they are the way they are because of society, they can change their lives significantly only by changing society. These feelings in turn create in each a consciousness of herself as a member of a group and the feeling of solidarity so necessary to any social movement. From this awareness comes the concept of "sisterhood."

The need for group solidarity explains why men have been largely excluded from women's rap groups. Sisterhood was not the initial goal of these groups, but it has been one of the more beneficial byproducts. Originally, the idea of exclusion was borrowed from the black power movement, which was much in the public consciousness when the women's liberation movement began. It was reinforced by the unremitting hostility of most of the new-left men at the prospect of an independent women's movement not tied to radical ideology. Even when this hostility was not evident, women in virtually every group in the United States, Canada, and Europe soon discovered that, when men were present, traditional sex roles reasserted themselves regardless of the good intentions of the participants. Men inevitably dominated the discussion and usually would talk only about how women's liberation related to men, or how men were oppressed by sex roles. In all-female groups, women found the discussions more open, honest, and extensive. They could learn how to relate to other *women*, not just to men.

While the male-exclusion policy arose spontaneously, the rap group did not develop without a struggle. The political background of many of the early feminists of the younger branch predisposed them against the rap group as "unpolitical," and they would condemn discussion meetings that "degenerated" into "bitch sessions." This trend was particularly strong in centers of new left activity. Meanwhile, other feminists, usually with a civil rights or apolitical background, saw that the "bitch sessions" obviously met a basic need. They seized on it and created the consciousness-raising rap group. Developed initially in New York and Gainesville, Florida, the idea soon spread throughout the country, becoming the paradigm for most movement organization.

THE SMALL GROUPS

The younger branch of the women's movement was able to expand rapidly in the beginning because it could capitalize on the new left's infrastructure of organizations and media and because its initiators were skilled in local community organizing. Since the primary unit was the small group and no need for national cooperation was perceived, multitudinous splits increased its strength rather than drained its resources. Such fission was often "friendly" in nature and, even when not, served to bring ever-increasing numbers of women under the movement's umbrella.

Unfortunately, these newly recruited masses lacked the organizing skills of the initiators, and, because the very ideas of "leadership" and "organization" were in disrepute, they made no attempt to acquire them. They did not want to deal with traditional political institutions and abjured all traditional political skills. Consequently, the growth of movement institutions did not go beyond the local level, and they were often inadequate to handle the accelerating influx of new people into the movement. Although these small groups were diverse in kind and responsible to no one for their focus, their nature determined both the structure and the strategy of the movement. The major, although hardly exclusive, activities of the younger branch were organizing rap groups, putting on conferences, putting out educational literature, running service projects such as bookstores and health centers, and organizing occasional marches against pornography or to "Take Back the Night." This branch contributed more in the impact of its ideas than in its activities. It developed several ideological perspectives, much of the terminology of the movement, an amazing number of publications and counter-institutions, numerous new issues, and even new techniques for social change.

Nonetheless, its loose structure was flexible only within certain limits, and the movement never transcended them. The rap groups were excellent for changing individual attitudes, but they were not very successful in dealing with social institutions. Their loose, informal structure encouraged participation in discussion, and their supportive atmosphere elicited personal insight; but neither was very efficient for handling specific tasks. Thus, although the rap groups were of fundamental value to the development of the movement, the more structured groups were more politically effective.

Individual rap groups tended to flounder when their members exhausted the virtues of consciousness raising and decided they wanted to do something more concrete. The problem was that most groups were unwilling to change their structure when they changed their tasks. They accepted the ideology of structurelessness without recognizing the limits on its uses.

Because structurelessness provided no means of resolving political disputes or carrying on ideological debates, the younger branch was racked by several major crises during the early seventies. The two most significant ones were an attempt by the Young Socialist Alliance (YSA), youth group of the Socialist Workers' Party (SWP), to take over the movement, and the so-called gay–straight split. The Trotskyist YSA saw the younger branch of the movement as a potential recruiting ground for socialist converts and directed its members to join with that purpose in mind. Although YSA members were never numerous, their enormous dedication and their contributions of time and energy enabled them to achieve positions of power quickly in many small groups whose lack of structure left no means of resisting. However, many new-left women had remained within the younger branch, and their past experience with YSA predisposed them to distrust it. Not only did they disagree with YSA politics, but they also recognized that, because YSA members owed their primary allegiance to a centralized national party, those members had the potential to control the entire movement. The battle that ensued can euphemistically be described as vicious, and it resulted in YSA being largely driven from the younger branch of the movement. (Several years later, in their SWP guise, YSA members began to join NOW, but NOW's structure made it more difficult to control.) However, the alienation and fragmentation this struggle left in its wake made the movement ill prepared to meet its next major crisis.

The gay–straight split occurred not because of the mere presence of lesbians in feminist groups but because a vocal group of those present articulated lesbianism as the essential feminist idea. They argued first that women should identify with, live with, and associate with women only, and eventually that a woman who actually slept with a man was clearly consorting with the enemy and could not be trusted. When this view met the fear and hostility many straight women felt toward homosexuality, the results were explosive.

The gay–straight struggle raged for several years and consumed most of the time and energy of the younger branch. By the time the tensions eased, most straight women had either become gay or had left the younger branch. Some joined NOW, some rejoined the new left, and many simply dropped out of women's groups altogether. After gay women predominated (by about four to one) in the small groups, their anger toward straight women began to moderate. However, the focus of both the gay and the straight women who remained was no longer directed at educating or recruiting nonfeminists into the movement but rather was aimed at building a "women's culture" for themselves. While a few groups engaged in outreach through public action on issues of concern to all women (e.g., rape) or even on issues concerning straight women exclusively (e.g., wife beating), most of the small groups concerned themselves with maintaining a comfortable niche for "women-identified women" and with insulating themselves from the damnation of the outside world. Consequently, while the small groups still exist throughout the country, most are hard for the uninitiated to locate and thus their impact on the outside world is now limited.

THE OLDER BRANCH

Older branch organizations have stayed with traditional forms of organization, including elected officers and national boards. Some have paid staff. All started as top-down organizations lacking a mass base. Only NOW and the NWPC subsequently developed a mass base, although not all wanted one. All have functioned largely as pressure groups, sometimes on the government, and sometimes within their professions. Collectively, these organizations have used the legal, political, and media institutions of the country with great skill, although there has been some specialization of function. Lawsuits have been largely handled by the Women's Rights Project of the ACLU and a couple of legal defense groups. NOW has organized many large marches. It, the NWPC, and several other groups maintain lobbyists on Capitol Hill.

As a result of their activities, the EEOC changed many of its originally prejudicial attitudes toward women. Numerous lawsuits were filed under the sex provision of Title VII of the 1964 Civil Rights Act. The Equal Rights Amendment passed Congress in 1972. The Supreme Court legalized most abortions. Complaints were filed against several hundred colleges and universities, as well as against many businesses, charging sex discrimination. Articles on feminism appeared in virtually every news medium, and a host of new laws were passed prohibiting sex discrimination in a variety of areas.

The organizations of the older branch have been able to sustain themselves longer than have those of the younger branch, but initially their structure hampered their development. NOW suffered three splits between 1967 and 1968. As the only action organization concerned with women's rights, it had attracted many different kinds of people with many different views on what to do and how to do it. With only a national structure and, at that point, no local base, individuals found it difficult to pursue their particular concerns on a local level; they had to persuade the whole organization to support them. This top-down structure, combined with limited resources, placed severe restrictions on diversity and, in turn, severe strains on the organization. Local chapters were also hampered by a lack of organizers to develop new chapters and the lack of a program into which they could fit.

These initial difficulties were overcome as NOW grew to become the largest single feminist organization. Although it never hired organizers to develop chapters, the enormous geographical mobility of its members and their desire to create chapters wherever they moved had the same results. NOW also benefited greatly from the publicity the movement received in the early seventies. Although much of that publicity was a response to the eye-catching tactics of the younger branch, or was aimed at creating "media stars" (none of whom were NOW leaders), NOW was often the only organization with a telephone and a stable address that incipient movement participants could find. Consequently, its membership grew at the same exponential rate that the younger branch had experienced in the late sixties.

With its first contested presidential election in 1974, NOW developed two major factions that fought for control of the organization and very nearly split it into two. Although these factions articulated their concerns ideologically, the fight in fact was not over issues but rather was a very ordinary attempt by "outs" to become "ins." By 1975, the insurgent faction had established solid control, and over the next few years this faction began to centralize NOW. A single office was located in Washington, the national bylaws were rewritten to provide for five paid officers, and state organizations were created that deprived local chapters of much of their autonomy.

While this centralization did drain resources and energy from the chapters, it allowed the national office to focus the organization's efforts and thus to increase its power on the national level. In the meantime, the issues surrounding the Equal Rights Amendment acquired a national prominence that had not developed when the amendment emerged from Congress in 1972. Therefore, when the ERA still lacked three states necessary for ratification one year from the March 22, 1979, deadline, NOW declared it would focus its efforts on the ERA to the virtual exclusion of anything else.

Unlike the suffrage campaign, however, the ERA campaign did not succeed. There is no consensus on why it failed, but certainly the fact that NOW started so late meant that it had an uphill battle. The suffrage movement had been actively pursuing state suffrage for a generation before it began the campaign for a federal amendment, and it began this campaign before Congress passed it to the states. Yet, even with an organization in place and troops ready, it almost failed. Getting the ERA out of Congress was not the idea of any specific feminist organization; when the campaign started in 1970, none of them had the resources to do that. Thus, none of the feminist organizations was prepared only two years later to replicate in the states the ad hoc lobbying effort that had been created at the national level.

States that already had a strong feminist movement (except Illinois) quickly ratified the ERA. However, they were less than the 75 percent necessary to add it to the Constitution. Then, in January 1973, a national "Stop ERA" campaign surfaced, headed by noted right-winger Phyllis Schlafly. Drawing on a network composed of readers of her newsletter, Republican women's clubs, and fundamentalist churches, she was able to bring to the anti-ERA campaign a political expertise the feminist organizations did not yet have. The kind of constituent pressure that congresspeople had felt at the national level local legislators felt at the state level—but for the opposite position.

By 1975, the major women's groups had realized that the ERA would require a long, hard political fight in southern and rural states. It took another three years to create viable, knowledgeable ERA coalitions in those states, largely, but not always, led by NOW. With only one year left until the seven-year deadline, ratification did not seem possible, so NOW asked Congress to extend the deadline. This request was totally unprecedented, and initial reactions were negative. But NOW responded with a professional lobbying organization backed by hundreds of local chapters collecting signatures on petitions and letters. On July 9, 1978, the first anniversary of the death of Alice Paul, NOW organized a march of over 100,000 women on the Capitol, despite so little publicity that many feminists did not know that the march was being planned. Within four months, the deadline had been extended by a little over three years.

The length of the extension had been a compromise, and it was a gamble the movement lost. At that point, there were no "undecideds" left among the current state legislators. Success for the ERA required the identification and electoral defeat of enough "antis" to gain the votes necessary when each state legislature met again. In most unratified states, there would be only one election before the new deadline. The nature of the U. S. political system makes it virtually impossible to change the composition of a legislature in only one election, absent an issue of overwhelming importance. Consequently, while a majority of the American population supported the ERA, the votes of seven legislators in three states kept it from being added to the Constitution.

The ERA campaign had several effects on NOW. The idea that women could oppose equal rights for women was initially something of a shock. Once the organization realized that radical rhetoric was threatening to some women and that the ERA was a surrogate issue for "destruction of the family," NOW sought to change its image. While active chapters were created in states that had previously seen little feminist activity, the NOW leadership also admonished all local chapters to devote themselves almost exclusively to the ERA, with the result that other areas of feminist activity atrophied, even in ratified states. To gain funds and the respectability of a large membership, the national organization actively solicited members but did not channel them into chapters; previously, recruitment had been a local function. Consequently, while the total membership grew, the number of local activists declined to the point where, even in major cities, chapter meetings were very small. Finally, NOW turned its attention to electoral politics, which it had previously eschewed. The need to replace state legislators convinced NOW that it could no longer neglect practical politics, and it joined the legions of other organizations that had formed political action committees to raise and distribute campaign funds.

This move brought its scope of activities into that previously carved out by the National Women's Political Caucus. The NWPC was formed in 1971 by prominent female politicians and other well-known feminists with the aim of getting more women elected and appointed to public office. Its organization mirrors that of the typical political party. The effective unit is the state organization. The national office primarily services rather than directs local chapters. Although the NWPC has a decidedly feminist bias, its membership is exceedingly diverse, with large numbers concerned chiefly with gaining office rather than pushing issues. On several occasions it and NOW have endorsed opposing candidates. The NWPC endorses only women (although not all women), whereas NOW will endorse men if it believes they will represent its interests. Although the NWPC does not command the same resources as NOW does, the national NWPC office has been an effective organizer of women's organizations in Washington to coordinate pursuit of their common interests, particularly the appointment of women to government positions. Although NOW is invited to the meetings, it has never been an active participant or engaged much in the usual political game playing of the Capitol, with the result that Washington politicians view NOW as less respectable than the NWPC.

THE NEXT REVOLUTION

The ERA dominated the women's liberation movement as it did the NWP, but that was more by accident than by intention. A Bill of Rights for Women proposed by NOW in 1968 contained eight planks, only one of which was the ERA. The younger branch never made a list of its demands, but in the many papers that appeared in its media, a constitutional amendment to achieve legal equality was not one of the articulated goals. At the first national feminist march, to commemorate the fiftieth anniversary of Suffrage on August 26, 1970, the three demands were equal opportunity in employment and education, free abortion on demand, and twenty-four-hour child-care centers. Even in 1977, when the ERA campaign was at its height, the National Women's Conference in Houston, Texas passed resolutions on twenty-five separate issues. By then, the three most controversial and visible issues were the ERA, abortion, and gay rights.

Of all these issues, the ERA captured the public imagination because it was the quintessential symbolic issue. It meant what people thought it meant, and all involved projected onto it both their fears and their hopes. But this time the emphasis was different from that of fifty years ago. The argument was not over the meaning of *equality*, but rather about the role of women. This time, the opponents rejected equality of any kind as desirable for women, favoring instead protection of women to pursue the traditional goals of wife and motherhood in a traditional way. To them, the ERA symbolized not equal legal rights, but the entire women's liberation movement, which they believed was, along with the other social movements of the sixties, a severe threat to their basic values and way of life.

Although not a new issue, the ERA became newly public at the end of a major period of social reform and at the beginning the women's movement. The timing could not have been worse. The sixties saw a major transformation in American society, and like previous social-reform movements, this one stimulated a backlash. The initial focus of that backlash was busing, but it quickly spread to encompass the new issues of feminism, abortion, and gay rights, all of which were interpreted as an attack on the family and the

American way of life. At the time the new right arose, feminism was still riding on the crest of enthusiasm that accompanies all new social movements. This enthusiasm was sufficient for the two-year Congressional campaign, but it was not uniform throughout the states. The new feminist organizations were not yet sufficiently organized to transfer resources to where they were most needed, or to deal with practical political problems. By the time they were ready, it was too late.

Nonetheless, the war fared better than did the battle. Feminism made the personal political and, in the process, raised everyone's consciousness about the importance of family issues, sexuality, and the role of women. It also stimulated major strides toward the legal equality that the ERA was originally written to achieve. Many state equal rights amendments were passed, discriminatory laws were changed, and the Supreme Court reinterpreted the basic premise against which laws affecting women were to be judged from one of protection to one of equal opportunity.

The ERA was ahead of its time in the 1920s. The NWP saw it as a legal revolution, but did not realize that an economic revolution had to come first. Women had only just won the right to work; they had not achieved the right for their work to be taken seriously. The real revolution of the contemporary women's movement is that the vast majority of the public no longer questions the right of any woman—married or unmarried, with or without children—to work for wages or to achieve her fullest individual potential.

The next revolution is a social one—a revolution in personal and family relationships. Although women have finally won the right to work, there is still a fundamental assumption that the principal social unit is the two-parent family, only *one* of whom is a primary wage earner. There is still a basic division of labor, in which men are expected to be the ''breadwinners'' and women are expected to focus their energies on the family, although each may ''help'' with the other's task.

The women's liberation movement began the social revolution with its critique of established sex roles. But it raised more questions than answers, and the backlash clearly indicates that, like the NWP in the 1920s, the movement is ahead of its time. Our society is not yet ready for the vast changes in the organization of work and in social policies that will be required to bring about this next step. These changes, like those that constituted the economic revolution, will probably accrue over time. They will come about as more women, and more men, adjust their lives to the conflicting pressures of family and work until a threshold of incompatibility is reached. At that time, as in the sixties, a new feminist movement will be needed to propose a new vision that can confront the problems of the social revolution.

Feminist Consciousness and Black Women

PAULINE TERRELONGE

Like the Populist movement at the turn of the century, and the Prohibition and Antiwar movements of subsequent decades, the contemporary feminist movement is having an enormous impact on black America. It is not so much that black people have embraced the feminist movement, or that they have even begun to identify with it. Rather its effect is seen in the controversy it has engendered within the race concerning the exact status of black males and females, and what the ideal role of each should be. A common (and, some would argue, the dominant) view within the black community at the present time is that blacks have withstood the long line of abuses perpetrated against them ever since their arrival in this country mainly because of the black woman's fortitude, inner wisdom, and sheer ability to survive. As a corollary to this emphasis on the moral, spiritual, and emotional strength of the black woman in offsetting the potential annihilation of the race, proponents of this view stress the critical role that she plays in keeping the black family together and in supporting black males. Indeed, many blacks regard the role of uniting all blacks to be the primary duty of the black woman, one that should supersede all other roles that she might want to perform, and certainly one that is essentially incompatible with her own individual liberation.[1] Pursuit of the latter is generally judged to be a selfish goal detrimental to the overall welfare of the race. In short, sexism is viewed by many blacks, both male and female, to be a factor of minimal importance in the overall oppression of the black woman. The brunt of culpability for her unequal condition is accorded to racism.[2]

The object of this essay is to challenge this point of view. It is my belief that the foregoing view of black female subordination expresses a narrow perspective on the nature of social oppression in American society, and, because of this, the solutions that are commonly proposed—e.g., correcting the imbalance in the black sex ratio, or building stronger black families—

are doomed to serve as only partial palliatives to the problems facing black women.

The first fact that must be grasped is that the black female condition in America has developed in a society where the dominant economic form is the market economy and the sole purpose of economic activity is the making of a profit on the part of large corporations. Because profit maximization is the superordinate goal to which all other social goals are merely subsidiary, labor is a premium. Labor must not only be made as highly productive as possible but also be obtained at the cheapest possible cost. The manipulation of the labor market is essential to attain these dual goals and provide for the effective functioning of the American economic order.

A major strategy for manipulating labor has been the maintenance of a sexual division of labor, i.e., a situation where certain roles are designated as male, others as female. The allocation of societal functions according to gender has been based on certain biological factors that objectively differentiate the sexes and the way those factors are interpreted through the ideology of sexism. The fact that women bear children has been used to justify their relegation to the domestic sphere. Their ability to reproduce has been made a duty, to which have been added the responsibilities of nurturing the offspring, serving the spouse, and performing or supervising all domestic-related chores. It is easy to see how the pattern of female responsibility for the domestic sphere is useful to the economic system; it has allowed certain critical societal functions to be performed without the need of providing monetary remuneration.[3]

It is generally recognized that the ideology of racism has functioned to maintain blacks in a subordinate economic state.[4] Less readily recognized, however, are the similarities of the process of racial subordination to that of female subordination. In both cases the rationale for subordination resides in characteristics ascribed by the large capitalist interests, which are almost totally white male. Moreover, both forces — sexism and racism — create an occupationally segregated labor market, thereby giving rise to a situation where there are male jobs and female jobs, white jobs and black jobs.

From a cursory view, the white female has appeared historically to enjoy a privileged status; after all, as a result of sharing the bedrooms of white males, to her fall many of the material privileges and benefits of the society. But it is essential to recognize that rarely has she achieved these amenities on her own merit; nearly always it has been through the efforts and good graces of her spouse. The apparent freedoms and material well-being enjoyed by many white women depend not on women earning them but on women fulfilling a nurturant and supportive role and, of course, maintaining a distinctive sexual identity through a socially defined image of female attractiveness. Thus, beauty and sexual attractiveness are essential to woman's economic survival, and maintaining these assets has become a major concern, second only to fulfillment of her domestic functions.

The cult of the home, like so many other aspects of white America, has unfortunately permeated the culture of Afro-America. While the cult in black society has been subjected to indigenous permutations,[5] in essence it bears close similarities to the white pattern, as would be expected in view of the fact that the economic forces affecting the larger society also impinge on the black subculture. Thus, within Afro-American culture (and I emphasize within), maleness creates privileges—that is, certain freedoms and rights are attached to being male. Certain sexually specific behaviors are part of the black socialization process. The result is that marriage among blacks is just as much a union of unequals as it is in the larger society; child rearing, domestic chores, and custody of children are largely female concerns. Hence, it is erroneous to argue that the domestic patterns of white society are not replicated in the black community. The "housewife" model may not fit completely, but it is closely approximated in the sense that black women must bear the brunt of the domestic-related chores, even when they also work outside the home.

What has historically differentiated black women from most white women is the peculiar way in which the racial and sexual caste systems have interfaced. Throughout their history in America, black women have had to face a condition of double dependency—(1) on their spouses or mates, and (2) on their employers. Although these dependencies have also been the lot of many employed white women, proportionately fewer of the latter faced both of them. Double dependency has practically always been the onus of black women. Moreover, because of the racial caste system, a significant proportion of black married women, both historically and contemporaneously, have not had the economic support of their husbands—because their husbands are either absent or underemployed or unable to find employment. What is significant about the fact that so many black women have had to contribute to their families' financial support is that society's reaction to their plight has been sexist. Because they are more economically independent of a male breadwinner than is the societal norm, many black women have been made to feel that they usurped the male role, as though they—and not society—were ultimately responsible for the black man's inability to be the main breadwinner.

It is sometimes argued that the black woman's lack of choice over whether she should or should not work renders her condition totally dissimilar to that of a white woman. While it is true that black men have had a more difficult time providing for their families than white men, and that this has forced more black women to be in the labor force than white women, it must be recognized that the roles of both groups of women were ultimately conditioned by larger economic forces: White women were conditioned not to work in the productive sector; black women were conditioned to work. Those white women who were forced by economic circumstances to work outside the home were made to feel that their behavior was somehow deviant, and in most cases they abandoned their occupational participation when it was no longer absolutely necessary to their families' financial well-being. Thus, neither group of women, white or black, had an option. Consequently, the behavior of both groups of women was a direct consequence of economic forces over which they exercised little or no control.

The foregoing picture of the different though mutually consistent roles played by black and white women has not remained static over the years. In the last twenty-five years, dramatic changes have taken place in the composition of the female labor force. Increasing numbers of married white women have sought paid employment and black women have made major gains in earnings. In short, the labor-force profiles of both groups of women have become more and more similar, especially for young women.[6]

The movement of white females into the labor sphere has been partially caused by inflation, which has made it increasingly difficult for white males to maintain a middle-class standard of living solely from their earnings. This situation bears stark similarity to the one that has traditionally prevailed in black society, where familial economic survival—in both the working and the middle classes—generally depends on both spouses' income.

For white women, like black women, labor-force participation has not relieved them of performing traditional female domestic chores. For both groups of women, this has had a significant impact on the nature of their occupational participation, as it is generally interpreted by employers as a sign of the inherent unreliability of female labor—i.e., as a source of potential absenteeism and turnover—and is used as an added rationale for relegating women to the least prestigious, least financially remunerative, and most menial tasks. Even working women who are not wives or mothers find their occupational destinies affected by employer expectations that they do or will perform dual roles.

The entrance of more women into the productive sphere of the society has not brought about the demise of occupational segregation based on sex; indeed, economists reveal that occupational segregation based on sex is highly resistant to change.[7] Thus, women continue to predominate in those jobs that are least secure; least subject to unionization; least lucrative in terms of compensation, working conditions, and fringe benefits; and least conducive to career advancement.[8] So the influx of women into the labor market has not appreciably reduced the chances of males to find employment in a labor market that continues to be occupationally segregated. Women can be absorbed by the economy as a result of the fact that in the past thirty years there has been a phenomenal increase in some traditional female jobs, primarily in the clerical and service sectors of the economy.

Women are judged by employers to be particularly suited for clerical and service jobs for three basic reasons: (1) because of their socialization, they are assumed to prefer these jobs despite the low wages;[9] (2) female socialization trains them to display the attitudes of docility and compliance essential to the functioning of bureaucracies; and (3) because women are assumed to be ultimately supported by men, employers think they will not resist being shunted into or out of the economy according to its boom and bust cycle. The latter is particularly detrimental to black women, since a considerable proportion of them are the sole or major suppliers of family income.

What is interesting about most female-dominated jobs is that they increasingly demand two credentials that are more difficult for black women than white to attain. One is a relatively high level of education, at least a high-school diploma. The other is the facility to read, write, and communicate verbally in mainstream English. Although it is not readily acknowledged, jobs such as telephone operator, typist, and secretary, commonly require an ability to use the language of white middle-class society. Because of their subcultural status and the low quality of education they receive, black women historically have been at a distinct disadvantage in manipulating the cultural symbols of the larger society. Thus, the deprecatory societal evaluation of black linguistic patterns and the institutional racism of the nation's educational system have worked to black women's disadvantage in the competition between black and white female workers for clerical jobs. In 1987 the proportions of black and white working women in administrative-support and clerical jobs were 26.4 and 29.5 percent respectively.[10] Nonetheless, the rapid infiltration of black women into the clerical sphere in recent years seems to indicate that the discrimination against black women holding clerical jobs is declining. Whether they are actually achieving total equality with white women in this sphere, or whether white women hold relatively more prestigious jobs, is a question that needs further investigation. What is clear is that the wage levels of black and white women workers have now almost completely converged.

Although black men are also victims of white ethnocentrism and poor education, their chances of earning higher pay than do black women are enhanced as racial barriers fall, because many high-paying male occupations — e.g., in craft unions, municipal services, and the military — do not place such demand on the communication skills that are the sine qua non for advancement in clerical jobs. Indeed, the military offers many black men the chance of making up the deficiencies they incurred in the nation's educational system, as well as the opportunity to gain significant social benefits that are, for many, the route to upward occupational mobility. The continued sexual stereotyping of positions in those areas that have belatedly opened up to blacks reduces the chances for black women to move out of the traditionally female, clerical jobs. Thus, the erosion of racial barriers in employment is working more to the advantage of black men than black women.[11]

It is important to recognize this point, because it contradicts the commonly held view that the black woman fares infinitely better in American society than does the black man. Those who advance this claim generally rest their arguments on two facts. First, a greater proportion of black women than men hold jobs that are designated *professional* in the Bureau of the Census classification schema, and, second, historically, black women were more likely to have graduated from high school and college than are black men.

Yet it must be recognized that black women have never held high-status professional jobs in any great numbers. This is because, even in the professional occupational category, rigid sex segregation persists. Black women are able to find relatively easy access to such female occupations as nursing and teaching, but have a hard time, particularly in comparison to black men, gaining access to higher-status occupations such as law, medicine, and dentistry.[12] The latter are just as much male fields among blacks as among whites.

Black women's greater educational attainment is similarly misleading.

First, in the society at large, women are more likely to have graduated from high school than are men, so that this is not an aberration among blacks. Moreover, although the number of black female college graduates has historically exceeded that of black male graduates,[13] this was not the case in all parts of the nation.[14] Since the advent of a whole gamut of minority programs designed to boost black college enrollment in the 1970s, black males have made strides in attaining a college education and are now 43.6 percent of all black students attending college.[15] Nor does attending college necessarily have the same impact on women as on men. A study of historically black colleges in the 1960s, containing half of all black college students, showed that the women significantly lowered their aspirations for professional achievement by the time they were seniors, whereas the men maintained or increased theirs.

> These black college-educated women appeared to be significantly limited by sexual constraints in their career aspirations. They consistently chose traditionally feminine occupations and very few planned to venture into occupations dominated by men. Even more significantly, perhaps, the women saw the "feminine" jobs they selected as having lower status and demanding less ability than the "masculine" occupations—a telling comment on how they viewed what they had to offer in the job world.[16]

The association of femaleness with a distinctive economic function transcends racial lines. This fact is often obscured by certain racial differences in female labor force participation, such as the higher unemployment rate of black women than of white women, as well as the tendency of black women to begin their careers in jobs lower in status, their greater expectations of working, and their tendency to value higher wages above job satisfaction.[17] Although these differences should not be underestimated, it is myopic to focus on them exclusively in assessing the black female condition. The observation by Gump and Rivers, based on an extensive review of the literature on black/white differences in labor force participation, is particularly poignant here:

> Much data has been presented portraying the black woman as more likely to enter the labor force, more interested in doing so, more likely to work full time and continuously, and more necessary to the financial welfare of her family. . . . While such facts suggest a woman much less constricted by the traditional role than her white counterpart, it is equally true that black women choose occupations traditional for women, are motivated perhaps more by a sense of responsibility than by achievement need, are much more traditional in their sex-role attitudes than are young white women, and to some extent seem burdened by the responsibility they carry.
> Thus it appears that black women have *not* escaped many of the constraints imposed upon white women, though they are free of some of them. . . . There are those who would assert too quickly the freedom of black women, and they must be reminded of her bondage.[18]

If there is much in the objective condition of black women that warrants the development of a black feminist consciousness, why have so many black women failed to recognize the patterns of sexism that directly impinge on their everyday lives? Why have they failed to address a social force that unremittingly thwarts their ability to compete on an equal basis in the society?

Five factors have contributed to this situation. The most formidable is that many black intellectuals and spokespeople have ignored the issue of sexism, largely because it has been viewed as a racially divisive issue. That is, a feminist consciousness has been regarded as a force that could generate internal conflict between black males and black females. It is this writer's firm conviction that, far from being a source of internecine conflict, a feminist consciousness would contribute to the welfare of the race in a variety of ways:

1. It would enable black men and women to attain a more accurate and deeper level of understanding of many of the social problems that are currently undermining the viability of the race. Such problems as the black male unemployment rate, the absence of the black male in the family, the large representation of black women among those on welfare, and the high black "illegitimacy" rate are just a few of the many social problems afflicting blacks that are, in part at least, attributable to the operation of sexism in our society.

2. Elimination of sexism on the interpersonal level within black culture would result in each sex developing its individual talents and capacities unhindered by societal definitions of appropriate sexual behavior, thus increasing the general pool of black abilities.

3. A feminist consciousness, in ridding black males and females of their socially conditioned anxieties concerning masculinity and femininity, would foster greater psychological well-being and thereby strengthen the interpersonal bonds that are constantly being eroded and loosened by the impact of interpersonal sexism.

A second factor that helps to explain the absence of feminist consciousness among black women is the ideology of racism. Racism is so ingrained in American culture, and so entrenched among many white women, that black females have been reluctant to admit that anything affecting the white female could also affect them. Indeed, many black women have tended to see all whites, regardless of sex, as sharing the same objective interest, and clearly the behavior of many white women vis-à-vis blacks has helped to validate this reaction.

A third factor is the message that emerged in the black social movement of the sixties. In one sense, this movement worked to the detriment of black women, because they were told in many different ways that the liberation of the black man was more important than was their own liberation. In fact, they were often given to believe that any attempt on their part to take an equal place with the black man in the movement would contribute to his emasculation.[19]

The idea of black matriarchy, another ideological ploy commonly introduced to academicians and policymakers, in a fourth factor that has suppressed the development of a feminist consciousness among black women. In a nutshell, this view holds that in their conjugal and parental relationships black women are more dominant than black men, and so black and white women relate to their mates in altogether different ways.[20] It is easy to see how this view of black women could be used by some to negate the fact of black female oppression: If the black woman were indeed found to be more dominant than is the black man, this could be construed as meaning that she is not dependent on him and thus not in need of liberation. In fact, scholarly exploration of the issue has revealed the idea of black matriarchy to be mythical and has shown that the relationship of black and white women to their mates is fundamentally similar. And even if a black matriarchy did exist, it would be fallacious to infer from this that the black woman is not sexually oppressed, for her subordination is a derivative of both her family-related role and her position in the productive sphere of the economy. Thus, single and married black women are both placed in positions of subservience whenever they seek employment. Both are subjected to the manipulative tactics that are used to keep all female laborers—white and black, married and unmarried—in a low economic state compared to male laborers.

What the participants in the debate on black matriarchy fail to recognize is the white bias of their viewpoints. Implicit in their arguments is the idea that any matriarchy is unnatural and deviant. To attach such a pejorative label to matriarchy, and to view the partriarchal form as a positive good or an index of normality, is to accept the normative standard of the larger white society. Given the role that the family plays in supporting and perpetuating existing unequal economic arrangements, it may be fitting for us to question whether it would not be in the best interests of blacks to work out familial relationships that deviate from the conventional patriarchal norm and approximate a more egalitarian pattern, thereby challenging the racial and sexual status quo.

A final factor that has inhibited the development of a feminist consciousness among women in American society in general, and black females in particular, has been the church. Biblical support for sexual inequality is as strong today as it ever was, and the Christian church has played a preeminent role in validating the patriarchal nature of Western culture.[21] This is as true in black churches as it is in white ones, although the role of black religion in enchaining black women has been little subject to discussion.[22] The persistence of patriarchal views in black churches is undoubtedly due in some measure to the fact that most of our noted black theologians are men. But a more important point is that it persists because of the deep religiosity of black people today and the fact that most black religions are basically Christian despite some deviations and modifications. For whatever reason, it is significant that the church is the most important social institution in the black community and the one in which black women (in contrast to black men) spend most of their time and energy. This dedication undoubtedly has contributed in no small part to the black female's passive acceptance of her subservient societal role. Even so-called black nationalist religions, which proffer a different view of the world and a substitute for the teachings of

Christianity, have failed to come to terms with the subordination of black women in our society. Indeed, some have even adopted theological preachments designed to stultify the development of female talents and to push women yet further into the traditional servile roles of mother and wife.[23]

In sum, black women in America have been placed in a dependent position vis-à-vis men. The source of their dependence is dual: It originates in the role they have been socialized to play in the family and the discrimination they face when they seek remunerative employment outside the home. Because sexual dependence works to the detriment of the entire race — both male and female — all blacks, regardless of sex, need to recognize the way in which their behavior, be it familial, marital, occupational, or otherwise, is subject to social control. From this realization they need to develop alternative behavioral norms for themselves and socialization patterns for their offspring that will challenge the distribution of power in America.

The view that racism is the sole cause of black female subordination in America today exhibits a very simplistic view of the black female condition. The economic processes of the society subordinate different groups of workers in different ways, but always for the same end. Because white supremacy and male chauvinism are merely symptoms of the same economic imperatives, it is facile to argue that white pigmentation is the sine qua non for the attainment of power in America, that white women share the same objective interests as white men, and that white women thus have nothing in common with black women. Although whiteness may be a contributory condition for the attainment of social privilege, sex and socioeconomic status are contingent conditions. Because color, gender, and wealth are at the present time collective determinants of power and privilege in America, it is almost impossible to disentangle their individual effects. Thus, those who would assert that the elimination of one type of social discrimination should have priority over all others display a naive conceptualization of the nature of power in American society and the multifaceted character of social oppression.

NOTES

1. Examples of literature supporting this perspective are Mae King, "Oppression and Power: The Unique Status of the Black Woman in the American Political System," *Social Science Quarterly*, 56 (1975), 116–28; Linda La Rue, "The Black Movement and Women's Liberation," *Black Scholar*, 1 (May 1970), 36–42; and Julia Mayo, "The New Black Feminism: A Minority Report," in *Contemporary Sexual Behavior: Critical Issues in the 1970's*, Joseph Zubin and John Money, eds. (Baltimore: Johns Hopkins University Press, 1973), 175–86.

2. Notable exceptions are Barbara Sizemore, "Sexism and the Black Male," *Black Scholar*, 4 (Mar.-Apr. 1973), 2–11; Aileen Hernandez, "Small Change for Black Women," *Ms.*, 3 (Aug. 1974), 16–18; Elizabeth Almquist, "Untangling the Effects of Race and Sex: The Disadvantaged Status of Black Women," *Social Science Quarterly*, 56 (1975), 129–42; Charmeyne D. Nelson, "Myths about Black Women Workers in Modern America," *Black Scholar*, 6 (Mar. 1975), 11–15; and William A. Blakey, "Everybody Makes the Revolution: Some Thoughts on Racism and Sexism," *Civil Rights Digest*, 6 (spring 1974), 11–19.

3. Margaret Bentsen, "The Political Economy of Women's Liberation," *Monthly Review*, 21 (Sept. 1970); Juliet Mitchell, *Women's Estate* (New York: Random House, 1971), 99–158; Paul

Baran and Paul Sweezy, *Monopoly Capital* (New York: Monthly Review Press, 1966); Gayle Rubin, ''The Traffic in Women: Notes on the 'Political Economy' of Sex,'' in *Toward an Anthropology of Women*, Rayna Reiter, ed. (New York: Monthly Review Press, 1975), 3; Jean Gardiner, ''Women's Domestic Labor,'' *New Left Review* 89 (Jan.-Feb. 1975), 47–59; Sheila Rowbotham, *Woman's Consciousness, Man's World* (Baltimore: Penguin Books, 1974).

4. See, among others, Harold Baron, ''The Demand for Black Labor: Historical Notes on the Political Economy of Racism,'' *Radical America*, 5 (Mar.-Apr. 1971), 1–46.

5. For further discussion of black sex-role socialization see, among others, Diane K. Lewis, ''The Black Family: Socialization and Sex Roles,'' *Phylon*, 34 (fall 1975), 221–37; Carlfred Broderick, ''Social Heterosexual Development among Urban Negroes and Whites,'' *Journal of Marriage and the Family*, 27 (May 1965), 200–3; Alice R. Gold and M. Carol St. Ange, ''Development of Sex-Role Stereotypes in Black and White Elementary Girls,'' *Developmental Psychology*, 10 (May 1974), 461; and Boone E. Hammond and Joyce Ladner, ''Socialization into Sexual Behavior in a Negro Slum Ghetto,'' in *The Individual, Sex, and Society*, Carlfred B. Broderick and Jesse Bernard, eds. (Baltimore: Johns Hopkins University Press, 1969), 41–52.

6. See Elizabeth Almquist's article in this book for more data on this point.

7. See Blau and Winkler, this volume.

8. See Blau and Winkler, this volume.

9. Edward A. Nicholson and Roger D. Roderick, *Correlates of Job Attitudes among Young Women* (Columbus: Ohio State University Research Foundation, 1973), 10.

10. *Employment and Earnings*, January 1988, 180.

11. Stuart H. Garfinkle, ''Occupation of Women and Black Workers, 1962–74,'' *Monthly Labor Review*, 98 (Nov. 1975), 25–35.

12. Elizabeth Almquist, ''Untangling the Effects of Race and Sex'' Marion Kilson, ''Black Women in the Professions, 1890–1970,'' *Monthly Labor Review*, 100 (May 1977), 38–41; Diane Nilsen Westcott ''Blacks in the 1970's: Did They Scale the Job Ladder?'' *Monthly Labor Review*, 105 (June 1982), 29–38.

13. Women are 54.7 percent of all black college graduates. Bureau of Labor Statistics, unpublished data from the March 1987 Current Population Survey. Part of the reason for this is that until recently blacks were basically a rural people and it is generally the case for farmer families to withdraw males from school to work the farm but not females, since farming is considered to be a male occupation. For further discussion of how this has contributed to present-day disparities in black male and female occupational status, see E. Wilbur Bock, ''Farmer's Daughter Effect: The Case of the Negro Female Professionals,'' *Phylon* (spring 1969), 17–26.

14. Andrew Billingsley, *Black Families in White America* (Englewood Cliffs, N.J.: Prentice-Hall, 1968), 79–82.

15. Bureau of Labor Statistics, unpublished data from the March 1987 Current Population Survey.

16. Patricia Gurin and Carolyn Gaylord, ''Educational and Occupational Goals of Men and Women at Black Colleges,'' *Monthly Labor Review*, 99 (June 1976), 13–14.

17. Patricia Cayo Sexton, *Women and Work*, Employment and Training Administration, R. & D. Monograph no. 46 (Washington, D.C.: Department of Labor, 1977), 15; Joyce O. Beckett, ''Working Wives: A Racial Comparison,'' *Social Work*, 21 (Nov. 1976), 463–71.

18. Janice Porter Gump and L. Wendell Rivers, *The Consideration of Race in Efforts to End Sex Bias* (Washington, D.C.: Department of Health, Education and Welfare, National Institute of Education 1973), 24–25.

19. Joyce A. Ladner, *Tomorrow's Tomorrow: The Black Woman* (Garden City, N.Y.: Doubleday and Co., 1971), 284; Robert Staples, *The Black Woman in America* (Chicago: Nelson-Hall Publishers, 1975), 174–76; Janice Gump, ''Comparative Analysis of Black Women's and White Women's Sex Role Attitudes,'' *Journal of Consulting and Clinical Psychology*, 43 (1975), 862–63; Cellestine Ware, *Woman Power: The Movement for Women's Liberation* (New York: Tower Publications, 1970), 75–99.

20. S. Parker and R. J. Kleiner, "Social and Psychological Dimensions of Family Role Performance of the Negro Male," *Journal of Marriage and the Family*, 31 (1969), 500–6; John H. Scanzoni, *The Black Family in Modern Society* (Boston: Allyn and Bacon, 1971); Katheryn Thomas Dietrich, "A Re-examination of the Myth of Black Matriarchy," *Journal of Marriage and the Family*, 37 (May 1975), 367–74; H. H. Hyman and J. S. Reed, "Black Matriarchy Reconsidered: Evidence from Secondary Analysis of Sample Surveys," *Public Opinion Quarterly*, 33 (1969), 346–54; Robert Staples, "The Myth of the Black Matriarchy," in *The Black Family*, Robert Staples, ed. (Belmont, Calif.: Wadsworth Publishing Co., 1971), 149–59; Alan Berger and William Simon, "Black Families and the Moynihan Report: A Research Evaluation," *Social Problems*, 33 (Dec. 1974), 145–61.

21. Simone de Beauvoir, *The Second Sex* (New York: Vintage Books, 1974); Susan Bell, *Women, from the Greeks to the French Revolution* (Belmont, Calif.: Wadsworth Publishing Co., 1973); Alan Cuming, "Women in Greek and Pauline Thought," *Journal of the History of Ideas*, 34 (Dec. 1973), 517–28.

22. Notable exceptions are Rosemary Reuther, "Crisis in Sex and Race: Black vs. Feminist Theology," *Christianity and Crisis*, 34 (Apr. 15, 1974), 67–73; "Continuing the Discussion: A Further Look at Feminist Theology," *Christianity and Crisis*, 34 (June 24, 1974), 139–43.

23. Barbara Sizemore, "Sexism and the Black Male," *Black Scholar*, 4 (Mar.-Apr. 1973), 2–11; Harry Edwards, "Black Muslim and Negro Christian Family Relationships," *Journal of Marriage and the Family*, 30 (Nov. 1968), 604–11.

Keep Us on the Pedestal: Women Against Feminism in Twentieth-Century America

SUSAN E. MARSHALL

In recent decades, a growing body of feminist research has delineated the structure, strategy, and political ideology of women's rights movements in the United States (Flexner 1973; Kraditor 1968, 1971; Freeman 1975; Cott 1987). We know surprisingly little, however, about the organization of opposition to proposed changes in female status. The astounding defeat of the Equal Rights Amendment (ERA) in 1982 (see Boles 1979; Berry 1986; Mansbridge 1986) underscores the continuing significance of antifeminist movements.

This article compares the American antisuffrage movement that flourished between 1910 and 1918 and the recent anti-ERA movement spearheaded by Phyllis Schlafly, to suggest a conceptual framework for understanding antifeminist movements in the United States. Much of the popular and scholarly work on American antifeminism has emphasized the powerful resistance of business interests to progress in women's rights for the purpose of maintaining an abundance of cheap female labor (Firestone 1970; Scott and Scott 1975; Carabillo 1978). While the profit motive may explain corporate financial contributions to the antifeminist cause, a large part of the organizing and lobbying activities has been performed by antifeminist females, many of whom are not in the labor force and thus not in a position to exploit directly members of their own sex (Brady and Tedin 1976; Tedin et al. 1977).

This analysis attempts to explain the emergence and growth of female countermovements to feminism through an examination of the rhetorical strategies used to define the movement, to establish goals, and to attract adherents. A comparison of female antisuffrage and anti-ERA literature

---

suggests that strikingly similar arguments have been utilized to justify the maintenance of traditional gender roles. In particular, the passage of legislation mandating gender equality was perceived as a threat to the privileged status of homemaker, which excuses women from the responsibilities of financial support, political participation, and military service. In both historical periods, the sacred symbols of family, God, and country were evoked frequently to emphasize the importance of female domestic roles for the perpetuation of American society. Conversely, this potent rhetoric discredited feminists as selfish, unpatriotic, irreligious, antifamily, and both antimale and antifemale. This article explores these common rhetorical themes and analyzes the two female antifeminist movements in terms of status politics (see Gusfield 1963; Lipset 1965).

HISTORICAL BACKGROUND

Although the first formal antisuffrage organization was established in the United States as early as 1872, organized antisuffrage activity remained sporadic and limited in scope until 1910, when suffragist victories began to mount in the form of state constitutional amendments giving women the vote. By 1913, there were sixteen state antisuffrage organizations and a National Association Opposed to Woman Suffrage. Many of these groups existed with acknowledged male financial support, but their leadership and membership were overwhelmingly female. Their activities included public speaking to advertise the cause, legislative lobbying at state and federal hearings on the suffrage issue, and the publication and distribution of antisuffrage literature. Their journals delineated the arguments against woman suffrage, reported the progress of antisuffrage campaigns, rejoiced at suffragists' defeats, and trivialized suffragists' victories. By 1918, however, the heyday of the antisuffrage movement had passed, weakened by the success of a suffrage amendment in the key eastern state of New York and the imminent ratification of the Susan B. Anthony amendment to the U.S. Constitution, which enfranchised 26 million women in 1920.

Similarly, the organization of contemporary antifeminists was in large part a response to the success of the women's movement in gaining state ratification of the ERA. Twenty-eight states ratified the ERA in 1972, the first year of eligibility. During that year, a countermovement began to coalesce, dedicated to halting ratification in additional states and rescinding the amendment where it had already been ratified. Reportedly backed by corporate interests, the countermovement nonetheless had a rank and file predominantly composed of women. Local and regional groups appeared, with such attention-getting names as Eve Reborn, HOT DOG (Humanitarians Opposed to Degrading Our Girls), AWARE (American Women Are Richly Endowed), and POW (Protect Our Women), but the most prominent national antifeminist organization was clearly Phyllis Schlafly's STOP-ERA, an offshoot of Eagle Forum, a conservative organization that Schlafly also founded. The contemporary antifeminist movement proved more successful than its predecessor. After 1977, no additional states ratified the ERA, several states voted to rescind ratification, and the lapse of the June 30, 1982, deadline found the ERA three states short of the thirty-eight needed to add it to the U.S. Constitution.

THE IDEOLOGY OF ANTIFEMINISM

Why would women organize to oppose actively a women's rights movement? A comparative historical analysis of American antisuffrage and anti-ERA literature suggests that the ideology of antifeminism embodies three related arguments: reaffirmation of divinely ordained sex differences, support for the traditional family as a necessary basis for the continuation of society, and alignment of antifeminism with unselfish patriotism. Issues of women's rights have been recast as a moral battle over the basic institutions and values of American society.

Nature's Plan: Specialization by Sex

Antifeminist arguments for the maintenance of differential laws by sex rest ultimately on a belief in inherent and hence immutable sex differences. By this argument, the superior intellectual and physical endowments of men intend them for the public sphere, the world of economics and politics, as the providers and protectors of women and children. Women, by contrast, are guided by sentiment rather than reason and are thus designed for the domestic sphere of childbearing and childrearing, keeping the home, and instilling morality. This specialization of function, it is argued, is ordained by God and nature, as supported by both scientific theories of evolution and religious tenets. Impertinent feminists who wish to tamper with the laws of nature thus threaten the continuation of civilization.

The antisuffragist view of woman's role was a reflection of middle-class values — "to be tender, loving, pure, and inspiring in her home, . . . to raise the moral tone of every household, to refine every man, . . . to mitigate the harshness and cruelty and vulgarity of life everywhere" (*Anti-Suffragist* 1908d, 8). The delicate female nervous system renders woman without "staying qualities, continuity of purpose, or affinity for the rough and tumble warfare in political life" (*Anti-Suffragist* 1910b, 2). Moreover, "woman does not think, she feels, she does not reason, she emotionalizes," and hence a female electorate is likely to "do injury to itself without promoting the public good" (*Woman's Protest* 1915c, 15; 1915e, 19). Because they believed in these inherent limitations, antisuffragists believed that feminists were asking not for equality but for special favors. "Women cannot consistently ask for a place in men's political race and then insist that they be helped over all the hurdles because they are naturally handicapped in the contest by their sex and their mission as mothers" (Heron 1915, 6). Paradoxically, however, antisuffragists repeatedly insisted: "We acknowledge no inferiority to men. We claim to have no less ability to perform the duties which God has imposed upon us than they have to perform those imposed upon them" (*Illinois Association* 1909, 3).

Contemporary antifeminists assert similar "fundamental inherent differences between men and women" (Schlafly 1977, 21). Male intellectual and physical superiority and female maternal instinct "must be recognized as part of the plan of the Divine Architect for the survival of the human race through the centuries" (p. 11). By opposing such sex-based roles, the women's movement and the ERA are "opposing Mother Nature herself" (p. 87). Specifically, legal mandates for equal employment opportunity rapidly degenerate into "reverse discrimination," given their blatant disregard for "the inadequacy of female qualifications" (p. 131). Gender-free laws will also remove traditional female protections from physically demanding jobs, thus increasing female injury and unemployment, and women's athletic opportunities will be virtually eliminated if they have to compete with men because of legal challenges to sex-segregated sports programs. While insisting that attempts to eradicate inherent sex differences cannot succeed, antifeminists also predict that experiments that undermine the traditional sex-based division of labor will "further confuse a generation already unsure about its identity," ominously conjuring up the specter of rampant homosexuality (p. 22).

In both countermovements, antifeminists portrayed themselves as women who accepted these sex differences and embraced their femaleness. Antisuffragists were "women who are proud of their womanhood and their relationship to men" (*Woman's Protest* 1915a, 3). They were the true ladies, the "patient, self-sacrificing women" who carry on their work "quietly and unostentatiously," with "grace of manner, dignity of bearing, purity of spirit, and nobility of conduct" (*Anti-Suffragist* 1908b, 5; Sebring 1915, 11; George 1915, 5). These qualities are also cited in more recent antifeminist literature, such as Andelin's *Fascinating Womanhood* (1966), Morgan's *Total Woman* (1973), and Schlafly's "Positive Woman," who "understands that men and women are different, and that these differences provide the key to her success as a person, and fulfillment as a woman" (Schlafly 1977, 9).

In sharp contrast, feminists have been characterized as malcontents, women who have failed at being women and are trying, somewhat childishly, to spoil the happiness of others of their sex. In the early decades of this century, suffragists were variously called "Amazons," "mannish," "unwomanly," "vulgar," and "viragoes"; in short, they were a disgrace to "Fair Womanhood" (*Anti-Suffragist* 1909a, 3; 1912a:2; 1912b, 7; White 1915b, 9; *Woman's Protest* 1915e, 19). According to Schlafly, feminists are "disgruntled," "whining," "straggly-haired" women who downgrade their sex and ultimately reject it, as evidenced by their campaign to adopt male prerogatives and jobs (Schlafly 1977, 34, 35, 37). Paradoxically, the sexual stereotypes of dependence and emotionality embraced by antifeminists are the very ones used to further discredit their adversaries. Feminists are "hysterical"; they are "howling dervishes" who "cry copiously" about supposed injustices and seek "silly" corrective measures such as the elimination of sexist words from laws and textbooks (*Anti-Suffragist* 1909c, 5; *Woman's Protest* 1915b, 7; Schlafly 1977, 28, 45). The use of the diminutive term *suffragette* is a notable example of the derogatory application of feminine stereotypes.

The Cult of Domesticity

To antifeminists, immutable sex differences dictate a traditional family structure, in which male breadwinners support female homemakers. Patriarchal marriage is the ultimate goal for the normal woman. "Marriage and motherhood give a woman new identity and the opportunity for all-round fulfillment as a woman" (Schlafly 1977, 56), and "if she does not think and plan to this end herself someone does it for her" (Bannister 1910, 6). Comparing domestic and career roles, they argued that motherhood offers the satisfaction of achievement at an early age, while marriage provides a boss (the husband) who is more tolerable than a supervisor or an office manager (Schlafly 1977, 57, 60). Feminist demands are perceived as a threat to this fundamental social order. Increased female participation in the economic and political spheres causes women to neglect their domestic responsibilities and erodes patriarchal power, which "will tend to the disintegration of the home and the hurt of the nation and the race" (Anti-Suffragist 1909b, 2).

Antisuffragists claimed that the female vote was unnecessary and redundant, for male family heads adequately represented the wishes of their wives. Moreover, women had considerable political influence through their charity work and especially through motherhood. "Raise good and able men and in one generation the world will be governed by good and able men," counsels one antisuffragist (Arnold 1915, 14). If women adequately perform their domestic duties, there is no time for active political participation. It is thereby implied that good wives and mothers are disinterested in the vote. Conversely, voting females neglect their family responsibilities, producing ill-mannered or delinquent children and exacerbating antagonism between the sexes to the point of marital dissolution. Political activity also strains the delicate female reproductive organs, "making [women] childless or mothers of a weak-kneed race" (Anti-Suffragist 1911, 7). This, of course, is the greatest threat to the continuance of society.

Contemporary antifeminists contend that the equal employment opportunity platform of the women's liberation movement "deliberately degrades the homemaker" (Schlafly 1977, 86). Equality of treatment under the ERA "would wipe out the most basic and precious legal right that homemakers now enjoy: the right to be a full-time homemaker" (p. 98). The ERA was labeled "an elitist upper-middle class cause" (p. 149), perpetrated by selfish professionals who "betray" other women for a "brief high" or "fix" of political power (Schlafly 1973, 12). Feminists' destructive antifamily activities harm both sexes. The eradication of sex-discriminatory employment practices eliminates protection for females from overtime work, making it more difficult for women to perform their domestic duties. In addition, feminist pressure for "reverse discrimination . . . means that employers are being forced to hire and train inexperienced single women with no dependents in order to achieve some arbitrary quota . . . rather than a more qualified man with dependents" (Schlafly 1977, 118). This unjust displacement of married males presumably forces more wives out of the home and into the labor force. Women's liberation thus represents a concerted attack on the family, on female homemakers, and on male providers.

In both historical periods, feminists have been cast as the antithesis of the generous, self-sacrificing maternal figure. They are possessed of "intense egotism" and driven by "personal indulgence," promoting a "do your own thing" attitude that "is eroding the fabric of our families" and inculcating dangerous, individualistic values in our children (Armstrong 1915, 3; Brazzil 1915, 18; Schlafly 1977, 77). Feminists are "marital misfits" whose refusal to have babies is responsible "for the apparent disintegration of the institution of marriage" (Schlafly 1977, 65, 212). At the extreme, suffragists were portrayed as advocates of un-Christian and un-American lifestyles, supporting activities such as free love and communal childrearing (*Anti-Suffragist* 1909d, 8; *Illinois Association* 1911, 1). Schlafly similarly charged that feminist support of abortion on demand represents an ominous revitalization of Hitler's genocidal policies (1977, 11) and that "lesbianism is logically the highest form in the ritual of women's liberation" (p. 208). "NOW [the National Organization for Women] is for prolesbian legislation giving perverts the same legal rights as husbands and wives — such as the rights to get marriage licenses, to file joint income tax returns, and to adopt children" (p. 228).

Pro Patria

The explicit intentions of suffragists and ERA advocates to alter U.S. laws for the attainment of gender equality enabled antifeminists to monopolize the sacred symbols of God, family, and country in defense of the status quo. The two countermovements adopted the role of patriot and portrayed feminists as radical socialists who would overthrow the government in their single-minded desire to press their minority views on an unwilling electorate. Paradoxically, while condemning feminists for their "enshrinement of individuality," antifeminists explained their own rejection of constitutional amendments as the patriotic defense of individual and state rights from the imposition of federal mandate (Schlafly 1977, 77). During both eras, feminists were charged with duplicity for demanding equal rights when they were unable or unwilling to shoulder equal responsibilities of citizenship.

Antisuffragists were quite insistent that the female vote would cause the downfall of democracy. The cult of domesticity does not prepare women for the job of running the country. With little knowledge of finance, protected by their husbands from taxpaying responsibilities, enfranchised women would presumably support expensive referenda and ultimately bankrupt the government (Tucker 1911, 6; White 1915a, 9). The greater emotionality of females would prompt them to cast impulsive votes for candidates and issues. "National obligations would be piled up under some outburst of pity. . . . International alliances and menaces would be 'happy thoughts' of some moment of great excitement. And without intending it or providing against it, the nation would be plunged into war" (*Anti-Suffragist* 1908c, 8). Not only would this be unjust to males, who are singularly burdened with the duties of military service, but it would also threaten democratic rule. "To extend suffrage to women would be to introduce into the electorate a vast noncombatant party incapable of enforcing its own rule. . . . To make possible a majority which a minority could safely defy would be to overthrow the idea of Republican Government" (*Anti-Suffragist* 1908a, 3). During this wave of feminism, however, neither suffragists nor their adversaries debated the issue of female participation in warfare. Both sides expected women to support the war effort from the sidelines via voluntary relief work and temporary employment in defense industries.

The contemporary feminist movement has recast the issue of female military duty. The exclusion of women from combat positions is viewed as an example of sex discrimination in employment. The ERA would make women subject to a draft and to equal participation in warfare. The countermovement claims that this issue demonstrates the hypocrisy of feminists. "They will exercise *their* freedom of choice to avoid military service" — through legal loopholes such as age restrictions, conscientious objector status, etc. — "but they are willing to inflict involuntary military duty on all other eighteen-year-old girls" (Schlafly 1977, 124). In contrast, antifeminists are true patriots. "It is the task of the Positive Woman to keep America Good" — that is, in accordance with the principles of "Judeo-Christian civilization" (pp. 213, 219). This includes support for capitalist free enterprise and freedom from excessive government intervention. Schlafly supports local control of educational facilities that honor the traditional family; the right of employers to prefer, among equal job candidates, wage earners with dependents; the right to life of all innocent persons from conception to natural death; and the right of society to protect itself by designating different roles for males and females in the military, police, and fire protection services. The ERA is thus viewed as a "federal grab for power," an undemocratic erosion of the rights of individual citizens and states (p. 166).

The antithesis of God-fearing, democratic society is socialism, and feminists are frequently portrayed as seditious radicals who "agitate and demonstrate and hurl demands at society" (Schlafly 1977, 10). Antisuffragists made much of the political alliance between women's suffrage organizations and the Progressive and Socialist parties, as well as the feminist establishment of a Woman's Peace Party during World War I (*Illinois Association* 1913; Conroy 1915; *Woman's Protest* 1915f; Repplier 1915). The continuation of militant suffragist activity during the war years was further evidence of the tendency of feminists to place self above country, in contrast to the patriotic contributions of antisuffrage organizations to the war effort (*Woman's Protest* 1915d). During both eras, feminist attacks on the traditional patriarchal institutions of marriage, work, and politics were perceived as evidence of "the rabid determination of militant radicals" to "evade" their domestic responsibilities at the expense of increased government "spending and control" (Schlafly 1977, 27, 204, 206). For antifeminists, socialism represents the greatest danger to women. Its emphasis on equality ignores inherent sex differences and makes the individual rather than the family the fundamental unit of society, thus reducing not only male power but also male responsibility for female dependents.

ANTIFEMINISM AS STATUS POLITICS

The antisuffragist and anti-ERA literature illustrates how countermovements to feminism frequently embrace masculine and feminine stereotypes to legitimate the preservation of sex-discriminatory legislation. Females should not vote because they do not have the emotional, cognitive, or physical abilities necessary for active political participation, and they cannot compel obedience to their mandate via military force. The ERA should not be passed because it legalizes "reverse discrimination," the displacement of male workers by less qualified females. In both periods, female advocates of gender equality were derided for their lack of competence in the male sphere as well as for their loss of femininity.

However, the antifeminist belief in a rigid sexual division of labor admits no inequality with males. Females are uniquely suited for their domestic duties of home maintenance and child care, and conversely the domination of the public sphere by males is justified by males' inherently superior aggressive, analytical, and logical abilities. This ideology of "separate but equal" means that feminists who complain of gender inequality in American society are guilty of derogating their own sex. Antifeminist rhetoric thus adeptly reversed the images of women's liberation and antifeminism. The former now represents dog-in-the-manger negativism, while the latter promises hope and fulfillment.

Both countermovements carried this argument one step further. Females not only have attained equality with males but also enjoy special privileges, which are threatened by feminist pressures to integrate traditional male and female roles. These asymmetrical rights and responsibilities are derived directly from the gender-based division of labor. As breadwinners, males are required to support their families and must pay their wives alimony in the event of divorce. As the stronger and more aggressive sex, males must also go to war. The physical inferiority of females thus works to their advantage, for women are spared the drudgeries and responsibilities of the male role. The insulation of females within the home preserves their special feminine qualities of gentleness, purity, and morality. It keeps them on the pedestal, above the harshness and vulgarity of the masculine public domain.

American antifeminist movements can thus be explained with reference to Gusfield's (1963) concept of status politics. Countermovements to feminism represent a defense of the dominant status of homemaker, which is perceived as threatened by demands to tear down the rigid separation of male and female spheres. Thus, antisuffragists warn that, "if women claim equality, they must lose their privileges" (*Anti-Suffragist* 1910a, 8). Schlafly's STOP-ERA organization was reportedly an acronym for "Stop Taking Our Privileges" (Solomon 1978, 49), and Schlafly labeled the ERA the "Extra Responsibilities Amendment" (Schlafly 1977, 104). The Nineteenth Amendment and the ERA thus became symbolic battlegrounds for the issue of which female lifestyles will dominate American society (Scott 1985; Marshall 1986). It is not surprising, therefore, that the rhetoric of antifeminism is so saturated with the sacred myths of God, family, and country. As Gusfield observed, the language of status politics is the language of moral issues. At stake is the "symbolic conferral of respect upon the norms of the victor and disrespect upon the norms of the vanquished" (1963, 174). Antifeminist movements represent the attempt of one group to legitimate publicly its concept of woman's proper place in the social order.

Despite the rhetorical similarities of the two antifeminist movements, significant social changes during this century have given each movement a distinct historical context, manifested by the differences in membership of the groups. In 1910, the status defense of the homemaker was led by wealthy, elite women, the wives of eminent eastern politicians and industrialists, such as Mrs. Elihu Root, Mrs. Schuyler Van Renssalaer, and Mrs. Lowell Putnam. The founder and first president of the National Association Opposed to Woman Suffrage, Mrs. Arthur M. Dodge, traced her American ancestry to the first colonists, and her husband was reported at the time to be New York's wealthiest merchant. Newspaper accounts of mass antisuffrage fund-raisers described the assemblage as "prosperous-looking" and reported large donations in response to requests from the dais to "forgo theatre or opera tickets" for the defeat of suffrage ("Suffragists" 1914, 20; "Mormons" 1915, 5). Antisuffrage publications made frequent reference to the social imperative for the "redemptive influence of a lady" to "displace vulgarity with refinement, bad taste with propriety," and "bad manners with fine breeding" during these trying times of social upheaval (Sebring 1915, 11). Not surprisingly, corporate contributors to the antisuffrage cause reportedly included liquor, railroad, and oil interests, and northern legislators who led the fight against suffrage in the U.S. Senate were also well-known spokespersons for the interests of big business (Flexner 1973, 297–305).

The status conflict that spawned the antisuffrage movement may be better understood within a broader class context as an attempt to preserve the cultural hegemony of the eastern industrial elite from the onslaughts of uneducated foreign immigrants and western pioneers. A common argument used against suffrage by these organizations, for example, was the deleterious consequence of expanding the political power of the foreign-born by granting the vote to immigrant women (Scott 1909, 1; *Woman's Protest* 1915g, 7). It is interesting to note that antisuffrage leader Dodge founded the National Federation of Day Nurseries for the dual purpose of alleviating the burdens of the working woman while achieving the broader social goal of inculcating American middle-class values in immigrant children. Moreover, the parallel growth of support for woman suffrage and political reform in the western states was denounced as irrelevant to the East, which contained, after all, the bulk of the American population and its moral center. While racist and classist rhetoric was not exclusive to one side of the suffrage issue (see Kraditor 1971, Chapters 6–7), the antisuffragists went further in their efforts to define motherhood and female domesticity as the solution to the political and cultural threat facing native-born Americans. Furthermore, although the predominantly middle-class suffrage movement also received its share of support from wealthy eastern socialites, the suffragists made greater efforts to reach working-class women. They courted prominent union leaders, spoke in immigrant neighborhoods, passed resolutions in support of women workers, and held public rallies to support female strikers and to protest poor working conditions in the wake of disasters, such as the Triangle Fire of 1911, which killed 146 women garment workers in New York City (see Gompers 1920; Schaffer 1962). While one might argue that the suffragists' motives were primarily instrumental, the suffragists were noticeably more likely than were the antisuffragists to target appeals to employed women of the lower classes.

In the contemporary era, antifeminism appears to receive its greatest support from a different segment of society. Surveys have generally found that female anti-ERA activists are more likely to come from lower-class backgrounds and to have lower levels of educational attainment than members of the pro-ERA movement; they are also less likely to have spouses with professional occupations (Tedin et al. 1977; Arrington and Kyle 1978). Female antifeminist activists are also less likely to be employed and, when employed, are less likely to be found in professional occupations than are pro-ERA activists (Mueller and Dimieri 1982). Other surveys assessing the correlates of women's attitudes about the ERA have similarly found that ERA opponents tend to be less educated (Huber, Rexroat, and Spitze 1978) and are less likely to be employed (Scott 1985) than those favoring the proposed amendment.

While the evidence is inconclusive, due to the small number of empirical studies, it does suggest that contemporary antifeminism is more likely to receive support among working-class, nonemployed women. Perhaps the attraction of this ideology lies in its defense of the traditional middle-class family with male as provider and female as homemaker, long a symbol of upward mobility in the United States. Seen in this light, the movement's charges that affirmative action programs threaten the male breadwinner role and force wives into the labor force to support families contain a powerful class appeal. Anti-ERA rhetoric portrayed feminists as "smooth-talking college women who have never seen a factory production line" and are thus far removed from and little concerned with the economic problems of working-class women (Schlafly 1977, 148, 145). Significantly, Phyllis Schlafly herself came from a modest family background, grew up during the Depression, worked her way through college, and achieved upward mobility through marriage to a successful attorney (Felsenthal 1981).

These divergent historical circumstances of the status politics of antifeminism point to tentative explanations for the failure of the antisuffragists to halt ratification of the Nineteenth Amendment in one era and the success of the anti-ERA movement fifty years later. During the second decade of this century, the status conflict favored the rising middle classes, as other popular reform movements—such as temperance, labor rights, and progressivism—joined with suffrage in chipping away at the hegemony of the eastern industrial elite. In addition, political support for the suffrage amendment increased after 1918, in recognition of women's contribution to the war effort and the embarrassing absence of female political rights in the aftermath of President Wilson's pledge to make the world safe for democracy. Suffragist leaders highlighted these incongruities in the media. They also demonstrated considerable political expertise when, after two decades of campaigns for the passage of state woman suffrage referenda, during which time an effective network of state organizations was developed, they followed up with a coordinated national effort single-mindedly focusing on the issue of the vote. (It has been suggested, however, that this single-issue strategy ultimately impeded expansion of the movement to other feminist concerns after suffrage was secured.)

By contrast, the success of the contemporary stop-ERA movement may be traced partly to the economic problems of the 1970s, which engendered a backlash against affirmative action programs designed to promote employment opportunities for women and minorities. Given the membership composition of the anti-ERA movement, it is likely that what is perceived as threatening to the male breadwinner role may concomitantly be seen as endangering the position of the female as homemaker as well as the family's middle-class status. One survey, for example, found that both sexes were more likely to oppose the ERA if they believed that its passage would make it harder for males to find good jobs, and the authors predicted that a stagnating economy would have deleterious effects on ratification (Huber, Rexroat, and Spitze 1978). This is indeed what happened. According to national opinion surveys, public support for the ERA generally declined throughout the 1970s, although a majority of Americans continued to support it (Daniels, Darcy, and Westphal 1982). Interestingly, 1980 marked the nadir of ERA support, the same year that the Republican party withdrew its long-standing support of the amendment at its national convention and nonetheless swept the presidential elections later that year. In the rising conservative political tide, antifeminist leaders such as Schlafly wasted no time in integrating the anti-ERA movement with other powerful New Right political movements, such as the Moral Majority. Feminists, on the other hand, may inadvertently have weakened support for the ERA by addressing a broad spectrum of issues, including the right to abortion, during the ratification struggle. The stop-ERA movement adeptly seized the opportunity to recruit new members through local churches and antiabortion groups (Brady and Tedin 1976; Mueller and Dimieri 1982). Postmortems conducted in the wake of the June 1982 ratification deadline identified other strategic errors by the pro-ERA movement—most notably, the failure to develop cohesive state organizations until the opposition had already mobilized, redefined the amendment, and scored some impressive state legislature defeats of the ERA (see Marshall and Orum 1986). The proponents had lost momentum as early as 1974, and they "were essentially fighting a rearguard action" (Boles 1982, 576). By the time the National Organization for Women (NOW) finally took charge of a focused national ratification campaign in the latter 1970s, it may have already been too late for the ERA.

Since defeating the ERA in 1982, STOP-ERA has ceased to be active, but its umbrella organization, Eagle Forum, monitors the feminist movement and stands ready to mobilize antifeminists should another ERA threaten to be passed in Congress. In the meantime, Schlafly's campaign against feminism has targeted the principle of comparable worth, which she views as unfair to the traditional family and a danger to the American economy (see Schlafly 1986).

The arduous and unsuccessful campaign for passage of the ERA marked a serious setback for the American feminist movement. Journalists speculated that feminism died with the amendment, and even Betty Friedan, a founder of NOW, wrote of the "profound paralysis of the women's movement" (Friedan 1985). NOW's leadership divided over the question of beginning a new ratification campaign, with many feminists arguing that there were more pressing issues for the movement to address. NOW ultimately announced a second ERA drive, and the proposed amendment has been reintroduced in Congress. The feminist movement has also reacted to the anti-ERA appeal by directing more attention to the problems of homemakers, emphasizing freedom of choice for alternative female lifestyles (including marriage and motherhood), and attempting to downplay its elitist image. Although the efficacy of the strategy has yet to be tested, these policy shifts illustrate strikingly the mutual influences of social movements and countermovements.

REFERENCES

Andelin, Helen B. 1966. *Fascinating Womanhood: A Guide to a Happy Marriage.* San Luis Obispo, Calif: Pacific Press.

Anti-Suffragist. 1908a. 1, 1 (July): 3.

———. 1908b. "Salutatory," 1, 1 (July): 4–5.

———. 1908c. 1, 2 (Dec.): 3.

———. 1908d. 1, 2 (Dec.): 8.

———. 1909a. "The Suffragettes' Midnight Raid." 1, 3 (Mar.): 3.

———. 1909b. "Extracts from Papers Read at Albany, N.Y., February 24, 1909." 1, 4 (June): 1–8.

———. 1909c. 2, 1 (Sept.): 5.

———. 1909d. 2, 1 (Sept.): 8.

———. 1910a. "Madame Bell-Ranske." 2, 3 (Mar.): 8.

———. 1910b. "Statement of Miss Phoebe W. Couzins, LL.B., in Opposition to Woman Suffrage." 2, 4 (June): 2.

———. 1911. "Australia." 3, 5 (Sept.): 7.

———. 1912a. "The Taste of Woman Suffrage." 4, 1 (Jan.): 2.

———. 1912b. "Subjects for the Alienist." 4, 2 (Apr.): 7.

Armstrong, Eliza D. 1915. "Woman Suffrage and the Saloon." *Woman's Protest* 7, 1 (May): 3.

Arnold, Mrs. George F. 1915. "Ignorance of the Real Issues at Stake." *Woman's Protest* 6, 6 (Apr.): 14.

Arrington, Theodore S., and Patricia A. Kyle. 1978. "Equal Rights Amendment Activists in North Carolina." *Signs* 3, 3 (Spring): 666–80.

Bannister, Lucy E. 1910. "Extracts from Paper Read before Judiciary Committee." *Anti-Suffragist* 2, 4 (June): 6.

Berry, Mary Frances. 1986. *Why ERA Failed.* Bloomington, Ind.: Indiana University Press.

Boles, Janet K. 1979. *The Politics of the Equal Rights Amendment: Conflict and Decision Process*. New York: Longman.

———. 1982. "Building Support for the ERA: A Case of 'Too Much, Too Late'" *PS* 15, 4 (Fall): 572–77.

Brady, David., and Kent L. Tedin. 1976. "Ladies in Pink: Religion and Political Ideology in the Anti-ERA Movement." *Social Science Quarterly* 56, 4 (Mar.): 564–75.

Brazzil, Ruth. 1915. "The False Foundation of the Suffrage Argument." *Woman's Protest* 7, 2 (June): 17–18.

Carabillo, Toni. 1978. "The New Right." *National NOW Times* (Mar.): 6.

Conroy, George R. 1915. "An Indissociable Alliance: Socialism, Suffragism, Feminism." *Woman's Protest* 7, 3 (July): 8–9.

Cott, Nancy F. 1987. *The Grounding of Modern Feminism*. New Haven: Yale University Press.

Daniels, Mark R., Robert Darcy, and Joseph W. Westphal. 1982. "The ERA Won—at Least in the Opinion Polls." *PS* 15, 4 (Fall): 578–84.

Felsenthal, Carol. 1981. *The Sweetheart of the Silent Majority: The Biography of Phyllis Schlafly*. Garden City, N.Y.: Doubleday.

Firestone, Shulamith. 1970. "The Women's Rights Movement in the U.S.: A New View." In *Voices from Women's Liberation*, ed. Leslie B. Tanner, pp. 433–43. New York: Signet (New American Library).

Flexner, Eleanor. 1973. *Century of Struggle: The Women's Rights Movement in the United States*. New York: Atheneum.

Freeman, Jo. 1975. *The Politics of Women's Liberation*. New York: Longman.

Friedan, Betty. 1985. "How to Get the Women's Movement Moving Again." *New York Times*, Nov. 3, Sec. 6, 26.

George, Mrs. A. J. 1915. "Why We Are Anti-Suffragists." *Woman's Protest* 7, 6 (Oct.): 5–6.

Gompers, Samuel. 1920. "Labor and Woman Suffrage." *American Federationist* 27 (Oct.): 936–39.

Gusfield, Joseph R. 1963. *Symbolic Crusade: Status Politics and the American Temperance Movement*. Urbana, Ill.: University of Illinois Press.

Heron, Mrs. John B. 1915. "Feminism a Return to Barbarism." *Woman's Protest* 6, 6 (Apr.): 5–6.

Huber, Joan, Cynthia Rexroat, and Glenna Spitze. 1978. "A Crucible of Opinion on Women's Status: ERA in Illinois." *Social Forces* 57, 2 (Dec.): 549–65.

Illinois Association Opposed to Woman Suffrage. 1909. *To the Voters of the Middle West*. 1 (Sept.).

———. 1911. *Man for the State; Woman for the Home*. 8 (June).

———. 1913. *Woman Suffrage a Socialist Movement*. 17 (May).

Kraditor, Aileen S., ed. 1968. *Up from the Pedestal: Selected Writings in the History of American Feminism*. New York: Quadrangle/New York Times.

———. 1971. *The Ideas of the Woman Suffrage Movement, 1890–1920*. New York: Anchor/Doubleday.

Lipset, Seymour Martin. 1965. "The Sources of the Radical Right." In *The New American Right*, ed. Daniel Bell, pp. 166–234. New York: Criterion.

Mansbridge, Jane J. 1986. *Why We Lost the ERA*. Chicago: University of Chicago Press.

Marshall, Susan E. 1986. "In Defense of Separate Spheres: Class and Status Politics in the Antisuffrage Movement." *Social Forces* 65, 2 (Dec.): 327–51.

Marshall, Susan E. and Anthony M. Orum. 1986. "Opposition Then and Now: Countering Feminism in the Twentieth Century." In *Research in Politics and Society*. vol. 2, eds. Gwen Moore and Glenna D. Spitze, pp. 13–34. Greenwich, Conn.: JAI Press.

Morgan, Mirabelle. 1973. *The Total Woman*. Old Tappan, N.J.: F. H. Revell.

"Mormons Control Eight Suffrage States." 1915. *New York Times*, Jan. 15, 5.

Mueller, Carol, and Thomas Dimieri. 1982. "The Structure of Belief Systems among Contending ERA Activists." *Social Forces* 60, 3 (Mar.): 657–75.

Repplier, Agnes. 1915. "Women and Peace." *Woman's Protest* 7, 6 (Oct.): 5–6.

Schaffer, Ronald. 1962. "The New York City Woman Suffrage Party, 1909–19." *New York History* 43 (July): 268–87.

Schlafly, Phyllis. 1973. *Phyllis Schlafly Report* 6 (July): 2, 12.

———. 1977. *The Power of the Positive Woman*. New York: Jove, HBJ Books.

———. 1986. "Comparable Worth: Unfair to Men and Women." *Humanist* 46 (May/June): 12–13.

Scott, Anne F., and Andrew M. Scott. 1975. *One-Half of the People: The Fight for Woman Suffrage*. Philadelphia: Lippincott.

Scott, Wilbur J. 1985. "The Equal Rights Amendment as Status Politics." *Social Forces* 64, 2 (Dec.): 499–506.

Scott, Mrs. William Forse. 1909. "Extracts from Papers Read at Albany, N.Y., Feb. 24, 1909." *Anti-Suffragist* 1, 4 (June): 1–2.

Sebring, Emma G. 1915. "The Call of the New Lady." *Woman's Protest* 6, 6 (Apr.): 10–11.

Solomon, Martha. 1978. "The Rhetoric of STOP ERA: Fatalistic Reaffirmation." *Southern Speech Communication Journal* 44 (fall): 42–59.

"Suffragists Spice Anti Mass Meeting." 1914. *New York Times*, Jan. 9, 20.

Tedin, Kent L., David W. Brady, Mary E. Buxton, Barbara M. Gorman, and Judy L. Thompson. 1977. "Social Background and Political Differences Between Pro- and Anti-ERA Activists." *American Politics Quarterly* 5, 3 (July): 6.

Tucker, Gilbert M. 1911. "Female Taxpayers Should Object." *Anti-Suffragist* 3, 3 (Mar.): 6.

White, Mrs. George P. 1915a. "Taxation without Representation—Misapplied." *Woman's Protest* 6, 4 (Feb.): 8–9.

White, Mrs. George P. 1915a. "Taxation without Representation—Misapplied." *Woman's Protest* 6, 4 (Feb.): 8–9.

———. 1915b. "The Recent Rejection of Radicalism." *Woman's Protest* 7, 1 (May): 8–9.

Woman's Protest. 1915a. "Must All Women Bear the Burden of the Ballot to Give Some Women Political Prominence?" 6, 3 (Jan.): 3.

———. 1915b. "The Futility of a Woman's Peace Party." 7, 1 (May): 5–7.

———. 1915c. "New Suffragist Plea—Give Us Jury Duty." 7, 2 (June): 14–15.

———. 1915d. "The Rise of Militancy in America." 7, 2 (June): 16–17.

———. 1915e. "A Noisy and Selfish Propaganda." 7, 2 (June): 19.

———. 1915f. "The Suffragist Peace Party Fiasco." 7, 3 (July): 6–7.

———. 1915g. "Cold Logic Applied to 'Inalienable Rights.'" 6, 6 (Apr.): 6–7.

From Pedestals to Partners: Men's Responses to Feminism

MICHAEL S. KIMMEL

"Are you a Feminist?" we asked the stenographer.

She said she was.

"What do you mean by Feminism?"

"Being like men," she answered.

"Now you are joking!"

"No, I'm not. I mean mental independence. And emotional independence too—living in relation to the universe rather than in relation to some other person."

"All men are not like that," we said sadly.

"Then they ought to join the Feminist movement!"

That exchange was reported in the March 1914 issue of *The Masses*, and was reported by young Max Eastman, the secretary of the Men's League for Woman Suffrage (Eastman, 1914: 7). It illustrates that men have responded to the feminist movement in a variety of ways, contrary to the common assumption that men have been united in their opposition to feminist demands, from Seneca Falls to the campaign for the Equal Rights Amendment.

Three types of men's responses can be identified from their speeches, sermons, pamphlets, and magazine articles, as well as from political organizations and voluntary associations in both the nineteenth and twentieth centuries.[1] The *antifeminist* response relied on traditional religious ideas to demand women's return to the private sphere of home and hearth. Antifeminist men yearned nostalgically for the traditional separation of spheres that had kept women from explicitly challenging men's dominance in the public sphere. "Get back to the home, where you belong!" might have served as the antifeminist battle cry. A *masculinist* response, by contrast, was less concerned with women's participation in the public sphere than with her dominance in the private realm. Masculinists claimed that women's control over childhood socialization had "feminized" American manhood, and they tried to develop islands of untainted virility so that boys could once again grow up to be "real men." Finally, a *pro-feminist* response provided support for women's increased participation in the public realm, joining with women in agitating for educational, labor, and political reforms. Many men also supported women's demands for changes in the private realm, such as in marriage and sexual relations; these men tried to live in their personal lives the alternative the women were demanding. Pro-feminists believed that feminism would benefit men as well as women, because relating to equals was healthier, and, as one pro-feminist man put it simply, "more fun" (O'Neill, 1978: 50).

These three responses did not simply emerge the moment feminist women began to agitate for changes. Rather, they reflected several longer-term changes in the organization of work, social mobility, and political rights that had fundamentally altered the traditional psychological and social foundations of masculinity. One pillar of nineteenth-century masculinity was economic autonomy, as a shopkeeper, farmer, or independent craftsperson. Owning the shop, being one's own boss, and controlling the labor process were central, but rapid industrialization and the closing of the frontier led to these men's replacement in the late nineteenth century with factory workers and dispossessed farm laborers. Before the Civil War, almost nine-tenths of American men were farmers or self-employed businesspersons; by 1870, that figure had dropped to two-thirds, and by 1910, less than one-third were independent (Trachtenberg, 1982). In Kansas alone, there were over 11,000 foreclosures on independent family farms from 1889 to 1893 (Shannon, 1945: 313). At the same time, women's entry into the work force and the professions and the rise of women's colleges all had a dramatic impact on the traditional definition of femininity. In 1880, 2.6 million women were employed. That figure more than doubled by 1900 (5.3 million), and, by 1920, it had climbed to 8.5 million (*Abstract of the Fourteenth Census*, 1920: 481). No longer were women supposed to manifest "learned helplessness." They could be as competent and capable as any man.

These trends have continued in our own era, as plant closings and the decline of the small shopkeeper and the American family farm have continued to erode the possibility of economic autonomy. Simultaneously, women have been flooding the labor force, the professions, and higher education. And just as the closing of the frontier eliminated the physical space in which men could test and prove their manhood, contemporary movements to impel military withdrawal from Vietnam, Iran, and other countries suggest a closing of the global imperial frontier. When President John F. Kennedy labeled his program "The New Frontier," could he have known what was at stake for American manhood?

THE ANTIFEMINIST RESPONSE

Although the crisis in American masculinity had its roots in the structural transformation of the American economy and political arena, some men

have confused women's simultaneous claims for a larger presence in the public sphere with the cause of their problems. Feminism, they believe, has caused the collapse of the "natural" order, which guaranteed them the superior position over women, and they seek to reverse this trend. In the nineteenth century, men often opposed women's suffrage on biological grounds. One writer claimed that women would be physiologically damaged if they got the vote, growing larger, developing heavier brains, and losing their unique feminine mannerisms and features (Bushnell, 1870). It was not so much that women should be deprived of the vote as that they should be *exempted* from it, because of their lofty position:

> The privilege of voting for and holding public elective offices is not denied to the women of this country for being inferior in intellect to the men, or for ranking lower as human beings than the men, or because the principle of equal rights to all in matters of public concern was not as applicable to them as to the men, but solely for *natural reasons*, nature having assigned the home and not the State to woman as her sphere. America's women would gain nothing by the suffrage; on the contrary they would lose their peace and happiness by it. *Womanhood* teaches them this. (Hertwig, 1883: 11–12.)

Another writer fused military service and the franchise, arguing that "no one should take part in government who was not ready to defend, by force, if necessary, the institutions of the country" (Frothingham, 1894: note on 1). This position was best summed up by one anonymous antifeminist, who argued in a debate about the question in Sacramento, California in 1880:

> I am opposed to woman's sufferage [sic] on account of the burden it will place upon her. Her delicate nature has already enough to drag it down. Her slender frame, naturally weakened by the constant strain attendant upon her nature is too often racked by diseases that are caused by a too severe tax upon her mind. The presence of passion, love, ambition, is all too potent for her enfeebled constitution and wrecked health and early death are all too common. (California Historical Society Library, San Francisco, ms. #2334.)

(The debate was decided in favor of the opponents to suffrage.)

Men also used the "natural" division between the sexes as the justification for opposition to women's education. "I think the great danger of our day is forcing the intellect of woman beyond what her physical organization will possibly bear," wrote John Todd in 1867; he counseled giving women "all the advantages and all the education which her organization, so tender and delicate, will bear; but don't try to make the anemone into an oak, nor to turn the dove out to wrestle with storms and winds, under the idea that she may just as well be an eagle as a dove" (Todd, 1867: 23, 25). And female labor-force participation was attacked on similar grounds. "The growing demand for female labor is an insidious assault upon the home; it is the knife of the assassin aimed at the family circle and the divine injunction. It excludes women from nature's dearest impulse," wrote Edward O'Donnell in 1897 (O'Donnell, 1897: 186).

Medical texts abounded with details of the horrors of women's equal participation in the public world. "Certain women seek to rival men in manly sports, and the strongminded ape them in all things, even in dress," observed Dr. Alfred Stillé in his presidential address to the American Medical Association in 1871. "In doing so, they may command a sort of admiration such as all monstrous productions inspire, especially when they tend towards a higher type than their own" (cited in Ehrenreich and English, 1979; 65).

Today's antifeminist argument differs little. Biology is still destiny and women's presumed "natural" function is to produce children. Feminism has duped women into abandoning marriage and children, argue contemporary antifeminists, who elevate women onto the proverbial pedestal. Women ought to be exempted from public participation because they are the bearers of morality, and only they can constrain men's antisocial amoral impulses. "No man with gumption wants a woman to fight his nation's battles," noted General William C. Westmoreland, one of the architects of America's Vietnam War (cited in Freedman, 1985: 110). And conservative theorist George Gilder writes that "a woman may even do more good without a job than with one" (1986: 41). "I'd just as soon keep her at home dependent on me rather than be dependent on her bringing in so much a week," one working man told a journalist, while another expressed fears at the consequences of women's entry into the work world, when he commented that, "If women work and they're married, they get too independent. Before long there's trouble at home" (Astrachan, 1986: 96).

Contemporary antifeminists also rely on a strange reading of anthropological literature to inveigh against women for their challenges to "the inevitability of patriarchy" (Goldberg, 1975; Amneus, 1979). If men have historically oppressed women in most cultures, they argue, there must be something natural and inevitable about patriarchy, which is therefore sacrosanct and unchallengeable.

Feminist arguments for equality are countered by antifeminists who point to areas in which equality would socially challenge the biological imperative. In employment, for example, C. H. Freedman attempts to frighten readers, asserting that "the forcing of the fire departments of this country to lower their standards to accommodate women amounts to nothing less than the offering of human sacrifices" (Freedman, 1985: 109). Many leaders of the religious right wing, including Jerry Falwell's Moral Majority, campaigned vigorously against the Equal Rights Amendment, because, they argued, woman would be forced to relinquish the rights and privileges she now possesses. One antifeminist man called Phyllis Schlafly "the most outstanding American in our history" for leading the fight against that "irresponsible and dangerous" amendment (Freedman, 1985: 250).

Organizationally, the National Organization for Men (NOM), led by divorce lawyer and *Playboy* columnist Sidney Siller, opposes feminism, which it claims is "designed to denigrate men, exempt women from the draft and to encourage the disintegration of the family" (Siller, 1984). NOM opposes affirmative action, imprisonment of men for nonpayment of alimony, and preference to women on child-custody issues. In the antifeminist scheme, it's time for men to stand up to the "libbers' stridency and the brain damaged man-hating" that characterizes modern feminism (cited in Freedman, 1985: 284).

Another group of men have been less distressed about women's increased power than with men's reduced significance. They mourned the disappearance of "real men" from the political scene, and sought frantically to reassert a vigorous virility in a world that "feminized" manhood. A century ago, as well as today, American men were concerned about "wimps."

The masculinist response differed from the antifeminist response in several important ways. Antifeminists saw women as the cause of men's problems, and sought to press women back into the private sphere where, they argued, women belonged. Masculinists were often indifferent to women in the public sphere, and sought instead to dislodge women's dominance in the home, and especially in the raising of young boys. It was here that boys were distracted from becoming men.

It was the presence of girls that distracted them. Masculinists believed there was "something enervating in feminine companionship," so the separation of boys and girls was essential to retrieve masculinity from women's clutches (Dubbert, 1979: 97). Several childrearing manuals cautioned against mixed dancing, coed classrooms, and even feather beds for boys, since these beds' softness and warmth led to impure thoughts (Barker-Benfield, 1976: 232). At the same time, a new "muscular Christianity" hailed a remasculinized Jesus: he was "no lick-spittle proposition," proclaimed preacher Billy Sunday in the 1890s, but "the greatest scrapper who ever lived" (cited in Douglas, 1977: 327). Thomas Hughes's *The Manliness of Christ* (1880) and Carl Case's *The Masculine in Religion* (1906) echo this theme.

Masculinists were terrified that men were turning into women; that is, that men were becoming "inverts." Throughout their writings, both then and now, one senses a terror of male homosexuality, which supposedly saps the virility of the nation. This fear is a response to the increased visibility, since the late nineteenth century, of a viable gay subculture in American cities. Today's gay and lesbian urban subculture provokes irrational hatred and fear among many, even as their contribution to American culture grows. One antidote was homosociality, a rigorously enforced single-sex social life. If the sexes mingled, it was reasoned, the boys would become feminized, and hence homosexual.[2] As G. Stanley Hall argued in his 1904 textbook, *Adolescence*, familiarity and camaraderie produced a disenchantment and diluted the "mystic attraction of the other sex" (Hall, 1904: 641). Such notions also fueled masculinist arguments against coeducation and against women's education in general. An article in *Educational Review* (1914: 109) blamed women teachers for creating a "feminized manhood, emotional, illogical, noncombative against public evils."

But perhaps the most significant answer to the perceived feminization of American boyhood was the number of organizations devoted to a boy's proper upbringing that sprang up around the country. The YMCA, the Boy's Club, and the Boy Scouts of America were devoted to reclaiming American boyhood from the feminizing influences of women, who were turning "robust, manly, self-reliant boyhood into a lot of flat chested cigarette smokers with shaky nerves and doubtful vitality" according to Ernest Thompson

Seton, the founder of the Boy Scouts of America in 1910 (cited in Macleod, 1983: 49). The Boy Scouts celebrated a masculinity tested and proven against nature and other boys. Here was a "boy's liberation movement to free young males from women, especially from mothers" (Dubbert, 1979: 152). If boys could be provided with a haven away from all feminizing influences, a place to redirect male anxieties and to sublimate adolescent sexual yearnings, then these boys could become the "real men" required by early-twentieth-century industrial capitalism.

The symbolic hero to the masculinist cause was President Theodore Roosevelt, whose triumph over youthful frailty and transformation into a robust vigorous warrior served as a template for a revitalized American social character. Roosevelt elevated compulsive masculinity and military adventurism to the level of national myth, and "symbolized a restoration of masculine identity at a time . . . when it appeared to be jeopardized" (Dubbert, 1980: 313).

These themes resonate through the contemporary masculinist response. Some masculinists seek to dislodge women's primacy in the private sphere, whereas others offer male camaraderie and support for men who are "wounded" in the struggle to constantly exude an aura of virility in the public sphere. Men's challenges to women's perceived parental monopoly come from "men's rights" groups such as the Coalition for Free Men, Mens Rights International, and Men Achieving Liberation and Equality (MALE). These groups often deny that men have any power in society, arguing that male supremacy is an illusion, along the lines of the illusion of the chauffeur: "he's dressed in the uniform and he looks like he's in the driver's seat," writes Warren Farrell, "but from his perspective someone else is giving the orders" (cited in Woldenberg, 1986: 10). Some writers claim that men, too, are oppressed, at least by "the system" if not by women, and rail against institutionalization of female privileges, such as exemptions from the draft and advantages in alimony, child custody, and child support (Haddad, 1979; Baumli, 1986). As one critic of this position summed it up,

> Men, they say, are emotionally and sexually manipulated by women, forced into provider roles where they work themselves to death for their gold-digger wives, kept from equal participation and power in family life, and finally dumped by wives only to have courts and lawyers give all the property, money, and child custody to the women. (Messner, 1986: 32.)

One writer advises men who feel powerless in the face of divorce-court proceedings to "fight dirty and win" by exploiting their wives' vulnerabilities (Robinson, 1986: 175).

Not all masculinists are so vicious, however. Some seek to provide some support and solace for men, and offer moving accounts of male bonding in homosocial settings. Philip Caputo's *A Rumor of War* echoes earlier themes of male intimacy during wartime, an intimacy threatened by the integration of women into all arenas:

> The communion between men is as profound as any between lovers. Actually it is more so. It does not demand for its sustenance the reciproc-

ity, the pledges of affection, the endless reassurances required by the love of men and women. It is, unlike marriage, a bond that cannot be broken by a word, by boredom or divorce, or by anything other than death. Sometimes that is not strong enough. (Caputo, 1977: 174.)

Lest anyone confuse the imperatives of homosociality for homosexuality, Caputo echoed a late-nineteenth-century theme when he noted in an interview (Astrachan, 1986: 52) that the "emotion of camaraderie, is of its nature chaste. It may be more intense than what happens between male and female lovers, but it has to be nonsexual. It's not just women. Warriors can't be homosexual lovers either."

Some contemporary masculinists echo the Muscular Christianity movement by recasting Jesus as a religious Rambo. Televangelist Jerry Falwell, for example, insists the "Christ wasn't effeminate. . . . The man who lived on this earth was a man with muscles. . . . Christ was a he-man!" (cited in Fitzgerald, 1986: 166). And other masculinists still insist that the separation of the sexes is the only way to preserve what is different (and interesting) about either men or women. The Century Club, founded in the late nineteenth century as a protected male island, away from the world of women and the demands of family life, is today battling to retain its character as a homosocial haven away from those demands. As member Lewis Lapham wrote in the *New York Times*, men's clubs are an example of the way in which

> nature divides the whole of its creation into opposing forces (proton and electron, positive and negative, matter and antimatter, masculine and feminine) in order that their dynamic symmetries might decode and organize the unlicked chaos. The clarity of gender makes possible the human dialectic. Let the lines of balanced tension go slack and the structure dissolves into the ooze of androgyny and narcissism. (Lapham, 1983.)

The masculinist often does not care what women are doing with their lives, as long as they leave him alone to be a real man among other men.

THE PRO-FEMINIST RESPONSE

Although less visible and less influential than their antifeminist or masculinist counterparts, both in the late nineteenth century and today, some American men have openly embraced feminist principles, believing that women's increased public participation—symbolized by suffrage or the ERA, women's increased personal autonomy, and women's right to birth control and sexual freedom—would be a significant gain for both women and men. In every feminist struggle, from Seneca Falls through the campaign for the ERA, pro-feminist men have supported women's demands. Some have even examined their own lives, and have struggled to develop more egalitarian and mutually supportive relationships.

In the mid-nineteenth century, pro-feminist men supported women's suffrage. Several men were signers of the original Declaration of Sentiments in 1848, among them Frederick Douglass, the celebrated black abolitionist.

Other abolitionists, such as William Lloyd Garrison, Samuel Gridley Howe, and Thomas Wentworth Higginson, also campaigned actively for women's rights. Many mid-century communal-living experiments were organized by men, such as Robert Dale Owen, John Humphrey Noyes, and Moses Harmon, who saw the communes as retreats from female sexual slavery and as locations to develop new relations between women and men and new forms of family organization based on mutuality and equality. And many of the men who founded and led the new women's colleges, such as Matthew Vassar, William Allan Neilson and Joseph Taylor (both of Smith College), and Henry Durant (of Wellesley), as well as the men who supported coeducation at Cornell, Oberlin, Wesleyan, and other schools, believed that men would also benefit from the ability to relate to strong, whole people, capable of complementary relations. Durant wrote that the "real meaning" of higher education for women was "revolt against the slavery in which women are held by the customs of society — the broken health, the aimless lives, the subordinate position, the helpless dependence, the dishonesties and shams of so-called education. The Higher Education of Women . . . is the cry of the oppressed slave. It is the assertion of absolute equality" (cited in Horowitz, 1984: 44).

By the end of the nineteenth and the beginning of the twentieth centuries, many men actively participated in the state campaigns for woman suffrage, believing that political equality might relieve the world of oppressively masculine politics. (What the masculinists wanted to restore, the pro-feminists wanted to eliminate.) The Men's League for Woman Suffrage had both American and English branches. In the United States, it was headed by Oswald Garrison Villard, publisher of the *New York Evening Post*, and Rabbi Stephen Wise, and was administered by the young Greenwich Village radical, Max Eastman. His pamphlet "Is Woman Suffrage Important?" linked a socialist economic critique of the leisured class with a feminist-inspired analysis of male–female relationships; capitalism and sexism had turned women's "enforced feebleness into a holy thing" (Eastman, 1916: 8).

Pro-feminist men also marched in suffrage demonstrations. An editorial from *La Follette's* in May 1911 praised the eighty-five "courageous and convinced men" who marched in a suffrage demonstration in New York City. One marcher counted being "booed and hissed down the Avenue a very thrilling and inspiring experience," and indicated his determination that "if I can help to that end, there shall be a thousand men in line next year." And he was not far off target. An article in the *New York Times* the next year estimated that about 800 men marched in a suffrage demonstration in New York (*New York Times*, 11 May 1912, p. 15), although Eastman's estimate was much higher, considering the Men's League took up five blocks of marchers, four abreast (Eastman, 1936: 351).

Within the growing labor movement, women's rights also found support, especially from Eugene V. Debs. In his pamphlet "Woman — Comrade and Equal," published by the Socialist Party (undated), Debs proclaimed himself "glad to align myself with a party that declares for absolute equality between the sexes. Anything less than this is too narrow for twentieth century civilization, and too small for a man who has a right conception of manhood'' (Debs, 1948: 454). Debs concluded by linking the social emancipation of women to the end of male violence against women and the transformation of masculinity:

> Under our brutal forms of existence, beating womanhood to dust, we have raged in passion for the individual woman, for use only. Some day we shall develop the social passion for womanhood, and then . . . we shall life woman from the mire where our fists have struck her, and set her by our side as our comrade and equal, and that will be love indeed.

Within the personal sphere, turn-of-the-century pro-feminist men supported women's claims for autonomy in marriage and demands for sexual freedom, including divorce and birth control. William Sanger, husband of birth-control advocate Margaret Sanger, was arrested in 1915 for distributing his wife's pamphlet, *Family Limitation*. At home, he was equally supportive. ''You go ahead and finish your writing,'' she quotes him as saying that year, ''and I'll get the dinner and wash the dishes'' (cited in Forster, 1985: 252). (Apparently, she used to draw the curtains in their apartment when he did so, lest anyone take notice of this gender reversal [Reed, 1977: 136].)

Many of the young radicals who clustered around Greenwich Village in the first two decades of the century supported women's equality and wrestled with these issues in their own lives. Max Eastman and Ida Rauh caused a scandal when they married in 1911 and she retained her own name on the mailbox of their Greenwich Village apartment. Perhaps the most articulate of these radicals was Floyd Dell, who argued that the liberation of women from the oppressive bonds of traditional femininity implied the liberation of men from the restrictive trappings of traditional masculinity. Feminism was more than ''a revolt of women against conditions which hamper their activities; it is also a revolt of women and men against the type of woman created by those conditions'' he wrote in 1921 (Dell, 1921: 349). In ''Feminism for Men,'' Dell made this clear:

> The home is a little dull. When you have got a woman in a box, and you pay rent on the box, her relationship to you insensibly changes character. It loses the fine excitement of democracy. It ceases to be companionship, for companionship is only possible in a democracy. It is no longer the sharing of life together—it is a breaking of life apart. Half a life—cooking, clothes, and children; half a life—business, politics and baseball. . . . It is in the great world that a man finds his sweetheart, and in that narrow little box outside of the world that he loses her. When she has left that box and gone back into the great world, a citizen and a worker, then with surprise and delight he will discover her again and never let her go (1914: 32).

To Dell, the woman's movement signaled the hope of all humankind, because it included both women and men; he wrote in 1913:

> If the woman's movement means anything, it means that women are demanding everything. They will not exchange one place for another, nor give up one right to pay for another, but they will achieve all rights to which their bodies and brains give them an implicit title. They will have a larger political life, a larger motherhood, a larger social service, a

larger love, and they will reconstruct or destroy institutions to that end as it becomes necessary. They will not be content with any concession or any triumph until they have conquered all experience (Dell, 1913: 51).

Today's feminist woman also has male allies, some of whom recall their century-old forebears. For example, organization such as Men Allied Nationally for the Equal Rights Amendment (MAN for ERA) sponsored rallies, and marched in ERA demonstrations behind a banner, just as the Men's League for Woman Suffrage had done in suffrage parades. And many prominent American men campaigned for the amendment. Predictably, men long identified with feminist causes, such as Phil Donahue and Alan Alda, were visibly supportive. Alda argued that men would benefit from the passage of the ERA, as wider role options available to women can relieve men of a lot of pressure:

> as women fill traditionally male roles as police chiefs, gas station attendants, baseball players, and bankers, we may also begin to realize that wisdom, aggressiveness, and physical courage are not solely male attributes. The pressure to provide these qualities all by ourselves will be taken from men's shoulders. We can still be strong and brave, but we won't have to feel we're the only ones who are. (Alda, 1976: 93.)

Men will benefit from feminism, Alda contends, because current standards of masculinity are often pathological, locking men into behavior that is destructive to women, to children, and to other men. As a prisoner of masculinity, as a sufferer of "testosterone poisoning," a man is "not someone you'd want to have around in a crisis—such as raising children or growing old together" (Alda, 1975: 16).

If appeals to men's self-interest do not convince, however, Alda resorts to moral arguments as well. "How long can we stand by and watch qualified people excluded from jobs or denied fair payment for their labor? How long can we do nothing while people are shut out from their fair share of economic and political power merely because they're women?" (Alda, 1976: 93). Moral claims also convinced journalist Howard Cosell, the sportscaster American fans most love to hate, who stated that he supported the ERA

> because, simply, it's right and necessary. It relates to the betterment of society, it relates to the principles upon which the nation was supposed to be founded, principles which have not been lived up to. You do what is right and you stand for what is right. And the way you do that is with your mind, your heart, your vocalizations, and your general influence. It's very simple (Cosell, 1975: 78).

Several organizations work with men around some area identified as important to the feminist movement. Several, such as R.A.V.E.N. in St. Louis (which stands for Rape and Violence End Now), EMERGE in Boston, and MOVE in San Francisco, are devoted to ending men's violence against women, both by supporting the battered-women's movement and by counseling violent men. Many cities have established men's centers or have ongoing men's support groups to help men understand and support women's demands. And the National Organization for Changing Men (NOCM) is a network of pro-feminist men across the country who are involved in every-thing from pro-feminist men's music and art to political organizing about rape and violence.[3] The organization applauds "the insights and positive changes that feminism has stimulated for both women and men" and op-poses continued economic and legal discrimination, rape, domestic violence, and sexual harassment (NOCM, 1986). Pro-feminist magazines such as *Changing Men* provide personal and analytic articles about these issues to both male and female readers.[4]

A number of pro-feminist men are also academic men, and their re-search on the history of masculinity (Dubbert, 1979; Filene, 1976; Kimmel, 1987a, 1987b, 1987c; Pleck and Pleck, 1980), on the formulation of the male sex role (Pleck, 1981, 1986; Brannon and David, 1976), on masculinity and sports (Fine, 1987; Messner, 1987), and on themes of masculinity in litera-ture (Morgan, 1987; Murphy, 1987) have all challenged the notion of mas-culinity, taking a feminist perspective. Often, male students pick up the feminist message as well. One national fraternity, for example, recently produced a poster against date rape (Pi Kappa Phi, 1985). Others are running workshops on date rape and sexual harassment (see Scher, Stevens, Goode and Eichenfeld, 1987).

In many different arenas, contemporary pro-feminist men are confront-ing prevailing notions about the ways women and men should relate, are opening up and are learning how to listen to their women friends and lovers, and are trying to integrate feminist ideas into their own lives. And some-times, they are even trying to talk with other men about these ideas. In breaking ranks with men's silence about the position of women in American society, pro-feminist men also face hostility and isolation from other men. But pro-feminist men believe that the social changes already accomplished by feminism, and the changes that feminism will bring, contain significant and desirable changes for men as well, and that the feminist vision of sexual equality and gender justice is both practically and morally a vision of a world in which we would want to live.

NOTES

1. This essay is based on an ongoing research project on men's responses to feminism in the United States. Earlier essays have been published in *The Making of Masculinities: The New Men's Studies*. Harry Brod, ed. 1987. Boston: Allen and Unwin; Barbara Risman and Pepper Schwartz, eds. 1987. *Gender in Intimate Relationships: A Microstructural View.* Belmont, CA: Wadsworth; and *Gender & Society* 1(3), 1987. I am grateful to Harry Brod, Martin Duberman, Cynthia Fuchs Epstein, Jo Freeman, John Gagnon, Judith Gerson, Frances Goldin, Cathy Greenblat, Meredith Gould, Barbara Laslett, Judith Lorber, Gina Morantz-Sanchez, Tom Mosmiller, Joseph Pleck, and Catharine Stimpson for comments and criticisms on earlier drafts.

2. Such insistence on homosociality as insurance against possible homosexual behavior is ironic, especially when one recalls that, as Kinsey revealed in his classic studies (Kinsey, 1948), most men who have had homosexual experiences first did so precisely in these homosocial realms, such as summer camp, Boy Scouts, the military, or religious institutions.

3. Contact the National Organization for Changing Men at Box 451, Watseka, IL 60970.

4. Contact *Changing Men* at 306 N. Brooks St., Madison, WI 53715.

Feminism

Alda, Alan. 1975. "What Every Woman Should Know about Men," *Ms.*, October.

Alda, Alan. 1976. "Alan Alda on the ERA," *Ms.*, July.

Amneus, Daniel. 1979. *Back to Patriarchy*. New Rochelle, NY: Arlington.

anonymous editorial. 1914. "The Woman Peril," *Educational Review*, 47, February.

anonymous participant in debate held at Elk Grove, Sacramento, California. 22 January 1880. California Historical Society Library, San Francisco, Ms. 2334.

Astrachan, Anthony. 1986. *How Men Feel*. Garden City, NY: Anchor Books.

Barker-Benfield, G.J. 1976. *The Horrors of the Half Known Life: Male Attitudes Toward Women and Sexuality in 19th Century America*. New York: Harper and Row.

Baumli, Francis, ed. 1986. *Men Freeing Men: Exploding the Myth of the Traditional Male*. Jersey City, NJ: New Atlantis Press.

Brannon, Robert and Deborah David, eds. 1976. *The Forty-Nine Percent Majority*. Reading, MA: Addison-Wesley.

Caputo, Phillip. 1977. *A Rumor of War*. New York: Holt, Rinehart and Winston.

Cosell, Howard. 1975. "Why I Support the ERA," *Ms.*, October.

Debs, Eugene. 1948. *Writings and Speeches of Eugene V. Debs,* edited by Arthur Schlesinger, Jr. New York: Hermitage Press.

Dell, Floyd. 1913. *Woman as World Builders — Contemporary Studies*. Chicago: Forbes.

Dell, Floyd. 1914. "Feminism for Men" *The Masses*, July.

Dell, Floyd. 1921. "Feminism and Socialism" *New Masses*.

Douglas, Ann. 1977. *The Feminization of American Culture*. New York: Alfred Knopf.

Dubbert, Joe. 1979. *A Man's Place: Masculinity in Transition*. Englewood Cliffs, NJ: Prentice-Hall.

Dubbert, Joe. 1980. "Progressivism and the Masculinity Crisis," pp. 303–320 in *The American Man*, edited by E. Pleck and J. Pleck. Englewood Cliffs, NJ: Prentice-Hall.

Eastman, Max. 1914. "What Do You Know About This?" *Masses* 5(6), March.

Eastman, Max. 1915. "Revolutionary Birth Control." *The Masses* 6:21–2.

Eastman, Max. 1916. "Is Woman Suffrage Important?" New York: Men's League for Woman Suffrage.

Eastman, Max. 1936. *The Enjoyment of Living*. New York: Harper and Row.

Ehrenreich, Barbara and Deirdre English. 1979. *For Her Own Good: 150 Years of Medical Advice to Women*. New York: Anchor Books.

Filene, Peter. 1976. *Him/Her Self: Sex Roles in Modern America*, New York: Harcourt, Brace (revised edition, Baltimore: Johns Hopkins University Press, 1986).

Filene, Peter. 1980. "In Time of War," pp. 321–335 in *The American Man*, edited by E. Pleck and J. Pleck. Englewood Cliffs, NJ: Prentice-Hall.

Filene, Peter. 1984. "Between a Rock and a Soft Place: A Century of American Manhood." Unpublished.

Fine, Gary Alan. 1987. *With the Boys*. Chicago: University of Chicago Press.

Fitzgerald, Frances. 1986. *Cities on a Hill*. New York: Simon and Schuster.

Forster, Margaret. 1985. *Significant Sisters: The Grassroots of Active Feminism*. New York: Alfred Knopf.

Freedman, C.H. 1985. *Manhood Redux: Standing Up to Feminism*. Brooklyn, NY: Samson Publishers.

Frothingham, O. B. 1890. "The Real Case of the Remonstrance against Woman Suffrage." *The Arena* 2 (July): 124–127.

Frothingham, O. B. 1894. *Woman Suffrage: Unnatural and Inexpedient*. Boston: privately printed.

Gilder, George. 1986. *Men and Marriage*. Gretna, LA: Pelican.

Goldberg, Steven. 1975. *The Inevitability of Patriarchy*. New York: Morrow.

Haddad, Richard. 1979. *The Men's Liberation Movement: A Perspective*. Columbia, MD: Coalition for Free Men.

Hall, G. Stanley. 1904. *Adolescence* vol. II. New York: Appleton.

Hantover, Jeffrey, P. 1980. "The Boy Scouts and the Validation of Masculinity," pp. 285–302 in *The American Man*, edited by E. Pleck and J. Pleck. Englewood Cliffs, NJ: Prentice-Hall.

Hertwig, John George. 1883. "Woman Suffrage." Washington, D.C.: Eckler Printers.

Horowitz, Helen L. 1984. *Alma Mater: Design and Experience in the Women's Colleges from their 19th Century Beginnings to the 1930's*. New York: Alfred Knopf.

Kimmel, Michael S., ed. 1985. "Men Confronting Pornography," special issue of *Changing Men*, 15.

Kimmel, Michael S. 1987a. "The 'Crisis' of Masculinity in Historical Perspective," pp. 121–154 in *The Making of Masculinities: The New Men's Studies*, edited by Harry Brod. Boston: Allen and Unwin.

Kimmel, Michael S. 1987b. "The Cult of Masculinity: American Social Character and the Myth of the Cowboy" pp. 235–249 in *Beyond Patriarchy: Essays by Men on Pleasure, Power, and Change*, edited by Michael Kaufman. New York: Oxford University Press.

Kimmel, Michael S., ed. 1987c. *Changing Men: New Directions in Research on Men and Masculinity*. Beverly Hills, CA: Sage Publications.

Kimmel, Michael S. and T. Mosmiller, eds. In press. *Against the Tide: A Documentary History of Pro-Feminist Men in America*. Boston: Beacon.

Lapham, Lewis. 1983. "La Difference" *New York Times*, March 4, p. 33.

Leach, William. 1980. *True Love and Perfect Union: The Feminist Reform of Sex and Society*. New York: Basic Books.

Macleod, David. 1983. *Building Character in the American Boy: The Boy Scouts, YMCA, and their Forerunners, 1870–1920*. Madison, WI: University of Wisconsin Press.

Marshall, Susan E. 1985. "In Defense of Separate Spheres: Class and Status Politics in the Antisuffrage Movement." Paper presented at the Annual Meeting, American Sociological Association, San Antonio, TX.

Marshall, Susan E. and A. Orum. 1986. "Opposition Then and Now: Countering Feminism in the Twentieth Century." Unpublished.

Messner, Michael. 1986. Book review of *Men Freeing Men*, in *Changing Men*, 16.

Messner, Michael. 1987. "The Life of a Man's Seasons: Sports and Masculinity in the Lifecourse of the Jock" pp. in *Changing Men: New Directions in Research on Men and Masculinity*, edited by Michael S. Kimmel. Beverly Hills, CA: Sage Publications.

Morgan, David. 1987. "Masculinity and Violence in American Fiction." Paper presented at Third International Interdisciplinary Congress on Women, Dublin, Ireland, July.

Murphy, Peter. 1987. *John Hawkes: Toward a Radical Theory of Male Heterosexuality*. Ph.D. dissertation, Dept. of English, S.U.N.Y. at Buffalo, NY.

New York Times. 1912. "The Heroic Men" editorial, May 11.

O'Donnell, Edward. 1897. "Women as Bread Winners—The Error of the Age" *The American Federationist*, October.

O'Neill, William L. 1978. *The Last Romantic: A Life of Max Eastman*. New York: Oxford University Press.

Pi Kappa Phi (fraternity) 1985. "Statement of Position on Sexual Abuse" and poster "Today's Greeks Call It Date Rape."

Pleck, Joseph. 1981. *The Myth of Masculinity*. Cambridge, MA: MIT Press.

Pleck, Joseph. 1986. *Working Wives/Working Husbands*. Beverly Hills, CA: Sage Publications.

Pleck, Joseph and Elizabeth Pleck, eds. 1980. *The American Man.* Englewood Cliffs, NJ: Prentice-Hall.

Reed, James. 1977. *From Private Vice to Public Virtue: The Birth Control Movement and American Society Since 1830.* New York: Basic Books.

Robinson, G. P. 1986. "When All Else Fails and the War is On: How to Fight Dirty and Win" pp. 174–176 in *Men Freeing Men,* edited by Francis Baumli. Jersey City, NJ: New Atlantis Press.

Rosenthal, Michael. 1984. "Recruiting for Empire: Baden-Powell's Boy Scout Law" *Raritan* 4: 67–84.

Rosenthal, Michael. 1986. *The Character Factory: Baden-Powell's Boy Scouts and the Imperatives of Empire.* New York: Pantheon.

Scher, Murray, Stevens, Mark, Goode, Glenn, and Greg Eichenfield, eds. 1987. *Handbook on Counseling and Therapy with Men.* Newbury Park, CA: Sage Publications.

Shannon, Fred A. 1945. *The Farmer's Last Frontier: Agriculture, 1860–1897.* New York: Holt, Rinehart.

Strauss, Sylvia. 1983. *Traitors to the Masculine Cause: The Men's Campaign for Women's Rights.* Westport, CT: Greenwood Press.

"Thomas Wentworth Higginson: Early Advocate of Equal Suffrage." 1911. *La Follette's,* May. p. 17.

Todd, John. 1867. *Woman's Rights.* Boston: Lee and Shepard.

Trachtenberg, Alan. 1982. *The Incorporation of America: Culture and Society in the Guilded Age.* New York: Hill and Wang.

Trimberger, Ellen Kay. 1984. "Feminism, Men and Modern Love: Greenwich Village, 1900–1925," in *Powers of Desire: The Politics of Sexuality,* edited by A. Snitow, C. Stansell and S. Thompson. New York: Monthly Review Press.

United States Bureau of the Census, 1920. *Abstract of the Fourteenth Census.*

Woldenberg, Susan. 1986. "Modern Man Is Revolting!" *Los Angeles Reader.* December 5, p. 1.

Name Index

Subject Index